A FIELD GUIDE

TO THE

BIRDS OF BRAZIL

A FIELD GUIDE TO THE

Birds
of Brazil

BER VAN PERLO

OXFORD
UNIVERSITY PRESS
2009

OXFORD
UNIVERSITY PRESS

Oxford University Press, Inc., publishes works that further
Oxford University's objective of excellence
in research, scholarship, and education.

Oxford New York
Auckland Cape Town Dar es Salaam Hong Kong Karachi
Kuala Lumpur Madrid Melbourne Mexico City Nairobi
New Delhi Shanghai Taipei Toronto

With offices in
Argentina Austria Brazil Chile Czech Republic France Greece
Guatemala Hungary Italy Japan Poland Portugal Singapore
South Korea Switzerland Thailand Turkey Ukraine Vietnam

Published by Oxford University Press, Inc.
198 Madison Avenue, New York, New York 10016

www.oup.com

Oxford is a registered trademark of Oxford University Press

Library of Congress Cataloging-in-Publication Data
Perlo, Ber van.
A field guide to the birds of Brazil / Ber van Perlo.
    p.   cm.
Includes bibliographical references and index.
ISBN 978-0-19-530154-0; 978-0-19-530155-7 (pbk.)
1. Birds—Brazil—Identification. I. Title.
QL689.B8P44   2009
598.0981—dc22   2008018823

9 8 7 6 5 4 3 2

Printed in China
on acid-free paper

Contents

List of Plates

1. Diomedeidae (Albatrosses)
2. Diomedeidae (Albatrosses) & Procellariidae (Giant-petrels)
3. Procellariidae (Prions and Petrels) & Pelecanoididae (Diving-petrel)
4. Procellariidae (Shearwaters and Petrels)
5. Procellariidae (Shearwaters and Petrels)
6. Hydrobatidae (Storm-petrels) & Phaethontidae (Tropicbirds)
7. Sulidae (Boobies) & Fregatidae (Frigatebirds)
8. Spheniscidae (Penguins) & Podicipedidae (Grebes)
9. Phalacrocoracidae (Cormorants), Anhingidae (Darter) & Threskiornithidae (Ibises)
10. Ardeidae (Herons)
11. Ardeidae (Herons)
12. Ardeidae (Herons), Ciconiidae (Storks) & Threskiornithidae (Spoonbills)
13. Anhimidae (Screamers), Pelecanidae (Pelicans), Phoenicopteridae (Flamingos) & Anatidae (Swans)
14. Anatidae (Whistling-ducks, Goose, Ducks, Pochards, and Merganser)
15. Anatidae (Teals, Wigeon, Shoveler, Pintails, and Duck)
16. Cathartidae (New World Vultures and Condor)
17. Pandionidae (Osprey) & Accipitridae (Kites and Harriers)
18. Accipitridae (Kites)
19. Accipitridae (Kites and Hawks)
20. Accipitridae (Hawks)
21. Accipitridae (Hawks)
22. Accipitridae (Hawks)
23. Accipitridae (Eagles)
24. Falconidae (Kestrels, Falcons, and Caracaras)
25. Falconidae (Forest-falcons and Caracaras)
26. Rheidae (Rheas) & Tinamidae (Tinamous)
27. Tinamidae (Tinamous)
28. Tinamidae (Tinamous), Psophiidae (Trumpeters), Aramidae (Limpkin) & Opisthocomidae (Hoatzin)
29. Cracidae (Guans)
30. Cracidae (Chachalacas), Odontophoridae (New World Quails), Cariamidae (Seriema) & Chionidae (Sheathbill)
31. Cracidae (Curassows), Phasianidae (Junglefowl) & Numididae (Guineafowl)
32. Rallidae (Crakes and Rails) & Jacanidae (Jacana)
33. Rallidae (Crakes and Rails)
34. Rallidae (Wood-Rails, Gallinules, and Moorhens)
35. Rallidae (Coots), Eurypygidae (Sunbittern), Heliornithidae (Sungrebe), Haematopodidae (Oystercatcher), Recurvirostridae (Stilt), Burhinidae (Thick-knee), Glareolidae (Pratincole) & Thinocoridae (Seedsnipe)
36. Scolopacidae (Dowitchers, Godwits, Curlews, Yellowlegs, and Willet)
37. Scolopacidae (Turnstone, Sandpipers, and Redshank) & Charadriidae (Plovers)
38. Charadriidae (Plovers) & Scolopacidae (Phalaropes)
39. Charadriidae (Knot, Sanderling, and Sandpipers) & Scolopacidae (Ruff)
40. Rostratulidae (Painted-snipe), Scolopacidae (Snipes), Sternidae (Terns) & Rynchopidae (Skimmer)
41. Sternidae (Terns)
42. Sternidae (Tern) & Laridae (Gulls)
43. Stercorariidae (Jaegers and Skuas)
44. Columbidae (Ground-doves and Quail-doves)
45. Columbidae (Doves and Pigeons)
46. Psittacidae (Pigeons and Macaws)
47. Psittacidae (Macaws and Parakeets)
48. Psittacidae (Parakeets)
49. Psittacidae (Parakeets)
50. Psittacidae (Parakeets and Parrots)
51. Psittacidae (Parrotlets)
52. Psittacidae (Parakeets and Parrots)
53. Psittacidae (Parrots)
54. Psittacidae (Parrots)
55. Cuculidae (Anis, Cuckoos, and Ground-cuckoos)
56. Cuculidae (Cuckoos)
57. Strigidae (Screech-owls and Pygmy-owls)
58. Strigidae (Owls)
59. Strigidae (Owls), Tytonidae (Barn Owl), Nyctibiidae (Potoos) & Steatornithidae (Oilbird)
60. Caprimulgidae (Nightjars and Nighthawks)
61. Caprimulgidae (Nighthawks, Pauraque, Poorwill, and Nightjars)
62. Caprimulgidae (Nightjars) & Apodidae (Swifts)
63. Apodidae (Swifts)
64. Trochilidae (Hermits)
65. Trochilidae (Hermits and Barbthroats)
66. Trochilidae (Hermit, Lancebill, Sabrewings, Violet-ears, and Mangos)
67. Trochilidae (Jacobins, Woodnymphs, Sapphires, and Emeralds)
68. Trochilidae (Awlbill, Plovercrest, Hummingbird, Coquettes, and Thorntail)

Note: the plates in this book are mainly aimed at showing together similar-looking species or species from the same area or habitat, but are not based on an accepted sequence of species or a systematic classification in families. Yet it might be worthwile to mention that recently, based on DNA research, several genera were transported, for instance, from the familiy of Thraupidae to Cardinalidae, and from Emberizidae to Thraupidae. This is not yet reflected in the English names; therefore it might be possible that in the future, for example, the name of finches now placed in the family of the tanagers might be changed to "tanager-finches."

Preface and Acknowledgments

This book should be treated as a field guide in which the information needed to identify a bird at the moment you observe it is given in a condensed form. The book's low weight and compact size make it easy to carry around and consult in the field. Help in identifying difficult species can be found in more detailed regional bird books, which can be consulted at home or on the road. Sound recordings from commercial CDs and DVDs transferred to your iPod or other MP3 player can be an important supplementary aid in the field.

To compose a work like this single-handedly, you need the support and help of dedicated friends. I was very lucky to find people willing to coach me through the process of composing the book, comment on its structure, supply basic and additional information about the avifauna and geography of Brazil, send hundreds of reference photos, both of living birds and museum specimens, point out important websites, and suggest improvements, corrections, and additions to plates, maps, and draft text. It is, however, not their responsibility but mine if the book contains errors.

My heartfelt thanks go to Rasmus Bøgh in Denmark, my indefatigable supporter in every respect, who solved taxonomic puzzles, found difficult-to-trace articles, provided many photos, and supplied numerous contributions especially to the sections on identification features and habitats.

I am also extremely thankful to my Brazilian friends: to Fabio Olmos, who helped revise this guide with the support of the Wetlands Trust/UK and the Museu de Zoologia da Universidade de São Paulo (MZUSP), for his prompt, authoritative comments on draft text and plates and for the many photos of museum specimens and Brazilian landscapes; and to Fernando C. Straube and Alberto Urben-Filho, who sorted out systematic riddles and gave extensive suggestions for improvement of text and plates.

I thank Doug Stotz for his comments on my draft text and plates; Andy Foster, bird guide and owner of the Serra dos Tucanos lodge, who introduced me to the wonderful Brazilian bird world; Nicholas Locke, President of R.E.G.U.A. (Reserva Ecologica de Guapi Assu, which protects one of the last stands of tropical rainforest left in the severely depleted Atlantic Rainforest), whose help is greatly appreciated; and Bernard Geling, owner of the site www.birdsounds.nl, for his contributions.

Research was done at the British Museum of Natural History in Tring, where the support and assistance of the staff, especially of Robert Prys-Jones and Katrina Cook, was very helpful. In going through the collection in Tring, Krys Kazmierczak, my old friend from *A Fieldguide to the Birds of the Indian Subcontinent*, lent me a hand; his help and his other contributions to this work are very much appreciated.

I am also grateful to Peter J. Prescott, senior editor at Oxford University Press, who made the achievement of this work possible, and to Kaity Cheng, Alycia Somers, Tisse Takagi, editorial assistants, and to all the other people at Oxford University Press that I came into contact with for all their help and their patience with me.

Eu sou muito grato a Sra. Sonia Silva Maia de Cachoeiras de Macacu pela ajuda com as traduções para o português.

Last, but first in my heart, I thank Riet Nelen, my wife, who thought that—(now we have both retired) I would start working less, but who sees me doing more and yet endures with patience, support, and encouragement.

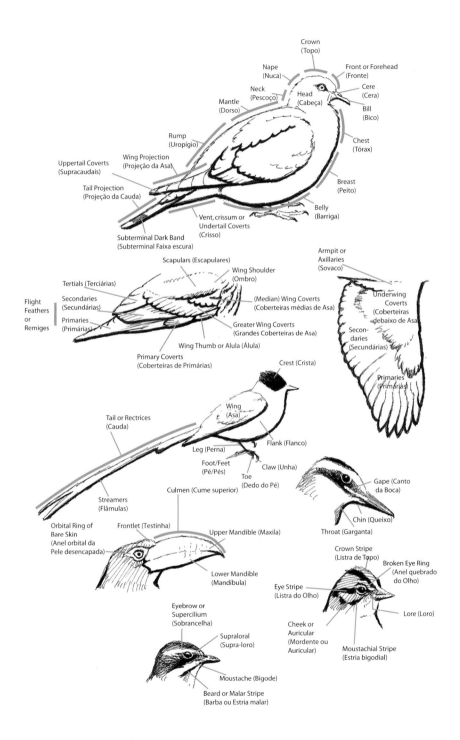

Crown
(Topo)

Nape
(Nuca)

Front or Forehead
(Fronte)

Neck
(Pescoço)

Cere
(Cera)

Mantle
(Dorso)

Head
(Cabeça)

Bill
(Bico)

Rump
(Uropígio)

Chest
(Tórax)

Wing Projection
(Projeção da Asa)

Uppertail Coverts
(Supracaudais)

Tail Projection
(Projeção da Cauda)

Breast
(Peito)

Vent, crissum or
Undertail Coverts
(Crisso)

Belly
(Barriga)

Subterminal Dark Band
(Subterminal Faixa escura)

Armpit or
Axillaries
(Sovaco)

Scapulars (Escapulares)

Wing Shoulder
(Ombro)

Tertials (Terciárias)

Underwing
Coverts
(Coberteiras
debaixo de Asa)

Flight
Feathers
or
Remiges

Secondaries
(Secundárias)

(Median) Wing Coverts
(Coberteiras médias de Asa)

Secon-
daries
(Secundárias)

Primaries
(Primárias)

Greater Wing Coverts
(Grandes Coberteiras de Asa)

Wing Thumb or Alula (Álula)

Primaries
(Primárias)

Primary Coverts
(Coberteiras de Primárias)

Crest (Crista)

Tail or Rectrices
(Cauda)

Wing
(Asa)

Leg (Perna)

Flank (Flanco)

Foot/Feet
(Pé/Pés)

Claw (Unha)

Toe
(Dedo do Pé)

Gape (Canto
da Boca)

Culmen (Cume superior)

Streamers
(Flâmulas)

Chin (Queixo)

Throat (Garganta)

Orbital Ring of
Bare Skin
(Anel orbital da
Pele desencapada)

Frontlet (Testinha)

Upper Mandible (Maxila)

Crown Stripe
(Lista de Topo)

Broken Eye Ring
(Anel quebrado
do Olho)

Lower Mandible
(Mandíbula)

Eye Stripe
(Listra do Olho)

Eyebrow or
Supercilium
(Sobrancelha)

Lore (Loro)

Supraloral
(Supra-loro)

Cheek or
Auricular
(Mordente ou
Auricular)

Moustachial Stripe
(Estria bigodial)

Moustache (Bigode)

Beard or Malar Stripe
(Barba ou Estria malar)

A FIELD GUIDE

TO THE

BIRDS OF BRAZIL

Introduction

1 BRAZIL: THE AREA COVERED

1.1 Country Profile

Brazil is a very large country—the world's fifth in surface area (3.3 million square miles or 8.5 million square km)—with a population of probably greater than 190 million (sixth largest in the world). Most people live in the eastern parts of the country, especially in the states of São Paulo and Rio de Janeiro. The federative republic of Brazil can be divided into five major regions (Sul, Centro-Oueste, Sudeste, Nordeste, and Norte) comprising 26 states and the Distrito Federal of Brasilia (figure 1).

FIGURE 1 Overview of Brazil

1.2 Biogeography

This paragraph gives a short overview of the factors that determine the presence and distribution of bird species in Brazil.

1.2.1 CLIMATE

Based on temperature and rainfall (figure 2), it is possible to distinguish several regions in Brazil with different climatic conditions.

Equatorial zone. In the equatorial zone in the north the annual average temperature lies between 24° and 27° C with little seasonal variation, while the annual average rainfall is high (> 3000 mm). In the eastern subregion (where the equator enters the country near Belém), the rainfall in the wet season (January–May) is 10 times higher (± 500 mm per month) than in the dry season (± 50 mm per month in September–November). In the western subregion (where the equator crosses the border with Columbia), the average rainfall per month is 275 mm throughout the year.

Tropical zone. The parts of the Amazon basin south and north of the equatorial zone have a tropical climate with a similar annual average temperature as the equatorial zone, but a somewhat lower average annual rainfall of 1500–2500 mm. This rainfall is not evenly distributed over the year: south of the equatorial zone there is a dry season (May–October) during which the large rivers return to their beds, to rise again in the wet season (December–May) to about 10 m above the dry-season level, flooding the surrounding forests. In the tropical climate zone north

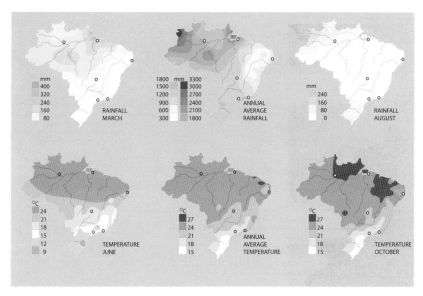

FIGURE 2 Climate in Brazil

of the equatorial zone at the border of Venezuela, the situation is different in that September–November is the dry season and April–June is the wet season.

Pantanal. In Pantanal the annual rainfall is 1500–2000 mm, with a pronounced dry season from May to October.

Central plateau. The central plateau can be subdivided in two parts: (a) the northeast, which is the driest area of the country, with annual rainfall less than 500 mm and temperatures that can rise above 40° C, (b) the grassy central area between the Pantanal and the dry northeast that has a dry "winter" from May to November with temperatures that are lower than those in the tropical zone and a wet, warm "summer" from November to March.

Coastal belt. The coastal belt along the Atlantic Ocean has the same average annual rainfall as the Pantanal, but the rain is evenly spread over the year, and there is also less variation in the average annual temperature, which is about 22–23° C.

Temperate zone. The Tropic of Capricorn crosses Brazil near São Paulo. The area south of this tropic lies in the temperate zone, with a distinct summer–winter rhythm. In the winter (June–July) the temperature can drop below 0° C at night, and in the mountains it might even snow; in the summer (January–March) the temperature can rise to above 35° C. The average annual rainfall of about 2000 mm is more or less evenly dispersed over the year.

1.2.2 GEOMORPHOLOGY

The topography of Brazil (figure 3) can be subdivided in two great plateaus and three plains.

Plateau of Guyana. The plateau of Guyana, north of the Amazon basin, embraces a loose array of table mountains, also known as *tepuis*. They include the Pico da Neblina, which with an altitude of 3014 m forms the highest peak in Brazil. The tepuis, survivors of erosion, form the watershed between the Orinoco and the Amazon.

Brazilian plateau. The Brazilian plateau, a tableland varying in altitude from 300 to 1500 m, is broken by low mountain ranges and cut by deep valleys. The edge of the plateau in the east rises steeply, forming an escarpment with several peaks of up to 2500 m or more.

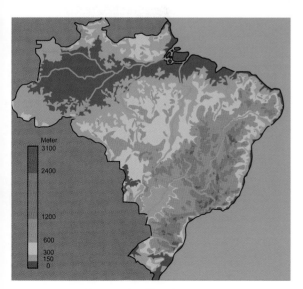

FIGURE 3 Topography of Brazil

FIGURE 4 Várzea and Terra Firme

Amazon lowlands. The Amazon lowlands lie between the Guyanan and Brazilian plateaus. This is a landscape of gently undulating hills, rarely rising to more than 150 m above sea level, crossed by many water courses that converge in the Amazon. Some of these, like the Amazon itself, are white-water rivers, thus called because of the suspended pale-colored mud particles from the Andes and other mountainous areas, from where they originate. Others, like the Rio Negro, are known as black-water rivers after their color of weak tea, brought about by decaying organic matter from lowland forests. Parts of the Amazon lowlands along the rivers are called *várzea* (figure 4); they are annually flooded north of the Amazon from April onward and south of the river from December. The higher parts above flood level are called *terra firme* ("solid ground"). Other small habitat subtypes in the lowlands are oxbow lakes (cut off river meanders) and wetlands.

Pantanal. The Pantanal, is a very large, gently sloping wetland area (150,000 km²) that floods in the wet season, when eventually up to 80% is covered with water. After the wet season the Pantanal dries out, and only a few small puddles in the lowest lying areas remain.

Coastal plain. The coastal plain, a belt along the Atlantic Ocean of up to 80 km wide in the south, widens to 200 km in the north and has a variety of habitat types such as lagoons with mangrove banks, protected from the ocean by sandstone and coral reefs, sand dunes, white-sand beaches, swamps, and *restinga*. This is however also the main area of settlement, containing Brazil's two largest cities, São Paulo and Rio de Janeiro.

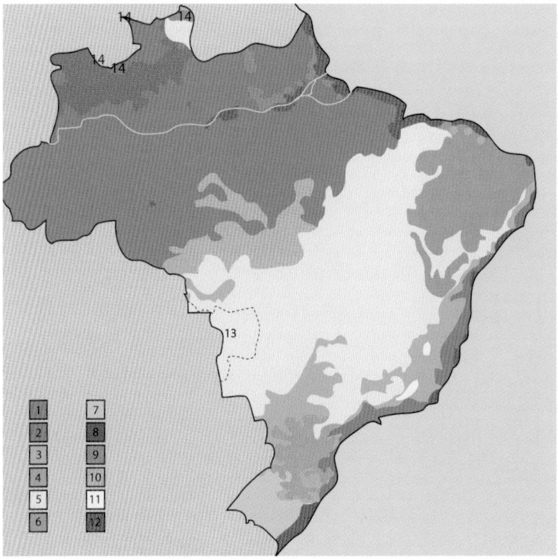

FIGURE 5 Natural Vegetation in Brazil

1.2.3 NATURAL VEGETATION

The natural vegetation of Brazil (figure 5) can be classified into 14 different types:

1. *Amazon rainforest* (figure 7C): various forest types united by high humidity and limited temperature variations. Exact timing of dry season varies. Large expanses remain but are being cleared rapidly.

2. *Atlantic tropical rainforest:* like the Amazon rainforest, but in a rather narrow belt along the Atlantic coast.

3. *Atlantic tropical seasonal forest:* occurs generally at elevations above 600 m. Seasonal forests are characterized by the loss of leaves by 10–60% of the tree species in the dry season. For both types of Atlantic forest, only 6% of the original range remains, mainly in national parks and other protected areas.

4. *Former araucaria forest* (figure 6B): almost wiped out and replaced by high-altitude crops and farms.

5. *Cerrado* (figure 8B): savanna; mosaic of grassland and woodland. Due to large-scale cutting of woodland, only parts of true *cerrado* remain.

6. *Caatinga* (figure 8A): dry woodland with numerous succulents (e.g., cacti).

7. *Southern campos:* grassy plains (often marshy) and hills with scattered bushes and trees.

8. *Campinaranas:* forest (often thorny) and savanna mosaics growing on poor soils. The large Rio Negro and Rio Branco campinaranas are shown on the map. Smaller areas of campinaranas exist elsewhere in the Amazon but are not shown on the map.

9. *Savanna–rainforest mosaic.*

10. *Savanna–rainforest–seasonal forest mosaic.*

11. *Alpine campos:* shrubby areas with low trees or bushes at high altitude above 1900 m.

12. Vegetation types of sea coast and river borders: (a) *Mangrove*—main areas indicated on the map, but locally as far south as Santa Catarina and along various rivers in the Amazon. (b) *Restinga* (not shown on the map)—woodland and scrub found locally in a narrow strip along the entire Brazilian coast.

13. *Pantanal* (figure 8C): Seasonal wetland (high-water season December–April).

14. *Tepuis* (figure 6A): table mountains with slopes covered in humid cloud forest, while the higher parts mainly have low, shrubby vegetation.

Some Notes *Terra firme* (figure 7D) is used to describe forests (mainly in the Amazon) that are never flooded. The trees are typically very high, forming a dense

FIGURE 6

(A) Tepui

(B) Araucaria angustifolia

(C) Atlantic Forest

FIGURE 7

(A) Cecropia

(B) Heliconia

(C) Bamboo Thicket

(D) Terra Firme

(E) Varzea (flooded)

FIGURE 8

TOP (A) Caatinga   **MIDDLE** (B) Cerrado

(C) Pantanal from the air

(D) Mauritia

canopy 30–50 m up. Relatively little light penetrates the canopy, resulting in relatively less life at lower levels. This situation changes dramatically when an old tree falls, leaving a light gap that is rapidly utilized by new plants. Species diversity is generally very high, but the majority of birds are only infrequently found below the subcanopy, except at the forest edge. Terra firme is very diverse (both locally and regionally), and exact borders between this and várzea can rarely be drawn. An important subhabitat that is common in terra firme are bamboo thickets (figure 7C) of species such as *Guadua*. These thickets are of great importance for a wide range of birds such as the Peruvian Recurvebill, Dusky-cheeked Foliage-gleaner, Bamboo Antshrike, and Manu Antbird. Bamboo thickets are typically found near clearings, forest edges, or light gaps, but they can also be seen in the interior. Bamboo thickets are generally not found in extensively flooded várzea, but some can survive low flooding. Bamboo thickets are also found in a wide range of non-Amazonian habitats, where species such as the Purple-winged Ground-Dove, Blackish-blue Seedeater, and Buffy-fronted Seedeater are associated with them. Large patches of bamboo often flower simultaneously, leading to the sudden appearance of relatively rare bamboo-associated birds (especially certain seedeaters), but this is a mixed blessing as the bamboo typically dies shortly after flowering.

Várzea (figure 7E) is forest that is periodically flooded, typically by white water. "White water" is used to refer to water that contains a high level of sediments and nutrients, resulting in it being rather muddy and murky. Depending on the type of sediments, it may appear almost whitish in color (as suggested by its name). For comparison, forest that is flooded throughout the year by stationary black water is called *igapó*. Black water contains relatively few sediments, is relatively poor in nutrients, and therefore often appears clearer. However, as suggested by its name, it is often stained dark, almost tea-colored, by leaves. In addition to stationary water that lacks the movements to pick up sediments, black water can be found in rivers that flow through white-sands regions. An example of this is the Rio Negro (as also suggested by its name). The water in this river originates in far northwestern Brazil and adjacent parts of Colombia and Venezuela. The soils in these regions are often dominated by white sands where nutrients rapidly are washed out by the rain, leaving relatively few sediments a river could pick up. The extensive areas of nutrient-poor white sands is also one of the explanations behind the large Rio Negro and Rio Branco campinaranas, as "typical" Amazonian trees are unable to grow on these soils. Várzea and igapó are generally not as species rich as terra firme, but a number of species are strictly found in these habitats. To minimize the risk of confusion, the term "várzea" in this book refers to any type of forest that is flooded.

Mauritia spp. (Moriche palm trees, figure 8D) are commonly seen in várzea. They can also be seen in a wide range of other habitats (e.g., the cerrado). They are very important for many birds such as the Point-tailed Palmcreeper, Moriche Oriole, Sulphury Flycatcher, and Red-bellied Macaw. Numerous other genera of palms exist in Brazil, of which one species, *Copernicia alba*, is among the commonest trees in the Pantanal.

Cecropia spp. (figure 7A) are distinctive trees with very large leaves. They are common along rivers and lakes in the Amazon (and in the Atlantic forest). They grow fast and are therefore also one of the first tall trees to emerge in the river island cycle (the first plants to dominate new river islands are dense grasses and bushes). Their large fruits are favored by many birds.

Many *Heliconia* spp. (figure 7B) exist, and the vast majority have striking red, orange, or yellow leafy flowers. Many hermit hummingbirds are associated with *Heliconia* ssp. Several commonly grow together in stands near forest edge, with hermits buzzing by regularly. Most other hummingbirds with relatively long bills will also feed on heliconias, but they are not as strongly associated with them as some of the hermits are.

2 BRAZIL: THE BIRDS

2.1 Classification and Names

Scientific and Portuguese names follow the first, second, and third list of the *Lista das Aves do Brasil* published by the Comitê Brasileiro de Registros Ornitológicos. Species on the second list (occurrence probable, but not yet sufficiently substantiated) are indicated in the text by placing their names in brackets, while species on the third list (occurrence suggested by various sources, but improbable) are preceded by a question mark. With a few exceptions (see, e.g., 126.9, 152.4, and 152.5), English names follow *A Classification of the Bird Species of South America* published by the SACC (South American Checklist Committee, list created by Sjoerd Mayer). Alternative English names are often mentioned. Sequence of families and species is more or less traditional, but adapted to include about 10 similar-looking species (sometimes from different families) in one plate.

2.2 Field Identification

2.2.1 PLATES

The 187 plates, each with up to 10 (rarely 11 or 12) species, show the birds in a more or less standardized stance. If the birds had been painted in more varied stances, the artistic value of the plates might have been greater, but standardizing the stance makes it easier to compare similar species. In general, the birds on any given plate are painted to the same scale, except flight silhouettes, which are normally shown smaller. If males and females have different visual features such as coloring or dimensions of body parts (e.g., tail length), both are illustrated, unless the differences are small (e.g., a slightly duller color in the female). Juveniles, immatures, and/or first-winter plumages are shown when the birds are often seen in these plumages. Nonbreeding plumages are shown if the birds may be seen as such in Brazil; migrants such as waders and wood warblers, which are normally seen in nonbreeding plumage, are shown in this plumage on the foreground of the plates. If several subspecies of a species occur in Brazil that differ by distinctive features, these are in many (but not in all) cases illustrated.

An effort has been made to show the birds in their typical "jizz"; what birders call jizz is a difficult-to-define combination of size, relative proportions, and body carriage of a bird. Part of a bird's jizz can be, for example, its stance (the angle of its body to a horizontal line).

2.2.2 CAPTIONS

The information for each species is given in this order:

1. *The English name* in bold capitals
2. *The Portuguese name* in parentheses
3. *The scientific name* in italics
4. *Length* in inches and centimeters, measured from tip of bill to tip of tail (L) or between the tips of spread wings (W)
5. *Identification notes* with emphasis on the main features, or those that are not visible in the plates (e.g., the color pattern of opened wings) or those that are most important for distinguishing it from similar species. Notes on behavior are sometimes added when important for identification.
6. *Habitat* (the preferred surroundings of a bird species) preceded by the symbol ♣; only simple terms are used, such as forest, woodland, marsh, plantations, savanna. There are, however, several habitats that are so specific that their identifying term could not been avoided; these are várzea, terra firme, caatinga, and cerrado (see section 1.2.3, "Natural Vegetation"). The habitat type "second growth" indicates a habitat that is developing at places where the original natural forest has disappeared. A "riverine belt" in this book is any growth along a river or stream that is richer in trees, bush, or other vegetation than its surroundings. The most lush form is tropical gallery forest, which resembles rainforest.
7. *Voice,* preceded by the symbol ♪; when possible, a distinction has been made between "call" and "song" as being the basic vocalizations of birds. "Call" is any short, probably unrestrainable sound given by a bird to indicate its presence to himself or other animals, and "song" is the modus in which a male (sometimes also a female) advertises its possession of a territory or its mood (anger, nervousness, contentment, togetherness). Only in a few cases is a further distinction, such as "flight call," "loud song,"

or "dawn song" given (many species sing only or mainly at or just before dawn, singly or in groups). The basic unit of a bird call or song in this book is called a "note" (so the transcription "wir-wir-wheer" has 3 notes). Attention is further paid to

- Pitch, using a subjective scale (very low, low, mid-high, high, very high, very/extremely high, extremely high), wherein "very low" and "extremely high" indicate vocalizations that are just or partially audible and "mid-high" indicates the normal pitch of an average man's voice if he uses his voice to try to imitate the vocalization

- Loudness, described as soft, weak, loud, ringing, and so on. Parts of transcriptions written in capitals are (much) louder

- Structure, described by terms such as accelerated, lowered, gliding, crescendo, and staccato

- Quality, described in terms of harsh, shrieking, mewing, and so on

- Length of a vocalization, which is given in seconds

- Speed, expressed in the number of notes per time unit (that which can be measured by a speedometer) and described as very slow, slow, calm, rapid, hurried, fast, very fast

- Tempo, which is defined by the "length" between the notes (i.e., what can be measured with a metronome) and indicated by terms such as almost-rattle, almost-trill, rattle, and trill and by the use of spaces (e.g., "peep peep peep" in which the notes are well separated), hyphens (e.g., "peep-peep-peep" in which the notes are almost connected, like when saying "red-billed"), or absence of spaces (e.g., "peeppeeppeep" in which the notes are uttered in one flow). An apostrope (as in the transcription "t'wooh" or "k'reeh") is used to indicate a small but just audible separation between the foregoing and following consonant. Note that hyphens in nonword descriptors are mainly used to aid readability (e.g., "rih-tjew-tjew-tjuh").

- Transcriptions. Though transcriptions are kept as simple as possible, it should be borne in mind that different people will transcribe bird vocalizations using different vowels and consonants (compare, for example, the way that different bird guides transcribe the chirping of a house sparrow). It is also true that differences exist between written and spoken text in different languages (Portuguese speakers will transcribe a sound differently from Dutch or English speakers).

  To keep transcriptions short, use is made of the indication "-" (as in "tjee tjee tjee -") when the foregoing note or group of notes is repeated 1–3 times. The indication "- -" within a transcription (as in "tjee tjee- - ronc-ronc") or at the end (as in "vrivri - -") means that the foregoing note or group of notes is repeated > 3 times; the indication "---" (without spaces, as in "tritritri---") indicates repetitions that are given in a high tempo.

The diacritic grave like in "rèh-rèh rèh" is used to indicate that the "e" sounds as the "e" in "red" and the "ò" sounds as the "o" in "pot"; an acute on a vowel like in "póor" indicates that that part of the vocalization is accented; capitalized parts are uttered (much) louder.

Note: You cannot expect to identify a bird solely on the basis of the description of voice in this or any book, but your identification based on other features (visual, behavior, habitat) can be supported by the description of voice.

For the description of voice in this book mainly use is made of tapes, CDs, DVDs, and of the voice recordings on the Web site http://www.xeno-canto.org/perc_map.php. For certain species voice is not described in the accounts if these sources did not provide sufficient information. For other species (such as migrants) it might contribute to identification to know that they are silent in Brazil; this is mentioned in the species accounts.

2.2.3 DISTRIBUTION MAPS

Information about range, seasonality, and occurrence can be an important aid to identification. In the distribution maps attention is paid to these factors, expressed in the following key:

KEY TO DISTRIBUTION MAPS (Chave dos mapas de Distribuição)	Resident	Austral "Summer"	Austral "Winter"	Transient	Chance of seeing species in its range and habitat	Symbol in text
Common to Frequent (Comum - Freqüente)	■	■	■		60 - 100%	
Frequent to Uncommon (Freqüente - incomum)	□	□	□		10 - 60%	
Uncommon to Rare (Incomum - raro)	□	□	□		Very small (Muito pequeno)	
Isolated Population or only a few records at indicated location (População isolada)	✳	✳	✳		Difficult to indicate (Difícil de indicar)	
Rare to Vagrant (Raro - viajante)		+	+		Negligible (Insignificante)	R
Hypothetical or questionable occurence (Acontecimento Hipotético)		?	?			?

Map sources:

- *Handbook of the Birds of the World* (del Hoyo et al., 1992–2007)
- *The Birds of South America* (Ridgely and Tudor, 1989, 1994), volumes 1 and 2
- The web site (http://www.xeno-canto.org/perc_map.php)
- The periodicals and journals *Revista Brasileira de Ornitologia* (formerly *Nattereria*), *Atualidades Ornithológicas*, *The Auk*, the *Bulletin of the British Ornothological Club*, and *Cotinga*
- Data supplied by Rasmus Bøgh and found in various site reports.

2.3 Endemism

An endemic is an organism that occurs only in an area with well-defined boundaries, such as a habitat, island, or country. So it is possible to distinguish the endemics of the Atlantic rainforest (a habitat type found in western Brazil, Northern Paraguay, and North Argentina) and the endemics of Brazil (a political unity). Among the bird species of Brazil there are 218 endemics in 30 families. These are listed in appendix 1, "The Endemics of Brazil," and indicated in the plate captions by their names being set in a blue font and the addition "En."

2.4 Short Introduction to Selected Bird Groups and Families

Section 2.4.1 describes some bird families and groups that occur in most or all continents of the world, and section 2.4.2 presents families and groups that are totally or largely restricted to the American continents. Numbers in **BOLDFACE** refer to plate numbers.

2.4.1 Worldwide Families and Groups

PETRELS, 1–6. Truly marine birds that only come to land to breed. Size between wingspans of > 3 m to < 40 cm. Most are soberly colored black, white, gray, and/or brown. Many but not all species follow ships. Often found at beach wrecks.

TROPICBIRDS, 6. Graceful birds from tropical waters. Normally fly at heights of 10 m above sea surface from where they plunge-dive for food.

BOOBIES AND GANNETS, 7. Seabirds with long pointed wings, tail, and bill. Perform spectacular plunge-dives.

FRIGATEBIRDS, 7. Skilful flyers with very large wings and a relatively small body. They take food from other seabirds or catch flying fish.

GREBES, 8. Waterbirds that only come to land to clamber to their nests.

CORMORANTS, 9. Eat fish, which are caught under water. Often seen drying their outstretched wings.

LARGE WADING BIRDS. Ibises, **9,** have a long decurved bill, used for probing in soft, wet ground for insects and crustaceans. Spoonbills, **12,** have straight, spatulated bills that are swept to and fro through the water surface to catch small prey. Herons, **10–12,** are long-necked and long-legged birds that fly with retracted neck. Storks, **12,** are large birds that fly and soar with extended necks. Flamingos, **13,** are characterized by their pink color and long, curved necks.

PELICANS, 13. Very large birds, best known for their pouch, which is used for catching fish.

DUCKS, GEESE, AND SWANS, 13–15. A varied group of birds, all with a broad bill and webbed feet.

OSPREY, 17. A rather large, white and blackish bird that hovers and plunges to catch fish.

RAPTORS. A very diverse group of diurnal predators, all with a hooked bill and claws. Two families exist: hawklike raptors (*Accaipitridae,* **17–23,** including, e.g., kites, harriers, buzzards, hawks, and eagles) and falcons and caracaras (*Falconidae,* **24–25,** including falcons, forest falcons, and caracaras).

RAILS AND COOTS, 32–35. Rails are secretive birds mainly of marsh and damp grass. Bodies are narrow and toes are long. Coots, **35,** forage on the water surface or graze openly.

GULLS AND TERNS. Gulls, **42**, are more robust and heavier billed than the more elegant, relatively longer-winged terns, **40–42**.

JAEGERS, 43. Strong seabirds, which predate other birds. Most species are characterized by a white flash in the wings.

WADERS. Include oystercatchers, **35** (noisy; long, heavy bills and legs), jacanas, **32** (extremely long toe nails), pratincoles, **35** (plover-like on ground, ternlike in flight), godwits, curlews, and allies, **36** (waders with long legs and bills), plovers, **37–38** (stop-and-run birds of mud and sand plains), sandpipers, **39** (walk or run, probing "tic-tic-tic" for food), phalaropes, **38** (found at the coast or out on the sea).

PIGEONS AND DOVES, 44–46. Heavy-bodied birds with small bills; arboreal or terrestrial; all with fast flight.

PARROTS, 46–54. Highly varied: from the large, splendid macaws, **46–47**, to the tiny, green parrotlets, **51**. All have a strong, hooked bill, fly fast, and are very social.

OWLS, 57–59. Birds of prey with forward-looking eyes. Normally, but not always, hunt at dusk or night.

SWIFTS, 62. Aerial, generally somber-colored birds, with sickle-formed wings and tiny feet (like hummingbirds). Not related to swallows.

TROGONS, 72. Sluggish, but very beautiful birds with a long tail and upright, hunched stance.

KINGFISHERS, 73. Characterized by a very long, heavy bill.

BARBETS, 76. Shortish birds, often in pairs, with beautiful colored plumage and a heavy bill.

WOODPECKERS, 81–85. Highly varied in size and coloring, but united by chisel-formed bill. Cling to bark, supporting themselves by the tail, except the tiny piculets, **81–82**.

PIPITS, 128. A group of very similar-looking species. Slender-bodied, long-tailed, and many with long nail to hind toe.

SWALLOWS AND MARTINS, 156–157. Aerial insect-catchers with graceful, often buoyant flight; many with blue gloss above.

THRUSHES, 160–161. Forage hopping on the ground, but sing from a high perch.

JAYS, 180. Noisy, intelligent, lively, and social birds with smart plumage, often with a crest.

SISKINS, 187. Small, striking yellow and black representatives in the Neotropics of a very large, worldwide group.

INTRODUCED SPECIES, 175. House Sparrow, from the Old World, Goldfinch and Greenfinch, from Europe, Waxbill, from Africa.

2.4.2 TYPICAL AMERICAN FAMILIES AND GROUPS

Only a handful of species that can be seen in the Neotropics also occur elsewhere in the World, such as the Black-crowned Night-Heron, **10**, Great Egret, **11**, Peregrine, **24**, some coastal waders, **35-39**, a few ducks, **14-15**, jaegers and skuas, **43**, gulls and terns, **40-42**, Barn Owl, **59**, Barn Swallow, **156**, Common Waxbill, **175**, House Sparrow, **175**, and a few other introduced species. In addition, there are many bird groups that do not occur north of Mexico, such as tinamous, screamers, trumpeters, hoatzin, potoos, motmots, jacamars, puffbirds, toucans, ovenbirds, wood-creepers, antbirds, antthrushes, antpittas, tapaculos, cotingas, and manakins. Following is a survey of these groups, which are restricted to or have their main distribution in the Neotropics.

In the text column, the (**BOLDFACED**) numbers indicate the plate numbers, the addition A indicates that the group or family occurs solely in America, and TA indicates that it only occurs in tropical America; the numbers in the thumbnail column refer to the numbers of the species on the plates.

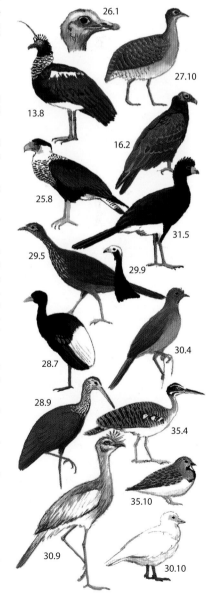

RHEA (**26**, TA) Large, gray bird resembling an ostrich.

TINAMOUS (**26-28**, TA) Shy, hunched, chickenlike, terrestrial birds; compactly built, almost tail-less with a rather long neck and small head. Vocal.

SCREAMERS (**13**, TA) Heavy-bodied birds with slightly webbed, large feet, small, crested heads on rather long necks and gray or blackish plumage.

NEW WORLD VULTURES (**16**, A) Large birds, mainly black or black and white, eating carrion.

CARACARAS (**24-25, 6**, A) A group of long- and broad-winged raptors, seen alone or in groups. As group related to true falcons.

GUANS (**29-31**, TA) Long-tailed and long-necked birds with relatively heavy legs. Mainly in forest and woodland. Curassows, **31**, are robust, mainly black or rufous forest birds with a swollen or otherwise accentuated bill base. The brownish to blackish guans, **29**, have a vivid red, naked throat. Piping-guans, **29**, are black with colorful dewlaps and white crests and wing-patches. The drab-brown chachalacas, **30**, have rufous in the tail and are less susceptible to hunting than the larger curassows and guans.

TRUMPETERS (**28**, TA) Beautiful, hunch-backed, terrestrial birds, mainly velvety black with iridescent neck feathers. Eat fallen fruits, large insects, small reptiles, and amphibians. Run fast.

LIMPKIN (**28**, A) An ibislike bird with long legs and neck and long, relatively heavy bill. Eats snails, which it seeks in marshes.

SERIEMA (**30**, TA) A terrestrial bird with long legs, long neck, and a frontal crest. Far-carrying call.

SHEATHBILL (**30**, TA) White, pigeonlike bird from southern areas, where it scavenges in mammal and penguin colonies.

SUNBITTERN (**35**, TA) A slim, long-billed, long-necked, and long-tailed bird that walks along forest streams. Unfolds a striking wing and tail pattern in flight or in display.

SEEDSNIPE (**35**, TA) Gregarious, terrestrial bird with long, pointed wings and relatively short tail. Mainly Andean in distribution, with only a single record from Brazil.

NEW WORLD CUCKOOS (55-56). Medium to large birds with long tails. Generally furtive, with a notable exception being the Squirrel Cuckoo.

ANIS (55, A) Gregarious, long-tailed cuckoos, breeding and raising young communally. Not shy.

GROUND-CUCKOOS (55, TA) Long-tailed, crested cuckoos. The three ground-cukoos are terrestrial, but the Striped, Pavonine, and Pheasant Cuckoo are mainly found in dense growth. All are elusive and, except for Striped Cuckoo, are rare. The Pavonine, Pheasant, and Striped Cuckoos are the only parasitic cuckoos in the Americas.

HOATZIN (28, TA) Peculiar bird with long, broad tail, long neck, and fierce, staring eyes. Lives in dense vegetation at water courses. Eats mainly leaves and shoots of mangroves. Noisy, rather tame; poor flyers.

OILBIRD (59, TA) Rufous-brown, nightjar-like bird, by day roosting and nesting in caves, at night feeding on fruits, sometimes very far from cave.

POTOOS (59, TA) Nocturnal and solitary birds that by day perch upright at the end of a branch or stump and are therefore very difficult to detect. Produce memorable, spooky vocalizations at night.

NIGHTHAWKS (60-61, A) **AND NIGHTJARS (60-62).** There is not a sharp division between nightjars and nighthawks. Nighthawks tend to have longer, more pointed wings and catch insects in active pursuit in the evening, whereas nightjars have rounder wing tips, larger heads, and longer tails and sally from a perch to catch passing insects at night. Only the Common Nighthawk is a vagrant outside the Americas.

HUMMINGBIRDS (64-71, A) No similar group of birds in the world (the superficially similar sunbirds of the Old World are not related and rarely hover). Two subfamilies: hermits, **64-66,** which are rather dull and congregate at loose leks, and typical hummingbirds, **66-71,** most of which (but not all) are tiny and have brilliant, iridescent colors. Highly accomplished fliers with tiny feet. Solitary and often aggressive, but many may gather at hummingbird feeders.

MOTMOTS (73, TA) Medium-sized, sluggish, bright-colored birds with a strong bill and a long tail, that often ends in raquets. May perch motionless for long periods in the forest subcanopy.

JACAMARS (74-75, TA) Attractive, bee-eater–like birds with long, pointed bills. They sally from perches to catch flying insects.

PUFFBIRDS (75-78, TA) Medium to small birds with relatively large heads and thick bills. Most are inactive, thickset, and with brownish or black-and-white plumage, but the more active and often gregarious nunbirds, **77,** and Swallow-wing, **76,** are mainly blackish.

TOUCANS, TOUCANETS, AND ARACARIS (79-80, TA) Medium to large bill with long tail. Not related to Old World hornbills.

PICULETS (81-82) Small, compact, mainly neotropical woodpeckers, which glean insects while clinging to and hopping over bark, twigs, and vines without support of their tail.

OVENBIRDS (TA) Three subfamilies: the terrestrial, short-tailed, brownish leaftossers, **100**, and miners, **91**, the typical ovenbirds, **90–100**, with an highly variable nest structure, as, for instance the distinctive, vaguely ovenlike, mud nests made by the horneros, **91.9** (for which these birds, and ultimately the family, are named) and the woodcreepers, **86–89**, a group of brownish, vaguely woodpecker-like birds. Bills of woodcreepers are often relatively long. Typically seen climbing on vertical tree-trunks using their long, pointed-tipped tails as support. Woodcreepers were previously placed in a family of their own.

ANTBIRDS (**101–117**, TA) A large, diverse group of arboreal to terrestrial species. Most are brownish, grayish, and blackish with darkish wing-coverts often tipped pale. The sexes of many species differ. No fixed rules exist, but the groups are roughly divided based on size, with antshrikes, **101–104**, typically being large and heavy-billed, antbirds, **111–117**, being intermediate, and antwrens, **105–110**, being the smallest. Some species are closely associated with swarming army ants. The two antpipits, **128**, are in the family *Tyrannidae*.

ANTTHRUSHES (**117–118**, TA) Inconspicuous but vocal birds that walk (not hop) the forest floor. Short tails commonly held cocked. Previously, the antpittas were included in this family.

ANTPITTAS (**119**, TA) Erect, short-tailed birds which run, walk or hop the forest floor on long legs. As antthrushes inconspicuous, more heard than seen.

GNATEATERS (**118**, TA) Small, roundish, long-legged birds, which feed on small insects. Found on or near the ground in densely vegetated areas in forest or woodland. Inconspicuous. ("Gnats" are a group of tiny to small insects, some of which with a painful bite.)

TAPACULOS (**120**, TA) Small, evasive, terrestrial birds, many with tail commonly held cocked. More heard than seen. *Scytalopus*-tapaculos, **120**, run like mice through low, dense vegetation and are very difficult to detect. Taxonomy very complex with several recently described species. The Bamboowren, **118**, and bristle-fronts, **120**, are tapaculos, but the Crescent-chest, **120**, is now placed in its own family.

TYRANT FLYCATCHERS (**131–151**, A) A huge, very diverse family, occurring in every possible habitat, except on water bodies. Dominating colors in most species are gray, brown, yellow, olive, or blackish, and many have spots, bars, or edging on wing-coverts. Most are fairly inconspicuous (with exceptions; e.g., kiskadees and kingbirds, **148**, monjitas, **146**, and Vermilion Flycatcher, **144**), and identification using visual features can be difficult (voice often useful). The two antpipits (which are tyrants in the conventional sense of the word) are shown in plate **128** next to the true pipits.

COTINGAS (121–124, TA) A very heterogenous group of extremely beautiful and/or bizarre-looking birds, though most females and in some cases both sexes are dull (e.g., the Screaming Piha, **124.2**). Some are essentially silent, but others have remarkable voices. A few form leks. The plantcutters, **124.1**, with their strange, serrated bill, are among the very few herbivorous birds.

MANAKINS (123–127, TA) Small, basically olive-green, short-tailed birds; males of many species, however, are brilliantly colored, and a few have elongated tail feathers. The males of many species perform delightful, communal dances at fixed places in the forest. Unlike the "typical manakins," the sexes are essentially identical in the tyrant-manakins, **127,** which are further characterized by quiet, upright perched stance. Included are also the piprites, **128,** thick-headed, large-eyed birds, often seen in mixed flocks.

TITYRAS, BECARDS, AND ALLIES (129–130, TA) A group of small- to medium-sized birds, previously spread over families *Tyrannidae, Cotingidae,* and *Pipridae.* Most are rather thickset. They are generally found at canopy level (Tityras, **129;** Purpletufts, **129**), the interior of forest (Schiffornis, **129;** Elegant Mourner, **130**), or both, including more open habitats (Becards, **130;** Xenopsaris, **130**).

VIREOS, GREENLET, PEPPERSHRIKE, SHRIKE-VIREO (154–155, A) Medium to small birds ranging from the warblerlike greenlets, **155,** and vireos, **154,** to the heavier-billed, thickset Peppershrike, **154.4,** and Shrike-Vireo, **154.5.** Except for the active greenlets, **155,** the members of this family are generally fairly slug-gish. Mainly from canopy to mid-level, although some species can be seen lower.

DONACOBIUS (158, TA) A single highly distinctive species, previously considered a wren or a mockingbird but now placed in a family of its own. Found in marshy and wet grassy areas. In pairs of small family groups. Very vocal.

MOCKINGBIRDS (161, A) Slender, long-tailed, thrushlike birds with mainly grayish plumage. Behave boldly and are good songsters.

WRENS (158–159, only one species in the Old World). A rather diverse group of birds, most with barred tail, wings, and/or under-parts, slender bills, and tail often held cocked. Many have very beautiful songs.

GNATCATCHERS (179, A) Small, slender, long-tailed birds with predominantly gray plumage and often with tail held cocked. Active insect gleaners in middle and higher strata at forest borders.

GNATWRENS (159, TA) Found in the undergrowth. Resemble wrens without barring.

WOOD WARBLERS (152–154, A) Attractive, small, lively birds of woodland or forest that forage in the canopy, lower strata, or on the ground. About half of the species in Brazil are migrants from North America.

TANAGERS (166–173, A) A large group consisting of small- to medium-sized, colorful and/or strikingly patterned species. Some are duller, being overall blackish, olive, or brown. Almost all are poor songsters and feed on insects, fruits, and nectar. The flowerpiercers, **178,** in Brazil are restricted to tepui highlands and have bills that are adapted to piercing flower bases to get at nectar. The dacnises, **176,** conebills, **178,** and long-billed honeycreepers, **176,** also belong in this family, but the "tanagers" of the genera *Piranga*, **173,** *Habia*, **173,** and *Mitrospingus*, **173,** were recently transferred to the next group of grosbeaks and saltators. Additionally, the Bananaquit (**173,** previously in monotypic family), *Paroaria* cardinals, **172,** and *Tiaris* grassquits (**173,** both previously in emberizine finches) are now considered members of the tanager family.

(A wide range of other more or less finchlike birds, which traditionally are placed in the family of emberezine finches, **181–187,** recently have been transferred to the tanager family. Therefore. it is possible that the English name will be changed to "Tanager-finches" in the future.)

CARDINAL (173, A). The only representative of this family is the Yellow Cardinal, **173.10.** Despite their names, the other cardinals, **172.6–10,** belong to the family of the tanagers.

SALTATORS (175, TA) Bills relatively thick. They are mainly black, gray, brown, olive, or blue, but a few are primarily yellow or red. Heads often distinctly patterned. Include the "tanagers" of the genera *Piranga*, *Habia*, and *Mitrospingus*, which have more normal bills and are primarily red, yellowish, olive, or brown.

EUPHONIAS AND CHLOROPHONIA (177–178, TA) Small, stubby-billed and thickset birds that previously were considered tanagers. The euphonias are predominantly blue-black and yellow (males) or yellow-olive (females). Chloroponia, **178.4,** is bright green, yellow, and blue. Generally fairly conspicuous.

EMBERIZINE FINCHES (181–187, A) A large group, varying in size and coloring. Most have conical bills, adapted to eat seeds. Most live in grasslands, a few in the understory of woodland and forest.

AMERICAN ORIOLES AND BLACKBIRDS (162–165, A) A group of birds with pointed bills and colors ranging from mainly black (often iridescent), over brown and olive, to pale gray-brown; many with yellow, orange, or red plumage parts. Some species are solitary, other colonial; many weave hanging, pouchlike nests for breeding, and others (**163.5–7**) are brood parasites. Many have distinctive voices.

Symbols, Abbreviations, and Glossary

♣	Habitat; a set of environmental factors that is preferred by a bird species (um conjunto de fatores ambientais, que é preferido por um pássaro)
♪	Vocalization (canto)
Basic (plumage)	The plumage of a bird outside the breeding period (a plumagem usada por um pássaro fora do período produzindo)
1st W	First basic plumage; the plumage of a juvenile in the 1st winter after hatching (primeiro plumagem básica; a plumagem de um juvenil no primeiro inverno após chocar)
2nd W	Second basic plumage; the plumage of a species in its 2nd winter (segunda plumage básica; a plumagem de uma espécie em seu segundo inverno)
1st S	Plumage in 1st summer after hatching (a plumagem no primeiro verão após chocar)
Br.	Breeding (produzindo)
N-br.	Nonbreeding (não-produzindo)
C	Central
cf.	Compare to (compare a)
En	Endemic; not occurring outside Brazil (não ocorrendo fora do Brasil)
esp.	Especially (especialmente)
extr.	Extreme, extremely (extremo, extremamente)
I	Introduced (introduzido)
Ad.	Adult (adulto)
Imm.	Immature (imaturo)
Incl.	Inclusive; including (inclusivo; incluir)
Juv.	Juvenile (juvenil)
L	Length in inches/centimeters (cumprimento no polegadas/centímetros)
♂	Male (macho)
♂♂	Males (machos)
♀	Female (fêmea)
♀♀	Females (fêmeas)
N, E, S, W	North(ern), east(ern), south(ern), west(ern); also in combinations (norte/do norte, leste, sul, oeste; também nas combinações)
Nom.	Nominate; the race of a species that was the first one described (a raça de uma espécie que foi a primeira a ser descrita)
Pl.	Plate (gravura)
R	Rare (garo)
Ri.	River (rio)
sec	Seconds

SL	Sea level
Ssp.	Subspecies (singular)
Sspp	Subspecies (plural)
V	Vagrant (nômade)
W	Wingspan in inches/centimeters (medida das asas abertas cumprimento no polegadas/centímetros)

Araucaria Large umbrella-shaped coniferous tree

Caatinga Dry woodland with cacti and other succulents

Cerrado Mosaic of grassland and woodland

Escapees Cage and water birds that have escaped from captivity and sometimes settle in the wild (os pássaros da gaiola e de água que escaparam do captiveiro e estabelecem-se às vezes no selvagem)

Forest A tall, multilayered habitat in which high trees dominate; the canopy is continuous and closed (um habitat multi-camadado em que árvores elevadas dominam e o dossel é contínuo e fechado)

Jizz Typical silhouette and stance of a species (silhueta típica e postura de uma espécie)

Lek Established place where males perform in ritual fights, dances, or/and in song contests to attract the attention of a female (lugar estabelecido onde os machos executam um ritual de lutas ritual, danças ou/e em competições da canções para atrair a atenção de uma fêmea)

Oxbow lake A cut-off meander of a river with stagnant water (um meandro de um rio com água estangada)

Restinga Woodland and scrub patches at the coast

Riverine belt Any growth along a river or stream that is higher and greener than the surroundings; a riverine belt that is dominated by trees is often called a gallery forest. (Qualquer crescimento ao longo de um rio ou córrego, que é mais elevado e mais verde do que dos arredores mais distantes)

Rufescent Tinged with red or rufous color (ligeiramente colorindo com cor vermelha ou vermelha marronzada)

Savanna In this book, any (large) area with a continuous cover of (high) grasses, interrupted by shrub and with a tree canopy of 5–30%. (qualquer área grande com uma cobertura contínua das gramas, interrompidas pelo arbusto e com um dossel da árvore pelo de 5–30%)

Second growth New natural forest developing in places where the original forest has disappeared (nova floresta natural desenvolvendo-se em lugares onde a floresta original desapareceu)

Speculum Patch of color on the wing contrasting with that of the rest of the wing (mancha na cor na asa que contrasta com a do resto da asa)

Taxon/taxa Systematic group(s): families, genus, species, subspecies (grupo sistemático, por exemplo família, gênero, espécie, raça)

Tepuis Mountains with flat tops (table mountains) at the border of Roraima with Venezuela

Terra firme Area above the highest flood level of Amazon rivers

Várzea Forest that is flooded in the Amazon wet season

White-sands Infertile tropical soil composed mainly of quartz sand and supporting a distinctive vegetation, varying from open savanna to closed forest, and characterized by many hard-leaved tree and other plant species, low diversity, and high endemism (solos tropicais inférteis compostos principalmente da areia de quartzo e suportam uma vegetação peculiar que varia do savanna aberto à floresta fechada, muitos caracterizado por árvores de folhagem dura e por outra espécie da planta, pela diversidade baixa e pelo endemism elevado)

Woodland A habitat in which trees dominate, but the canopy is not closed (um habitat em que as árvores dominam, mas o dossel não é fechado)

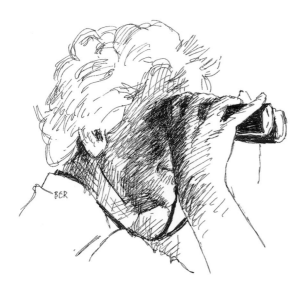

Plate 1

1.1 WANDERING ALBATROSS (Albatroz-gigante) *Diomedea exulans* W 130 in./330 cm. All albatross species are difficult to identify for two reasons: they often closely resemble each other (e.g., **1.1–1.4**) and they go through different color stages before attaining full Ad. plumage. **1.1** goes through at least 6 color stages, the last one often attained only after 16 years. In Brazil probably mainly Imms. are seen. Juv. is distinctively chocolate brown; in all other stages differs from **1.3** and **1.4** by lack of thin black line along cutting edge of bill. ♣ Offshore, accidentally at coast.

1.2 TRISTAN ALBATROSS (Albatroz-gigante) *Diomedea dabbenena* (Albatroz-de-tristão) W 130 in./330 cm. Can't be reliably separated from **1.1** in the "field," although the bill of some individuals can look positively shorter and stubbier compared to **1.1**. Ad. ♂ differs from Ad. ♀ by more solid black upperwings and less blotched body plumage. Juv. as Juv. **1.1** but grayer. Imm. shows blotchy body plumage. All age stages differ (like **1.1**) from **1.3** and **1.4** mainly by lack of thin black line along cutting edge of bill. ♣ Offshore.

1.3 NORTHERN ROYAL ALBATROSS (Albatroz-real-do-norte) *Diomedea sanfordi* W 130 in./330 cm. Not separable from **1.1** and **1.2** except by black line along cutting edge of bill. Head and underparts of Ad. as Ad. **1.4**, but upperwings are mainly dark. There is no brown Juv. plumage as for **1.1** and **1.2**. Molts directly into full Ad. plumage. Imm. plumage with some black on crown and with almost solid-black upperwings. ♣ Off coast, but keeps to shelf waters; follows ships. V.

1.4 SOUTHERN ROYAL ALBATROSS (Albatroz-real) *Diomedea epomophora* W 130 in./330 cm. Ad. head and underparts as **1.3**, but upperwings extensive white. Head of Imm. without black on crown. Note white flashes on upperwings of Imm. ♣ Keeps to shelf waters; accidently at coast. Follows ships.

1.5 SHY ALBATROSS (Albatroz-arisco) *Thalassarche* *cauta* W 98 in./250 cm. Very similar to **1.6**, but bill browner. Black underwing lining very narrow. Note diagnostic black patch where leading edge on underwing meets body. Imm. similar to Ad, except dark bill mark and some mottling to underwing. ♣ Offshore. V.

1.6 BLACK-BROWED ALBATROSS (Albatroz-de-sobrancelha) *Thalassarche melano-* *phris* (or *melanophrys*) W 90 in./225 cm. From **1.5** by broad underwing lining, esp. along leading edge. Juvs. (seen far more than adults) have all-dark underwings. ♣ Fairly abundant at southern coast.

Plate 2

2.1 YELLOW-NOSED ALBATROSS (Albatroz-de-nariz-amarelo) *Thalassarche chlororhynchos* W 79 in./200 cm. Less hooded than slightly larger **2.2**; also differing by narrower dark rims to underwing and lack of yellow edge to lower mandible. Note slender wings. Imm. shares all-black bill with Imm. **2.2** but always has white underwing as shown by adult. ♣ Offshore, normally not seen along the coast.

2.2 GRAY-HEADED ALBATROSS (Albatroz-de-cabeça-cinza) *Thalassarche chrysostoma* W 87 in./220 cm. Cf. **2.1**. Distinctive gray hood and broad black margins to underwing diagnostic. Juv. shows more or less uniform black underwings, which become in immature stages progressively white, streaked with black. ♣ Offshore. V.

2.3 LIGHT-MANTLED ALBATROSS (Piau-de-costas-claras) *Phoebetria palpebrata* W 85 in./215 cm. Unmistakable by elongated jizz, angled wings, and pale mantle. Also cf. **2.4**. Flies fast on bended, angular wings. Pale stripe along lower mandible is pale bluish, but yellowish in **2.4** (only visible at very close range). ♣ Offshore. V.

2.4 SOOTY ALBATROSS (Piau-preto) *Phoebetria fusca* W 79 in./200 cm. Jizz as **2.3**, but mantle always same color as wings; in Juv. stage and in worn plumage neck can become pale, but always distinctly separated from dark mantle. Juvs. of **2.3** and **2.4** lack white stripe on lower mandible and don't have white primary shafts. ♣ Offshore. V.

2.5 SOUTHERN (or Antarctic) **GIANT-PETREL** (Petrel-gigante) *Macronectes giganteus* W 77 in./195 cm. Size of an albatross but with shorter, broader wings, massive bill, and different, characteristic hump-backed jizz. In most plumages resembles **2.6** and therefore often not safely separable; only white-headed (**a**) and all-white (**b**) forms safely identifiable as Southern Giant-Petrel. Note difference in coloring of bill tip, greenish in this species and pinkish in following species, but this feature not always distinctive. Dark brown form exists. All-black Imm. (not separable from Imm. **2.6**) becomes progressively paler blotched. Color of eyes varies, probably depending on age and on individual and/or geographical variation. As **2.6** with heavy flight on stiff wings in glides, interspersed with 4–5 flaps. ♣ Open sea, seashore, harbors. Follows ships. R.

2.6 NORTHERN (or Hall's) **GIANT-PETREL** (Petrel-gigante-do-norte) *Macronectes halli* W 75 in./190 cm. Brown form (**a**) and pale form (**b**) shown. No pure white form known and normally not with distinctive white head as **2.5**. ♣ As **2.5**.

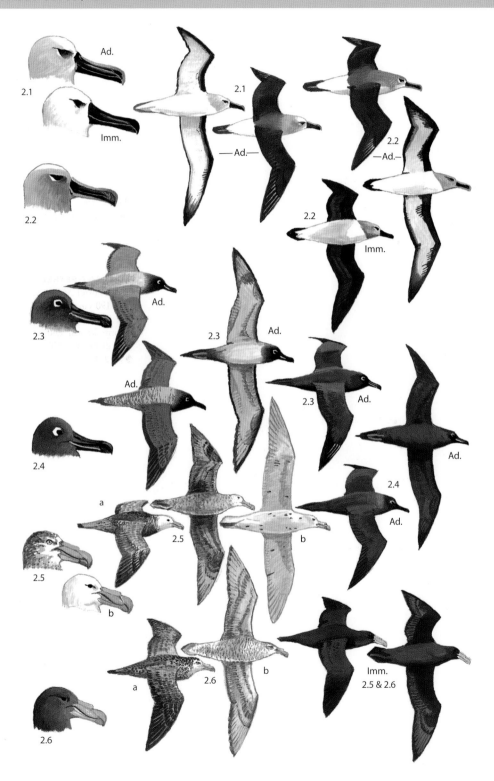

Plate 3

3.1 BROAD-BILLED PRION (Faigão-de-bico-largo)

Pachyptila vittata W 23.6 in./60 cm. Prions are very difficult to separate; bill width is not a reliable field mark. From **3.2–3.4** by massive head, steep forehead, broad bill; slightly darker than **3.2–3.4**; flight slower and less erratic. ♣ Offshore. V.

3.2 DOVE (or Antarctic) **PRION** (Faigão-rola) *Pachy-*

ptila desolata W 23.6 in./60 cm. Bill width midway between that of **3.1** and **3.4**. Flight fast, erratic, and high over water with glides and bursts of wing beats. ♣ Open sea. R.

3.3 SLENDER-BILLED PRION (Faigão-de-bico-fino)

Pachyptila belcheri W 23.6 in./60 cm. Paler plumaged than **3.1**, **3.2**, and **4** with less distinct M-mark over wings (darkest part round scapulars and across rump). Sides of slender bill (when seen from above) bent inward. Gregarious. ♣ Open sea; occasional wrecks along most of Brazilian coast; has been found, for instance, on the beach at Marajó Island, mouth of the Amazon.

3.4 ? FAIRY PRION (Faigão-de-bico-curto) *Pachyptila*

turtur W 22 in./55 cm. Note broad black tail band and restricted gray at breast sides. Flight low over sea with shallow wing beats. ♣ Open sea. (Probably not in Brazil.)

3.5 MAGELLANIC DIVING-PETREL (Petrel-mergul-

hador-de-magalhães) *Pelecanoides magellani* W 13.8 in./35 cm. Vibrant flight low over sea, but normally seen swimming and diving, resembling small penguin. ♣ Offshore. V.

3.6 CAPE (or Pintado) **PETREL** (Pomba-do-cabo)

Daption capense W 33.5 in./85 cm. Unmistakable by pattern on upperparts. ♣ Offshore. Follows ships.

3.7 KERGUELEN PETREL (Grazina-de-bico-curto)

Lugensa (or *Aphrodroma*) *brevirostris* W 31.5 in./80 cm. Flies fast on narrow wings, may arch to great heights. Note silvery reflections on underwing. Characteristically thick necked. ♣ Offshore. R.

3.8 BLUE PETREL (Petrel-azul) *Halobaena caerulea*

W 23.6 in./60 cm. From **3.1–3.4** by conspicuous white tip of tail and black marks on face. ♣ Offshore.

Plate 4

4.1 GREATER SHEARWATER (Bobo-grande-de-sobre-

branco) *Puffinus gravis* W 43 in./ 110 cm. *Puffinus* species (**4.1–4.6**) have long, thin, black bills. This species is distinctively marked by dark cap, pale horseshoe rim to uppertail coverts, and darkish belly patch. From **5.1** by more distinct underwing pattern and black bill. Strong flight with powerful slow wing beats and long glides, occasionally banking close to surface. ♣ May occur in large flocks along coast in spring and autumn; occasionally wrecks on coast from NE Brazil south to Paraná.

4.2 SOOTY SHEARWATER (Bobo-escuro) *Puffinus gri-*

seus W 39 in./100 cm. Note slim posture and distinctive underwing pattern. Agile, fast flight; alternating long glides with strong wing beats. ♣ Occasionally in loose flocks during southern winter. R.

4.3 SHORT-TAILED SHEARWATER (Bobo-de-cauda-curta) *Puffinus tenuirostris* W 37 in./95 cm. Very similar to **4.2**, but bill generally shorter, forehead steeper, and head slightly more hooded. Underwing grayer, but much overlap with **4.2**. ♣ In 2007 a beach-washed specimen was found in Bahia. (No map.) V.

4.4 MANX (or Common) **SHEARWATER** (Bobo-

pequeno) *Puffinus puffinus* W 31.5 in./ 80 cm. From smaller **4.5** by more pointed wings, less narrow borders to underwing, uniform black upperwings. Flies with stiff wing beats, alternating with long glides. ♣ Offshore in N winter.

4.5 [LITTLE SHEARWATER (Pardela-pequena) *Puffi-*

nus assimilis] W 23.6 in./60 cm. May concern ssp. *elegans* from Tristan da Cunha group, accounting for some records off SE and S Brazil. This ssp. is quite distinctive and is considered as a full species in some taxonomic arrangements. It has silvery gray upperparts, white lower parts, cap reaching the eye. and white-edged upperwing coverts. Flight is characterized by more wing flapping in longer series than **4.4**.

4.6 AUDUBON'S SHEARWATER (Pardela-de-asa-

larga) *Puffinus lherminieri* W 27.5 in./ 70 cm. Flight is with more glides than **4.4**. Difficult to distinguish from larger **4.4**, which has more pointed wings. Most (but not all) birds have dark vent and the cap reaches to the eye. Note also incomplete breast band. ♣ Nests on Fernando de Noronha; at sea there are records S to São Paulo and N Paraná. ♪ Nervous twittering and croaking at colony.

4.7 [BULWER'S PETREL (Alma-negra) *Bulweria bul-*

werii] W 25.5 in./65 cm. Note characteristic jizz with long wings held well forward. Striking wing bars. Buoyant flight, normally not higher than 2–3 m above sea surface. ♣ Off coast; generally does not follow ships.

4.8 GRAY PETREL (Pardela-cinza) *Procellaria cinerea*

W 47 in./120 cm. *Procellaria*-petrels (**4.8–4.10**) have mid-long, distinctively "fragmented" bills. Note uniform pale brown upper- and underwings and bulky jizz with relatively short wings. Flies with long, effortless glides, interspersed by a few shallow wing beats. ♣ Off coast. Follows ships. V.

4.9 WHITE-CHINNED PETREL (Pardela-preta) *Procel-*

laria aequinoctialis W 55 in./140 cm. White chin difficult to see. Large and bulky with long wings, uniform black with silvery reflections to underwings. Powerful flight, slow wing beats, alternating with long glides. ♣ Offshore, but might be seen closer to coast. Follows ships.

4.10 SPECTACLED PETREL (Pardela-de-óculos) *Pro-*

cellaria conspicillata W 57 in./145 cm. From **4.9** by facial markings. Powerful flight interspersed with slow wing beats and glides. ♣ In flocks offshore, often over deeper and warmer waters than **4.9**. Follows ships.

Plate 5

5.1 CORY'S SHEARWATER (Bobo-grande) *Calonectris*

diomedea W 45 in./115 cm. Probably concerns ssp. *edwardsii* Cape Verde Shearwater. Large, grayish brown jizz; long bill yellow-ochraceous with dark tip. Note scalloped pattern of upperparts, esp. of scapulars. Often soars rather high; also long glides close to water surface. ♣ Open sea, but occasionally near coast.

5.2 SOUTHERN FULMAR (Pardelão-prateado) *Ful-*

marus glacialoides W 45 in./115 cm. From gulls by compact build, wing pattern (lacking black at wing tips), flight behavior (long glides on stiff, straight wings, interspersed by short series of rapid wing beats). ♣ Open sea. Follows trawlers.

5.3 HERALD PETREL (Grazina-de-trindade) *Ptero-*

droma arminjoniana W 37 in./95 cm. Underparts vary from dark (**a**) to pale (**b**). Note typical black bill, shared with **5.4–5.9**. Rather uniform brown above. Underwings with large white patch at base of primaries, normally extending to base of secondaries. Unlike most other seabirds diurnal, hence easily observed near breeding grounds. Long glides interspersed with some calm, deep wing beats. Rarely follows ships. ♣ Breeds on Ilha Trindade. R.

5.4 GREAT-WINGED PETREL (Fura-bucho-de-cara-

cinza) *Pterodroma macroptera* W 37 in./95 cm. Uniform brown with paler patch at base of primaries. From other all-dark petrels (except **5.3**) by lack of white primary shafts on upperwings. ♣ Offshore. R.

5.5 WHITE-HEADED (or -hooded) **PETREL** (Grazina-

de-cabeça-branca) *Pterodroma lessonii* W 43 in./110 cm. Unmistakable by size, white head and tail, M-mark across upperwings. Very strong flight. May inspect ships. ♣ Offshore. R.

5.6 SOFT-PLUMAGED PETREL (Grazina-mole)

Pterodroma mollis W 35.5 in./90 cm. Pale (**a**) and dark (**b**, even rarer than **a**) forms shown. Resembles **5.5** and prions (**3.1–3.4**), but with different tail coloring and paler M-mark across wings. Rather compact, with bulging forehead. ♣ Open sea. R.

5.7 [BLACK-CAPPED PETREL (Grazina-de-coroa-

preta) *Pterodroma hasitata*] W 37 in./ 95 cm. Unmistakable by white collar and rump. Note underwing pattern. ♣ Offshore.

5.8 KERMADEC PETREL (Petrel-de-kermadec) *Ptero-*

droma neglecta W 35.5 in./90 cm. Dark (**a**) and pale (**b**) forms shown, both characterized by white flash on upperwing formed by primary shafts. Head paler than mantle, often almost white. ♣ Offshore.

5.9 ATLANTIC (or Hooded) **PETREL** (Grazina-de-

barriga-branca) *Pterodroma incerta* W 41 in./105 cm. Striking white belly, sharply demarcated from dark brown plumage parts. Wings uniform blackish brown. Strong and fast flight, often with 1–2 beats at peaks of glides. May follow ships ♣ Open sea. R.

Plate 6

6.1 WILSON'S STORM-PETREL (Alma-de-mestre) *Oceanites oceanicus* L 6.7 in./17 cm. From similar dark-bellied **6.3** and **6.6** by less angled, more straightly held wings, more distinctive wing bars, and slightly protruding feet. Is capable of long, sustained glides on stiff, flat wings. ♣ Open sea, occasionally in flocks.

6.2 WHITE-FACED STORM-PETREL (Painho-de-ventre-branco) *Pelagodroma marina* L 7.9 in./20 cm. Unmistakable by facial pattern, rather pale plumage, rounded wings, and long dangling legs. Sails low over sea on stiff, flat wings. ♣ Offshore. R.

6.3 [BAND-RUMPED STORM-PETREL (Paínho-da-ilha-da-Madeira) *Oceanodroma castro*] L 7.9 in./20 cm. Most similar to **6.6**, but tail less forked and shape of rump-patch different. Flies with sharp twists and short glides. ♣ Offshore.

6.4 BLACK-BELLIED STORM-PETREL (Painho-de-barriga-preta) *Fregetta tropica* L 7.9 in./20 cm. Normally with broad black band from breast over belly to vent (as shown); there is, however, much variation in underparts, which may vary between almost completely dark to almost all-white; ssp. *melanoleuca* (from island Cough in southern Atlantic; not shown) is all-white below. ♣ Offshore. V.

6.5 WHITE-BELLIED STORM-PETREL (Painho-de-barriga-branca) *Fregetta grallaria* L 7.9 in./20 cm. Not safely separable from ssp. *melanoleuca* of **6.4**, but differing by nonprotruding feet and paler upperparts. Note absence of distinctive paler wing bar in **6.4** and **6.5**. ♣ Open sea. Follows ships. R.

6.6 LEACH'S STORM-PETREL (Painho-de-cauda-furcada) *Oceanodroma leucorhoa* L 7.9 in./20 cm. Note rather large size and long, arched wings. Strong flyer; powerful wing beats interspersed with short glides. ♣ Offshore, occasionally inshore.

6.7 RED-BILLED TROPICBIRD (Rabo-de-palha-de-bico-vermelho) *Phaethon aethereus* W 41 in./105 cm. Adults (**6.7–6.9**) unmistakable, Imms. differ in bill color and pattern of outerwings. ♣ Offshore over warm seas. Nests only on Fernando de Noronha and Abrolhos islets (Bahia); likely to be seen only near those islands.

6.8 RED-TAILED TROPICBIRD *Phaethon rubricauda* W 41 in./105 cm. Cf. **6.7**. ♣ Warm seas. Only one record from Abrolhos islets (southern Bahia). V.

6.9 WHITE-TAILED TROPICBIRD (Rabo-de-palha-de-bico-amarelo) *Phaethon lepturus* W 35.5 in./90 cm. Cf. **6.7**. ♣ Offshore over warm seas. Nests mostly on Fernando de Noronha, only a few birds in Abrolhos.

Plate 7

7.1 AUSTRALASIAN GANNET (Atobá-australiano)

Morus serrator W 67 in./170 cm. Very difficult to separate from **7.2**, but Ad. and Imms. always show some white tail feathers, while black throat stripe is half as long as shown for **7.2**. Juv. paler, esp. its head. ♣ Normally at open sea. V.

7.2 CAPE GANNET (Atobá-do-cabo) *Morus capensis*

W 65 in./165 cm. Ad. and Imms. normally with black tail feathers. Throat stripe (see **b**) much longer than that of **7.1**. Normally at open sea. V.

7.3 MASKED BOOBY (Atobá-grande) *Sula dactylatra*

W 59 in./150 cm. From larger **7.1** and **7.2** by different wing pattern (black running from wing tip to body). Imm. with white neck collar. ♣ Open sea; approaches some capes and other coastal points.

7.4 BROWN BOOBY (Atobá-pardo) *Sula leucogaster*

W 55 in./140 cm. Ad. unmistakable by all-dark head and neck. Note in Imm. absence of white rump and uppertail coverts. ♣ Near islands, beaches, and rocks.

7.5 RED-FOOTED BOOBY (Atobá-de-pé-vermelho)

Sula sula W 59 in./150 cm. White-tailed white form (**a**, uncommon) and white-tailed brown form (**b**, most common) shown. All-brown form and white-headed, white-tailed brown form (rare in Brazil) not shown. The dark-tailed, white form does not occur in Brazil. ♣ Offshore. Nests only on Fernando de Noronha.

7.6 MAGNIFICENT FRIGATEBIRD (Tesourão) *Fregata magnificens*

W 90 in./230 cm. Frigatebirds are difficult to identify. Most common (**7.6**) is largest species; ♂ shows all-dark upperwings; ♀ often with white freckling in armpit; Juv. normally without white running up into armpit. ♣ All along coast, but best seen near breeding colonies on Fernando de Noronha, Abrolhos, and several islands off Rio, São Paulo, and Paraná. Largest South Atlantic colony in Alcatrazes (São Paulo), with > 6.000 birds. ♪ Nasal cackling at colony.

7.7 ? ASCENSION FRIGATEBIRD (Tesourão-de-ascensão) *Fregata aquila*

W 79 in./200 cm. ♀ ♀ in all-dark (**a**) and in partly white (**b**) forms. ♂ and ♀ (**b**) not safely separable from **7.6**. Young, normally with collar closed over breast, are quite variable and may have more rufous than pictured in the plate. Adults of both sexes have horn-colored bills, which are however very rosy on the sides. ♣ Rarely seen more than 150 km from Ascension. (Improbable record.)

7.8 GREAT FRIGATEBIRD (Tesourão-grande) *Fregata minor*

W 85 in./215 cm. Note pale wing bar of ♂; no white to underparts. Note white chin of ♀; Juv. not safely separable from other frigatebirds. ♣ Now restricted to Ilha da Trindade, where extr. R.

7.9 LESSER FRIGATEBIRD (Teoursão-pequeno) *Fregata ariel*

W 73 in./185 cm. ♂ with characteristic white bars in armpits. ♀ not safely separable from ♀ ♀ **7.6** and **7.7**; Juv. not separable from Juv. **7.8**. ♣ Now restricted to Ilha da Trindade, where extr. R.

Ad.

Imm.

7.1

Ad.

Imm.

7.2

b

Juv.

Juv.

7.3

Imm.

7.5

a

b

Imm.

7.3

7.4

7.4

Imm.

♂

♀

7.8

♀

Imm.

7.5

Imm.

♀

♂

Imm.

7.6

♀

Imm.

7.9

♂

♂

7.7

♀ b

Imm.

♀ a

Imm.

♂

Plate 8

8.1 KING PENGUIN (Pingüim-rei) *Aptenodytes patagonicus* L 37.5 in./95 cm. Unmistakable by size, bill shape, and head pattern. ♣ Found once on the beach. V.

8.2 MAGELLANIC PENGUIN (Pingüim-de-magalhães) *Spheniscus magellanicus* L 27.5 in./ 70 cm. Unmistakable by black and white bands across chest and upper breast. ♣ Incidentally found in flocks near coastline, even invading bays. R.

8.3 MACARONI PENGUIN (Pingüim-de-testa-amarela) *Eudyptes chrysolophus* L 27.5 in./ 70 cm. Plumes connected across forehead. Note white tail base. ♣ Occasional wanderer to coast. V.

8.4 ROCKHOPPER PENGUIN (Pingüim-de-penacho-amarelo) *Eudyptes chrysocome* L 23.6 in./60 cm. Note yellow line over eyes and plumes sprouting from behind eyes. No white tail base. ♣ Occasionally found dead on the coast. V.

8.5 LEAST GREBE (Mergulhão-pequeno) *Tachybaptus* *dominicus* L 9.8 in./25 cm. Small and compact. Yellow eyes diagnostic. ♣ Any water body with floating vegetation, sheltered ponds, quiet rivers; often together with **8.7**. ♪ Call: nasal gabbling in chorus; also occasionally a very or extr. high "fih."

8.6 WHITE-TUFTED GREBE (Mergulhão-de-orelha-branca) *Rollandia rolland* L 11.8 in./ 30 cm. Note white sides of face contrasting with black crown, throat, and neck, visible from long distance. Underparts and flanks rufous. ♣ Lakes, streams, marshes, ponds.

8.7 SILVERY GREBE (Mergulhão-de-orelha-amarela) *Podiceps occipitalis* L 9.8 in./25 cm. Small, red-eyed, and with silvery gray plumage. Black stripe through middle of nape visible from long distance. ♣ Open water, even at the sea coast. V.

8.8 PIED-BILLED GREBE (Mergulhão-caçador) *Podilymbus* *podiceps* L 13.8 in./35 cm. Unmistakable by heavy bill. Note absence of bill ring in N-br plumage. ♣ Sheltered ponds of any size, lake margins with floating vegetation, quiet rivers. ♪ Usually silent; occasional nasal cackling in hurried series of low "weh" and "cah" notes.

8.9 GREAT GREBE (Mergulhão-grande) *Podiceps major* L 23.6 in./60 cm. Unmistakable by jizz with long thin neck. ♣ Any larger water body, in winter even in sea (surf line). ♪ Call: high "keh kah" in series.

8.1

8.2 Imm.

8.3

8.4

8.5 N-br.

8.6 N-br.

8.7

8.8 N-br.

8.9 N-br.

Plate 9

9.1 ANHINGA (Biguatinga) *Anhinga anhinga* L 33.5 in./ 85 cm. Unmistakable by size, jizz, wing pattern, and plumes hanging from scapulars and back. ♣ Any calm water in woodland. ♪ Call: varied; e.g., series of low, froglike grunts.

9.2 NEOTROPIC CORMORANT (Biguá) *Phalacrocorax* *brasilianus* L 25.6 in./65 cm. Unmistakable by jizz and overall blackish coloring. Note white line, accentuating beak corner. ♣ Any fresh or saline water. ♪ Generally silent; low grunts at nest.

9.3 ANTARCTIC SHAG (Biguá-das-shetland) *Phalacro-* *corax bransfieldensis* L 29.5 in./75 cm. Marine. Unmistakable by color pattern. Larger than **9.2**. ♣ Remains found once in Bahia. V.

9.4 SCARLET IBIS (Guará) *Eudocimus ruber* L 23.6 in./ 60 cm. Unmistakable. Imm. also shown in flight. ♣ Mangroves and nearby mud flats. ♪ Usually silent; occasionally very low, nasal "orgh" or "ac-ac."

9.5 BARE-FACED (or Whispering) **IBIS** (Tapicuru-de- cara-pelada) *Phimosus infuscatus* L 21.5 in./55 cm. Very slender jizz. From **9.6** in flight by legs not projecting beyond tail. ♣ Shallow water, marshes with nearby open habitats, incl. newly plowed fields. ♪ Call: high "wuh-wurup" in irregular series.

9.6 WHITE-FACED IBIS (Caraúna-de-cara-branca) *Plegadis chihi* L 21.5 in./55 cm. Wings with green reflections diagnostic. Legs project beyond tail in flight. White facial outline is not present outside Br season. ♣ Marshes and other habitats with shallow water such as ricefields. ♪ Call: low, nasal, croaking "rèh-rèh rèh."

9.7 SHARP-TAILED IBIS (Trombeteiro) *Cercibis oxy- cerca* L 27.5 in./70 cm. No other ibis with such long tail. ♣ Open grassy areas near rivers, marshes, lakes. ♪ Call: mid-high "tut tuterup tut tot tuterup" (as from toy trumpet) or, in flight, repeated, drawn-out "tuuut - -"

9.8 PLUMBEOUS IBIS (Maçarico-real) *Theristicus caer- ulescens* L 29.5 in./75 cm. Note large size, pale eyes, and shaggy neck feathers. ♣ Marshes. ♪ Call: often in duet; high, rapid, nasal "tutututu-tut---"

9.9 BUFF-NECKED IBIS (Curicaca) *Theristicus caudatus* L 27.5 in./70 cm. Unmistakable. ♣ Dry open areas, including burnt ground and air fields. Very common in campos in Pantanal and southern Brazil. ♪ Call: falsetto "cree cree-cru" in flight; high, rapid, nasal/hoarse "crucrucru- -" in chorus at roost.

9.10 GREEN IBIS (Coró-coró) *Mesembrinibis cayen- nensis* L 21.5 in./55 cm. No other similar large black bird with down-curved bill in Brazil. Note striking manes and iridescent green neck feathers. ♣ Lagoons, forest streams, marshes, and muddy pools in and at woodland. ♪ Call: low, hollow roaring as if starting a moped.

9.1

♂

♀

Br.

Imm.

N-br.

9.2

N-br.

Br.

9.3

N-br.

Br.

Imm.

9.4

Imm.

Imm.

9.9

N-br.

9.6

9.5

9.10

9.7

9.8

Plate 10

10.1 LEAST BITTERN (Socoí-vermelho) *Ixobrychus exilis* L 11.8 in./30 cm. Unmistakable by small size and plumage pattern. From **10.2** by pattern of back and more extensive blackish crown. ♣ Freshwater marshes. ♪ Call: low, soft "róar" or "póor."

10.2 STRIPE-BACKED BITTERN (Socoí-amarelo) *Ixobrychus involucris* L 13.8 in./35 cm. Striping of back diagnostic. ♣ Reed beds, sedges, long grass. ♪ Call: mid-high, nasal "who" and low "wow."

10.3 PINNATED BITTERN (Socó-boi-baio) *Botaurus pinnatus* L 25.6 in./65 cm. Note rufous-streaked foreside of neck (not barred as Imm. **10.9** and **10.10**) and contrasting dark flight feathers when flying. ♣ In tall vegetation in and at freshwater and brackish marshes, lagoons, inundated grassland, rice fields, ditches. ♪ Call/song: low "woo woo woo woo - -" in slightly irregular series (about 3 ×/2 sec).

10.4 ZIGZAG HERON (Socoí-zigue-zague) *Zebrilus undulatus* L 11.8 in./30 cm. From **10.9** and **10.10** by very small size and compact build. ♣ Dense vegetation under tree cover at streams, lagoons, and other water bodies. ♪ Call/song: high, forcefully exhaled "ooh" at 3- to 4-sec intervals.

10.5 BLACK-CROWNED NIGHT-HERON (Savacu) *Nycticorax nycticorax* L 23.6 in./60 cm. Ad. unmistakable; Imm. differs from Imm. **10.6** by shorter legs and yellower bill. ♣ Wooded edges of fresh waters, but also in mangrove. ♪ Call: high, rather barking "wuc-wur worc - -" in flight.

10.6 YELLOW-CROWNED NIGHT-HERON (Savacu-de-coroa) *Nyctanassa violacea* L 23.6 in./60 cm. Unmistakable. Note long legs of Imm. ♣ Mainly at coastal waters, in mangrove, occasionally at fresh waters. ♪ Call: hoarse, throaty "wur wur - -."

10.7 BOAT-BILLED HERON (Arapapá) *Cochlearius cochlearius* L 19.7 in./50 cm. Unmistakable. Note large, dark eyes. ♣ Same habitat as **10.6**. ♪ Call: accelerating and decelerating series of mid-high, froglike "rac-rac-rac---" notes.

10.8 STRIATED HERON (Socozinho) *Butorides striata* L 15.7 in./40 cm. Unmistakable; mostly seen with retracted neck. Note streaking below of Imm. ♣ Near any water body with some fringing vegetation, but can also been seen on the open sea shore. ♪ Generally silent, but when flushed might utter, sharp, slightly hoarse "tjuw."

10.9 FASCIATED TIGER-HERON (Socó-boi-escuro) *Tigrisoma fasciatum* L 25.6 in./65 cm. From **10.10** by distinctive barring of upperparts and rufous lower belly and vent. Imm. not safely separable from Imm. **10.10**. ♣ Fishes from rocks in or at fast-running mountain streams.

10.10 RUFESCENT TIGER-HERON (Socó-boi) *Tigrisoma lineatum* L 27.5 in./70 cm. Ad. with no or little barring. ♣ In forest near streams, ponds, swamps. ♪ Call: low, barking "wrof-wrof- -." or "wuf."

10.1

10.2

10.3

Ad.

Imm.

10.4

Imm.

10.5

10.6

Imm.

10.7

Imm.

Imm.

10.8

Imm.

10.9

Imm.

10.10

Plate 11

11.1 WHISTLING HERON (Maria-faceira) *Syrigma sibi-* *latrix* L 21.5 in./55 cm. Unmistakable; note red, black-tipped bill and golden finely streaked wing coverts. ♣ Grasslands, fields, rice plantations. ♪ Call: series of joined, high, reedy/fluted "tueeeh" notes.

11.2 TRICOLORED HERON (Garça-tricolor) *Egretta* *tricolor* L 25.6 in./65 cm. Unmistakable by very slender jizz and striking white underparts. ♣ Mangrove and other wet habitats near coast. ♪ Generally silent, but might utter low, nasal, complaining "uuuh" notes in series.

11.3 LITTLE BLUE HERON (Garça-azul) *Egretta caeru-* *lea* L 25.6 in./65 cm. Ad. all darkish blue; white Imm. differs from other white herons by greenish legs and pinkish bill. ♣ Any fresh and saline water with some fringing vegetation; also on tidal mud flats. ♪ Generally silent.

11.4 SNOWY EGRET (Garça-branca-pequena) *Egretta* *thula* L 23.6 in./60 cm. Note full bushy crest and very yellow lores. Yellow of feet often runs up the backside of legs. ♣ Fresh and brackish waters, shores, coast, mud flats. ♪ Generally silent, but might utter low "gwa-gwa."

11.5 GREAT EGRET (Garça-branca-grande) *Ardea alba* L 37.5 in./95 cm. Note size. Black feet diagnostic. ♣ At marshes, lake edges, river margins, estuaries, mud flats. ♪ Call: may utter very low, belching "burr."

11.6 LITTLE EGRET *Egretta garzetta* (Garça-branca-* pequena-européia) L 23.6 in./60 cm. Note bluish lore in N-br plumage. In Br plumage differs from slightly smaller **11.4** by thin plume (only two feathers). Forehead less steep than that of **11.4**. ♣ Normally in swamps and marshes with some open water. V.

11.7 WESTERN REEF HERON *Egretta gularis* L 23.6 in./ 60 cm. Dark form (**a**) and head of white form (**b**) shown. White chin of dark form diagnostic. Note in white form heavy bill with yellowish lower mandible ♣ Rocky shores and reefs. All-white birds have been recorded in Fernando de Noronha. ♪ Generally silent. V.

11.8 CATTLE EGRET (Garça-vaqueira) *Bubulcus ibis* L 19.7 in./50 cm. Br plumage unmistakable. Compacter build than other white herons. Feeds very characteristically at feet of cattle, catching the flushed insects. ♣ Normally associated with cattle. ♪ Generally silent.

11.9 SQUACCO HERON (Garça-caranguejeira) *Ardeola* *ralloides* L 17.7 in./45 cm. Striking difference between white silhouette in flight and cryptic coloring when perched. ♣ Vagrant from Eurasia, where it occurs in reedy vegetation near water. Several records (including a number of birds together from Fernando de Noronha). V.

11.10 CAPPED HERON (Garça-real) *Pilherodius pileatus* L 21.7 in./55 cm. Unmistakable by black cap. ♣ Near wood patches at shallow waters, marshes, river edges. ♪ Generally silent.

11.1

Imm.

11.2

Imm.

11.3

N-br.

11.5

Br.

N-br.

11.4

N-br.

Br.

11.7

a

b

11.8

Br.

N-br.

Br.

11.9

N-br.

N-br.

11.10

Plate 12

12.1 GREAT BLUE HERON (Garça-azul-grande) *Ardea*

herodias L 47 in./120 cm. Dark (**a**) and white (**b**) forms shown. Intermediate forms (e.g., with only white head and neck) are possible. ♣ May be found at any type of fresh or saline water. In Brazil so far only seen in the Anavilhanas Archipelago. ♪ Call: low, raucous "fraaah." V.

12.2 GRAY HERON (Garça-real-européia) *Ardea cinerea*

L 39 in./100 cm. From larger **12.1** by white, not rufous thighs. From **12.3** by purple-gray, not white, neck and white forehead and streak through crown. ♣ Vagrant from Europe, where seen in grasslands near water, in marshes, and in other open country. ♪ Call: sudden, high "wrah." V.

12.3 COCOI (or White-necked) **HERON** (Garça-moura)

Ardea cocoi L 43 in./110 cm. White neck of Ad. diagnostic. Imm. shows striking resemblance with Ad. **12.2** but note white crown of Ad. **12.2**. From Imm. **12.2** by blacker crown (but probably not safely separable). ♣ Marsh, river edges. ♪ Call: deep "vrah" in flight.

12.4 PURPLE HERON (Garça-roxa) *Ardea purpurea*

L 35 in./90 cm. Unmistakable by coloring, slender jizz, and secretive behavior. Note brownish-gray plumage of Imm. ♣ Vagrant from Europe, where occurs in large marshes. V.

12.5 AGAMI (or Chestnut-bellied) **HERON** (Garça-da-mata)

Agamia agami L 29.5 in./75 cm. Ad. unmistakable by dark colors except striking white stripe down throat, broadening to breast. Note rufous stripe down throat of Imm. ♣ Forest streams and swamps. ♪ Call: very low "wuh wuh -" and "wudrdrdr."

12.6 WOOD STORK (Cabeça-seca) *Mycteria americana*

L 37.5 in./95 cm. Unmistakable by white plumage, bare gray head and neck, and heavy bill. Note black primaries and secondaries in flight. Gregarious. Perches in trees. ♣ Wooded marsh, mangrove. ♪ Normally silent.

12.7 MAGUARI STORK (Maguari) *Mycteria americana*

L 47 in./120 cm. Unmistakable by size, yellow eyes, and black-and-white plumage. ♣ Wet areas with tall vegetation.

12.8 JABIRU (Tuiuiú) *Jabiru mycteria* L 51 in./130 cm.

Unmistakable by red collar and large size. ♣ Open woodland at edges of rivers and lakes. ♪ Normally silent.

12.9 ROSEATE SPOONBILL (Colhereiro) *Platalea ajaja*

L 31.5 in./80 cm. Unmistakable by pink plumage and bill shape. ♣ Mangrove, wet woodland, muddy beaches. ♪ Call: low, barking grunts.

12.10 EURASIAN SPOONBILL (Colhereiro-europeu)

Platalea leucorodia L 33.5 in./85 cm. Unmistakable by shape and coloring of bill. ♣ Vagrant from Europe to Ilha Fernando de Noronha. V.

12.1 a b

12.6

Imm.

12.7

12.2 Imm.

12.3 Imm.

Imm.

12.4

12.8

12.5 Imm.

12.9

12.10

Plate 13

13.1 ? AMERICAN WHITE PELICAN (Pelicano-branco) *Pelecanus erythrorhynchos* L 55 in./ 140 cm, W 270 cm. Unmistakable by white plumage with black flight feathers. Very large. ♣ Normally found at open, rather shallow water. (Improbable record.)

13.2 BROWN PELICAN (Pelicano-pardo) *Pelecanus occi-* *dentalis* L 49 in./125 cm, W 79 in./ 200 cm. Unmistakable by coloring and bill shape. ♣ River mouths. V.

13.3 GREATER FLAMINGO (Flamingo) *Phoenicopterus* *ruber* L 51 in./130 cm. Largest of the four flamingo species, differing from **13.4** by uniform pink legs and from **13.6** by larger, differently patterned bill. ♣ Wide, brackish shallow lakes and lagoons. ♪ Low gabbling in groups when feeding; gaggling in flight.

13.4 CHILEAN FLAMINGO (Flamingo-chileno) *Phoe-* *nicopterus chilensis* L 39 in./100 cm. Note the contrasting pink leg joints. ♣ Prefers brackish shallow lakes and lagoons. Can be found almost year-round in Lagoa do Peixe (Ri. Grande do Sul). ♪ Call: very low "goorc." R.

13.5 ANDEAN FLAMINGO (Flamingo-grande-dos- andes) *Phoenicopterus andinus* L 43 in./ 110 cm. Characterized by yellow legs and large black area, visible in folded wings. ♣ Rare winter visitor in brackish shallow waters. V.

13.6 PUNA FLAMINGO *Phoenicoparrus jamesi* (flamin- go-da-puna) L 35 in./90 cm. Note small size, black eyes, small bill, dark, uniform pink legs. ♣ High montane areas. There is only one record of this flamingo in Brazil, coming from Acre. Either an escapee or a very lost bird. V.

13.7 SOUTHERN SCREAMER (Tachã) *Chauna torquata* L 31.5 in./80 cm. Corpulent, large legs, fluffy plumage. Gregarious. Note white-and-black collar. As **13.8** with white underwing coverts. ♣ Grassland, wet savanna, marsh. Perches in trees. ♪ Call: very high or falsetto "we-weeér" (2nd part steeply upslurred); song: often in duet; loud, resounding, falsetto, drawn-up shrieks.

13.8 HORNED SCREAMER (Anhuma) *Anhima cornuta* L 31.5 in./80 cm. Unmistakable by general jizz and color pattern. Note thin quill. White underwing coverts. ♣ Marsh, wet savanna, swamps, and ponds in forest. ♪ Call: low "ong!"; song: series of excited, hurried, muffled yet far-carrying "UH-who" vocalizations in excited duets.

13.9 COSCOROBA SWAN (Capororoca) *Coscoroba* *coscoroba* L 39 in./100 cm. Unmis- takable by large size, white plumage, and pink bill. ♣ Lakes and lagoons. ♪ Call; high, nasal "wút wr-hawa"; may also be transcribed as "cós- co-roba."

13.10 BLACK-NECKED SWAN (Cisne-de-pescoço- preto) *Cygnus melanocoryphus* L 47 in./ 120 cm. Unmistakable. ♣ Shallow fresh and brackish marshes. ♪ Gen- erally silent.

13.7

13.8

13.1

Ad.

13.2

Imm.

13.2

Br.

N-br.

Imm.

13.3

13.5

13.6

13.4

13.9

13.10

Plate 14

14.1 BLACK-BELLIED WHISTLING-DUCK (Asa-

branca) *Dendrocygna autumnalis* L 19.7 in./50 cm. Whistling-ducks (**14.1–14.3**) are characterized by their upright stance. Sp. **14.1** unmistakable by pink bill and legs and by white in wings. Crepuscular. ♣ Open, shallow water, large marshes. ♪ Call: very high, fluted, mellow or sharp "tuweé" (2nd part stressed).

14.2 WHITE-FACED WHISTLING-DUCK (Irerę) *Den-*

drocygna viduata L 17.7 in./45 cm. Unmistakable by head pattern. ♣ Marsh, flood plains. ♪ Call: very high, thin, whistled "swée-wee-lee."

14.3 FULVOUS WHISTLING- (or Tree-) **DUCK**

(Marreca-caneleira) *Dendrocygna bicolor* L 19.7 in./50 cm. Distinctive by sickle-shaped flank feathers, barred back, white uppertail coverts, and black collar. ♣ Wet, low grassland, flood plains. ♪ Call: very high, sharp, whistled "feee-ih" and very high, musical, wheezy, twittering, like "pitpit-weeÉH-pitpit."

14.4 ORINOCO GOOSE (Pato-corredor) *Neochen jubata*

L 21.5 in./55 cm. Unmistakable by dark wings and whitish head and neck. ♣ Rocky beaches. ♪ Call: typical, gooselike gaggling "wukwuk-OOOR-OOOR-wuk wuk - -." R.

14.5 MASKED DUCK (Marreca-de-bico-roxo) *Nom-*

onyx dominicus L 13.8 in./35 cm. This and **14.6** unmistakable by compact jizz, strong bill, and often—when swimming—by cocked tail. From **14.6** by back streaks, rufous hindcrown, and white wing speculum. ♣ Marsh, flood plains, secluded ponds.

14.6 LAKE DUCK (Marreca-pé-na-bunda) *Oxyura vit-*

tata L 15.7 in./40 cm. Cf. **14.5**. ♣ Lakes; open water in marshes. ♪ Generally silent.

14.7 MUSCOVY DUCK (Pato-do-mato) *Cairina*

moschata L 31.5 in./80 cm (♂), 25.5 in./65 cm (♀). Unmistakable. Escapees are "fatter," heavier, have white at other places (head, neck, and/or underparts) than only at upper- and underwing and normally have more warts. Amount of white on wings of wild birds varies (♀ ♀ sometimes have no white, and Imms. never do). ♣ Any water (including marsh) in woodland or forest. ♪ Generally silent.

14.8 AMERICAN COMB DUCK (Pato-de-crista)

Sarkidiornis sylvicola L 27.5 in./70 cm (♂), 24 in./60 cm (♀). Unmistakable, esp. ♂; as in **14.7** the ♀ is significant smaller than ♂. ♣ Marshes in open or wooded country. ♪ Generally silent. *Note:* by SACC treated as ssp. of Comb Duck *S. melanotos.*

14.9 ROSY-BILLED POCHARD (Marrecão) *Netta*

peposaca L 21.5 in./55 cm. ♂ unmistakable; note in ♀ peaked crown, dark cheeks, whitish vent. ♣ Well-vegetated lakes and marshes in open country. ♪ Generally silent.

14.10 SOUTHERN POCHARD (Paturi-preta) *Netta*

erythrophthalma L 17.7 in./45 cm. Dark ♂ normally unmistakable, esp. if chestnut flanks and red eyes can be seen; note facial pattern of ♀. ♣ Rather deep fresh and saline waters. ♪ Generally silent.

14.11 BRAZILIAN MERGANSER (Pato-mergulhão)

Mergus octosetaceus L 21.5 in./55 cm. Unmistakable; differs from cormorants by white in wings. ♣ High-country rivers with rapids. ♪ Call: low (or mid-high), barking "wrah" in slow series. R.

14.1

Imm.

14.1

14.2

14.3

14.4

14.5

♀

14.6

♀

14.7

♀

14.8

♀

14.9

♀

14.10

♀

14.11

Plate 15

15.1 RINGED TEAL (Marreca-de-coleira) *Callonetta leucophrys* L 11.8 in./30 cm. Unmistakable by general color pattern and small size. Note pattern of ♀ face sides. ♣ Marshes, ponds, lagoons in woodland, flooded forest. ♪ Generally silent.

15.2 BRAZILIAN TEAL (Pé-vermelho) *Amazonetta brasiliensis* L 15.7 in./40 cm. Unmistakable by red bill of ♂ and facial pattern. Note triangular white speculum at rear of wing in flight and characteristic spots on breast sides. ♣ Among vegetation in lakes, ponds, pools. ♪ Call: in flight, very high, sweet, fluted "fweé-tje" or "wu-wít" (stressed 2nd part much higher).

15.3 CHILOE (or Southern) **WIGEON** (Marreca-oveira) *Anas sibilatrix* L 19.7 in./50 cm. Unmistakable by color pattern, size, white rump, and white forewing. ♣ Prefers open country with scattered lakes; also along streams and ponds in woodland. ♪ Call: very high, rather sharp babbling, like "wuut-wuut-wuutwut - -."

15.4 BLUE-WINGED TEAL (Marreca-de-asa-azul) *Anas discors* L 15.7 in./40 cm. ♂ is unmistakable by white crescent in front of eyes; ♀ very similar to ♀**15.5**, but shows more distinct eye stripe and has less spatulated bill. ♣ Ponds, marshes, flood plains. ♪ Generally silent, but might utter very high, thin "fjit fjit - -" in flight. V.

15.5 CINNAMON TEAL (Marreca-colorada) *Anas cyanoptera* L 15.7 in./40 cm. ♂ unmistakable; for ♀ cf. **15.4**; both have rather spatulated bill (similar to **15.6**). ♣ Shallow water with emergent vegetation. ♪ As **15.4**. V.

15.6 RED SHOVELER (Marreca-colhereira) *Anas platalea* L 19.7 in./50 cm. Unmistakable 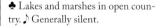 by shape of bill. Note pale eye of ♂. ♣ Lakes and marshes in open country. ♪ Generally silent.

15.7 SPECKLED TEAL (Marreca-pardinha) *Anas flavirostris* L 15.7 in./40 cm. Like larger **15.10**, but flanks hardly speckled. Wing pattern different, showing one buff and one white stripe. ♣ Marshes, lakes, ponds, streams, rivers. ♪ Call: very high, clear, whistled "preep."

15.8 WHITE-CHEEKED PINTAIL (Marreca-toicinho) *Anas bahamensis* L 13.8 in./35 cm. Unmistakable by bicolored head and pointed white tail. ♣ Fresh and saline waters. ♪ Generally silent.

15.9 NORTHERN PINTAIL (Arrabio) *Anas acuta* L 23.6 in./60 cm (♂), 21.7 in./55 cm (♀). Note elegant, slender jizz. Br ♂ unmistakable, N-br ♂ from ♀ by gray, black-bordered bill. Note unmarked head of ♀. ♣ Ponds, lakes, marshes, estuaries. ♪ Call: mid-high, nasal "uhh uh-uh-uh - -," given by ♀. V.

15.10 YELLOW-BILLED PINTAIL (Marreca-parda) *Anas georgica* L 23.6 in./60 cm. From smaller **15.7** by pointed, not rounded, tail feathers. ♣ Lakes, rivers, marshes, estuaries, coastal waters. ♪ Call: sudden, very high "tjew!"

15.11 SILVER TEAL (Marreca-cricri) *Anas versicolor* L 15.7 in./40 cm. From smaller **15.7** by flank barring and bill color. ♣ Shallow pools and ponds in open country. ♪ Call: high, mellow, hurried, fluted "wit t'weérwih."

15.12 BLACK-HEADED DUCK (Marreca-de-cabeça-preta) *Heteronetta atricapilla* L 13.8 in./35 cm. Rather featureless, but with distinctive jizz (long body, thick neck); note pink spot at bill base of Br ♂. ♣ Lakes, marshes, pools with fringing vegetation in open country. ♪ Generally silent.

15.1 ♀

15.1

15.2

15.2 ♀

15.3

15.3 ♀

15.4 ♀

15.4

15.5 ♀

15.5

15.6 ♀

15.6 ♀

15.7

15.7

15.8

15.8

15.9   ♂ N-br.   ♂ Br.   ♀

15.9 ♀

15.10

15.10   15.11   15.12

15.11

15.12 ♀

Plate 16

16.1 BLACK VULTURE (Urubu-de-cabeça-preta) *Cora-* *gyps atratus* W 57 in./145 cm. Characterized by gray, naked head and upright stance; 6 outer primaries mainly white. Flight on flat wings, steady, without rocking, in glides, interspersed by a few wing flaps. ♣ Any type of country (including towns and refuse dumps) except true forest. ♪ Usually silent.

16.2 TURKEY VULTURE (Urubu-de-cabeça-vermelha) *Cathartes aura* W 75 in./190 cm. Stance more horizontal than **16.1**; flight mainly gliding, rocking from side to side, the wings held in a shallow V shape. Coloring brown-black, naked skin of head red (this obscured in Imm.). ♣ More or less wooded country, rarely in forests. ♪ Usually silent.

16.3 LESSER YELLOW-HEADED VULTURE (Urubu- de-cabeça-amarela) *Cathartes burro-vianus* W 23.6 in./60 cm. Very similar to larger **16.2**, but blacker with head mainly yellow, black stripe through eye, and in flight with more distinct white shafts of primaries. Note that wings tips normally exceed tail length. Soars and glides on wings held in V shape. ♣ Wooded grassland, marsh, river margins. ♪ Usually silent.

16.4 GREATER YELLOW-HEADED VULTURE (Uru- bu-da-mata) *Cathartes melambrotus* W 83 in./210 cm. Very similar to distinctive smaller **16.3** with wing tips reaching tail tip. Soars on flat wings (unlike **16.3**). Note the long tail and the diagnostic dark primaries, contrasting with paler secondaries in flight. Bluer face than **16.3**. ♣ Lowland forest with adjacent grassland. ♪ Usually silent.

16.5 KING VULTURE (Urubu-rei) *Sarcoramphus papa* W 75 in./190 cm. Unmistakable by colorful head and black-and-white plumage. Note the short tail (of Ad. and Imm.), giving triangular flight silhouette. ♣ Prefers forest away from settlements, but may wander to more open areas. ♪ Usually silent.

16.6 [ANDEAN CONDOR (Condor-dos-andes) *Vultur* *gryphus*] W 118 in./300 cm. Unmistakable by large size. Upperwing pattern of Ad. diagnostic. Juv. is brown, not black, with buff ruff; if Juv. is seen flying at a distance, it can be distinguished from **16.2**, **16.3**, and **16.4** by paler upperwing coverts and spread, shorter tail. Imms. are intermediate between Ad. and Juv., after each molt showing more white on upperwing, before reaching adulthood after 4–6 years. ♣ Hilly, wooded country with cliffs. ♪ Usually silent. V.

16.1

16.1

16.2

Imm.

16.3

16.2

16.3

Imm.

16.4

16.4

Imm.

16.5

Imm.

16.6

♀

Imm.

16.6

Plate 17

17.1 OSPREY (Águia-pescadora) *Pandion haliaetus*

W 61 in./155 cm. Unmistakable by crisp black-and-white plumage and by habitat. In flight has characteristically kinked wings. Imm. differs from Ad. by narrow streaks on hindcrown and neck. ♣ Any type of clear, quiet, open water. ♪ Rather silent, but might give a rapid series of staccato "tjuw" notes and slower, faster, clear or squeaky variations thereof.

17.2 SWALLOW-TAILED KITE (Gavião-tesoura)

Elanoides forficatus W 47 in./120 cm. Unmistakable. Gregarious. ♣ Over forest. ♪ Call: occasionally a rapid, fluted series of "tuweét" notes and very high "see-see," often together as "see-see-tuweet-tuweet-tuweet- -."

17.3 WHITE-TAILED KITE (Gavião-peneira) *Elanus*

leucurus W 35.5 in./90 cm. Unmistakable by black shoulders and underwing pattern. ♣ Open areas, fields, savanna, marsh. ♪ Generally silent, but might give a thin, hissing, rising "sweeeeeé."

17.4 PEARL KITE (Gaviãozinho) *Gampsonyx swainsonii*

W 22 in./55 cm. Unmistakable by size (hardly larger than a thrush) and by black stripe (or patch) to breast sides. N rufous-flanked ssp. *leonae* (**a**) shown and C and S Nom. (**b**, paler). ♣ Open woodland, palm groves, savanna. ♪ Rather silent, but in flight might give a very high, sharp, staccato "chip-chip - -."

17.5 CINEREOUS HARRIER (Gavião-cinza) *Circus*

cinereus W 43 in./110 cm. Harriers (**17.5** and **17.6**) are identifiable by jizz (long and slender), flight (long, slender wings, bent at wrist, held in V shape) and by owl-like face mask. ♂ and ♀ differ from **17.6** by smaller size, shorter wings, and finely barred breast and belly; Imm. differs from Imm. **17.6** mainly by different, shorter-winged jizz. ♣ Reed beds, marsh, pastures. ♪ Usually silent.

17.6 LONG-WINGED HARRIER (Gavião-do-banhado)

Circus buffoni W 47 in./120 cm. Pale form (**a**, perched ♂ and Imm.) shown and dark form (**b**, Ad. ♂ and Imm. in flight). Pale ♂ and ♀ unmistakable by white breast and belly; dark form by sooty black (♂) or dark brown (♀) underparts and underwings. Long-winged jizz of Imm. diagnostic. All Ad. forms have umber, seemingly dark eyes. In all plumages (incl. Imm.), base of bill has little or no visible yellow. Perches mainly on ground. ♣ Over marsh, wet savanna. ♪ Generally silent.

17.1

Imm.

17.1

17.2

17.3

Imm.

a

b

17.4

17.5

♂

♀

17.5

Imm.

Imm.

♂

♀

Imm.

17.5

♂ b

17.6

♀

♂ a

17.6

♀

Imm. a

Imm. b

Plate 18

18.1 SNAIL KITE (Gavião-caramujeiro) *Rostrhamus* *sociabilis* W 43 in./110 cm. As **18.2** with very distinctive slender bill, but differing by red eyes, longer wings, and by tail pattern. ♂ and ♀ have different plumages as shown (unlike **18.2**). Imm. as ♀ but feathers of upperparts edged paler. ♣ Marsh, wetlands. ♪ Call: series of 4–7 low, rapid, raspy notes, like "kurre-kurre-ki-ki."

18.2 SLENDER-BILLED KITE (Gavião-do-igapó) *Heli-* *colestes (or Rostrhamus) hamatus* W 43 in./110 cm. Note yellow eyes and short tail and wings. Imm. shows narrow white tail bars. ♂ and ♀ have similar plumages. ♣ At shallow waters in forest. ♪ Call: high, mewing "WÍ-eèuw" or "wirr-WÍ-èw-wirr-WÍ-èw."

18.3 DOUBLE-TOOTHED KITE (Gavião-ripina) *Har-* *pagus bidentatus* W 27.5 in./70 cm. Rufous restricted to breast and belly. Note the diagnostic median throat stripe of **18.3** and **18.4** (though this feature not always very evident); both species may be mistaken for an *accipiter*-hawk, but these are more slender, with longer legs, more fierce expression, shy behavior, and different hunting technique. Forages (catching insects and lizards) clambering and hopping at mid-levels and in canopy. ♣ Forest, tall second growth. ♪ Call: very high, inhaled, swiftlike "sueeé-eh" or very high, whistled "fju-oweé" (as if produced by someone wolf-whistling through his fingers).

18.4 RUFOUS-THIGHED KITE (Gavião-bombachinha) *Harpagus diodon* W 29.5 in./75 cm. Rufous restricted to underwings and thighs. Resembles **19.7**, which shows the typical *accipiter*-hawk features. ♣ Open forest, woodland. ♪ Call: reported to be a very high trisyllabic whistle.

18.5 MISSISSIPPI KITE (Sauveiro-do-norte) *Ictinia* *mississippiensis* W 35.5 in./90 cm. As **18.6** with very long, narrow wings (widest at wrists). May show some rufous in primaries, but always far less than **18.6**. Note white secondaries. Imm. differs from Imm. **18.6** by rufous-brown markings below. ♣ Migrates (normally in groups) over woodland. ♪ Call: very high, thin, steeply lowered "séee-juw" whistle. R.

18.6 PLUMBEOUS KITE (Sovi) *Ictinia plumbea* W 35.5 in./90 cm. Rufous in wings and barred tail diagnostic. ♣ All types of woodland (including mangrove), esp. near rivers, but may hunt over open country. Up to 2600 m. ♪ Call: generally silent, but might give a mid-high, drawn-out, mournful whistle.

18.1

♀

18.1—

18.2

Imm.

18.2

18.3

♂

♀

18.3

Imm.

Imm.

18.4

Imm.

18.4

Imm.

18.5

Imm.

18.5

Imm.

Imm.

18.6

18.6

Imm.

Imm.

18.6

Imm.

Plate 19

19.1 GRAY-HEADED KITE (Gavião-de-cabeça-cinza)

Leptodon cayanensis W 39 in./100 cm. Ad. distinctively patterned black and white with gray head. Note black underwing coverts in flight. Imm. variable with underparts white (**a**) or densely streaked (**b**); intermediates possible. Imm. **a** differs from larger Ad. **23.6** by unfeathered legs, yellow, not black, lores, and brown upperparts. ♣ Forest and adjacent areas, mangrove. ♪ Song: low, excited, hurried, level or ascending series of nasal "u-wic" notes (2–4 sec).

19.2 WHITE-COLLARED KITE (Gavião-de-pescoço-

branco) *Leptodon forbesi* W 39 in./100 cm. From Ad. **19.1** by white neck and chin and, in flight, by white underwing coverts; differs from pale Imm. **19.1** by different underwing and undertail pattern. ♣ Atlantic rainforest. E, R.

19.3 HOOK-BILLED KITE (Caracoleiro) *Chondrohierax*

uncinatus W 35.5 in./90 cm. Normal form (**a**) and uncommon blackish form (**b**) shown. Note heavy, conspicuously hooked bill, facial pattern, and pale, staring eyes. From **18.1** by yellow, not red, bare parts. ♣ Forest and woodland with marsh, ponds, streams. ♪ Song: high, sharp, shivering, rapid series of slightly lowered "wic" notes.

19.4 GRAY-BELLIED HAWK (Tauató-pintado) *Acci-*

piter poliogaster W 31.5 in./80 cm. Distinctively bicolored with extensively yellow, bare face parts. Cheeks black or gray, eyes yellow or orange; cf. forms **a** and **b**. Imm. differs from much larger Ad. **23.7** by unfeathered legs and lack of crest. ♣ Lowland forest, dense woodland, riverine belts.

19.5 TINY HAWK (Gavião-miudinho) *Accipiter (or*

Hieraspiza) superciliosus W 19.7 in./50 cm. Red eyes and fine barring below diagnostic. Imms. (finely barred below as adults) in several color forms, brown or rufous (**b**, shown). Catches even hummingbirds. ♣ Forest, tall second growth. ♪ Call: very high, rapid, sharp, and piercing series of whinnying "weet" notes.

19.6 SHARP-SHINNED HAWK (Gavião-miúdo) *Acci-*

piter striatus W 19.7/60 cm. In SE Brazil ssp. *erythronemius* RUFOUS-THIGHED HAWK (**a**, with solid rufous flanks) and in W ssp. *ventralis* PLAIN-BREASTED HAWK, latter in different color forms; rare dark form (**b**) and rufous (**c**, in flight) form shown. Not shown is form with almost uniform creamy underparts. Extent of rufous on flanks is quite variable in same geographical area, but thighs always rufous, showing darker streaking. Imms. of this and **19.7C** are only *accipiter* species in Brazil with streaked underparts. ♣ Woodland, second growth, plantations. ♪ Call of ♀: very high, rapid series of staccato "tjew" notes, as "weéh-tjewtjew---tjuw"; ♂ calls slightly higher "tictic---tic."

19.7 BICOLORED HAWK (Gavião-bombachinha-

grande) *Accipiter bicolor* W 27.5 in./70 cm. Cf. **18.4**. Underparts unmarked or faintly barred, neck almost concolor with face sides. Shown are S ssp *guttifer* (**a**, with pale brown, faintly barred underparts and pale underwing coverts) and C ssp *pileatus* (**b**, gray below with rufous underwing coverts). Not shown is Nom., resembling **b**, but with white underwings. Imm. variable, from almost white and streaked below (**c**) to uniform buff (**d**). Note mottled crown of Imm.; thighs of Imm's and adults variable from streaked to solid rufous. ♣ Edges and clearings of forest and tall second growth. ♪ Normally silent.

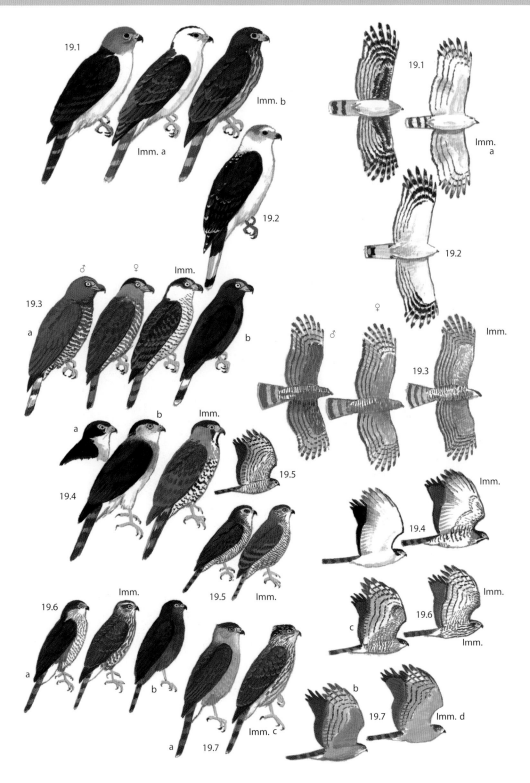

19.1

Imm. a

Imm. b

19.2

19.1

Imm. a

19.2

19.3

a

♂ ♀ Imm.

b

♂ ♀ Imm.

19.3

a

b Imm.

19.4

Imm.

19.5

19.4

19.5 Imm.

Imm.

19.5 Imm.

19.6

a

b

c

19.6

Imm.

Imm.

b

Imm. c

a 19.7

19.7 Imm. d

Plate 20

20.1 CRANE HAWK (Gavião-pernilongo) *Geranospiza* *caerulescens* W 39 in./100 cm. Shown are widespread *gracilis* group (perched) and Amazonian Nom. (flying). Unmistakable by slender jizz, distinctive tail pattern and single (adult) or double (Imm.) wing band across underside of wings. Versatile in its hunting techniques; most spectacular might be the use of its double-jointed legs, with which it can feel around in tree hollows, hanging nests, or large bromeliads. ♣ Forest edge, swampy woodland, mangrove. ♪ Call: explosive, lowered "Wéeeuw." *Note*: Almost certainly 2 species are involved, differing in saturation of gray body plumage and in color of pale tail bands (white in one, orange-rufous in other species).

20.2 SLATE-COLORED HAWK (Gavião-azul) *Leucopternis schistaceus* W 39 in./100 cm. Ad. distinctive by all-gray feathering and white band across tail. Very similar to Snail Kite (**18.1**), but with shorter wings and less slender bill. ♣ Forested edges of rivers and lakes. ♪ Call: high, level, drawn-out whistle, like "tjuuuuw."

20.3 BLACK-FACED HAWK (Gavião-de-cara-preta) *Leucopternis melanops* W 39 in./100 cm. From **20.6** in same range by black mask, yellow cere, shorter wings, absence of white on rim of wings, and different tail pattern. Probably not in range of **20.4**. ♣ Forest edge and clearings, mangrove. ♪ Call: very high, rather sharp, steeply descending "piuuuh."

20.4 WHITE-BROWED HAWK (Gavião-vaqueiro) *Leu-* *copternis kuhli* W 39 in./100 cm. From **20.3** by dark crown and distinctive white eyebrow. ♣ Wet forest. ♪ Call: very high, mournful "piuuuh."

20.5 WHITE-NECKED HAWK (Gavião-pombo-pequeno) *Leucopternis lacernulatus* W 45 in./115 cm. Not in range of **20.6**. From larger **20.7** by black subterminal band across tail and by less spotting and barring to mantle and scapulars. Usually seen in the understory; may come to the ground at army-ant swarms. ♣ Atlantic forest, woodland. En, R.

20.6 WHITE HAWK (Gavião-branco) *Leucopternis albi-* *collis* W 49 in./125 cm. No similar raptor in range, except **20.3** and Black-and-white Hawk Eagle (**23.6**), which differs by slender, long-tailed jizz, yellow cere, and black hindcrown. ♣ Forest and adjacent swamps. ♪ Call: very high, level, squeaky, slightly hoarse "wees wees wees."

20.7 MANTLED HAWK (Gavião-pombo-grande) *Leucopternis polionotus* W 49 in./125 cm. Note distinctive tail pattern (lacking black on underside and barred broadly white on upperside). Commonly seen fully exposed in the canopy. ♣ Atlantic forest, less in plantations. ♪ Call: long, very high, upslurred whistle, like "wueeeeeh." R.

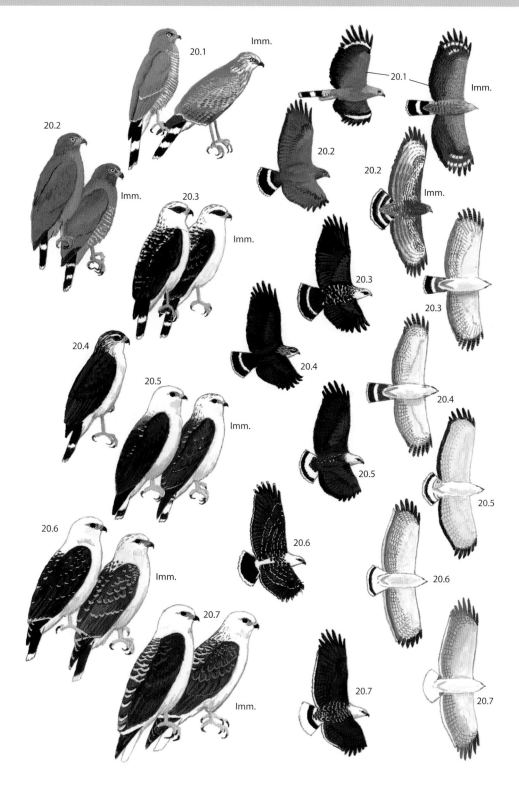

Plate 21

21.1 GRAY (or Gray-lined) **HAWK** (Gavião-pedrês)

Buteo nitidus W 35.5 in./90 cm. Compact build and combination of gray plumage and distinctive tail pattern diagnostic. South American forms have yellow eyes as shown. Note white face sides of Imm. with distinctive moustache and chin stripe, and pearl-shaped dark spots on clean buff underparts. Perches well exposed in canopy. ♣ Normally near water (e.g., in riverine belts), but also in open woodland. ♪ Call: typical buteolike "Wéee-uh" whistle; song: "wéeuh-wéeuh-wéeuh - -."

21.2 BROAD-WINGED HAWK (Gavião-de-asa-larga)

Buteo platypterus W 33.5 in./85 cm. Compact buzzard with dark upperparts, rufous-barred underparts (running together in more or less solid breast collar), and distinctive tail pattern. Perches in canopy as well as well-exposed. ♣ Forest edge, open woodland, plantations; often near water. ♪ Call: very high, thin, piercing "t'weeeéh."

21.3 WHITE-RUMPED HAWK (Gavião-de-sobre-

branco) *Percnohierax* (or *Buteo*) *leucorrhous* W 33.5 in./85 cm. Rather narrow white band across rump diagnostic (both in Ad. and Imm.). Ad. unmistakable by color pattern, esp. of underparts, and by yellow eyes. Note tail pattern of Imm. if seen from below. ♣ Montane forest. ♪ Call: very/ extr. high, thin, nasal "p'tuuuh" or downslurred "féeeuh."

21.4 SHORT-TAILED HAWK (Gavião-de-cauda-curta)

Buteo brachyurus W 35.5 in./90 cm. Pale form unmistakable by blackish upperparts and all-white underparts. All-black form (**a**) difficult to distinguish from other all-dark buzzards if white forehead cannot be seen. Imm. as Ad. but head narrowly streaked and wing feathers scaled paler. All-dark Imm. densely streaked and blotched below. Most seen when soaring because normally concealed in foliage when perched. ♣ Forest, woodland, mangrove. ♪ Call: very high, downslurred, slightly sharp/nasal "niuuuuuh."

21.5 SWAINSON'S HAWK (Gavião-papa-gafanhoto)

Buteo swainsoni W 49 in./125 cm. Gregarious, N migrant, more Imms. than adults seen in Brazil. Note straight back, giving the species its characteristic jizz. Imms. of normal form (**a**) often have distinctive pale throat bordered by dark markings. Variable; some forms (**b** and **c**) shown. All forms long winged as **21.6**, but with different tail pattern. ♣ Open country. ♪ Call: probably mid-high, descending, nasal "tithjoouw."

21.6 WHITE-TAILED HAWK (Gavião-de-rabo-branco)

Buteo albicaudatus W 51 in./130 cm. Pale form (**a**) unmistakable by rufous scapulars; dark form (**b**) differs from dark **21.7** by darker plumage. Sub-Ad. (**c**, plumage in 2nd year before molting in full Ad. plumage) has black, not white, throat and blacker head and mantle. Note dark field on underwing, formed by darker inner primaries. ♣ Open and lightly wooded areas. ♪ Call: high, squeaky "vree tuwee tuee" (each note "pushed out" and slightly upslurred); song: slightly ascending, rapid series, like "tuuh tuweh-tuweh-tuweh - -."

21.7 [RED-BACKED HAWK (Aquilucho Común) *Buteo*

polyosoma] W 45 in./115 cm. Highly variable (**a, b, c, d**). Birds with gray upperparts (**a**) or all-dark plumage (**c**) are normally ♂♂, forms with rufous mantle (**b**) or dark brown mantle and underparts (**d**) are often ♀♀. Note rounded wings (not attenuated to tip as **21.5** and **21.6**, unless gliding; cf. flying **c**). Note lack of black patches at wrists, distinguishing this species from pale **21.5** and **21.6**. ♣ From S and W South America. Prefers open, scarcely wooded country, but might be seen near river belts and forest edges. ♪ Normally silent, but might give a high, strong, rapid series of 4–9 ringing "keek" notes. (Records in coastal Rio de Janeiro [Cabo Frio] and possibly Mato Grosso do Sul.)

21.1
Imm.
21.3

Imm.

21.2
21.2
Imm.
21.4
21.3

a
Imm.
Ad. a

21.4

Ad.
Imm. a

b
Imm. c
Ad. c
Imm.

Imm. a
21.5 a
Imm.

21.5 c

21.5

a
b

Imm.
a
b
Imm.

c
21.6

21.6

a
b
Imm.

21.7
Imm.
a
c

21.7

a
b
c
d

Imm.

Plate 22

22.1 ZONE-TAILED HAWK (Gavião-de-rabo-barrado)

Buteo albonotatus W 51 in./130 cm. In flight very similar to **16.2**, but differing by black-and-white tail pattern and fine barring at underside of flight feathers. Note white spots in plumage of Imm. and its different tail pattern. ♣ Open areas, but also in a great variety of other habitats, such as humid forest and overgrown marshes. ♪ Call: drawn-out "keeer"; song: very high, "sawing" series of slightly undulating, sharp "wee" notes (10 sec).

22.2 ROADSIDE HAWK (Gavião-carijó) *Rupornis (or*

Buteo) magnirostris W 29.5 in./75 cm. Several sspp.; N Nom. (**a**; gray with gray to rufescent barring below), SE *magniplumis* (**b**; brown-gray with rufescent barring below), *saturatus* (**c**; Pantanal region; with dark head and cinnamon barring below), and Juv. shown. Adults with yellow eyes, plain/faintly streaked chest and rufous wing-patch. Juv. with brown eyes, streaked chest, barred/scaled underparts and reduced wing-patch. Note short wings with rufous panels, best seen in upperwings. Aptly named. ♣ Open forest, woodland, ranchland, fields, riverine belts. Normally seen perched on fence poles or power pylons. ♪ Call: high, descending, mewing, peevish-sounding "wée-yur."

22.3 SAVANNA HAWK (Gavião-caboclo) *Heterospizias*

(or *Buteogallus) meridionalis* W 37 in./95 cm. Resembles **22.2** in its rufous tinges and habitat. Ad. unmistakable by rufous plumage and tail and, in flight, dark blotches on sides of chest and dark thighs. Imm. differs from Imm. of **22.6** by some rufescent coloring to wings and by wing tip reaching tail tip. ♣ Wooded savanna, marsh, mangrove. Often hunts walking on the ground. ♪ Call: buteolike, very high, down-gliding "mièèèh."

22.4 [COMMON BLACK-HAWK (Gavião-carangue-

jeiro-preto) *Buteogallus anthracinus*] W 45 in./115 cm. Very similar to Great Black Hawk (**22.6**), but smaller, relatively shorter legged, and with longer primary projection when perched. White flashes at base of outer primaries, seen from below in flight, diagnostic. Imm. differs from Imm. **22.6** by beard stripes and fewer tail bars. ♣ At large (sometimes smaller) water bodies near forest, woodland, wooded swamps, mangrove. ♪ Call: series, starting very high, then slowing down and descending "wuwuwée-wéek-week week wuh."

22.5 RUFOUS CRAB-HAWK (Caranguejeiro) *Buteogallus aequinoctialis* W 35.5 in./90 cm.

Ad. is darker above than **22.3** and has short tail. Imm. has large black patches on breast sides and is otherwise distinctively marked by black spots and streaks. Species strictly restricted to coast. ♣ All low-lying habitats at sea coast, such as mangrove. Hunts crabs on mud flats. ♪ Call: very high, pinched, nasal, 3-noted "wee-chí-chee"; middle note highest.

22.6 GREAT BLACK-HAWK (Gavião-preto) *Buteogallus urubitinga* W 49 in./125 cm.

Large, thickset, all black except distinctively banded tail. Note wing pattern of perched Imm. ♣ Forest edge at water. ♪ Call: long, very high, sharp, fluted "ueeeeeeeeeeee."

22.7 HARRIS'S (or Bay-winged) **HAWK** (Gavião-asa-de-telha) *Parabuteo unicinctus*

W 43 in./110 cm. Pale rufous wing-shoulder diagnostic. Note slender, long-tailed jizz and white tail base. ♣ Normally in dry but also in wet open areas with thorn scrub and scattered trees. ♪ Call: prolonged, low, raucous "fraaaaah."

22.8 BLACK-COLLARED HAWK (Gavião-belo) *Busarellus nigricollis* W 49 in./125 cm.

Unmistakable by white head and black patch to upper breast. ♣ Wetlands, mangrove. ♪ Call: very high, hoarse, fluted, falsetto, gull-like "w'reeeeee w'reeeeeeh-wrih."

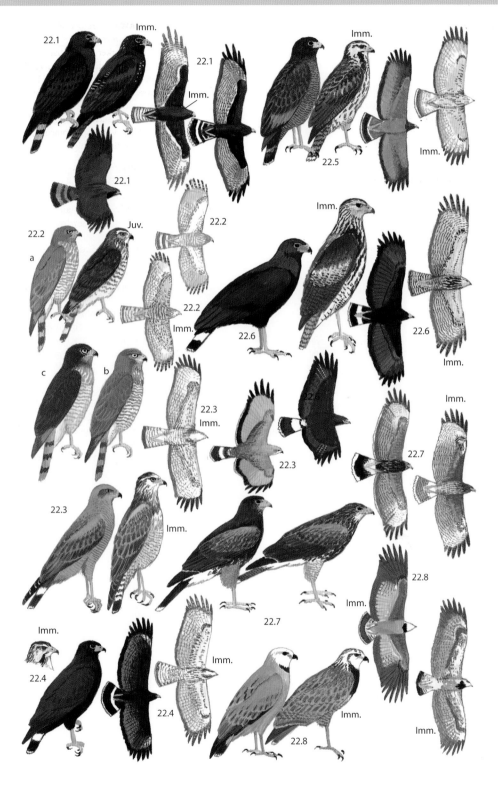

Plate 23

23.1 BLACK-CHESTED BUZZARD-EAGLE (Águia-

chilena) *Buteo (or Geranoaetus) melanoleucus* W 73 in./185 cm. S Nom. (**a**) and E ssp. *australis* (**b**, with thin barred underparts) shown. Bulky, small-headed jizz with long-pointed wings. Note distinctive upperwing pattern of Ad. and pale breast/upper belly of Imm. (see flight silhouette). Imm. longer-tailed than Ad. and therefore confusingly similar to some Imm. hawks on Pl. **22**. ♣ Open, montane areas. ♪ Call: slow series of 3 well-separated, rising "weet weet weet" notes or high, rapid "kiu-kiu-kiu- -."

23.2 CROWNED (Solitary-) **EAGLE** (Águia-cinzenta)

Harpyhaliaetus coronatus W 75 in./ 190 cm. Ad. all gray with short, distinctively patterned tail. Note absence (or very indistinct) barring of flight feathers, both in Ad. and Imm. ♣ Open woodland, dry wooded grassland. ♪ Call: very high, drawn-out, nasal, double-fluted "fwuuuuh" or gull-like, almost falsetto "t'weeeeeuh" (starting with "t'w" stepping up to very high "-euh"). R.

23.3 CRESTED EAGLE (Uiraçu-falso) *Morphnus guian-*

ensis W 73 in./185 cm. Pale (**a**) and dark (**b**) forms shown. Smaller than **23.4** with more slender bill and unmarked underwing coverts. ♣ Forest, riverine belts. ♪ Call: very high, loud, resounding "Wew-Wew-Wew - -." R.

23.4 HARPY EAGLE (Gavião-real) *Harpia harpyja*

W 80 in./205 cm. Very large with huge talons. Note diagnostic black breast band. In flight, note black marks and patches on underwings. Imm. very pale, each year becoming darker, starting by acquiring black flight feathers after 1st molt, reaching full Ad. plumage in 4th year. ♣ Tall forest. ♪ Call: sharply fluted "tí-juww," starting very high and gliding down. R.

23.5 BLACK HAWK-EAGLE (Gavião-pega-macaco)

Spizaetus tyrannus W 55 in./140 cm. Unmistakable in its habitat. Note indistinct demarcation between black breast and white-speckled belly and the black streak through eyes of Imm. ♣ Fragmented habitat, forest edge and clearings, riverine belts, semiopen woodland. ♪ Call: high, loud, resounding "WEEuw."

23.6 BLACK-AND-WHITE HAWK-EAGLE (Gavião-

pato) *Spizaetus (or Spizastur) melanoleucus* W 51 in./130 cm. Unmistakable by plumage pattern and bright yellow eyes, cere, and feet. Indistinct crest, but black streak through crown. Imm. as Ad. but slightly browner and with more dark tail bars. ♣ Forest edge and clearings, esp. near rivers. Also in riverine belts.

23.7 ORNATE HAWK-EAGLE (Gavião-de-penacho)

Spizaetus ornatus W 51 in./130 cm. Ad. unmistakable by color pattern. Imm. mostly whitish below with striped thighs and some mottling on underwing coverts. ♣ Prefers continuous forest. ♪ Call: high, ringing "Wéew"; song: high "wu-wúutwu-wu-wu- -" in unstructured series.

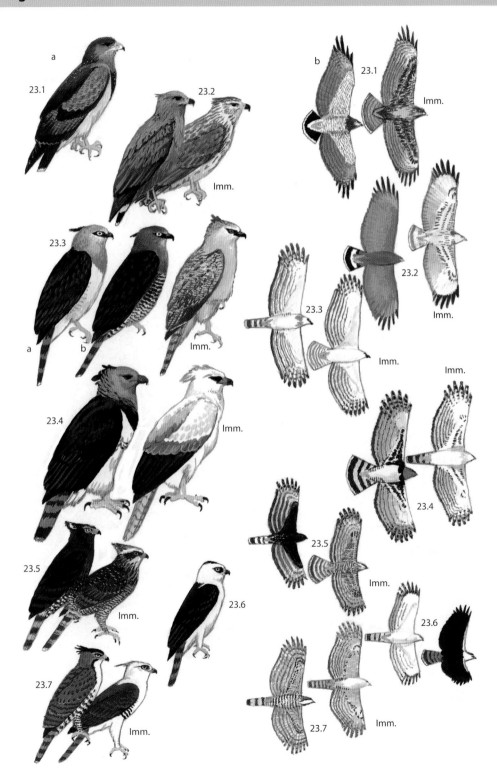

Plate 24

24.1 AMERICAN KESTREL (Quiriquiri) *Falco sparver-*

ius L 9.8 in./25 cm. Unmistakable by small size, distinctive head pattern, and general coloring. ♣ Open landscape, savanna. Perches on poles and wires, but also hovers if breeze is strong enough. ♪ Not very vocal, but might give a rapid series of 5–10 "kli" notes as "klikliklikli---"

24.2 EURASIAN KESTREL *Falco tinnunculus* (Penei-

reiro-de-dorso-malhado) L 13.8 in./35 cm. From smaller **24.1** by all-rufous wings of ♂ and less distinctive head pattern of ♂ and ♀. ♣ Open or lightly wooded country. ♪ Might give a rapid series of 5–10 very high, loud, sharp "kli" notes as "klikliklikli---" (louder and sharper than **24.1**). V.

24.3 APLOMADO FALCON (Falcão-de-coleira) *Falco*

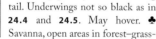

femoralis L 15.7 in./40 cm. Very distinctive by pale eyebrow and long tail. Underwings not so black as in **24.4** and **24.5**. May hover. ♣ Savanna, open areas in forest–grass-land mosaics. ♪ Generally silent, but might give a sudden high, sharp "wic!" V.

24.4 ORANGE-BREASTED FALCON (Falcão-de-

peito-laranja) *Falco deiroleucus* L 13.8 in./35 cm. From smaller **24.5** by less compact, longer-tailed jizz. Rufous rim to black at neck sides and upper breast diagnostic. ♣ Open forest, esp. at water. ♪ Call: long string of very high "kip" notes.

24.5 BAT FALCON (Cauré) *Falco rufigularis* L 9.8 in./

25 cm. Small and compact. Normally with white breast and neck sides, but some birds do have rufous on chest, causing confusion with larger, less compactly built **24.4**. ♣ Forest, woodland, riverine belts, wooded savanna, town parks. ♪ Call: long string of very high, weak, slightly shrill "wee" notes.

24.6 MERLIN (Esmerilhão) *Falco columbarius* L 9.8 in./

25 cm. Small and compact. Hunts flying birds in fast flight. ♣ Vagrant from the N hemisphere, where found in open woodland. ♪ Usually silent. V.

24.7 PEREGRINE FALCON (Falcão-peregrino) *Falco*

peregrinus L 15.7 in./40 cm. Occurrence of at least 2 sspp. in Brazil possible: *anatum* (**a**, shown perched and in flight) and *tundrius* (**b**, with narrower stripe down eyes). ♣ Often near cliffs and outcrops in open woodland, savanna, rocky coasts, high buildings. ♪ Generally silent, though "kek" (single or in series) might be given.

24.8 SPOT-WINGED FALCONET (Falcão-de-asa-

pintada) *Spiziapteryx circumcincta* L 11.8 in./30 cm. Unmistakable by head pattern and, in flight, white rump. Note yellow eyes. ♣ Open, dry areas. ♪ Probably rather silent away from breeding grounds in Argentina and Bolivia. V. to São Pedro and São Paulo Archipelago.

24.9 LAUGHING FALCON (Acauã) *Herpetotheres*

cachinnans L 19.7 in./50 cm. Unmistakable by large size, black mask, big-headed jizz, and buff-rufous in spread wings. ♣ Forest edge, riverine belts, large trees in savanna. ♪ Call: slow series of mid-high, nasal "wow" notes (1 ×/ 2–3 sec); song: very long, slow series of high, nasal "wah" notes, as "wah wah wah - -," or strings of joined "who" notes (neither particularly laughing).

24.10 BLACK CARACARA (Gavião-de-anta) *Daptrius*

ater W 35.5 in./90 cm. Forest dweller, living and foraging in groups in canopy, understory, and on ground. Not shy. Noisy. From larger **24.11** by lack of white in plumage. Note yellow bare skin at head of Imm. (shown in flight). ♣ Forest edge and clearings near rivers, riverine belts, mangrove. ♪ Call: high, drawn-out, raucous, downslurred shriek.

24.11 RED-THROATED CARACARA (Gralhão) *Ibycter*

americanus W 41 in./105 cm. White belly and vent diagnostic. ♣ Forest edge and adjacent areas. ♪ Call/song: raucous, unnerving, loud, far-carrying "è'è'aaohw" in chorus.

24.1

24.2

24.3

24.4

24.5

24.6

24.7

24.7

24.8

24.9

24.10

24.11

Imm.

a

b

Plate 25

FOREST-FALCONS: Infrequently seen, but often heard. Differ from *Accipiter* hawks by graduated tail with white bands (not squarish with pale gray bands), more extensive bare skin around the eyes, and, often, by eye color.

25.1 BARRED FOREST-FALCON (Falcão-caburé)

Micrastur ruficollis L 13.8 in./35 cm. The Amazonian ssp. *concentricus* only occurs in a gray form (**a**), while the SE Nom. (**b**) only occurs as brown form; **a** separable from **25.2** and **25.3** by brown, yellow, or ochre eyes, three white tail bars, and denser barring below, extending to vent. Imm. not safely separable from Imm. **25.2** (which may have white spots on uppertail coverts). ♣ Understory and middle levels of forest and second growth. ♪ Call/song: varies per region; may be a slow series of mid-high "tjew---" or "tjow---" notes (2 ×/3 sec).

25.2 LINED FOREST-FALCON (Falcão-mateiro) *Mic-*

rastur gilvicollis L 13.8 in./35 cm. Note white eyes of adult, double tail bar and—in most cases—lack of barring to vent. Imm. may show white spots to uppertail coverts. No rufous form. ♣ Understorey of wet forest. ♪ Call/song: generally similar to **25.1**; also series as "tooh tuh tuh."

25.3 CRYPTIC FOREST-FALCON (Falcão-críptico)

Micraster mintoni L 13.8 in./35 cm. From **25.1–2** by single broad tail bar and restricted barring to underparts. Extent of barring below variable from almost absent to extending from chin to belly. Legs of **25.2** and **25.3** are pale yellow, not yellow or pink as shown. ♣ Forest. ♪ Call/song: mid-high, nasal "tjow," single-noted or in series.

25.4 COLLARED FOREST-FALCON (Falcão-relógio)

Micrastur semitorquatus L 19.7 in./50 cm. Variable; three color forms (**a, b, c**) shown. Form **a** is very similar to **25.5** (which is smaller and has shorter legs). Scaling and barring of underparts of Imm. extend over belly to vent. ♣ Forest, dry woodland, riverine belts, mangrove. ♪ Call: peacock-like "owl."

25.5 BUCKLEY'S (or Traylor's) **FOREST-FALCON**

(Falcão-de-buckley) *Micraster buckleyi* L 17.7 in./45 cm. Cf. **25.4**. Ad. may have some white spots on secondaries; Imm. without markings on lower belly and vent. ♣ Forest and second growth. ♪ Call/song: high, slightly nasal, pitiful "au-auw-auw."

25.6 SLATY-BACKED FOREST-FALCON (Tanatau)

Micrastur mirandollei L 15.7 in./40 cm. Note dark eyes. Ad. without barring of underparts; Imm. scaled, not barred below. ♣ Forest and secondary growth near rivers, normally in understory. ♪ Call: high, nasal, mourning "aah-aah-aah- - oh'aah."

25.7 CRESTED (Northern) **CARACARA** (Caracará-do-

norte) *Caracara (or Polyborus) cheriway* W 51 in./130 cm. Imm. is browner than Ad. and lacks barring on chest. ♣ Ranchland, fields, savanna, plantations, marsh, fragmented forest. ♪ Generally silent.

25.8 SOUTHERN CARACARA (Caracará) *Caracara (or*

Polyborus) plancus W 51 in./130 cm. From **25.7** by mainly brownish, often lightly barred scapulars and densely pale-barred lower back. ♣ Wooded open country, fields, pasture land, marsh. ♪ Generally silent.

25.9 YELLOW-HEADED CARACARA (Carrapateiro)

Milvago chimachima W 37 in./95 cm. Unmistakable by creamy body and characteristic black line starting behind eye. In flight, notice conspicuous white panels in wings. Imm. differs from rather similar **25.10** by distinctive streaking, while **25.10** appears more or less uniform gray-brown. ♣ Savanna, fields, ranchland. ♪ Call; screechy, steeply downslurred shriek that starts very high, like "shréeeeeeah."

25.10 CHIMANGO CARACARA (Chimango) *Milvago*

chimango W 35.5 in./90 cm. Rather featureless when perched or walking but with white panel in wings when flying. From Imm. **25.9** by more uniform gray-brown underparts and nearly unbarred tail. ♣ Open areas, agricultural land, wetlands, beaches, developed areas. ♪ Call: screechy, rather thin, steeply downslurred shriek, that starts very high, like "kéeeeeah."

Plate 26

26.1 GREATER RHEA (Ema) *Rhea americana* H 43 in./ 110 cm. Unmistakable. ♣ Savanna, dry scrubland. ♪ Silent. R.

26.2 DWARF TINAMOU (Inhambu-carape) *Taoniscus* *nanus* L 5.9 in./15 cm. Coloring variable, whitish below, as shown, or deep buff. Very small, recalling small dove or Old World quail. ♣ Thornscrub, savanna, secondary forest. ♪ Call/song: extr. high "tírri-tih - -" in irregular series. R.

26.3 GRAY TINAMOU (Azulona) *Tinamus tao* L 17.7 in./ 45 cm. Note large size, grayish plumage. and freckled-white stripes to sides of neck. ♣ Forest, second growth, riverine belts in scrubland. ♪ Song: often in duet; high, clear, level "whuuu" (at long intervals).

26.4 GREAT TINAMOU (Inhambu-de-cabeça-vermelha) *Tinamus major* L 17.7 in./45 cm. Note large size and rufescent head ♣ Seasonally flooded forest. ♪ Song: varied, often a series of beautiful, clear, long, whistled notes that slightly rise and follow each other closely or with short intervals.

26.5 SOLITARY TINAMOU (Macuco) *Tinamus solitar-* *ius* L 17.7 in./45 cm. As **26.3** but brownish, not gray, and in different range. ♣ Forest, preferable without undergrowth. ♪ Song: series of about 4 long, clear, calmly descending, whistled notes, with a longer interval after the 1st note "whu whu-whu-whu" (3 sec). R.

26.6 WHITE-THROATED TINAMOU (Inhambu- galinha) *Tinamus guttatus* L 13.8 in./ 35 cm. Note distinct spotting to wings, back, and rump. ♣ Terra firme. ♪ Song: a few slow, eerie, slightly descending, fluted notes at up to 2-sec intervals.

26.7 RED-WINGED TINAMOU (Perdiz) *Rhynchotus* *rufescens* L 15.7 in./40 cm. Unmistakable by general color pattern. Note long, curved bill. ♣ Humid habitats such as wet grassland; also in savanna woodland. ♪ Song: short, slightly descending series of high, fluted "wJWRjuh wirju-ju" ("JWR" transposed one octave higher).

26.8 SPOTTED NOTHURA (Codorna-amarela) *Nothura* *maculosa* L 9.8 in./25 cm. Color highly variable between much darker than shown and much paler. Legs dull. Only nothura with both webs of flight feathers barred (inner webs uniformly dark in **26.9** and **26.10**). ♣ Ranchland, savanna, scrubland. ♪ Song: high, crescendoing "wir-rrrrrur" trill (4 sec), that might be followed by sharp, double-fluted "wíh wíh wíh - - tjutjutju tjuh."

26.9 LESSER NOTHURA (Codorna-mineira) *Nothura* *minor* L 7.5 in./19 cm. Very similar to **26.8**, but smaller and generally more rufescent coloring. ♣ Grassland and shrub at 700–1000 m. Generally avoids areas with short grasses (unlike **26.8**). En, R.

26.10 WHITE-BELLIED NOTHURA (Codorna-do- nordeste) *Nothura boraquira* L 9.8 in./ 25 cm. Often with conspicuous whitish belly and dark crown. Bright yellow legs diagnostic. ♣ Dry grassland, sparsely wooded savanna. ♪ Song: high, fluted "fuuu-wíh" (2nd part short and slightly higher).

26.1

26.2

26.3

26.4

26.5

26.6

26.7

26.8

26.9

26.10

Plate 27

27.1 CINEREOUS TINAMOU (Inhambu-preto) *Crypturellus cinereus* L 11.8 in./30 cm.

Characterized by unmarked dark gray plumage with pinkish legs. May show some white speckling to throat. ♣ Forest, wooded savanna, plantations. ♪ Song: very calm series of single, high, very pure, fluted notes (2 birds may sing together at different pitches).

27.2 BLACK-CAPPED TINAMOU (Inhambu-de-coroa-preta) *Crypturellus atrocapillus* L 11.8 in./30 cm.

No other tinamou with combination of densely barred plumage and pink-red legs in (restricted) range. ♣ Forest, flood plains in forest. ♪ Song: rather low, fluted, fast "wu'oh'wo" ("oh" higher, 1 ×/sec).

27.3 BROWN TINAMOU (Inhambuguaçu) *Crypturellus obsoletus* L 11.8 in./30 cm.

From smaller **27.7** by grayish throat and barred vent (often not easily seen). Belly pale buff-gray in ssp. *griseiventris* (Santarém region) ♣ Humid forest, second growth. Up to 1800 m in SE, but in lowlands in Amazon. Where overlaps with **27.7** in E, restricted to highlands. ♪ Song: series of high, loud, vehement, fluted notes "TJUR-Tjur-WUtWUtWUtWUT" (last long phrase may be continued and upslurred).

27.4 UNDULATED TINAMOU (Jaó) *Crypturellus undulatus* L 11.8 in./30 cm.

Several sspp.; W *yapura* (**a**) and *undulatus* (**b**; Pantanal region) shown; remaining sspp. most like **a**. Note whitish throat, faintly scaled vent, rather plain back (finely vermiculated if seen well), and lack of bright/contrasting head in **a**; **b** is only *Crypturellus* in range with conspicuously barred upperparts. ♣ Forest, riverine belts, dry scrub, forest remains. ♪ Song: sequence of three high, pure, fluted notes; last one slightly higher, like "fjuu fjuu-fjuu?"

27.5 VARIEGATED TINAMOU (Inhambu-anhangá) *Crypturellus variegatus* L 11.8 in./30 cm.

Characterized by blackish crown and face sides and by heavy, dark barring of upperparts. From **28.2** mainly by darker cap. ♣ Forest edge and clearings. ♪ Song: calm, slightly rising series of about 5–7 high, fluted notes, 1st one longest, the others rising or lilting up.

27.6 RED-LEGGED TINAMOU (Inhambu-de-perna-vermelha) *Crypturellus erythropus* L 11.8 in./30 cm.

Overall dark rufous plumage with pale and dark barred upperparts, mouse-gray breast, and crimson legs. ♣ Open forest, open woodland, thorn scrub, slightly wooded grassland with some bush. ♪ Song: calm series of 3 low, slightly rising, fluted notes, last one shortest or missing.

27.7 LITTLE TINAMOU (Tururim) *Crypturellus soui* L 9.8 in./25 cm.

Strength of colors variable; ♂ ♂ of Amazon sspp. generally duller than typical ♀ (as shown); both sexes of Atlantic ssp. intermediate. Note small size, gray head (dark-capped in N), whitish throat, and plain upperparts. ♣ Forest, dense woodland. Mainly in humid regions, but locally extending into nearby drier areas. ♪ Song: high, fluted "fjuu-wirrr" or "fjuuuwi-wurrrr"; last part always as tremolo.

27.8 YELLOW-LEGGED TINAMOU (Jaó-do-sul) *Crypturellus noctivagus* L 11.8 in./30 cm.

No similar barred tinamou in range. Note distinctive pale eyebrow. ♣ Forest, wooded savanna, riverine belts, thorn scrub. ♪ Song: series of 4 low, mournful "wooh wuwúwu" notes. En, R.

27.9 GRAY-LEGGED TINAMOU (Inhambu-de-pe-cinza) *Crypturellus duidae* L 11.8 in./30 cm.

Very restricted range and not in range of other pale-barred tinamous. ♣ Dense forest, woodland with bush. ♪ Song: mid-high, drawn-out and slightly rising, fluted "fuuuuuúh?"

27.10 BRAZILIAN TINAMOU (Inhambu-relogio) *Crypturellus strigulosus* L 11.8 in./30 cm. ♂ shows distinct barring of tail and tail coverts. Pattern of ♀ barring more "wavy" than other tinamous. ♣ Dense humid forest. ♪ Song: 3 high, fluted notes, merging into each other, the 1st very long, 2nd long and higher, 3rd short (almost like the sound of a wet finger over the rim of a glass).

Plate 28

28.1 RUSTY TINAMOU (Inhambu-carijo) *Crypturellus* *brevirostris* L 9.8 in./25 cm. Barring of wings coarser than on rest of body. ♣ Flood plains in dense forest.

28.2 BARTLETT'S TINAMOU (Inhambu-anhangai) *Crypturellus bartletti* L 9.8 in./ 25 cm. Overall browner plumage and fainter barring than other barred tinamou in range. ♣ Dense forest. ♪ Song: series of high, beautiful, short, fluted notes, which might rise 1 note after the 1st few.

28.3 SMALL-BILLED TINAMOU (Inhambu-chororo) *Crypturellus parvirostris* L 9 in./ 23 cm. Difficult to distinguish from slightly larger **28.4**, but is overall browner with dark red, not purplish, legs and has different (softer) voice. No other tinamou with red bill but **28.4**. ♣ Forest, scrubby grassland, riverine belts, open woodland. ♪ Song: odd series, that starts with one or more high, sharp, stressed, well-separated, staccato "TRIH" notes, then rapidly accelerates in a descending almost-trill, to end in a few low "tjuuh" notes.

28.4 TATAUPA TINAMOU (Inhambu-chintã) *Cryp-* *turellus tataupa* L 9.8 in./25 cm. Cf. **28.3**. ♣ Wet places at forest edge. ♪ Song: a very short version of **28.3** like "frrúh frrúhfruhfruhfru."

28.5 ? BARRED TINAMOU *Crypturellus casiquiare* L 9.8 in./25 cm. Unmistakable by bright orange-rufous head and barred upperparts. ♣ Dense forest. ♪ Song: very long, slightly rising, then lowering and decelerating series of high, short, fluted notes, at the end again and again another note, long after you think the series has stopped. (Occurs just outside Brazil in Columbia and Venezuela.)

28.6 GRAY-WINGED TRUMPETER (Jacamim-de- costas-cinzentas) *Psophia crepitans* L 19.7 in./50 cm. Jizz of trumpeters is unmistakable. Each species has its own range. This species differs from **28.7** and **28.8** by orange band across mantle. ♣ Dense, moist forest away from settlements. ♪ Alarm call: loud, harsh "GRAH" notes; song: very low humming, like "wuh-wuh-wuh wuh wuh - -."

28.7 PALE-WINGED TRUMPETER (Jacamim-de-cos- tas-brancas) *Psophia leucoptera* L 19.7 in./50 cm. CW Nom. (**a**, with white lower back) and NW ssp. *ochroptera* (**b**, with orange-buff lower back) shown. ♣ Dense, moist forest away from settlements. ♪ Alarm call: loud, harsh "KRETCH" notes; song: very low "wuh wuh wuh - -," as from a dog giving warning growls.

28.8 DARK-WINGED TRUMPETER (Jacamim-de- costas-verdes) *Psophia viridis* L 19.7 in./ 50 cm. The three sspp. C Nom. (**a**, with dusky back), green-backed C *viridis* (**b**), and all-black NE *obscura* (**c**) are to be split in separate species. ♣ Dense, moist forest away from settlements. ♪ Call: high "Tsets" notes.

28.9 LIMPKIN (Carão) *Aramus guarauna* L 27.5 in./ 70 cm. From ibises by straight bill. ♣ Wooded, scrubby marsh, thick vegetation at edges of lakes in woodland. ♪ Call: high, wailing, cranelike "wreeer wreeer wreeer."

28.10 HOATZIN (Cigana) *Opisthocomus hoazin* L 23.5 in./ 60 cm. Unmistakable by general jizz and color pattern. Clambers among branches near or over water, the Juvs. aided to do so by "prehistoric" claws at wing bend. ♣ Prefers tall vegetation (esp. the calla-lily–like *Montrichardia arbore-scens*) at the edge of lakes and rivers. ♪ Call: hoarse grunts, like "vruuh" or, in series, "w'vruh vrih wi-vruh."

28.1

28.2

28.3

28.4

28.5

28.6

28.7

a b

28.8

a b c

28.9

28.10

Plate 29

29.1 WHITE-CRESTED GUAN (Jacupiranga) *Penelope*

pileata L 31.5 in./80 cm. Contrasting rich rufous below and dark brown above. Note that rufous extends to neck and crown. Not in range of **29.2–29.7**. ♣ Dense forest. ♪ Call: low, raucous yelping "EhUh" or "u'u'u'u'u." En, R.

29.2 CHESTNUT-BELLIED GUAN (Jacu-de-barriga-

castanha) *Penelope ochrogaster* L 27.5 in./70 cm. Less contrasting colors than **29.1**, with neck brown, same as color of rest of upperparts. Not in range of **29.1** and **29.3–29.7**. ♣ Wet spots in woodland, woodland at water and swamps, riverine belts. En, R.

29.3 WHITE-BROWED GUAN (Jacucaca) *Penelope*

jacucaca L 25.6 in./65 cm. Overall dark with distinctive white eyebrow. Not in range of other guans. ♣ Dry woodland and forest patches. ♪ Call: low, harsh cackling; song: low, raucous, barking "wrah-wrah- -." En, R.

29.4 MARAIL GUAN (Jacumirim) *Penelope marail*
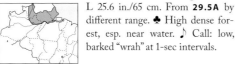
L 25.6 in./65 cm. From **29.5A** by different range. ♣ High dense forest, esp. near water. ♪ Call: low, barked "wrah" at 1-sec intervals.

29.5 RUSTY-MARGINED GUAN (Jacupemba) *Penel-*

ope superciliaris L 25.6 in./65 cm. Typically with narrow white eyebrow (**b**), but this greatly reduced in S (**a**), or rufous in NE (not shown). Diagnostic rusty edging of tertials sometimes worn off, but only *Penelope* guan without whitish edging to mantle or wing coverts. ♣ Often at edges of lakes and rivers in forest, woodland, riverine belts. ♪ Call: low, barked "wruh-wruh- -."

29.6 SPIX'S GUAN (Jacu-de-spix) *Penelope jacquacu*

L 27.5 in./70 cm. Resembles **29.2** but with less contrasting face sides. No other guan in range. ♣ Humid forest, forest edges, clearings, riverine belts. ♪ Call: very low, forcefully exhaled "orc orc - -."

29.7 DUSKY-LEGGED GUAN (Jacuaçu) *Penelope*

obscura L 27.5 in./70 cm. Legs dusky. Typically with broad white forehead (shown), but this is reduced in S. Only *Penelope* guan in range with whitish edging to wing coverts and mantle. ♣ Tall forest, woodland and forest patches in grassland. ♪ Call: very high, fluted/yelping "wuut-wuut-wuut- -"; song: high, rapid, nasal "wee-wu wee-wu - -."

29.8 RED-THROATED PIPING-GUAN (Cujubi) *Abur-*

ria (or *Pipile*) *cujubi* L 29.5 in./75 cm. NC Nom. (**a**) and S and W ssp. *nattereri* (**b**, with smaller dewlap and not uniform white crest) shown. Not in range of **29.10**. Some hybridization with **29.9** where their ranges meet. (The evidence for the split is weak, and **29.8** and **29.9** are perhaps better treated as conspecific). ♣ Forest, riverine belts.

29.9 BLUE-THROATED PIPING-GUAN (Jacutinga-

de-garganta-azul) *Aburria* (or *Pipile*) *cumanensis* L 25.5 in./65 cm. NW Nom. (**a**) and SW ssp. *grayi* (**b**, with mainly white dewlap) shown. ♣ Forest in steep, hilly country away from settlement; also in riverine belts. ♪ Song: calm series of up to 10 rising, clear, piped/whistled "peeé-peeé--peeé" notes.

29.10 BLACK-FRONTED PIPING-GUAN (Jacutinga)

Aburria (or *Pipile*) *jacutinga* L 27.5 in./70 cm. White eyering in black face sides diagnostic. ♣ Near streams and rivers in Atlantic forest. R.

Plate 30

30.1 SPECKLED CHACHALACA (Aracuã) *Ortalis guttata* L 19.7 in./50 cm. W Nom. (**a**) and E ssp. *araucuan* (**b**, whitish below, head chestnut, dark legs) and heads of sspp. *squamata* (**c**, darkest), *remota* (**d**, only one specimen known) and *subaffinis* (**e**, as **a**, but with brown face sides) shown. Not in range of **30.2–30.4**. ♣ Low woodland, palm groves, second growth, sometimes at forest edge. ♪ Dawn song: cacophony of communal cackling, based on "wírre-wò."

30.2 VARIABLE CHACHALACA (Aracuã-pequeno) *Ortalis motmot* L 19.7 in./50 cm. Note rufous color of head. Not in ranges of **30.1**, **30.3**, and **30.4**. ♣ In dense undergrowth at edges of open spaces in forest and woodland. ♪ Voice as **30.1**, but more vehement and more based on "wUrre-wò." May also cackle like a frightened chicken or utter harsh "whut whut wruh-Wrah-WRAAH-WRAAh - -."

30.3 BUFF-BROWED CHACHALACA (Aracuã-desobrancelhas) *Ortalis superciliaris* L 17.7 in./45 cm. Buff brow diagnostic. There is some N–S variation in this species: birds near the coast look lighter, esp. on the chest, which can be quite brownish gray. Not in range of **30.1, 30.2,** and **30.4**. ♣ Thickets. ♪ Dawn song: harsh, cackled, repeated "TJURRE-wruh." En.

30.4 CHACO CHACHALACA (Aracuã-do-pantanal) *Ortalis canicollis* L 21.5 in./55 cm. Head and neck slightly darker, but otherwise same color as rest of upperparts. Not in range of **30.1– 30.3**. ♣ Swampy forest, riverine belts, dry, open woodland, second growth. ♪ Dawn song: hoarse, harsh cackling "fruh frudder't' Truh."

30.5 CRESTED BOBWHITE (Uru-do-campo) *Colinus cristatus* L 7.5 in./19 cm. Unmistak- 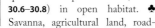 able by crest, rufous cheek spots, spotted underparts and (unlike **30.6–30.8**) in open habitat. ♣ Savanna, agricultural land, roadsides, woodland edges. ♪ Song: 3 very high, rising, well-separated, nasal notes "uh uh u'Wéet," (middle note often omitted, so that the remainder may sound as "bob White").

30.6 MARBLED WOOD-QUAIL (Uru-corcovado) *Odontophorus gujanensis* L 9.8 in./ 25 cm. As other wood-quails a forest dweller, differing from tinamous by compact build and short legs. Note overall fine barring between rufous blotches. Normally with distinct, off-white patch behind eye (not shown). ♣ Tall forest floor, second growth. ♪ Song: sustained, fast, high, rolling, piped "toot-oh-wi-toot-oh-wi - - -" in duet ("wi" given by partner), after some time slightly losing in speed and pitch as if the birds get tired.

30.7 SPOT-WINGED WOOD-QUAIL (Uru) *Odonto-* *phorus capueira* L 11.8 in./30 cm. Characterized by uniform gray underparts. ♣ Atlantic forest, second growth. ♪ Song: high, piped, clear "wéer-wrur wéer-wrur - -."

30.8 STARRED WOOD-QUAIL (Uru-de-topete) *Odon-* *tophorus stellatus* L 9.8 in./25 cm. Mainly rufous below. Pale rump accentuated by dark mantle and wings. Bare facial skin yellowish. ♣ Forest floor. ♪ Song: high, piped, hurried "coo-currucoo" of pair.

30.9 RED-LEGGED SERIEMA (Seriema) *Cariama cris-* *tata* L 35 in./90 cm. Unmistakable by size, jizz, and voice. Shy. ♣ More or less dry areas; open woodland, scrub, savanna. ♪ Song: calm series of nasal, well-separated, and accentuated "hah-hah" notes, lilting up and then down again.

30.10 SNOWY (or Pale-faced) **SHEATHBILL** (Pomba-antártica) *Chionis albus* L 15.7 in./ 40 cm. Unmistakable by white color and pigeonlike proportions. ♣ Patrols rocky and sandy shores, esp. near seabird colonies. V.

c
d
a
b
30.1
e
30.2
30.5 ♀
30.6
30.3
30.7
30.4
30.8
30.9
30.10

Plate 31

31.1 NOCTURNAL (or Rufous) **CURASSOW** (Urumu-tum) *Nothocrax urumutum* L 21.5 in./ 55 cm. No similar bird in range. Note black crest and pale tips of outer tail feathers. Sings at night. ♣ Moist or partially flooded forest. ♪ Song: very low, humming series of short "mum" notes, sustained for hours at night "mum mum-mum-mum mum-mum mum - -."

31.2 ALAGOAS CURASSOW (Mutum-do-nordeste) *Mitu mitu* L 33.5 in./85 cm. Virtually extinct in the wild; remaining birds are in two private collections as part of a captive-breeding project under supervision of the Brazilian wildlife agency (IBAMA). Breeding has been successful and birds are to be spread among other collections soon (2007). Note bare skin around ear and pale brown tips of tail feathers. ♣ Forest. En.

31.3 RAZOR-BILLED CURASSOW (Mutum-cavalo) *Mitu tuberosum* L 33.5 in./85 cm. Only curassow with all tail feathers tipped white. Note large bill. ♣ Forest, usually in lowlands. ♪ Song: very low, almost inaudible growled "wur-wur-wúr-wuhr-wuhr."

31.4 CRESTLESS (or Lesser Razor-billed) **CURASSOW** (Mutum-do-norte) *Mitu tomentosum* L 31.5 in./80 cm. From other curassows by combination of chestnut belly and tail tips. ♣ Thick undergrowth in forest. ♪ Song: very low, almost inaudible, growled "wur-wur-wúr-wuhr-wuhr."

31.5 BLACK CURASSOW (Mutum-poranga) *Crax alec-**tor* L 35 in./90 cm. In Brazil 2 sspp., yellow-billed NE Nom. (**a**) and orange-red-billed NW *erythrognatha* (**b**). From **31.8** by different range and all-black tail. ♣ Thick undergrowth at forest edge, riverine belts. ♪ Song: very low, almost inaudible, hollow "wuuh wut-wut-wut."

31.6 WATTLED CURASSOW (Mutum-de-fava) *Crax* *globulosa* L 33.5 in./85 cm. From other curly-crested curassows by different range and larger wattles at bill base (♂) or red and black bill (♀). ♣ Forest (often at wet places), riverine belts, forest patches in flood plains. ♪ Song: modest, descending whistle, starting very high "weeeeiuw" (1 sec). No low booming by this species known. R.

31.7 RED-BILLED CURASSOW (Mutum-de-bico-vermelho) *Crax blumenbachii* L 33.5 in./ 85 cm. Cf. **31.6**. ♣ Undergrowth of tall forest near water and at edges and clearings. ♪ Call: low "oop" notes. En, R.

31.8 BARE-FACED CURASSOW (Mutum-de-penacho) *Crax fasciolata* L 31.5 in./80 cm. Cf. **31.5** and **31.6**. Note small white tips of outer tail feathers (♂). Two sspp., differing in ♀♀, heavily barred Nom. (**a**) and thinly waved, critically endangered *pinima* (**b**, restricted to Pará and Maranhão east of the Tocantins R.). ♣ Forest, woodland, riverine belts. ♪ Song: low, hoarse "e-ur" notes of pair, like grunting of domestic pigs.

31.9 RED JUNGLEFOWL (Galinha-doméstica) *Gallus gallus* L 27.5 in./70 cm (♂), 17.7 in./45 cm (♀). Shown is original wild Junglefowl from Asia; birds seen walking about in rural areas are very variable, usually long-legged and long-necked. No established feral population in Brazil. ♣ Prefers edge of moist forest and second growth. (No map). I.

31.10 HELMETED GUINEAFOWL (Fraca-da-guiné) *Numida meleagris* L 21.5 in./55 cm. Ssp. *galeata*. Unmistakable by jizz and spotting. ♣ Prefers dry natural and cultivated areas with tree and shrub cover. (No map.) I.

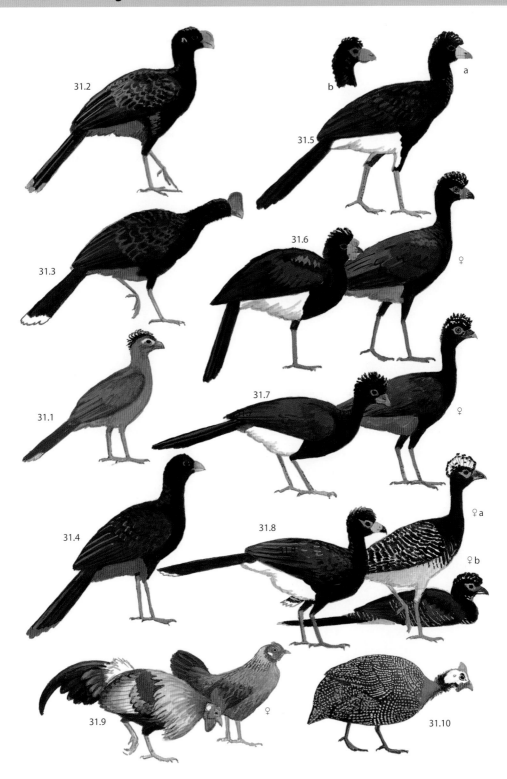

Plate 32

32.1 SPECKLED RAIL (Pinto-d"água-carijó) *Coturnicops notatus* L 5.5 in./14 cm. Very dark overall, narrow pale area from chin to vent (**32.8** and **33.3** are dark gray to black below, narrowly barred white). In flight, shows white wing patch formed by secondaries. ♣ Wet grassland, marsh, swamps, rice fields. ♪ Soft calls and song, barely audible from some distance.

32.2 OCELLATED CRAKE (Maxalalagá) *Micropygia schomburgkii* L 5.9 in./15 cm. Unmistakable by orange plumage with rows of black-margined white drop-shaped spots. ♣ More or less muddy areas in dense grassland with some scrub and tree cover. ♪ Call: high, wailing "uVéeeer" shriek. as from a crying baby.

32.3 CHESTNUT-HEADED CRAKE (Sanã-de-cabeça-castanha) *Anurolimnas castaneiceps* L 7.9 in./20 cm. From **32.4** and **32.5** by greenish yellow bill and legs. ♣ Forest, tall second growth, dense thickets. ♪ Song: in duet: one bird gives high, clear, two-syllable "ú-weet" note, the other cuts in with low "tée tr'rutter." R.

32.4 RUSSET-CROWNED CRAKE (Sanã-castanha) *Anurolimnas* (or *Laterallus) viridis* L 6.7 in./17 cm. Note black bill, red legs, buff streak through eyes, unmarked flanks. ♣ Dense vegetation at woodland, roadsides, cultivation; normally not in marsh. ♪ Song: beautiful yet strange, dry rattling like the sound of a seashell wind chime or someone going through a bead curtain.

32.5 BLACK-BANDED CRAKE (Sanã-zebrada) *Anurolimnas* (or *Laterallus) fasciatus* L 7.5 in./19 cm. Black-barred, buff posterior underparts diagnostic. ♣ Tall vegetation in wet places. ♪ Song: in duet; two parallel running, long, very high, whinnying series of sharp, shivering notes, which gradually change to a descending trill.

32.6 RUFOUS-SIDED CRAKE (Sanã-parda) *Laterallus melanophaius* L 6.3 in./16 cm. From **33.1** by dark olive crown, darker greenish bill, buff vent, and olive-brown legs and from **33.2** (with very restricted range) by uniform olive wings. ♣ Dense vegetation at marshes, tall wet grassland. ♪ Very varied vocalizations. Call: may be a very high "trrriuh"; song: 3–5 sec long, thin, gradually lowered, shivering series "sriririr--- riri" or series of low, toneless rasps "grrra-grrrra-grrra- -."

32.7 GRAY-BREASTED CRAKE (Sanã-do-capim) *Laterallus exilis* L 5.9 in./15 cm. Unmistakable by head-neck color pattern. ♣ Tall to short grass at water edge, rice fields. ♪ Call: very high, angry "ti-tju-tju"; song: seemingly long, dry, downslurred rattle (2–4 sec).

32.8 BLACK RAIL (Açanã-preta) *Laterallus jamaicensis* L 5.5 in./14 cm. Unmistakable by very dark color pattern. Not in range of **33.3**. ♣ Fresh and saline marshes and grassland with scattered small pools. ♪ Probably silent in South America. V.

32.9 UNIFORM CRAKE (Saracura-lisa) *Amaurolimnas concolor* L 7.9 in./20 cm. From **32.3** by brown forecrown, more extensive rufous underparts and by generally different range, from **32.4** by longer, green, not black, bill. ♣ Flooded forest, wooded swamps, edges of mangrove, dense thickets. ♪ Song: series of about 5–10, high, fluted, upslurred "tu-eeh" notes (last few slightly lower).

32.10 WATTLED JACANA (Jaçanã) *Jacana jacana* L 9.8 in./25 cm. Unmistakable by very long toes and nails and by color pattern. ♣ Wetland with floating vegetation and adjacent grassland. ♪ Call: high, nasal chattering "wit-wit-wit-wee-wee-wit- -"; song: as call, but slower.

Plate 33

33.1 RED-AND-WHITE CRAKE (Sană-vermelha) *Laterallus leucopyrrhus* L 5.9 in./15 cm. Cf. **33.2**. ♣ Marshy areas, tussocky grassland with puddles.

33.2 RUFOUS-FACED CRAKE (Sană-de-cara-ruiva) *Laterallus xenopterus* L 5.5 in./14 cm. From **32.6** and **33.1** by extensive wing barring. ♣ Flooded, tussocky marsh areas. R.

33.3 DOT-WINGED CRAKE (Sană-cinza) *Porzana spiloptera* L 5.9 in./15 cm. Unmistakable in its range by very dark coloring. ♣ Fresh and salt marshes, wet to dry grassland. R.

33.4 ASH-THROATED CRAKE (Sană-carijó) *Porzana albicollis* L 7.9 in./20 cm. From **33.6** by scalloped patterning of upperparts and uniform greenish bill ♣ Drier parts of marshy areas, grassland, roadsides, second growth. ♪ Song: varied; e.g., series of mid-high, slightly descending "prrraauw."

33.5 YELLOW-BREASTED CRAKE (Sană-amarela) *Porzana flaviventer* L 5.1 in./13 cm. Note very small size and distinctive head pattern. ♣ Marsh, lake edges, flood plains, rice fields.

33.6 PAINT-BILLED CRAKE (Turu-turu) *Neocrex erythrops* L 7.5 in./19 cm. Red ring at base of pale green bill diagnostic. ♣ Tall vegetation in more or less wet places such as reed beds, marsh, pastures. ♪ Call: very low, muttered series of joined or disconnected "toc" notes, like "toctoc-toc---toc." Song: varied; e.g., series of repeated, high, fluted "tjúh tjuppetjup" notes; also very low "toc" notes that are gradually transformed into high, loud, sharp "KITS" notes.

33.7 CLAPPER RAIL (Saracura-matraca) *Rallus longirostris* L 13.8 in./35 cm. No other rail with similar barred rear parts with such a long, decurved, red bill. ♣ Prefers mangrove. ♪ Song: rapid series of scratchy, almost toneless "kreh" notes.

33.8 PLUMBEOUS RAIL (Saracura-do-banhado) *Pardirallus sanguinolentus* L 13.8 in./35 cm. Very similar to smaller **33.9** but differing by more pronounced dark feather centers of upperparts and by orange spot at base of bill. ♣ Wet places, ponds, ditches, often in agricultural surroundings. ♪ Song: not rail-like; slightly hoarse, almost thrushlike "tju-wéer" in a descending series of about 4–7 notes.

33.9 BLACKISH RAIL (Saracura-sană) *Pardirallus nigricans* L 11.8 in./30 cm. Cf. **33.8**. ♣ Wet areas with dense vegetation. ♪ Song: series of steeply upslurred "ruweét" notes, often in duets, with added bouncing down "tit-titter-ur-ur-wu."

33.10 SPOTTED RAIL (Saracura-carijó) *Pardirallus maculatus* L 9.8 in./25 cm. Ad. easily recognizable by overall striping, barring, and spotting in combination with long, orange-based bill. Imms. occur in pale and dark (shown) color form, the latter differs from larger adults (**33.8** and **33.9**) mainly by paler legs and by some sparse white spotting. ♣ Swamps, marsh, rice fields, wet grassland.

Plate 34

34.1 LITTLE WOOD-RAIL (Saracura-do-mangue) *Aramides mangle* L 11.8 in./30 cm. From other wood-rails by all-gray head and neck, from larger **34.3** also by rufous breast and orange spot at base of bill. ♣ Mangrove, coastal and inland marsh. En.

34.2 RED-WINGED WOOD-RAIL (Saracura-de-asa-vermelha) *Aramides calopterus* L 11.8 in./30 cm. Note gray belly and reddish wing patch. From **34.4** by different range. ♣ Periodically inundated forest.

34.3 GRAY-NECKED WOOD-RAIL (Saracura-três-potes) *Aramides cajanea* L 13.8 in./ 35 cm. Head and neck all gray except rufous hindcrown. ♣ At swamps, streams, and other wet places in forest, second growth, woodland, mangrove, rice fields. ♪ Song: laborious, nasal "áhák oh" in descending series, in duet or chorus, becoming a cacophony (some low notes sound like a baby sobbing).

34.4 SLATY-BREASTED WOOD-RAIL (Saracura-do-mato) *Aramides saracura* L 13.8 in./ 35 cm. Only gray-bellied wood-rail in range. ♣ Prefers wet places at or near forest and woodland. ♪ Song: cacophonic chorus based on high, loud, fluted "WéehWéeh woh."

34.5 GIANT WOOD-RAIL (Saracuruçu) *Aramides ypecaha* L 17.7 in./45 cm. From simi- lar rufous-necked **34.2** (different range) and from **34.4** by rufous, not gray, belly. ♣ Wet, slightly wooded areas near water, such as swamps and riverine belts. ♪ Song: unstructured shrieking, based on "WRAAh-terrah" or "WRAAh-Tratah" in chorus.

34.6 SPOT-FLANKED GALLINULE (Frango-d'água-carijó) *Gallinula melanops* L 9.8 in./ 25 cm. Unmistakable by green bill, black foreface, and by white flank spots. Differing from crakes, for example, by frequenting open areas (normally seen swimming at edge of water). ♣ Any water with floating vegetation, wet savanna, reed beds. ♪ Call: soft, low "wut wut - -."

34.7 LESSER MOORHEN *Gallinula angulata* (Frango-d'água-menor) L 9.8 in./25 cm. From larger **34.8** by color pattern of bill and lack of reddish leg garters. ♣ Swamps and inundations with fringing and floating vegetation. V.

34.8 COMMON (Moorhen or) **GALLINULE** (Frango-d'água-comum) *Gallinula chloropus* L 13.8 in./35 cm. Unmistakable by white line along flanks and yellow-tipped red bill. ♣ At edges of any type of water with fringing vegetation. ♪ Call: low, snappy, nasal "wuh wuh - -."

34.9 AZURE GALLINULE (Frango-d'água-pequeno) *Porphyrio flavirostris* L 9.8 in./25 cm. Azure-blue wings and pale blue neck and head diagnostic. Imm. differs from Imm. **34.10** by white underparts and blue in wings. ♣ Well-vegetated marsh, rice fields, wet savanna, ponds with floating vegetation. ♪ Rather silent, occasionally uttering mid-high, nasal "u'wúr" notes in descending, slow series.

34.10 PURPLE GALLINULE (Frango-d'água-azul) *Porphyrio martinica* L 11.8 in./ 30 cm. Unmistakable; no similar shining blue bird in Brazil. ♣ Well-vegetated wetlands, grassy swamps, water with floating and emergent plants. ♪ Call: nasal chattering.

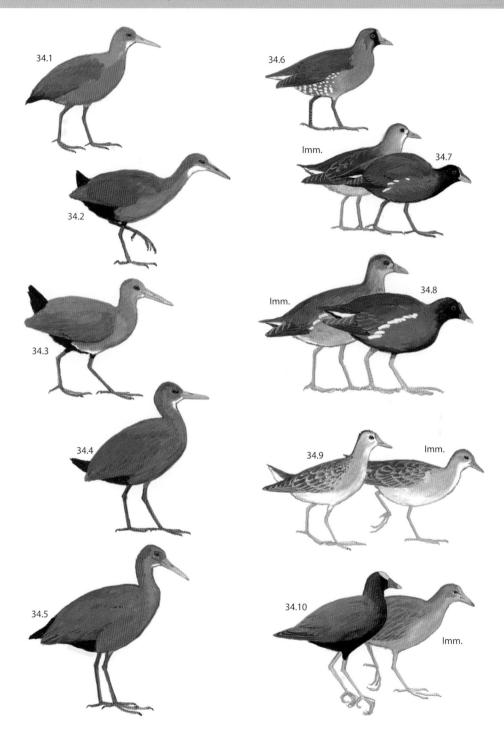

34.1

34.2

34.3

34.4

34.5

34.6

Imm. 34.7

Imm. 34.8

34.9 Imm.

34.10 Imm.

Plate 35

35.1 RED-GARTERED COOT (Carqueja-de-bico-manchado) *Fulica armillata* L 17.7 in./ 45 cm. Bill pattern diagnostic. ♣ Waters with submerged and floating vegetation along edges. ♪ Call: high, quick "whit"; song: mid-high, nasal "wurt't'wurt't'wurt't'wurt'the."

35.2 RED-FRONTED COOT (Carqueja-de-escudo-vermelho) *Fulica rufifrons* L 15.7 in./ 40 cm. Bill pattern diagnostic. ♣ Among vegetation in lakes and marshes. ♪ Call: typical cootlike "kruh"; song: nasal, descending "pútput---pat-pat pa."

35.3 WHITE-WINGED COOT (Carqueja-de-bico-amarelo) *Fulica leucoptera* L 15.7 in./ 40 cm. Lack of red in bill diagnostic. In flight, white seam to secondaries. ♣ Waters with submerged plants and short-grassed shores. ♪ Song: unstructured barks as from a small dog: "wit wu wu wit-wut wu - -."

35.4 SUNBITTERN (Pavãozinho-do-pará) *Eurypyga helias* L 17.7 in./45 cm. Unmistakable in its habitat. ♣ At forest rivers and streams. ♪ Song: high, level or lowered, whistled "fj'wooooh" or "fjuuuuu'wíh."

35.5 SUNGREBE (Picaparra) *Heliornis fulica* L 11.8 in./ 30 cm. Unmistakable. Pumps head as it swims. ♣ Near and under overhanging vegetation at edges of forest rivers, streams, and lakes. ♪ Call: raucous, barking, and snapping "wuhwuh-wroo-Wàh"; song: short, rapid series of "ooh-ke-oohke- -" (5–6×).

35.6 AMERICAN OYSTERCATCHER (Piru-piru) *Haematopus palliatus* L 17.7 in./45 cm. Unmistakable by general color pattern and long, red bill. ♣ Sandy and pebbled beaches, mud flats, salt marsh. ♪ Noisy. Call: very high, sharp, staccato "peet peet pit peet - -" or, in flight, "peet-peet-peereweet-peet- -."

35.7 BLACK-NECKED STILT (Pernilongo-de-costas-negras) *Himantopus mexicanus* L 15.7 in./40 cm. Nom. (**a**) and white-crowned ssp. *melanurus* (**b**, White-backed Stilt [Pernilongo-de-costas-brancas]) shown. ♀♀ have brown upperparts, which are shiny blue in ♂. ♣ Shallow water. ♪ Can be noisy. Call: high, mewing "wew-wew-wew-witwit-wew- -."

35.8 DOUBLE-STRIPED THICK-KNEE (Téu-téu-da-savana) *Burhinus bistriatus* L 17.7 in./ 45 cm. Distinctive by high stance, yellow, staring eyes, and long tail and wings. Note color pattern of wings in flight. Crepuscular. ♣ Open to sparsely wooded dry grassland. ♪ Call: quiet at day, noisy at night; loud, high, yelping "rrr rr wer-wer-were-wer-wer-wer- -," cacophonic if in chorus.

35.9 COLLARED PRATINCOLE (Perdiz-do-mar) *Glareola pratincola* L 9.8 in./25 cm. Sternlike, but brown and with distinctive face pattern. Wings very dark underneath. ♣ Open fields and savanna, normally near water. ♪ Call: high, sharp, rather nasal "kerreu." Recorded on Atol das Rocas. V.

35.10 [LEAST SEEDSNIPE (Agachadeira-mirim) *Thinocorus rumicivorus*] L 7 in./18 cm. Not unlike a quail or ground-dove. Note "waistcoat" as if buttoned over breast. Underwing coverts black. (♀ same size as ♂, but is painted larger to show details). ♣ Open, dry, sparsely vegetated, stony areas. ♪ Call: soft, high "wic-wic-wic."

35.1

35.2

35.3

Imm.

35.6

35.7

35.7

♂ a

♀

♂ b

35.8

35.4

35.9

N-br.

Br.

35.5

♀

35.10

♂

♀

Plate 36

36.1 ? LONG-BILLED DOWITCHER (Maçarico-de-bico-comprido) *Limnodromus scolopaceus* L 11.8 in./30 cm. Not safely separable from **36.2** except by flight call. Bill length of both dowitchers variable (bill length of **36.1** might even be shorter than that of **36.2**). Note color of legs, striping of flanks, and rather heavy bill. ♣ Mainly at freshwater sites, but also at salt marshes and mud flats. ♪ Call: in flight, very high, whinnying, rapid "wi-wi-wi" (1–5× "wi"). Erroneous record.

36.2 SHORT-BILLED (or Common) **DOWITCHER** (Maçarico-de-costas-brancas) *Limnodromus griseus* L 9.8 in./25 cm. Cf. **36.1**. ♣ Mud flats near mangrove; also at pools in brackish marsh. ♪ Call (in flight or when flushed): high, rather sharp, rapid "tu-tu-tu" (2–3× "tu").

36.3 HUDSONIAN GODWIT (Maçarico-de-bico-virado) *Limosa haemastica* L 15.7 in./40 cm. Under- and upperwing pattern diagnostic. From **36.10** by pink-based bill. ♣ Shallow saline lakes and estuaries. ♪ Call: very high, nasal, thin "wut-wéet-wit" (last "wit" may be missing).

36.4 BAR-TAILED GODWIT (Fuselo) *Limosa lapponica* L 15.7 in./40 cm. From **36.3** and **36.5** in N-br plumage by patterned upperparts. Note tail barring and lack of wing bar. ♣ Normal winter habitat is wetlands close to sea coast. ♪ Call: mid-high, loud, nasal "wut-wut wut-wut-wut." V.

36.5 [MARBLED GODWIT (Maçarico-marmóreo) *Limosa fedoa*] L 17.7 in./45 cm. Cinnamon coloring of wings, esp. of unmarked underwing, diagnostic. Note upturned bill. ♣ Mainly coastal. ♪ Call: high, gull-like "weuh-weuh-weuh querre-querre-querre."

36.6 ESKIMO CURLEW (Maçarico-esquimó) *Numenius borealis* L 11.8 in./30 cm. Smaller than **36.7**, with relatively thinner and shorter bill, buffier plumage, and less pronounced stripes on sides of crown. ♣ Pampa. R (probably extinct; worldwide no confirmed records since 1963).

36.7 WHIMBREL (Maçarico-galego) *Numenius phaeopus* L 17.7 in./45 cm. American ssp. *haemastica* (**a**) HUDSONIAN CURLEW (Maçarico-do-bico-torto) without white to rump and Eurasian Nom. (**b**), with white rump wedge, shown. ♣ Coastal beaches, mud flats, mangrove swamp. ♪ Call: high, level, rapid, liquid-sounding "bibibibi" (up to 7× "bi").

36.8 GREATER YELLOWLEGS (Maçarico-grande-de-perna-amarela) *Tringa melanoleuca* L 11.8 in./30 cm. Note yellow legs and thin bill, which is longer than head. Neck sides in N-br plumage more conspicuously streaked and head proportionally larger than **36.9**. ♣ Coastal flats and lagoons, also in inland pastures and at streams and pools. ♪ Call: high, loud, nasal "tjeew-tjeew-tjeew - - -" or, in flight, high, nasal, falsetto "fjeet-fjee-wuh."

36.9 LESSER YELLOWLEGS (Maçarico-de-perna-amarela) *Tringa flavipes* L 9.8 in./25 cm. From **36.8** by shorter bill (about length of head). Looks more elegant than **36.8**. ♣ Normally on mud flats and lagoons, but may be seen inland. ♪ Call: high, staccato "tjew-tjew-tjew- -" or, in flight, high, slightly nasal "tiwtiwtiw."

36.10 WILLET (Maçarico-de-asa-branca) *Tringa (or Catoptrophorus) semipalmata* L 15.7 in./40 cm. From **36.3** by shorter, straight, heavier bill, rather plump jizz, and, in flight, by less black in tail pattern. ♣ Salt marshes, mud flats near mangrove. ♪ Call: very high, excited shrieks and screams, like "klee-li" or "willet," often running together to very high, sharp, often falsetto "weer-wee-wee" or musical, ascending and descending "weedl-weedl-willet."

N-br.

36.1

36.2

N-br.

36.6

36.7

36.7

b a

N-br.

N-br.

36.3

N-br.

36.8

N-br.

36.4

N-br.

36.9

N-br.

36.5

N-br.

N-br.

36.10

Plate 37

37.1 RUDDY TURNSTONE (Vira-pedras) *Arenaria interpres* L 9.8 in./25 cm. Dark crescents on breast sides diagnostic. Note drawn-in head and short legs. ♣ At sea coast on rocky shores, sandy beaches with seaweed heaps, exposed reefs. ♪ Flight call: high, rapid, staccato "djidjidji" or "tju-tjutjutju."

37.2 UPLAND SANDPIPER (Maçarico-do-campo) *Bartramia longicauda* L 11.8 in./30 cm. Thin neck and long tail diagnostic. Resembles other buff-brown waders but differs by relatively short, pink-yellow bill and yellow legs. Note pale central part of wing. ♣ Open grassland, bare fields, burned areas. ♪ Call: high, rattling trill "wirrrrrrrrrr" or, in flight, high, fast, fluted "weetweet."

37.3 SPOTTED SANDPIPER (Maçarico-pintado) *Actitis* (or *Tringa*) *macularius* L 7.5 in./19 cm. Tail protruding beyond tail. Note white indent before wing (when perched). ♣ Vegetation at muddy or stony river edges, mangrove. ♪ Call: hurried, clear "weét weét-weét-weét."

37.4 SOLITARY SANDPIPER (Maçarico-solitário) *Tringa solitaria* L 7.9 in./20 cm. Note squarish head, distinct eyering, and greenish legs. Dark underwing diagnostic. ♣ Near streams and other small bodies of waters in savanna. Rare at coast. ♪ Call: very high, thin, soft "peet peet - -"; song: very high, sharp, slightly descending "Pit-pee-wee."

37.5 TEREK SANDPIPER *Xenus cinereus* L 9.8 in./25 cm. Note characteristic upturned bill, dark V-mark on back (which is fainter in N-br plumage), and, in flight, white trailing edge to inner wings. ♣ Seashore, muddy lakes, creeks, and river edges. V.

37.6 COMMON REDSHANK (Maçarico-de-perna-vermelha) *Tringa totanus* L 19.7 in./50 cm. Broad white trailing edge to wings in flight diagnostic. Note red legs and bill base, which are also shown by some ruffs, but these have normally pale base to shorter bill. ♣ Short grass at edge of water bodies. ♪ Call: high, clear "teúhuuh" or "túwee."

37.7 PIED LAPWING (Batuíra-de-esporão) *Vanellus cayanus* L 7.9 in./20 cm. Note conspicuous black and white V on mantle and striking wing pattern. ♣ Open places at savanna ponds, forest rivers, sea coast. ♪ Call; mid-high, piped "wurt" (1–3×) together as angry-sounding, nasal, rapid "wurtwurtwurt."

37.8 SOUTHERN LAPWING (Quero-quero) *Vanellus chilensis* L 13.8 in./35 cm. Unmistakable. Note long, thin crest. ♣ Short-grazed ranchland, fields, wetlands, tidal flats. ♪ Flight call: high, nasal "éuw-éuw-éuw- -."

37.9 AMERICAN GOLDEN-PLOVER (Batuiruçu) *Pluvialis dominica* L 9.8 in./25 cm. From N-br **37.10** by smaller size, slimmer build, some golden speckling on upperparts, less distinct wing bar, more distinct white eyebrow, and unmarked armpits. ♣ Short-grazed ranchland, fields, wetlands, tidal flats. ♪ Call: very high, sharp, rising, fluted "t'tlueeét" (higher-pitched than **37.10**).

37.10 BLACK-BELLIED (or Gray)**PLOVER** (Batuiruçu-de-axila-preta) *Pluvialis squatarola* L 11.8 in./30 cm. Black armpits in N-br plumage diagnostic. Note white vent of Br plumage. ♣ Coastal mud flats and sandy beaches, also at inland waters. ♪ Call: very high, clear, rising "plueeét."

N-br.

37.1

37.2

N-br.

37.3

37.4

37.5

37.6

37.7

37.8

37.9

N-br.

37.10

N-br.

Plate 38

38.1 SEMIPALMATED PLOVER (Batuíra-de-bando)

Charadrius semipalmatus L 7 in./ 18 cm. Note thin eyering, indistinct white eyebrow, starting behind eye, and rather narrow collar without bulges at breast sides. Differs little from slightly larger **38.2**; best to distinguish by voice. Webbed (semipalmated) feet not visible in the field. ♣ Beaches and shores free from vegetation, sandbanks, mud flats. ♪ Call: high, nasal "tuwée."

38.2 ? COMMON RINGED PLOVER (Borrelho-

grande-de-coleiro) *Charadrius hiaticula* L 6.3 in./16 cm. Cf. **38.1**. ♣ Seashore, lake edges, river banks. ♪ Call: high "peep peep peep - -." (Rare vagrant from Eurafrica to the Americas, not yet seen in Brazil.)

38.3 PIPING PLOVER (Batuíra-melodiosa) *Charadrius*

melodus L 7 in./18 cm. From **38.1** by much paler plumage and stockier build. ♣ Normally on sandy beaches. ♪ Call: high "pip pip - -." V.

38.4 WILSON'S (or Thick-billed) **PLOVER** (Batuíra-

bicuda) *Charadrius wilsonia* L 7 in./ 18 cm. Note heavy bill and rosy legs. ♣ Barren sandy beaches of islands and lagoons. Breeds in Brazil; status of migrant population in country, if any, remains to be established. ♪ Call: very high "kwit" or "kwirrit."

38.5 COLLARED PLOVER (Batuíra-de-coleira) *Char-*

adrius collaris L 5.9 in./15 cm. Characterized by lack of hind collar, small size, and pink legs. ♣ Sandy beaches, estuaries, open, sandy savanna. ♪ Call: high, musical "pirrt pirrit kwit-kwit - -."

38.6 TWO-BANDED PLOVER (Batuíra-de-coleira-dupla)

Charadrius falklandicus L 7.5 in./ 19 cm. Rather large with black legs; normally with two breast bands as shown, but upper one sometimes not closed over breast. ♣ Sandy and stony seashores, wet savanna, gravel near streams and ponds. ♪ Flight call: "prit."

38.7 RUFOUS-CHESTED DOTTEREL (or Plover)

(Batuíra-de-peito-tijolo) *Charadrius modestus* L 7.5 in./19 cm. From other plovers by lack of any white to chin and throat in Br and N-br plumage. Note plain wings in flight. ♣ Flooded and eroded grassland, marsh, mud flats, rocky shores. ♪ Call: slightly lowered "puwee."

38.8 TAWNY-THROATED DOTTEREL (Batuíra-de-

papo-ferrugíneo) *Oreopholus ruficollis* L 9.8 in./25 cm. Unmistakable by color pattern and upright stance. ♣ Fields, grassland. ♪ Usually silent.

38.9 WILSON'S PHALAROPE (Pisa-n'água) *Phalaro-*

pus tricolor L 9.8 in./25 cm. Note long, thin bill, white rump without central stripe, and, in flight, uniform wings. Yellow legs (blackish in Br plumage) often visible because species forages more often on land than **38.10**, which is normally seen swimming offshore. ♣ Coastal waters. ♪ Call: mid-high, muffled "wuh-wuh-wuh-wuh -" and low, muffled cackling.

38.10 RED PHALAROPE (Falaropo-de-bico-grosso)

Phalaropus fulicarius L 7.9 in./20 cm. Habitat and blackish ear streak (N-br plumage) diagnostic. ♣ Offshore, occasionally inshore. ♪ Call: low, nasal, and slightly scratchy "éuw éuw éuw - -." V.

38.1 N-br.

38.2 N-br.

38.3 N-br.

38.4 N-br.

38.5 N-br.

N-br. 38.6

N-br. 38.7

38.8

38.9 ♀ ♂

N-br. ♂

N-br. ♂ 38.10 ♂ ♀

Plate 39

39.1 RED KNOT (Maçarico-de-papo-vermelho) *Calidris canutus* L 9.8 in./25 cm. Rather

large, short-legged, plump. In N-br plumage almost uniform gray with greenish legs. Note grayish (actually finely barred) rump and thin white wing stripe. Incomplete Br plumage shown (full Br plumage has more extensive rufous on sides of face). ♣ Beaches, mud flats. ♪ Usually silent.

39.2 SANDERLING (Maçarico-branco) *Calidris alba*

L 7.9 in./20 cm. In N-br plumage distinctive pale gray (almost white) with dark wing shoulder. Striking white wing bar in flight. Runs along the water's edge, being chased by each advancing wave. ♣ Sandy beach at the water line. ♪ Call; very high, thin, hurried "tjuwtjuwtjuw---."

39.3 SEMIPALMATED SANDPIPER (Maçarico-

rasteirinho) *Calidris pusilla* L 5.5 in./14 cm. In N-br plumage more uniform gray than other small sandpipers. Note rather deep bill base. ♣ Mud flats, sandy beaches, occasionally in salt marsh. ♪ Call: high "tri" and short twitters.

39.4 LEAST SANDPIPER (Maçariquinho) *Calidris

minutilla* L 5.5 in./14 cm. From **39.3** and **39.5** by yellowish legs. Full breast band normally well defined. Thin bill slightly curved. ♣ Mainly freshwater mud flats with some low vegetation. ♪ Call: very high, thin "sree sree -sreesree - -."

39.5 WHITE-RUMPED SANDPIPER (Maçarico-de-

sobre-branco) *Calidris fuscicollis* L 6.7 in./17 cm. Note long wing projection, extending beyond tail at rest, and flesh-colored bill base. White rump in flight diagnostic. ♣ Open mud flats at inland and coastal waters.

39.6 BAIRD'S SANDPIPER (Maçarico-de-bico-fino)

Calidris bairdii L 6.3 in./16 cm. Wings project beyond tail. Legs blackish. Note the rather flattened body if seen from behind. Avoids wading. ♣ Dry mud flats, grassland, marsh. ♪ Call: very high, lonely-sounding "tueeh teeeh-teeeh?"

39.7 PECTORAL SANDPIPER (Maçarico-de-colete)

Calidris melanotos L 7.9 in./20 cm. Note slender jizz, slightly decurved, flesh-colored base of bill, and pale yellowish legs. Striped breast and white belly sharply demarcated. ♣ Mainly at edges of freshwater lakes, flood plains, marsh. ♪ Call: mid-high "churr churr -."

39.8 STILT SANDPIPER (Maçarico-pernilongo) *Calidris himantopus* L 7.9 in./20 cm. Note

distinctive long, dull yellow legs, white rump and thin wing bar in flight. ♣ Fresh- and saltwater mud flats. ♪ Usually silent.

39.9 BUFF-BREASTED SANDPIPER (Maçarico-

acanelado) *Tryngites subruficollis* L 7.9 in./20 cm. Prefers dry terrain. Rather plump with thin, black bill, fine spotting on breast sides, sandy-buff plumage. ♣ Short grassland, flood plains. ♪ Usually silent. R.

39.10 [RUFF (Combatente) *Philomachus pugnax*]

L 11.8 in./30 cm (♂), 9.8 in./25 cm (♀). Normally seen in flocks with ♂♂ distinctly larger than ♀. Note plump body with rather small head. ♂♂ esp. variable, even in N-br plumage (some variants of Br plumage shown). Often has pale ring at base of bill, as if smoking a black cigarette. ♣ Shallow water, wet grassland, marsh, flood plains. ♪ Usually silent.

N-br.

39.5

39.1

39.2

N-br.

Br.

Imm.

39.6

N-br.

Br.

Imm.

39.3

N-br.

Br.

N-br.

Imm.

39.7

39.8

N-br.

Br.

Imm.

39.4

N-br.

Br.

Imm.

39.10

39.9

N-br. ♂

♀

Br.

Plate 40

40.1 SOUTH AMERICAN (or Magellan) **SNIPE** (Narceja-sul-americana) *Gallinago paraguaiae* L 11.8 in./30 cm. From **40.2** by yellowish legs and higher forehead. Variable; darker specimens than shown possible. In flight shows

rufous in tail. ♣ Wet savanna. ♪ Call: low, rapid "tsjac-tsjac-tsjac"; song: produced in aerial dive by outer feathers of spread tail, sounds like "wh'wh'wh-wh-wh-wuh wuh wih-wih" (1st half as vibrating, toneless rattle).

40.2 GIANT SNIPE (Narcejão) *Gallinago undulata* L 17.7 in./45 cm. Note large size, gray legs, and broad base to bill ♣ Tall grass, marsh, flood plains. ♪ Call (display call in flight): as **40.1**, but even lower-pitched, shorter, and without vibrations.

40.3 SOUTH AMERICAN PAINTED-SNIPE (Narceja-de-bico-torto) *Nycticryphes semicollaris* L 7.9 in./20 cm. Unmistakable by dark plumage, contrasting with white "brazes," wing spots, and belly. Note pale yellow, down-curved bill. ♣ Open marsh, rice fields, short grassland.

40.4 SOOTY TERN (Trinta-réis-das-rocas) *Onychoprion fuscatus* (or *Sterna fuscata*) L 15.7 in./40 cm. Unmistakable by pied pattern of Ad. and spotted plumage of Imm. ♣ Offshore islands.

40.5 BLACK TERN (Trinta-réis-negro) *Chlidonias niger* L 9.8 in./25 cm. Note in N-br and in Imm. plumages short, shallowly forked tail, compact, short-billed jizz, and dark smudge in front of folded wing. ♣ In winter mainly over coastal waters. ♪ Call: very high, sharp "sreét." V.

40.6 LARGE-BILLED TERN (Trinta-réis-grande) *Phaetusa simplex* L 15.7 in./40 cm. Unmistakable by large size, heavy, yellow bill, and wing pattern. ♣ Beaches, mangrove, estuaries. ♪ Call: mid-high, loud "mew."

40.7 BROWN NODDY (Trinta-réis-escuro) *Anous stolidus* L 15.7 in./40 cm. From smaller **40.8** by less distinct division between white crown and dark neck, also by paler underwing and by contrasting bar over upperwing. ♣ Offshore islands.

40.8 BLACK (or Lesser) **NODDY** (Trinta-réis-preto) *Anous minutus* L 13.8 in./35 cm. Cf. **40.7**. ♣ Offshore islands.

40.9 WHITE (or Fairy) **TERN** (Grazina) *Gygis alba* L 11.8 in./30 cm. Unmistakable by pure white plumage, seemingly large eyes, and short, pointed bill. ♣ Coral islands.

40.10 BLACK SKIMMER (Talha-mar) *Rynchops niger* L 17.7 in./45 cm. Unmistakable by bill shape and fishing method (ploughs, in fast flight, with lower mandible through surface of water, until it touches fish, upon which bill immediately snaps shut). ♣ Open coastal waters and rivers. ♪ Call: nasal cackling.

40.1

40.2

40.3

40.4

40.4

Imm.

40.5

N-br.

Imm.

40.5

N-br.

40.6

40.7

40.8

40.9

N-br.

40.10

Br.

Plate 41

41.1 ROYAL TERN (Trinta-réis-real) *Thalasseus maximus* (or *Sterna maxima*) L 19.7 in./50 cm. Large size and orange bill diagnostic. ♣ Coastal waters, estuaries. ♪ Call: very high "trrreér" or "kree-ur."

41.2 SANDWICH TERN (Trinta-réis-de-bando) *Thalasseus* (or *Sterna*) *sandvicensis* L 15.7 in./40 cm. Sspp. *acutiflavida* (**b**, N migrant with black, yellow-tipped bill) and *eurygnatha* Cayenne Tern (**a**, South American breeder with all-yellow bill). Bill color diagnostic but cf. **40.6**. Cayenne Tern may have yellow (**c**) or black legs. ♣ Beaches, coral flats, estuaries. ♪ Call: very high "kreejik."

41.3 ROSEATE TERN (Trinta-réis-róseo) *Sterna dougallii* L 15.7 in./40 cm. Note pale color of upperparts. Bill color partly red (**a**) at start of breeding season, changing to black within a few weeks (**b**). The long tail with white outer rectrices is diagnostic; **41.5** has the outer rectrices with gray edges. ♣ Coastal waters, estuaries. ♪ Call: very high "kreee-er." R.

41.4 SOUTH AMERICAN TERN (Trinta-réis-de-bico-vermelho) *Sterna hirundinacea* L 15.7 in./40 cm. In all Ad. plumages has all-red bill (occasionally with small dark tip). From **41.5**, by tail reaching beyond wingtips when perched; differs from **41.6** and **41.7** by more uniform gray upperwing, larger size, heavier bill, longer tail, and less pelagic habitat. ♣ Coastal waters, estuaries, harbors.

41.5 COMMON TERN (Trinta-réis-boreal) *Sterna hirundo* L 13.8 in./35 cm. Characteristic black tip to red bill in Br plumage. Tail not projecting. Strong dark accent to wing bend in N-br and Imm. plumage. Note wing pattern in 1st W with rather dark secondaries. ♣ Coastal and inland along large rivers. ♪ Call; very high "kreeeeejur" ("jur" lower in pitch).

41.6 ARCTIC TERN (Trinta-réis-ártico) *Sterna paradisaea* L 13.8 in./35 cm. From **41.5** by shorter legs, rounder head, shorter bill, and large translucent-looking areas at rear wing. S plumages of **41.6** and **41.7** (gray overall with narrow white cheek) unlikely to be seen in Brazil. W plumages of **41.6** (acquired in N winter) and **41.7** (in austral winter) not safely separable from each other, but forewing of **41.6** darker and bill slightly shorter. ♣ Offshore; rare near coast. ♪ Call: as **41.5**, but even higher pitched.

41.7 ANTARCTIC TERN (Trinta-réis-antártico) *Sterna vittata* L 13.8 in./35 cm. Cf. **41.6**. Bill color variable, but all red (as shown) only for a short period, at beginning of Br season (May–June). Note differences in patterning of upperwing in Imms. **41.6** and **41.7**. ♣ Mainly pelagic. ♪ Call: high "bic-bic beec - -." V.

41.8 SNOWY-CROWNED (or Trudeau's) **TERN** (Trinta-réis-de-coroa-branca) *Sterna trudeaui* L 13.8 in./35 cm. Rather large, stocky, and with heavy bill. Very pale gray with white head. Never shows a full cap, only a smear through eye. ♣ Fresh- and saltwater wetlands. May feed over fields.

41.9 LEAST TERN (Trinta-réis-miúdo) *Sternula* (or *Sterna*) *antillarum* L 9.8 in./25 cm. From similar small-sized **41.10** by smaller bill, which is black with yellow tip in Br plumage and all black in N-br plumage. Imm. differs from Imm. **41.10** by darker band across forewing and all-black bill. ♣ Water bodies close to the sea. ♪ Call: very high, nasal "kreeh-kreeh-krih - -."

41.10 YELLOW-BILLED TERN (Trinta-réis-anão) *Sternula* (or *Sterna*) *superciliaris* L 9.8 in./25 cm. Bill all yellow in all plumages. 1st 5 primaries are black, whereas **41.9** has only 1 or 2 primaries black. ♣ Coastal waters. ♪ Call: very high, mewing "tsip - -."

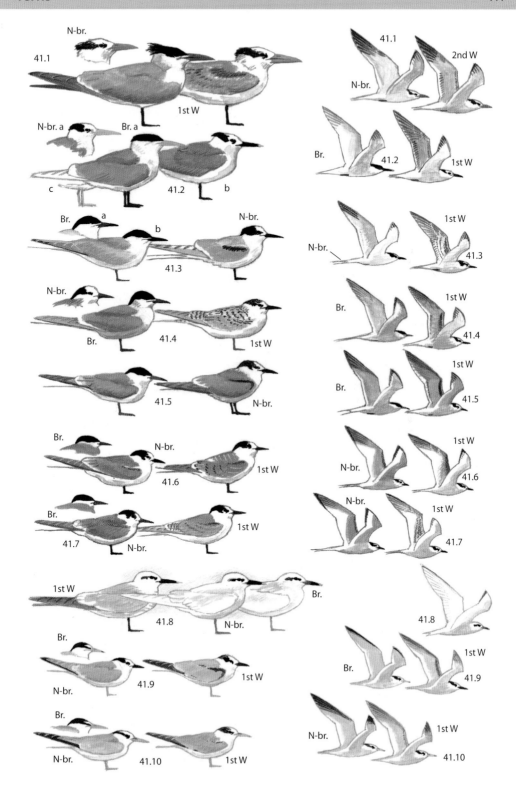

41.1 N-br.

2nd W

N-br.

1st W

41.1 N-br. a Br. a c 41.2 b

Br. 41.2 1st W

Br. a b N-br. 41.3

N-br. 1st W 41.3

N-br. Br. 41.4 1st W

Br. 1st W 41.4

41.5 N-br.

Br. 1st W 41.5

Br. N-br. 41.6 1st W

N-br. 1st W 41.6

Br. 41.7 N-br. 1st W

N-br. 1st W 41.7

1st W 41.8 N-br. Br.

41.8

Br. N-br. 41.9 1st W

Br. 1st W 41.9

Br. N-br. 41.10 1st W

N-br. 1st W 41.10

Plate 42

42.1 GULL-BILLED TERN (Trinta-réis-de-bico-preto)

Gelochelidon (or Sterna) nilotica L 15.7 in./40 cm. Very pale. Short, thick bill and long legs diagnostic. N-br and Imm. birds have little black behind eyes. Does not plunge-dive, but picks small insects and such from ground or water surface; often seen picking crabs from mud flats while in flight. ♣ Coastal waters (incl. nearby lakes/marshes), estuaries. ♪ Call: mewing, nasal "w'Wèt" or bleating "meh-eh-heh."

42.2 OLROG'S GULL (Gaivota-de-Olorg) *Larus*

atlanticus L 21.5 in./55 cm. In W with white, brown-freckled head; smaller than **42.3**, with differently patterned bill. Head is darker in 1st W than head of **42.3** in 1st W. ♣ Sea coast, estuaries, river banks. R.

42.3 KELP GULL (Gaivotão) *Larus dominicanus* L

23.6 in./60 cm. Black mantle and wings with characteristic pattern at wing tip diagnostic. Note barring of mantle in 1st W. 2nd W (perched) has extensive gray in mantle and wings and blackish subterminal tail band and white uppertail coverts. ♣ Coastal waters. ♪ Call: hoarse, slightly downslurred "wru'uh" or high, staccato, resounding, nasal "wic-wic-wir-wir- -."

42.4 LESSER BLACK-BACKED GULL (Gaivota-de-

asa-escura) *Larus fuscus* L 19.7 in./50 cm. Three sspp. could wander to Brazil: Nom. (**a**, upperparts as black as those of **42.3** but with smaller white tips to primaries, thinner bill, yellow-orange legs, and more slender jizz), *intermedius* (**b**, with outer wing deeper black than inner wing), and *graelsii* (not shown, with gray upperparts). 2nd W differs from that of **42.3** (not shown in flight) by darker secondary coverts and little or no contrast between inner and outer primaries. ♣ Sea coast and estuaries. ♪ Call: very high, loud, raucous, descending "eeer-tjouw-tjouw- -." V.

42.5 GRAY-HOODED (or -headed) **GULL** (Gaivota-

de-cabeça-cinza) *Chroicocephalus* (or *Larus*) *cirrocephalus* L 15.7 in./40 cm. Note pale eyes. Br head as gray as mantle. Perched W birds generally not unlike **42.6**, but with completely different and diagnostic upper- and underwing pattern. ♣ Coastal and inland waters. ♪ Call: mid-high, nasal shrieks, like "sruw" or "wreer."

42.6 BROWN-HOODED GULL (Gaivota-maria-velha)

Chroicocephalus (or *Larus*) *maculipennis* L 17.7 in./45 cm. White wedge on outerwing diagnostic. 1st W, like Ad. plumage, shows much white in outer area of upperwing. ♣ Coastal and inland waters, harbors. ♪ Call: downslurred "aoch aoch aoch."

42.7 LAUGHING GULL (Gaivota-alegre) *Leucophaeus*

(or *Larus*) *atricilla* L 15.7 in./40 cm. Small white primary tips. Note black at wing tips merging gradually in dark gray upperwing and mantle. W plumage with gray wash from neck to flanks. 1st W differs from other Imm. gulls by grayish neck. ♣ Strictly coastal. ♪ Call/song: high, nasal "ka-weck" and "kakaka-kaka-ka-kèèf."

42.8 FRANKLIN'S GULL (Gaivota-de-franklin) *Leu-*

cophaeus (or *Larus*) *pipixcan* L 13.8 in./35 cm. White wing tip diagnostic. Note black and gray separated by white in wings; extensive dark hood in N-br and 1st W plumage. ♣ ♪ Coastal and inland waters, marshes, fields, grassland, refuse dumps. ♪ Call: very high, sharp, nasal, descending series of "naJaah Jaah - --." V.

42.9 RING-BILLED GULL (Gaivota-de-bico-manchado)

Larus delawarensis L 19.7 in./50 cm. Bill pattern and pale eyes diagnostic. Note upperwing pattern without white between black wing tip and gray rest of wing. Imms. have pink, not yellow-green, bills; 1st W with gray mantle, 2nd W with row of black spots at end of tail. ♣ Coastal and inland waters, fields, grassland, refuse dumps. ♪ Call: very high, desperate-sounding "pieeew" (single or in descending series) or "puweeé." V.

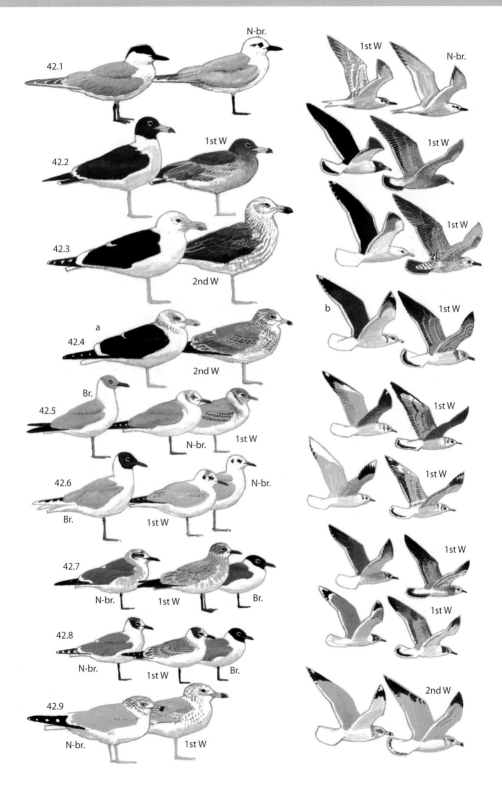

42.1 N-br. 1st W N-br.

42.2 1st W 1st W

42.3 2nd W 1st W

42.4 a 2nd W b 1st W

42.5 Br. N-br. 1st W 1st W

42.6 Br. 1st W N-br. 1st W

42.7 N-br. 1st W Br. 1st W

42.8 N-br. 1st W Br. 1st W

42.9 N-br. 1st W 2nd W

Plate 43

43.1 PARASITIC (or Arctic) **JAEGER** (Mandrião- parasítico) *Stercorarius parasiticus* L 15.7 in./40 cm (excl. tail stream- ers). Pale (**a**) and dark (**b**) forms shown. Note pale spot between lore and bill base. Pointed tail feathers (shorter than **43.2**) diagnostic. Neck sides solid gray (extending around upperbreast like a paler-colored collar), not speckled as in **43.3**. Imm. rather rufous overall. ♣ Off- shore and coastal. Accidental inland along large rivers.

43.2 LONG-TAILED JAEGER (Mandrião-de-cauda- comprida) *Stercorarius longicaudus* L 15.7 in./40 cm (excl. tail streamers). Ad. without white flash in wings; chest band weak or missing. Imm. cold gray and white wing flash small or missing. ♣ Offshore. Accidental near the coast. R.

43.3 POMARINE JAEGER (Mandrião-pomarino) *Ster-* *corarius pomarinus* L 17.7 in./45 cm (excl. tail streamers). Normal (**a**) and dark (**b**) forms shown. Length- ened, twisted, blunt tail feathers diagnostic, but these often missing in worn plumage. Neck sides speckled. Bill pinkish. Note pattern of double white patch on outer underwing of Imm. ♣ Offshore. Accidental near the coast and inland along large rivers.

43.4 GREAT SKUA (Mandrião-grande) *Stercorarius* (or *Catharacta*) *skua* L 21.5 in./55 cm. Ad. distinctively striped overall with dark eye patches. Upperwing in flight (not shown) two-toned with blackish secondaries and primaries and much paler coverts. Overall warmer toned than **43.5**. Pattern of darker eye patches retained in dark form, which has all-dark wings. Imm. rather rufous, with darker head (not with only dark cap as **43.6** Imm.). ♣ Offshore. Rarer near the coast. R.

43.5 SOUTH POLAR SKUA (Mandrião-do-sul) *Sterco-* *rarius* (or *Catharacta*) *maccormicki* L 21.5 in./55 cm. Pale (**a**) and dark (**b**) forms shown. Less warm toned than **43.4** and not striped below. Imm. dark steel-gray. ♣ Offshore. Rarer near coast.

43.6 CHILEAN SKUA (Mandrião-chileno) *Stercorarius* (or *Catharacta*) *chilensis* L 21.5 in./ 55 cm. Distinctively patterned and colored with dark cap and rufous cheeks. Note bicolored bill of adult. Imm. (not shown) as Ad. but mantle and wings barred, not striped. ♣ Offshore. Rarer near the coast.

43.7 BROWN (Southern or Falkland) **SKUA** (Mandrião- antártico) *Stercorarius* (or *Cathar- acta*) *antarcticus* L 23.5 in./60 cm. Ssp. *hamiltoni* Tristan Skua (**a**, from Tristan da Cunha) and paler Nom. Falkland Skua (**b**, from Falkland Islands) shown. Not shown ssp. *lonnbergi* Subantarctic Skua (largest skua, dark brown, with irregular, pale blotch- ing on mantle and often some scattered white spots on forehead and crown). May resemble **43.4**, but with less contrast in wings and without dark eye patches. ♣ Off- shore. Rarer near the coast. *Note*: The variation in plum- age, esp. among Imms. is much greater than can be shown or described.

43.1   1st W   Br.   a.   Br.   b.   N-br. a   Imm.

43.2   1st W   Br.   Br.   N-br.   Imm.

43.3   1st W   Br.   a.   N-br.   Br.   b.

43.4   Imm.   Imm.

43.5   Imm.   Ad. a   Ad. b   43.4   43.5

43.6   43.6

43.7   a.   b.   43.7

Plate 44

44.1 COMMON GROUND-DOVE (Rolinha-cinzenta)

Columbina passerina L 6.7 in./17 cm. From other Ground-Doves by scaling of chest and head. ♣ Virtually any open to semiopen habitat (even in towns). ♪ Song: mid-high, hollow, pushed-out "oowhò" in long series.

44.2 PLAIN-BREASTED GROUND-DOVE (Rolinha-de-asa-canela) *Columbina minuta* L

5.9 in./15 cm. ♂ with pink flush to chest and gray cap and rump. ♀ resembles **44.3** ♀. ♣ Arid areas with scrub, some trees, and bare patches; savanna, fields. ♪ Song: long, monotonous series of mid-high, hollow "whoop" notes.

44.3 RUDDY GROUND-DOVE (Rolinha-roxa) *Columbina talpacoti* L 6.3 in./16 cm. ♂

unmistakable by gray crown contrasting with vinaceous-rufous body. ♀ differs from smaller **44.2** ♀ by longer tail, browner plumage, rufescent rump, black underwing coverts (rufous in **44.1** and **44.2**), and black wing spots (no violet iridescence). ♣ Semiopen habitats, incl. lightly wooded country, forest edge, savanna, riverine growth, scrubby areas, fields, towns. Prefers humid areas. ♪ Song: long, monotonous series of mid-high, hollow "whuc" notes or "t't'wooh."

44.4 PICUI GROUND-DOVE (Rolinha-picui) *Columbina picui* L 7 in./18 cm. Unmistak-

able by wing and tail pattern. ♣ Savanna, grassland, forest edge, towns. Mainly in arid areas. ♪ Song: series of about 5 "u'Loh" notes.

44.5 BLUE-EYED GROUND-DOVE (Rolinha-do-planalto) *Columbina cyanopis* L 6.3

in./16 cm. Sexes similar. From **44.3** ♂ by whitish vent and no gray on crown. ♣ Grassland within cerrado. Very rare, possibly extinct. En, R.

44.6 BLUE GROUND-DOVE (Pararu-azul) *Claravis*

pretiosa L 7.9 in./20 cm. ♂ with black outer rectrices and wing spots (latter often forming bands). ♀ with chestnut wing-spots and rufous rump and central rectrices. ♣ In or near forest, woodland, scrubby areas. ♪ Song: slow series of 5–7 deep "oop" notes at 1-sec intervals.

44.7 PURPLE-WINGED GROUND-DOVE (Pararu-es-

pelho) *Claravis godefrida* L 7.9 in./ 20 cm. ♂ differs from **44.6** ♂ by broader, blackish purple wing bars and white outer rectrices. ♀ differs from **44.6** ♀ by broader, darker wing bars and less rufescent central rectrices and rump. ♣ Humid forest, mainly in hilly areas. Associated with flowering bamboo. R.

44.8 [SAPPHIRE QUAIL-DOVE (Juriti-safira) *Geotry-*

gon saphirina] L 9.8 in./25 cm. Unmistakable by contrasting head pattern and bluish rump. ♣ Terra firme. ♪ Song: long series of 2-noted "u-cróo" ("u" hard to hear). *Note*: Not confirmed in Brazil, but likely to occur.

44.9 VIOLACEOUS QUAIL-DOVE (Juriti-vermelha)

Geotrygon violacea L 9.8 in./25 cm. Bill red. Face whitish (no contrasting dark moustache). Creamy whitish underwing coverts diagnostic. ♣ Humid forest and nearby second growth/plantations. Rather arboreal. ♪ Song: slow series of high, deep "pooo" notes.

44.10 RUDDY QUAIL-DOVE (Pariri) *Geotrygon mon-*

tana L 9.8 in./25 cm. From **44.9** by more distinct face pattern. Note violaceus wash to nape and neck. ♣ Humid forest and nearby second growth/plantations. ♪ Song: slow, very low monotonous series of deep, hollow "cooo" notes.

44.1

44.2

44.3

44.4

44.5

44.6

44.7

44.8

44.9

44.10

Plate 45

45.1 SCALED DOVE (Fogo-apagou) *Columbina squam-* *mata* L 7.9 in./20 cm. Unmistakable by scaling (reduced in Imm.), rufous flash in wings, and long, pointed tail. ♣ Dry savanna with scrub and some tree cover, cultivation, settlements, cities. ♪ Call/song: very high, piped "whu papá" in long series.

45.2 LONG-TAILED GROUND-DOVE (Rolinha-vaque- ira) *Uropelia campestris* L 6.7 in./ 17 cm. Unmistakable by black and white wing bars, yellow eyering, and long tail. ♣ Grassland, savanna, woodland edge. Mainly in drier regions.

45.3 EARED DOVE (Pomba-de-bando) *Zenaida auri-* *culata* L 9.8 in./25 cm. Note wedge-shaped tail, black spots on wings, and two streaks on ear coverts. No rufous in wings. ♣ Wide range of open to semiopen habitats, incl. towns. Spreading due to deforestation. ♪ Song: low, gloomy-sounding "whoo coocoo coo."

45.4 WHITE-TIPPED DOVE (Juriti-pupu) *Leptotila* *verreauxi* L 9.8 in./25 cm. Bill black. Crown to upper mantle tinged gray. Note broad white tips to tail (mainly visible from below) and extensive rufous in underwing. Cf. **45.5**. ♣ Woodland, second growth, forest edge (avoids interior of humid forest), plantations. Prefers drier habitats than **45.5**. ♪ Song: varies by region; e.g., mid-high, mournful, single "oooh" note, slightly gaining in strength, level or slightly lowered and rising.

45.5 GRAY-FRONTED DOVE (Juriti-gemedeira) *Lep-* *totila rufaxilla* L 11.8 in./30 cm. Resembles **45.4**, but with narrower white tips to tail, purplish tinge to upper mantle, and bluish gray central crown that contrasts clearly with hindcrown/nape. ♣ Forest and nearby second growth. Generally avoids arid areas. ♪ Song: varies by region; e.g., mid-high, mournful, single "oooh" note, slightly gaining in strength at 4- to 5-sec intervals.

45.6 ? EURASIAN TURTLE-DOVE (Rola-turca) *Streptopelia decaocto* L 11.8 in./30 cm. No other dove with black bar across neck. Long, slender, rather pale. ♣ Completely dependent on human surroundings. ♪ Call: nasal, high, querelous "kruuur"; song: high "coocoo cu" repeated at 0.5-sec intervals.

45.7 ROCK (Dove or) **PIGEON** (Pombo-doméstico) *Columba livia* L 13.8 in./35 cm. Ancestor from the Old World of all feral pigeons; in most of these the basic ancestral features such as bars across wings, white rump, terminal tail bar, and neck coloring retained. ♣ Towns, occasionally at cliffs. I.

45.8 PALE-VENTED PIGEON (Pomba-galega) *Pata-* *gioenas cayennensis* L 9.8 in./25 cm. Note vinaceous shoulder, grayish white belly, and gray rump. ♣ Edge of humid forest, woodland, tree stands in savanna. Often near rivers. ♪ Song: high, soft, cooing "óot-ke-toóh," repeated 6–7 × without intervals.

45.9 PLUMBEOUS PIGEON (Pomba-amargosa) *Pata-* *gioenas plumbea* L 13.8 in./35 cm. From smaller **45.10** by grayer (less vinaceous) color, slightly longer bill and, in area of overlap, whitish eyes (Juv. and SE sspp. with reddish eyes). ♣ Canopy and borders of forest; also nearby second growth. ♪ Song: varies per region; might be a high, piped, slightly irregular "oot oot Oót coo-coór."

45.10 RUDDY PIGEON (Pomba-botafogo) *Patagioenas* *subvinacea* L 11.8 in./30 cm. Iris reddish to pale yellowish, but from a distance eyes appear dark due to red eyering. Cf. **45.9**. ♣ Canopy and borders of humid forest. ♪ Song: high, mellow "oot wuoo-coocoo."

Plate 46

46.1 SCALED PIGEON (Pomba-trocal) *Patagioenas* *speciosa* L 11.8 in./30 cm. Scaling diagnostic. Note yellow-tipped red bill and white vent contrasting with dark tail. ♣ Canopy and edge of forest, woodland. Will fly over open areas to reach suitable habitats. ♪ Song: very low "oo-loúah ooh ooh" (only "lou" higher pitched).

46.2 PICAZURO PIGEON (Pombão) *Patagioenas pica-* *zuro* L 13.8 in./35 cm. Scaly neck diagnostic, but this featutre is not always well developed. Note white rim along upperwing coverts and black terminal tail bar. ♣ Woodland, riverine belts, savanna, towns. ♪ Song: typical pigeonlike, high "oo Oó koo-kwoo," repeated up to 6 × without intervals.

46.3 SPOT-WINGED PIGEON (Pomba-do-orvalho) *Patagioenas maculosa* L 13.8 in./35 cm. Extensive spotting on wings diagnostic. Tail as **46.2**. ♣ Dry open woodland, cultivation. ♪ Song: very low, hoarse, laborious "ucch uch-uch-uch-ucch uch-uch-uch ucch," repeated 2–4 ×.

46.4 BAND-TAILED PIGEON (Pomba-de-coleira- branca) *Patagioenas fasciata* L 15.7 in./40 cm. Note neck pattern, pale gray terminal half of tail, and yellow legs and bill. ♣ Humid forest and shrubbery from 800 to 2000 m. ♪ Song: low, regular, deep, "pumped out" or sawing "ooh ooh - -," up to 10 ×.

46.5 CHESTNUT-FRONTED MACAW (Maracanã- guaçu) *Ara severus* L 19.7 in./50 cm. Note white face, maroon frontlet, and lack of red on belly. Red underwing diagnostic. ♣ Edge of humid forest (mainly várzea; infrequently flying over terra firme), riverine belts, second growth with scattered trees. ♪ Call: high, hoarse "WRAA-WRAA-WRAA" or chattering "chew-chew-chiw-chew - -."

46.6 RED-BELLIED MACAW (Maracanã-do-buriti) *Orthopsittaca manilata* L 19.7 in./50 cm. Note yellowish face, red on belly, and lack of red/maroon on forehead. Underwing yellowish as in **46.8** and **46.9**. ♣ Clearings and borders of humid forest (will fly over dense forest), riverine belts, savanna, plantations. Associated with *Mauritia* palms. ♪ Call: high, muttering "wreh" and very high, shrieking "weer-eh-weer-wir."

46.7 BLUE-HEADED MACAW (Maracanã-de-cabeça- azul) *Primolius* (or *Propyrrhura*) *couloni* L 15.7 in./40 cm. Note gray facial skin and bicolored bill, but be aware of Imm. with white face and all-dark bill. No red/maroon on forehead or belly. ♣ Forest edge and clearings, esp. at rivers and streams. ♪ Call: nasal, clenched "tjèhtjèr," "wrrrèh" or "wrèh-wrèh-wrèh." R.

46.8 BLUE-WINGED MACAW (Maracanã-verdadeira) *Primolius* (or *Propyrrhura*) *maracana* L 15.7 in./40 cm. Resembles **46.6**, but with red forehead and patch on lower back. Face yellowish or white. ♣ Forest edge, plam groves, and riverine belts in caatinga. ♪ Call: e.g., high, shrieking "WÈH-WÈH-WÈH- -." R.

46.9 YELLOW- (or Golden-) **COLLARED MACAW** (Maracanã-de-colar) *Primolius* (or *Propyrrhura*) *auricollis* L 15.7 in./40 cm. Yellow collar diagnostic. Yellowish underwing as **46.6** and **46.8**, but note lack of red on belly. ♣ More or less wooded savanna, cerrado. ♪ Loud, rasping "WRUH-WRUH-WRUH- -."

46.10 RED-SHOULDERED MACAW (Maracanã- pequena) *Diopsittaca nobilis* L 11.8 in./30 cm. Three sspp.: *cumanensis/lon-gipennis* (**a**, widespread S of Ri. Amazon; with pale upper mandible) and Nom. (**b**, N of Ri. Amazon; all-dark bill). Note red underwing coverts, white face, and lack of red on belly. Smallest macaw, easily mistaken for **48.1** or **48.2**. ♣ Savanna and marsh with palm stands, riverine belts, woodland. ♪ Call: loud, rasping "Urc" or "WRUH-WRUH-WRUH."

Plate 47

47.1 HYACINTH MACAW (Arara-azul-grande) *Anodorhynchus hyacinthinus* L 39 in./100 cm.

Largest macaw. Note narrow yellow lappet which stretches when bill is open. Not in range of **47.2** and **47.3**. ♣ Near palm stands at forest edge, savanna, and open woodland. ♪ Call: rather low, rattling "AARRah- AARRah- -" in long series. R.

47.2 INDIGO (or Lear's) **MACAW** (Arara-azul-de-lear)

Anodorhynchus leari L 29.5 in./75 cm. Not in range of **47.1** and **47.3**. Note large, roundish, yellow lappets at bill base. ♣ Caatinga with palms. Roosts and breeds on cliffs. ♪ Call: rather low, raucous, slightly crowlike "wraah." En, R.

47.3 GLAUCOUS MACAW (Arara-azul-pequena) *Anodorhynchus glaucus* L 27.5 in./70 cm.

Not in range of bluer **47.1** and **47.2**. ♣ Presumably open to semiopen areas with palms. Probably extinct. R.

47.4 SPIX'S (or Little Blue) **MACAW** (Ararinha-azul)

Cyanopsitta spixii L 21.5 in./55 cm. Note pale head contrasting with bluish body. Facial skin gray; white in Imm. ♣ Gallery woodland in caatinga. Extinct in the wild; a captive population exists. En, R.

47.5 BLUE-AND-YELLOW MACAW (Arara-canindé)

Ara ararauna L 33.5 in./85 cm. Unmistakable by color pattern. ♣ Várzea, riverine belts, woodland, savanna with scattered trees, cerrado. ♪ Call: mid-high, scraping "wrraah-wrraah-wrraah" and nasal "WREH-WRAH-Wreh wreh - -."

47.6 SCARLET MACAW (Araracanga) *Ara macao* L 33.5 in./85 cm.

From larger **47.7** by yellow bar across upperwing and less distinct red lines in white face. ♣ In or near humid forest, mainly terra firme. Locally also humid wooded savanna. ♪ Call: nasal "E'Eèh," "sraAAh," or "wrEH."

47.7 RED-AND-GREEN (or Green-winged) **MACAW**

(Arara-vermelha-grande) *Ara chloropterus* L 37.5 in./95 cm. No yellow in wing. Virtually all red from below (as **47.6**, but darker). ♣ Forest (mainly humid, but locally even caatinga), riverine belts, wooded savanna. ♪ Call: mid-high, groaning "ih-urre-urre," "wireh," "kraaAH" or "WRAAAH," often changing to falsetto.

47.8 GOLDEN PARAKEET (Ararajuba) *Guarouba guarouba* L 13.8 in./35 cm.

Note pale bill. ♣ Terra firme and clearings with scattered trees. ♪ Call: high, slightly hoarse, upslurred "kree-krree-kree-kree" or "krueh." En, R.

47.9 SUN PARAKEET (Jandaia-amarela) *Aratinga solstitialis* L 11.8 in./30 cm.

From **47.10** (note range) by more yellow and orange. Imm. with greenish head and mantle. ♣ Foothill forest. Will cross more open habitat (e.g., savanna) to reach other forested areas. ♪ Call: very high, loud, gull-like shrieking, "zeet-zeet-zeet- -." (Introduced to Fernando de Noronha.) R.

47.10 SULFUR-BREASTED PARAKEET (Cacaué) *Aratinga pintoi* L 11.8 in./30 cm.

Resembles **47.9**, but suffused with green and with less orange; Imms. of the two spp. alike. A recently described species. ♣ Open to semiopen areas, gallery forest. ♪ Call: sharp, very high shrieking, like "eeuwt-uht-uht."

47.1

47.2

47.3

47.4

47.5

47.6

47.6

47.7

47.8

Imm.

47.9

47.10

Plate 48

48.1 BLUE-CROWNED PARAKEET (Aratinga-de-testa-azul) *Aratinga acuticaudata* L 13.8 in./35 cm. Two sspp.; Nom. (**a**, in far SW; lower mandible black, crown and cheeks bluish) and widespread *haemorrhous* (**b**; all-pale bill and bluish crown). Note lack of red in plumage, except at base of undertail. ♣ Woodland, cerrado, open areas with scattered trees, cultivated areas. ♪ Call: magpie-like, shrieking "wrah" or "sreehsreeh" In flight more nasal "tjaw-tjaw" or gull-like "weeh-wéehweéh."

48.2 WHITE-EYED PARAKEET (Periquitão-maracanã) *Aratinga leucophthalma* L 13.8 in./35 cm. Bill pale. Underwing primary coverts and random speckling on neck/head red (lacking in Juv.). Note absence of blue. Cf. also **48.1**, **46.10**, and **49.2**. ♣ Woodland, savannalike habitats, riverine belts, forest edge, várzea, mangrove. Will fly over terra firme to reach suitable habitats. ♪ Song/call: very high, nasal shrieking "r'teet-r'teet-tiw- -" or "sreet-sreet- -."

48.3 JANDAYA PARAKEET (Jandaia-verdadeira) *Aratinga jandaya* L 11.8 in./30 cm. Note orange-yellow head (lightly suffused green in Imm.) unlike **48.4**; hybrids occur in the limited area of overlap. No overlap with **47.9** and **47.10**. Typical upperwing pattern (**a**) rather similar in **47.9** and **48.4–48.9**. ♣ Forest edge, woodland, and pastures and fields with tree stands. ♪ Call: very high, shrieking "uht-uht-uht- -." En.

48.4 GOLDEN-CAPPED PARAKEET (Jandaia-de-testa-vermelha) *Aratinga auricapillus* L 11.8 in./30 cm. Note orange/red belly (extend varies) and reddish ocular region and underwing coverts. May have yellow-tinged cheeks. Cf. **48.3** and **48.6**. ♣ Mainly semideciduous forest. Also edge of humid forest and nearby secondary growth and agriculture. ♪ Call: loud, shrieking "uht-uht tuw." En, R.

48.5 DUSKY-HEADED PARAKEET (Periquito-de-cabeça-suja) *Aratinga weddellii* L 11.8 in./30 cm. Head gray. Chest green (not brownish olive as in **48.6–48.8**). ♣ Borders and clearings of humid forest, incl. forest remnants surrounded by open habitats; also plantations. ♪ Call: high, shrieking "weet-weet wit-wit -," less loud and piercing than other *Aratinga* parakeets.

48.6 PEACH-FRONTED PARAKEET (Periquito-rei) *Aratinga aurea* L 9.8 in./25 cm. Note yellow-orange forehead (smaller in Imm.) and lime-green belly. ♣ Semiopen to open habitats with trees (locally even in towns). Avoids dense humid forest. ♪ Call: rolling "vreet vreet-vreet-vreet-vreet," irregularly breaking from low to very high pitched.

48.7 BROWN-THROATED PARAKEET (Periquito-de-bochecha-parda) *Aratinga pertinax* L 9.8 in./25 cm. Three ssps: NW *chrysogenys* (**a**, crown greenish, sometimes tinged blue), *chrysophrys* (**b**, N Roraima; paler than **a**, and forehead yellowish-brown), and *paraensis* (**c**, S Pará; resembles **b**, but forehead bluish). Note brownish chest. Orange to mid-belly and yellow to ocular region often lacking. No overlap with **48.8**. ♣ Dry and arid savanna with tree stands and woodland remains or mangrove, forest edge, cultivation. ♪ Call: shrill, very high "vrreeh vreevreeh vrivri - -."

48.8 CACTUS (or Caatinga) **PARAKEET** (Periquito-da-caatinga) *Aratinga cactorum* L 9.8 in./25 cm. From **48.6** by wing pattern, yellow/orange belly, and lack of orange in head. No overlap with **48.5** and **48.7**. ♣ Caatinga, cerrado, and degraded pastures. ♪ Call: very high, hurried "vreevree---" or shrill "tu-tjeew-tjeew." En.

48.9 NANDAY (or Black-hooded) **PARAKEET** (Periquito-de-cabeça-preta) *Nandayus nenday* L 13.8 in./35 cm. Unmistakable by contrasting black hood and blue-black flight feathers. Chest tinged blue. ♣ Gallery forest, woodland, savanna. ♪ Call: Very high, shrieking "wri-uuh," "srree-srree-srree- -," or "rruh rruh ruh."

a

b

48.1

48.6

48.2

a   b   c

48.3

48.7

a

48.4

48.8

48.5

48.9

Plate 49

PYRRHURA PARAKEETS: Long-tailed with upperside of primaries bluish. Chest scaly (except in **49.1** and **49.8**) and belly maroon (reduced/lacking in Ad. **49.4** and **50.5–50.7** and in Juv. of all). Red rump in **49.1**, **49.7–49.10**, and **50.1–50.4**. Noisy in flight, where typically close to the canopy or, when crossing open space, the ground. Generally silent and difficult to see when perched. Little or no overlap between most, but cf. *Aratinga* parakeets (Pl. **48**).

49.1 BLUE-THROATED (or Ochre-marked) **PARAKEET**

(Tiriba-grande) *Pyrrhura cruentata* L 11.8 in./30 cm. Note distinctive facial pattern and blue chest. ♣ Canopy and edge of humid forest. Locally in shaded plantations and selectively logged forest. Up to 950 m. ♪ Call: nasal twittering "tr tr tjer-tjer-tjer- -" or "tjeh-tjeh- -." En, R.

49.2 BLAZE-WINGED PARAKEET (Tiriba-fogo) *Pyr-*

rhura devillei L 9.8 in./25 cm. Note yellowish green uppertail and grayish brown crown. Red and yellow underwing coverts (reduced in Juv.), unlike other *Pyrrhura* parakeets in range (cf. **48.2**). ♣ Riverine belts in Pantanal and adjacent areas. ♪ Call: very high, rather shrill "wreet-je," or "sree-eh-sree-sree"-type notes.

49.3 MAROON-BELLIED (or Reddish-bellied) **PARA-**

KEET (Tiriba-de-testa-vermelha) *Pyrrhura frontalis* L 9.8 in./25 cm. Forecrown greenish; usually with maroon frontlet. Two ssps.: N Nom. (**a**; uppertail green with maroon tip) and S *chiripepe* (**b**; uppertail yellowish green). ♣ Forest (incl. *Araucaria*), gallery woodland, city parks. Up to 2000 m. ♪ Call: very high, sharp, nasal "wuut-tjeet-tjeet," "tirr," or "terrre-terre-tjurk-tjurk."

49.4 PEARLY PARAKEET (Tiriba-pérola) *Pyrrhura*

lepida L 9.8 in./25 cm. Nom ssp. *lepida* (**a**, with red underwing coverts and blue tinge to cheeks, chest, and thighs) and *anerythra* (**b**, W part of range; with less blue and no red in wing). Little or no red on belly. Cf. **50.1** (only other *Pyrrhura* in range) and *Aratinga* parakeets (Pl. **48**). ♣ Canopy and edge of terra firme, second growth. ♪ Call: very high, nasal, "wih-chew" or chattering "wic-wic-wic- -." En, R.

49.5 CRIMSON-BELLIED PARAKEET (Tiriba-de-

barriga-vermelha) *Pyrrhura perlata;* L 9.8 in./25 cm. Unmistakable by red underparts (reduced in Juv.). ♣ Canopy and edge of humid forest (locally in drier areas), second growth. ♪ Call: high, rapid "wrr'wur-wir-wir-wir." Also a strange, slightly toy-trumpet–like "peeéh" at 1- to 3-sec intervals.

49.6 GREEN-CHEEKED PARAKEET (Tiriba-de-cara-

suja) *Pyrrhura molinae* L 9.8 in./25 cm. Uppertail maroon. Crown brownish-gray. A rare yellow form (**a**) exists. Cf. **48.2**, **48.3**, and **50.7**. ♣ Woodland, forest (mainly deciduous), riverine belts. ♪ Call: very high, shrieking "sit-sit-sit- -," "peer-wit" or "puhr-weet," often with quality of a squeaky wheel.

49.7 WHITE-EARED (or Maroon-faced) **PARAKEET**

(Tiriba-de-orelha-branca) *Pyrrhura leucotis* L 9.8 in./25 cm. Note dark cheeks. Often includes **49.8–49.10** and **50.1–50.4** as sspp., but no overlap with **50.1–50.7**. ♣ Humid forest and adjacent areas with tree stands. Sometimes in cocoa plantations. Up to 500 m. ♪ Call: very high, rather thin, rapid "wee-wee-wee- -" or "tic-tic-tic- -." En, R.

49.8 MADEIRA PARAKEET *Pyrrhura snethlageae*

(Tiriba-do-madeira) L 7.9 in./20 cm. Note pale chest with diagnostic narrow markings. *Note*: Should probably be considered a ssp. of **50.1** (intermediates are known). ♣ Humid forest and adjacent clearings, mainly in lowlands.

49.9 GRAY-BREASTED PARAKEET *Pyrrhura anaca*

(or *griseipectus*) (Tiriba-de-peito-cinza) L 7.9 in./20 cm. Only *Pyrrhura* parakeet in its limited range. Often considered a ssp. of **49.7**, but chest and neck-sides grayer (without green), and never shows blue in crown. ♣ Humid to semihumid forest and nearby clearings. Generally above 500 m. ♪ Call: piercing, fast, chattering "t'kreet-kreet-wih-kreet-krit." En, R.

49.10 RED-CROWNED PARAKEET *Pyrrhura rosei-*

frons (Tiriba-de-cabeça-vermelha) L 7.9 in./20 cm. Facial color pattern distinctive. ♣ Humid forest and adjacent clearings, mainly in lowlands.

49.1

49.6
a

49.2

49.7

49.3
b
a

49.8

49.4
b
a

49.9

49.5

49.10

Plate 50

50.1 SANTAREM (or Hellmayr's) **PARAKEET** (Tiriba-de-hellmayr) *Pyrrhura amazonum* L 7.9 in./20 cm. Resembles **50.3** (limited area of contact), but blue in forecrown narrower and little or no red in wing. Also cf. **49.8**. ♣ Humid forest and adjacent clearings, mainly in lowlands. ♪ Call: very high, slightly rising, irregular "pic-pic-pic picpic - -." En.

50.2 DEVILLE'S PARAKEET (Tiriba-de-deville) *Pyrrhura lucianii* L 7.9 in./20 cm. Note absence of pure red in head and wings. Not in range of **49.7, 49.9, 50.1**, or **50.3–50.4**. ♣ Humid forest and nearby clearings, mainly in lowlands. En.

50.3 PAINTED PARAKEET (Tiriba-de-testa-azul) *Pyrrhura picta* L 7.9 in./20 cm. Often includes **49.8, 49.10**, and **50.1–50.2** as sspp. (of these, limited contact with **50.1** only), but with extensive blue in forecrown and red in shoulder. ♣ Humid forest and nearby clearings with scattered trees. Mainly lowlands; rarely to 1800 m. ♪ Call: rapid, nasal twittering.

50.4 PFRIMER'S PARAKEET (Tiriba-de-pfrimer) *Pyrrhura pfrimeri* L 9.8 in./25 cm. Note dark head. Only *Pyrrhura* parakeet in limited range and habitat. ♣ Exclusively in dry, deciduous forest. ♪ Call: high, nasal, sharp "turre-weét-weétweét." En, R.

50.5 FIERY-SHOULDERED PARAKEET (Tiriba-de-cauda-roxa) *Pyrrhura egregia* L 9.8 in./25 cm. In limited range/habitat only parakeet with red and yellow underwing coverts and leading edge of wing, but cf. **48.2**. ♣ Humid forest on the tepuis at 700–1800 m.

50.6 MAROON- (or Black-) **TAILED PARAKEET** (Tiriba-fura-mata) *Pyrrhura melanura* L 9.8 in./25 cm. Note dark maroon uppertail (base green) and red/yellow in primary coverts (often hard to see when perched). May have red in loral region. Cf. **50.5** and **50.7**. ♣ Canopy and edge of humid forest, second growth. Mainly in lowlands. ♪ Call: very high, rather strident "tjuw wITwIT - -," "ee-eh-uw," "wut-wut," or "kreEh-krEeh."

50.7 BLACK-CAPPED (or Rock) **PARAKEET** (Tiriba-rupestre) *Pyrrhura rupicola* L 9.8 in./25 cm. Note red in wing (often difficult to see when perched), blackish gray crown, and green uppertail. ♣ Terra firme and várzea. ♪ Call: falsetto "weeh," "wuh," or "wureet-wureet"-type notes.

50.8 MONK PARAKEET (Caturrita) *Myiopsitta monachus* L 11.8 in./30 cm. Note gray forehead, throat, and chest. ♣ Savanna, woodland, riverine belts, ranchland, towns. Large colonial stick nest placed in tree or on pylon. ♪ Call: very high, rasping "krrih krrih-krrih-krruh- -."

50.9 RED-FAN (or Hawk-headed) **PARROT** (Anacã) *Deroptyus accipitrinus* L 13.8 in./35 cm. S ssp. *fuscifrons* (**a**) and N Nom. (**b**) shown. Note erect stance with long tail, giving rather *Accipiter*-hawk–like jizz. Neck feathers can be raised to spectacular fan. ♣ Terra firme, also in forest patches in savanna. ♪ Call: high, slurred, nasal "tu-rút túwut tureét -."

50.10 BLUE- (or Purple-) **BELLIED PARROT** (Sabiá-cica) *Triclaria malachitacea* L 11.8 in./30 cm. All green with bluish belly in ♂. Note pale bill and long tail. ♣ Atlantic forest. Rarely plantations and parks. Up to 1000 m. ♪ Song: unparrotlike, almost thrushlike, very high, fluted "fiuw fi-fi fjew - -" ("fi-fi" staccato; "fjew" gliding down). R.

Plate 51

PARROTLETS: Small, with short, slightly wedge-shaped tails (**51.5** and **51.6**), or clearly wedge-shaped tails (**51.1–51.3**); some illustrated with fanned tails to show patterns. *Forpus* parrotlets (**51.7–51.9**) have an undulating flight somewhat similar to certain *Brotogeris* parakeets (see **52.4–52.6**), but unlike straighter flight of other parrotlets.

51.1 GREEN-RUMPED PARROTLET (Tuim-santo)

Forpus passerinus L 5.1 in./13 cm. ♂ only parrotlet with blue in wings and a bright emerald rump (rump never pure blue as in **51.2** and **51.3** ♂♂). All-green ♀ very similar to **51.2a** ♀ (no overlap with **51.2b**), but with head yellower (**a**) in limited area of contact (head greener in Roraima). ♣ Various semiopen wooded areas, even mangrove and parks. Avoids interior of dense humid forest. ♪ Call: very/extr. high, sharp, finchlike, staccato "Twéet" in series.

51.2 BLUE-WINGED PARROTLET (Tuim) *Forpus*

xanthopterygius (or *crassirostris*) L 5.1 in./13 cm. Three ssp's; ♂ of green-headed W *crassirostris* (**a**) and yellow-headed NE *flavissimus* (**b**) shown; not shown S Nom., which is intermediate. Note blue rump and bar over wing in ♂♂. ♀♀ of all ssp's lack blue. Cf. **51.1** and **51.3**. ♣ Open to semi-open areas, incl. savanna, Caatinga, forest borders, riverine growth, parks. Avoids interior of dense humid forest. ♣ Riverine belts, forest edge and adjacent more open areas, including pastures and settlement. ♪ Call: very high, bickering "tsip-tsip-tsip- - -" and irregular chirping.

51.3 DUSKY-BILLED PARROTLET (Tuim-de-bico-

escuro) *Forpus modestus* (or *sclateri*). L 5.1 in./13 cm. Mainly dark upper mandible diagnostic (bill all pale in **51.1** and **51.2**). ♣ Várzea and other lowland forest, preferring edge and clearings. ♪ Call: very/extr. high, staccato "dzip-dzip-dzip- - ."

51.4 TEPUI PARROTLET (Periquito-dos-tepuis) *Nan-

nopsittaca panychlora L 5.5 in./14 cm. Note small range. Yellow markings near eyes diagnostic. No pure blue in plumage. ♣ Humid forest up to 2200 m. ♪ Call: very/extr. high, soft chirping.

51.5 AMAZONIAN PARROTLET (Periquito-da-

amazônia) *Nannopsittaca dachilleae* L 5.5 in./14 cm. Note small range. Overall green with pale blue forecrown. ♣ Edge and clearings of humid forest, wooded areas. Mainly near rivers. ♪ Call: very high, sharp chirps. R.

51.6 SCARLET-SHOULDERED PARROTLET (Apuim-

de-asa-vermelha) *Touit huetii* L 6.3 in./16 cm. Note blue to wing bend and red underwing coverts (the latter unlike other parrotlets [**51.1–51.5**]). ♀ with black-tipped green uppertail. ♣ Humid forest, mainly terra firme. ♪ Call: very high "tjoot-tjoot-tjoot- -" mixed with "tjer tjer -."

51.7 SAPPHIRE-RUMPED PARROTLET (Apuim-de-

costas-azuis) *Touit purpuratus* L 7 in./18 cm. Widespread Nom. (**a**) and ssp. *viridiceps* (**b**, upper Ri. Negro area; without or with reduced brown in crown). ♀ with narrow green subterminal band in tail. Note brown scapulars. No overlap with **51.8** and **51.9**. ♣ Humid forest, locally to 1200 m. ♪ Call: mid-high or high, nasal "wec wec werrec werrec werc-werc-werc- -."

51.8 BROWN-BACKED (or Black-eared) PARROTLET

(Apuim-de-costas-pretas) *Touit melanonotus* L 5.9 in./15 cm. Brown back and reddish outer rectrices diagnostic. ♣ Humid forest. Mainly 500–1200 m, locally 0–1700 m. ♪ Call in flight: very high, liquid-sounding "wicwicwic- -" or chattering "bibibihihi---." En, R.

51.9 GOLDEN-TAILED PARROTLET (Apuim-de-cau-

da-amarela) *Touit surdus* L 6.3 in./16 cm. Note brownish-olive scapulars and yellow (♂) or greenish (♀) outer rectrices. Tail feathers of ♀ (**a**) yellowish with green tips and margins. No overlap with **51.6** and **51.7**. ♣ Humid forest up to 1000 m. ♪ Call: falsetto "kree-kree-kree-kruh- -" or shrieking "k'reeéh." En, R.

51.1

♀

♂

51.2

a

b

a

♂

♀

51.3

♀

♀

♂

51.4

51.5

51.6

♂

♀

51.7

a

b

♂

♀

51.8

51.9

a

♀

♂

♂

Plate 52

52.1 PLAIN PARAKEET (Periquito-rico) *Brotogeris* *tirica* L 9.8 in./25 cm. Rather uniform green with brown tinge to shoulder. In flight note blue outerwing from above. A rare pale bluish mutation exists. ♣ Forest edge and canopy, plantations, semiopen areas with scattered trees, incl. parks and city plazas. ♪ Call very/extr. high, shrill "cricri." En.

52.2 CANARY (or White) **-WINGED PARAKEET** (Periquito-de-asa-branca) *Brotogeris* *versicolurus* L 7.9 in./20 cm. Unmistakable by striking wing pattern. Normally some white visible in wing of perched birds. ♣ Várzea, river islands, secondary forest. ♪ Call: very high, nasal/piped "tjutju-tju-tju."

52.3 YELLOW-CHEVRONED PARAKEET (Periquito-de-encontro-amarelo) *Brotogeris* *chiriri* L 9.8 in./25 cm. From **52.2** by range and lack of white in wing. ♣ Savannalike habitats (e.g., cerrado), riverine belts in open country, woodland, caatinga, parks. ♪ Call: very high, shrill "weeweet wee weewitwit -."

NOTE: The following parakeets (**52.4–52.6**) have rather short, wedge-shaped tails similar to smaller *Forpus* parrotlets (Pl. **51.1–51.3**).

52.4 COBALT-WINGED PARAKEET (Periquito-de-asa-azul) *Brotogeris cyanoptera* L 7 in./ 18 cm. Small orange chin spot. Frontlet (usually) tinged yellowish. Also differs from **52.5** and **52.6** by more blue in wing and bluish central tail. ♣ Canopy and edge of humid forest. ♪ Call: high, sharp phrases, like "teeweet teeweert," and communal twittering.

52.5 GOLDEN-WINGED PARAKEET (Periquito-de-asa-dourada) *Brotogeris chrysoptera* L 6.3 in./16 cm. Several sspp.; N Nom. (**a**, with dark frontlet and orange chin spot and wing band), *tuipara* (**b**, E part of range; as **a**, but frontlet orange), and *chrysosema* (**c**, SW part; resembles **b**, but only ssp. with yellow, not orange, wing band) shown. Wing band difficult to see when perched, and lacking in Juv. ♣ Humid forest, woodland, urban areas with trees. ♪ Call: very high, excited twittering and hurried, scratchy-sounding "vrit-vrit-vrit- -."

52.6 TUI PARAKEET (Periquito-testinha) *Brotogeris* *sanctithomae* L 6.7 in./17 cm. Nom. (**a**, widespread in W) and *takatsukae* (**b**, E of Manaus). Note contrasting yellow forehead (also postocular streak in **b**), rather dark bill and lack of pure blue in upperwing (underwing primary coverts blue). ♣ Second growth, trees and scrub along rivers, edges of várzea. ♪ Call: very high, "tirwit tirwitwit - -"; also excited, level chattering and a raspy, rattlelike vocalization.

NOTE: *Amazona* Parrots: Fly with distinctive shallow wing strokes. Tails rather short and square (some illustrated with fanned tails to show patterns). Most species, except **52.10**, **53.1**, and **53.5–53.7**, show a similar upperwing pattern.

52.7 ORANGE-WINGED PARROT (or Amazon) (Curica) *Amazona amazonica* L 11.8 in./30 cm. Distinguished by blue line through eye between yellow crown and cheeks. Extent of yellow on crown variable, sometimes fully replaced by pale blue (**a**). ♣ Lowland areas, from terra firme to town parks, wherever there are tall trees except in várzea. ♪ Call: very high, piercing "tjee-tjee tjee -" or "treer-treer - -," often changing to falsetto.

52.8 KAWALL'S (or White-faced) **PARROT** (or Amazon) (Papagaio-dos-garbes) *Ama-* *zona kawalli* L 13.8 in./35 cm. From **52.9** by white at base of bill, gray eye ring, and no red at leading edge of wing. ♣ Humid forest; mainly near rivers and flooded areas. ♪ Call: high, mewing "tjew-tjew-tjew-tjuw" or high, dry "tjaw-raw-ruw-rèh- -." En.

52.9 MEALY PARROT (or Amazon) (Papagaio-moleiro) *Amazona farinosa* L 15.7 in./40 cm. Large with a distinctly bicolored tail and broad white eyering. Diagnostic powdery effect to nape/back can be difficult to see, as can the red on leading edge of wing. Small yellow crownpatch often missing. Cf. **52.8** and **53.9b**. ♣ Canopy and borders of humid forest. Locally in plantations and gallery woodland. ♪ Call: extensive repertoire; very high, biting "tjee-tjee- - jtjeewah-krr-krr-ronk-ronk."

52.10 VINACEOUS (or -breasted) **PARROT** (or Amazon) (Papagaio-de-peito-roxo) *Ama-* *zona vinacea* L 11.8 in./30 cm. Note purple chest and red forehead, wing-speculum, and pale-tipped bill. Cf. **53.1** and **54.10**. ♣ Prefers forest with *Araucaria*, but also other forest types (incl. secondary). Up to 2000 m. ♪ Call: loud, high "wout-wout- -" or "wi-rout wi-rout." R.

52.1

52.4

a
b
c

52.2

52.5

a

b
a

52.3

52.6

a

52.7

52.9

52.8

52.10

Plate 53

53.1 RED-SPECTACLED PARROT (or Amazon) (Papagaio-charão) *Amazona pretrei* L 11.8 in./30 cm. Note red on face and leading edge of wing. No wing speculum. ♣ *Araucaria* and other types of forest; breeds in open woodland. ♪ Call: mid-high and very high nasal communal cackling en route to and at roosts. Single birds may call nasal "tjertjer." R.

53.2 RED-LORED (or Yellow-cheeked) **PARROT** (or Amazon) (Papagaio-diadema) *Amazona autumnalis* L 13.8 in./35 cm. Note red wing-speculum and large spot on lores. Crown and nape edged blue. Cf. **53.6**. ♣ Gallery woodland; edge and clearings of humid forest. Locally also plantations. ♪ Call: very/extr. high notes, like "tjirc tjirc -," "ti erc-erc" ("ti" extr. high), "njec-njec- njec," or "wrec-j'wreck."

53.3 [BLUE-CHEEKED PARROT (or Amazon) (Papagaio-de-bochecha-azul) *Amazona dufresniana*] L 13.8 in./35 cm. Cheeks blue. Lores and wing speculum yellow-orange. ♣ Humid forest up to 1700 m. ♪ Call: salvos of "wrecwrec---" or very high "fwic-fwic - -" notes (each "fwic" upslurred).]

53.4 RED-BROWED PARROT (or Amazon) (Chauá) *Amazona rhodocorytha* L 13.8 in./35 cm. Cheeks blue. Lores and wing speculum yellow-orange. ♣ Humid forest up to 1700 m. ♪ Call: very high, hurried, nasal series of "tjuw" notes. En, R.

53.5 RED-TAILED PARROT (or Amazon) (Papagaio-de-cara-roxa) *Amazona brasiliensis* L 13.8 in./35 cm. Note red forecrown, bluish ear coverts, purple throat, and lack of wing-speculum. More red in tail than **53.4** (best visible when tail is spread or when viewing from below). ♣ Coastal forest, mangrove. Mainly below 300 m. ♪ Call: very high, rather sharp, chattered "tièh-tjeh-tjeh-tjeh - -" and low grunts. En, R.

53.6 FESTIVE PARROT (or Amazon) (Papagaio-da-várzea) *Amazona festiva* L 13.8 in./35 cm. Note narrow maroon frontal band, blue postocular patch, and lack of red in wings. Red rump diagnostic, but difficult to see when perched and reduced in Imm. Cf. **53.2** and **54.8**. ♣ Forest and woodland at/near water (rivers, flooded areas). ♪ Call: e.g., mid-high "rèh-rèh-rèh- -" (as barking of small dog), often changing to falsetto. Also, in flight, "wrah-wrah-wrah- -."

53.7 YELLOW-FACED (Amazon or) **PARROT** (Papagaio-galego) *Alipiopsitta* (or *Amazona*) *xanthops* L 9.8 in./25 cm. Extent of yellow in head, underparts, and wings very variable (sometimes almost lacking). Note small size, bone-yellow bill (culmen usually dark), orange flanks (often only visible in flight), and lack of wing-speculum. ♣ Cerrado, caatinga, riverine belts. ♪ Call: very high, slightly mewed, sharp "pjee-peer-e'pjeer." R.

53.8 BLUE- (or Turquoise-) **FRONTED PARROT** (or Amazon) (Papagaio-verdadeiro) *Amazona aestiva* L 13.8 in./35 cm. Head pattern variable (two variants, **a** and **b**, shown), but with some yel- low to ocular region and some blue to forecrown. Shoulder is yellow or red (often difficult to see when perched). Wing speculum red. ♣ Woodland, savannalike habitats, gallery forest, caatinga. Locally in wooded urban areas. ♪ Call: rather low "uw-uww- -," higher "euw-euw-euw- -," or "reuh-reuh- -."

53.9 YELLOW-CROWNED PARROT (or Amazon) (Papagaio-campeiro) *Amazona ochrocephala* L 13.8 in./35 cm. Three sspp.: *xantholaema* (**a**, Ilha do Marajó; with extensive yellow to head) and widespread Nom/*nattereri* (**b**; with variable amount of yellow to crown); **a** is distinctive in its range, **b** differs from **52.9** by size, narrower white eye ring, red to the shoulder (often hard to see), and usually more yellow to crown. Also cf. **53.8**. ♣ Canopy and borders of humid forest, wooded areas (even in towns), mangrove. ♪ Call: low, high, or very high, slow, often drawn-out "urr-urr-wurr" or "ur-re-wur."

53.10 DUSKY PARROT (Maitaca-roxa) *Pionus fuscus* L 9.8 in./25 cm. Characterized by dark plumage with distinctive facial pattern and red vent. ♣ Humid forest, mainly terra firme. ♪ Call: high, shrieking, pushed-out "ERK" or "we-ERK." In flight, "wu-erk -wu-erk- -."

Plate 54

54.1 WHITE-BELLIED PARROT (Marianinha-de-cabeça-amarela) *Pionites leucogaster* L 9.8 in./25 cm. C ssp. *xanthurus* (**a**)

and green-thighed E Nom. (**b**) shown; W *xanthomeria* (not shown) with green tail and yellow thighs. Note pale bill and lack of black (Imm. with black-tinged crown). ♣ Canopy and edge of humid forest. Locally in drier forest. ♪ Call: varied series of very high, loud shrieks, like "tweet-tweet-sreet," "vrrruh," or piped "pur-prur" or "weert-weert-pirr."

54.2 BLACK-HEADED PARROT (Marianinha-de-cabeça-preta) *Pionites melanocepha-lus* L 9.8 in./25 cm. Virtually unmistakable. No overlap with **54.1**. ♣ Canopy and edge of várzea and

terra firme. ♪ Song: varied, mostly very high, repeated, shrill, squeaky, nasal (or even melodious) shrieks, most of these single, some repeated.

54.3 RED-CAPPED (or Pileated) **PARROT** (Cuiú-cuiú) *Pionopsitta pileata* L 7.9 in./20 cm. Rather small and short-tailed, but larger and longer-tailed than *Touit* parrotlets. Faint brownish ear patch of ♀ lacking in Imm. ♣ Humid for-

est, incl. *Araucaria* and forest remnants. Up to 1500 m. ♪ Call: very high, piercing shrieks, like "tjeéreweét." In flight, high "tjer-tjer'tjer- -."

54.4 ORANGE-CHEEKED PARROT (Curica-de-bochecha-laranja) *Pyrilia barrabandi* L 9.8 in./25 cm. Nom. (**a**, N of Ri. Amazon, with yellow cheek and trousers) shown and ssp. *aurantii-*

gena (**b**, S of Ri. Amazon, with more orange in plumage). Both sspp. with red underwing coverts. ♣ Terra firme, less in várzea, also in woodland.

54.5 CAICA PARROT (Curica-caica) *Pyrilia caica* L 9.8 in./25 cm. Unmistakable by complete absence of red in plumage and by black head, bordered by golden, scalloped collar. ♣ Mainly terra

firme. ♪ Call: e.g., loud, nasal "scet scet scet-wetwet," "pureét" or very high, sharp "wit."

54.6 VULTURINE PARROT (Curica-urubu) *Pyrilia vulturina* L 9.8 in./25 cm. Unmistakable by color pattern of head. Juv. with feathered green head ♣ Várzea

and terra firme. ♪ Call: calm, rather quiet, nasal or falsetto "u-weeét tjuw," "seep," and other sounds at any pitch, some of these gliding up or down. In flight, noisy "uh-ro-weét," for example. En.

54.7 BALD (or Orange-headed) **PARROT** (Papagaio-de-cabeça-laranja) *Pyrilia aurantio-cephala* L 9.8 in./25 cm. Unmistakable by bald, orange head. Juv. with feathered green head. ♣ Várzea and

terra firme. En.

54.8 SHORT-TAILED PARROT (Curica-verde) *Gray-didascalus brachyurus* L 9.8 in./25 cm. Note very short tail and large head. Lores dark and shoulder reddish-brown (often difficult to

see). ♣ Tree stands near rivers/lakes (esp. river islands), várzea; locally also plantations and mangroves. ♪ Call: might be loud, rasping, rapid "ki-kri-kris-kree- -."

54.9 BLUE-HEADED PARROT (Maitaca-de-cabeça-azul) *Pionus menstruus* L 9.8 in./25 cm. NE Nom. (**a**, with bicolored

bill and green breast) shown and E. ssp. *reichenowi* (**b**, with pale bill and bluish breast, merging in green lower belly). Both unmistakable by blue head and red vent. ♣ Humid forest and woodland. Locally in plantations and drier woodland (incl. cerrado). Up to 1500 m. ♪ Call: e.g., rising "prrr-tjer-ti-TJEET." In flight, "tjeet tjeet treet" or very high, sharp, loud "tjerre-tjer tjer-tjerre - -."

54.10 SCALY-HEADED PARROT (Maitaca-verde) *Pio-nus maximiliani* L 9.8 in./25 cm. Three sspp.: SE *melanoblepharus* (**a**, with dark cap) and NE Nom. (**b**, with white eyering and paler cap).

SW *siy* (not shown) resembles **a**, but eyering white. Note bluish chest and red vent. ♣ Mainly dry to semihumid woodland and forest; also more humid forest in SE (incl. *Araucaria*). Up to 1600 m. ♪ Call: cacophony of very high, shrill "teer-teer-teer- -."

54.1 a b

54.6

54.2

54.7

54.3 ♂ ♀

54.8

54.4 a b

54.9 a b

54.5

54.10 a b

Plate 55

55.1 GREATER ANI (Anu-coroca) *Crotophaga major* L

17.7 in./45 cm. Larger, longer-billed, and glossier than **55.2**. Eyes pale, but be aware of dark-eyed Imm. As **55.2** and **55.3**, usually in groups. ♣ At wet forest edge and clearings, riverine belts, mangrove, tree stands, and thickets at marsh. ♪ Call: low, hollow "OH" or "tjork"; song: high, rapid, descending, gobbling "crocro-júww" in chorus, supported by growls, rattles, and hisses from other group members.

55.2 SMOOTH-BILLED ANI (Anu-preto) *Crotophaga*

ani L 13.8 in./35 cm. Eyes dark. Bill stubbier than **55.1** and with less glossy plumage. ♣ Virtually any semiopen habitat with trees or thickets, incl. small-scale cultivation, woodland, mangrove, forest edge. ♪ Call: "jueeéh," steeply ascending; song: varied; e.g., high, resounding, slow series of about 20 "ou" notes, each note emphasized, second half of series gradually descending, or slow series of very high, fluted trill (police whistle), mewing "tueét" and low "tsec" notes.

55.3 GUIRA CUCKOO (Anu-branco) *Guira guira*

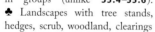

L 13.8 in./35 cm. Note crest, orange-yellow bill, and white rump. Often in groups (unlike **55.4**–**55.6**). ♣ Landscapes with tree stands, hedges, scrub, woodland, clearings in forests, ranchland. ♪ Call/song: slow series of 5–7 slightly piped double notes ("gee-rah"), calmly descending and changing into an indignant-sounding growl; also a long, very high, rather sharp, chattering rattle "bibibi---," that rises or lowers slightly in pitch.

55.4 PAVONINE CUCKOO (Peixe-frito-pavonino) *Dro-*

mococcyx pavoninus L 11.8 in./30 cm. Peculiar tail usually fanned as in **55.5**, but note rufous-buff eyebrow and unmarked rufous throat and chest. Very secretive. ♣ High- and lowland forest with thick undergrowth. ♪ Song: high series of 5 clear, beautiful, fluted notes "wu-wee-pe'wiwi" (almost level, "wu" and "pe" slightly lower).

55.5 PHEASANT CUCKOO (Peixe-frito-verdadeiro) *Dro-*

mococcyx phasianellus L 13.8 in./35 cm. From **55.4** by buff-white eyebrow and speckled chest. Very secretive. ♣ Undergrowth of forest and dense woodland. ♪ Song: 3-noted, slightly rising, melancholy "wu wi trrrih."

55.6 STRIPED CUCKOO (Saci) *Tapera naevia* L 9.8 in./

25 cm. Note narrow malar stripe and bold dark streaking on back and crest. ♣ Landscapes with tree stands, hedges, scrub, woodland, pastures, ranchland. ♪ Call/song: high, clear, fluted "wu wi" (2nd note higher).

NOTE: Ground-Cuckoos: Large, terrestrial cuckoos. Rare and inconspicuous. Sometimes at ant swarms, where bill-snaps are often loud. Limited area of overlap between species.

55.7 RUFOUS-VENTED GROUND-CUCKOO (Jacu-

estalo) *Neomorphus geoffroyi* L 19.7 in./ 50 cm. Note gray brown head and neck, distinctive black band across breast, and rufous vent. Nom. shown (S Amazon). Not shown, E ssp. *maximiliani* (as Nom., but tail purplish), SE *dulcis* (dark bluish wings and tail) and *australis* (may occur in far SW; resembles Nom.). ♣ Undisturbed humid forest. ♪ Song: mid-high "wóuw." Also castanetlike bill clapping.

55.8 SCALED GROUND-CUCKOO (Jacu-estalo-

escamoso) *Neomorphus squamiger* L 19.7 in./50 cm. From **55.7** by indistinct breast band. ♣ Undisturbed humid forest. En, R.

55.9 RUFOUS-WINGED GROUND-CUCKOO (Jacu-

estalo-de-asa-vermelha) *Neomorphus rufipennis* L 19.7 in./50 cm. Unmistakable by rufous wings and bluish-black head, chest and mantle. ♣ Undisturbed humid forest. ♪ Song: rather low, not loud, yet far carrying, lonely "wóuh" given at 5-sec intervals; also loud bill snapping.

55.10 RED-BILLED GROUND-CUCKOO (Jacu-estalo-

de-bico-vermelho) *Neomorphus pucheranii* L 19.7 in./50 cm. Note mainly red bill and black cap. ♣ Undisturbed humid forest.

55.1

55.2

55.3

55.4

55.5

55.6

55.7

55.8

55.9

55.10

Plate 56

56.1 MANGROVE CUCKOO (Papa-lagarta-do-mangue)

Coccyzus minor L 13.8 in./35 cm. From smaller **56.7** by heavier, bicolored bill. Note restricted range. ♣ Coastal habitats, esp. in mangrove, but also in dry scrub. ♪ Song: might be very low, rapid, didgeridoolike "è-è-è-è-è-o-o."

56.2 YELLOW-BILLED CUCKOO (Papa-lagarta-de-

asa-vermelha) *Coccyzus americanus* L 11.8 in./30 cm. Extensive rufous in wing diagnostic. Note gray or yellow eyering, large white tips to tail, and black and yellow bill. ♣ Various shrubby and wooded habitats. ♪ Silent in South America.

56.3 [DWARF CUCKOO (Papa-lagarta-de-papo-ferru-

gem) *Coccycua pumila*] L 7.9 in./20 cm. Small and relatively short tailed. Note contrasting rufous throat. ♣ Edge and clearings of forest, second growth, woodland, pastures with trees. ♣ Call: grating "trrr trrr trrr."

56.4 ASH-COLORED CUCKOO (Papa-lagarta-cinzento)

Micrococcyx cinereus L 9.8 in./25 cm. Note black bill, red eye ring, and squarish tail with grayish underside and narrow white spots at tip (be aware of new, still growing feathers). ♣ Woodland and scrubland, deciduous forest, riverine belts. ♪ Song: slightly descending series of up to 20 plaintive "cow" notes.

56.5 BLACK-BILLED CUCKOO (Papa-lagarta-de-

bico-preto) *Coccyzus erythropthalmus* L 11.8 in./30 cm. Bill black, usually with gray base to lower mandible. Eyering red. Little or no rufous in wing. Graduated tail with grayish underside and narrow white tips. Imm. with yellow eye ring and browner throat. ♣ Varied habitats from forest to scrubland up to 2000 m. ♪ Quiet in South America. V.

56.6 PEARLY-BREASTED CUCKOO (Papa-lagarta-

de-euler) *Coccyzus euleri* L 11.8 in./30 cm. Resembles slightly larger **56.2**, but no rufous in wing. ♣ Varied habitats from forest to scrubland up to 2000 m. ♪ Song: sustained, level series of downslurred, evenly spaced "úwl" notes.

56.7 DARK-BILLED CUCKOO (Papa-lagarta-acanel-

ado) *Coccyzus melacoryphus* L 9.8 in./25 cm. Note deep buff underparts, black mask, gray neck sides, and black bill. Cf. **56.1**. ♣ Varied; from deciduous forest, edge of humid forest and woodland to mangrove, ranchland and shrubbery. ♪ Song: low, rather weak, slightly hurried, and descending series of hollow "orl" or "cowl" notes.

56.8 LITTLE CUCKOO (Chincoã-pequeno) *Coccycua*

(or *Piaya*) *minuta* L 9.8 in./25 cm. From larger **56.10** by shorter tail and darker, less contrasting, underparts. ♣ Edge of humid forest, woodland, shrubby growth. Mainly near water. ♪ Call: high, dry "wic"; song: mid-high, dry, almost rattle or "uuuh we-we-we-wih" (1st part drawn out and rising, 2nd part "we-we-we" a slightly rising almost-rattle, "wih" trailing off).

56.9 BLACK-BELLIED CUCKOO (Chincoã-de-bico-

vermelho) *Piaya melanogaster* L 15.7 in./40 cm. Note gray cap and red bill. ♣ Humid forest. Occasionally in wooded savanna. ♣ Canopy of lowland forest, woodland, shrubby growth. ♪ Dry, cackling "wih tit-trrWIT." Also might be a high, piped "puweéT-puw."

56.10 SQUIRREL CUCKOO (Alma-de-gato) *Piaya*

cayana L 17.7 in./45 cm. Large and long tailed with pale gray chest and dull greenish yellow bill. ♣ Wide variety of wooded habitats from forest and woodland to areas with scattered trees (even in gardens and mangrove). ♪ Call: 2 well-separated "weét wèè" notes, 1st note very high, short, and strident, 2nd much lower and drawn out; song: slow series of up to 20 very high, short, fluted "weep" notes, slowly rising at start and lowering at end (15 sec).

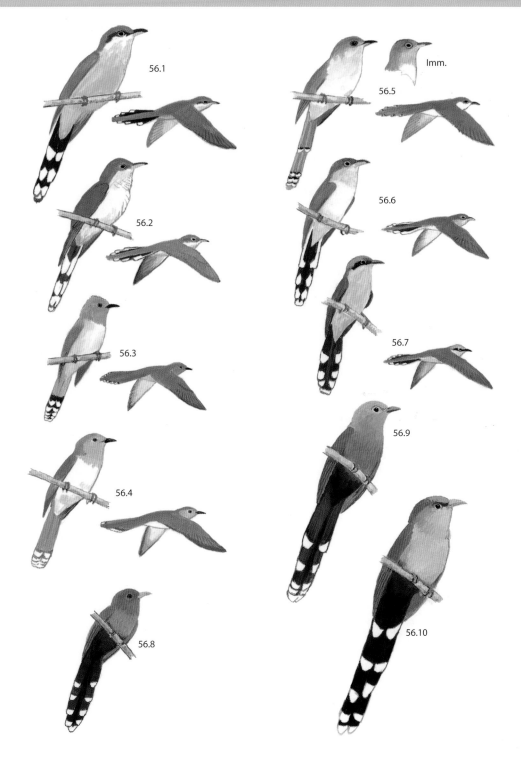

56.1

56.2

56.3

56.4

56.8

56.5

Imm.

56.6

56.7

56.9

56.10

Plate 57

57.1 TROPICAL SCREECH-OWL (Corujinha-do-mato)

Megascops (or *Otus*) *choliba* L 7.9 in./ 20 cm. Widespread. Gray (**a**) and rufous form (**b**) shown; a brown form and intermediates also occur. Nonreflective eyes yellow. Ear tufts smaller than in **57.2** and **57.6**, but these can be lowered in all screech-owls. ♣ Wide variety of wooded habitats from savanna and city parks to forest. Prefers more open habitats than most other screech-owls. Up to 2500 m. ♪ Song: short, level or slightly ascending almost-trill, followed by 1–3 slower, higher "drrrrrrwc-wec" notes.

57.2 BLACK-CAPPED (or Variable) **SCREECH-OWL**

(Corujinha-sapo) *Megascops* (or *Otus*) *atricapilla* L 9.8 in./25 cm. Gray (**a**) and rufous forms (**b**, most common) shown; a brown form also occurs. Nonreflective eyes dark brown or yellow. Crown more uniform dark than in **57.1** and **57.6**. From **57.6** by range and by voice. ♣ In or near humid forest. Mainly below 600 m. ♪ Song: long, low, slow, level trill, gradually gaining in strength (up to 18 sec). *Note*: population found in higher elevation Atlantic forest in eastern Pernambuco and Alagoas may be an undescribed species.

NOTE: The SACC maintains the combination of the following two species (**57.3** and **57.4**) in one species, Tawny-bellied Screech-Owl *Megascops (or Otus) watsonii*.

57.3 SOUTHERN TAWNY-BELLIED SCREECH-OWL

(Corujinha-relógio) *Megascops* (or *Otus*) *usta* L 7.9 in./20 cm. Black facial rim less contrasting than in **57.1** and nonreflective eyes brownish to amber. From **57.4** by darker crown, heavier streaks to breast, and esp. by song. ♣ In or near humid forest up to 500 m. ♪ Song: long, slow, slightly rising series of mid-high "oo" notes, gaining in strength, at the end slightly lower ("ou" 3 ×/sec, total 16 sec).

57.4 NORTHERN TAWNY-BELLIED SCREECH-OWL

(Corujinha-orelhuda) *Megascops* (or *Otus*) *watsonii* L 7.9 in./20 cm. Very similar to **57.3**. Locally some overlap in ranges. ♣ Lower story of humid forest interior; also, but less so, at edge. ♪ Song: as **57.3**, but much faster and not lowered at the end but somewhat undulating.

57.5 VERMICULATED (or Roraima) **SCREECH-OWL**

(Corujinha-de-roraima) *Megascops* (or *Otus*) *guatemalae* (or *roraimae*) L 7.9 in./20 cm. Brown form shown; also occurs in a rufous form. Very similar to **57.1**, but with less distinct dark facial rim and vertical black lines in underpart pattern fewer and less distinct. No overlap with **57.2** and **57.6**. ♣ Humid forest. Mainly at 500–1800 m. ♪ Song: short to long, high, fast, slightly lowered trill, like "rrrr---uw."

57.6 LONG-TUFTED SCREECH-OWL (Corujinha-do-sul) *Megascops* (or *Otus*) *sanctae-catarinae* L 9.8 in./25 cm. Brown

form shown; also occurs in a rufous form. Nonreflective eyes yellow; occasionally brown. Larger than **57.1**. ♣ Wooded areas (incl. *Araucaria*), forest edge. Generally avoids interior of dense forest. Mainly below 1000 m. ♪ Song: varied; e.g., a long series, which rises rather steeply before it is lowered at the end and stops suddenly, "rrrr---ruh!" (20 sec), or a very low, barking series of 3–5 sec, which gradually is lowered in pitch.

NOTE: Pygmy-owls show a "pseudo-face" on back of head, except in Imms. (and possibly Ad. **57.9**). Active day or night. Small birds often respond aggressively to their calls.

57.7 AMAZONIAN (or Hardy's) **PYGMY-OWL** (Caburé-da-amazônia) *Glaucidium hardyi*

L 5.5 in./14 cm. Grayish head contrasts with browner back and chest markings. Note 3–4 visible white bars in tail (incl. tip) and spotted crown (sometimes plain). Cf. **57.10**. ♣ Upperstory of humid forest. ♪ Song: high, lowered, shivering almost-trill (3 sec).

57.8 LEAST PYGMY-OWL (Caburé-miudinho) *Glaucidium minutissimum* L 5.5 in./

14 cm. Resembles **57.7** (no overlap), but head slightly browner. Cf. **57.10**. ♣ Canopy and edge of humid forest. Locally also in nearby brushy areas. ♪ Song: mid-high, piped "tooh tooh."

57.9 PERNAMBUCO PYGMY-OWL (Caburé-de-pernambuco) *Glaucidium mooreorum*

L 5.5 in./14 cm. From **57.8** mainly by range and voice. ♣ Canopy and edge of humid forest. En, R.

57.10 FERRUGINOUS PYGMY-OWL (Caburé) *Glaucidium brasilianum* L 6.7 in./17 cm.

Widespread. From **57.7–57.9** by streaked (not spotted) crown (occasionally plain) and longer tail with at least 5 (rarely 4) visible white tail-bars (incl. tip) in gray form (**a**) or no white in tail in rufous form (**b**). ♣ Cerrado, savanna, scrub, second growth, parks, woodland and forest (avoids interior of terra firme). Prefers deciduous to semihumid regions. ♪ Song: mid-high, hurried series of about 7–12 "hoot-hoot- -" notes.

57.1 a b

57.2 a b

57.3

57.4

57.5

57.6

57.7

57.8

57.9

57.10 a b

Plate 58

58.1 BURROWING OWL (Coruja-buraqueira) *Athene* *cunicularia* L 7.9 in./20 cm. Long-legged terrestrial owl with barring below and spotting above. Juv. all white below. ♣ Dry open areas, savanna, ranchland, pastures, grassy areas (even in towns or airports). Rather social. ♪ Song: very high, rapid series of about 15–20 sharp "tjíp" notes, preceded by inhaled or sharp "tjuuch."

58.2 BUFF-FRONTED OWL (Caburé-acanelado) *Aego-* *lius harrisii* L 7.9 in./20 cm. Unmistakable small owl with rich buff underparts, cheeks, and forecrown. ♣ Humid forest and woodland. Locally also in wooded caatinga and cerrado. ♪ Song: low, often crescendoing, rolling "rrrrrrrur" (5–6 sec).

58.3 STRIPED OWL (Coruja-orelhuda) *Rhinoptynx* (or *Pseudoscops*) *clamator* L 13.8 in./ 35 cm. S ssp. *midas* shown; N and C Nom. has more tawny underparts. Note buffy-white face boldly bordered by black rim, streaked underparts, and long ear tufts. ♣ Forest, second growth, riverine belts, woodland to cerrado, caatinga, agricultural areas, suburbs, and plantations. ♪ Song: very high, descending, single-noted, nasal "pieeeuw" (1 sec).

58.4 STYGIAN OWL (Mocho-diabo) *Asio stygius* L 15.7 in./40 cm. Long, close-set ear tufts. Upperparts and face very dark (forehead pale). ♣ Woodland, open areas with trees, forest (avoids interior of dense humid lowland forest). ♪ Song: low, dull, far-carrying "hóow" at 40-sec intervals.

58.5 SHORT-EARED OWL (Mocho-dos-banhados) *Asio flammeus* L 13.8 in./35 cm. Note streaked underparts, tiny ear tufts (often not visible), and yellow eyes. ♣ Grassland, marshes, farmland, savanna, open woodland. Roosts on the ground. Diurnal and nocturnal. ♣ All types of open country. ♪ Generally silent.

58.6 GREAT HORNED OWL (Jacurutu) *Bubo virgin-* *ianus* L 21.5 in./55 cm. Largest owl in Brazil. Note barred underparts and distinct ear tufts. ♣ Open forest (incl. Caatinga), woodland, savanna, open areas with wooded patches. ♪ Song: very low, hollow "oohóo," muffled as if swallowing something.

58.7 RUSTY-BARRED OWL (Coruja-listrada) *Strix* *hylophila* L 13.8 in./35 cm. Lack of ear tufts, dark eyes, and barring below diagnostic. ♣ Forest and second growth. ♪ Song: high, exhaled "èèèèèuh," like a car stopping abruptly (1 sec). R.

58.8 MOTTLED OWL (Coruja-do-mato) *Strix* (or *Cic-* *caba*) *virgata* L 13.8 in./35 cm. Overall color rather variable; Amazonian type shown. Note dark nonreflective eyes and lack of ear tufts. Belly typically streaked as shown, but may appear more barred in N. Birds from the Atlantic forest are bigger, and the ground color of the belly is light rufous to dark buff; they also lack the white tail bars visible in N birds. ♣ Wide range of forest types, woodland, savanna, plantations; sometimes even in city parks. ♪ Song: surprised-sounding, steeply ascending and descending "ouuúuw."

58.9 BLACK-BANDED OWL (Coruja-preta) *Strix* (or *Ciccaba*) *huhula* L 13.8 in./35 cm. Unmistakable by overall black and white barring. ♣ Humid forest (incl. *Araucaria*). Occasionally in plantations. ♪ Song: varied; e.g., short series of "oo" notes in 2 well-separated parts, 1st part a 3-noted, rapidly ascending, laughing "oo-oo-oo," 2nd part low "oouw"; or "oo-oo Oow" (last syllable higher); or ascending "oouw" at 1-sec intervals.

58.10 CRESTED OWL (Coruja-de-crista) *Lophostrix* *cristata* L 15.7 in./40 cm. Unmistakable by long, white eyebrows. ♣ Humid forest (mainly in interior). Locally in dense tall second growth. ♪ Song: extr. low, short "rooh" at 4-sec intervals.

Plate 59

59.1 SPECTACLED OWL (Murucututu) *Pulsatrix per-spicillata* L 19.7 in./50 cm. SE ssp. *pulsatrix*, Short-browed Owl (**a**, with yellowish amber eyes and broken breast band; likely to be considered a full species), and widespread Nom. (**b**, with yellow eyes and paler underparts) shown. Juv. has a black face set in further all-white head; eyes as adult. Cf. **59.2**. ♣ Forest, open areas with scattered trees, riverine belts, plantations. ♪ Song: very low, rapid series of about 5–6 "oo" notes. Also low, rapid "wuc-wuc-duc-d-t."

59.2 TAWNY-BROWED OWL (Murucututu-de-barriga-amarela) *Pulsatrix koeniswaldiana* L 17.7 in./45 cm. From larger **59.1** by bare, not feathered, toes, creamy buff (not white) facial markings, and dark eyes. Juv. differs from Juv. **59.1** by brown face and dark eyes. ♣ Humid forest, *Araucaria* forest, woodland. ♣ ♪ Song: often duets, with one bird giving very low "wuwuwuwu," answered by the other by the same series, but an octave higher.

59.3 BARN OWL (Coruja-da-igreja) *Tyto alba* L 13.8 in./35 cm. Unmistakable by white to rich buff underparts and heart-shaped face. ♣ Wide variety of open to semiopen habitats (even in towns). ♪ Call in flight: very high, hoarse/squeaky "shru-eeeh."

NOTE: Potoos: Feed nocturnally on flying insects caught by sallying out from perch. Difficult to spot during daytime, but easily identified as Potoos by upright manner of perching on top of tree stumps, for example.

59.4 WHITE-WINGED POTOO (Urutau-de-asa-branca) *Nyctibius leucopterus* L 9.8 in./25 cm. Smaller than **59.6–59.8**. Large white patch on wing coverts diagnostic. ♣ Canopy of terra firme. ♪ Call: high, slightly upslurred, mellow "wueet"; song: long, down-gliding, fluted, melancholy-sounding "fuuuu---u" (5 sec).

59.5 RUFOUS POTOO (Urutau-ferrugem) *Nyctibius bracteatus* L 9.8 in./25 cm. Generally unmistakable by overall deep rufous color, but cf. larger **59.9**. ♣ Terra firme and swampy palm forest. ♪ Song: high, rapid, bouncing-down series of "wup-wuwuwu---wu" notes (2–3 sec).

59.6 LONG-TAILED POTOO (Mãe-da-lua-parda) *Nyctibius aethereus* L 19.7 in./50 cm. Rather rufescent. Slender. Very long tail (ca. half total length) diagnostic. ♣ Lowland forest, mainly humid. ♪ Song: strange series; raucous at start, upslurred, and slightly lowered at end, together sounding as "ràooúuul."

59.7 COMMON (or Gray) **POTOO** (Mãe-da-lua) *Nyctibius griseus* L 15.7 in./40 cm. L 13.8 in./35 cm. Overall color varies from grayish (shown; most common) to rufescent. ♣ Savanna, woodland, forest edge, second growth. ♪ Song: strange, calm, mournful series of 3–6 piped/fluted, descending, eerie-sounding notes; 1st one normally longest.

59.8 GREAT POTOO (Mãe-da-lua-gigante) *Nyctibius grandis* L 19.7 in./50 cm. Large and bulky. Typically pale gray; occasionally browner. Overall vermiculated/barred (not streaked). Eyes dark, but reflect orange-red in torch light as in other potoos. ♣ Forest, riverine belts in more open areas (incl. cerrado), tall second growth. Esp. at rivers or lakes. ♪ Song: very low, hoarse, spooky-sounding "wòòòòuw."

59.9 OILBIRD (Guácharo) *Steatornis caripensis* L 17.7 in./45 cm. Virtually unmistakable. ♣ In or near humid forest up to 2600 m. Roosts and nests colonially in caves, but can be seen up to 150 km from these roosts during nocturnal foraging. Feeds exclusively on fruits taken in flight. ♪ Clicks (sounding as static on radio) for echolocation in cave; low "krèèh-krèèh-krèèh- -" as contact call.

Plate 60

60.1 SICKLE-WINGED NIGHTJAR (Curiango-do-

banhado) *Eleothreptus anomalus* L 7.5 in./19 cm. Overall pale grayish brown. From other small nightjars in range (Pl. **61**) by short tail, lack of a large throat patch/crescent (only a buff chin), and essentially no nuchal collar. ♂ with long, white-tipped primaries; ♀ with very rounded wings and barring near primary-tips. ♣ Grassland, savanna, woodland, and gallery forest. Often near water. ♪ Song: series of dry, twittered "trrrrr trr-trr trr" trills. R.

60.2 WHITE-WINGED NIGHTJAR (Bacurau-de-rabo-

branco) *Eleothreptes* (or *Caprimulgus*) *candicans* L 7.9 in./20 cm. Small. Pale grayish brown overall. ♂ with extensive white in tail, underparts, and wing (almost all white from below); ♀ with barring almost reaching primary-tips. Both sexes with dark ocular area contrasting with broad whitish moustache and eyebrow; no nuchal collar (cf. **61.10** and **62.1**). ♣ Open cerrado and grassland. ♪ Short, soft wing purr; also vocal sounds like short, undulating whistle. R.

60.3 SCISSOR-TAILED NIGHTJAR (Bacurau-tesoura)

Hydropsalis torquata (or *brasiliensis*) L 11.8 in./30 cm. (+ up to 13.8 in./ 35 cm of tail extensions in ♂). Overall buffy gray with a three-pointed tail tip (may appear forked when perched). From **60.5** by tawny (buff in S) nuchal collar, lack of white wing bars, and longer tail in ♂. Also cf. **60.4** and **61.4** ♣ Lowland forest, woodland, savanna, grassland, parks. ♪ Song: calm series of very/extr. high, piercing, doublets "FEé-tje - -" without intervals.

60.4 LONG-TRAINED NIGHTJAR (Bacurau-tesoura-

gigante) *Macropsalis forcipata* (or *creagra*) L 11.8 in./30 cm. (+ up to 24 in./60 cm of tail extensions in ♂). From smaller **60.3** by darker upperparts and forked tail; ♂ also differs by longer tail. ♣ Humid forest. Locally in woodland and second growth; 500–1800 m (to SL in S part of range). ♪ Song: soft, rapid "pi-pi-t'pru" ("pi-pi" very high and thin, "t'pru" descending much lower) repeated once, followed by some low mumbled "pr" notes.

60.5 LADDER-TAILED NIGHTJAR (Acurana) *Hydro-

psalis climacocerca* L 9.8 in./25 cm. ♂ pale grayish with extensive white on undertail, belly, and wing band; ♀ buffier (incl. belly and wing band) without white in tail. Little or no nuchal collar. Note three-pointed tail tip (may appear forked when perched). Cf. **60.3**, **61.4**, and **61.9**. ♣ Humid forest, woodland, second growth. Usually near rivers or lakes. ♪ Call/song: series of well- but irregularly spaced, very/extr. high "tjip" notes.

NOTE: Nighthawks: Wings pointed (except in **60.10**) and extending to or beyond tail tip when perched. Tails squarish, notched in center. Hunt insects in sustained flight. Crepuscular (**61.1**–**61.3** more nocturnal).

60.6 LEAST NIGHTHAWK (Bacurauzinho) *Chordeiles*

pusillus L 6.7 in./17 cm. Resembles larger **60.9**, but darker overall, wing band closer to wing tip and with distinctive white or buff trailing edge of wings (cf. **61.1** and **61.2** without white throat and wing bands). ♣ Grassy areas with trees and scrub, cerrado, caatinga. Roosts on ground or rarely lengthwise on branch. ♪ Song: rattling series of about 5–6 × "pu" or "djuk," followed by suddenly upslurred "puwEE," together as "pupupupupuwEE."

60.7 SAND-COLORED NIGHTHAWK (Bacurau-da-

praia) *Chordeiles rupestris* L 7.9 in./ 20 cm. Pale buff-gray with white throat and underparts (incl. most of underside of wings and tail). ♣ Near sandbars along rivers or oxbow lakes; less so on rocky river islands and marshy areas. Roosts on ground or low branches. Social. ♪ Song: raucous "tr-TRAAA TRAAA - -."

60.8 LESSER NIGHTHAWK (Bacurau-de-asa-fina)

Chordeiles acutipennis L 7.9 in./20 cm. Very similar to **60.9**, but wing band closer to wing tip (and buff in ♀), barring on underwing extends to inner primaries and wings project almost to tail tip when perched. Also cf. **60.6**. ♣ Wide variety of open to semiopen habitats, incl. grassland, farmland, savanna, shrubby areas, open woodland, towns. Rarer in marsh, mangrove, forest edge. Roosts on ground or lengthwise along branches. Sometimes in small groups. ♪ Song: level, toadlike trill, slightly increasing in strength (4–6 sec).

60.9 COMMON NIGHTHAWK (Bacurau-norte-

americano) *Chordeiles minor* L 9.8 in./ 25 cm. Overall brownish gray with white subterminal band in undertail (lacking in ♀). White wing band intersects leading edge of wing about halfway between wing tip and wing bend ("wrist"). Wings often project beyond tail when perched. Cf. **60.6** and **60.8**. ♣ Habitat and roosting behavior as **60.8**, but usually flies higher and is commoner in humid habitats. ♪ Silent in South America.

60.10 NACUNDA NIGHTHAWK (Corucão) *Podager*

nacunda L 11.8 in./30 cm. Contrasting white below, sharply demarcated from brown chest. Rounded wings with dark primaries and white band. ♣ Grassland, marshes, savanna. Locally also at forest edge, seashore, towns. Roosts on the ground. Often in groups. ♪ Call: soft "Wee?"; song: very low "roo-coo," sometimes followed by much lower "do."

Plate 61

61.1 BAHIAN (or Plain-tailed or Caatinga) **NIGHT-**

HAWK (Bacurau-do-são-francisco) *Nyctiprogne* (or *Chordeiles*) *vieillardi* L 7 in./18 cm. Note small range. Overall rather dark chestnut (no white/buff in tail, on throat, or wing bar; cf. **60.6** and **60.8**). ♣ Riverine woodland and brush. Roosts crosswise on low branches. Social. ♪ Call: soft "weet-weet." En, R.

61.2 BAND-TAILED NIGHTHAWK (Bacurau-de-cauda-

barrada) *Nyctiprogne leucopyga* L 7 in./18 cm. Dark brownish overall. No wing bands. Note white tail band (visible from below). No throat-patch, but often with a small spot on either side of lower throat. ♣ Forest, woodland, or areas with dense brush. Always near water. Perches crosswise on branches. Social. ♪ Song: mid-high, soft, mellow "tjow" or slightly guttural "wuc-wói wuc wuc."

61.3 SHORT-TAILED (or Semi-collared) **NIGHTHAWK**

(Tuju) *Lurocalis semitorquatus* L 9.8 in./25 cm. Dark overall (no wing band or white in tail). Long wings extend well beyond very short tail when perched. ♣ Wide variety of habitats with trees; from forest to woodland and wooded savanna. Roosts lengthwise on canopy branches. ♪ Song: varies per region; e.g., piped, lifted "tu-wút" or "tuit."

61.4 COMMON PAURAQUE (Bacurau) *Nyctidromus*

albicollis L 11.8 in./30 cm. Large, long-tailed nightjar with gray-brown (**a**) and rufous (**b**) forms. ♂ with extensive white on outer rectrices (only near tip in ♀). Wing band white (♂) or whitish buff (♀). Note uniform chestnut cheeks and buff-edged black spots on scapulars. White crescent on lower throat often reduced. ♣ Virtually any habitat, but prefers wooded areas. ♪ Song: high "weé-ur," sometimes as "weé-ur-wo" ("wo" low and weak).

61.5 OCELLATED POORWILL (Bacurau-ocelado) *Nyc-*

tiphrynus ocellatus L 7.9 in./20 cm. A rather uniform sooty brown (♂) or rufous (♀) nightjar with black spots on scapulars and white spots on belly. Outer rectrices broadly tipped white (mainly visible from below). ♣ Forest, mainly humid. ♪ Song: clear, sweet, trilled "prrrír-uh" ("uh" lower).

NOTE: Nightjars (incl. **60.1–60.5**, **61.4**, **61.5**, and **61.6–61.10**): Tails squarish or rounded (except in **60.3–60.5**) and wings less pointed than in most nighthawks. Depending on species, tail extends well beyond or slightly past wing tips when perched. Roosts on or near the ground (e.g., on low branches or rocks), occasionally on roofs. Hunts insects by sallying out from ground or branch (**60.1**, **60.2**, **61.9**, and **61.10** will also hunt in low, sustained flight). More strictly nocturnal than nighthawks.

61.6 RUFOUS NIGHTJAR (João-corta-pau) *Caprimul-*

gus rufus L 11.8 in./30 cm. Large and generally rufous-brown. Narrow whitish band on lower throat. ♂ with large white spots on inner webs of outer 3 rectrices (difficult to see when perched; buff from below). Both sexes with rufous tail corners. Faint buff nuchal collar. No wing bands, but barring to near primary tips. Cf. **61.7** and **61.4b**. ♣ Wide variety of habitats, incl. forest, riverine belts, woodland, cerrado, second growth, large gardens. Roosts on ground or low perch. ♪ Song: clear, rapid "tjuw-wutwut-wiúr."

61.7 SILKY-TAILED NIGHTJAR (Bacurau-rabo-de-

seda) *Caprimulgus sericocaudatus* L 9.8 in./25 cm. Resembles **61.6** (incl. wing pattern), but more blackish brown overall, chest blacker, and ♂ with white tail corner (both webs). ♣ Forest and densely wooded areas (mainly, but not exclusively, humid). ♪ Song: "tju-wú"wuír" (2nd half of 2nd part gliding up and forcefully exhaled).

61.8 BAND-WINGED NIGHTJAR (Bacurau-da-telha)

Caprimulgus longirostris L 7.9 in./20 cm. Overall rather dark brownish gray. Nuchal collar rufous. Wing bands and crescent on throat white/buff (♂/♀). ♂ has broad white tail corners (distinct when tail is spread or from below). ♣ Grassland, rocky and shrubby areas, woodland, forest edge, cities. Mainly above 1000 m, but to SL in SE. ♪ Song: very/extr. high, sharp "seeeuh-si" (1st part gliding down).

61.9 WHITE-TAILED NIGHTJAR (Bacurau-de-cauda-

branca) *Caprimulgus cayennensis* L 7.9 in./20 cm. ♂ overall pale gray-buff with white belly, throat, wing band, and in tail (tail almost all white from below). Darker and buffier ♀ lacks white in tail, has cinnamon wing band and buff throat usually speckled black. Both sexes with cinnamon nuchal collar and rather pointed corners to the squarish tail. ♣ Grassland, shrub, savanna, forest edge, pastures. Up to 1500 m. ♪ Song: very/extr. high, downgliding "sjeeeuh."

61.10 SPOT-TAILED NIGHTJAR (Bacurau-de-rabo-

maculado) *Caprimulgus maculicaudus* L 7.9 in./20 cm. Small. Dark crown and face contrast with buff eyebrow, malar, and throat. Nuchal collar cinnamon. Prominent spots on wing coverts and scapulars whitish buff. ♂ with white tail-corners; undertail with broad white tips and spots on basal half (**a**). Cf. **61.9**, **62.1**, **60.1** ♀, and **60.2** ♀. ♣ Savanna and grassland with scattered trees and thickets, but also along woodland edges. Lowlands. ♪ Song: very high, rather sharp "p'teét," repeated every 3–4 sec.

Plate 62

62.1 LITTLE NIGHTJAR (Bacurau-chintă) *Caprimulgus*

parvulus L 7.9 in./20 cm. Small and stubby. Overall brownish gray. Nuchal collar cinnamon and throat white/whitish buff (♂/♀). ♂ has white wing band and spots on inner webs of all, except central tail-feather tips (distinct from below). From **62.2** also by less contrasting facial pattern (esp. eyebrow) and chest more barred (less spotted). ♣ Open wooded country, forest edge, savanna, thickets in grassland, pastures. Lowlands. ♪ Song: warbling "turéÉÉt-wruwruwruwru" (1st part rapidly upslurred from low to very high, 2nd part as a warbling, level twitter). *Note:* The N ssp. *heterurus* might be a seperate species, SANTA MARTA NIGHTJAR, separable (from S Nom.) by its more level-pitched song: "tjib-djub-djebdjebdjeb" ("djub slightly lower).

62.2 BLACKISH NIGHTJAR (Bacurau-de-lajeado)

Caprimulgus nigrescens L 7.9 in./20 cm. Small, with wings almost reaching tail tip when perched. Overall dark with a white crescent on lower throat (often reduced to small white spots on either side of the lower throat). No nuchal collar. ♂ with white tail corners (mainly visible from below) and small wing bar. ♣ Clearings and edge of humid forest, esp. near rocky outcrops. Up to 1200 m. ♪ Song: sudden scream, repeated every 3–6 sec, like "tréeuw."

62.3 RORAIMAN NIGHTJAR (Bacurau-dos-tepuis)

Caprimulgus whitelyi L 7.9 in./20 cm. Very similar to **62.2** (note altitude), but ♂ with whitish spots on wing coverts and both sexes with white on inner web of outer tail feathers (less in ♀; in both sexes mainly visible from below). From larger **61.8** by lack of nuchal collar, wings almost reaching tail tip when perched, and white to tail in both sexes. ♣ Densely vegetated clearings and edges of montane forest (1200–1800 m). R.

62.4 PYGMY NIGHTJAR (Bacurauzinho-da-caatinga)

Caprimulgus hirundinaceus L 7 in./18 cm. Very small. Both sexes with white wing bars. ♂ with white tips to outer two tail-feathers. From **62.1** by overall paler, sandy color (except in darker ssp. *villiardi* from Espírito Santo) and no large white/buff-edged black scapular spots. ♣ Caatinga and openings in deciduous woodland. Ssp. *villiardi* in rocky areas. ♪ Song: very high, mellow, fluted "wíew" or "wíuw"; also low "wúw"; all in series with 3- to 4-sec intervals. En.

62.5 [WHITE-CHINNED SWIFT (Taperuçu-de-mento-branco) *Cypseloides cryptus*]

L 5.9 in./15 cm. Large, with short, squarish tail. Rather uniform blackish (whitish chin often hard to see); roosts and nests behind waterfalls. ♣ Forest on or near the tepuis. ♪ Calls: very high, hoarse twittering. Might also give staccato clicks.

62.6 [WHITE-CHESTED SWIFT (Taperuçu-de-peito-branco] *Cypseloides lemosi* L 5.5 in./

14 cm. Unmistakable by white chest mark (reduced, occasionally even lacking, in ♀ and Juv.) and shallowly forked tail. ♣ Secondary forest and scrub.

62.7 SOOTY SWIFT (Taperuçu-preto) *Cypseloides*

fumigatus L 5.9 in./15 cm. From larger **62.8** by darker, blackish brown color without whitish tinge to head. ♣ Roosts and breeds near waterfalls. Feeds in small groups over nearby habitats, mainly humid forest, second growth.

62.8 GREAT DUSKY SWIFT (Taperuçu-velho) *Cypsel-*

oides senex L 7 in./18 cm. Large. Overall brown with whitish tinge to head (esp. forehead). Cf. **62.7**. ♣ Roosts and breeds near waterfalls. Feeds over nearby habitats, mainly forest. More gregarious than **62.7**.

62.9 TEPUI SWIFT (Taperuçu-dos-tepuis) *Strepto-*

procne phelpsi L 6.7 in./17 cm. Unmistakable by mainly orange head. ♣ Humid forest and grassland. Up to 2500 m. ♪ Call: rather low "tjip-tjip-tjip" or very high, scratchy "twui-twui- -."

62.10 WHITE-COLLARED SWIFT (Taperuçu-de-

coleira-branca) *Streptoprocne zonaris* L 7.9 in./20 cm. Very large with shallowly forked tail. White collar diagnostic, but incomplete and/or scaly in Juv. ♣ Roosts and breeds in caves or near waterfalls (often with **62.8**). Flies over a wide range of habitats (e.g., forest, savanna, towns). Up to 2500 m. ♪ Call: very high, sharp "seep-seep- -."

62.11 BISCUTATE SWIFT (Taperuçu-de-coleira-falha)

Streptoprocne biscutata L 7.9 in./20 cm. Very large with shallowly forked tail. White collar diagnostic, but incomplete and/or scaly in Juv. ♣ Roosts and breeds in caves or near waterfalls (often with **62.8**). Flies over a wide range of habitats (e.g., forest, savanna, towns). Up to 2500 m. ♪ Call: as **62.10**, but may be less sharp, more sounding like "weep-weep- -."

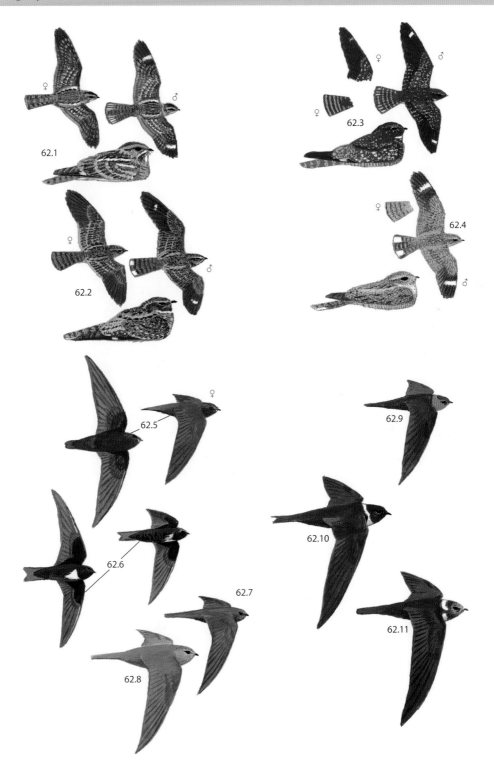

Plate 63

63.1 BAND-RUMPED SWIFT (Andorinhão-de-sobre-

branco) *Chaetura spinicaudus* L 4.3 in./
11 cm. Small. Narrow and clearly
defined whitish rump band diagnostic. Pale throat contrasts with
dark chest and belly. ♣ Forest
(mainly humid) and adjacent clearings. Up to 1000 m.
♪ Song: extr. high, soft "sreeuw sreeuw -."

63.2 PALE-RUMPED SWIFT (Taperá-de-garganta-

branca) *Chaetura egregia* L 5.1 in./
13 cm. Resembles smaller **63.3**, but
rump and uppertail coverts whitish,
and pale throat contrasts with sooty
chest and belly. ♣ Humid lowland
forest and adjacent clearings. ♪ Call: extr. high "siw-siw-
siw-tjee-tjee- -."

63.3 GRAY-RUMPED SWIFT (Andorinhão-de-sobre-

cinzento) *Chaetura cinereiventris*
L 4.3 in./11 cm. Gray (paler in E)
rump and uppertail coverts contrast
sharply with glossy blackish back,
head, and wings. Gray underparts
with dark vent and undertail. Smaller, less bulky, and
grayer rump patch contrasts more than in **63.4–63.6** and
63.8. ♣ Humid forest and nearby clearings. Up to 1500 m.
♪ Call: very high, sharp, staccato "chi chi chi-chi chi - -" or
"vrriuw vrriuw."

63.4 [CHIMNEY SWIFT (Andorinhão-migrante)

Chaetura pelagica] L 5.1 in./13 cm.
Resembles **63.8** (note "opposite"
season in area of possible overlap),
but rump barely contrasts with back.
♣ Forest, second growth. ♪ Call:
extr. high sharp "sreee" and "tji" notes (single or as trills).

63.5 CHAPMAN'S SWIFT (Andorinhão-de-chapman)

Chaetura chapmani L 5.5 in./14 cm.
L 5.1 in./13 cm. Rump and long
uppertail coverts brownish gray;
contrasting somewhat with glossy
black upperparts. Lacks contrasting
pale throat of **63.4** and **63.8**. From **63.6** only by range. ♣
Humid lowland forest and nearby surroundings. ♪ Call:
rapid series of extr. high, piercing, almost chattering
"tji" notes.

63.6 AMAZONIAN SWIFT *Chaetura viridipennis*

(Andorinhão-da-amazônia) L 5.5 in./
14 cm. Often considered a ssp. of
similar **63.5**. ♣ Humid lowland
forest and nearby (incl. towns).

63.7 SHORT-TAILED SWIFT (Andorinhão-de-rabo-

curto) *Chaetura brachyura* L 3.9 in./
10 cm. Pale vent, rump, and uppertail coverts almost cover very short
tail. Note bulging mid-wing, lack of
pale throat, and floppy-winged
flight. ♣ Forest (esp. in clearings and along rivers), woodland, towns, mangrove. Mainly in humid regions. Lowlands. ♪ Call/song: mixture of very high twittering and
rolls.

63.8 SICK'S (or Ashy-tailed or Ashy-throated) **SWIFT**

(Andorinhão-do-temporal) *Chaetura
meridionalis* L 5.5 in./14 cm. Rump
and long uppertail coverts brownish
gray; contrasts somewhat with sooty
blackish back and head. Pale
throat usually contrasts with dark brownish underparts.
Cf. **63.3–63.6**. ♣ Forest, savanna, second growth, towns.
Virtually any habitat during migration. ♪ Calls: very/extr.
high twittering "tjit-tjit-tjuw-tjittjit- -."

63.9 WHITE-TIPPED SWIFT (Andorinhão-serrano)

Aeronautes montivagus L 5.1 in./
13 cm. From **63.11** by white tail tips
(lacking in ♀), shorter, shallowly
forked tail (often appears square)
and lack of white neck collar. ♣
Over forest, second growth, open slopes between 600 and
2000 m. ♪ Call/song: sustained extr. high, undulating (in
pitch and strength), fast rattling.

63.10 FORK-TAILED PALM-SWIFT (Andorinhão-do-

buriti) *Tachornis squamata* L 5.1 in./
13 cm. Unmistakable by long, deeply
forked tail (often held together in a
point) and extensive white to underparts. ♣ Various open to semiopen
habitats (even towns) near palms. Up to 1000 m. ♪ Call:
irregular series of extr. high, piercing, joined "zeeee"
notes.

63.11 LESSER SWALLOW-TAILED SWIFT (Ando-

rinhão-estofador) *Panyptila cayennensis* L 5.1 in./13 cm. Unmistakable
by long, deeply forked tail (often
held together in a point) and white
neck collar. ♣ Mainly forest. Locally
also woodland, cultivated areas, towns. Mainly in humid
regions. Up to 1000 m. ♪ Normally flies so high that voice
is not heard.

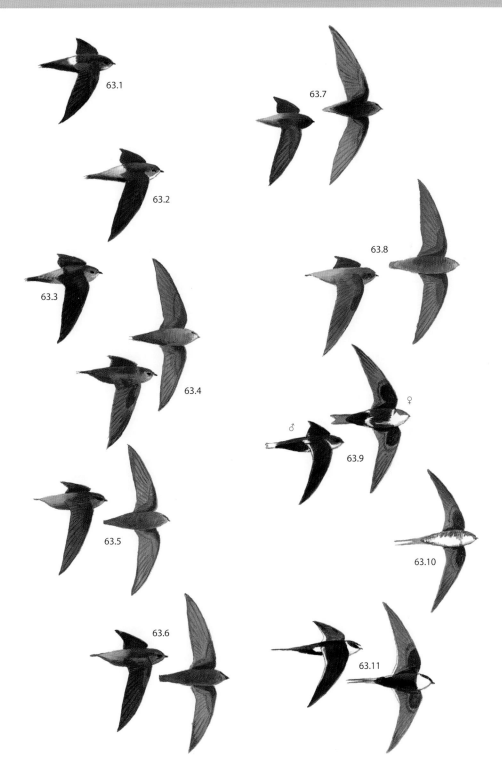

63.1

63.2

63.3

63.4

63.5

63.6

63.7

63.8

♀

♂ 63.9

63.10

63.11

Plate 64

64.1 EASTERN LONG-TAILED HERMIT (Rabo-branco-de-bigodes) *Phaethornis superciliosus* L 5.5 in./14 cm. Large. Chest pale grayish tinged buff; remaining underparts dull buff. Both sexes with whitish buff gular stripe. Cf. **64.2**. ♣ Forest, second growth, riverine belts, plantations. Mainly in humid regions (extends into nearby semideciduous areas locally). Up to 1200 m. ♪ Call: high "wueet-wueet- -" (without intervals) in flight; staccato, strong "tzic-tzic- -" at lek.

64.2 GREAT-BILLED HERMIT (Besourão-de-bico-grande) *Phaethornis malaris* L 5.9 in./ 15 cm. (6.3 in./16 cm in NE). NE Nom. (shown) only ssp. to overlap with **64.1**, but larger, underparts darker, chest grayer (not clearly tinged buff), and gular stripe faint/absent in ♂. Sspp. not shown: NW *insolitus* (as Nom), SW *ochraceiventris* (ochre below), and C *bolivianus* (buff below; cf. **64.10**). ♣ Humid lowland forest and second growth. ♪ Call/song: single- or double sounding, upslurred, very high, sharp "t'sjic-t'sjic-t' sjic- -."

64.3 MARGARETTA'S HERMIT (Rabo-branco-de-margarette) *Phaethornis margarettae* L 5.9 in./15 cm. Only large hermit in range without dark scaling on throat (see **64.4**) or contrasting rump patch (see **64.10**). No overlap with **64.1** or **64.2**. ♣ Humid lowland forest and nearby second growth. En.

64.4 SCALE-THROATED HERMIT (Rabo-branco-de-garganta-rajada) *Phaethornis eurynome* L 5.5 in./14 cm. Only large hermit with distinctly pale-scaled dark throat. Cf. **64.8**. ♣ Forest, tall second growth. Prefers humid regions. Up to 2250 m; in N part of range mainly in highlands. ♪ Call at lek: very high, sharp "tsju." Song: varied; may be very high, thin "fee-fjee tuh"("tuh" lower).

64.5 WHITE-BEARDED HERMIT (Rabo-branco-cinza) *Phaethornis hispidus* L 5.1 in./ 13 cm. Underparts and scaling to rump grayish. Distinct white gular stripe and malar. ♣ Várzea, swamp forest, riverine growth, forest edge, overgrown plantations. Up to 1000 m. ♪ Call/song: very high "tju-tju- -" without intervals.

64.6 STRAIGHT-BILLED HERMIT (Rabo-branco-de-bico-reto) *Phaethornis bourcieri* L 5.1 in./13 cm. Bill almost straight (other *Phaethornis* hermits, except **64.7**, have curved bills). Grayish below. ♣ Mainly terra firme; occasionally in várzea, thickets, plantations. Up to 1500 m. ♪ Call/song: insectlike, extr. high "tzee-tzee" notes.

64.7 NEEDLE-BILLED HERMIT (Rabo-branco-amarelo) *Phaethornis philippii* L 4.7 in./ 12 cm. Bill almost straight as in **64.6**, but underparts orange-tawny. ♣ Humid lowland forest, plantations.

64.8 DUSKY-THROATED HERMIT (Rabo-branco-pequeno) *Phaethornis squalidus* L 4.3 in./11 cm. From larger **64.4** by browner (less gray) chest, and throat appears more uniform dark (less scaled). From smaller **64.9** ♂ by longer tail and buffier underparts. ♣ Humid forest and dense second growth up to 2250 m. ♪ Call/song: at lek, may be a rhythmic, rapid melody, like "wit weet whut-whutwhut wit weet, zjew zjew" (fluted "wit" very high, "weet" slightly lower, nasal "wut" mid-high, reverberating "zjew" very low). En.

64.9 STREAK-THROATED (or Rupurumi) **HERMIT** (Rabo-branco-do-rupurumi) *Pha-* *ethornis rupurumii* L 4.3 in./11 cm. Medium-small. Dingy grayish below (sometimes tinged buff), throat mottled black (sometimes hard to see). ♣ Humid to semideciduous woodland and forest (esp. borders), riverine growth. ♪ Song: e.g., "fee-fee-t'tjuh" notes (1st part extr. high, "tjuh" much lower).

64.10 PLANALTO HERMIT (Rabo-branco-acanelado) *Phaethornis pretrei* L 5.5 in./14 cm. Large. Cinnamon-buff below. Contrasting orange-rufous rump. Tail broadly tipped white. Cf. **65. 2**. ♣ Wide variety of semiopen habitats, incl. woodland, forest edge, caatinga, riverine growth, wooded areas in savanna, second growth, gardens. Up to 2250 m. ♪ Song: irregular series of very high "tsee" and "tseree" notes, with few or no intervals.

64.1

64.6

64.2

64.7

64.3

64.8

64.4

64.9

64.5

64.10

Plate 65

65.1 BUFF-BELLIED HERMIT (Rabo-branco-de-barriga-fulva) *Phaethornis subochraceus* L 4.7 in./12 cm. Lacks uniform contrasting rump patch of **64.10**, **65.2**, and **65.3**. Tail broadly tipped white, and 2nd pair of rectrices elongated (as in **64.10**, but unlike **64.2**). ♣ Dry to semideciduous forest, woodland, shrub. ♪ Song (at lek): "tjuw-tjék" in rapid series.

65.2 CINNAMON-THROATED HERMIT (Besourão-de-sobre-amarelo) *Phaethornis nattereri* L 3.9 in./10 cm. Resembles larger **64.10**, but outer rectrices tipped buff. ♣ Semideciduous forest, riverine growth, caatinga, cerrado, second growth. Lowlands. ♪ Song (at lek):, series with notes as extr. high "tweettweet," "tsjeeh," and low "weeh-oh-wee."

NOTE: 65.2 ♂ plumage as shown is now considered to be a separate species, MARANHAO HERMIT (Rabo-branco-do-maranhão) *Phaethornis maranhaoensis*. Resembles **65.2** ♀ as shown, but with darker, richer throat color and shorter tail. Cf. paler-throated **65.3** ♀. ♣ Forest, woodland, second growth. Lowlands. En.

65.3 REDDISH HERMIT (Rabo-branco-rubro) *Phaethornis ruber* L 3.5 in./9cm. Tiny. Rump and underparts orange-rufous; chin whitish to pale ochre. ♂ with black chest patch (faint/absent in ♀). Tail rather wedge shaped; outer rectrices tipped rufous, color of central pair vary. ♣ Forest (humid to semideciduous), woodland (incl. cerrado), second growth, wooded savanna. Up to 1200 m. ♪ Song: irregular series of "fee," "fjee," and "fiuw" notes, all at extr. high but varying pitch.

65.4 GRAY-CHINNED HERMIT (Rabo-branco-de-garganta-cinza) *Phaethornis griseogularis* L 3.5 in./9 cm. Note small range. Very similar to **65.3** ♀, but chin gray and lacks coppery tinge to green upperparts. ♣ Humid forest at 800–1800 m. ♪ Call/song: calm but slightly irregular series of extr. high "feeuh" notes.

65.5 MINUTE HERMIT (Rabo-branco-mirim) *Phaethornis idaliae* L 3.1 in./8 cm. Tiny. White-tipped tail rather wedge-shaped (longer in ♀). Underparts grayish. Throat dark brown in ♂ (cf. **64.8**), orange-rufous in ♀ (cf. **65.3** ♀). ♣ Humid forest, wooded areas near the coast, old second growth. Lowlands. ♪ Call: in flight, very/extr. high, ascending "tuh-wéeh tuh-wéeh." En.

65.6 BROAD-TIPPED HERMIT (Rabo-branco-de-cauda-larga) *Anopetia gounellei* L 4.3 in./11 cm. Pale brownish buff below. Rump often tinged buff. Tail broadly tipped white, and 2nd pair of rectrices as long as central pair. Cf. *Phaethornis* hermits (Pl. **64** and **65**). ♣ Caatinga, shrubby areas, semideciduous forest. ♪ Song: slow series of repeated, very high, downslurred, chirping "twut" notes. En.

65.7 RUFOUS-BREASTED (or Hairy) **HERMIT** (Balança-rabo-de-bico-torto) *Glaucis hirsutus* L 4.3 in./11 cm. Rounded tail rufous with dark subterminal band and white tips. Underparts brownish rufous. Cf. localized **65.10** and **66.4**. ♣ Wide variety of shrubby and wooded habitats, incl. forest (mainly at edge; avoids interior of primary terra firme), woodland, riverine belts, thickets, overgrown plantations, mangrove. Up to 1000 m. ♪ Call in flight: very high "seep"; song: e.g., rapid "seep-seep-seep."

65.8 SOOTY BARBTHROAT (Balança-rabo-escuro) *Threnetes niger* L 4.3 in./11 cm. Two sspp. Nom. (**a**, N Amapá; with all-dark tail and faint or no rufous throat collar) and ssp. *loehkeni* (**b**, Bronze-tailed Barbthroat, S and C Amapá, with pale tip to tail and distinct rufous throat collar). Cf. **65.9**. ♣ Edge of lowland forest (mainly humid) and second growth. ♪ Call: extr. high "tsuw."

65.9 PALE-TAILED BARBTHROAT (Balança-rabo-de-garganta-preta) *Threnetes leucurus* L 4.3 in./11 cm. Note distinct throat collar. Three sspp. (all sometimes considered sspp. of **65.8**): widespread Nom. (**a**, with white in tail), W *cervicauda* (**b**, with buff in tail), and intermediate *medianus* (not shown, from S Pará). From **65.8b** by tail pattern. ♣ Edge of forest (mainly humid), second growth, brushy pastures, overgrown plantations. Up to 1000 m. ♪ Song: extr. high, hurried hissing (just audible).

65.10 HOOK-BILLED HERMIT (Balança-rabo-canela) *Glaucis dohrnii* L 5.1 in./13 cm. Resembles **65.7**, but with white-tipped bronzy green tail and straighter bill. ♣ Humid lowland forest. En, R.

Plate 66

66.1 SAW-BILLED HERMIT (Beija-flor-rajado) *Ram-* *phodon naevius* L 5.9 in./15 cm. Size, tail pattern, and broad streaks to breast (narrow on belly) diagnostic. ♣ Understory of Atlantic forest. ♪ Song: very high, chattering twitter. Also a sustained, rapid series of very high "bic" notes or a descending series of 3 slow, well-separated "seee" notes. En, R.

66.2 BLUE-FRONTED LANCEBILL (Bico-de-lança) *Doryfera johannae* L 4.3 in./11 cm. Note long, very slightly upcurved bill and coppery tinge to nape. ♣ Humid forest at 900–1800 m, locally lower.

66.3 GRAY-BREASTED SABREWING (Asa-de-sabre- cinza) *Campylopterus largipennis* L 5.5 in./14 cm. Large with gray underparts and broad white corners to rounded tail. Cf. **67.3** ♀, **69.8**, **71.2**, and **71.9** ♀. ♣ Humid forest (avoids interior of terra firme), second growth, thickets, plantations. Mainly lowlands, but at 1000–1500 m. in SE. ♪ Call: high, strong "tjew" irregularly at 1 ×/sec.

66.4 RUFOUS-BREASTED SABREWING (Asa-de- sabre-canela) *Campylopterus hyper-ythrus* L 4.7 in./12 cm. Note rufous underparts and outer rectrices (tail appears all rufous from below). ♣ Edge of humid forest, shrub; 1200–2600 m. ♪ Call: in flight, high, nasal "wit wirrit wit - -."

66.5 BUFF-BREASTED SABREWING (Asa-de-sabre- de-peito-camurça) *Campylopterus duidae* L 4.7 in./12 cm. Tail pattern and wing shape diagnostic. ♣ At streams in humid Atlantic forest. ♪ Call: very high, nasal, irritated-sounding "tir tirre-tirre-trit."

66.6 BROWN VIOLET-EAR (Beija-flor-marrom) *Colibri* *delphinae* L 4.7 in./12 cm. Unmistakable by overall dull grayish brown color, cinnamon tinge to rump, and violet-blue ears. ♣ Forest, woodland, second growth, shrubby areas; 700–2000 m. ♪ Call: very/extr. high, strident "zeep" notes in irregular series; song: series of very high "seep" notes, slightly irregular in tempo and pitch.

66.7 SPARKLING VIOLET-EAR (Beija-flor-violeta) *Colibri coruscans* L 5.5 in./14 cm. Unmistakable in small range (no overlap with **66.8**) by violet-blue ears and central belly and by throat and breast pattern. Tail with dark subterminal band. ♣ Forest edge and clearings, woodland; 1200–2400 m. ♪ Song: short series of 4–7 extr. high, strident, staccato "tseet" notes.

66.8 WHITE-VENTED VIOLET-EAR (Beija-flor-de- orelha-violeta) *Colibri serrirostris* L 5.1 in./13 cm. Unmistakable by white vent and blue-violet ears. ♣ Wide range of semiopen habitats, incl. savanna, grassland, shrub, second growth, gardens, open forest. Up to 2700 m. ♪ Song: high to very high, 2-noted, sharp "tí-tju tí-tju - -."

66.9 GREEN-THROATED MANGO (Beija-flor-de- veste-verde) *Anthracothorax viridigula* L 4.7 in./12 cm. Resembles **66.10**, but ♂ with green throat, while ♀ shows stronger coppery red tinge to upperparts (esp. rump) than **66.10** ♀. Many (all?) ♀♀ with white band on the lower throat, clearly dividing black stripe in two. Juv. ♂ as **66.10** ♀, but line below is green on the throat. ♣ Mangrove, forest (avoids interior of dense forest), woodland, savanna. Mainly near water. Lowlands. ♪ Song: very high, slightly descending trill, like "f'srrrrrih-tjew tjuh."

66.10 BLACK-THROATED MANGO (Beija-flor-de- veste-preta) *Anthracothorax nigricollis* L 4.7 in./12 cm. Note tail pattern and distinctive black stripe below (chest section often irregular and faint in ♀ and Imms.). Cf. **66.9** and **68.1**. ♣ Wide variety of open to semiopen habitats (even in towns). Lowlands. ♪ Call: very high "chip chip -."

Plate 67

67.1 WHITE-NECKED JACOBIN (Beija-flor-azul-de-rabo-branco) *Florisuga mellivora* L 4.7 in./12 cm. Note white nape, belly, and undertail in ♂. ♀ variable; typically as shown (belly and scaling to throat and vent white) or similar, but with bluer throat and/or more white to tail, or ♂-like. ♣ Forest, woodland, plantations, second growth, riverine belts. Mainly in humid regions. Up to 1500 m. ♪ Call: extr. high, thin "fiw fiw -."

67.2 BLACK JACOBIN (Beija-flor-preto) *Florisuga fusca* L 5.1 in./13 cm. Unmistakable by black and white pattern. Imm. (**a**) with rufous malar and less white to tail. ♣ Forest, woodland, gardens. Up to 1500 m.

67.3 FORK-TAILED WOODNYMPH (Beija-flor-tesoura-verde) *Thalurania furcata* L 3.9 in./10 cm (♂), 3.1 in./8 cm (♀). Glittering parts almost velvety. ♂ with blue underparts and green back (often with blue neck collar). ♀ with whitish underparts and slightly forked tail; outer rectrices with greenish gray basal half, broad blue-black subterminal band and white tips (cf. **66.3**, **67.5** ♀, and **71.9** ♀). ♣ Forest, woodland, tall second growth, plantations, gardens. Up to 2000 m. ♪ Call: dry, toneless pistollike "tic" notes or very high "tjuw-tjuw- -."

67.4 LONG-TAILED WOODNYMPH (Beija-flor-de-costas-violetas) *Thalurania watertonii* L 5.1 in./13 cm. L 5.1 in./13 cm (♂), 3.9 in./10 cm (♀). ♂ differs from **67.3** ♂ by longer tail, all-blue mantle, and more green to underparts. ♀ as smaller **67.3** ♀, but note range. ♣ Forest and other wooded habitats. En.

67.5 VIOLET-CAPPED WOODNYMPH (Beija-flor-de-fronte-violeta) *Thalurania glaucopis* L 3.9 in./10 cm (♂), 3.1 in./8 cm (♀). ♂ with diagnostic blue cap. ♀ resembles **67.3** ♀, but green usually extends more onto neck sides and flanks and greenish gray base of outer rectrices narrower. ♣ Forest (incl. edge), wooded areas, gardens, parks. Up to 850 m (rarely to 1500 m). ♪ Call/song: series of dry, ticking rattles.

67.6 GOLDEN-TAILED SAPPHIRE (Beija-flor-de-cauda-dourada) *Chrysuronia oenone* L 3.9 in./10 cm. Note reddish base to lower mandible and goldish copper tail. ♂ with blue hood. ♣ Humid forest (prefers edge), tall second growth. ♪ Song: irregular series of joined, extr. high "tjeé" and very high "tjuw" notes.

67.7 RUFOUS-THROATED SAPPHIRE (Beija-flor-safira) *Hylocharis sapphirina* L 3.5 in./9 cm. Note violet-copper tail, rufous chin, and rufous/buff (♂/♀) vent. ♂ with black-tipped red bill as **70.9**, but note blue throat. ♣ Canopy and edge of lowland forest, woodland, wooded savanna, plantations.

67.8 WHITE-CHINNED SAPPHIRE (Beija-flor-roxo) *Hylocharis cyanus* L 3.5 in./9 cm. Several sspp.: E Nom. (**a**, ♂) and darker Amazonian *viridiventris* (**b**, ♂ and ♀) shown. Blue-black tail (white-tipped in ♀) contrasts with coppery rump. ♂ with black-tipped red bill (only base red in Imm. ♂) and blue throat and forehead. ♀ whitish below with variable amount of green on flanks and blue throat-spots. ♣ Humid forest, gallery forest, woodland, second growth; 0–1200 m (0–500 m in SE). ♪ Song: sustained 2-noted series of joined, penetrating "feé" and "tju" notes like "fee-tjutjutju---."

67.9 WHITE-CHESTED EMERALD (Beija-flor-de-bico-preto) *Amazilia* (or *Agyrtria*) *brevirostris* L 3.9 in./10 cm. Note small range. Bill all-black (base of lower mandible fleshy red in **67.7** and **67.8** ♀) and rump and tail tinged coppery. ♣ Forest edge, second growth, riverine belts, scrub. Lowlands. ♪ Song: varied; may be a high chattering "pjuwpjuw---" or series of "pee-twtrrrr" notes ("pee" very high, "twtrrrr" a low twitter).

67.10 VERSICOLORED EMERALD (Beija-flor-de-banda-branca) *Amazilia* (or *Agyrtria*) *versicolor* L 3.5 in./9 cm. Crown green and throat green (**d**) to turquoise (**b**; white-scaled in ♀). Coastal SE Nom. (**c**; intermediates with **b**, **d** occur) and turquoise-crowned ssp. *milleri* (**a**, N of Ri. Amazon) have white throats. All with orange/pink base to lower mandible, white vent faintly spotted dusky green and coppery green tail with dusky blue subterminal band. ♣ Forest edge, riverine belts, cerrado, caatinga, shrub, gardens, parks, mangrove. Up to 1800 m. ♪ Song: extr. high (sometimes almost inaudible), sort of ticking "tuw tuw - -" (1 × "tuw"/sec).

67.1

67.2

Imm.

67.3

67.4

67.5

67.6 ♀

67.7 ♀

a   b

67.8 ♀

67.9

a   b

67.10

c

d

♀

Plate 68

68.1 FIERY-TAILED AWLBILL (Beija-flor-de-bico-virado)

Avocettula recurvirostris L 3.5 in./9 cm. Resembles larger **66.9**, but note upturned bill. ♣ Savannalike habitats, mainly near rocky outcrops. Sometimes also forest edge.

68.2 (Black-breasted) **PLOVERCREST** (Beija-flor-de-topete)

Stephanoxis lalandi L 3.5 in./9 cm. Small. Two sspp.: *loddigesii* (**a**) and Nom. (**b**, S part of range) shown. ♂ unmistakable; ♀♀ of the two sspp. similar, with pale gray underparts and white-tipped tail (mainly visible from below; cf. longer-billed ♀ **67.5**). ♣ Forest, woodland, wooded shrub. Prefers highlands in N part of range. ♪ Call/song: very high, slightly irregular, ticking "tjee-tjee-tjee- -."

68.3 RUBY-TOPAZ HUMMINGBIRD (Beija-flor-vermelho)

Chrysolampis mosquitus L 3.5 in./9 cm. ♂ unmistakable. Note tail pattern of ♀. ♣ Wooded and shrubby savanna, gardens, cultivation between SL and 1700 m. ♪ Call/song: very high, rather clear "tju-tju- -."

NOTE: COQUETTES and THORNTAILS: Small with distinctive pale rump-bands, leading to confusion with certain moths. Slow, weaving flight without the abrupt movements of most other hummingbirds.

68.4 DOT-EARED COQUETTE (Topetinho-do-brasil-central)

Lophornis gouldii L 2.8 in./7 cm. Whiskers white. Limited contact with **68.6**. ♣ Forest edge, savanna, cerrado.

68.5 TUFTED COQUETTE (Beija-flor-de-leque-canela)

Lophornis ornatus L 2.8 in./7 cm. No overlap with **68.4** and **68.6**. Note tawny-rufous whiskers in ♂ and rufous throat in ♀. ♣ Forest edge, riverine belts, plantations, savanna. Up to 1000 m.

68.6 FRILLED COQUETTE (Topetinho-vermelho)

Lophornis magnificus L 2.8 in./7 cm. Resembles **68.5**, but "whiskers" in ♂ fan shaped and rufous at the base. ♀ with spotty effect to throat (sometimes reduced), resembling uniform rufous throat of ♀ **68.5**. ♣ Forest edge, plantations, cerrado.

68.7 FESTIVE COQUETTE (Topetinho-verde)

Lophornis chalybeus L 3.1 in./8 cm. Two sspp.: SE Nom. (**a**) and W *verreauxii* (**b**; not shown ♀ is darker below than ♀ **a**). ♂ unmistakable. Underparts of ♀ grayish (often tinged buff) mottled dusky and with a dark spot on mid-throat (sometimes a 2nd on mid-chest), but lacks prominent flank patches and malar (if present) not clearly defined as in ♀♀ **68.9** and **68.10**. ♣ Humid forest and second growth. Locally in cerrado. Up to 1000 m.

68.8 PEACOCK COQUETTE (Rabo-de-espinho)

Lophornis pavoninus L 3.9 in./10 cm. ♂ unmistakable by black-spotted green whiskers. ♀ with whitish throat streaked blackish; chest and belly as throat or more uniform green. ♣ Humid forest and old second growth at 500–2000 m.

68.9 RACKET-TAILED COQUETTE (Bandeirinha)

Discosura longicaudus L 3.9 in./10 cm. ♂ unmistakable. ♀ resembles ♀ **68.10**, but tail-base gray (not dusky) and rump-band and belly buff-tinged. Also cf. ♀ **68.7**. ♣ Canopy and edge of humid forest, scrubby savanna.

68.10 BLACK-BELLIED THORNTAIL (Rabo-de-espinho-de barriga-preta)

Discosura (or *Popelairia*) *langsdorffi* L 5.1 in./13 cm. ♂ unmistakable. Note white malar and flanks in ♀. Cf. ♀♀ **68.7** and **68.9**. ♣ Mainly canopy and edge of humid forest; locally in wooded/shrubby habitats.

Plate 69

69.1 GLITTERING-THROATED EMERALD (Beija-flor-de-garganta-verde) *Amazilia* (or *Polyerata*) *fimbriata* L 3.5 in./ 9 cm (4.3 in./11 cm in SE). Resembles **67.10d**, but base of lower mandible red (sometimes pinkish), vent all white (spotted N of Ri. Amazon), and tail bluish black with greener base. ♀ with white-scaled throat. ♣ Virtually any open to semiopen habitat, incl. forest (avoids interior of terra firme), riverine belts, woodland, savanna (incl. cerrado), caatinga, plantations, gardens, parks, mangrove. ♪ Song: series of almost toneless, very short, rattling trills, like "trr" (2 ×/sec).

69.2 SAPPHIRE-SPANGLED EMERALD (Beija-flor-de-peito-azul) *Amazilia* (or *Polyerata*) *lactea* L 3.9 in./10 cm. As **69.1**, but throat violet-blue. ♣ Forest edge, riverine belts, cerrado, parks, gardens, plantations. Lowlands. ♪ Song: rapid series of a few extr. high "tzut" notes, like "tzut-tzut-tzut- -."

69.3 PLAIN-BELLIED EMERALD (Beija-flor-de-barriga-branca) *Amazilia* (or *Agyrtria*) *leucogaster* L 3.9 in./10 cm. Median underparts white. Outer rectrices blue-black, central ones bronze-green. ♣ Mangrove, shrub, forest edge, gardens, parks, plantations. Near SL.

69.4 WHITE-BELLIED HUMMINGBIRD (Beija-flor-verde-e-branco) *Amazilia* (or *Leucippus*) *chionogaster* L 4.3 in./11 cm. Note small range. Median underparts white. Tail green, basal half (and sometimes tips) of inner webs of outer rectrices white (best visible from below). ♣ Cerrado, shrub, thickets. ♪ Song: series of soft, very high twitters and dry, toneless rattles.

69.5 COPPER-TAILED HUMMINGBIRD *Amazilia* (or *Saucerottia*) *viridigaster* (Beija-flor-de-barriga-verde) L 3.5 in./9 cm. Note small range. Chest and head green, turning bronzy copper toward rump and rufous on tail. ♣ Humid forest and shrub; 700–2000 m, occasionally lower.

69.6 BLUE-GREEN EMERALD *Amazilia* (or *Agyrtria*) *rondoniae* (Beija-flor-de-cabeça-azul) L 3.5 in./9 cm. Note small range. Probably a variant of **67.10**, but with azure-blue crown. ♣ Lowland forest, riverine growth, cerrado.

69.7 BLUE-CHINNED SAPPHIRE (Beija-flor-de-garganta-azul) *Chlorestes notata* L 3.5 in./9 cm. Note red base to lower mandible and rather rounded blue-black tail. ♂ with small blue chin. Median underparts of ♀ whitish, throat variably spotted green. ♣ Edge and clearings of humid forest, woodland, plantations, gardens. Lowlands. ♪ Call/song: extr. high (barely audible) "zeet-zeet- -."

69.8 SOMBRE HUMMINGBIRD (Beija-flor-cinza) *Aphantochroa cirrochloris* L 4.7 in./ 12 cm. Fairly large and dull. Slightly curved black bill. Soot-gray below (faintly spotted green on throat) with white patch below legs. May show narrow white tail edging but not broad tips as in **66.3**, ♀♀ **67.3–67.5**, and **71.9**. ♣ Forest (esp. edge), second growth, gardens, plantations. En.

69.9 WHITE-TAILED GOLDENTHROAT (Beija-flor-de-bico-curvo) *Polytmus guainumbi* L 3.9 in./10 cm. Note curved bill, white postocular streak and malar, golden green upperparts, green (♂) or buff-white (♀) underparts and tail with white tips and outer webs (only on outermost rectrix in ♀). Imm. as ♀, but with no green below or spotting restricted to central throat. ♣ Savanna, cerrado, scrub, grassland, riverine growth. Often near water. Up to 1500 m. ♪ Call: very high, ticking "twit," given at irregular intervals.

69.10 GREEN-TAILED GOLDENTHROAT (Beija-flor-verde) *Polytmus theresiae* L 3.5 in./ 9 cm. Greener than **69.9**. ♂ lacks white tail-tips; ♀ with white tail-corner and scaling below. Two sspp.: NE Nom. (**a**) and W *leucorrhous* (**b**, ♀ shown; ♂ with green-spotted white vent). ♣ Forest edge, várzea, scrub, savanna. Lowlands. ♪ Song: hurried, rising and descending twitter, like "tutu---títititu" (3 sec).

Plate 70

70.1 FIERY TOPAZ (Topázio-de-fogo) *Topaza pyra* L 7.9 in./20 cm (♂, incl. tail), 5.5 in./ 14 cm (♀). Large. ♂ differs from ♂ **70.2** by red nape and extensive rufous in tail. ♀ (with coppery rufous throat) differs from ♀ **70.2** by mainly rufous outer rectrices (distinct from below). ♣ Humid forest, esp. near small streams. ♪ Call: series of staccato "tic" notes as singles or as short, fast rattles.

70.2 CRIMSON TOPAZ (Beija-flor-brilho-de-fogo) *Topaza pella* L 7.9 in./20 cm (♂, incl. tail), 5.5 in./14 cm (♀). Resembles **70.1**, but ♂ lacks rufous in tail and ♀ with rufous-buff restricted to outer web of outermost tail feather. ♣ Humid forest, esp. near small streams. ♪ Voice as **70.1**.

70.3 BLUE-TAILED EMERALD (Esmeralda-de-cauda-azul) *Chlorostilbon mellisugus* L 3.1 in./ 8 cm. ♂ resembles larger ♂ **69.7**, but bill all black. Combination of white postocular streak and all-black bill diagnostic in ♀. ♣ Edge of humid forest (esp. near rivers), shrub, savanna, gardens. Up to 1800 m. ♪ Call in flight: nervous, short twitter; from perch, soft, dry "tit-twit."

70.4 GLITTERING-BELLIED EMERALD (Besourinho-de-bico-vermelho) *Chlorostilbon lucidus* (or *aureoventris*) L 3.9 in./ 10 cm. ♂ with forked all-blue tail and black-tipped red bill. ♀ differs from smaller ♀ **70.3** by red base to bill. ♣ Virtually any open to semiopen habitat, incl. woodland, cerrado, caatinga, savanna, shrub, forest edge, grassland, gardens. Up to 2800 m. ♪ Call: high, almost toneless, rattling twitter; song: inhaled, hurried "tuit-tuit- -."

70.5 VELVET-BROWED BRILLIANT (Brilhante-veludo) *Heliodoxa xanthogonys* L 4.3 in./11 cm. Bill almost straight, base of lower mandible often orange. ♂ rather dark with green frontlet and violet-blue central throat. ♀ with green-spotted white underparts and white tail-corners. ♣ Humid forest; 700–2000 m. ♪ Song: very/extr. high, hurried twitter, followed by "twit tuit," together as "t'chwiwi twit tuit."

70.6 BLACK-THROATED BRILLIANT (Brilhante-de-garganta-preta) *Heliodoxa schreibersii* L 4.7 in./12 cm. Rather dark. Bill slightly curved. Throat and belly black (♂) or sooty (♀). Lower throat violet. Obvious pale malar in ♀. No overlap with **70.5**. ♣ Humid lowland forest (mainly interior).

NOTE: Not shown is PINK-THROATED BRILLIANT, *Heliodoxa gularis*, which probably does not occur in Brazil, but in NE Peru, NE Ecuador, and S Colombia. Bill almost straight, throat patch pink (smaller in ♀). White vent diagnostic. ♣ Forest interior and scrub; up to 1000 m or higher.

70.7 GOULD'S JEWELFRONT (Beija-flor-estrela) *Heliodoxa aurescens* L 4.7 in./12 cm. Unmistakable by extensive rufous in tail and broad orange-rufous chest-band. ♣ Humid lowland forest (incl. borders). ♪ Song: exreme high, thin "feee" (1 ×/sec).

70.8 BRAZILIAN RUBY (Beija-flor-rubi) *Clytolaema rubricauda* L 4.3 in./11 cm. Straight, black bill. ♂ with ruby throat and tail mainly bronzy rufous. ♀ with underparts and outer rectrices cinnamon. A melanistic form (**a**) occurs. ♣ Forest (incl. *Araucaria*), shrub, parks, plantations. ♪ Song: dry rattle, starting high pitched, changing from "ti" to "tu," together as "tititi--- titutu" En.

70.9 GILDED (Sapphire or) **HUMMINGBIRD** (Beija-flor-dourado) *Hylocharis chrysura* L 3.5 in./9 cm. Resembles ♂**67.7**, but no blue to throat and conspicuously tinged golden throughout. ♣ Savannalike areas, grassland, forest (avoids interior of humid forest), gardens, plantations (incl. eucalyptus). Mainly below 1000 m. ♪ Call: soft, dry rattles, like "trru trr-trr-trr."

70.10 WHITE-THROATED HUMMINGBIRD (Beija-flor-de-papo-branco) *Leucochloris albicollis* L 4.3 in./11 cm. Unmistakable by white throat, belly, and tail corners. ♣ Canopy and edge of forest, gardens, parks, plantations. Mainly below 1300 m. ♪ Call: irregular, dry "tjek-tjek tjek- -."

70.1 ♀

70.1

♀

70.2

70.2 ♀

♀

70.4

70.3

♀

♀

70.5

♀

a

70.8

♀

70.6

70.9

♀

70.7

70.10

♀

Plate 71

71.1 SWALLOW-TAILED HUMMINGBIRD (Beija-flor-tesoura) *Eupetomena macroura* L 6.3 in./16 cm. No similar hummer in Brazil, but cf. ♂ **67.5**. ♣ Forest, woodland, savannalike habitats, gardens, parks, plantations. Up to 1600 m.

♪ Call: e.g., in flight, mid-high, nasal "tjiw" in a slow or hurried series.

71.2 OLIVE-SPOTTED HUMMINGBIRD (Beija-flor-pintado) *Leucippus chlorocercus* L 4.7 in./12 cm. Note restricted range/habitat. Dull olive green above, whitish below. Tail dull greenish with pale grayish corners.

Bill blackish. From ♀ **67.3** by duller upperparts and distinct white postocular spot. Also cf. **67.10**, **69.1**, and ♀ **69.7**. ♣ Semiopen areas along large rivers (esp. on river islands). ♪ Song: extr. high "fee" followed by high "tju" or "tjutju," together as "feé-tju."

71.3 HOODED VISORBEARER (Beija-flor-de-gravata-vermelha) *Augastes lumachella* L 3.9 in./10 cm. Unmistakable in small range by head pattern and coppery red tail. ♣ Montane, rocky areas with cacti and low shrub; 900–

2000 m. ♪ Song: nasal, dry "tru weé tru zee - -." En, R.

71.4 HYACINTH VISORBEARER (Beija-flor-de-gravata-verde) *Augastes scutatus* L 3.5 in./9 cm. Unmistakable in small range by creamy white pectoral band and blue on sides of neck (also on belly in ♂). ♣ Open to semiopen shrubby

areas, gallery forest, montane forest; 900–2000 m. ♪ Song: series of high, dry "tjic," "whi," "zuzu," and other notes. En, R.

71.5 BLACK-EARED FAIRY (Beija-flor-de-bochecha-azul) *Heliothryx auritus* L 4.7 in./12 cm. Three sspp.: N Nom. (**a**, underparts all white), NW *phainolata* (**b**, with green throat) and S and C *auriculata* (not shown, with chin

and throat sides green). ♀♀ of all sspp. with white underparts (incl. throat) and long tail. Cf. ♀ **71.6**. ♣ Humid forest, second growth. Up to 1300 m. ♪ Call: very high, dry "tju tji twu twi -" notes.

71.6 HORNED SUNGEM (Chifre-de-ouro) *Heliactin bilophus* L 3.9 in./10 cm. ♂ unmistakable. ♀ differs from larger ♀ **71.5** (note habitat and range) by more golden upperparts (incl. upper-tail), partial white collar, and tail

pattern and /shape. ♣ Riverine belts, shrub, woodland, cerrado, grassland.

71.7 LONG-BILLED STARTHROAT (Bico-reto-cinzento) *Heliomaster longirostris* L 4.7 in./12 cm. Very long, almost straight bill. Throat patch pink in ♂, smaller, dusky, and often faintly scaled in ♀. Streak on back and tail-corners

white. ♣ Forest edge, woodland, riverine belts, second growth. Up to 1200 m. ♪ Call: high, strong, sharp "twic-tjic - -."

71.8 STRIPE-BREASTED STARTHROAT (Bico-reto-de-banda-branca) *Heliomaster squamosus* L 4.7 in./12 cm. Resembles **71.7**; ♂ with broad green flanks and more forked tail; ♀ with distinctly white-edged dark throat. N-br. ♂

has throat like ♀. ♣ Forest, woodland, riverine growth, parks. En.

71.9 BLUE-TUFTED STARTHROAT (Bico-reto-azul) *Heliomaster furcifer* L 5.1 in./13 cm. Very long, almost straight bill. Br. ♂ unmistakable. ♀ with broad white tail tips and underparts all whitish gray. N-br. ♂ as ♀, but with longer,

forked tail. ♣ Forest edge, woodland, savannalike areas, scrub.

71.10 AMETHYST WOODSTAR (Estrelinha-ametista) *Calliphlox amethystina* L 2.4 in./6 cm. Small; ♂ unmistakable. No other ♀ hummingbird with dark smear through eye and tawny flanks. ♣ Canopy and edge of humid forest.

♪ Call: low, very short rattle, like "trr."

71.1

71.2

71.3 ♀

71.4 ♀

71.5
a
b ♂ ♀ ♀

71.6 ♀ ♀

71.7 ♀

71.8 ♀

71.9 ♀

71.10 ♀

Plate 72

72.1 PAVONINE QUETZAL (Surucuá-pavão) *Pharo-* *machrus pavoninus* L 13.8 in./35 cm. Large, thickset, golden-emerald above. Note tail pattern of ♀. ♣ Middle and upper strata of terra firme. ♪ Song: high, slightly chivering, forlorn "fhuuuh," followed by low "tjup," together as "fhuuuh tjup"; 1st part slightly falling in pitch, but gaining in strength.

72.2 COLLARED TROGON (Surucuá-de-coleira) *Tro-* *gon collaris* L 9.8 in./25 cm. ♂ differs from ♂ **72.3** (note range) by broad tail-barring and narrower eye ring; ♀ with paler face and dusky culmen (bill all yellow in ♀ **72.3**). ♣ Mid-levels of humid to semihumid forest, tall woodland. Up to 2000 m (generally at lower altitudes than **72.3** in area of overlap). ♪ Song: slightly descending series of 4–8 mid-high, fluted, yet nasal "jtuw" notes.

72.3 MASKED TROGON (Surucuá-mascarado) *Trogon* *personatus* L 9.8 in./25 cm. Cf. **72.2**. ♣ In or near humid forest; 700–2000 m. ♪ Song: level series of 4–6 fluted "tjuw" notes.

72.4 BLACK-THROATED TROGON (Surucuá-de- barriga-amarela) *Trogon rufus* L 9.8 in./25 cm. N Nom. (**a**) shown and tails of W ssp. *sulphureus* (**b**, uppertail reddish) and SE *chrysochlorus* (**c**, uppertail as **a**, but barring below denser). Combination of yellow underparts and green (♂) or brown (♀) head diagnostic. ♣ Middle and lower levels of humid forest, tall second growth, dense woodland. ♪ Song: slow, level, or slightly descending series of 5–8 loud, fluted "woo" or "tjuw" notes.

72.5 BLACK-TAILED TROGON (Surucuá-de-cauda- preta) *Trogon melanurus* L 11.8 in./30 cm. Dark undertail diagnostic. ♣ Upper or middle levels of humid lowland forest and tall woodland. ♪ Call/song: rapid, yelping "wah-wah-wah- -," like barking of small dog or high, calm "wew-wew-wew- -." Also fast "prupruprupru."

72.6 (Amazonian) **WHITE-TAILED TROGON** (Surucuá- grande-de-barriga-amarela) *Trogon viridis* L 11.8 in./30 cm. From smaller **72.9** by different tail pattern in ♂ and complete bluish white eye ring in both sexes (yellowish or white in **72.9**). Also cf. **72.7b**. ♣ Upper to middle levels of humid forest (also in drier areas in E), woodland, second growth, plantations. ♪ Song: slow or rapid, high, crescendoing "tjuwtjuwtjuw- -" (6–7 sec).

72.7 SURUCUA TROGON (Surucuá-variado) *Trogon* *surrucura* L 9.8 in./25 cm. Two sspp.: Nom. (**a**, N to Rio de Janeiro; ♂ shown; ♀ as ♀ **b**, but red below) and *aurantius* (**b**, S to São Paulo); **a** resembles **72.8**; **b** differs from **72.6** by tail pattern and complete yellow (♂) or partial white (♀) eye ring. These sspp. seem to show limited overlap, and even hybridization, in the Itatiaia area. ♣ Mid-levels of forest and woodland up to 2000 m. ♪ Call: short, high, dry rattling trill; song: high "tuw-tuw-tuw- -" ("tuw" 10–15 ×), level or ascending at the end.

72.8 BLUE-CROWNED TROGON (Surucuá-de-barriga- vermelha) *Trogon curucui* L 9.8 in./25 cm. From **72.7a** (limited contact) by barring of undertail. Amount of white on chest and broadness of white tail tips variable. ♣ Forest (humid to dry), woodland, second growth, wooded savanna, scrub. ♪ Song: long, rapid series of "tju" notes, crescendoing and becoming more excited-sounding, at the end often downslurred in a slower chatter (up to 12 sec).

72.9 (Amazonian) **VIOLACEOUS TROGON** (Surucuá- pequeno) *Trogon violaceus* L 9.8 in./25 cm. Blue-headed ♂ with yellowish eye ring. Gray-headed ♀ with partial white eyering. Cf. **72.6**. No overlap with **72.7**. ♣ Upper levels of humid forest (esp. borders) and tall woodland. ♪ Song: slow series of up to 15 fluted/yelping "tjuw" notes, slowly rising in strength and pitch.

Plate 73

73.1 BROAD-BILLED MOTMOT (Udu-de-bico-largo) *Electron platyrhynchum* L 13.8 in./ 35 cm (incl. tail). From larger **73.2** by green chin, less rufous on underparts, and larger black central spot on breast. Often with racquets (like **73.2a**) in W. ♣ Humid forest and second growth up to 1100 m. ♪ Call: hoarse/pinched "Ouch" at 3- to 4-sec intervals.

73.2 RUFOUS MOTMOT (Juruva-ruiva) *Baryphthengus* *martii* L 17.7 in./45 cm (incl. tail). Note extensive rufous in underparts. With (**a**) or without tail rackets. ♣ Humid lowland forest and second growth. ♪ Song: high, muffled but resounding "óorúc" at 3-sec intervals.

73.3 RUFOUS-CAPPED MOTMOT (Juruva-verde) *Baryphthengus ruficapillus* L 15.7 in./ 40 cm (incl. tail). Note distinctive green head with rufous cap and lack of racquets. ♣ Humid forest, gallery forest, dense woodland. ♪ Song: short, high, muffled trill, like "urrrrc."

73.4 BLUE-CROWNED (or -diademed) **MOTMOT** (Udu- de-coroa-azul) *Momotus momota* L 15.7 in./40 cm (incl. tail). Head pattern diagnostic. ♣ Forest, woodland, second growth, plantations, gardens. ♪ Song: slow, owl-like, muffled, slightly descending trill (4 sec).

73.5 RINGED KINGFISHER (Martim-pescador- grande) *Megaceryle torquata* L 15.7 in./ 40 cm. Large size, bicolored bill, and gray coloring diagnostic. ♣ Open to semiopen areas near water (rivers, streams, lakes, marshes, lagoons, rocky coast, etc.). ♪ Call in flight: sustained, toneless, loud, dry rattle.

73.6 GREEN-AND-RUFOUS KINGFISHER (Martim- pescador-da-mata) *Chloroceryle inda* L 9.8 in./25 cm. All-rufous underparts diagnostic. ♣ Shaded perches at streams, swamps, mangrove. ♪ Call in flight: short "shreew."

73.7 AMAZON KINGFISHER (Martim-pescador- verde) *Chloroceryle amazona* L 11.8 in./ 30 cm. From smaller **73.9** by proportionally larger bill and streaking on flanks; flight-feathers only with white spotting to inner webs (not visible when perched). ♣ Open to semiopen area at rivers, lakes, larger ponds, lagoons, estuaries, mangrove. ♪ Call/ song: series of sharp, nasal "chaw" notes, dry rattles, descending "tewtewtew- -" and other notes.

73.8 AMERICAN PYGMY KINGFISHER (Martinho) *Chloroceryle aenea* L 5.1 in./13 cm. Note small size and rufous underparts with white central belly and vent. ♣ Densely vegetated areas at streams, pools, lagoons, swamps (incl. várzea), mangrove. ♪ Call: fast, descending, twittering trill or weak "weet" and other notes.

73.9 GREEN KINGFISHER (Martim-pescador- pequeno) *Chloroceryle americana* L 7.9 in./20 cm. Both webs of flight feathers spotted white (spots visible when perched). ♂ with green spotting on flanks; ♀ with two breast bands (lower often incomplete). Cf. **73.7**. ♣ Open to semiopen areas at streams, lakes, ponds, swamps (incl. várzea), marsh, mangrove, rocky coast. ♪ Call: dry, staccato, toneless "tictic."

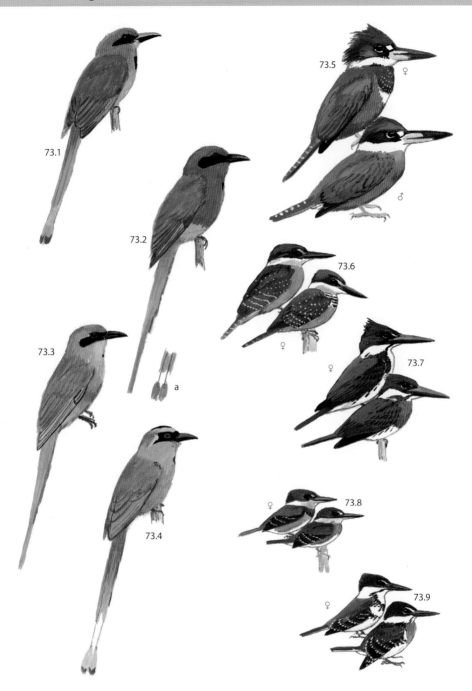

73.1

73.2

73.3

a

73.4

73.5 ♀

♂

73.6

♀

♀

73.7

73.8 ♀

73.9 ♀

Plate 74

74.1 YELLOW-BILLED JACAMAR (Ariramba-de-bico-amarelo) *Galbula albirostris* L 7.5 in./ 19 cm. Note yellow bill and lack of green on chest. ♂ with white throat (lacking in ♀). Cf. **74.2**. ♣ Understory of interior of humid forest and dense woodland. ♪ Call: high, staccato "pinc" notes; possible song: a nice, ascending series, immediately followed by a few accentuated, lilting "ping" notes, the total sounding like "tutu - - tutu-tu ti ping ping ping ping."

74.2 BLUE-CHEEKED (or-necked)**JACAMAR** (Ariramba-da-mata) *Galbula cyanicollis* L 7.9 in./20 cm. Resembles ♀ **74.1** (no overlap), but cheeks usually bluish. ♣ Understory of humid forest, gallery forest, and dense woodland. ♪ Call: very high, dry "kip-kip kipkip - -"; song: a rapidly accelerating and ascending series of "weep" notes, which at the end change into a very fast, dry, toneless rattle.

74.3 RUFOUS-TAILED JACAMAR (Ariramba-de-cauda-ruiva) *Galbula ruficauda* L 8.7 in./ 22 cm. From **74.8** and **74.9** by distinct white (♂) or rufous (♀) throat patch. Underside tail rufous as in **74.1, 74.2, 74.8,** and **74.9,** but unlike **74.10.** ♣ Wide range of habitats from lower growth of forest to woodland, riverine belts, cerrado, caatinga, second growth, plantations. ♪ Song: very high, fluted, ascending series of "wu" notes, which in the 2nd half accelerates to a descending, chattering almost-trill.

74.4 GREAT JACAMAR (Jacamaraçu) *Jacamerops aureus* L 11.8 in./30 cm. Large and robust. Heavy, curved bill diagnostic. ♣ Mid-levels to subcanopy of humid forest, second growth; woodland, gallery forest. ♪ Song: strange series of 3 descending, fluted notes, each one drawn out, the 2nd and 3rd slightly trilled, the 1st loudest.

74.5 PARADISE JACAMAR (Ariramba-do-paraíso) *Galbula dea* L 11.8 in./30 cm. Mainly dark blue-black. Very long central tail feathers diagnostic. ♣ Humid forest (locally in drier forest), gallery forest. Prefers the canopy, but to mid-levels at forest edge. ♪ Song: may be a descending series of 15–18 notes with increasing intervals, the 1st few rather nasal "djip" notes, then changing into level, more mournful "wheer" notes. Also series with even intervals between loud, ringing "weer" notes.

74.6 PURPLISH JACAMAR (Ariramba-violácea) *Galbula chalcothorax* L 7.9 in./20 cm. Rather dark. Note whitish (♂) or buff (♀) belly and lack of rufous in undertail. From smaller **74.7** by range and more purple (less rufous) reflections. ♣ Lower to mid-levels of terra firme and dense woodland. Often near rivers. ♪ Song: short series of nasal chattering with, e.g., querulous-sounding "treeeeeer."

74.7 BRONZY JACAMAR (Ariramba-bronzeada) *Galbula leucogastra* L 7.9 in./20 cm. Cf. **74.6.** ♣ Lower to mid-levels of humid forest, tall second growth, gallery forest, forest remnants in open regions. ♪ Song: varied series of musical, ascending, piping notes, like "pee-pee-peeh" (5–6 × and rising, ending suddenly) or nasal "vravravra" (3 ×, ending suddenly).

74.8 BLUISH-FRONTED JACAMAR (Ariramba-da-capoeira) *Galbula cyanescens* L 7.9 in./ 20 cm. White chin spot often lacking. Crown iridescent bluish to green. Cf. **74.3** and **74.9.** ♣ Lower to mid-levels of humid forest, second growth. Often near rivers/streams. ♪ Song: very high, fluted "fuu-fuu-fuu-fuu-fuu-w"wdrrrrrur," 1st part ascending, 2nd part trilling/bouncing-down.

74.9 WHITE-CHINNED JACAMAR (Ariramba-de-barba-branca) *Galbula tombacea* L 7.9 in./20 cm. From **74.8** (limited overlap) by larger spot on chin and dusky brown crown (often bluer toward rear). ♣ Lower to mid-levels of humid forest, second growth. Often near rivers/streams. ♪ Song: rising series of 2–8 accelerating, nasal shrieks, ending as downslurred, chattering trill.

74.10 GREEN-TAILED JACAMAR (Ariramba-de-cauda-verde) *Galbula galbula* L 7.9 in./ 20 cm. Tail green, duskier below (lacks rufous undertail of **74.1–74.3, 74.8,** and **74.9**). ♣ Lower to mid-levels of humid forest edge, riverine belts, woodland, plantations, mangrove. ♪ Song: rising series, starting very high of 2–8 accelerating shrieks, ending as downslurred, chattering trill, the total with piccolo-like quality.

74.1

74.2

♀

74.3

♀

74.4

♀

74.5

74.6

♀

74.7

♀

74.8

74.9

74.10

♀

Plate 75

75.1 WHITE-EARED JACAMAR (Ariramba-vermelha)

Galbalcyrhynchus leucotis L 7.9 in./ 20 cm. Unmistakable; resembles a reddish chestnut kingfisher. From **75.2** by white ear coverts. ♣ Humid forest, esp. at edge near water. ♪ Call: steeply lowered, fluted "péeeuh-péeeuh-péeeuh- -."

75.2 PURUS JACAMAR (Sovela-vermelha) *Galbalcy-*

rhynchus purusianus L 7.9 in./20 cm. Cf. **75.1**, which has different range. ♣ Humid forest, esp. at edge near water. ♪ Call: very high, sharp, slightly piped "tjeew"; song: series of very high, piercing, almost level "péeeu" (1 ×/sec).

75.3 BROWN JACAMAR (Ariramba-preta) *Brachygalba*

lugubris L 6.3 in./16 cm. Several sspp.: NE Nom. (**a**, with all-dark bill) shown and C and S ssp. *melanosterna* (**b**, with yellow basal half of lower mandible). White belly sometimes tinged buff. Cf. **75.5**. ♣ Canopy and edge of forest, woodland, wooded savanna (esp. near rivers). ♪ Call: very/extr. high, piped upgliding "pueeeeét"; song: may be a duet with an ascending, slightly nasal, very fast twitter from one bird continued in extr. high, tinkling "seeseesee---," combined with high "wheet-tweet-thweet - -" from the other (though difficult to assess what comes from each of the 2 birds).

75.4 WHITE-THROATED JACAMAR (Agulha-de-

garganta-branca) *Brachygalba albo-gularis* L 6.3 in./16 cm. Unmistakable by white throat and face (with remarkable blue eyes) and rufous belly. ♣ Near rivers in humid forest. ♪ Call: very high "tuweet."

75.5 THREE-TOED JACAMAR (Cuitelão) *Jacamaral-*

cyon tridactyla L 7 in./18 cm. From **75.3b** (limited contact possible) by whitish underparts extending over chest, gray flanks (flanks and chest blackish brown in **75.3**) and all-dark bill. ♣ Forest edge and woodland (even small patches) near earth banks (e.g., rivers). Locally in eucalyptus woods. ♪ Alarm call: high, shivering/chattering rattle, undulating in sharpness and in strength; song: calm series of very high "tree," "whu," "whee," fluted "weet," and nasal "prrrèh" notes and similar single notes. En, R.

75.6 RUSTY-BREASTED (or -throated) **NUNLET**

(Macuru) *Nonnula rubecula* L 5.9 in./ 15 cm. Several ssps: E and SE Nom. (**a**; somewhat variable) and NE *tapanahoniensis* (**b**) shown. Note white eye ring and belly. Chest cinnamon to rufous. Cf. **75.7**. As other nunlets, it is inconspicuous and resembles a large-billed flycatcher. ♣ Lower and mid-levels of humid forest (also in drier areas in EC), riverine woodland. ♪ Song: a crescendoing series of high, fluted "wuw" notes, at the end falling in pitch and strength (20 × "wuw"/8 sec).

75.7 FULVOUS-CHINNED NUNLET (Freirinha-ama-

relada) *Nonnula sclateri* L 5.9 in./ 15 cm. From **75.6** by orange-red eye ring and buffier belly. ♣ Lower and mid-levels of humid forest, esp. near bamboo.

75.8 RUFOUS-CAPPED (or Gray-cheeked) **NUNLET**

(Freirinha-de-coroa-castanha) *Nonnula ruficapilla* L 5.5 in./14 cm. Rufous cap diagnostic. ♣ Lower and mid-levels of humid forest and second growth, esp. near bamboo. ♪ Song: long, almost level series of very high, loud, resounding "tuw" notes (3 × "tuw"/sec) or short series of nasal "tjuwee" notes.

75.9 CHESTNUT-HEADED NUNLET (Freirinha-de-

cabeça-castanha) *Nonnula amaurocephala* L 5.9 in./15 cm. Distinctively colored rufous and olive. ♣ Low levels in or near flooded forest. En.

Plate 76

76.1 SCARLET-CROWNED BARBET (Capitão-de-coroa) *Capito aurovirens* L 7.5 in./ 19 cm. Note orange chest and throat. Crown red (♂) or white (♀). ♣ Canopy and edge of humid lowland forest and woodland often near water. ♪ Song: e.g., low, rhytmic "roo-roo-roo- -" (about 7 ×).

76.2 BLACK-SPOTTED BARBET (Capitão-de-bigode-carijó) *Capito niger* L 7 in./18 cm. Note red throat and forehead. Cf. **76.3** in limited area of possible contact (N Roraima). ♣ Canopy and edge of humid lowland forest, woodland, plantations. ♪ Song: slow series of low, hollow double-notes "woo-hoo woo-hoo woo-hoo - -."

76.3 GILDED BARBET (Capitão-de-fronte-dourada) *Capito auratus* L 7 in./18 cm. Variable; throat orange (S and NE part of range) to red (C and NW part); forehead buffy-orange to golden reddish. ♣ Canopy and edge of humid lowland forest, woodland, plantations. ♪ Song: rapid series of mid-high, hollow double notes "tooroót" (accent on 2nd part, 2 ×/sec).

76.4 BROWN-CHESTED (or Cinnamon-breasted) **BAR-****BET** (Capitão-de-peito-marrom) *Capito brunneipectus* L 7 in./18 cm. Note absence of red/orange in plumage. ♣ Canopy and edge of humid lowland forest. ♪ Song: mid-high, hollow accelerated trill, at the end running together as one downslurred note (3 sec). En.

76.5 BLACK-GIRDLED BARBET (Capitão-de-cinta) *Capito dayi* L 7 in./18 cm. Mainly black and white overall. Note red vent. ♣ Canopy and edge of humid lowland forest, woodland, plantations. ♪ Song: e.g., very low, accelerating series of "woo" notes, sometimes at the end bouncing down (5–6 sec).

76.6 LEMON-THROATED BARBET (Capitãode-bigode-limão) *Eubucco richardsoni* L 5.9 in./15 cm. Three sspp.: NW *nigriceps* (**a**, ♂) and S *auranticollis* (**b**, ♂ and ♀; similar *puruensis* not shown). Virtually unmistakable by facial pattern, but cf. ♀ **76.7**. ♣ Canopy and edge of humid lowland forest (esp. várzea), dense second growth. ♪ Song: almost-trill of "oop" notes.

76.7 SCARLET-HOODED BARBET (Capitão-de-colar-amarelo) *Eubucco tucinkae* L 6.7 in./17 cm. ♂ unmistakable. ♀ differs from ♂ **76.6b** by narrow yellow nuchal collar, narrow orange chest band and lack of red chin. ♣ Várzea, gallery forest, river islands.

76.8 COLLARED PUFFBIRD (Rapazinho-de-colar) *Bucco capensis* L 7.5 in./19 cm. Very roundish jizz. Note complete black collar. ♣ Terra firme. Locally in várzea. ♪ Song: high, fluted "wuh-weéh" in chorus.

76.9 SWALLOW-WINGED PUFFBIRD (Urubuzinho) *Chelidoptera tenebrosa* L 5.9 in./ 15 cm. Unmistakable by jizz, rufous belly (duller in SE) and white rump (**a**) and underwing coverts. ♣ Edge and clearings of forest, woodland, wooded savanna, tall second growth. Usually perches high on exposed branch. Nests on sandy bank. ♪ Song: very high, slightly descending, tinkling trill, like "srrrrrrri."

76.10 LANCEOLATED MONKLET (Macuru-papa-mosca) *Micromonacha lanceolata* L 5.5 in./14 cm. Small. Note densely streaked underparts and rather uniform upperparts (may appear faintly scaled). Prominent whitish bill base. ♣ Humid forest and nearby second growth. ♣ Edge and clearings in primary forest and second growth. ♪ Song: very/extr. high, accelerating series of up to 10 upslurred "fueeét" notes.

Plate 77

77.1 BLACK-FRONTED NUNBIRD (Chora-chuva-preto) *Monasa nigrifrons* L 9.8 in./25 cm. Only red-billed nunbird without white. ♣ Várzea, gallery forest, woodland, palm groves. Usually near water. ♪ Call: dry, bouncing-down "tidrdrrrrrr"; song: sustained, hurried series of "tuweét-notes (10 sec).

77.2 BLACK NUNBIRD (Chora-chuva-de-asa-branca) *Monasa atra* L 9.8 in./25 cm. Note range. Only red-billed nunbird with white on wing. ♣ Humid forest (local inside terra firme), tall second growth. Often near water. ♪ Call/song: repeated "tulút tirr," 1st part ascending.

77.3 WHITE-FRONTED NUNBIRD (Chora-chuva-de-cara-branca) *Monasa morphoeus* L 9.8 in./25 cm. Unmistakable by white at bill base. ♣ Prefers higher levels inside Atlantic forest or terra firme. Rarer in gallery forest, humid forest borders, tall second growth. ♪ Song: excited, unstructured, communal chattering, like "wur-wir-tcha-wawa- -."

77.4 YELLOW-BILLED NUNBIRD (Chora-chuva-de-bico-amarelo) *Monasa flavirostris* L 9.8 in./25 cm. Unmistakable by yellow bill. ♣ Humid forest, second growth, clearings with scattered trees. ♪ Song: series of high, stressed "Tjéeuw-wur" (1 ×/sec).

77.5 GUIANAN PUFFBIRD (Macuru-de-testa-branca) *Notharchus macrorhynchos* L 9.8 in./25 cm. Large and pied. Often considered conspecific with **77.6** (limited overlap possible), but with less white to forehead. ♣ Upper and mid-levels of forest (incl. clearings), tall second growth, woodland, plantations. ♪ Song: level, rapid series of high, loud, fluted "wuut" notes, slightly gaining in intensity.

77.6 WHITE-NECKED PUFFBIRD (Macuru-de-pescoço-branco) *Notharchus hyperrhynchus* L 9.8 in./25 cm. Cf. **77.5**. ♣ As **77.5**. ♪ Call: high, lonely-sounding "weeeeeh"; song: high, dry trill, like "wuirrrrrr" (3–6 sec).

77.7 BUFF-BELLIED PUFFBIRD (Macuru-de-barriga-castanha) *Notharchus swainsoni* L 9.8 in./25 cm. Unmistakable in range. ♣ Upper and mid-levels of humid forest and tall second growth.

77.8 BROWN-BANDED PUFFBIRD (Macuru-de-peito-marrom) *Notharchus ordii* L 7.9 in./20 cm. From **77.5** and **77.6** by brown mid-breast. ♣ Upper and mid-levels of humid forest (incl. clearings), tall second growth. Occasionally in drier forest near rocky outcrops. ♪ Song: high, fluted series, starting with "wú-wit" notes, that descend and change to "foo-li-lit" notes (7–8 sec).

77.9 PIED PUFFBIRD (Macuru-pintado) *Notharchus tectus* L 6.3 in./16 cm. From larger **77.5** and **77.6** by narrow white eyebrow, white scapulars, and lack of white neck-collar; also by white at base of tail and at tip (best seen from below). ♣ Upper and mid-levels of humid forest, tall second growth, woodland, mangrove, wooded savanna, plantations. ♪ Song: very high, slightly descending, sharp fluted, yet tinkling "tiritititi-wit-wit-wit-tuih-tuih-tuih."

77.1

77.2

77.3

77.4

77.5

77.6

77.7

77.8

77.9

Plate 78

78.1 CHESTNUT-CAPPED PUFFBIRD (Rapazinho-de-boné-vermelho) *Bucco macrodactylus* L 5.9 in./15 cm. Note facial pattern with white eyebrow and orange-rufous nuchal collar. Underparts faintly barred. Cf. **78.2**. ♣ Mid- to lower levels of humid forest and woodland. Prefers shrubby areas near water.

78.2 SPOTTED PUFFBIRD (Rapazinho-carijó) *Bucco tamatia* L 7 in./18 cm. Note black cheeks, white malar, and orange-rufous throat. Underparts black-spotted (often forming a pectoral band). Cf. **78.1**. ♣ Mid- to lower levels of várzea, borders of terra firme, mature second growth, woodland. Often near water. ♪ Song: varied; e.g., slighty rising, then lowering series of high, fluted "tuwereé," changing to "tuweé" notes.

78.3 WHITE-EARED PUFFBIRD (Joăo-bobo) *Nystalus chacuru* L 7.9 in./20 cm. Note white ear coverts, black cheeks, and red bill. ♣ Dry to semihumid forest, second growth, woodland, savanna-like areas (e.g., cerrado), scrub, open areas with trees. ♪ Song: high, fluted, rapid "wuh-weeh-wuh-wirreeh-wuh-wirreeh" ("wuh" lower).

78.4 SPOT-BACKED (or -bellied) **PUFFBIRD** (Rapazinho-dos-velhos) *Nystalus maculatus* L 7.5 in./19 cm. Note bill coloring, orange-rufous chest, and spotted underparts. Cf. **78.5**. ♣ Woodland, caatinga, savanna (incl. cerrado), second growth, palm groves. ♪ Song: high, fluted "tjurr-tjurre-truh." En.

78.5 STREAK-BELLIED (or Chaco) **PUFFBIRD** *Nystalus striatipectus* (Rapazinho-do-chaco) L 7.5 in./19 cm. Often considered a ssp. of **78.4** (limited contact possible), but underparts more streaked and chest-patch duller. ♣ Woodland, savanna, second growth, palm groves. ♪ Song: high, fluted, slightly descending "wuuh-tju-tju."

78.6 STRIOLATED PUFFBIRD (Rapazinho-estriado) *Nystalus striolatus* L 7.9 in./20 cm. Cheeks, chest, and flanks streaked. Bill yellowish dusky. ♣ Upper and mid-levels of humid forest, woodland. ♪ Song: high, fluted series of lonely-sounding "wruuuh-wruuuh" or "witwit-wuuuh wruuuh."

78.7 CRESCENT-CHESTED PUFFBIRD (Barbudo-rajado) *Malacoptila striata* L 7.5 in./19 cm. Note multicolored breast band and streaky head and back. No overlap with **77.8** and **77.9**. ♣ Lower and middle levels of humid forest (even small patches), second growth forest/woodland. ♪ Song: sustained series of joined, very high, loud, piercing "jeéew" notes (30 sec).

78.8 SEMICOLLARED PUFFBIRD (Barbudo-de-coleira) *Malacoptila semicincta* L 7.5 in./19 cm. From **78.9** by range and rufous nuchal collar. ♣ Lower and middle levels of humid forest (mainly terra firme).

78.9 WHITE-CHESTED PUFFBIRD (Barbudo-pardo) *Malacoptila fusca* L 7.5 in./19 cm. Overall streaked with dark-tipped orange bill. White chest band sometimes hidden. ♣ Lower and middle levels of humid forest (mainly terra firme). ♪ Song: slightly dovelike "wút coocoó."

78.10 RUFOUS-NECKED PUFFBIRD (Barbudo-de-pescoço-ferrugem) *Malacoptila rufa* L 7 in./18 cm. Two sspp.: *brunnescens* shown; W Nom. (not shown) has uniform rufous lores. Note grayish head and contrasting rufous cheeks and nuchal collar. ♣ Lower and middle levels of humid forest. Locally in nearby cerradolike areas. ♪ Song: very/extr. high, slightly undulating, thin trill (2–3 sec).

78.1

78.2

78.3

78.4

78.5

78.6

78.7

78.8

78.9

78.10

Plate 79

79.1 LETTERED ARACARI (Araçari-miudinho-de-bico-riscado) *Pteroglossus inscriptus*

L 13.8 in./35 cm. W ssp. *humboldtii* (**a**, ♂ and ♀) and C and E Nom. (**b**, ♂ shown; ♀ with brown head). Letter pattern on sides of upper mandible diagnostic. Red restricted to rump. ♣ Humid lowland forest, tall second growth, plantations. Locally in cerrado (mainly near palm groves or gallery woodland). ♪ Call: low "chak-chak shrek chek - -."

79.2 GREEN ARACARI (Araçari-miudinho) *Pteroglossus viridis* L 13.8 in./35 cm. Note bill

pattern. ♣ Humid lowland forest, tall second growth, riverine woodland, plantations. ♪ Call: high, dry "srek srek srrek srek - -."

79.3 RED-NECKED ARACARI (Araçari-de-pescoço-vermelho) *Pteroglossus bitorquatus*

L 15.7 in./40 cm. Three sspp.: *sturmii* (**a**; W part of range) and C *reichenowi* (**b**) shown. E Nom. resembles **a**, but bill pattern closer to **b**. Combination of bill pattern and red chest, nape, and mantle diagnostic. ♣ Humid lowland forest, tall second growth, riverine woodland. ♪ Call: exhaled "fu' Wheét" in unhurried series. Also irregular "tek" and "tuc-tuc" notes.

79.4 IVORY-BILLED ARACARI (Araçari-de-bico-de-marfim) *Pteroglossus azara* L 15.7 in./

40 cm. Two sspp.: Nom. (**a**, SE part of range) and *flavirostris* (**b**, NW part). Combination of bill pattern and double (red and black) chest band diagnostic, but cf. **79.6**. ♣ Humid lowland forest, tall second growth, riverine woodland. ♪ Call: low, slightly raucous "wekwuk" notes in chorus.

79.5 BLACK-NECKED ARACARI (Araçari-de-bico-branco) *Pteroglossus aracari* L 17.7 in./

45 cm. Note bill pattern, single red band on underparts, and black head (often with small brown patch on the ear coverts). ♣ Humid forest, second growth, riverine woodland, plantations. Locally in cerrado.

79.6 BROWN-MANDIBLED (or Maria's) **ARACARI** (Araçari-de-bico-marrom) *Pteroglossus mariae* L 15.7 in./40 cm.

Resembles **79.4b**, but with most of lower mandible brown. Often considered a ssp. of **79.4**; hybrids between the two are known. ♣ Humid lowland forest, tall second growth, riverine woodland. ♪ Song: falsetto "te-Swéer-swur."

79.7 CHESTNUT-EARED ARACARI (Araçari-castanho) *Pteroglossus castanotis* L 17.7 in./

45 cm. From **79.6** (limited overlap) by bill pattern, pale eyes, and extension of brown on head. ♣ Várzea, second growth, woodland, cerrado, plantations. ♪ Call: very/extr. high, piercing "SEúur."

79.8 MANY-BANDED ARACARI (Araçari-de-cinta-dupla) *Pteroglossus pluricinctus*

L 17.7 in./45 cm. Unmistakable by bill pattern, two bands across underparts, and pale eyes. ♣ Humid lowland forest (esp. terra firme) and nearby tall second growth. ♪ Call: high, crunching, almost staccato "wit wut wit-wit-wit tsing wut - -."

79.9 CURL-CRESTED ARACARI (Araçari-mulato) *Pteroglossus beauharnaesii* L 17.7 in./

45 cm. Unmistakable by whitish cheeks, bill pattern, and red mantle and belly band. Curly crown visible at close range. ♣ Humid lowland forest (esp. terra firme) and nearby tall second growth. ♪ Call: low, raucous "cha-cha-cha cha wruh cha - -."

79.10 SAFFRON TOUCANET (Araçari-banana) *Pteroglossus (or Baillonius) bailloni*.

L 13.8 in./35 cm. Unmistakable. ♣ Humid forest and nearby second growth. Up to 1600 m. R.

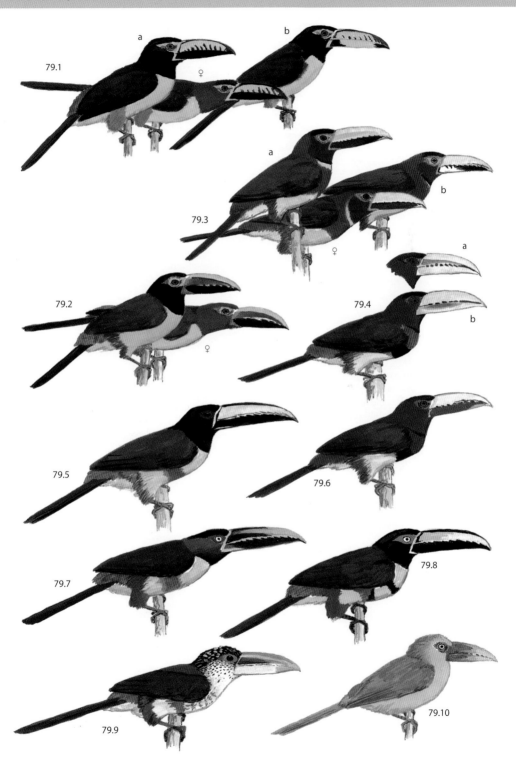

Plate 80

80.1 EMERALD (or Peruvian) **TOUCANET** (Tucaninho-

de-nariz-amarelo) *Aulacorhynchus prasinus* (or *atrugularis*) L 13.8 in./ 35 cm. Unmistakable in its small range. ♣ Humid forest and nearby second growth. ♪ Call/song: series of froglike croaks and high "wèh" notes (2–3 ×/sec).

80.2 CHESTNUT-TIPPED TOUCANET (Tucaninho-

verde) *Aulacorhynchus derbianus* L 13.8 in./35 cm. Unmistakable in its range. ♣ Humid forest and nearby second growth; 800–2400 m. ♪ Call/ song: very long series of "wah" notes, given at low or high pitch (3 ×/2 sec; "wah" sometimes sounding like a low, hoarse "wrah").

80.3 GUIANAN TOUCANET (Araçari-negro) *Selenidera*

piperivora (or *culik*) L 13.8 in./ 35 cm. Unmistakable in its range by black and red bill. Note gray underparts of ♀. ♣ Humid forest (esp. terra firme), riverine woodland. Up to 900 m. ♪ Call: toneless, dry rattle "krrru"; also may be a rather desperate sounding, high "euuuuúh."

80.4 GOULD'S TOUCANET (Saripoca-de-gould) *Sele-*

nidera gouldii L 13.8 in./35 cm. Resembles **80.5–80.7**, but with different bill pattern and range. ♣ Humid forest (locally into drier forest) and nearby second growth, riverine woodland. Up to 700 m. ♪ Call/song: very low, croaking "porc-porc-porc- -."

80.5 TAWNY-TUFTED TOUCANET (Saripoca-de-

bico-castanho) *Selenidera nattereri* L 11.8 in./30 cm. Bill pattern diagnostic. Whitish markings on lower mandible sometimes lacking. ♣ Terra firme, white-sand forest. ♪ Call/song: "ah-woóh" (1st part toneless, croaking, 2nd part high-pitched).

80.6 GOLDEN-COLLARED TOUCANET (Saripoca-

de-coleira) *Selenidera reinwardtii* L 13.8 in./35 cm. Only *Selenidera* toucanet in range. ♣ Humid lowland forest (esp. terra firme) and nearby second growth. ♪ Call: series of very low, pumped croaks, like "caooc," at 3 ×/2 sec.

80.7 SPOT-BILLED TOUCANET (Araçari-poca) *Sele-*

nidera maculirostris L 13.8 in./35 cm. Bill pattern diagnostic. Only *Selenidera* toucanet in range. ♣ Humid forest and nearby second growth, riverine woodland. Up to 1400 m. ♪ Call/song: very low croaking "cock-cock-cock- -."

80.8 CHANNEL-BILLED TOUCAN (Tucano-de-bico-

preto) *Ramphastos vitellinus* L 19.7 in./ 50 cm. Three sspp.: W and C *culminatus* (**a**, Yellow-ridged Toucan), E *ariel* (**b**, Ariel Toucan) and NE *vitellinus* (**c**); **b** and **c** unmistakable by bill and chest pattern; **a** very similar to larger **80.9a**, but bill shorter with a more keeled culmen. Intermediates between sspp. common where they meet, an example (**d** = **a** × **b**) shown. ♣ Humid forest and nearby second growth, riverine woodland, parks, plantations, forest patches in more open regions. Lowlands. ♪ Call/song: calm, almost level series of high, sharp, loud "Kéer" (or "Kéejr") notes.

80.9 WHITE-THROATED TOUCAN (Tucano-grande-

de-papo-branco) *Ramphastos tucanus* L 21.5 in./55 cm. Two sspp. (intermediates common where they meet): *cuvieri* (**a**, Cuvier's Toucan, W part of range) and Nom. (**b**, Red-billed Toucan, E part of range); **a** resembles **80.8a**; **b** unmistakable by brown tones in bill. ♣ Humid forest and nearby second growth, riverine woodland. Up to 1100 m. ♪ Call/song: mid/high, loud, clear "tu cléar," given in series of 2 ×/3sec.

80.10 RED-BREASTED (or Green-billed) **TOUCAN**

(Tucano-de-bico-verde) *Ramphastos dicolorus* L 19.7 in./50 cm. Unmistakable by color pattern of bill and extensive red in underparts. ♣ Prefers humid montane and submontane forest, but also in lowland forest, woodlots in more open regions, second growth, and plantations. ♪ Call/song: loud, raucous "WRèh" or "niuh," given in series of 2 ×/3sec.

80.11 TOCO TOUCAN (Tucanuçu) *Ramphastos toco*

L 23.6 in./60 cm. Unmistakable by color pattern of bill. ♣ Forest edge, woodland, tall second growth, palm groves, wooded savanna, plantations. Occasionally in gardens. ♪ Call/song: high, slightly raucous (gull-like) "wrreh" or low "wruh," given in series of 2 ×/3sec.

Plate 81

81.1 BAR-BREASTED (or Golden-fronted) **PICULET**

(Pica-pau-anão-dourado) *Picumnus aurifrons* L 3.1 in./8 cm. Several sspp.: *borbae* (**a**, NC part of range), *wallacii* (**b**, SW part of range) and *transfasciatus* (**c**, E part of range) shown. Combination of barred chest and streaked/spotted lower flanks diagnostic in most of range, but cf. **81.6**. ♣ Terra firme (esp. edge), also várzea and second growth. ♪ Call: extr. high, very thin "see-see-suw."

81.2 LAFRESNAYE'S PICULET (Pica-pau-anão-do-

amazonas) *Picumnus lafresnayi* L 3.9 in./10 cm. Note barred underparts; nape of ♂ is black, dotted white. Cf. **81.3** and **81.4**. ♣ Woodland, second growth, várzea, forest edge. Lowlands. ♪ Normally silent, occasionally extr. high "see-see."

81.3 ORINOCO PICULET (Pica-pau-anão-do-orinoco)

Picumnus pumilus L 3.5 in./9 cm. From larger **81.2** (limited contact possible) by plain back, brown, yellow-dotted nape, and darker ear coverts. Also cf. **81.4**. ♣ Edge of humid forest, gallery forest, riverine belts, thickets. Lowlands. Mainly up to 300 m.

81.4 GOLDEN-SPANGLED PICULET (Pica-pau-anão-

de-pintas-amarelas) *Picumnus exilis* L 3.9 in./10 cm. Note barred, yellowish white underparts, and scaled or spotted mantle. White spots on wing coverts sometimes reduced (esp. in Roraima). ♣ Humid forest, old second growth, riverine thickets, woodland. Up to 1900 m. ♪ Song: extr. high, thin "see see suw."

81.5 RUSTY-NECKED PICULET (Pica-pau-anão-

fusco) *Picumnus fuscus* L 3.9 in./10 cm. Very restricted range. Note warm buff tone of neck and underparts, which may be faintly barred as shown. ♣ Várzea. R.

81.6 WHITE-BELLIED PICULET (Pica-pau-anão-de-

pescoço-branco) *Picumnus spilogaster* L 3.5 in./9 cm. Throat barring and flank spotting often reduced, but no overlap with **82.6**. From **81.1c** (limited overlap) by whiter underparts, more spots (fewer streaks) on flanks, grayer upperparts, and red crown in ♂. ♣ Gallery forest, forest edge, woodland, mangrove. ♪ Call/song: extr./very high, descending, shivering, slow trill (2 sec).

81.7 SPOTTED PICULET (Pica-pau-anão-pintado)

Picumnus pygmaeus L 3.9 in./10 cm. Distinctively patterned and colored. ♣ Dry open woodland, caatinga. ♪ Call/song: very high, descending, fast, chivering trill "ttrrrruh" (2 sec). En.

81.8 VARZEA PICULET (Pica-pau-anão-da-várzea)

Picumnus varzeae L 3.5 in./9 cm. Only piculet in its limited range with dark underparts. ♣ Várzea, river islands. En.

81.9 OCHRE-COLLARED PICULET (Pica-pau-anão-

de-coleira) *Picumnus temminckii* L 3.9 in./10 cm. Ochre neck and barred underparts diagnostic, but cf. **82.1** and **81.10**. ♣ Forest, woodland, thickets. ♪ Song/call: may be a dry, toneless trill "trrrrruh" (1 sec).

81.10 WHITE-WEDGED (or -edged) **PICULET** (Pica-

pau-anão-escamado) *Picumnus albosquamatus* L 4.3 in./11 cm. Two sspp.: Nom. (**a**, the Pantanal; with black-scaled underparts) and widespread *guttifer* (**b**; with black spot at center of breast feathers and white-spotted back). Only piculet in range without barring on chest. Hybrids with **81.9** and **82.1** are known. ♣ Dense parts of cerrado, riverine thickets, dry to semiarid forest, woodland. ♪ Song: extr. high, slightly undulating, tinkling trill "tititi.... titi" (5 sec).

81.11 FINE-BARRED PICULET *Picumnus subtilis* L

3.5 in./9 cm. Underparts distinctly differing from **81.1** and **82.2** (the only other piculets in this part of Acre); note absence of streaking below. ♣ Humid forest.

81.1 a b c ♀

81.6 ♀

81.2 ♀

81.7 ♀

81.3 ♀

81.8 ♀

81.9 ♀

81.4 ♀

81.5 ♀

81.10 a b ♀

81.11 ♀

Plate 82

82.1 WHITE-BARRED PICULET (Pica-pau-anão-barrado) *Picumnus cirratus* L 3.9 in./10 cm. Note grayish brown upperparts (faintly barred in Roraima) and black-and-white barred underparts. N sspp. lack white upper border to ear coverts. Hybrids with **81.9** common; with **81.8** or **81.10** rarer. ♣ Forest edge, woodland, riverine thickets, dense scrub, parks, gardens. Up to 2100 m. ♪ Call/song: extr. high, dry, fast trill, like "trrrrriut."

82.2 RUFOUS-BREASTED PICULET (Pica-pau-anão-vermelho) *Picumnus rufiventris* L 3.9 in./10 cm. Unmistakable by extensive rufous on underparts and head. No overlap with **82.3**. ♣ Thick undergrowth (esp. with bamboo) of humid forest and woodland. ♪ Call/song: extr. high (just audible) "tsit-tsit-tsit- -."

82.3 TAWNY PICULET (Pica-pau-anão-canela) *Picumnus fulvescens* L 3.9 in./10 cm. Unmistakable by extensive tawny brown on underparts and head. No overlap with **81.5** or **82.2**. ♣ Deciduous to semideciduous second growth forest, caatinga, scrub. Up to 950 m. ♪ Call/song: extr. high "see-see-see -sisi-wi." En, R.

82.4 OCHRACEOUS PICULET (Pica-pau-anão-da-caatinga) *Picumnus limae* L 3.9 in./10 cm. Unmistakable by whitish buff underparts. No overlap with **82.6**. ♣ Semideciduous forest and nearby tall caatinga. Up to 1000 m. ♪ Call/song: extr/very high, piercing "tee-tee-tee-titiwi." En, R.

NOTE: Piculets in southern Ceará look intermediate between **82.3** and **82.4** and quite confusing; variation from whitish to fulvous belly may be clinal.

82.5 MOTTLED PICULET (Pica-pau-anão-carijó) *Picumnus nebulosus* L 4.3 in./11 cm. Note buff-brown collar and streaking of belly and flanks. ♣ Humid forest, *Araucaria* forest, riverine woodland. Often in bamboo. Up to 1400 m. R.

82.6 PLAIN-BREASTED PICULET (Pica-pau-anão-creme) *Picumnus castelnau* L 3.5 in./9 cm. Only piculet with unmarked whitish underparts in its limited range. ♣ Várzea and other forest/woodland near rivers. R.

82.7 WHITE-THROATED WOODPECKER (Pica-pau-de-garganta-branca) *Piculus leucolaemus* L 7.9 in./20 cm. Note yellow facial stripe, white throat, and pattern of chest and belly. ♣ Humid lowland forest. ♪ Call/song: high, hoarse/hissing "sraa-sraa-sraa- -" or drawn-out, hissing, lowered "wheeeeee" (sounding from some distance like an imitation of the wind through willows).

82.8 WHITE- (or Yellow-) **BROWED WOODPECKER** (Pica-pau-dourado) *Piculus aurulentus* L 7.9 in./20 cm. Note whitish yellow supercilium and line from lores to side of neck. Throat yellow. ♣ Humid forest and nearby second growth; 750–2000 m, locally lower in S. ♪ Song: slow or hurried series of 7–15 high "wuh" notes. R.

82.9 GOLDEN-OLIVE WOODPECKER (Pica-pau-oliváceo) *Colaptes (or Piculus) rubiginosus* L 7.9 in./20 cm. Only woodpecker in limited range with whitish face, plain golden-olive back, and barred underparts. Cf. **82.11, 83.8,** and *Veniliornis* woodpeckers (**83.1–83.7**). ♣ Humid forest and second growth; 700–2200 m. ♪ Song: e.g., high, sharp, angry, rattling trill (2–3 sec).

82.10 YELLOW-THROATED WOODPECKER (Pica-pau-bufador) *Piculus flavigula* L 7.9 in./20 cm. Three sspp.: *magnus* (**a**, S Amazon, ♂ and ♀), E *erythropis* (**b**, ♂) and Nom. (N Amazon, not shown; as **a**, but ♂ with red malar). ♂♂ with yellow ear coverts and face (also throat in **a**); ♀♀ with yellow forecrown, face, and throat (not shown ♀ **b** usually with some red on throat). ♣ Humid lowland forest; locally in drier forest; drier caatinga. ♪ Song: series of 1–7 high, hoarse, angry-sounding "vraah" notes.

82.11 GOLDEN-GREEN WOODPECKER (Pica-pau-dourado-escuro) *Piculus chrysochloros* L 9.8 in./25 cm (7.9 in./20 cm in C). Several sspp.: N *capistratus* (**a**, ♂), SE *polyzonus* (**b**, ♂ and ♀) and NE *paraensis* (**c**, ♂ and ♀) shown. Throat yellow (most of range), whitish (in W) or barred (in N). Combination of barred underparts, yellow line in face, and whitish blue eyes diagnostic. ♣ Humid forest, caatinga, woodland (even small patches), riverine forest, palm groves. ♪ Song: series of 15 almost toneless, hoarse "schraah" notes, sounding like a hysterically crying baby.

82.1

82.2

82.3

82.4

82.5

82.6

82.7

82.8

82.9

82.10

82.11

Plate 83

83.1 CHECKERED (or Chequered) **WOODPECKER** (Pica-pau-chorão) *Veniliornis (or Piciodes) mixtus* L 5.5 in./14 cm. Distinctively spotted/checkered blackish brown and white. Note dark mask. Small and without the yellow-green tones of **83.3** and **83.8** and **83.9**. ♣ Woodland, gallery forest, savanna, cerrado. ♪ Call/song: high, sharp, almost level, rapidly twittered "wutwitwit---wih."

83.2 LITTLE WOODPECKER (Picapauzinho-anão) *Veniliornis passerinus* L 5.9 in./15 cm. Several sspp.: S *olivinus* (**a**, ♂ and ♀), E *taenionotus* (**b**, ♂), and W *agilis* (**c**, ♀) shown. All sspp., except **c**, with eyebrow faint or lacking. E and C sspp. may show faint red spots on back. From **83.4–83.7** by lack of yellow on head. Also cf. larger *Piculus* woodpeckers (**82.7–82.11**). ♣ Forest edge, woodland (incl. caatinga), savanna, second growth, mangrove, river islands, plantations, gardens. ♪ Call/song: sharp, chattered, almost-rattle of "wuwu---," turning into "wiwi---" notes; 1st few notes rising.

83.3 WHITE-SPOTTED WOODPECKER (Picapauzinho-verde-carijó) *Veniliornis spilogaster* L 7 in./18 cm. Back barred dark olive-green and yellowish. Note long white eyebrow and malar. ♣ Forest (even small patches), woodland, shrub, parks. ♪ Call: e.g., "Tjup Tjiddur" notes; "dur" note lowered.

83.4 RED-RUMPED WOODPECKER (Pica-pau-de-sobre-vermelho) *Veniliornis kirkii* L 6.3 in./16 cm. Note small distribution and altitudinal range. Red rump diagnostic, but often hard to see. ♣ Humid forest and nearby second growth; 1400–1750 m. ♪ Call: unstructured series of high, nasal "trut" or very high "twit" notes.

83.5 GOLDEN-COLLARED WOODPECKER (Pica-pau-de-colar-dourado) *Veniliornis cassini* L 6.3 in./16 cm. Note yellow nuchal collar. No overlap with **83.6** and **83.7**, but cf. **83.2**, **83.4**, and *Piculus* woodpeckers (**82.7–82.11**). ♣ Canopy and edge of humid forest and nearby second growth. Up to 1500 m. ♪ Call: loud, upslurred, rattling trill (3 sec).

83.6 RED-STAINED WOODPECKER (Picapauzinho-avermelhado) *Veniliornis affinis* L 6.7 in./17 cm. Cf. **83.5**. Note yellow nuchal collar and faint red spotting on wing coverts (often hard to see). Cf. **83.2**, **83.7**, and *Piculus* woodpeckers (**82.7–82.11**). Shown is W ssp. *hilaris;* E Nom. (not shown) with no or reduced red stains on upperparts. ♣ Canopy and edge of humid lowland forest and nearby second growth, plantations. ♪ Call: high, sharp, slightly undulating, chattering rattle (5–7 sec).

83.7 YELLOW-EARED WOODPECKER (Picapauzinho-de-testa-pintada) *Veniliornis maculifrons* L 5.9 in./15 cm. Note yellow nuchal collar. No overlap with **83.4** and **83.5**, but cf. **83.2**, **83.6**, and *Piculus* woodpeckers (**82.7–82.11**). ♣ Humid forest edge, secondary forest, parks. Lowlands and hilly country. ♪ Call/song: high, nasal, rising then slightly falling, chattering rattle (5–7 sec). En.

83.8 SPOT-BREASTED WOODPECKER (Pica-pau-de-peito-pontilhado) *Colaptes punctigula* L 7.9 in./20 cm. Note whitish face and spotted underparts. Cf. **83.9** and **82.9**. ♣ Wide range of wooded habitats, incl. várzea (avoids interior of terra firme), woodland, second growth, wooded savanna, palm groves, mangrove. ♪ Call/song: may be a rapid, regular series of high, clear "wick" notes, like "wick-wickwick---" (3–4 sec).

83.9 GREEN-BARRED WOODPECKER (Pica-pau-verde-barrado) *Colaptes melanochloros* L 9.8 in./25 cm. Resembles smaller **83.8** (note range), but barring of upperparts pale yellowish (less bronze-green). There is much variation in the amount of spotting on the underparts. The back can be plain in some populations. Ssp. *nattereri* (not shown) from central Brazil is much smaller than the other forms. ♣ Forest, woodland, savannalike areas, open areas with some trees, second growth, caatinga, plantations, gardens, parks. ♪ Call: e.g., fast, nasal, staccato, descending "tidwurrr"; song: very high, short, clear, liquid "wikwikwik---" (about 10 × "wik," 1st two and last two notes rising or falling) or slow series of 6–7 high "wir" notes.

83.10 CAMPO FLICKER (Pica-pau-do-campo) *Colaptes campestris* L 11.8 in./30 cm. Shows lots of individual variation in amount and shape of markings on back and underparts. Two sspp.: S white-throated *campestroides* (**a**, FIELD FLICKER) and widespread black-throated Nom. (**b**). Unmistakable by orange-yellow collar and ear coverts. Rather terrestrial. ♣ Virtually any open to semiopen habitat, incl. grassland, farmland, savanna, woodland, forest edge, parks, gardens, second growth, shrub. ♪ Call: e.g., high, sharp, nasal "tih," "tir," or "wur"; song: e.g., rapid "wicwicwic---" (10–12 ×, 1st few rising, last few descending). Also a duet of high "wicwicwic," immediately answered by low "wucwuc."

83.1

83.2
a
b
♀ c
♀ a

83.3
♀

83.4
♀

83.5
♀

83.6
♀

83.7
♀

83.8
♀

83.9
♀

83.10
a
b
♀ b

Plate 84

84.1 SCALY-BREASTED WOODPECKER (Picapauz-

inho-chocolate) *Celeus grammicus* L 9.8 in./25 cm. Three sspp.: SW *latifasciatus* (**a**), NW Nom. (**b**), and C *subcervinus* (not shown, intermediate between **a** and **b**). Barring rather faint to strong (chest may appear almost all black), but tail and rump always unbarred (cf. **84.2**, **84.3**, and **84.9**). ♣ Upper levels of humid lowland forest; locally in nearby wooded savanna. ♪ Song: "fuweét-tjeeuh" (1st part loud and upswept, 2nd part soft and nasal).

84.2 WAVED WOODPECKER (Pica-pau-barrado)

Celeus undatus L 9.8 in./25 cm. Clearly barred above and below; chest may appear almost all black (cf. **84.9**). From **84.1b** (limited contact possible in Roraima) by barred rump (often also tail, **a**) and paler head and underparts. ♣ Upper levels of humid lowland forest; locally in nearby wooded savanna. ♪ Song: high, nasal "fuweét-eeuh."

84.3 CHESTNUT WOODPECKER (Pica-pau-choco-

late) *Celeus elegans* L 11.8 in./30 cm. Two sspp.: pale-crested NE Nom. (**a**) and chestnut-headed W and C *jumanus* (**b**). Only *Celeus* woodpecker without a black chest or barring to back and underparts (be aware that **84.1b** can appear uniform from afar). ♣ All levels of humid lowland forest; locally in nearby wooded savanna. Also riverine woodland, plantations. ♪ Song: may be a high, level, rapid, clear, piped "tjuuh-tjuuh-tjuuh-wuh."

84.4 PALE-CRESTED WOODPECKER (Pica-pau-

louro) *Celeus lugubris* L 9.8 in./25 cm. Rufescent-brown (**a**, N Nom.) to blackish brown below (**b**, S ssp. *kerri*). From **84.5** (also note range) by back pattern (mantle and wing coverts barred buff; flight feathers barred chestnut). ♣ Semideciduous forest, woodland, cerrado, palms groves. ♪ Song: may be a very high, slackening, fluted "twee-twee-tee-tee-tee."

84.5 BLOND-CRESTED WOODPECKER (Pica-pau-

de-cabeça-amarela) *Celeus flavescens* L 11.8 in./30 cm. Three races: SE Nom. (**a**), NE *ochraceous* (**b**), and EC *intermedius* (not shown; intermediate between **a** and **b**). Note mainly blackish underparts. ♣ Forest, woodland (incl. eucalyptus), second growth, cerrado, caatinga, parks, plantations. ♪ Song: e.g., loud, calm, ringing, piped "peep-peep-peep- -" (15 × "peep"), descending "weeh-weeh-weeh," or very high, sharp "weeh-weeh."

84.6 CREAM-COLORED WOODPECKER (Pica-pau-

amarelo) *Celeus flavus* L 9.8 in./25 cm. Of three sspp., Amazonian Nom. (**a**, amount of brown in wing variable) and E *subflavus* (**b**) shown. Overall mainly creamy yellow. ♣ Humid forest, woodland, gallery forest; occasionally in mangrove or plantations. ♪ Song: high, calm "wrih-wrih-wrih-wruh" (3–4 × "wrih," "wruh" lowered).

84.7 RUFOUS-HEADED WOODPECKER (Pica-pau-

lindo) *Celeus spectabilis* L 9.8 in./25 cm. Unmistakable by contrasting rufous head and wings, but cf. **84.8**. ♣ Lower and mid-levels of humid lowland forest and woodland, esp. near rivers and bamboo.

84.8 KAEMPFER'S (or Caatinga) **WOODPECKER**

(Pica-pau-do-parnaíba) *Celeus obrieni* L 9.8 in./25 cm. Often considered a ssp. of larger **84.7** (no overlap), but with less black barring. ♣ Cerrado, palm groves. Associated with bamboo. En, R. Possibly extinct.

84.9 RINGED WOODPECKER (Pica-pau-de-coleira)

Celeus torquatus L 11.8 in./30 cm. Three sspp.: NE Nom. (**a**), W and C *occidentalis* (**b**), and E *tinnunculus* (not shown; resembles **b**); **a** unmistakable by black collar and uniform cinnamon underparts; note barred tail and rump, black chest, and barred whitish buff belly in **b**. ♣ Humid lowland forest, riverine woodland. ♪ Song: high, clear, piped "peeh-peeh-peeh" (3–6 × "peeh").

Plate 85

85.1 WHITE WOODPECKER (Pica-pau-branco) *Mela-* *nerpes candidus* L 9.8 in./25 cm. Unmistakable. Social. ♣ Dry to semihumid forest and woodland, savanna, scrub, cultivations, palm groves, eucalyptus woods. ♪ Call/ song: very high, downslurred, ternlike "krreeerr."

85.2 YELLOW-FRONTED WOODPECKER (Benedito- de-testa-amarela) *Melanerpes flavi-frons* L 6.7 in./17 cm. Note stripe of white streaks through middle of otherwise black mantle. Social. ♣ Humid forest, second growth, cane fields, palm groves, cultivation. ♪ Call/song: rapid, nasal, slightly descending "weeweeweewit."

85.3 YELLOW-TUFTED WOODPECKER (Benedito- de-testa-vermelha) *Melanerpes cruentatus* L 7.5 in./19 cm. Two forms (**a**, **b**), both unmistakable. Note black back and white rump. Social. ♣ Canopy and edge of humid forest, tall second growth, plantations. ♪ Call/song: very fast, rattling, almost level or slightly ascending "wutwut---."

85.4 WHITE-FRONTED WOODPECKER (Pica-pau- de-testa-branca) *Melanerpes cactorum* L 6.7 in./17 cm. Virtually unmistakable. May have white throat (as shown in ♀). Social. ♣ Dry forest, gallery forest, woodland, savanna, palm groves. ♪ Call: may be a very high, nasal "wut-weetwut," repeated in a series in which "weetwut" is higher pitched each time.

85.5 HELMETED WOODPECKER (Pica-pau-de-cara- canela) *Dryocopus galeatus* L 9.8 in./ 25 cm. From larger **85.7a** by cinnamon face (no white line to bill) and creamy rump. Mantle always lacks white. ♣ Humid forest; sometimes also nearby forest patches and gallery forest. Up to 800 m. R.

85.6 ROBUST WOODPECKER (Pica-pau-rei) *Campe-* *philus robustus* L 13.8 in./35 cm. Unmistakable by pattern. Note creamy mantle and rump. ♣ Tall humid forest, *Araucaria* stands. Up to 1000 m. ♪ Call: high "kew."

85.7 LINEATED WOODPECKER (Pica-pau-de-banda- branca) *Dryocopus lineatus* L 13.8 in./ 35 cm. Two sspp.: large SE *erythrops* (**a**) and widespread Nom. (**b**). Note white line from bill down sides of neck. White markings on scapulars (often missing in **a** as shown, cf. **85.5**) never meet on lower back (cf. ♀ **85.9**). ♣ Forest (usually avoids interior of humid forest), woodland, cerrado, riverine woodland, second growth, plantations (incl. eucalyptus), gardens. Up to 2100 m. ♪ Call: high "kip"; song: "kip-wjurrrrr," 2nd part low,shivering, and fading out.

85.8 RED-NECKED WOODPECKER (Pica-pau-de- barriga-vermelha) *Campephilus rubricollis* L 11.8 in./30 cm. Three sspp.: N Nom. (**a**) and S *trachelopyrus/olallae* (**b**). Unmistakable by rufous-cinnamon underparts (also wing panel in **b**) and lack of white on back. ♣ Humid forest and nearby second growth. Also riverine woodland. Up to 1800 m. ♪ Call/song: low, nasal "ti'heeu."

85.9 CRIMSON-CRESTED WOODPECKER (Pica- pau-de-topete-vermelho) *Campephilus melanoleucos* L 13.8 in./35 cm. White scapular lines meet on lower back, forming a V shape. ♂: pale buff at bill. ♀: black on front runs op to top of crown and white line on face broader than **85.7**. ♣ Forest, woodland (incl. small patches, as long as tall trees are present), tall second growth, riverine woodland, palm groves, plantations. Up to 1600 m. ♪ Song: short, nasal, shivering "ti'wir" and "ti'd'wir."

85.10 CREAM-BACKED WOODPECKER (Pica-pau- de-barriga-preta) *Campephilus leuco-pogon* L 11.8 in./30 cm. Unmistakable by creamy back and black underparts. ♣ Woodland, savanna, groves. ♪ Call: low, nasal "tjuaw."

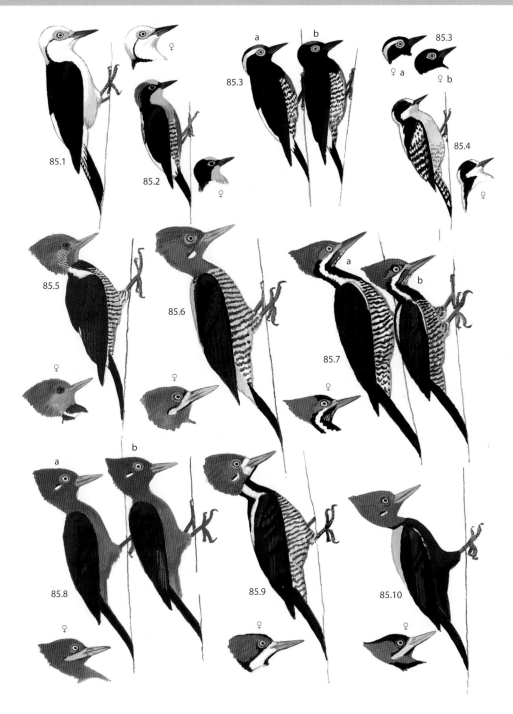

85.1

85.2 ♀

85.3 a b

85.3 ♀ a

85.3 ♀ b

85.4

85.4 ♀

85.5 ♀

85.6 ♀

85.7 a b

85.7 ♀

85.8 a b

85.8 ♀

85.9 ♀

85.10 ♀

Plate 86

86.1 PLAIN-BROWN WOODCREEPER (Arapaçu-pardo)

Dendrocincla fuliginosa L 7.9 in./ 20 cm. Sspp. distinguished by how pale the throat is, by the presence or absence of a buff-cinnamon superciliary and of some streaking/dotting in the upper chest; N Nom. (**a**, with buff mark behind eye) and NW ssp. *phaeochra* (**b**, with plain face) shown. Only plain woodcreeper in most of range. Often at ant swarms. ♣ Middle and lower levels of terra firme, less often várzea and plantations. ♪ Call: extr. high, sweeping "sweeuh"; song: long series of sweeping "weekwee-kweek---" notes, slightly lowered and slowed at end. There are also various rattles, such as a sustained, very high, slightly undulating "bicbic---."

86.2 THRUSH-LIKE (or Plain-winged) **WOOD-CREEPER** (Arapaçu-liso) *Den-*

drocincla turdina L 7.9 in./20 cm. Only *Dendrocincla* woodcreeper in range. ♣ Middle and lower levels of humid forest, mature second growth, riverine belts. ♪ Song: series (60 sec and more) of very high "keepkeepkeep---" notes, slightly undulating, fading, and crescendoing at random.

86.3 WHITE-CHINNED WOODCREEPER (Arapaçu-

da-taoca) *Dendrocincla merula* L 7 in./ 18 cm. From **86.1** by plain face and clearly defined white throat. Eyes usually pale bluish in S and W, but dark brown in N ♣ Terra firme, occasionally riverine belts and edge of várzea. Usually at ant swarms. ♪ Call: series of very high "bic bic - -" notes; song: simple, very high, twittering "titterit titterit - -."

86.4 LONG-TAILED WOODCREEPER (Arapaçu-rabudo)

Deconychura longicauda L ♂ 7 in./ 18 cm, ♀ 6.3 in./16 cm. Slender, with unmarked back. From very similar **86.5** by slightly larger size, longer bill, and more clearly spotted crown. ♣ Terra firme and várzea. Forest interior. Below 500 m. ♪ Song: varies geographically; N of Amazon, a high, distinctly descending, clear, rather plaintive "pee-pue-tue-tuh---" (7–8 notes).

86.5 SPOT-THROATED WOODCREEPER (Arapaçu-

de-garganta-pintada) *Deconychura stictolaema* L ♂ 7 in./18 cm, ♀ 6.3 in./ 16 cm. Cf. **86.4**. ♣ Interior and edge of terra firme and várzea. ♪ Song: high, short, staccato rattle, slightly rising and trailing off.

86.6 OLIVACEOUS WOODCREEPER (Arapaçu-verde)

Sittasomus griseicapillus L 6.3 in./ 16 cm. Sspp. fall into three groups: Amazonian *griseicapillus* group (**a**), SE *sylviellus* group (**b**), and E *reiseri* (not shown; as **b**, but brighter cinnamon-rufous above). All sspp. characterized by small size, small bill, and unstreaked plumage. ♣ Virtually any habitat with trees. ♪ Call: high, sweeping "weet"; song: four distinctive vocal variations in Brazil; in SE very high, loud, descending "weet weet weet - -" (5–20 ×, each "weet" slightly upturned) or a high rattling trill (>20 sec); in NE a high, fast, slightly rising "weeweewee---" (6–20 notes).

86.7 WEDGE-BILLED WOODCREEPER (Arapaçu-de-

bico-de-cunha) *Glyphorynchus spirurus* L 5.9 in./15 cm. Note distinctive chisel-shaped bill. Several current sspp., varying in amount of white streaking on chest and in throat color. Nom. from Amapá and N Pará (not shown) has conspicuous whitish throat and looks bigger. ♣ Mainly in terra firme, but also in várzea, riverine belts, palm swamp. ♪ Call: nervous, sneezing "tseets tseets tseets-tseets -"; song: varies geographically; in SE 2-noted plaintive "weep-weep"; in N fast, ascending, sweeping series of 3 notes.

86.8 SCIMITAR-BILLED WOODCREEPER (Arapaçu-

platino) *Drymornis bridgesii* L 11.8 in./ 30 cm. Unmistakable by bill, densely streaked underparts, and facial pattern. ♣ Woodland, scrub, savanna, suburbs. Often forages on the ground. ♪ Song: very high, loud but thin "feetfeetfeet---tuit" ("feet" up to 8 × and level, "tuit" lower and descending)

86.9 LONG-BILLED WOODCREEPER (Arapaçu-de-

bico-comprido) *Nasica longirostris* L 13.8 in./35 cm. Unmistakable by long bill, small head, and long neck. ♣ Várzea, forested swamps, and nearby terra firme. Locally in riverine belts in cerrado. ♪ Call: high, nasal "weetut" or "weet-erweet"; song: loud melancholy-sounding, drawn-out calls "wuuuueet wuuueeet - "(3–4 ×), each slightly rising and thereafter trailing off.

86.10 CINNAMON-THROATED WOODCREEPER

(Arapaçu-galinha) *Dendrexetastes rufigula* L 9.8 in./25 cm. Stout, pale bill. Overall plain except for distinct "collar" of white streaks (in E part of range; shown), white streaks on chest and sides of neck (SC part of range), or faint white streaks, restricted to chest (W part of range). ♣ Humid forest, river islands. Often in palms at forest edge. ♪ Song: very high loud series of ringing notes, sounding almost like a trill (7–8 sec).

86.1
a
b

86.2

86.3

86.4

86.5

a

86.4

b

86.7

86.8

86.9

86.10

Plate 87

87.1 BAR-BELLIED WOODCREEPER (Arapaçu-de-

barriga-pintada) *Hylexetastes stresemanni* L 11.8 in./30 cm. Characterized by heavy, red bill and bold barring below. ♣ Humid forest.

87.2 UNIFORM WOODCREEPER (Arapaçu-uniforme)

Hylexetastes uniformis L 11.8 in./30 cm. Heavy red bill as in **87.1**, **87.3**, and **87.4**, but no overlap in range. Cf. smaller **87.10b** and **88.2b**. ♣ Humid forest, esp. terra firme. Locally also semideciduous woodland. ♪ Song: loud series of about 6 "Weeah weeah - - weeh" notes.

87.3 BRIGIDA'S WOODCREEPER (Arapaçu-deloro-

cinza) *Hylexetastes brigidai* L 11.8 in./30 cm. Similar to **87.2**, but lores pale. Larger and heavier-billed than **87.10b**. ♣ Humid forest, mainly terra firme. ♪ Song resembles that of **87.2**. En.

87.4 RED-BILLED WOODCREEPER (Arapaçu-de-

bico-vermelho) *Hylexetastes perrotii* L 11.8 in./30 cm. Similar to **87.2** and **87.3**, but with whitish throat and face. No overlap in range. ♣ Humid forest, esp. terra firme. ♪ Song resembles that of **87.2**.

87.5 STRONG-BILLED WOODCREEPER (Arapaçu-

vermelho) *Xiphocolaptes promeropirhynchus* L 11.8 in./30 cm. Note large size, very large, pale, grayish horn-colored bill (dark in tepuis), pale lores, and streaked underparts. Dark malar not always visible. ♣ Mainly terra firme; sometimes várzea. ♪ Song: high, loud descending series of 5–7 paired "weetju weetju - -" notes.

87.6 CARAJÁS WOODCREEPER (Arapaçu-do-cara-

jás) *Xiphocolaptes carajaensis* L 11.8 in./30 cm. Often considered a ssp. of very similar but slightly larger **87.5**. No overlap in range. ♣ Primarily terra firme. ♪ Song as **87.5**, but possibly slightly faster. En.

87.7 WHITE-THROATED WOODCREEPER (Arapaçu-

de-garganta-branca) *Xiphocolaptes albicollis* L 11.8 in./30 cm. Large with long, black bill. Dark malar between whitish throat and streak from lores to lower ear patch. Back plain. Cf. **88.3**. *Note*: Two very distinctive forms from the hinterland forests of Bahia may well be full species with a very restricted range: the quite pale *villanovae* (only from Senhor do Bonfim) and *bahiae* (from Chapada Diamantina), the latter lacking ventral barring. ♣ Humid forest, second growth, riverine belts in cerrado. ♪ Song: slow, descending series of 4–6 high, sharp, double-noted whistles, like "witjuu witjuu - -."

87.8 MOUSTACHED WOODCREEPER (Arapaçu-do-

nordeste) *Xiphocolaptes falcirostris* L 11.8 in./30 cm. No woodcreeper with similar face pattern in range. ♣ Deciduous forest ("mata seca"), tall arboreal caatinga, and gallery forest. ♪ Call: whining, drawn-out "wèèè-tuh" (last part high and dry); song: varied; series of 4–7 double-notes, like "wèèè-TJUH wèèè-TJUH - -" ("wèèè-TJUH" often gradually changing to ringing "Tu-Tjuh"). En, R.

87.9 GREAT RUFOUS WOODCREEPER (Arapaçu-do-

campo) *Xiphocolaptes major* L 11.8 in./30 cm. Unmistakable by large size, massive pale bill, and dark lores. Big ssp. *remoratus* (not shown) from Mato Grosso has a more extensively streaked chest and a barred belly. ♣ Dry forest, woodland, riverine belts; also in cerrado and wooded savanna. ♪ Song: slightly descending series of 5–8 double-noted whistles, like "wéettuck - -."

87.10 AMAZONIAN   BARRED-WOODCREEPER

(Arapaçu-barrado) *Dendrocolaptes certhia* L 10.6 in./27 cm. Sspp. *radiolatus* (**a**; in NW) shown and *concolor* (**b**, Concolor Woodcreeper, Ri. Madeira to Ri. Tocantins; may have faint barring; **a** and other sspp. (resembling **a**, but barring less distinct) unmistakable by scalloped barring below and lack of streaking; **b** differs from **88.1** and **88.2b** by reddish bill. Also cf. **87.2**. ♣ Humid forest, savanna forest, gallery forest, and mangrove. Often at ant swarms. ♪ Call: "tjiew," accented at beginning, drawn-out at end; song: rapid, whinnying, run-together series of up to 12 notes, 1st rising than fading and falling off.

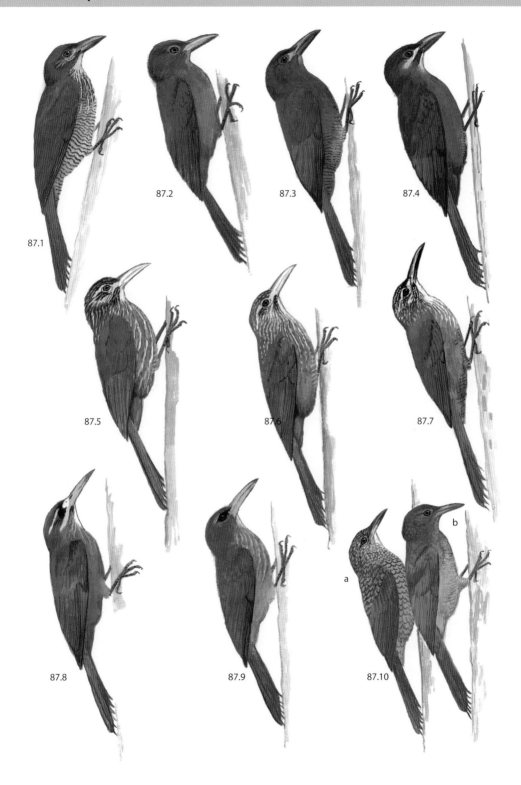

87.1

87.2

87.3

87.4

87.5

87.6

87.7

87.8

87.9

87.10

a

b

Plate 88

88.1 HOFFMANNS'S WOODCREEPER (Arapaçu-marrom) *Dendrocolaptes hoffmannsi* L 11 in./28 cm. From **87.10** and **88.2b** by black bill. ♣ Humid forest, tall second growth. Often at ant swarms. ♪ Song: level, rapid "wutwutwut---" (up to 20 ×). En.

88.2 BLACK-BANDED WOODCREEPER (Arapaçu-meio-barrado) *Dendrocolaptes picumnus* L 10.6 in./27 cm. Several sspp.: N Nom. shown (**a**, with barred underparts), less marked *pallescens* (**b**, the Pantanal) and *transfasciatus* (**c**, with streaked breast and barred belly). Follows army-ant swarms. *Note: picumnus* group (including Nom. and very similar *validus* from NW Amazon), *pallescens*-group, and ssp. *transfasciatus* may be full species. ♣ Terra firme and inundated várzea. Can also be seen in forested savanna and, rarely, in mangrove. ♪ Call: very high "tjieh"; song: rapid, descending series of sharp notes (SW); softer and less sharp in W Amazonia.

88.3 PLANALTO WOODCREEPER (Arapaçu-grande) *Dendrocolaptes platyrostris* L 9.8 in./25 cm. From larger **87.7** by shorter bill, little or no dark malar and, in SE part of range, finely streaked back. Back plain in N and W part of range, unlike **88.2a**. Belly and vent barred. Shown Nom. (**a**) and paler-headed ssp. *intermedius* (**b**). ♣ Humid forest, woodland, palm swamps, cerrado, and caatinga. ♪ Call: varied; may start with very high "i-i-i" continued with "weekweek---"; song: unmusical series of 5 or many more "tjew" notes, well-separated or run together, normally slightly rising, then trailing off.

88.4 STRAIGHT-BILLED WOODCREEPER (Arapaçu-de-bico-branco) *Xiphorhynchus picus* L 7.9 in./20 cm. Note plain back and whitish bill with straight or upturned culmen. Extensively marked white or buff head. ♣ Open habitats such as wooded savanna, riverine belts, swamps, mangrove, arid scrub, plantations, pastures with scattered trees. ♪ Call: simple, very high "twit twit - -"; song: rapid, descending series of "peecpicpitpit---" notes (lasting 2 sec).

88.5 ZIMMER'S WOODCREEPER (Arapaçu-ferrugem) *Xiphorhynchus kienerii* L 9.8 in./25 cm. Very similar to **88.4**, but tail longer. ♣ Mainly in interior of várzea. ♪ Song: very high, fast, almost level series of "i" notes.

88.6 STRIPED WOODCREEPER (Arapaçu-riscado) *Xiphorhynchus obsoletus* L 7.9 in./20 cm. Dense whitish buff streaking above and below. Pale bill (often dark at base of upper mandible) with slightly curved culmen. ♣ Várzea and wooded swamps. Locally also terra firme and riverine belts in cerrado. ♪ Call: very high, indignant-sounding "tic," often prolonged to a short twitter; song: very high, rising trill, like "wuhwuh---wihwih" (2–3 sec).

88.7 LESSER WOODCREEPER (Arapaçu-rajado) *Xiphorhynchus fuscus* L 6.7 in./17 cm. NE ssp. *atlanticus* (**a**) and SE Nom. (**b**) shown. Slender, curved bill. From **89.4**–**89.6** by spotted (not streaked or plain) crown and less boldly marked underparts. From **89.4** and **89.5** also by streaking on mantle (sometimes faint) ♣ Humid forest, incl. *Araucaria*. Inland in drier wooded areas. ♪ Call: very high, sharp "fieet fieet - -"; song: fast, sharp rattle, stuttered at end and (in Nom.) at beginning (2–3 sec).

88.8 OCELLATED WOODCREEPER (Arapaçu-ocelado) *Xiphorhynchus ocellatus* L 7.9 in./20 cm. Culmen/upper mandible dark; lower mandible pale. Mantle virtually plain (may be faintly streaked in NW). Breast spotted buff. ♣ Mainly in terra firme, sometimes várzea. ♪ Call: very high, fast "teettitteet"; song: short, fast, descending, rattling series of notes (up to 1 sec).

88.9 TSCHUDI'S WOODCREEPER (Arapaçu-) *Xiphorhynchus chunchotambo* L 7.9 in./20 cm. Back finely streaked. From very similar overlapping ssp. of **88.11** by larger spots on breast. ♣ Humid forest. ♪ Song: resounding, descending, whinnying series (2 sec).

88.10 SPIX'S WOODCREEPER (Arapaçu-de-spix) *Xiphorhynchus spixii* L 7.9 in./20 cm. Very similar to **88.6**, but voice different. Also cf. **88.8** and **89.2**. ♣ Humid forest, incl. montane. ♪ Song: very high, very fast trill, descending at beginning, level at end, last note higher (as a sort of "full stop"). En.

88.11 ELEGANT WOODCREEPER (Arapaçu-elegante) *Xiphorhynchus elegans* L 7.9 in./20 cm. (Includes ssp. *juruanus* JURUÁ WOODCREEPER from W Brazil, differing by voice.) Bill and markings below as **88.8**, but back clearly streaked. Streaking above and below finer in SW (cf. **88.9**). Also cf. **88.6** and **89.2**. ♣ Mainly terra firme, but occasionally in várzea, second growth, riverine belts. ♪ Call: characteristic 3-noted "tjictjicwuuuw," 1st 2 staccato, 3rd much lower and whining; song: descending series of "witwitwit---" notes; each note accentuated (3–5 sec and longer).

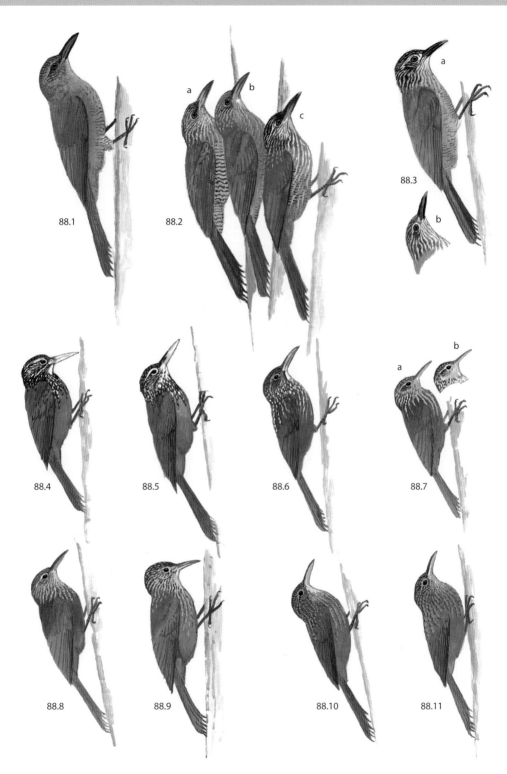

88.1

88.2
a
b
c

88.3
a
b

88.4

88.5

88.6

88.7
a
b

88.8

88.9

88.10

88.11

Plate 89

89.1 CHESTNUT-RUMPED WOODCREEPER (Arapa-çu-assobiador) *Xiphorhynchus pardalotus* L 7.9 in./20 cm. Bill black (only lowermost part of lower mandible pale). Throat and streaking fulvous. No overlap with most *Xiphorhynchus* woodcreepers, but cf. **89.2**. ♣ Forest, mainly terra firme. Locally also in wooded savanna. ♪ Call: unstructured series of chirps; song: level, clicking "tju-ptjup-tjuptjeetjee."

89.2 BUFF-THROATED WOODCREEPER (Arapaçu-de-garganta-amarela) *Xiphorhynchus guttatus* L 9.8 in./25 cm. Variable; *guttatoides* group Lafresnaye's Woodcreeper (**a**; W Amazon and Pantanal region; with buff streaking and throat and bill pale except for dark base to upper mandible), *eytoni* group Dusky-billed Woodcreeper (**b**; SE Amazon and Ceará; throat white and bill dark except for lowermost part of lower mandible), Nom. group (not shown; NE Amazon and E; as **a**, but upper mandible dark). Larger and heavier-billed than other *Xiphorhynchus* woodcreepers and lacks barring to vent and belly. ♣ Mainly humid forest. Locally in palm swamps, semideciduous forest, cerrado, and mangrove. ♪ Call: resounding, descending "weerweerwir" (3–6 notes); song: varies geographically; in W Amazonia: loud, resounding, crescendoing series of "wuut" notes, falling off at the end (3–6 sec); in Mato Grosso a very high, rising trill, decelerating and descending at the end.

89.3 NARROW-BILLED WOODCREEPER (Arapaçu-de-Cerrado) *Lepidocolaptes angustirostris* L 7.9 in./20 cm. Several sspp.: *angustirostris* (**a**) and *bahiae* (**b**, with plain, buffish underparts) shown. Unmistakable by head pattern. ♣ Open woodland, palm swamps, savanna, wooded areas in towns. ♪ Call: 1–3 squeaky notes; song: basically a series of 6–8 loud "peep" notes, which may vary in tempo, pitch, and strength.

89.4 SCALED WOODCREEPER (Arapaçu-escamado) *Lepidocolaptes squamatus* L 7.9 in./20 cm. Note plain mantle and nape and bold streaking below. No overlap with **89.5–89.8**, but cf. **88.7b**. ♣ Humid forest. ♪ Call: "péeir"; song: series of sharp, connected "pi" notes, slightly rising and slowing down and sharply falling off at end. En.

89.5 WAGLER'S WOODCREEPER (Arapaçu-de-wagler) *Lepidocolaptes wagleri* L 7.5 in./19 cm. Often considered a ssp. of **89.4**, but crown plainer and markings below less contrasting. No overlap with **89.4** or **89.6–89.8**, but cf. **88.7**. ♣ Woodland, dry to semideciduous forest. En.

89.6 SCALLOPED WOODCREEPER Arapaçu-escamado-do-sul) *Lepidocolaptes falcinellus* L 7.9 in./20 cm. Similar to **89.4**, but nape streaked (sometimes extends faintly into mantle). No overlap with **89.4**, **89.5**, or **89.7** and **89.8**, but cf. **88.7b**. ♣ Humid forest, *Araucaria* forest. Occasionally in semideciduous forest.

89.7 STREAK-HEADED WOODCREEPER (Arapaçu-listrado) *Lepidocolaptes souleyetii* L 7.9 in./20 cm. Similar to **89.8**, but head more streaked. ♣ Forest, woodland. ♪ Song: short, very high, sharp, shivering, downslurred trill.

89.8 LINEATED WOODCREEPER (Arapaçu-de-listras-brancas) *Lepidocolaptes albolineatus* L 7 in./18 cm. Note slender, curved bill. Appears plain except for streaked underparts (**b**), but NE Nom. (**a**) has indistinct spots on crown and nape. ♣ Canopy of terra firme; less in várzea and riverine belts. ♪ Song: series of about 15 fluted notes, falling in pitch and accelerated.

89.9 CURVE-BILLED SCYTHEBILL (Arapaçu-de-bico-curvo) *Campylorhamphus procurvoides* L 9.8 in./25 cm. Two groups: *multostriatus* group (shown; streaks with narrow, dark edging; S of Ri. Amazon) and Nom. group (not shown; as **89.10**, but mantle plain; N of Ri. Amazon). Both differ from **89.10** by slightly darker, more curved bill. ♣ Terra firme, bamboo stands. ♪ Song: varies per region; e.g., high fluted "wuuut wuutttttt" (2nd "wuut" changing to level or rising trill).

89.10 RED-BILLED SCYTHEBILL (Arapaçu-beija-flor) *Campylorhamphus trochilirostris* L 9.8 in./25 cm. Only scythebill in most of range. Note pinkish red bill, slight streaking to mantle, and lack of dark edges to streaks. ♣ Woodland, cerrado, caatinga, scrub, riverine belts, várzea, bamboo stands. ♪ Call: very high, excited, upslurred trill (or almost-trill); song: individually and regionally varied; in NW a rapid, descending, musical, whinnying series of up to 25 notes; in NE a short series of fluted notes "wuut wuut wit-wit-triffit" (last part ascending).

89.11 BLACK-BILLED SCYTHEBILL (Arapaçu-de-bico-torto) *Campylorhamphus falcularius* L 9.8 in./25 cm. Note black bill. ♣ Atlantic forest, second growth, bamboo stands. Mainly in highlands in N part of range. ♪ Call: very high, piercing "pjeetpjeet" (2–3 ×); song: level or descending, raspy "sree-sree-sree- -" (up to 5–6 ×).

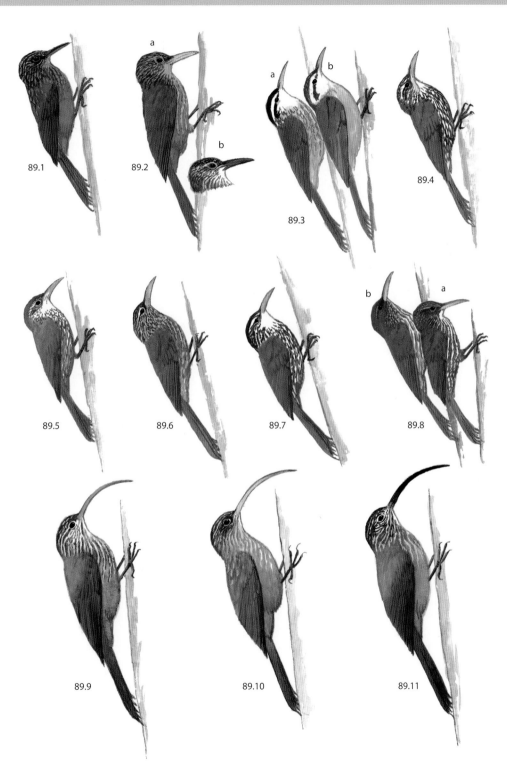

89.1

89.2 a b

89.3 a b

89.4

89.5

89.6

89.7

89.8 b a

89.9

89.10

89.11

Plate 90

90.1 TUFTED TIT-SPINETAIL (Rabudinho) *Leptas-* *thenura platensis* L 6.7 in./17 cm. Cf. **90.2**. ♣ Woodland, shrub. ♪ Song: 2–3 extr. high notes ending in very short trill.

90.2 STRIOLATED TIT-SPINETAIL (Grimpeirinho) *Leptasthenura striolata* L 6.3 in./ 16 cm. From **90.1** by range, streaked mantle, and more extensive streaking below. ♣ Forest edge (incl. *Araucaria*), woodland, tall second growth; 500–1200 m. ♪ Song: level, short, hurried series of 2–5 very high, thin or full notes, last one often slightly lower. En.

90.3 ARAUCARIA TIT-SPINETAIL (Grimpeiro) *Lept-* *asthenura setaria* L 7 in./18 cm. Unmistakable by streaked head, plain rufous mantle, and long tail. ♣ Canopy of *Araucaria*; 750–2000 m. ♪ Song: series (2–3 sec) of very high, thin notes changing in tempo between trill and rattle. R.

90.4 ITATIAIA (Thistletail or) **SPINETAIL** (Garrincha- chorona) *Oreophylax moreirae* L 7.5 in./ 19 cm. Note rufous chin (reduced in Juv.) and long, pointed tail. No similar bird in range and habitat. ♣ Low levels in thickets, shrub, bamboo, and tall grass. Above 1850 m. ♪ Call: low "piuw"; song: accelerating series of extr. high, slightly rising notes "you-tee-wiwiwiwi." En.

90.5 SHORT-BILLED CANASTERO (Lenheiro) *Asthenes* *baeri* L 5.9 in./15 cm. From **90.8** by shorter, heavier bill, grayer ear coverts and eyebrow, larger orange throat-patch, and shorter tail. ♣ Arid scrub and woodland. Up to 1300 m. ♪ Call: very high "weet weet - -." Normally sings (as the other canastero species) from exposed perch atop a bush.

90.6 CIPO CANASTERO (Lenheiro-da-serra-do-cipó) *Asthenes luizae* L 6.7 in./17 cm. Unmistakable in range and habitat. ♣ Brushy and grassy areas with rocks; 900–1500 m. ♪ Call: high "tjip"; song: descending series of about 12 notes "tseeptseep---." En, R.

90.7 HUDSON'S CANASTERO (João-platino) *Asthenes* *hudsoni* L 7 in./18 cm. Note streaked flanks. Tail edged whitish. Throat usually white (shown), but sometimes with orange chin. Crown not rufous, unlike **95.10** and **96.4**. ♣ Tall grass and sedges, esp. in marshy areas. Up to 950 m.

90.8 [SHARP-BILLED (or Lesser) **CANASTERO** (João-de-rabo-comprido) *Asthenes pyrrholeuca*] L 5.9 in./15 cm. Cf. **90.5**. ♣ Tall grass, marshy areas. ♪ Call: very high "weet weetweet - -." Not yet confirmed in Brazil.

90.9 CHOTOY SPINETAIL (Bichoita) *Schoeniophylax* *phryganophilus* L 7.9 in./20 cm. Unmistakable by combination of long tail, yellow chin, rufous shoulder, and streaked back. ♣ Open areas with scattered trees and bushes, riverine belts. ♪ Call: hurried "sreepsreeptrrit"; song: low, descending, "chop-chop-chop---," ending in a rattle.

Plate 91

91.1 CAMPO MINER (Andarilho) *Geositta poeciloptera* L 4.7 in./12 cm. Small. Note short tail, plain back, and rufous in wing (mainly in flight). No overlap with **91.2**, but cf. **91.9** and pipits (Pl. **128**). ♣ Open cerrado, grassland with scattered trees and bushes. Often in recently burned areas. Mainly terrestrial. ♪ Song (in display flight): high, level, hurried, rolling "turruturrut---" (15–20 sec). R.

91.2 COMMON MINER (Curriqueiro) *Geositta cunicu-* *laria* L 5.9 in./15 cm. Note dark-streaked chest, plain back, rather short tail, and rufous in wing (mainly in flight). Generally distinctive, but cf. **91.3** and **91.4** and pipits (Pl. **128**). ♣ Open grassy areas, shrub. Often in sandy coastal habitats. Terrestrial. ♪ Call: very high, sharp "fweet"or "fwit"; song: in low flight display, series of shrill notes.

91.3 BAR-WINGED CINCLODES (Pedreiro-dos-andes) *Cinclodes fuscus* L 6.7 in./17 cm. Cf. **91.4**. ♣ Grassland and other open habitats. Often near water. Terrestrial. ♪ Call: extr. high "tic" notes; song: given from perch (while flapping wings) or in flight, short, shrill, buzzing, like "srrrrrrih" or "srrrrruh."

91.4 LONG-TAILED CINCLODES (Pedreiro) *Cinclodes* *pabsti* L 7.9 in./20 cm. From smaller **91.3** (no known overlap) by longer tail, and uniform chest (no faint scalloping) ♣ Grassland and other open habitats. Often near water; 750–1700 m. Terrestrial. ♪ Song: from perch or in flight, very high, short, sharp, crescendoing rattle/trill. En.

NOTE: Horneros (**91.5–91.9**) are largely terrestrial. Except **91.9**, all have bright rufescent backs and well-defined eyebrows. The large, rounded mud-nests, for which they have received their name (*hornero* is Spanish for baker), is typically placed in a tree or other high structure. R.

91.5 LESSER HORNERO (Joãozinho) *Furnarius minor* L 5.1 in./13 cm. Small. In most of range only hornero with gray (not pinkish) legs, but cf. **91.7**. ♣ Low scrub on river islands. ♪ Call: sudden, mid-high "dzip"; song: high, very loud, resounding, harsh series "dipdipdip---," 1st 6–7 notes slightly descending (up to 8 sec).

91.6 WING-BANDED (or Band-tailed) **HORNERO** (Casaca-de-couro-da-lama) *Furnarius figulus* L 6.3 in./16 cm. From **91.7** and **91.8** by dark-tipped inner webs of tail feathers (mainly visible from below), outer primaries with two (not one) rufous bands, and paler underparts contrasting less with white throat. ♣ Woodland, second growth, parks, gardens, semiopen areas. Often near water; often near humans. ♪ Call: e.g., harsh "djeep-djeep- -"; song: series of 3–20 high, very loud staccato notes "djip-djip- -," sometimes run together. En.

91.7 PALE-LEGGED HORNERO (Casaca-de-couro- amarelo) *Furnarius leucopus* L 7 in./18 cm. Legs typically pinkish, but may be grayish in E. Tawny-ochraceous chest contrasts somewhat with white throat. ♣ Woodland, second growth, parks, gardens, semiopen areas. Often near water; often near humans. ♪ Song: slightly descending and slowing series of about 15 very loud staccato notes, the last 3–5 well accentuated.

91.8 PALE-BILLED HORNERO (João-de-bico-pálido) *Furnarius torridus* L 6.3 in./16 cm. Resembles **91.7**, but chest darker rich rufous-brown. Shy. ♣ Woodland and forest at rivers. ♪ Song: descending, hurried series of loud, fluted notes, ending in a tremolo (total 4–5 sec).

91.9 RUFOUS HORNERO (João-de-barro) *Furnarius* *rufus* L 7.9 in./20 cm. Rather featureless. Note contrasting rufous tail. Wing band rarely visible when perched. ♣ Virtually any open to semiopen habitat. Often near humans. ♪ Song: often in duet; chattering, sharp notes in 7–8 sec series, hurried and slightly undulating at start, leveling and slowing down in second half.

Plate 92

92.1 PINTO'S SPINETAIL (Tatac) *Synallaxis infuscata*

L 6.7 in./17 cm. Only *Synallaxis* spinetail in small range with all-rufous crown and tail. ♣ Dense undergrowth in lowland forest, woodland, second growth. ♪ Call/song: high, hurried, nasal "teh-tjeh teh-tjetjeh." Song may also sound like a fast, short, dry trill. En, R.

92.2 RUFOUS-CAPPED SPINETAIL (Pichororé) *Synallaxis ruficapilla*

L 5.9 in./15 cm. Only *Synallaxis* spinetail in range with rufous wings, tail, and cap. Note fine whitish eyebrow. ♣ Low levels of forest, woodland. Usually near bamboo. Up to 1400 m. ♪ Call: dry rattle, like "trrrrruh"; song: "tdrrrWit" ("Wit" much higher).

92.3 BAHIA SPINETAIL (João-baiano) *Synallaxis whitneyi*

L 6.3 in./16 cm. Only *Synallaxis* spinetail in small range with rufous wings, tail, and cap. ♣ Dense undergrowth of forest; 500–1000 m. ♪ Call: high, dry "rutrut-." En, R.

92.4 SOOTY-FRONTED SPINETAIL (Petrim) *Synallaxis frontalis*

L 5.9 in./15 cm. From most other spinetails in range by rufous wings and tail. From **92.1**– **92.3** by gray frontlet, paler face, and inconspicuous black throat-patch. ♣ Undergrowth of deciduous forest, riverine belts, savanna, thickets, plantations. ♪ Call: varied; may be an irregular, high, nasal "tjip tjip tjipjip - -"; song: very high 2-noted "du-Twee" (2nd note much higher).

92.5 PALE-BREASTED SPINETAIL (Uí-pi) *Synallaxis albescens*

L 5.9 in./15 cm. Note gray frontlet and dull brownish tail. Rufous in plummage restricted to crown and wing coverts. Note also pale underparts. ♣ Low levels in virtually any open or semiopen habitat with tall grasses and/or shrubs. ♪ Call: extr. high "tsweét"; song: unceasing, very high, shrill "zutsweet zutsweet - -."

92.6 SPIX'S (or Chicli) **SPINETAIL** (João-teneném) *Synallaxis spixi*

L 6.7 in./17 cm. Note rufous crown and wing coverts. Black chin patch larger than in **92.5** and underparts darker. ♣ Undergrowth of shrub, cerrado, woodland edge, grassy areas with shrub. Up to 2050 m. ♪ Call/song: 4- or 5-noted "wuh-wididit" ("wuh" lower).

92.7 DARK-BREASTED SPINETAIL (João-de-peito-escuro) *Synallaxis albigularis*

L 6.3 in./ 16 cm. No similar species in most of range, but in limited area of contact, cf. **92.5**. From very similar **92.8** (note range) by slightly paler, spikier tail. ♣ Areas with tall grass and shrubs. Mainly near water. Lowlands. ♪ Song: high, sharp "Dit-drrrr" ("Dit" higher).

92.8 CINEREOUS-BREASTED SPINETAIL (João-grilo) *Synallaxis hypospodia*

L 6.3 in./ 16 cm. Resembles **92.5**, but underparts grayer and wings (usually) more rufescent. Also cf. **92.7**. ♣ Open areas with tall grass and shrub. Often near water. Lowlands. ♪ Song: high, sharp "tut-Drrrrrrruh" (last part staccato and slightly descending).

92.9 MACCONNELL'S SPINETAIL (João-escuro) *Synallaxis macconnelli*

L 6.3 in./16 cm. No similar *Synallaxis* spinetail in range with all-rufous crown except paler **92.5**. ♣ Dense forest undergrowth. Up to 1900 m. ♪ Call: short, dry rattle, like "drrrr"; song: dry rattle, ending in a higher pitched, full-stop "drrrrrh-Tic."

92.10 CABANIS'S SPINETAIL (João-do-norte) *Synallaxis cabanisi*

L 6.7 in./17 cm. Darker than **92.5** and with all-rufous wings. ♣ Dense undergrowth in or near humid lowland forest. ♪ Call: low "zic"; song: hurried, chattered "tjet-jetjetjet - -," rather unstructured in pitch.

92.1

92.2

92.3

92.4

92.5

92.6

92.7

92.8

92.9

92.10

Plate 93

93.1 GRAY-BELLIED SPINETAIL (Pi-puí) *Synallaxis*

cinerascens L 5.9 in./15 cm. Only spinetail in range with gray underparts and no rufous on crown. ♣ Dense undergrowth in humid forest interior. Up to 1150 m. ♪ Song: very high, piercing "weeet-suweet" (1st note higher).

93.2 WHITE-BELLIED SPINETAIL (João-de-barriga-

branca) *Synallaxis propinqua* L 6.3 in./ 16 cm. From **93.3** by black throat-patch. ♣ Tall grass, thickets, and low bush at rivers. In lowlands. ♪ Song: strange, mechanical-sounding, scratchy shiver (5–6 sec).

93.3 PLAIN-CROWNED SPINETAIL (João-tenením-

becuá) *Synallaxis gujanensis* L 6.3 in./ 16 cm. From **93.4a** (note range) by lack of contrasting white lores. Also cf. **93.2**. ♣ Low levels in shrub, stands of cane, edge of forest and woodland. Near water. Lowlands. ♪ Song: varies geographically; in W Amazonia, "tjuh mcweet," 1st part slightly downslurred, "weet" much higher; in NE, 2 well-separated notes, 1st note high, sharp, explosive "Whip," 2nd note lower "wuh," together as "Whip wuh."

93.4 WHITE-LORED SPINETAIL (João-do-pantanal)

Synallaxis albilora L 6.3 in./16 cm. Two sspp. (Nom. and *simoni*), often treated as full species: (**a**) WHITE-LORED SPINETAIL (João-do-pantanal) *Synallaxis albilora*. Note distinct whitish lores; (**b**) **ARAGUAIA SPINETAIL** (João-do-araguaia) *Synallaxis simoni*; En. From **a** (no known overlap) by mostly white underparts and cinnamon-rufous back. ♣ Undergrowth of riverine belts. Up to 1000 m. ♪ Voices of the two ssspp. differ; *albilora* repeats sharp "keeew kiw-kweet" notes; *simoni* gives a series of evenly spaced "keeip" notes.

93.5 HOARY-THROATED SPINETAIL (João-de-

barba-grisalha) *Synallaxis kollari* L 6.3 in./16 cm. No similar bird in its restricted range. ♣ Dense undergrowth of riverine belts. ♪ Song/call: double-noted "tuh-tíh," second note higher. En, R.

93.6 OCHRE-CHEEKED SPINETAIL (Estrelinha-preta)

Synallaxis scutata L 5.5 in./14 cm. Note distinctive eyebrow and small black throat-patch. ♣ Undergrowth of dense, low forest in cerrado and caatinga. ♪ Song: extr. high, thin "fweeet puh-wit," 1st part upslurred, 2nd note lower pitched than 1st and 3rd. Constantly repeated at 1-sec intervals.

93.7 CHESTNUT-THROATED SPINETAIL (Puru-

chém) *Synallaxis cherriei* L 5.5 in./ 14 cm. Resembles **93.8a**, but wings not uniform and lacks black throat-patch. ♣ Dense undergrowth of humid lowland forest. Often in bamboo thickets. ♪ Song: "prruh-píh" (2nd note higher) in long series with short interruptions. R.

93.8 RUDDY SPINETAIL (João -tenením-castanho)

Synallaxis rutilans L 5.5 in./14 cm. Virtually all-rufous plumage combined with black throat-patch (**a**) diagnostic. Dark ssp. *omissa* (**b**; Juvs. of other sspp. similar) of far E has rufous wings. ♣ Undergrowth of humid lowland forest, mainly terra firme. ♪ Song: 2-noted "kéewoh" (2nd note lower), constantly repeated.

93.9 YELLOW-CHINNED SPINETAIL (Curutié) *Cer-*

thiaxis cinnamomeus L 5.9 in./15 cm. Unmistakable in most of its range by bicolored plumage, but cf. **93.10**, **94.6**, and **94.10**. Note whitish eyebrow. Diagnostic yellow chin lacking in Juv. ♣ Wetlands, marshes, mangrove, and other semiopen habitats near water. ♪ Alarm call: low "tjew"; song: loud rattle, like "t-t-trrrrrr." *Note*: An undescribed taxon with more uniform upperparts and chin lacking yellow occurs together with this species near Ri. Araguaia.

93.10 RED-AND-WHITE SPINETAIL (João-da-canarana)

Certhiaxis mustelinus L 5.9 in./15 cm. Conspicuously bicolored. From **93.9** by lacking an eyebrow and having a white chin. ♣ Marsh at rivers in forest. ♪ Call: dry "chuk chuk-chuk"; song: loud, dry, irregularly undulating rattle.

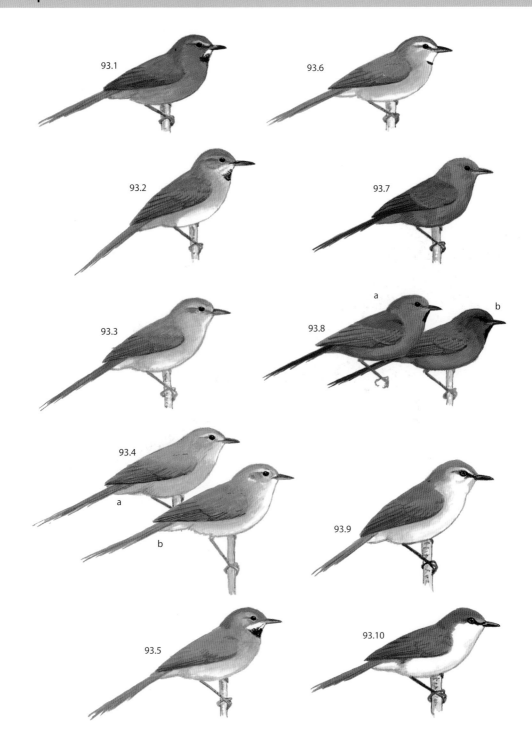

Plate 94

94.1 PALLID SPINETAIL (Arredio-pálido) *Cranioleuca* *pallida* L 5.9 in./15 cm. Combination of white eyebrow and rufous crown, wings, and tail diagnostic. Juv. resembles **94.4**, but with all-rufous wings. ♣ Upper levels of forest, woodland, tall second growth; 700–2150 m. ♪ Song: extr. high, slightly descending series of about 5 "seetseet--tut" notes (often accelerated to a trill at the end). En.

94.2 TEPUI SPINETAIL (João-do-tepui) *Cranioleuca* *demissa* L 5.9 in./15 cm. Note eyebrow and rufous crown, wings, and tail. No similar *Cranioleuca* in range, but cf. **92.9**. ♣ Mid- to upper levels of forest and woodland above 1100 m. ♪ Call: high, short, dry rattle; song: fast, short series, starting extr. high, ending in a high rattle, like "zizi---zrr" (1–2 sec).

94.3 STRIPE-CROWNED SPINETAIL (Arredio) *Cran-* *ioleuca pyrrhophia* L 5.9 in./15 cm. Streaked crown bordered by white eyebrow diagnostic. Grayer (less buff) below than **94.1** and **94.4**. ♣ Deciduous forest, woodland, second growth. ♪ Call: "wrrru"; song: extr. high "tit-tit-srrrru," downslurred at end.

94.4 OLIVE SPINETAIL (Arredio-oliváceo) *Cranioleuca* *obsoleta* L 5.5 in./14 cm. Note dull brown crown and rufous wing coverts. Cf. **94.1** and **94.3**. ♣ Mid- to upper levels of forest, second growth, *Araucaria* woodland. Up to 1000 m. ♪ Call: soft, dry, hurried trill; song: short series, at first extr. high and hesitant "tzit-tzit-tzit-," and then a short trill ending in a very high "-sfeet-sfeet-sfeet."

94.5 GRAY-HEADED SPINETAIL (João-de-cabeça-cinza) *Cranioleuca semicinerea* L 5.9 in./15 cm. Unmistakable in range. ♣ Forest, woodland. Mainly in dry regions; locally at borders of humid forest; 500–850 m. ♪ Call: high "trwit"; song: extr. high "tsit-tsit-tsit-" then bouncing down as rattle. En.

94.6 RUSTY-BACKED SPINETAIL (Arredio-do-rio) *Cranioleuca vulpina* L 6.3 in./16 cm. Differs from **93.9** and **93.10** by pale (not black) lower mandible and gray-buff (less white) underparts. Cf. **94.10**. ♣ Mid- to low levels of riverine belts, várzea, thick vegetation near water. ♪ Song: series of descending, scolding notes "scew-scew-scew- -" (2–3 sec).

94.7 SCALED SPINETAIL (João-escamoso) *Cranioleuca* *muelleri* L 5.9 in./15 cm. Scalloped underparts diagnostic. ♣ Mid-levels to subcanopy of humid lowland forest. En.

94.8 SPECKLED SPINETAIL (João-pintado) *Cranio-* *leuca gutturata* L 5.5 in./14 cm. Speckled underparts diagnostic. ♣ Várzea and terra firme with dense vines. Below 400 m, occasionally much higher. ♪ Alarm call: short, low rattle; song: extr. high "sreet-steer - -" (almost inaudible).

94.9 SULPHUR-THROATED (or -bearded) **SPINE-** **TAIL** (Arredio-de-papo-manchado) *Cranioleuca sulphurifera* L 6.3 in./16 cm. Note habitat, wing-pattern, faintly streaked throat, and yellow chin. ♣ Marshes with tall grasses or reeds.

94.10 PARKER'S SPINETAIL (Arredio-de-peito-branco) *Cranioleuca vulpecula* L 5.5 in./14 cm. Differs from very similar **94.6** by paler chest and less distinct eyebrow. ♣ Shrub and woodland at rivers; esp. river islands. ♪ Song: high "tjuw-tjuw-tjerrr" (last note a trill, rapidly descending).

Plate 95

95.1 RED-SHOULDERED SPINETAIL (João-chique-chique) *Gyalophylax hellmayri* L 7.5 in./19 cm. No similar bird in its range. ♣ Arid, scrubby woodland. ♪ Alarm call: high, shrill "quebéc." En, R.

95.2 STRIATED SOFTTAIL (Rabo-amarelo) *Thripophaga macroura* L 7.1 in./18 cm. Note extensive streaking and orange chin. Cf. larger **97.10**. ♣ Mid- to lower levels of humid forest, esp. in dense vine tangles. Up to 1000 m. ♪ Song: unstructured mixture of short rattles, "tjew-tjew-tjew" notes, and sparrowlike chatters (often in duet). En, R.

95.3 PLAIN SOFTTAIL (João-liso) *Thripophaga fusciceps* L 6.7 in./17 cm. Dark; no streaking. Note rufous wings and tail. ♣ Várzea. Mainly in dense vines. ♪ Song: very rhythmic chattering with rattles in tune, given in duet.

95.4 RUFOUS-FRONTED (or Common) **THORNBIRD** (João-de-pau) *Phacellodomus rufifrons* L 6.7 in./17 cm. Rather featureless, but note rufous front. Shows contrasting rufous remiges in far NE. ♣ At low levels in a wide range of habitats with thickets, but generally avoids forest interior. Mainly below 1300 m. ♪ Call: extr. high, sharp "zipzipzip-zip-"; song: rather unstructured series of very high, mewing "tsjew" notes, rising, falling, and repeating.

95.5 FRECKLE-BREASTED THORNBIRD (Tio-tio) *Phacellodomus striaticollis* L 7.1 in./18 cm. Note freckled breast and pale eyes. Wings and tail brownish rufous. ♣ Near water in riverine belts, lowland scrub, and marsh. Up to 700 m. ♪ Song: series of about 8–10 well-spaced notes, 1st 3–4 mid-high and nasal, last 5–6 high, sharp and loud.

95.6 GREATER THORNBIRD (Graveteiro) *Phacellodomus ruber* L 7.9 in./20 cm. Note yellow (not white) eyes and contrasting rufous wings and cap. Cf. **95.5** and **99.9**. ♣ Undergrowth of riverine belts, marshes, woodland, and shrub near water. Up to 1100 m. ♪ Call: loud, high "djeub-djeb-djebdjed"; song: series of up to 20 loud, sharp, resounding notes, starting very high and explosive, thereafter slightly accelerating and gradually descending.

95.7 ORANGE-EYED THORNBIRD (João-botina-da-mata) *Phacellodomus erythrophthalmus* L 6.7 in./17 cm. Dark with contrasting rufous throat and forecrown. Eyes orange, which may seem black when seen in shadow. ♣ Undergrowth of humid forest. ♪ Song: slow, descending series of up to 15 sharp, ringing notes. En.

95.8 RED-EYED THORNBIRD (João-botina-do-brejo) *Phacellodomus ferrugineigula* L 6.7 in./17 cm. Differs from **95.7** by larger rufous areas on forecrown and breast, duller and darker central tail, and duller reddish eyes. ♣ Undergrowth of forest, woodland, second growth, marsh. ♪ Song: as **95.7**, but less sharp, sounding more like "tjirp tjirp tjirp - -."

95.9 CANEBRAKE GROUNDCREEPER (Cisqueiro) *Clibanornis dendrocolaptoides* L 8.7 in./22 cm. Note white throat and scalloping between cheeks and chin. ♣ Bamboo and other dense undergrowth of forest. Often near streams. Up to 1200 m. ♪ Short to long series of loud, staccato "chet" notes, often interspersed with harsh chatters. R.

95.10 BAY-CAPPED WREN-SPINETAIL (Boininha) *Spartonoica maluroides* L 5.1 in./13 cm. Note small size, rufous crown, and streaked back. Cf. **94.9**, **90.7**, and **96.4**. ♣ Marshes and other wet areas with tall grasses. ♪ Song: very dry trill (2–3 sec). R.

Plate 96

96.1 WREN-LIKE RUSHBIRD (Bate-bico) *Phleocryptes* *melanops* L 5.5 in./14 cm. Note white throat and boldly patterned wimp and face sides. ♣ Bamboo and other dense undergrowth of forest; often near streams. Up to 1200 m. ♪ Song: curious mechanical-sounding series of tics (sounds like an idling motor, with the throttle occasionally opened), sustained for long periods.

96.2 CURVE-BILLED REEDHAUNTER (Junqueiro-de-bico-curvo) *Limnornis curviro-* *stris* L 6.3 in./16 cm. Curved bill diagnostic. ♣ Marshes with tall grasses or reeds. Up to 1100 m. ♪ Song: fast rising and thereafter descending series, reminiscent of guineafowl cackling; also a very long rattle, abruptly changing in pitch.

96.3 STRAIGHT-BILLED REEDHAUNTER (Junqueiro-de-bico-reto) *Limnoctites rectirostris* L 6.7 in./17 cm. Note habitat and long bill. Note virtually straight bill, gray-tinged crown, and spikier tail. ♣ Marshes and other wet areas with spiny Eryngos (*Eryngium spp*). ♪ Song: long series, alternating between a low, slightly undulating trill and a very high rattle. R.

96.4 FIREWOOD-GATHERER (Cochicho) *Anumbius* *annumbi* L 7.5 in./19 cm. Note rufous frontlet, white throat edged by black-spotted malars, and broadly white-tipped tail (mainly visible from below). ♣ Grassland, shrub, lightly wooded areas, tree-stands near farms. ♪ Song: strong, very high series of 2–3 hurried, staccato notes, followed by short, slightly descending rattle, like "djip-djip-drrrr."

96.5 LARK-LIKE BRUSHRUNNER (Corredor-crestudo) *Coryphistera alaudina* L 6.3 in./16 cm. Note crest. Virtually unmistakable. ♣ Open woodland, semiopen areas with shrub and scattered trees. ♪ Varied vocalizations, e.g., very high "sreeh" and descending "sreeweewee."

96.6 ORANGE-FRONTED PLUSHCROWN (João-folheiro) *Metopothrix aurantiaca* L 4.3 in./11 cm. Virtually unmistakable. Juv. lacks orange crown. Note orange legs. ♣ Woodland, second growth, várzea, edge of terra firme. ♪ Song: slightly descending series of 3–5 high, thin notes (2 sec).

96.7 RORAIMAN BARBTAIL (João-de-roraima) *Roraimia* *adusta* L 5.9 in./15 cm. No similar bird in its range. ♣ Humid forest; 1200–2500 m. ♪ Call: very high, inquiring "whit?"

96.8 PINK-LEGGED GRAVETEIRO (Acrobata) *Acro-* *batornis fonsecai* L 5.5 in./14 cm. Unmistakable by combination of gray plumage and pink legs. Juv. differs from Ad. by the gray plumage parts being brownish. ♣ Cacao plantations shaded by taller trees. ♪ Song: extr. high, excited twittering. En, R.

96.9 POINT-TAILED PALMCREEPER (Limpa-folha-do-buriti) *Berlepschia rikeri* L 7.9 in./ 20 cm. Unmistakable. ♣ Palm groves (mainly *Mauritia*) in forest, swamp, or savanna. ♪ Song: very high, loud series of 12–15 "weet-weetwitwitwit---" notes, up to 5 sec, rising, getting sharper, and falling off at the end.

96.10 WHITE-BROWED FOLIAGE-GLEANER (Limpa-folha-miúdo) *Anabacerthia amaurotis* L 6.3 in./16 cm. Throat and broad eyebrow creamy white. Back plain. Cf. **97.4**. ♣ Understory of forest, tall second growth. Mainly at 600–1500 m; locally lower. ♪ Call: extr. high, thin "tseep tseep seepseep -"; song: e.g., a short, accelerated, ascending and descending series of very/extr. high "seep" notes. R.

Plate 97

97.1 CAATINGA CACHOLOTE (Casaca-de-couro-da-

caatinga) *Pseudoseisura cristata* L 9.8 in./25 cm. Large and mostly rufous. Note crest. No overlap with **97.2** and **97.3**. ♣ Caatinga, deciduous forest. Often near humans. ♪ Duets in which one bird gives a long series of well-spaced, very loud, piercing "tjew" notes, the other intermixes with 1-sec rattles. En.

97.2 BROWN CACHOLOTE (Coperete) *Pseudoseisura*

lophotes L 9.8 in./25 cm. Unmistakable in its range. ♣ Deciduous forest, woodland, shrub, gardens. ♪ Unmusical duet of well-spaced, grating notes, intermixed with soft, descending "tjew" notes.

97.3 RUFOUS (or Gray-crested) **CACHOLOTE** (Casaca-

de-couro-de-crista-cinza) *Pseudoseisura unirufa* L 7.9 in./20 cm. Very similar to **97.1** (no overlap in range), but often with grayer crown. ♣ Flood plains, riverine belts, woodland. Often near humans. ♪ Duet of sustained, loud, accelerating, slightly descending "chew" notes mixed with chattering and rattles, finishing with combined cackling.

97.4 BUFF-BROWED FOLIAGE-GLEANER (Trepador-

quiete) *Syndactyla rufosuperciliata* L 7.1 in./18 cm. Differs from **97.10** by narrower buff eyebrow and more olive (less rufescent) mantle. ♣ Lowland forest, riverine belts, second growth up to 2000 m. ♪ Call: very high, sharp, snarling "tsjeep tsjeep -"; song: short series of high-pitched, loud, sharp notes, slightly ascending, then bouncing down "dzeepdzeep---."

97.5 PERUVIAN RECURVEBILL (Limpa-folha-de-bi-

co-virado) *Simoxenops ucayalae* L 7.9 in./20 cm. Unmistakable by dark rufous-brown plumage and by bill shape. ♣ Low levels in bamboo thickets in humid forest. ♪ Song: short, loud, harsh, ascending rattle (2–3 sec), last note(s) sometimes lowered. R.

97.6 CHESTNUT-WINGED HOOKBILL (Limpa-fol-

ha-picanço) *Ancistrops strigilatus* L 7.1 in./18 cm. Unmistakable by strongly contrasting rufous wings and densely streaked underparts and mantle. Cf. **97.7** and foliage-gleaners (Pl. **98–99**). ♣ Mainly in upper levels of terra firme; locally in várzea. ♪ Call: "teetjuw" (second part often lower); song: sustained, gently undulating, slightly angry-sounding rattle (up to 35 sec).

97.7 EASTERN STRIPED WOODHAUNTER (Limpa-

folha-riscado) *Hyloctistes subulatus* L 7.1 in./18 cm. Differs from foliage-gleaners in range (Pl. **98–99**) by blurry streaking of underparts and mantle. Eyering less distinct than in **99.2**. ♣ Low to mid-levels of humid forest, old second growth. ♪ Call: high, sharp "kreeut"; song: monotone, nasal "tjeutjeu tjeutjeutjeu" or undulating or descending "djepdjep---" (up to 8 sec).

97.8 WHITE-COLLARED FOLIAGE-GLEANER (Tre-

pador-coleira) *Anabazenops fuscus* L 7.9 in./20 cm. Relatively large. Note white collar. Wings brown, not rufous. ♣ Forest and second growth with extensive bamboo; 350–1200 m. ♪ Call: high, nasal, hurried "wjew-wjew---" (up to 8 ×); song: high, musical, slightly lowered "djepdjep---" (up to 11 ×; sometimes some notes doubled). En.

97.9 DUSKY-CHEEKED (Bamboo or Crested) **FOLI-**

AGE-GLEANER (Barranqueiro-de-topete) *Anabazenops dorsalis* L 7.5 in./19 cm. As **99.2**, but underparts grayer, upperparts more rufescent, and eyebrow more prominent. ♣ Mid- and low levels in humid forest, second growth; Esp. esp. near water and/or bamboo. Up to 1000 m. ♪ Song: series of about 7–8 well-separated, slightly accelerated, nasal "tjew" notes.

97.10 PALE-BROWED TREEHUNTER (Trepador-so-

brancelha) *Cichlocolaptes leucophrus* L 8.7 in./22 cm (N part of range), 7.1 in./18 cm (S part of range). Relatively large. Note strong streaking below and less distinct streaking of back. Tail rufous (shown; S part of range) or cinnamon (N part). Lacks orange chin of **95.2**. ♣ Humid montane and lowland forest. ♪ Call: very high, sharp, grating "shreew"; song: loud, sweeping "wip wip - -" or "sreep sreep - -" (up to 6–7 ×), sometimes interspersed by some chattering. En.

Plate 98

98.1 RUFOUS-TAILED FOLIAGE-GLEANER (Limpa-folha-de-cauda-ruiva) *Philydor rufi-caudatum* L 6.7 in./17 cm. Smaller, slenderer, and with finer bill than *Automolus* foliage-gleaners. Note faint streaking to breast and vent. Cf. **99.1**. Also cf. **98.2**. ♣ Mid- to upper levels of terra firme; locally also várzea. Up to 900 m. ♪ Call: dry, very short rattle, like "krrreh"; song: high, staccato "wicwic-wic---," lowered at the end (up to 2 sec).

98.2 CINNAMON-RUMPED FOLIAGE-GLEANER (Limpa-folha-vermelho) *Philydor pyrrhodes* L 5.9 in./15 cm. Unmistakable by contrasting dark wings and crown. ♣ Understory of humid forest; often near palms. Up to 500 m. ♪ Call: fast "tjaktjaktjak"; song: low or very high, long, dry, gradually rising trill, ending with a full stop.

98.3 RUSSET-MANTLED (or Planalto) **FOLIAGE-GLEANER** (Limpa-folha-do-brejo) *Syndactyla dimidiata* L 6.7 in./17 cm. Rather uniform rufescent color overall. Cf. **98.4** with paler underparts and gray-tinged crown. Also cf. **98.6**. ♣ Low to mid-level of forest and woodland; up to 1200 m. ♪ Song: rather short or very long series of "tsjek" notes, ascending, starting and ending with some stuttering (the total reminiscent of a small, slowly starting motorbike).

98.4 RUFOUS-RUMPED FOLIAGE-GLEANER (Limpa-folha-de-sobre-ruivo) *Philydor erythro-cercum* L 6.7 in./17 cm. From **98.1** by rufous rump and lack of even faint streaking. ♣ Mid- to upper levels of terra firme; locally also várzea; up to 1300 m. ♪ Song: hurried series of 4–5 very high, piercing notes.

98.5 CHESTNUT-WINGED FOLIAGE-GLEANER (Limpa-folha-de-asa-castanha) *Philydor erythropterum* L 7.1 in./18 cm. Note contrasting rufous wings and ochre-orange chin and lores. Lacks streaking of **97.6**. ♣ Mid- to upper levels of terra firme; locally also várzea. Up to 500 m; locally higher. ♪ Song: very high, ringing, buzzing trill, slightly rising and falling.

98.6 OCHRE-BREASTED FOLIAGE-GLEANER (Limpa-folha-ocráceo) *Philydor lichtensteini* L 6.3 in./16 cm. Note gray-brown crown and ochraceous underparts. ♣ Mid- to upper levels of forest, tall second growth. Up to 800 m. ♪ Call: short, very high, inhaled trill; song: series of up to 10 extr. high, piercing "zipzip---" notes.

98.7 BUFF-FRONTED FOLIAGE-GLEANER (Limpa-folha-de-testa-baia) *Philydor rufum* L 7.5 in./19 cm. Buff forehead diagnostic. ♣ Mid- to upper levels of forest, second growth. Up to 1200 m; locally higher.

98.8 BLACK-CAPPED FOLIAGE-GLEANER (Limpa-folha-coroado) *Philydor atricapillus* L 6.7 in./17 cm. Unmistakable by facial pattern. ♣ Forest, tall second growth; up to 1000 m. ♪ Call: very high, metallic-sounding "zic - -"; song: rapid series of 6–8 very high notes, the 1st 2 lower (as if taking a run-up), the last 2 slightly lower still.

98.9 ALAGOAS FOLIAGE-GLEANER (Limpa-folha-do-nordeste) *Philydor novaesi* L 7.1 in./18 cm. Unmistakable in its tiny range. ♣ Humid forest, old second growth. En, R.

98.10 SHARP-TAILED STREAMCREEPER (João-porca) *Lochmias nematura* L 5.5 in./14 cm. Unmistakable by scaling below. ♣ Woodland, forest. Always near streams or small rivers. Mainly in highlands; also in lowlands in S. ♪ Call: extr. high, sharp, indignant "tsiterit" or "tsitit"; song: series of extr. high, loud, piercing notes, slightly stuttering at first, then accelerating and slightly rising.

98.1

98.6

98.2

98.7

98.3

98.8

98.4

98.9

98.5

98.10

Plate 99

99.1 BUFF-THROATED FOLIAGE-GLEANER (Bar-ranqueiro-camurça) *Automolus ochrolaemus* L 7.5 in./19 cm. Note faintly flammulated breast, distinct broad eyering, relatively faint eyebrow, and buff throat. ♣ Mid- and low levels in humid forest, second growth, plantations. Up to 1000 m. ♪ Call: downslurred, dry "krèeh"; song: series of 3–4 well-separated, descending "keh-keh-keh-kreh" notes.

99.2 OLIVE-BACKED FOLIAGE-GLEANER (Barran-queiro-pardo) *Automolus infuscatus* L 7.5 in./19 cm. Note brown-olive face sides and upperparts. White throat often puffed out. ♣ Undergrowth of lowland forest. Up to 700 m. ♪ Call: high, sharp, decisive "tjíwah"; song: short, descending trill "terrrruh."

99.3 PARA FOLIAGE-GLEANER (Barranqueiro-do-pará) *Automolus paraensis.* L 7.5 in./19 cm. Differs from **99.2** by broader dark margins to feathers of crown and cheeks. ♣ Mainly Terra firme, also in várzea. Up to 700 m. ♪ Nasal "wheet wheet - -"; song: very high, penetrating, sharp "kreet-kreetkrititit," slightly descending. En.

99.4 WHITE-EYED FOLIAGE-GLEANER (Barran-queiro-de-olho-branco) *Automolus leucophthalmus* L 7.9 in./20 cm. Virtually unmistakable in range and habitat. Note white (not yellow) eyes. ♣ Low to mid-levels of forest, tall second growth. Mainly up to 1000 m; locally higher. ♪ Call: high, sharp, nasal "itiew"; song: fast, rhythmic, liquid or grating "tlewtlew---."

99.5 WHITE-THROATED (or Tepui) **FOLIAGE-GLEANER**(Barranqueiro-de-roraima) *Automolus roraimae* L 7.1 in./18 cm. Characterized by contrasting white throat and eyebrows. ♣ Montane forest, merging in wind-clipped woodland; 1100–2500 m. ♪ Song: short, very dry, upslurred rattle (almost like bleating of a goat).

99.6 BROWN-RUMPED FOLIAGE-GLEANER (Bar-ranqueiro-escuro) *Automolus melanopezus* L 6.7 in./17 cm. Note pale ochre-orange throat and reddish-orange eyes. Also cf. **99.7**. ♣ Undergrowth of várzea, esp. with bamboo. Up to 500 m. ♪ Song: short series in 3 parts, starting with "wet weet," continued with fast, liquid "wiwiwiwi," and ending with lower dry rattle.

99.7 RUDDY FOLIAGE-GLEANER (Barranqueiro-ferrugem) *Automolus rubiginosus* L 7.1 in./18 cm. Dark. Deep rufous throat and chest. ♣ Undergrowth of humid lowland forest. ♪ Song: varies geographically; in N, 2-noted "tutwuuh" (2nd note higher), in W, a mournful, upslurred "ttweuuuh."

99.8 CHESTNUT-CROWNED FOLIAGE-GLEANER(Barranqueiro-de-coroa-castanha) *Automolus rufipileatus* L 7.5 in./19 cm. Note yellow-orange eyes. Crown slightly more chestnut than remaining upperparts. ♣ Low levels in várzea; less so in terra firme. Often near bamboo. Up to 500 m; locally higher. ♪ Call: grating "krih-krih- -"; song: short, shivering, staccato trill "kriiiiiih" (1.5 sec).

99.9 CHESTNUT-CAPPED FOLIAGE-GLEANER (Fura-barreira) *Hylocryptus rectirostris* L 7.9 in./20 cm. Note yellowish eyes. Crown and wings contrast less with mantle and with less white to central underparts than in shorter-billed and longer-tailed **95.6**. ♣ Riverine belts, woodland, up to 1000 m. ♪ Call: dry, cackling "kjep -kjep - -"; song: as call, but accelerating to a rattle, in total lasting 2–3 sec.

99.10 SHARP-BILLED TREEHUNTER (Trepador-zinho) *Heliobletus contaminatus* L 5.1 in./13 cm. Small. Differs from **96.10** by buff (not whitish) eyebrow, throat, and cheeks. Streaked upper back from São Paulo southward. Also cf. **97.4**. ♣ Mid- to upper levels of forest, incl. *Araucaria*. Mainly in highlands in N part of range. ♪ Song: extr. high, twittering rattle, 1st 3–4 notes lower, then upslurred. *Note*: An undescribed *Heliobletus* sp. occurs in SE Bahia.

99.1

99.2

99.3

99.4

99.5

99.6

99.7

99.8

99.9

99.10

Plate 100

100.1 TAWNY-THROATED LEAFTOSSER (Vira-fol-ha-de-peito-vermelho) *Sclerurus mexicanus* L 6.3 in./16 cm. Differs from other leaftossers by tawny-rufous throat. Note long, curved bill. ♣ Humid forest. Up to 1100 m. ♪ Call: very high, simple "tsik"; song: very high, piercing series of 4–6 descending "tess-tsee-tsee---tsee" notes (last "tsee" often back to level of 1st note).

100.2 SHORT-BILLED LEAFTOSSER (Vira-folha-de-bico-curto) *Sclerurus rufigularis* L 6.3 in./16 cm. From **100.1** by shorter bill and paler throat. ♣ Terra firme up to 500 m. ♪ Call; extr. high "siew siew -"; song: short, descending series of 4–5 very high, piercing notes, preceded by 2–4 × "tjup."

100.3 GRAY-THROATED LEAFTOSSER (Vira-folha-de-garganta-cinza) *Sclerurus albigularis* L 6.7 in./17 cm. Whitish gray throat contrasts with rufous chest. Cf.**100.4**; no overlap with **100.5**. ♣ Humid lowland forest. ♪ Song: series of 2–5 level or rising notes, often followed by level, lower "tjutjut-" (2–3 × "tjut).

100.4 BLACK-TAILED LEAFTOSSER (Vira-folha-pardo) *Sclerurus caudacutus* L 6.7 in./17 cm. Two groups; NE Amazonian *insignis* group (**a**) and widespread *brunneus* group (**b**). Note whitish chin in **a** and whitish chin with faint scaling in **b**. Lacks contrasting rufous chest and rump of **100.5**. ♣ Terra firme. Mainly in lowlands; to 1100 m in tepuis. ♪ Song: loud series of hurried, descending, clear notes (2–3 sec), often ending in a rising double note or a short canarylike roll.

100.5 RUFOUS-BREASTED LEAFTOSSER (Vira-folha) *Sclerurus scansor* L 7.5 in./19 cm. NE ssp. *cearensis* (**a**; with white throat) and widespread Nom. (**b**; faintly scaled throat). ♣ Forest, tall second growth. Up to 1500 m. ♣ Terra firme. Mainly in lowlands; to 1100 m in tepuis. ♪ Call: very high, thin "títs"; song: varied; e.g., a very high, slightly descending, sharp trill, like "vrrrrr-tri-trit" (3 sec).

100.6 RUFOUS-TAILED XENOPS (Bico-virado-da-copa) *Xenops milleri* L 4.3 in./11 cm. Differs from **100.7–100.9** by lack of white malar and all-rufous tail. Note straight bill. ♣ Mainly canopy and subcanopy of terra firme, but also várzea. Up to 600 m. ♪ Song: rising and descending trill (2 sec).

100.7 SLENDER-BILLED XENOPS (Bico-virado-fino) *Xenops tenuirostris* L 3.9 in./10 cm. Differs from **100.9** by less streaking below and black extending to outer webs of some tail feathers. ♣ Canopy and subcanopy of humid forest. Up to 600 m. ♪ Song: very high, level, fast, lashing "tseep---" (4–6 ×).

100.8 PLAIN XENOPS (Bico-virado-miúdo) *Xenops* *minutus* L 4.7 in./12 cm. Plumage not streaked. Wing pattern as other xenops. ♣ Humid forest; locally also deciduous and gallery forest. Up to 1500 m. ♪ Call: very high, upslurred "sweep"; song: extr. high, hurried series of 5–10 × "seep---."

100.9 STREAKED XENOPS (Bico-virado-carijó) *Xen-**ops rutilans* L 4.7 in./12 cm. Note upturned bill, streaking below, and white malar. Only inner web of 3rd feather from outer tail feathers is black. ♣ Forest, woodland. Up to 2400 m. ♪ Song: hurried series of 5–8 extr. high notes, 1st and last lower pitched.

100.10 GREAT XENOPS (Bico-virado-da-caatinga) *Megaxenops parnaguae* L 6.3 in./16 cm. Unmistakable by bill shape and bright rufous plumage. ♣ Caatinga and semihumid woodland; up to 1100 m. ♪ Song: long, very high, loud, nervous, unstructured series of chattering or liquid "toc-toc-" and "Wicwic-" notes, rising and falling with sudden crescendos. En, R.

100.1

100.2

100.3

100.4
a
b

100.5
a
b

100.6

100.7

100.8

100.9

100.10

Plate 101

101.1 FASCIATED ANTSHRIKE (Papa-formiga-bar-rado) *Cymbilaimus lineatus* L 7.1 in./ 18 cm. Note heavy bill and red eyes. ♀ crown rufous. ♣ Dense parts of mid-level humid forest. Up to 1200 m. ♪ Song: simple, slow series of about 4–5 high, evenly spaced "weh" notes, increasing in strength.

101.2 BAMBOO ANTSHRIKE (Choca-do-bambu) *Cym-bilaimus sanctaemariae* L 6.7 in./ 17 cm. Differs from **101.1** by dark eyes, longer crest (often held flat); ♀ also by black rear-crown and deeper buff underparts with less barring. ♣ Extensive bamboo stands in humid lowland forest. ♪ Song: simple series of 8–10 very high, well-spaced chipping notes.

101.3 SPOT-BACKED ANTSHRIKE (Chocão-carijó) *Hypoedaleus guttatus* L 7.9 in./20 cm. Unmistakable in range. Often whiter below than shown. ♣ Dense vines in upper strata of humid lowland forest. ♪ Song: very high, slow, at first rising then descending, shivering rattle (4–5 sec).

101.4 GIANT ANTSHRIKE (Matracão) *Batara cinerea* L 11.8 in./30 cm. Unmistakable. ♣ Dense understory of humid forest, esp. near bamboo. Up to 2200 m. ♪ Song: series that starts with a short trill and continues with a fast series of notes that increase in strength and pitch, leveling out and decelerating at the end.

101.5 TUFTED ANTSHRIKE (Borralhara) *Mackenzi-aena severa* L 7.9 in./20 cm. Cf. **101.6**. Not in range of **101.7**. ♣ Dense undergrowth of forest, esp. near bamboo. Locally in overgrown plantations. Up to 1400 m. ♪ Call: sudden rising shriek, like "sreeew"; song: short, slow, slightly accelerating series of 6–8 very high, slightly rising, strident "sreek" notes.

101.6 LARGE-TAILED ANTSHRIKE (Borralhara-asso-biadora) *Mackenziaena leachii* L 9.8 in./25 cm. ♂ unmistakable. ♀ from ♀ **101.5** by spotted back and lack of uniform rufous crest. ♣ Dense understory of humid forest, esp. near bamboo. Up to 2200 m. ♪ Call: downslurred, sharp "sree"; song: hurried, slightly slowing down, at first rising then descending series of about 15 very high, strident "sweep" notes (4 sec).

101.7 BLACK-THROATED ANTSHRIKE (Borralhara-do-norte) *Frederickena viridis* L 7.9 in./20 cm. Large, with heavy bill and red eyes. Note black head and chest of ♂. ♀ unmistakable in range by rufous upperparts and densely barred underparts. ♣ Dense understory of lowland forests. ♪ Song: slow series of 10–15 first rising, then leveling out, fluted "tuh" notes (6–7 sec).

101.8 UNDULATED ANTSHRIKE (Borralhara-ondu-lada) *Frederickena unduligera* L 9.8 in./ 25 cm. Large and essentially dark (♂) or rufous (♀). SW *pallida* (**a**) and NW Nom. (**b**) shown. ♣ Dense undergrowth of humid lowland forest. ♪ Call: long, suddenly starting, gliding-down "Weeeew"; song: short series of 8–13 directly connected "wuiw" notes, increasing in strength and pitch. Birds in SW Amazonia may sing differently.

101.9 GREAT ANTSHRIKE (Choró-boi) *Taraba major* L 7.9 in./20 cm. Unmistakable by color pattern and red eyes. ♣ Undergrowth of virtually any habitat with thickets. ♪ Song: low, accelerating series of nasal notes, running up to the end or up to halfway, often ending in one (or regionally in a repeated) snarl.

Plate 102

102.1 BLACK-CRESTED ANTSHRIKE (Chorá-boi)

Sakesphorus canadensis L 5.9 in./15 cm. Far N ssp. *fumosa* (**a**) and widespread *loretoyacuensis* (**b**) shown. Distinctive in range. ♂**a** superficially similar to ♂ **103.5**. ♣ Low to mid-levels of woodland, várzea, riverine belts. ♪ Song: accelerating series of level or ascending, bouncing, nasal notes (3–4 sec).

102.2 SILVERY-CHEEKED ANTSHRIKE (Choca-do-nordeste)

Sakesphorus cristatus L 5.5 in./ 14 cm. ♂ unmistakable in range. ♀ with all-brown tail and no white on scapulars. ♣ Lower levels of deciduous forest, woodland, caatinga. ♪ Song: short series of chopped, nasal notes, accelerating and trailing off to a growling sound (3–4 sec). En.

102.3 GLOSSY ANTSHRIKE (Choca-d"água)

Sakesphorus luctuosus L 6.7 in./17 cm. Note crest (rufous in ♀) and white tail-tips. ♣ Low to mid-levels of várzea, woodland and shrub near rivers. ♪ Song: short, accelerating series of 10–15 high, nasal "ah" notes. En.

102.4 WHITE-BEARDED ANTSHRIKE (Papo-branco)

Biatas nigropectus L 7.1 in./18 cm. ♂ unmistakable. ♀ with rufous wings. ♣ Extensive bamboo in forest and second growth between 500 and 1200 m. ♪ Song: slow series of 6–8 mournful, yet melodious notes, first rising, then lowering in pitch at the end. R.

102.5 PEARLY ANTSHRIKE (Choca-pintada)

Megastictus margaritatus L 5.1 in./13 cm. Unmistakable by large spots on wings, incl. tertials. ♣ Lower levels of humid forest, woodland. Up to 1200 m. ♪ Call: very high "wit-wit- -," 1st "wit" stressed; song: probably a duet, starting with 2–3 "wuit" notes from ♂, answered by low, rapid, grating "wr-wr-wr-wred" from ♀.

102.6 SATURNINE ANTSHRIKE (Uirapuru-selado)

Thamnomanes saturninus L 5.5 in./ 14 cm. ♂ with diagnostic black throat and upper chest. ♀ from ♀ **102.7** by whiter throat (note range). Also cf. ♀ **102.8**. ♣ Understory of humid forest; esp. terra firme. ♪ Song: accelerated, ascending series of notes, at first grating, then gradually changing to sharp and piercing.

102.7 DUSKY-THROATED ANTSHRIKE (Uirapuru-de-garganta-preta)

Thamnomanes ardesiacus L 5.5 in./14 cm. ♂ with small/no black throat-patch; when lacking cf. ♂♂ **102.8**, **103.7**, and **103.8**. ♀ paler below than ♀ **102.8b**; also cf. ♀ **102.6**. ♣ Understory of humid forest; esp. terra firme. ♪ Song: very high, sometimes slow series of about 10–12 rising, fluted notes, often accelerated at the end.

102.8 CINEREOUS ANTSHRIKE (Ipecuá)

Thamnomanes caesius L 5.5 in./14 cm. ♂ always lacks black to throat; from ♂ **102.7** by more erect posture and longer tail. Also cf. ♂♂ **102.9**, **103.7**, and **103.8**. ♀ variable; E Nom. (**a**, only vent cinnamon) and N Amazonian *glaucus* (**b**; underparts rich tawny-rufous; SC sspp. similar) shown; SE Amazon *hoffmannsi* paler below (not shown). ♣ Low to mid-levels of humid forest. ♪ Song: series, starting with some slow, sharply rising notes, then descending as a short rattle.

102.9 BLUISH-SLATE ANTSHRIKE (Uirapuru-azul)

Thamnomanes schistogynus L 5.5 in./ 14 cm. ♂ as ♂ **102.8** (note range). ♀ unmistakable by contrasting underparts. ♣ Low to mid-levels of humid forest. ♪ Song: hurried series of a few very high, fluted notes, then accelerating to a rather long, downslurred rattle.

102.10 SPOT-WINGED ANTSHRIKE (Choca-cantadora)

Pygiptila stellaris L 5.1 in./ 13 cm. Stocky with short, plain tail. ♂ with white-spotted wings. ♀ unmistakable. ♣ Mid- to upper levels of humid forest. Up to 700 m. ♪ Song: short, dry rattle, ending in high "tuw," together as "tdrrrrTiúw."

Plate 103

103.1 BAND-TAILED ANTSHRIKE (Choca-de-cauda-pintada) *Thamnophilus (or Sakesphorus) melanothorax* L 6.7 in./17 cm. Note broad white tail-tip in ♂. ♀ unmistakable. ♣ Dense tangled vegetation in forest understory, dense thickets at rivers and in swampy places. ♪ Song: slow, slightly accelerating series of 7–9 low, hollow "ah" notes.

103.2 BARRED ANTSHRIKE (Choca-barrada) *Thamnophilus doliatus* L 6.3 in./16 cm. Unmistakable by pale eyes and overall barred plumage (♂) or streaked face (♀). ♣ Low to mid-levels of woodland, second growth, shrub, riverine belts. ♪ Song: high, bouncing down series of 10–15 nasal notes, ending in emphatic "tjaw."

103.3 CHESTNUT-BACKED ANTSHRIKE (Choca-listrada) *Thamnophilus palliatus* L 6.7 in./17 cm. Both sexes with pale eyes, barred underparts, and rufous back (also rufous crown in ♀). ♣ Forest edge, várzea, woodland, second growth, shrub (even in gardens and parks), overgrown plantations. Up to 1000 m. ♪ Song: high, accelerating, descending series of 10–15 nasal notes, ending in emphatic "tjaw" (slightly higher and shorter than **103.2**).

103.4 CAATINGA BARRED ANTSHRIKE *Thamnophilus capistratus* L 6.7 in./17 cm. Differs from **103.2** by reddish eyes, blacker crown in ♂, and faint barring to chest in ♀. ♣ Caatinga, restinga, sometimes in forest edge. *Note*: This species was recently split from **103.1**; the English name was in 2008 not yet official. En.

103.5 BLACKISH-GRAY ANTSHRIKE (Choca-preta-e-cinza) *Thamnophilus nigrocinereus* L 6.7 in./17 cm. Several sspp.: *tschudii* (**a**; Ri. Madeira) and *cinereoniger* (**b**; in NW) shown. ♂♂ of E. sspp. as ♂ **a**, but somewhat paler below; ♀♀ as ♀ **b**, but darker above. Note white-edged (not spotted) wing coverts of ♂. ♀ distinctive, but cf. ♀♀ **114.5** and **114.6** with cinnamon wing spots and finer bill. ♣ Mid- to lower levels of várzea, woodland and shrubby growth near rivers, mangrove. Up to 350 m. ♪ Song: series of about 10 low, descending, hooted notes.

103.6 CASTELNAU'S ANTSHRIKE (Choca-selada) *Thamnophilus cryptoleucus* L 6.7 in./17 cm. ♂ from ♂ **103.5a** by more uniform black plumage. ♀ lacks white on wing coverts and does not have blue eyering. ♣ Mid- to lower levels of várzea, woodland, and tall second growth near rivers. ♪ Song: series of about 10 low, descending, hooted notes (as **103.3**, but even lower and notes more barked).

103.7 WHITE-SHOULDERED ANTSHRIKE (Choca-lisa) *Thamnophilus aethiops* L 6.3 in./16 cm. ♂ from ♂ **103.8** by small, white shoulder spots and black/dusky crown. Plumage varies; E of Ri. Tocantins (**a**) crown gray and wing spots (often difficult to see); cf. smaller and finer-billed ♂ **102.8**. Also cf. ♂♂ **102.10, 114.2, 114.5–114.7**, and **115.7**. Rufous ♀ distinctive. ♣ Undergrowth of humid forest; up to 900 m. ♪ Song: slow series of about 6 evenly spaced, almost level hooted notes.

103.8 PLAIN-WINGED ANTSHRIKE (Choca-de-oho-vermelho) *Thamnophilus schistaceus* L 5.5 in./14 cm. ♂ from ♂ **102.8** by heavier bill with most of lower mandible gray (not blackish). Wings not spotted as ♂♂ **103.7** and **103.9**. ♀ olive-brown or rufous-brown with contrasting rufous crown. ♣ Mid-levels of humid forest; up to 900 m. ♪ Song: hurried, accelerating series of high hooted "tjaw" notes.

103.9 MOUSE-COLORED ANTSHRIKE (Choca-murina) *Thamnophilus murinus* L 5.5 in./14 cm. Eyes pale grayish (not reddish as in **103.8**). NE ssp. *cayennensis* (**a**; wings brown), S *canipennis* (**b**; wings with narrow white edging), and NW Nom. (not shown; wings intermediate between **a** and **b**). ♀♀ of all sspp. dull with rufescent crown. ♣ Mid-levels of humid forest; mainly terra firme and white-sand forests. Up to 1300 m. ♪ Song: high, slow, simple series "tja tja tja ta-tjow"; "tjow" lower.

103.10 STREAK-BACKED ANTSHRIKE (Choca-de-roraima) *Thamnophilus insignis* L 6.7 in./17 cm. White nape diagnostic. Also note rufous crown of ♀. ♣ Low to mid-levels of humid forest, woodland, dense shrub; above 900 m. ♪ Song: slightly rising, accelerating series of nasal "ahn" notes, ending in upslurred "tonight."

Plate 104

104.1 AMAZONIAN ANTSHRIKE (Choca-canela) *Tham-*

nophilus amazonicus L 5.5 in./
14 cm. Sspp. *cinereiceps* (**a**; NW part
of range, crown gray) and *obscurus*
(**b**; Ri. Tapajós–Ri. Tocantins; back
almost all-black) shown. ♂♂ of
other sspp. inseparable from ♂♂ **104.6** and **104.7**.
Orange-headed ♀♀ of all sspp. unmistakable (belly often
more orange than shown). ♣ Low to mid-levels of humid
lowland forest, dense second growth. In S often near bamboo; in NE also in savanna woodland. ♪ Song: rapid, at first
slightly rising, then descending series of chattering notes.

104.2 ACRE ANTSHRIKE (Choca-de-acre) *Thamno-*

philus divisorius 5.9 in./15 cm. Note
hooded appearance and lack of
white shoulder spots. ♀ unmistakable. ♣ Low levels of stunted forest
at ca. 500 m.

104.3 RUFOUS-CAPPED ANTSHRIKE (Choca-de-

chapéu-vermelho) *Thamnophilus
ruficapillus* L 6.3 in./16 cm. Note
barred chest and rufous cap of ♂. ♀
very like ♀ **104.4** (note range), but
wings duller. ♣ Understory of thick-
ets, woodland, shrub, second growth; up to 2400 m. ♪
Song: slightly accelerating series of 12–15 "tjew" notes.

104.4 RUFOUS-WINGED ANTSHRIKE (Choca-de-asa-

vermelha) *Thamnophilus torquatus* L
5.5 in./14 cm. Note black crest of ♂.
♀ resembles ♀ **104.3**. ♣ Understory of semideciduous woodland,
cerrado, thickets, second growth; up
to 1750 m. ♪ Song as **104.2**, but notes at the end more
bouncing down.

104.5 VARIABLE ANTSHRIKE (Choca-da-mata)

Thamnophilus caerulescens L 5.9 in./
15 cm. Typical ♂ and ♀ (**a**), ♂ S *gil-
vigaster* (**b**; lower underparts washed
ochre-cinnamon), ♀ NE *cearensis*
(**c**; with narrow or no wing bars),
and ♀ C *ochraceiventer* (**d**; crown blackish) shown. From
104.8–104.10 (no overlap with **104.1** or **104.6–104.7**)
by narrow gray-white (♂) or buff (♀) edge on outer webs
of tertials (broad white edge in both sexes of **104.6–
104.10**); ♀ also differs from these species by rich ochre-
cinnamon lower underparts and dusky/dull dark brown
(not rufescent) tail. Also cf. **102.2** and **103.5**. ♣ Low to
mid-levels of forest, woodland, second growth, riverine
belts. Avoids arid habitats. Up to 1500 m; locally higher.
♪ Song: high, hurried series of 4–5 notes "au-au-au-au,"
last one slightly lower.

104.6 NORTHERN (Guianan or Eastern) **SLATY-
ANTSHRIKE** (Choca-bate-cabo)

Thamnophilus punctatus L 5.5 in./
14 cm. No overlap in range with
104.5, **104.7**, or **104.8**, but cf.
104.1. ♀ unmistakable in range by
wing pattern and rufous crown. ♣ Low to mid-levels of
white-sand forest, edge of other forest types, woodland,
old second growth. Up to 1200 m. ♪ Song: series of 9–10
nasal notes, starting very slowly, but accelerating and rising very sharply.

104.7 NATTERER'S SLATY-ANTSHRIKE (Choca-de-

natterer) *Thamnophilus stictocephalus*
L 5.9 in./15 cm. For ♂ cf. **104.1**. ♀
generally unmistakable. Differs
from **104.8** and **104.9** by less white
(♂) or less buff (♀)underparts. ♣
Low to mid-levels of white-sand forest, semideciduous
forest, edge of other forest-types, woodland. Up to 700 m.
♪ Song: series of level, nasal notes, starting slowly, but
accelerating to a level, bouncing rattle (3–4 sec).

104.8 BOLIVIAN SLATY-ANTSHRIKE (Choca-da-

bolívia) *Thamnophilus sticturus* L
5.5 in./14 cm. Eyes usually pale. See
104.5. Also cf. **104.7** and **104.9**. ♣
Low to mid-levels of semideciduous
forest, riverine woodland, second
growth. Up to 600 m. ♪ Song: series of level, nasal notes,
starting low, but accelerating and sharply rising to a very
high, sharp rattle.

104.9 PLANALTO SLATY-ANTSHRIKE (Choca-do-

planalto) *Thamnophilus pelzelni* L
5.5 in./14 cm. Cf. **104.5**. Belly of ♂
whiter than that of ♂♂ **104.7** and
104.10 and eyes usually darker than
104.8. Mantle of ♀ more rufescent
than in ♀♀ **14.8** and **104.10**. ♣ Low to mid-levels of
deciduous and semideciduous forest, edge of humid forest, riverine belts. Up to 1100 m. ♪ Call: downslurred,
cackling "krrrruh"; song: short, rising, cackling series, finishing as rattle, the last note lower pitched (2–3 sec). En.

104.10 SOORETAMA SLATY-ANTSHRIKE (Choca-

de-sooretama) *Thamnophilus ambiguus* L 5.9 in./15 cm. Cf. **104.5** and
104.9. ♣ Low to mid-levels of forest, woodland, second growth. Up to
700 m. ♪ Call: level, high, cackling
"witwitwit" or "witrrr"; song: cackling series, starting high
and rising, then finishing as a short, sometimes descending rattle (3 sec). En.

104.1   a   ♀   b

104.2   ♀

104.3   ♀

104.4   ♀

104.5   ♂a   ♀a   ♀c   ♂b   ♀d

104.6   ♀

104.7   ♀

104.8   ♀

104.9   ♀

104.10   ♀

Plate 105

105.1 BLACK BUSHBIRD (Choca-preta) *Neoctantes* *niger* L 6.3 in./16 cm. Stocky with short, plain tail. ♀ unmistakable. ♣ Mid- to upper levels of humid forest. Up to 700 m. ♪ Song: rhythmic series of high, even-pitched, pumped "wuúh" notes, sustained at least for 10–15 sec.

105.2 RONDONIA BUSHBIRD (Choca-de-garganta- preta) *Clytoctantes atrogularis* L 6.7 in./ 17 cm. ♂ unmistakable. ♀ with black tip, unlike **97.5**. ♣ Dense undergrowth in humid forest. En, R.

105.3 SPOT-BREASTED ANTVIREO (Choquinha-de- peito-pintado) *Dysithamnus sticto-thorax* L 4.7 in./12 cm. ♂ distinctive by spotted underparts and face sides. ♀ from ♀ **105.4** by spotted face sides. ♣ At edges of lower levels of forest up to 1250 m. ♪ Call: low "churr"; song: rather hurried series of some 20 mellow, slightly staccato, rising and falling notes, the last 3–5 accelerated. R.

105.4 PLAIN ANTVIREO (Choquinha-lisa) *Dysitham-* *nus mentalis* L 4.7 in./12 cm. 4 sspp.: shown is EC and SE Nom. (**a**; NE *emiliae* similar) and C ssp. *affinis* (**b**; N *spodoniatus* similar). Small and short-tailed with dark face (♂) or rufous crown and white eyering (♀). ♣ Undergrowth of forest, woodland. Up to 2500 m. ♪ Call: high "tjuw"; song: series of 4 high, staccato notes, followed by a short, downslurred roll.

105.5 RUFOUS-BACKED ANTVIREO (Choquinha-de- asa-ferrugem) *Dysithamnus xanthop-terus* L 4.7 in./12 cm. Unmistakable by rich rufous back. ♣ Mid- to upper levels of humid forest; 750–1700 m. ♪ Song: very high, rapid series of a descending, shivering, whistled rattle. En.

105.6 PLUMBEOUS ANTVIREO (Choquinha-chumbo) *Dysithamnus plumbeus* L 5.1 in./ 13 cm. Note size and wing spots. ♣ Understory of humid lowland forest. ♪ Song: slow series of 6–8 evenly spaced, rising and falling, sad-sounding notes. En, R.

105.7 PYGMY ANTWREN (Choquinha-miúda) *Myr-* *motherula brachyura* L 3.1 in./8 cm. Both sexes have yellow belly. Throat white (♂) or buff-tinged white (♀). ♣ Mid- to upper levels of humid forest, woodland; esp. at edge. Up to 900 m. ♪ Call: e.g., high, falling "mew"; song: short, rising, accelerating series of very high, sharp notes, at start well separated and gradually changing to a descending rattle/trill (3–4 sec).

105.8 MOUSTACHED (or Short-billed) **ANTWREN** (Choquinha-de-bico-curto) *Myr-motherula (ignota) obscura* L 3.1 in./ 8 cm. Resembles **105.7**, but malar broader and upperparts blacker. ♣ Upper levels of humid lowland forest. ♪ Call: high "tjew"; song: rapid, level series of staccato notes, accelerated and downslurred at the end (3–4 sec).

105.9 SCLATER'S ANTWREN (Choquiha-de-garganta- amarela) *Myrmotherula sclateri* L 3.1 in./8 cm. Resembles **105.7** and **105.8**, but both sexes yellow-throated, ♂ with yellow face and ♀ with streaking extending more onto chest. ♣ Canopy in interior of humid lowland forest. ♪ Song: short, slow series of 4–6 well-separated "peuw" notes.

105.10 YELLOW-THROATED ANTWREN (Choquinha- de-coroa-listrada) *Myrmotherula ambigua* L 3.1 in./8 cm. ♂ from ♂ **105.4** by yellow throat; ♀♀ insepa-rable from **105.7**. ♣ Mid- to upper levels of lowland forest; esp. in white-sand areas. ♪ Song: monotone, slow, very high "pew-pew- -" (5–7 ×).h

Plate 106

106.1 KLAGES'S ANTWREN (Choquinha-do-tapajós) *Myrmotherula klagesi* L 3.9 in./ 10 cm. ♂ resembles ♂ **106.2**. ♀ as ♀ **106.4**, but less extensive streaking below. ♣ Upper levels of várzea and other forests near rivers. ♪ Call: high, dry "tzik-tzik tzik -"; song: short series of double notes "teWíc - -" notes (5–7 ×). En, R.

106.2 AMAZONIAN STREAKED ANTWREN (Choquinha-estriada-da-amazônia) *Myrmotherula multostriata* L 3.9 in./ 10 cm. ♂ with semiconcealed white interscapular patch, unlike ♂♂ **106.1** and **106.4**. ♀ with rich-ochre head and white belly. Differs from **106.3** mainly by range. ♣ Low to mid-levels of várzea, shrubby areas near rivers. ♪ Call: funny-sounding, repeated series of about 6 fluted notes, 1st 3 stepping up, 3rd and 4th level, 4th–6th stepping down; song: short, musical, at start slightly rising rattle (4–5 sec).

106.3 GUIANAN STREAKED ANTWREN (Choquinha-estriada) *Myrmotherula surinamensis* L 3.9 in./10 cm. Cf. **106.2**. ♣ Low to mid-levels of várzea, shrubby areas near rivers, mangrove. ♪ Call: dry "mew" or "mew-kjew"; song: short, sharp, level trill "d-rrrrr," "d-" slightly lower.

106.4 CHERRIE'S ANTWREN (Choquinha-de-peitoriscado) *Myrmotherula cherriei* L 3.9 in./10 cm. ♂ from ♂♂ **106.1**– **106.3** by black (not pale gray) lower mandible and thicker black streaking below. ♀ from ♀♀ **106.2** and **106.3** by buff head and belly. ♣ Low to mid-levels in várzea, low shrubby forest in white-sand areas, shrubby areas near rivers. Lowlands. ♪ Call: high, nasal "tjeew" or "teetjuw"; song: short, very high, sharp, rattling trill, slightly rising at start.

106.5 PLAIN-THROATED ANTWREN (Choquinhade-garganta-clara) *Myrmotherula hauxwelli* L 3.5 in./9 cm. Note tiny size, very short tail, and distinct tertial spots. No overlap with **106.6**. ♣ Low levels in humid lowland forest, esp. terra firme. ♪ Call: very high, strident "wic"; song: series of very high, crescendoing, slightly accelerating "weec" notes (8–11 sec).

106.6 RUFOUS-BELLIED ANTWREN (Choquinha-debarriga-ruiva) *Myrmotherula guttata* L 3.5 in./9 cm. Note tiny size, very short tail, and distinct tertial spots. ♣ Low levels in humid lowland forest; esp. terra firme. ♪ Alarm call: low, rattling "trru"; song: very/extr. high, almost level series of 15–20 piercing, well-separated "tzeet" notes, first few slightly drawn out.

106.7 STAR-THROATED ANTWREN (Choquinha-degarganta-pintada) *Myrmotherula gularis* L 3.5 in./9 cm. No similar species in its range. ♣ Dense understory of humid forest up to 1550 m. ♪ Call: low "tzeet-tzeet -"; song: extr. high, slightly lowered "tzew-tzew - -," ("tzew" about 6 ×). En.

106.8 BROWN-BELLIED ANTWREN (Choquinha-debarriga-parda) *Epinecrophylla* (or *Myrmotherula) gutturalis* L 3.9 in./ 10 cm. ♂ unmistakable by throat pattern in most of range (cf. rufousbacked ♂ **106.10** in small area of contact). Dull ♀ with buff-dotted wing coverts. ♣ Understory of humid forest up to 1000 m. ♪ Song: extr. high, thin, shivering, descending "t-srrrrruw."

106.9 WHITE-EYED ANTWREN (Choquinha-de-olhobranco) *Epinecrophylla* (or *Myrmotherula) leucophthalma* L 3.9 in./ 10 cm. As in **106.8** and **106.10**, eye color variable, but usually rather pale. Lacks rufous back of **106.10**, except in ssp. *phaeonota* (not shown; Ri. Madeira–Ri. Tapajós), where separated by more edged (less spotted) wing coverts, less crisp throat pattern in ♂, and plain throat in ♀. Cf. ♀ **107.1b**. ♣ Undergrowth of humid lowland forest. ♪ Song: very high, very thin, slightly descending "tsitsitsituw."

106.10 STIPPLE-THROATED ANTWREN (Choquinha-de-garganta-carijó) *Epinecrophylla* (or *Myrmotherula) haematonota* L 3.9 in./10 cm. Note rufous mantle. ♀ with flammulated throat (shown), except in NW. Cf. **106.9** and **107.1**. ♣ Undergrowth of humid lowland forest, esp. terra firme.♪ Song: extr. high, very thin, descending, rapid shiver "tsititi---" (2–3 sec).

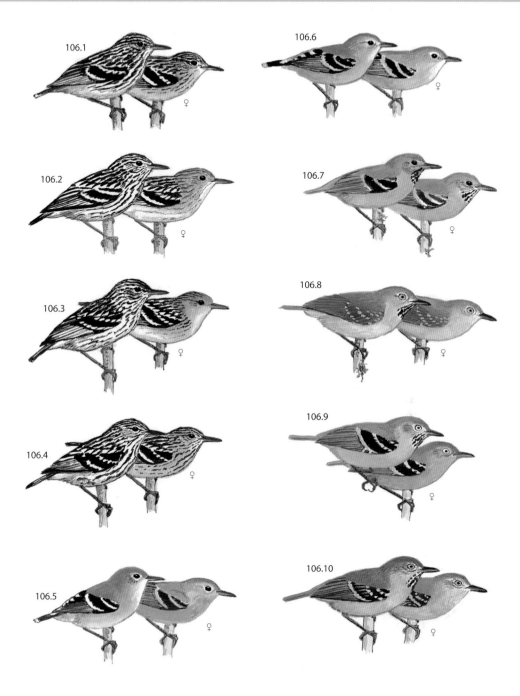

106.1

106.2

106.3

106.4

106.5

106.6

106.7

106.8

106.9

106.10

Plate 107

107.1 ORNATE ANTWREN (Choquinha-ornada)

Epinecrophylla (or *Myrmotherula*) *ornata* L 3.9 in./10 cm. W ssp. *meridionalis* (**a**) and C and E Nom. (**b**) shown. Note small throat-patch in ♂♂. ♀ **a** distinctive, but cf. **106.10**. ♀ **b** from ssp. *phaeonota* of **106.9** by gray-brown (not rufescent-brown) tail and more spotted (less edged) wing coverts. ♣ Low to mid-levels of humid forest up to 900 m. ♪ Call: grating "zee-zee-zee-"; song: extr. high, thin, rattling trill (2 sec).

107.2 RUFOUS-TAILED ANTWREN (Choquinha-de-

cauda-ruiva) *Epinecrophylla* (or *Myrmotherula*) *erythrura* L 4.3 in./11 cm. Rufous tail diagnostic. Black spots on throat of ♂ indistinct or lacking. ♣ Mainly terra firme but also in várzea; up to 600 m. ♪ Call: very/extr. high, ascending and descending, slow rattle; song: unmusical, extr. high, slightly descending "seep-seep-seep- -" (up to 10 ×).

107.3 WHITE-FLANKED ANTWREN (Choquinha-de-

flanco-branco) *Myrmotherula axillaris* L 3.9 in./10 cm. NW *melaena* (**a**) and E *luctuosa* (**b**) shown. ♂♂ of remaining sspp. resemble ♂ **b** with more white to flanks; ♀♀ as ♀ **a**. Regularly flicks wings, revealing diagnostic whitish flanks. ♣ Low to mid-levels of humid forest; up to 1200 m. ♪ Song: high, nasal series of "Iew" notes at irregular intervals.

107.4 RIO DE JANEIRO ANTWREN (Choquinha-

fluminense) *Myrmotherula fluminensis* L 3.9 in./10 cm. ♂ lacks whitish flanks of ♂ **107.3b**; underparts much more black than those of ♂ **107.7**. Very rare: ♀ unknown. ♣ Possibly forest or woodland at low elevations. ♪ Not known. En, R, possibly extinct.

107.5 RIO SUNO ANTWREN (Choquinha-do-oeste)

Myrmotherula sunensis L 3.5 in./9 cm. Small range. ♂ darker, shorter tailed, and with smaller wing spots than ♂ **107.6**. ♀ less gray above than ♀ **107.6b** and ♀ **108.3a** ♣ Low to mid-levels of humid lowland forest. ♪ Song: very/extr. high, nasal, slightly descending "swee-swee-swee."

107.6 LONG-WINGED ANTWREN (Choquinha-de-

asa-comprida) *Myrmotherula longipennis* L 3.9 in./10 cm. In range, white scapulars (often hard to see) distinguish it from all but pale-flanked ♂ **107.3**. ♀ variable: N Nom. (**a**; white belly diagnostic), SW *garbei* (**b**; upperparts grayer than ♀ **107.5**, but less gray than in ♀ **108.4a**), SC *ochrogyna* (**c**; cf. ♀ **108.4b**), and SE *paraensis* (**d**; face sides buffier than ♀ **108.4c**). SC *transitiva* (not shown) resembles **c**. Flick wings, but does not wag tail sideways as do **107.8** and **107.9**. ♣ Mainly in understory of terra firme, but also in várzea. ♪ Song: varied; e.g., slow series of high, nasal "suee" notes or very high, rising "tui-tui- -" (5–6 × "tui").

107.7 SALVADORI'S ANTWREN (Choquinha-pequena)

Myrmotherula minor L 3.5 in./9 cm. Short tailed. Lacks whitish flanks and, in ♂, less extensive black bib than **107.3b**. ♀ with gray crown, unlike ♀ **107.9**. Also cf. **108.2**. ♣ Low to mid-levels of forest and old woodland; up to 900 m. ♪ Song: short twittering, starting extr. high, completed by liquid "tyweet-tweet-tueet." En, R.

107.8 IHERING'S ANTWREN (Choquinha-de-ihering)

Myrmotherula iheringi L 3.5 in./9 cm. ♂ from ♂ **107.6** by black bib extending onto malar, and lack of white tail-tip. ♀ with distinctive ♂-like wing-pattern. ♣ Low to mid-levels of humid lowland forest. ♪ Song: resounding series of slightly rising, evenly spaced "peep" notes (5–25).

107.9 UNICOLORED ANTWREN (Choquinha-cinzenta)

Myrmotherula unicolor L 3.9 in./10 cm. Plain-winged ♂ unmistakable in range. ♀ from ♀ **107.7** by shorter tail and at most a gray tinged crown. Also cf. ♀ **107.3b**. ♣ Mid- to lower levels of lowland forest, old woodland. ♪ Song: irregular series of very high, sharp, drawn-out, well-separated "Seeep" notes. En, R.

107.10 ALAGOAS ANTWREN (Choquinha-de-alagoas)

Myrmotherula snowi L 3.9 in./10 cm. Virtually unmistakable in tiny range (cf. **107.3b**; often found in same flocks). ♣ Mid- to lower levels of semihumid forest; 400–550 m. ♪ Song: irregular series of very high, sharp, drawn-out, well-separated "seeup" notes, each "seeup" descending. En, R.

107.1

107.2

107.3

107.4

107.5

107.6

107.7

107.8

107.9

107.10

Plate 108

108.1 LEADEN ANTWREN (Choquinha-da-várzea)

Myrmotherula assimilis L 3.9 in./ 10 cm. ♂ with diagnostic gray (no black) wing coverts edged white. ♂ with semiconcealed white dorsal patch, unlike ♂ **108.4**. Note buff bars in ♀. ♣ Low to mid-levels of várzea, forest and shrub near rivers. ♪ Song: short, melodious series starting with two stuttered notes, followed by slightly rising rattle, which changes into a desending trill (4–5 sec).

108.2 PLAIN-WINGED ANTWREN (Choquinha-de-

asa-lisa) *Myrmotherula behni* L 3.5 in./ 9 cm. Plain-winged ♂ unmistakable in range. Dull ♀ lacks whitish belly of ♀ **107.6a**, whitish flanks of ♀ **107.3a**, and grayish back of ♀ **108.4a**. ♣ Low to mid-levels of humid forest; 1000–1800 m. ♪ Song: series of high, simple, slightly downslurred "tiuw" notes.

108.3 BAND-TAILED ANTWREN (Choquinha-de-ra-

bo-cintado) *Myrmotherula urosticta* L 3.9 in./10 cm. Broad white tail-tip diagnostic, but cf. **107.3b** with narrow tip, larger black bib, and whitish flanks. ♣ Low to mid-levels of lowland forest. ♪ Song: short series of 4–5 very high, nasal, well-separated, sharply upslurred "tjeuwi" notes. En, R.

108.4 GRAY ANTWREN (Choquinha-de-garganta-

cinza) *Myrmotherula menetriesii* L 3.5 in./9 cm. Short-tailed. ♂ with throat black (**a**; in SW and SC part of range) or plain (**b**; N and E range). ♀ with gray (**a**; W range), grayish olive (**b**; E range) or rufescent (**c**; Ri. Madeira–Ri. Tapajós) back. Cf. **106.5** and **107.6**. ♣ Mid- to upper levels of humid forest up to 1000 m. ♪ Song: ascending series of 6–8 eerie, two-syllabled "wueeih" notes.

108.5 BANDED ANTBIRD (Tovaquinha) *Dichrozona*

cincta L 3.9 in./10 cm. Lower wing bar and white/buff (♂/♀) rump form unique band. ♣ Low levels of terra firme up to 800 m. Rather terrestrial. ♪ Song: slow, gradually rising series of about 15–20 drawn-out, loud, very sharp "tueét" notes.

108.6 STRIPE-BACKED ANTBIRD (Piu-piu) *Myr-

morchilus strigilatus* L 6.3 in./16 cm. Recognizable by terrestrial behavior and streaked mantle. ♣ Low levels in woodland and scrub; up to 1100 m. ♪ Very/extr. high, sharp "sreet-soweét," sometimes immediately followed by strident, slightly descending "sreet-sreet-sreet-sruw-sruw."

108.7 DOT-WINGED ANTWREN (Papa-formiga-de-

bando) *Microrhopias quixensis* L 4.7 in./12 cm. Black ♂♂ of all sspp. with white wing markings and long tail with large white tips (may appear all-white from below). ♀ unmistakable; C *bicolor* (**a**; W and NE sspp. similar, but with blacker upperparts) and SE *emiliae* (**b**) shown. ♣ Mid- to lower levels of humid lowland forest. ♪ Song: may vary according to ssp. and even to sex; e.g., very high, sharp "tu-TwéeTwée-tdrrr" (2nd part much higher and louder) or very high, loud "tutweetwee-tdrrrrr," 1st part slow and descending, followed by rattling 2nd part, which is longer and higher.

108.8 STREAK-CAPPED ANTWREN (Zidedę) *Terenura*

maculata L 3.9 in./10 cm. Virtually unmistakable in range, but cf. ♀ **109.9**. ♣ Upperstory of Atlantic forest and second growth. Up to 1250 m. ♪ Call: very high, sharp, hurried "pichée-pichée- -"(3–4 ×); song: high, sharp, ringing rattle, like "trrrrr" (3 sec).

108.9 ORANGE-BELLIED (or Alagoas) **ANTWREN**

(Zididę-do-nordeste) *Terenura sicki* L 3.9 in./10 cm. Unmistakable in tiny range. ♣ High levels of semi-humid forest; 200–700 m. ♪ Song: e.g., very high, very sharp "tewée-tuwée-titititi," diminishing in strength, or very/extr. high "srrrr" (3 sec). En, R.

108.10 CHESTNUT-SHOULDERED ANTWREN (Zidedę-

de-encontro) *Terenura humeralis* L 3.9 in./10 cm. Virtually unmistakable in range. ♣ Canopy of humid lowland forest, esp. terra firme. ♪ Song: very high, thin, slightly descending, gradually accelerating to a "fuh-fuh-weet-weet-d-rrrr" rattle.

108.11 ASH-WINGED ANTWREN (Zidedę-de-asa-

cinza) *Terenura spodioptila* L 3.9 in./ 10 cm. ♣ Virtually unmistakable. Vaguely similar to some *Myrmotherula* antwrens (Pl. **107** and **108**). ♣ Canopy of humid forest, esp. terra firme. Up to 1100 m. ♪ Song: very high, thin, bouncing, descending, trilled rattle ending in 3 well-separated notes, like "tsee-tsee-tsee-tsititrtrtr-tuut-tuut-tuut."

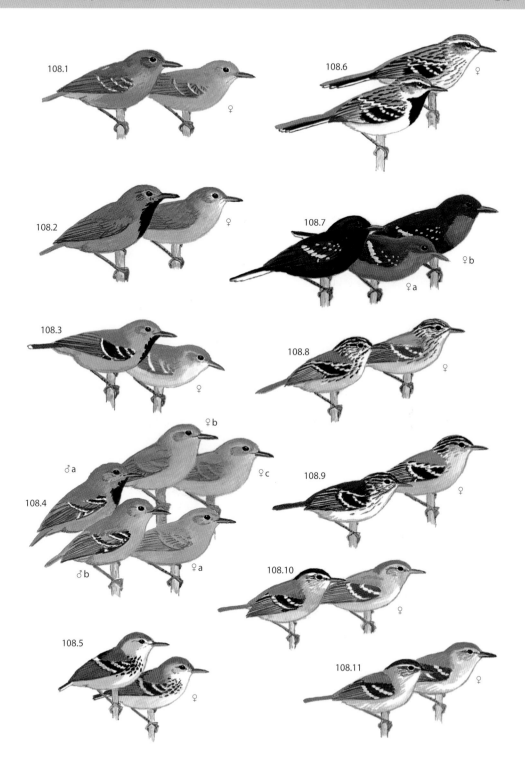

108.1

108.2 ♀

108.3

108.4 ♀b ♂a ♀c ♂b ♀a

108.5 ♀

108.6 ♀

108.7 ♀b ♀a

108.8 ♀

108.9 ♀

108.10 ♀

108.11 ♀

Plate 109

109.1 BAHIA (or Pileated) **ANTWREN** (Corozinho-de-boné) *Herpsilochmus pileatus* L 4.3 in./ 11 cm. ♂ virtually inseparable from ♂ **109.2** (note range). ♀ is ♂-like with less buff below than ♀ **109.2**. ♣ Mid- to upper levels of coastal woodland. ♪ Song: fast series of very high, rising "toot" notes, accelerating to a rattle (2–3 sec). En, R.

109.2 BLACK-CAPPED ANTWREN (Chorozinho-de-chapéu-preto) *Herpsilochmus atri-capillus* L 4.7 in./12 cm. Cf. **109.1**. ♣ Middle and lower forest strata, riverine belts, caatinga woodland, normally below 800 m. ♪ Song: very high, slightly rising, "tuh-wrrrrrrih," 1st note almost inaudible, 2nd part descending at the end.

109.3 SPOT-TAILED ANTWREN (Chorozinho-de-cauda-pintada) *Herpsilochmus stic-* *turus* L 3.9 in./10 cm. ♂ with all-black crown. ♀ with rufous streaks on crown (not easily seen). Cf. **109.4**. ♣ Mid- to upper levels of humid forest; esp. near water. Up to 550 m. ♪ Song: short, very high, staccato series changing to a rattle (1st 2–4 notes slightly rising).

109.4 TODD'S ANTWREN (Chorozinho-de-cabeça-pintada) *Herpsilochmus stictocephalus* L 4.3 in./11 cm. ♂ from very similar ♂ **109.3** by tiny white spots on forehead; ♀ from **109.3** by white streaks on crown and buff chest (at most a faint tinge in ♀ **109.3**). ♣ Canopy of humid forest up to 700 m. ♪ Song: short, high, rapid series of about 12 notes, which descend and slow down at the end.

109.5 SPOT-BACKED ANTWREN (Chorozinho-de-costas-manchadas) *Herpsilochmus* *dorsimaculatus* L 4.7 in./12 cm. No similar species in range and habitat. Resembles **109.4**, but back blacker and ♀ with deeper, more extensive buff. ♣ Mid- and upper levels of humid forest. Up to 600 m. ♪ Song: very high, fast, slightly rising, then descending and fading, trilling "wiwiwurrrrrrr" series (2 sec).

109.6 RORAIMAN ANTWREN (Chorozinho-de-roraima) *Herpsilochmus roraimae* L 5.1 in./13 cm. Crown unspotted. Note tail pattern. Resembles **109.4**, but tail longer and with more spots. ♣ Mid- to upper levels of humid forest; 700–2000 m. ♪ Song: very high, loud, fast, chipping series of about 12 notes, the last 3–4 descending and decelerating.

109.7 PECTORAL ANTWREN (Chorozinho-de-papo-preto) *Herpsilochmus pectoralis* L 4.7 in./12 cm. ♂ with diagnostic black spot on chest. ♀ duller and smaller than ♀ **109.8** (note range). ♣ Deciduous forest, woodland, caatinga, riverine growth. Up to 850 m. ♪ Song: high, very fast chattering series of "tututjdrrrrrr" notes, which rise rather sharply at the start and may finish slightly falling-off to an abrupt ending (2–3 sec). En, R.

109.8 LARGE-BILLED ANTWREN (Chorozinho-de-bico-comprido) *Herpsilochmus lon-* *girostris* L 5.1 in./13 cm. Large with relatively heavy bill. ♂ with diagnostic faint gray spots on underparts, esp. chest. Bright ♀ distinctive. ♪ ♣ Dry to deciduous forest, palm groves. Up to 1100 m. ♪ Song: high, fast, chattering series, rising at start, descending and decelerating at end, given by ♂, immediately echoed by ♀.

109.9 RUFOUS-WINGED ANTWREN (Chorozinho-de-asa-vermelha) *Herpsilochmus* *rufimarginatus* L 4.7 in./12 cm. SE Nom. (**a**) and widespread *frater/scapularis* (**b**) shown. Rufous wing-patch diagnostic. ♣ Mid- to upper levels of forest, woodland. Up to 1500 m. ♪ Song: high, descending series of "jupjup" notes, replaced in the middle by a rattling "jup-jup-jrrrr-jup-jup" trill. Other chattering variations include one in which the rattle in the middle is sharply raised and the last part is shortened to 1 note.

109.10 CAATINGA ANTWREN (Chorozinho-da-caatinga) *Herpsilochmus sellowi* L 4.3 in./ 11 cm. ♂ resembles ♂ **109.2**, but cheek cleaner. ♀ with faintly buff-mottled crown. ♣ Mid- to upper levels of caatinga (absent from the driest parts), semideciduous forest, woodland. Up to 1100 m. ♪ Song: very high, short, fast rattle, like "wrrrrru"; somewhat rising at start and lowered at end. En, R.

Plate 110

110.1 NARROW-BILLED ANTWREN (Formigueiro-do-nordeste) *Formicivora iheringi* L 4.7 in./12 cm. Virtually unmistakable, but cf. short-tailed **107.3b**. ♣ Low to mid-levels of deciduous forest; 250–1100 m. ♪ Song: series of very high, loud "tiúw" notes (2/sec over 8 sec). En, R.

110.2 WHITE-FRINGED ANTWREN (Papa-formiga-pardo) *Formicivora grisea* L 5.1 in./13 cm. ♂ from ♂ **110.3** by narrower white eyebrow and broader white flanks. ♀ distinctive. ♣ Woodland, caatinga, second growth, shrub. Up 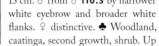 to 1000 m. ♪ Song: crescendoing series of high, harsh "piuw" notes (3/sec over 8 sec).

110.3 BLACK-BELLIED ANTWREN (Formigueiro-de-barriga-preta) *Formicivora melanogaster* L 5.1 in./13 cm. ♂ resembles ♂ **110.2**. ♀ distinctive in range. ♣ Low to mid-levels of deciduous forest, woodland, caatinga, tall shrub. Up to 1050 m. ♪ Song: slow series of high, nasal "tjew" notes (2/sec over 8 sec).

110.4 SERRA ANTWREN (Formigueiro-da-serra) *Formicivora serrana* L 5.1 in./13 cm. Nom. (**a**, N part of range) and S ssp. *interposita* (**b**) shown. Not in range of **110.3** and **110.5**. ♣ Low levels at edge of semihumid forest, woodland, shrub, eucalyptus plantations. Up to 1550 m. ♪ Song: rapid series of high, dry notes (3–4/sec over 3–4 sec). En.

110.5 RESTINGA ANTWREN (Formigueiro-do-litoral) *Formicivora littoralis* L 5.5 in./14 cm. Unmistakable in range and habitat. ♣ Low levels in coastal shrub and thickets. ♪ Song: low, rattling, level series of "tjatjatja---"notes (2 sec). En, R.

110.6 BLACK-HOODED ANTWREN (Formigueiro-de-cabeça-negra) *Formicivora erythronotos* L 4.3 in./11 cm. Unmistakable in restricted range. ♣ Undergrowth of secondary forest, shrub, and abandoned banana plantations near the coast. ♪ Song: high, level, rattling "tjotjotjo---" (2–3 sec). En, R.

110.7 RUSTY-BACKED ANTWREN (Papa-formiga-vermelho) *Formicivora rufa* L 5.1 in./13 cm. Note rusty upperparts and ochre-buff flanks. ♣ Undergrowth of cerrado, savanna with scattered trees and shrub, open forest, wet grassland, scrub. ♪ Song: high, nasal, nervous-sounding rattles and trills.

110.8 SINCORÁ ANTWREN (Papa-formiga-do-sincorá) *Formicivora grantsaui* L 5.1 in./13 cm. Differs from **110.7** by less rufescent upperparts, brown flanks, and gray-and-white (not plain white) underwing coverts. ♣ Low scrub in eroded areas at rocky slopes and ridges above 800 m. ♪ Song: slow (2 notes/sec) series of very short, very high "tjew" notes. En.

110.9 PARANA ANTWREN (or Long-billed or Marsh Antbird) (Bicudinho-do-brejo) *Stymphalornis (or Formicivora) acutirostris* L 5.5 in./14 cm. Unmistakable in small range. ♣ Marsh with tall grasses and shrub, wet fields, mangrove swamps. ♪ Song: slow, leisurely series of 2–4 high "tjew" notes or slow series of high, double-noted "kreTif- -" notes (5–6 ×). En, R.

110.10 SAO PAULO ANTWREN (Bicudinho-do-brejo-paulista) L 5.5 in./14 cm. Unmistakable in small range. ♣ Marsh with tall grasses and shrub. *Note:* Recently discovered; still undescribed. En.

110.1

110.6 ♀

110.2 ♀

110.7 ♀

110.3 ♀

110.8 ♀

b   a

110.4

110.9 ♀

110.5 ♀

110.10 ♀

Plate 111

111.1 FERRUGINOUS ANTBIRD (Trovoada) *Drymo-*

phila ferruginea L 5.1 in./13 cm. ♂ from ♂ **111.2** by blacker back and darker rufous underparts, extending farther down (only lower belly and vent paler and browner). ♀ with pale-streaked black crown (all brown in ♀ **111.2**). ♣ Bamboo stands in/near humid forest, woodland. Up to 1200 m (infrequently to 1600 m). ♪ Song: very high, loud, sharp "tit-tuweéh" (1 × or 3 × without interval). En.

111.2 BERTONI'S ANTBIRD (Trovoada-de-bertoni)

Drymophila rubricollis L 5.1 in./13 cm. Cf. **111.1**. ♣ Bamboo stands in/near humid forest. Up to 2000 m, in N only above 900 m. ♪ Song: series of about 6–10 thin, sharp notes, starting very high, descending steeply, and accelerating to drawn-out last two notes.

111.3 RUFOUS-TAILED ANTBIRD (Choquinha-da-

serra) *Drymophila genei* L 5.5 in./14 cm. Rufous tail diagnostic. ♣ Bamboo stands in/near humid forest; 800–2200 m. ♪ Song: series of 6–7 notes, starting with very high "sih," then jumping to lower nasal "theéh" notes, the total as "síhtjeéh-tjeéh-tjeéh." En, R.

111.4 OCHRE-RUMPED ANTBIRD (Choquinha-de-

dorso-vermelho) *Drymophila ochro-pyga* L 5.1 in./13 cm. Combination of streaked chest, ochre-rufous lower underparts, and mainly black tail diagnostic. ♣ Bamboo and vines in montane forest; 300–1950 m. ♪ Song: 2-noted "Tí-zzzzèh," 1st note very high and sharp, 2nd drawn-out and hoarse. En, R.

111.5 STRIATED ANTBIRD (Trovoada-listrada) *Dry-*

mophila devillei L 5.5 in./14 cm. Two sspp.: W Nom. (**a;** ♀ shown) and E *subochracea* Xingu Antbird (**b;** ♀ as ♀ **a**, but underparts virtually un-streaked ochre-buff). No relatives in range, but cf. **113.6**. ♣ Bamboo thickets in forest; up to 1000 m. ♪ Song: very high, strident ""wic-Wic-Wic-tidrrrrn," last part bouncing down.

111.6 DUSKY-TAILED ANTBIRD (Choquinha-carijó)

Drymophila malura L 5.5 in./14 cm. Note uniform gray/brown (♂/♀) tail and faint eyebrow. ♣ Dense undergrowth of humid forest and woodland. Up to 1400 m, locally to 1900 m. ♪ Song: very high series starting with "tsip tsip", then accelerating and slightly descending to a rattling trill (4 sec). ♀ may chime-in with similar but weaker song.

111.7 SCALED ANTBIRD (Pintadinho) *Drymophila*

squamata L 5.1 in./13 cm. Spotted pattern and tail barring distinctive. ♣ Dense undergrowth of forest and woodland up to 1100 m. ♪ Extr. high, calm series of 4–7 sharp, pushed-out, descending notes. En.

111.8 WHITE-BACKED FIRE-EYE (Papa-taoca) *Pyri-*

glena leuconota L 6.7 in./17 cm. ♀♀ variable; typical form (**a**) and sspp. *maura* (**b**; Pantanal region) and *similis* (**c**; SC Amazon) shown. Note bright red eyes of all sspp. No over-lap with **111.9, 111.10,** or **115.8**. ♣ Understory of forest, woodland, riverine belts. Up to 900 m. ♪ Call: nasal "tjew-tjew"; song: rapid, slightly rising, then descending series of very high, staccato "weet---" notes (2 sec).

111.9 WHITE-SHOULDERED FIRE-EYE (Papa-taoca-

do-sul) *Pyriglena leucoptera* L 6.7 in./17 cm. Unmistakable in range. 2nd white wing bar near shoulder of ♂ often concealed (as shown). ♣ Understory of forest, old second growth, plantations. Often near bamboo. Up to 1300 m. ♪ Call: very high, chipping "tjew tjew -"; song: slow, short series of about 5 descending, fluted notes.

111.10 FRINGE-BACKED FIRE-EYE (Papa-taoca-da-

bahia) *Pyriglena atra* L 6.7 in./17 cm. Unmistakable in small range. ♣ Understory of forest edge, tall sec-ond growth. ♪ Call: very high, piped "peek"; song: hurried, descending series of about 6 "peeh---" notes. En, R.

Plate 112

112.1 GRAY ANTBIRD (Chororó-pocuá) *Cercomacra* *cinerascens* L 5.5 in./14 cm. Gray/ rather dull (♂/♀) with broad white tail-tips. Faint or no wing spots in N. ♣ Subcanopy with understory vine tangles in humid lowland forest, tall second growth. ♪ Song: strange, rather toneless, froglike "krísh-wruh" or "wruh-krísh" (3 ×).

112.2 RIO DE JANEIRO ANTBIRD (Chororó-cinzento) *Cercomacra brasiliana* L 5.5 in./14 cm. Only *Cercomacra* antbird in range.♣ Thick undergrowth of forest, second growth. Up to 950 m. ♪ Song: low, soft "crunk - -" (4–6 ×). En, R.

112.3 DUSKY ANTBIRD (Chororá-escuro) *Cercomacra* *tyrannina* L 5.5 in./14 cm. Two sspp.; W Nom. shown. In E *saturatior*, ♂ usually with a few white bars to vent; ♀ with ear-patch chestnut-rufous (not olive-gray). In dark gray ♂♂ of both sspp., note narrow white wing edging and tail tip (latter sometimes worn off). Cf. **112.1**, **112.4**, and **112.10**. ♣ Thick undergrowth of humid forest; esp. at edge; up to 1200 m. ♪ Song: very high, rapid series of rather liquid notes, the 1st 1–2 lower, the last 3–5 bouncing down.

112.4 BLACKISH ANTBIRD (Chororó-negro) *Cerco-* *macra nigrescens* L 5.9 in./15 cm. ♂ dark gray with plain tail and narrow white wing edging. ♀ with rich rufous underparts and forecrown. Cf. **112.1**, **112.3**, **112.6**, and **112.10**. ♣ Thick undergrowth of humid forest, woodland, thickets. Up to 900 m. ♪ Song of ♂: musical "pur-tidrrrr," 2nd part bouncing and much higher, often answered by ♀ with series of 8–10 sharp, steeply rising notes.

112.5 BANANAL ANTBIRD (Chororó-de-goiás) *Cerco-* *macra ferdinandi* L 6.3 in./16 cm. No similar species in small range. Broad white tail tips. ♀ with faint white streaks on throat and chest. ♣ Mid- to low levels of humid forest and woodland near water. ♪ Call: very fast, very high "wididi"; song: hurried, squeaky "tudr-tudr-tudr" randomly combined with call. En.

112.6 BLACK ANTBIRD (Chororó-preto) *Cercomacra* *serva* L 5.5 in./14 cm. ♂ blacker (esp. chest) than ♂ **112.4**. Tail plain. ♀ from ♀ **112.4** by lack of broad rufous forecrown. ♣ Dense undergrowth of humid lowland forests, second growth. ♪ Song: slow series of 8–10 well-spaced, slightly accelerating, rising "wrut wrut wrut-writ-writwit-reetreet" notes (the last two at same pitch).

112.7 RIO BRANCO ANTBIRD (Chororó-do-rio- branco) *Cercomacra carbonaria* L 5.9 in./15 cm. Unmistakable in small range. ♣ Low to mid-levels of thickets in forest, woodland, second growth. Always near rivers. ♪ Song: low, slow, short series of 4–5 pairs of mewing double "kurih-kurih- -" notes (with "ku" sounding as clicking pebbles). R.

112.8 MANU ANTBIRD (Chororó-de-manu) *Cercoma-* *cra manu* L 5.9 in./15 cm. Unmistakable in small range. ♣ Low to mid-levels of thickets in forest, woodland, second growth. Always near rivers. ♪ Song: low, short series of 2–4 rather laborious, cackled double notes, often together with slightly higher-pitched, unsynchronized counter-song of ♀.

112.9 MATO GROSSO ANTBIRD (Chororó-do-panta- nal) *Cercomacra melanaria* L 6.3 in./ 16 cm. Virtually unmistakable in range. Note rather long, white-tipped tail. ♣ Dense undergrowth of deciduous forest, gallery forest, woodland. Often near water. Lowlands. ♪ Song: Very low, very dry, froglike "krokreééh-tjow," often together with high, strident "chip-chip- -" of ♀.

112.10 WILLIS'S ANTBIRD (Chororó-didi) *Cercomacra* *laeta* L 5.5 in./14 cm. Three sspp.: *waimiri* (**a**; W part of range), *sabinoi* (**b**; E part) and Nom. (not shown; C part). ♂♂ of **b** and Nom. have narrow white tail tips and are virtually unmistakable in range (cf. **112.1**). ♂ **a** from very similar ♂ **112.4** by broader white wing edging. Lacks narrow white tail tip and edging to vent of overlapping ssp. of **112.3**. ♀ **a** with diagnostic dark-gray wing coverts with distinct cinnamon-brown edge. ♣ Dense undergrowth of humid lowland forest, woodland, second growth. Overlaps with **112.3**, esp. in shrubby, wet section of white-sand woodland. ♪ Song: very high, short, very sharp "puh-wéedi-wéedi-wéedih" ("wéedi" 2–5 ×).

Plate 113

113.1 SLENDER ANTBIRD (Gravatazeiro) *Rhopornis ardesiaca* L 7.5 in./19 cm. Unmistakable in small range. Note long tail.

♣ Low in dense, dry forest near patches of terrestrial bromeliads. At 100–1000 m. ♪ Very high, loud, increasing series of 7–9 rather sharp "peer" notes without intervals. En, R.

113.2 [BLACK-TAILED ANTBIRD (Formigueiro-de-rabo-preto) *Myrmoborus melanurus*]

L 5.1 in./13 cm. ♂ is dark gray with slightly blacker head. Note dusky mask of ♀. ♣ Várzea. ♪ Song: descending, accelerating series of loud, resounding notes, which bounce down (3 sec).

113.3 WHITE-BROWED ANTBIRD (Papa-formiga-de-sobrancelha) *Myrmoborus leucophrys*

L 5.1 in./13 cm. Eyebrow distinct. Wings plain (♂) or only faintly marked (♀). ♣ Low levels of humid forest edge, várzea, thickets. Up to 1000 m. ♪ Song: very high, loud, slightly descending, hurried series of ringing notes (3 sec).

113.4 ASH-BREASTED ANTBIRD (Formigueiro-liso) *Myrmoborus lugubris* L 5.1 in./13 cm.

♀♀ variable; E Nom. (**a**; with strong contrast between white underparts and brown upperparts), W ssp. *berlepschi* (**b**, with pale gray belly), and C *stictopterus/femininus* (**c**). ♣ Dense undergrowth of humid lowland forest near rivers; mainly on river islands. ♪ Song: as **113.3**, but slower (notes countable) (4–5 sec).

113.5 BLACK-FACED ANTBIRD (Formigueiro-de-cara-preta) *Myrmoborus myotherinus*

L 5.1 in./13 cm. Several sspp., all with wing bars, black mask, and red eyes, varying in color of underparts; E *ochrolaema* (**a**) and C *ardesiacus* (**b**) shown. ♣ Dense undergrowth of humid forest (mainly terra firme) and nearby habitats. Up to 900 m. ♪ Song: short, slow, descending series of 5 rather sharp, evenly spaced "zree-zree-zree-zrut-zrut" notes.

113.6 WARBLING ANTBIRD (Papa-formiga-cantador) *Hypocnemis cantator* L 4.7 in./12 cm.

Plain tail far shorter than superficially similar **111.5**. ♣ Dense undegrowth of lowland forest and woodland.

NOTE: 113.6 is recently split on voice and plumage features into 6 species (no overlap between species, except **c** and **d**): **113.6a**: GUIANAN WARBLING ANTBIRD *Hypocnemis cantator*, shown. **113.6b**: IMERI WARBLING ANTBIRD *Hypocnemis flavescens*, not shown; as **a**, but pale yellowish below. **113.6c**: PERUVIAN WARBLING ANTBIRD *Hypocnemis peruviana*, not shown; as **a**, but with stronger black markings in both sexes. **113.6d**: YELLOW-BREASTED WARBLING ANTBIRD *Hypocnemis subflava*, ♂ shown; ♀ with more olive back and buffier wing spots. **113.6E**: RONDONIA WARBLING ANTBIRD *Hypocnemis ochrogyna*, not shown; resembles **a**. **113.6F**: SPIX'S WARBLING ANTBIRD *Hypocnemis striata* En, not shown; resembles **a**.

113.7 YELLOW-BROWED ANTBIRD (Cantador-amarelo) *Hypocnemis hypoxantha* L 4.7 in./12 cm. W Nom. (**a**) and E ssp. *ochraceiventris* (**b**).

Note in both yellow (not white) eyebrow and rather plain back. ♣ Dense undergrowth of lowland forest and nearby shrub. ♪ Song: descending, decelerating series of about 5–8 notes, fluted at first, but gradually becoming more scratchy; slower and starting higher pitched than that of **113.6**.

113.8 BLACK-CHINNED ANTBIRD (Solta-asa-do-norte) *Hypocnemoides melanopogon* L 4.7 in./12 cm. Cf. **113.9** ♣ As **113.9**.

♪ Song: series of 8–12 high, accentuated "few" notes, 1st 2–3 evenly-spaced and rising, then as "djew" notes accelerating and bouncing down.

113.9 BAND-TAILED ANTBIRD (Solta-asa) *Hypocnemoides maculicauda* L 4.7 in./12 cm. Very similar to **113.8** (note range), but white tail tip slightly broader and semiconcealed white interscapular patch. Superficially similar ant-

wrens (Pl. **105–108**) smaller, lack pale gray eyes, and have narrower white tail tip. ♣ Undergrowth of várzea, swamps, forest and woodland near water. Lowlands. ♪ Song: strong, accelerating series of loud raspy notes, rising in strength and pitch to a sharp rattle, then falling and decelerating (5–6 sec).

113.10 BLACK-AND-WHITE ANTBIRD (Formigueiro-preto-e-branco) *Myrmochanes hemileucus* L 4.3 in./11 cm. Small and almost unmistakable, but cf. seed-eaters (Pl. **181** and **182**). ♣ Low levels of thickets, shrub and woodland

edge on river islands. ♪ Song: very short "tiderrru," bouncing down.

Plate 114

114.1 SILVERED ANTBIRD (Papa-formiga-do-igarapé)

Sclateria naevia L 5.9 in./15 cm. Legs pinkish. Three sspp.: W *argentata* (**a**), NE Nom. (**b**), and SE *toddi* (not shown; ♂ 'intermediate between **a** and **b**, ♀ as ♀ **a**, but less white below). ♂ **a** resembles ♂ **115.4**. ♀ **a** and ssp. *toddi* paler below (esp. on throat and mid-belly) than ♀♀ **114.6A**. ♣ At edges and in thickets of streams and rivers in várzea, esp. under overhanging vines; also in marsh, swampy areas. ♪ Song: very high, rapid series of "jip---" notes, after a short stutter lowered in pitch, then rising in pitch and strength, trailing off at the end (4–5 sec).

114.2 SLATE-COLORED ANTBIRD (Formigueiro-cinza) *Schistocichla* (or *Percnostola*)

schistacea L 5.5 in./14 cm. ♂ from ♂ **114.6A** ssp. *subplumbea* by gray (not brown) eyes and black (not gray) lower mandible. Differs from **114.6B** by gray legs and rufous ear coverts in ♀. ♣ Understory of terra firme. ♪ Song: slow, short series of high, loud, piercing "teew" notes, increasing in strength and slightly in pitch.

114.3 AMAZONAS ANTBIRD (Formigueiro-de-pelzeln)

Percnostola minor L 5.5 in./14 cm. Often includes **114.4** as a ssp., but eyes gray (not reddish). Note wing edging (not spotting), black crown of ♂ and rufous head of ♀. ♣ Undergrowth of lowland forest, old woodland. ♪ Song: as **114.4**, but slightly faster.

114.4 BLACK-HEADED ANTBIRD *Schistocichla* (or *Percnostola*) *rufifrons* (Formigueiro-de-cabeça-preta) L 5.5 in./14 cm. ♂

from ♂ **114.3** by red, not gray, eyes. May show slight crest. ♀ from ♀ **114.3** by red eyes. ♣ Low forest with dense undergrowth. ♪ Song: high, calm, decelerating series of loud sharp "tieew" notes.

114.5 CAURA ANTBIRD (Formigueiro-do-caura) *Schistocichla* (or *Percnostola*) *caurensis* L

7.5 in./19 cm. Larger and less dark than **114.7**. ♣ Open understory and floor of humid forest up to 1500 m. ♪ Song: very high, loud, descending series of about 10 piercing, lilting, descending "sreek" notes.

114.6A SPOT-WINGED ANTBIRD (Formigueiro-de-asa-pintada) *Schistocichla* (or *Percnostola*) *leucostigma* L 5.9 in./15 cm.

Three sspp.: NE Nom. (**a**, legs pinkish), NW *infuscata* (**b**, legs gray), and SW *subplumbea* (not shown; as **a**, but legs gray and wing spots of ♂ smaller). Note white/

cinnamon (♂/♀) spots (not edging) on wings. Cf. **114.2**, **114.5**, **114.6B**, **114.7**. ♣ Understory of humid forest, esp. terra firme; up to 700 m. *Note*: Traditionally **114.6B**, **114.6C**, and **114.7** included as sspp. ♪ Song: in SW, series of rather sharp "chi---" notes, 1st 2–3 level and very high, then gradually shivering-down (2–3 sec); in NE, very high, level, powerful, sharp almost-rattle (4 sec).

114.6B HUMAITA ANTBIRD *Schistocichla* (or *Percnostola*) *humaythae* L 5.9 in./15 cm. Contact with **114.6A** possibly in Ri. Javarí region. Note pink (not gray) legs, unlike **114.2** and W sspp. of **114.6A**. ♀ lacks whitish throat and central underparts of ♀ **114.1a**. ♣ Understory of humid lowland forest, esp. terra firme.

114.6C RUFOUS-FACED ANTBIRD *Schistocichla* (or *Percnostola*) *rufifacies* L 5.9 in./15 cm. Note pinkish (not gray) legs. ♂ as ♂ **114.6B**, but no overlap in range. ♀ lacks white throat and central belly of ♀ **114.1** ssp. *toddi*. ♣ Understory of humid lowland forest, esp. terra firme. En.

114.7 RORAIMAN ANTBIRD *Schistocichla* (or *Percnostola*) *saturata* (Formigueiro-de-roraima)

L 5.9 in./15 cm. Resembles **114.6Ab** (note altitude), but ♂ more uniform dark and ♀ darker overall with grayer ear patch. ♣ Understory of humid lowland forest above 700 m. ♪ Song: series of slowly starting, accelerating notes, sharply lowered in pitch at end.

114.8 WHITE-LINED ANTBIRD (Formigueiro-do-bambu) *Percnostola lophotes* L 5.5 in./

14 cm. Both sexes with conspicuous crest. ♣ At low levels of bamboo thickets near rivers or forest edge. Occasionally in other dense thickets near rivers. ♪ Song: descending series of "toot" notes, starting very high and hesitantly, but then accelerating and going down. R.

114.9 WHITE-PLUMED ANTBIRD (Papa-formiga-de-topete) *Pithys albifrons* L 4.7 in./

12 cm. Unmistakable. ♣ At ant swarms in humid forest; up to 1350 m. ♪ Call: a low, very high, or extr. high, grating "sreew"; song, very high "tjeeeew," dropping in pitch (1/4 sec).

114.10 PALE-FACED (Bare-eye or) **ANTBIRD** (Mãe-de-taoca-dourada) *Skutchia borbae* L

6.7 in./17 cm. Unmistakable by facial pattern. ♣ At ant swarms in understory of humid lowland forest, esp. terra firme. ♪ Song: 2–3 very high, long, slightly descending notes, the last one esp. rather mournful. En.

Plate 115

115.1 WHITE-BELLIED ANTBIRD (Formigueiro-de-barriga-branca) *Myrmeciza longipes* L 5.9 in./15 cm. Virtually unmistakable. Note small dark (not pale) wing spots of ♀. ♣ Ground and lowest levels in woodland, riverine belts, shrubby forest borders; normally below 700 m. ♪ Song: rapid, compact, descending series of shivering, rather sharp "weew---" notes, decelerating at the end (3–4 sec).

115.2 WHITE-BIBBED ANTBIRD (Formigueiro-asso-biador) *Myrmeciza loricata* L 5.9 in./15 cm. ♂ unmistakable by color pattern; note buff throat of ♀. ♣ Floor of humid forest and tall second growth; 700–1300 m. ♪ Call: very/extr. high, very fast "trititititi"; song: extr. high, descending, rapid series of 3–5 whispered, sawing double "siweesiwee-see" notes. En.

115.3 SQUAMATE ANTBIRD (Papa-formiga-de-grota) *Myrmeciza squamosa* L 5.9 in./15 cm. Differs from **115.2** by narrower eyebrow, white wing spots, lack of large white chest-patch in ♂, and faintly scaled whitish underparts of ♀. ♣ Floor of humid forest, woodland (locally also drier). Up to 1000 m. ♪ Song: like that of **115.2**, but even higher pitched and faster. En.

115.4 YAPACANA ANTBIRD (Formigueiro-de-yapac-ana) *Myrmeciza disjuncta* L 5.1 in./13 cm. Note range. Legs pinkish gray. ♂ from larger ♂ **114.1** by pale lower mandible. ♂ with very narrow white tail tips. ♣ Undergrowth of stunted woodland. Lowlands. ♪ Song: curious, rapid sequence of 1 or 2 almost toneless, rising gratings, immediately followed by very high "pipip" or "pi," the total as "grrrrrr-pipip-grrrrrr-pi."

115.5 GRAY-BELLIED ANTBIRD (Formigueiro-de-barriga-cinza) *Myrmeciza pelzelni* L 5.5 in./14 cm. Note range. ♂ resembles ♂ **116.1**. ♀ unmistakable by pattern below. ♣ Low levels of white-sand forest and woodland. Lowlands. ♪ Song: level series of about 15 very/extr. high "sree" notes without intervals.

115.6 SOUTHERN CHESTNUT-TAILED ANTBIRD (Formigueiro-de-cauda-castanha) *Myrmeciza hemimelaena* L 4.7 in./12 cm. Note gray legs, grayish head, and rufescent upperparts and tail. Cf. **116.1** and **114.6**. ♣ Undergrowth of humid forest and nearby overgrown clearings. Up to 900 m. ♪ Song: short, rapid series of loud rather sharp "tee" notes, the 1st 2 level pitched, then rapidly descending (1–1.5 sec).

115.7 PLUMBEOUS ANTBIRD (Formigueiro-chumbo) *Myrmeciza hyperythra* L 6.7 in./17 cm. Combination of wing spots and blue eyering diagnostic. ♣ Low levels of humid lowland forest, esp. várzea. ♪ Song: at first rising, then leveling-out series of rattling "wee---" notes (2–3 sec).

115.8 WHITE-SHOULDERED ANTBIRD (Formigueiro-grande) *Myrmeciza melanoceps* L 6.7 in./17 cm. ♂ from ♂ **115.10** by blacker plumage, narrower blue eyering, and white shoulder (often not easily seen). ♀ Unmistakable. ♣ Low levels of várzea, forest edge. Mainly near water. ♪ Call: short, very high, rather liquid twitter; song: loud, musical series of about 6–8 pure notes, the 1st 2 as mid-high, hurried "fewfew," the last 4–6 high, decelerating, and sounding like "fiuw - -."

115.9 GOELDI'S ANTBIRD (Formigueiro-de-goeldi) *Myrmeciza goeldii* L 6.7 in./17 cm. No similar species in range with red eyes. ♂ with semiconcealed white interscapular patch. ♂ shorter tailed than ♂ **111.8** (note range). ♣ Low levels of várzea, forest edge, second growth woodland, bamboo hickets. Lowlands. ♪ Song: high, level, fluted series of about 10 loud notes, starting as stuttered "drd," followed by slightly decelerating "yuh - -", together as "drd-yuh-yuh - -."

115.10 SOOTY ANTBIRD (Formigueiro-de-taoca) *Myrmeciza fortis* L 6.7 in./17 cm. ♀ distinctive; ♂ sooty black with white along wing edge (often hard to see). Cf. **115.8**. ♣ Low levels of humid lowland forest, mainly terra firme. ♪ Song: very high, level series of 8–10 loud "tjuh" notes, which increase slightly in strength (3 sec).

115.1

115.2 ♀

115.3 ♀

115.4 ♀

115.5 ♀

115.6 ♀

115.7 ♀

115.8 ♀

115.9 ♀

115.10 ♀

Plate 116

116.1 BLACK-THROATED ANTBIRD (Formigueiro-de-peito-preto) *Myrmeciza atrothorax* L 5.5 in./14 cm. Legs gray, tail black, and upperparts rather dull. Typically (**a**; ♂ often lacks faint white chest-spotting; in SW black on underparts more extensive) with fine wing spots, but dark NW *tenebrosa* (**b**) with all black/rufescent underparts (♂/♀) and wing spots barely visible. ♣ Understory of humid forest, woodland. Up to 1200 m. ♪ Song: very high, slightly decelerating series of 4–8 very sharp "chee" notes, starting with a stuttered "tutu," then slightly rising in strength and in pitch, together as "tutu-chee-cheé- -."

116.2 FERRUGINOUS-BACKED ANTBIRD (Formigueiro-ferrugem) *Myrmeciza ferruginea* L 5.9 in./15 cm. Unmistakable. ♣ Floor of humid lowland forest (esp. terra firme) and woodland. ♪ Song: short, very high, increasing, decelerating "tjutju-tee-tee-teeh," level pitched after "tjutju."

116.3 SCALLOPED ANTBIRD (Formigueiro-de-cauda-ruiva) *Myrmeciza ruficauda* L 5.9 in./15 cm. Differs from **115.3** by buff (not white), indistinct eyebrow. ♣ Floor of humid to semihumid forest and woodland. Up to 950 m. ♪ Song: very high, sharp, almost level, rattling trill. En, R.

116.4 RUFOUS-THROATED ANTBIRD (Mãe-de-taoca-de-garganta-vermelha) *Gymnopithys rufigula* L 4.7 in./12 cm. Unmistakable. Note bright rufous throat and bold bare eyering. ♣ At ant swarms in understory of humid forest, esp. terra firme. Up to 900 m. ♪ Song: complicated; starts with some very high, level, fluted "weee" notes, which accelerate and descend, becoming a short rattle before leveling-out and decelerating as low grating "sree-sree-sree" notes (5 sec).

116.5 WHITE-THROATED ANTBIRD (Mãe-de-taoca-de-cauda-barrada) *Gymnopithys salvini* L 5.1 in./13 cm. Unmistakable. Note barred tail in both sexes and black-barred back of ♀. ♣ At ant swarms in understory of humid forest. Up to 450 m. ♪ Song: slow, resounding series of 3–4 descending, long, upslurred "weeih" notes.

116.6 DOT-BACKED ANTBIRD (Guarda-várzea) *Hylophylax punctulatus* L 3.9 in./10 cm. Differs from **116.7** by partly whitish cheeks, spotted (not plain) rump, and gray (not pinkish) legs. ♣ Understory of várzea; dense vegetation at water. ♪ Song: very high, sharp "sreébeer" or "sree-Beér," constantly repeated (1 ×/2 sec).

116.7 SPOT-BACKED ANTBIRD (Guarda-floresta) *Hylophylax naevius* L 4.3 in./11 cm. Cf. **116.6**. ♂ with gray crown in S. ♣ Undergrowth of humid forest and nearby second growth. Up to 1300 m. ♪ Very/extr. high, slightly descending series of 10–12 strident, run together "tjuwit-" notes; depending on region, "tjuwit" sounding as double note or reduced to "tWít---."

116.8 SCALE-BACKED ANTBIRD (Rendadinho) *Dichropogon* (or *Hylophylax*) *poecilinotus* L 5.1 in./13 cm. Several sspp.: NW *duidae* (**a**; ♂ as ♂ **b**), NE Nom. (**b**), SE *nigrigula* (**c**), far E *vidua* (**d**; ♀ as ♀ **c**), SW and SC *griseiventris* (**e**; ♂ as ♂ **c**) and WC *gutturalis* (not shown; ♂ as ♂ **c**, ♀ as ♀ **a**). ♂♂ of all sspp. and ♀♀ of most sspp, with diagnostic scaly back. Plain-backed ♀♀ (**c**, **d**, **e**) with diagnostic contrasting brown upperparts and gray underparts. ♣ Understory of terra firme up to 1350 m. Locally also in várzea. ♪ Song: very high, sharp series of about 10 "tweeh" notes with little intervals, each note and total series slightly increasing in pitch and speed.

116.9 BLACK-SPOTTED BARE-EYE (Mãe-de-taoca) *Phlegopsis nigromaculata* L 6.7 in./17 cm. Unmistakable. ♣ At low levels near ant swarms in humid lowland forest. ♪ Call: starlinglike, downslurred "sriuuw"; song: 3–4 leisurely "tieuw srew - -" (2nd and 3rd or 4th notes slightly lower pitched).

116.10 REDDISH-WINGED BARE-EYE (Mãe-de-taoca-avermelhada) *Phlegopsis erythroptera* L 7.1 in./18 cm. Unmistakable. ♣ At low levels near ant swarms in humid lowland forest. ♪ Song: series of 4–7 descending, well-separated, shrill notes.

Plate 117

117.1 WING-BANDED ANTBIRD (Pinto-do-mato-carijó) *Myrmornis torquata* L 5.9 in./15 cm. Unmistakable. ♣ Floor of humid forest up to 900 m. ♪ Song: series of 2–30 gradually rising, stressed, ringing "weew" notes.

117.2 BICOLORED (or White-cheeked) **ANTBIRD** (Mãe-de-taoca-bochechuda) *Gymnopithys leucaspis* L 5.5 in./14 cm. Unmistakable by bicolored plumage, bold bare eyering, and black from ear patch to upper flanks. ♣ At ant swarms in understory of humid lowland forest and old woodland. ♪ Song: hurried series starting with very high, fluted "weeh weeh" notes, becoming sharp and higher before hurrying down to a few low snarls 3–4 sec).

117.3 HARLEQUIN ANTBIRD (Mãe-de-taoca-arlequim) *Rhegmatorhina berlepschi* L 5.9 in./15 cm. No similar bird in range. ♣ At ant swarms in understory of humid lowland forest, esp. terra firme. ♪ Song: very high, slightly descending series of loud, sharp notes, the 1st drawn out, the rest becoming shorter. En. *Note*: Insert (**a**) shows a form of unclear affinities known from SW Pará.

117.4 CHESTNUT-CRESTED ANTBIRD (Mãe-de-taoca-cristada) *Rhegmatorhina cristata* L 5.9 in./15 cm. Unmistakable by overall rufous color and bold bare eyering. ♣ At ant swarms in understory of humid lowland forest, esp. terra firme. ♪ Song: slow, slightly accelerating series of 8–10 fluted notes, the 1st slightly lower, the following higher and drawn out, then calmly descending.

117.5 HAIRY-CRESTED ANTBIRD (Mãe-de-taoca-cabeçuda) *Rhegmatorhina melanosticta* L 5.9 in./15 cm. Unmistakable by pale crown and bold bare eyering. ♣ At ant swarms in understory of humid lowland forest, esp. terra firme. ♪ Song: slow series, starting with a few very high, sharp, fluted notes, then descending to a few drawn-out, grating notes.

117.6 WHITE-BREASTED ANTBIRD (Mãe-de-taoca-papuda) *Rhegmatorhina hoffmannsi* L 5.9 in./15 cm. Unmistakable. Note white extending over breast (unlike **117.3a**). ♣ At ant swarms in understory of humid lowland forest, esp. terra firme. ♪ Song: much as **117.5**, but may be less sharp and slightly faster. En.

117.7 BARE-EYED (or Santarem) **ANTBIRD** (Mãe-taoca-de-cara-branca) *Rhegmatorhina gymnops* L 5.5 in./14 cm. Unmistak- able by color and bold bare eyering. ♣ At ant swarms in understory of humid lowland forest, esp. terra firme. ♪ Song: 4–5 very high, descending notes, each one drawn out. En.

117.8 RUFOUS-CAPPED ANTTHRUSH (Galinha-do-mato) *Formicarius colma* L 7.1 in./18 cm. Two forms, **a** with rufous forehead and **b** (in N and W) with black forehead. Color pattern of head with bright rufous reaching mantle diagnostic. ♣ On ground in terra firme, locally in várzea. Up to 1100 m. ♪ Call: very high, decisive "tjew"; song: rapid series of high, musical, run-together notes, 1st slightly descending, then ascending (4–5 sec).

117.9 BLACK-FACED ANTTHRUSH (Pinto-do-mato-de-cara-preta) *Formicarius analis* L 6.7 in./17 cm. Note black throat sharply demarcated from gray breast. ♣ On ground in humid for- est up to 1000 m. ♪ Call: very high, ascending "twuh"; song: melodious "tjuh tididi-tududu" (1st and 2nd part well separated, middle part one note higher pitched).

117.10 RUFOUS-FRONTED ANTTHRUSH (Pinto-domato-de-fronte-ruiva) *Formicarius rufifrons* L 7.1 in./18 cm. Differs from **117.8** by olive crown and nape. ♣ Thickets and bamboo at edges of swampy forest. ♪ Song: series of high, melodious, evenly spaced notes, the middle part 1 note higher pitched, the the last part falling off at the end. R.

Plate 118

118.1 SHORT-TAILED ANTTHRUSH (Tovaca-cam-

painha) *Chamaeza campanisona* L 7.9 in./20 cm. Note olive-brown back, dark-marked rich-buff vent and tail with dark subterminal band, and narrow (often not visible) buff-white tip. Faint spots on throat diagnostic (**118.3** and **118.4** may have spots on malar). ♣ On ground in forest and woodland. Up to 1000 m; mainly below **118.3** and **118.4** in area of overlap. In tepuis up to 1500 m. ♪ Call: high, liquid "wic"; song: hurried series of melodious fluted notes, slightly rising and descending, and ending in some liquid or bubbling notes (also sounding like cackling laughter or like a cymbal roll).

118.2 STRIATED (or Noble) **ANTTHRUSH** (Tovaca-

estriada) *Chamaeza nobilis* L 8.7 in./22 cm. Only *Chamaeza* antthrush in range. ♣ On ground in humid lowland forest; esp. terra firme with sparse undergrowth. ♪ Call: long, accelerating, slightly descending series of low, hollow "hoot" notes, ending in 3–4 lazy barks.

118.3 SUCH'S (or Cryptic) **ANTTHRUSH** (Tovaca-

cantadora) *Chamaeza meruloides* L 7.5 in./19 cm. Resembles larger **118.1**, but tail-tip buff (often not visible) and throat and vent essentially unmarked. ♣ On ground in humid forest. Up to 1500 m. ♪ Song: very beautiful, exceptionally long series of well-accentuated, rising, increasing notes (30 sec). En.

118.4 RUFOUS-TAILED (or Brazilian) **ANTTHRUSH**

(Tovaca-de-rabo-vermelho) *Chamaeza ruficauda* L 7.5 in./19 cm. Resembles **118.1**, but back rufous-brown, tail all-brown, and throat unspotted. ♣ On ground in humid forest and woodland at 600–2200 m. Mainly above **118.1** and **118.3** in area of overlap. ♪ Song: exactly as that of **118.3**, but much faster (6 sec).

118.5 RUFOUS GNATEATER (Chupa-dente) *Conopo-*

phaga lineata L 4.7 in./12 cm. 3 sspp. Shown are ♂ of EC and NE Nom. (**a**; white chest-patch often not visible; SE ssp. *vulgaris* similar) and ♀ of *cearae*, CEARÁ GNATEATER (**b**). Cf. **118.9** (only other gnateater in range). ♣ Undergrowth of humid to semihumid forest, woodland. 300–2400 m. ♪ Call: sharp, thin "tsiew"; song: simple almost-rattle of about 10 notes, the last 2–5 higher pitched.

118.6 CHESTNUT-BELTED (or -bellied) **GNATEATER**

(Chupa-dente-de-cinta) *Conopophaga aurita* L 4.7 in./12 cm. Two groups: Nom. group (**a**; N and W part of range; belly often buffier; ♀ as ♀ **b**) and *snethlageae* group SNETH-LAGE'S GNATEATER (**b**). ♀ from ♀ **118.8** by absence of spots on wings. ♣ Dense undergrowth of terra firme. Up to 700 m. ♪ Song: a short, extr./very high, very sharp rattle.

118.7 HOODED GNATEATER (Chupa-dente-de-capuz)

Conopophaga roberti L 4.7 in./12 cm. Unmistakable in range. ♣ Undergrowth of lowland forest, woodland. ♪ Song: a short, very high, ascending rattle. ♪ Song: short, high, musical almost-rattle, upslurred at the end (2 sec). En.

118.8 ASH-THROATED GNATEATER (Chupa-dente-

do-peru) *Conopophaga peruviana* L 4.7 in./12 cm. Wing spotting diagnostic in range. ♣ Undergrowth of terra firme.

118.9 BLACK-CHEEKED GNATEATER (Cuspidor-de-

máscara-preta) *Conopophaga melanops* L 4.3 in./11 cm. ♂ unmistakable. ♀ from **118.5** by all-black bill (no pale lower mandible), spots on wings, and whitish chin. ♣ Undergrowth of mainly, but not exclusively, humid forest. Up to 800 m. ♪ Call: very sharp "tsitsit"; song: very high, musical, hurried trill (2 sec). En.

118.10 BLACK-BELLIED GNATEATER (Chupa-dente-

grande) *Conopophaga melanogaster* L 5.9 in./15 cm. Unmistakable in range. ♣ Dense undergrowth of humid lowland forest. ♪ Call: angry-sounding low grunts and short rattles; song: slow series of up to 5 high, dry, well-separated, short rattles (1 rattle/sec). En.

118.11 SPOTTED BAMBOOWREN (Tapaculo-pintado)

Psilorhamphus guttatus L 5.1 in./13 cm. Distinctively patterned and spotted. ♣ Low levels in extensive bamboo at edge of humid forest and woodland, esp. in vines; 600–1000 m. ♪ Song: a hurried, level (or slightly rising) soft series of mid-high, hooted "to-to---" notes (8–15 sec). R.

Plate 119

119.1 VARIEGATED ANTPITTA (Tovacuçu) *Grallaria* *varia* L 7.5 in./19 cm. SE *imperator* (**a**) and NE Nom. (**b**) shown. Unmistakable in most of range, but cf. **119.3**. ♣ On ground in humid forest, woodland. Up to 650 m in most of range; up to 1400 in SE. ♪ Song: 3-part series of low-pitched, mournful notes, middle 4–6 pitched 1 note higher and slightly faster than 1st 6 and last 2 notes.

119.2 ELUSIVE ANTPITTA (Tovacuçu-xodó) *Grallaria* *eludens* L 7.5 in./19 cm. Unmistakable in range by broad black streaks below. ♣ On ground in terra firme. ♪ Song: low 3-noted series of "Tuuh tju-eh" notes (2nd note begins with an abrupt rise).

119.3 ? SCALED ANTPITTA (Tovacuçu-corujinha) *Grallaria guatimalensis* L 6.7 in./17 cm. Note range and habitat. Differs from **119.1** by more crescentlike (sometimes reduced) patch on lower throat, lack of narrow, pale shaft-streaks on back, and, in E part of range, darker underparts. ♣ On ground in humid forest above 650 m. ♪ Song: low, hollow, hurried series, increasing in volume and pitch, the last 2 notes slightly falling off (length about 15–30 notes). (Record is probably based on wrong identification.)

119.4 SPOTTED ANTPITTA (Torom-carijó) *Hylopezus* *macularius* L 5.5 in./14 cm. Note head pattern with diagnostic buff eyering. ♣ Dense undergrowth of lowland forest. ♪ Song: low, laborious "whoak-whoak-whoak-who-who" (the last 2 notes falling off).

119.5 AMAZONIAN ANTPITTA (Torom-torom) *Hylo-* *pezus berlepschi* L 5.9 in./15 cm. Note rather plain sides of face and streaking of breast. ♣ Dense undergrowth of lowland forest. ♪ Song: 3 (or 4) mid- to high, well-separated, hollow "Uh" notes.

119.6 WHITE-BROWED ANTPITTA (Torom-do-nor- deste) *Hylopezus ochroleucus* L 5.5 in./14 cm. Unmistakable in range. ♣ On ground in woodland, caatinga; esp. in dense growth. ♪ Song: series in 3 parts, 1st ascending, 2nd with double-noted notes, last 3-noted, sounding like "piupiu-piupiu tetju tetju tetju tetjutu." En, R.

119.7 SPECKLE-BREASTED ANTPITTA (Pinto-do-mato) *Hylopezus nattereri* L 5.5 in./14 cm. Unmistakable in range. ♣ On ground in humid forest, woodland; esp. in dense growth. ♪ Song: short, fairly fast, beautiful, fluted series of about 10 notes increasing in volume and pitch.

119.8 TEPUI ANTPITTA (Torom-de-peito-pardo) *Myr-* *mothera simplex* L 6.3 in./16 cm. Differs from **119.9** by absence of streaks on breast. ♣ Thick undergrowth in dense forest and woodland; 600–2400 m. ♪ Song: rather slow series of 7–10 well-accentuated, low notes, level at first, last 2–4 somewhat rising.

119.9 THRUSH-LIKE ANTPITTA (Tovaca-patinho) *Myrmothera campanisona* L 5.9 in./15 cm. Brownish chest faintly streaked whitish. ♣ Thick undergrowth of humid forest up to 800 m. ♪ Song: often level series of up to 6–7 low, hollow notes.

Plate 120

120.1 RUSTY-BELTED (or -bellied) **TAPACULO** (Corneteiro-da-mata) *Liosceles thoracicus*

L 7.5 in./19 cm. Unmistakable. Ssp. *dugandi* of far NW (**a**) and widespread Nom. (**b**) shown. ♣ On ground in terra firme. ♪ Low, descending, at the end slightly accelerating, leisurely series of about 7–15 mellow, hooted notes (5 sec).

NOTE: *Scytalopus* tapaculos: inconspicuous but vocal. Little or no overlap in range of most species. Juv. brownish overall; often with some dark scaling; Imm. with brownish, often dark-scaled rear parts and faint edging to wing coverts. Taxonomy very complex.

120.2 SERRA DO MAR (or Mouse-colored) **TAPACULO**.

(Tapaculo-do-espinhaço) *Scytalopus speluncae* (or *notorius*) L 3.9 in./ 10 cm. Note dark gray underparts of both sexes; ♀ with dark, brown-barred lower flanks. ♣ Dense undergrowth of humid forest; often in bamboo stands; 1000–2500 m. ♪ Call: sharp, nasal, hurried "jepjepjep"; song: a long, rapid series of "tjep" notes, sustained for 6–30 sec. En.

120.3 PLANALTO TAPACULO *Scytalopus pachecoi*

(Tapaculo-ferreirinho) L 3.9 in./ 10 cm. Medium gray below. Both sexes with dark-barred lower flanks; ♀ (not shown) browner above. ♣ Dense undergrowth of forest, incl. *Araucaria*. Up to 1500 m.

NOTE: Next to **120.2** and **120.3** there might be a third

species involved: ESPINHAÇO TAPACULO, with plumage and song very similar to **120.2**, and occurring in Espinhaço Mts. in Minas Gerais. It may be an undescribed species, or, possibly, correctly labeled according to systematic rules, *Scytalopus speluncae*, in which case **120.2** becomes *notorius*.

120.4 MARSH (or Tall-grass Wetland) **TAPACULO**

(Macuquinho-da-várzea) *Scytalopus iraiensis* L 3.9 in./10 cm. Unbarred flanks. Note habitat. ♣ Treeless wet places with rushes and grass between 750 and 950 m. ♪ Song: long series of high, hooted, chipped notes, starting slowly and hesitantly, then gradually accelerating and and rising with a more staccato quality (may last for > 30 sec). En, R.

120.5 DIAMANTINA TAPACULO (Tapaculo-da-chapada-

diamanina) *Scytalopus diamantinensis* L 4.3 in./11 cm. Restricted to the Chapada Diamantina. Not in range of **120.2** and **120.3**. Differs from **120.4** by rufous, black-barred underparts. ♣ Forest and second growth with dense layers of dead leaves, fallen stems, ferns, and bamboo; 850–1600 m. En.

120.6 BAHIA (or Chestnut-sided) **TAPACULO** (Macuquinho-baiano) *Scytalopus psychopompus* L 4.3 in./11 cm. Differs from

120.7 by range and unbarred flanks. ♣ Thick vegetation in lowland forest. ♪ Voice unknown. En, R, possibly extinct.

120.7 WHITE-BREASTED TAPACULO (Macuquinho) *Scytalopus indigoticus* L 4.3 in./11 cm.

Note extensive white underparts. Sexes alike. ♣ Dense undergrowth of humid forest. Up to 1500 m; mainly in highlands in far N part of range. ♪ Song: low, soft, short, upslurred, froglike roll (3 sec). En, R.

120.8 BRASILIA TAPACULO (Tapaculo-de-brasília) *Scytalopus novacapitalis* L 4.3 in./ 11 cm. Resembles **120.6** and **120.7**,

but underparts whitish gray. ♣ Undergrowth of forest and woodland near water; 800–1000 m. ♪ Song: simple, calm, sustained series of well-separated staccato "chip" or "chet" notes (about 1 × "chip"/sec). En, R.

120.9 COLLARED CRESCENT-CHEST (Tapaculo-de-

colarinho) *Melanopareia torquata* L 5.5 in./14 cm. Unmistakable. ♣ Stony cerrado with scattered bush and low trees. ♪ Song: simple repetition of single high, sharp "tuw" note (1 ×/sec, up to 30 sec).

120.10 SLATY BRISTLEFRONT (Entufado) *Merulaxis*

ater L 7.1 in./18 cm. Plumes diagnostic. Virtually unmistakable, but cf.**120.11**. ♣ Mainly in undergrowth of montane forest and second growth; 400–1800 m, locally down to 100 m. ♪ Song: starting with a slow series of very high, sharp, stressed "click" notes (1 ×/sec), followed by a long, chattering laugh, which starts very high, bounces down, and glides up and down at the end (10 sec). En, R.

120.11 STRESEMANN'S BRISTLEFRONT (Entufado-baiano) *Merulaxis stresemanni* L 7.5 in./19 cm. Restricted range. ♂

from ♂ **120.10** by lack of brown tones in plumage; ♀ brighter chestnut-brown below. ♣ Undergrowth of humid lowland forest. ♪ Song: as **120.10**, but lower pitched. En, R.

Plate 121

121.1 WHITE-WINGED COTINGA (Anambé-de-asa-branca) *Xipholena atropurpurea* L 7.5 in./19 cm. Not in range of **121.2** and **121.3**. ♣ Humid forest; also in low, often scrubby woodland. Up to 900 m. ♪ Call: high, barking "weh"; does not sing, but wing-whirs. En, R.

121.2 WHITE-TAILED COTINGA (Anambé-de-rabo-branco) *Xipholena lamellipennis* L 7.9 in./20 cm. ♂♂ unmistakable by white tail; ♀ probably not separable from ♀ **121.3** (note range). ♣ Canopy of humid forest up to 400 m. ♪ Call: high "wic." En.

121.3 POMPADOUR COTINGA (Anambé-pompadora) *Xipholena punicea* L 7.9 in./20 cm. ♂ with dark tail unmistakable in range. ♀ rather uniform, unmottled gray below. ♣ Canopy of humid forest up to 1300 m. ♪ Call/song: high, staccato "weh."

121.4 SPANGLED COTINGA (Anambé-azul) *Cotinga cayana* L 7.9 in./20 cm. Dark eyes and black wings distinctive. ♀ as ♀ **121.5**, but eyes always dark and with less ochre below. ♣ Canopy of humid forest up to 600 m. ♪ Silent.

121.5 PLUM-THROATED COTINGA (Cotinga-azul) *Cotinga maynana* L 7.5 in./19 cm. Cf. **121.4**. ♀ may have dark eyes. ♣ Canopy of forest, esp. várzea. ♪ Silent.

121.6 PURPLE-BREASTED COTINGA (Anambé-de-peito-roxo) *Cotinga cotinga* L 7.1 in./18 cm. ♂ unmistakable by dark cobalt blue color, ♀ from ♀♀ **121.4** and **121.5** by distinct scaling and spotting below. ♣ Canopy of humid forest up to 800 m. ♪ Silent.

121.7 PURPLE-THROATED COTINGA (Cotinga-de-garganta-encarnada) *Porphyrolaema porphyrolaema* L 7.1 in./18 cm. ♂ unmistakable, ♀ with distinct barring below. ♣ Humid forest up to 400 m. ♪ Silent.

121.8 BANDED COTINGA (Crejoá) *Cotinga maculata* L 7.9 in./20 cm. Unmistakable; not in range of **121.4**–**121.6**. ♣ Canopy of humid forest up to 200 m. Occasionally also in second growth. ♪ Silent. En, R.

121.9 BLACK-FACED COTINGA (Anambé-de-cara-preta) *Conioptilon mcilhennyi* L 9.8 in./25 cm. Unmistakable by white-rimmed, black face sides. ♣ Várzea and swampy forest at lake and river margins. ♪ Song: short, surprised-sounding "wuèèèèh," gliding up to three notes higher.

121.10 GUIANAN COCK-OF-THE-ROCK (Galo-da-serra) *Rupicola rupicola* L 11.8 in./30 cm. Unmistakable. ♣ Near rocky outcrops in humid forest up to 1200 m, occasionally much higher. ♪ Call: at lek, downslurred, aggressive "Wèh" and other hoarse sounds, such as a laborious "èh-uh"; song: peacocklike "wèèhow," 1st part upslurred, 2nd shorter and lower.

Plate 122

122.1 BLACK-NECKED RED-COTINGA (Saurá-de-

pescoço-preto) *Phoenicircus nigricollis* L 7.9 in./20 cm. ♂ with blackish throat and upperparts unmistakable. ♀ from ♀ **122.2** (note range) by redder underparts ♪ "Sings" at lek, along with 5–20 other males, by uttering at intervals a sneezing "twèh"; also produces cricketlike trill with its wings.

122.2 GUIANAN RED-COTINGA (Saurá) *Phoenicircus*

carnifex L 7.9 in./20 cm. Brown, not black, mantle and dark red wings. ♀ less bright orange below than ♀ **122.1**. ♣ Humid forest up to 600 m. ♪ Call at dawn: described as "pee-chew-eet." At lek, produces mechanical trill produced by wing whirring.

122.3 BLACK-AND-GOLD COTINGA (Saudade)

Tijuca atra L 9.8 in./25 cm. ♂ unmistakable. ♀ resembles **122.4**. ♣ Forest; 1200–2000 m. ♪ Song: curious high, sharp, eerie "suuuuuwíii," increasing in strength, upslurred midway (4 sec). En, R.

122.4 GRAY-WINGED COTINGA (Saudade-de-asa-

cinza) *Tijuca condita* L 9.8 in./25 cm. Brighter below and grayer face and wings than ♀ **122.3**. ♣ Forest, woodland; 1350–2000 m. ♪ Song: very/extr. high, sharp, slow "tue-twée" or "t-twée-tee-deedeé." En, R.

122.5 [RED-BANDED FRUITEATER (Anambé-de-

whitely) *Pipreola whitelyi*] L 6.7 in./17 cm. Unmistakable. ♣ Mossy forest and dense stunted woodland; 1300–2250 m. ♪ Extr. high (just within ear reach), upslurred, slightly lowered and rising "seeeeeh" as one note or slow trill. Not confirmed in Brazil, but likely to occur.

122.6 AMAZONIAN UMBRELLABIRD (Anambé-

preto) *Cephalopterus ornatus* L 19.7 in./50 cm (♂), 15.7 in./40 cm (♀). Unmistakable. ♣ Várzea, humid forest and woodland along rivers. Often near *Cecropia* trees. Up to 300 m. ♪ Song: strange, very low, exhaled "boooh," as if from a didgeridoo.

122.7 CAPUCHINBIRD (Maú) *Perissocephalus tricolor*

L 13.8 in./35 cm. Unmistakable. ♣ Mid- to upper levels of humid forest up to 600 m. ♪ Song: at lek: series of 3 very low notes, starting with a long, inhaled, toneless, growling, "frrrroh," then an exhaled, drawn-out, bleating "waòòòòòòòw," and a short, lower "woh" (the total as the weirdest sound you will ever hear coming from a bird).

122.8 WHITE BELLBIRD (Araponga-da-amazônia)

Procnias alba L 11.8 in./30 cm. ♂ is unmistakable. Note that crown of ♀ is the same color as mantle and throat, streaked olive. ♣ Canopy of humid forest up to 1250 m. ♪ Song: 2-noted, resounding "dzong-dzíng," ("dzing" higher) reminiscent of a gong or the closing of an iron gate.

122.9 BEARDED BELLBIRD (Araponga-do-nordeste)

Procnias averano L 11.8 in./30 cm. ♂ virtually unmistakable, but cf. **122.10**. ♀ with dusky crown. ♣ Canopy of forest, woodland. Up to 1900 m. ♪ Song: 1-noted, low, loud, sudden "kRuh."

122.10 BARE-THROATED BELLBIRD (Araponga)

Procnias nudicollis L 11.8 in./30 cm. ♂ unmistakable. ♀ with blackish crown. ♣ Canopy of forest up to 1000 m. ♪ Song: 1-noted, high, loud, sudden "kríh," with the same quality as described for **122.8**. R.

Plate 123

123.1 BARE-NECKED FRUITCROW (Anambé-pombo) *Gymnoderus foetidus* L 9.8 in./25 cm. Unmistakable. ♣ Canopy of várzea and humid lowland forest along rivers/lakes. ♪ Silent.

123.2 PURPLE-THROATED FRUITCROW (Anambé-uma) *Querula purpurata* L 11.8 in./30 cm. Note pale, stumpy bill and short legs. No overlap with **123.4**. ♣ Humid forest and second growth up to 750 m.

123.3 CRIMSON FRUITCROW (Anambé-militar) *Haematoderus militaris* L 13.8 in./35 cm. Unmistakable. ♣ Canopy of humid forest up to 200 m. ♪ Call/song: noisy, high, mellow, nasal, repeated "tjiward."

123.4 RED-RUFFED FRUITCROW (Pavó) *Pyroderus scutatus* L 17.7 in./45 cm (♂), 15.7 in./40 cm (♀). Unmistakable. ♀ has darker bill. ♣ Humid forest (incl. *Araucaria*), woodland. Up to 1900 m. ♪ Song at lek: very low, pumped-out "voovooh," as from didgeridoo.

123.5 HELMETED MANAKIN (Soldadinho) *Antilophia galeata* L 5.5 in./14 cm. Unmistakable. Note enlarged frontlet and long tail of ♀. ♣ Low levels in riverine belts, palm groves, woodland; 500–1000 m. ♪ Call/song: high, "whueEE-pur" ("whueEE" exhaled and gliding-up to a very high pitch) or nervous, very fast "wudr-wudr-weéte-hweét," last part rising very steeply.

123.6 ARARIPE MANAKIN (Soldadinho-do-araripe) *Antilophia bokermanni* L 5.9 in./15 cm. Unmistakable. Differs from **123.5** by small and different range. ♣ Low levels in tall, second growth forest at ca. 800 m. Prefers humid areas. ♪ Call: slightly different from **123.5**; "widr weéteh-weét" (1st and 2nd part well separated). En, R.

123.7 PIN-TAILED MANAKIN (Tangarazinho) *Ilicura militaris* L 5.1 in./13 cm. Note gray face, dull orange eyes, and elongated central tail feathers in ♀. ♣ Humid forest and second growth up to 1400 m; in N part of range not in lowlands. ♪ Call: extr. high, thin, hurried "see-see- -" ("see" 4–6 ×). En.

123.8 FLAME-CROWNED (or–crested) **MANAKIN** (Coroa-de-fogo) *Heterocercus linteatus* L 5.5 in./14 cm. ♂ unmistakable in range. ♀ resembles ♀ **125.9**, which see. ♣ Low levels of humid lowland forest.

123.9 YELLOW-CROWNED (or -crested) **MANAKIN** (Dançarino-de-crista-amarela) *Heterocercus flavivertex* L 5.5 in./14 cm. Both sexes with more contrasting gray cheeks than respective sexes of **123.8** (no overlap), but ♀♀ barely separable. ♣ Low to mid-levels of várzea and other forests/woodlands near rivers. ♪ Call: 3 parts; extr. high, long, upslurred "seeee," exploding "tSIT," and drawn-out, gliding-down "seeh," together as "seeee-tSITseeh."

123.10 [ORANGE-CROWNED MANAKIN (Dançarino-de-crista-laranja) *Heterocercus aurantiivertex*] L 5.5 in./14 cm. Very similar to **123.9** (no overlap), but cf. **123.8**. ♣ Middle and lower levels in várzea. ♪ Song: very high, slightly falling and rising trill (2–3 sec).

Plate 124

124.1 WHITE-TIPPED PLANTCUTTER (Corta-ramos)

Phytotoma rutila L 7.5 in./19 cm. Unmistakable. Note bill shape. ♣ Accidental in Brazil. ♪ Song: strange, toneless series of 1–5 long "creee" sounds, stressed in the middle (as if dragging a fingernail over a comb). V.

124.2 SCREAMING PIHA (Cricrió) *Lipaugus vociferans*

L 9.8 in./25 cm. Rather uniform gray. Note upright stance. Cf. very similar **150.1**. ♣ Humid forest up to 500 m. ♪ Song: very characteristic, loud, far-carrying, explosive, lashing sound, like "Wít-wítjuh" ("tjuh" low-pitched).

124.3 CINNAMON-VENTED PIHA (Tropeiro-da-serra) *Lipaugus lanioides* L 9.8 in./

25 cm. As **124.2**, but wings, tail, and vent browner. ♣ Montane humid forest between 500 and 1000 m, locally higher. ♪ Song: low, calm, nasal, staccato "tu-téhtjuh" or "tutu-téhtjutju"; middle-note higher. En, R.

124.4 ROSE-COLLARED PIHA (Cricrió-de-cinta-vermelha) *Lipaugus streptophorus*

L 7.9 in./20 cm. ♂ unmistakable, chestnut vent of ♀ diagnostic. ♣ Humid forest; 1000–1800 m.

124.5 KINGLET CALYPTURA (Tietę-de-coroa) *Calyptura cristata* L 3.1 in./8 cm. Unmis-

takable by color pattern and very small size. ♣ Humid forest and second growth up to 900 m. Virtually unknown. Only a single confirmed recent record. En, R.

124.6 SWALLOW-TAILED COTINGA (Tesourinha-da-mata) *Phibalura flavirostris* L 7.9 in./

20 cm. Unmistakable by long, forked tail. ♀ (not shown) as ♂, but with lower underparts scaled, not spotted. ♣ Forest borders, lightly wooded areas, gardens; SL–2000 m. ♪ Usually silent. R.

124.7 SHARPBILL (Araponga-do-horto) *Oxyruncus cristatus* L 6.7 in./17 cm. Unmistak-

able by pointed bill, general coloring, and spotting below. ♣ Upper levels of humid forest; SL–1100 m. ♪ Song: long, calm "fiuuuu--uh," just audible at the beginning, then gliding down almost 5 notes.

124.8 HOODED BERRYEATER (Corocochó) *Carpornis cucullata* L 9.8 in./25 cm. Unmistak-

able by color pattern. Note brown back. ♣ Mid-levels to subcanopy of humid forest, palm groves; 400–1600 m. ♪ Song: soft, mellow "wrat? what-now." En, R.

124.9 BLACK-HEADED BERRYEATER (Sabiá-pimenta) *Carpornis melanocephala* L 7.9 in./

20 cm. Differs from **124.8** (which occurs at higher altitudes) by red eyes and plain olive-green upperparts. ♣ Mid-levels to subcanopy of humid forest up to 500 m. ♪ Song: high, gliding-down, indignant-sounding "njauow." En, R.

124.1

124.2

124.3

124.4 ♀

124.5 ♀

124.6

124.7

124.8 ♀

124.9

Plate 125

125.1 CRIMSON-HOODED MANAKIN (Uirapuru-vermelho) *Pipra aureola* L 4.3 in./ 11 cm. Note black flanks in ♂. ♀ with pale eyes and yellow throat and belly; inseparable from ♀ **125.2** (note range). ♣ Low levels of várzea, woodland, second growth, mangrove. Below 300 m. ♪ Call: plaintive, gliding-down "eeeuw."

125.2 BAND-TAILED MANAKIN (Uirapuru-laranja) *Pipra fasciicauda* L 4.3 in./11 cm. ♂ unmistakable. Note white in tail. Cf. **125.1**. ♣ Low levels of forest, gallery woodland. Up to 600 m. ♪ Song: downslurred, slightly sharp "wieeèr."

125.3 WIRE-TAILED MANAKIN (Rabo-de-arame) *Pipra filicauda* L 4.7 in./12 cm. ♂ and ♀ unmistakable by tail wires. ♣ Low levels in riverine belts, streams in open woodland. Below 300 m. ♪ Song: downslurred, thin "wieeèr."

125.4 GOLDEN-HEADED MANAKIN (Cabeça-de-ouro) *Pipra erythrocephala* L 3.5 in./ 9 cm. ♂ unmistakable. ♀ as ♀ **125.5** (no overlap), but bill usually paler. ♣ Low levels in humid forest, second growth. ♪ Call: e.g., "Tíew" note; song: series of 6 notes with distinct pause after 4th, like "Pééterru-tjip prrrtip" ("Péé" higher and stressed).

125.5 RED-HEADED MANAKIN (Cabeça-encarnada) *Pipra rubrocapilla* L 3.9 in./10 cm. ♂ unmistakable. Small ♀ dull olive overall with very short tail. No overlap with **125.4**, but cf. **125.6**. ♪ Call/song: hoarse, nasal, level "gekker" or "krits."

125.6 ROUND-TAILED MANAKIN (Dançador-de-cauda-graduada) *Pipra chloromeros* L 4.3 in./11 cm. Very like **125.5**, but tail rounded, not square, and ♂ with yellow, not red, thighs. ♣ Low levels in humid lowland forest. ♪ Song: high, very hurried "Teeh-tje-Zwee-wir-wur" or other hurried combinations of these notes.

125.7 SCARLET-HORNED MANAKIN (Dançador-de-crista) *Pipra cornuta* L 4.7 in./12 cm. ♂ unmistakable. ♀ dull, rather long tailed, with slight crest and flesh-brown legs; cf. **123.10**. ♪ Song: short combinations of shrill "sreet," run-together "titjurrr," and toneless, grating "kreekree" in fast series of 4–7 notes.

125.8 WHITE-BEARDED MANAKIN (Rendeira) *Manacus manacus* L 4.3 in./11 cm. ♂ unmistakable. Bright orange (not pinkish) legs of ♀ diagnostic. ♣ Undergrowth of forest, second growth. Up to 1000 m. ♪ Call: very high, rather dry "kirrp" (repeated with irregular intervals).

125.9 FIERY-CAPPED MANAKIN (Uirapuru-cigarra) *Machaeropterus pyrocephalus* L 3.5 in./ 9 cm. Color of crown and back diagnostic in ♂. ♀ with purplish legs and blurry streaking below. ♣ Low levels of humid lowland forest, woodland. ♪ Call: very high, sharp, lonely-sounding "plee" with rather long intervals.

125.10 OLIVE MANAKIN (Dançarino-oliváceo) *Xenopipo uniformis* L 5.1 in./13 cm. Slightly similar to **123.9** (no overlap), but cf. **123.8**. ♣ Low levels of shrubby forest (incl. várzea), woodland. Up to 1200 m. Call: extr. high, gliding-up "wseeeeeé" (< 1 sec).

125.11 BLACK MANAKIN (Pretinho) *Xenopipo atronitens* L 5.1 in./13 cm. ♂ resembles ♂ **135.3**, but more thickset and with stubbier bill. ♀ virtually inseparable from **125.10**. ♣ Woodland, stunted forest on sandy soils, riverine belts. ♪ Calls: varied; e.g., very high, chirping "writ wit wit," varying in pitch.

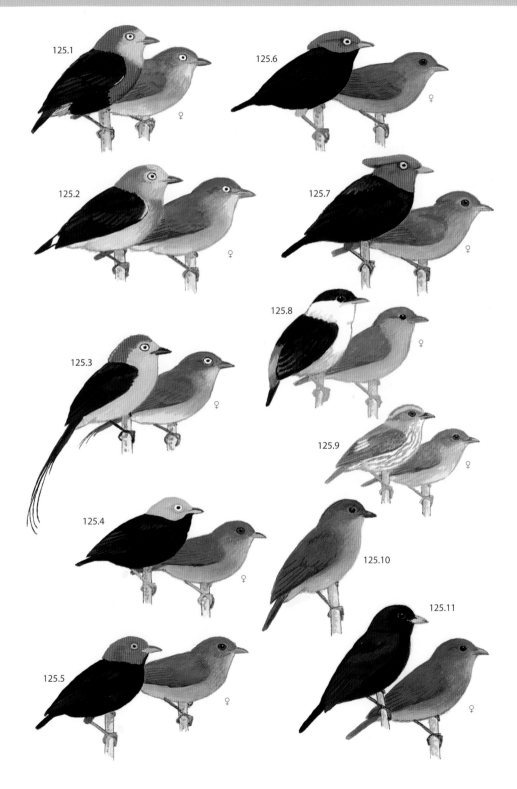

125.1

125.6 ♀

125.2 ♀

125.7 ♀

125.3 ♀

125.8 ♀

125.9 ♀

125.4 ♀

125.10

125.11

125.5 ♀ ♀

Plate 126

126.1 WHITE-CROWNED MANAKIN (Cabeça-branca)

Dixiphia (or *Pipra*) *pipra* L 3.9 in./ 10 cm. Ad. ♂ unmistakable. Note red eyes and grayish face of ♀. ♣ Low levels in humid forest, second growth. Up to 1500 m. ♪ Call: low, downslurred, nasal "njew."

126.2 BLUE-CROWNED MANAKIN (Uirapuru-de-

chapéu-azul) *Lepidothrix coronata* L 3.5 in./9 cm. NW ssp. *carbonate* (**a**) and SW *caelestipileata* (**b**; ♀ as ♀ **a**) shown. ♂♂ unmistakable in range. Note bright green of ♀. ♣ Humid forest, second growth, normally below 1000 m. ♪ Call: 2-noted "piRééh," with toneless or sharp "pi" merged in "R."

126.3 WHITE-FRONTED MANAKIN (Uirapuru-estrela)

Lepidothrix (or *Pipra*) *serena* L 3.5 in./ 9 cm. Both sexes resemble **126.4**. ♣ Low levels in interior and at edge of humid forest. Up to 500 m. ♪ Call: high, fluted "wuéew."

126.4 ORANGE-BELLIED (or Tepui) **MANAKIN** (Dan-

çador-do-tepui) *Lepidothrix* (or *Pipra*) *suavissima* L 3.5 in./9 cm. ♂ from ♂ **126.3** by range and no yellow patch on black breast. ♀ from ♀ **126.2** (little overlap) by bluish frontlet. ♣ Low levels of humid forest up to 1800 m. ♪ Call: high, slightly nasal, short "wíh."

126.5 OPAL-CROWNED MANAKIN (Cabeça-de-

prata) *Lepidothrix* (or *Pipra*) *iris* L 3.5 in./9 cm. Bright green with yellow belly and pale eyes. Crown bluish in ♂; pure green (as shown; W part of range) or blue-tinged (E part of range) in ♀. No overlap with **126.2, 126.6**, and **126.7**, but cf. **126.1**. ♣ Low levels of humid lowland forest (esp. terra firme), second growth. ♪ Call: very (almost extr.) high upslurred "feer," repeated with short intervals. En.

126.6 GOLDEN-CROWNED MANAKIN (Dançador-

de-coroa-dourada) *Lepidothrix* (or *Pipra*) *vilasboasi* L 3.5 in./9 cm. Note tiny range. Crown yellow (♂) or pure green (♀). ♣ Low levels of humid lowland forest. En, R.

126.7 SNOW-CAPPED (or -crowned) **MANAKIN**

(Uirapuru-de-chapéu-branco) *Lepidothrix* (or *Pipra*) *nattereri* L 3.5 in./ 9 cm. ♂ with white crown and rump. Crown of ♀ pure green (N part of range) or blue-tinged (S part of range; shown). No overlap with **126.5** and **126.6**, but cf. **126.1**. ♣ Low levels of humid lowland forest; esp. terra firme. ♪ Call: high, slightly grating, steeply ascending "tuWeét."

126.8 BLUE-BACKED MANAKIN (Tangará-falso)

Chiroxiphia pareola L 4.7 in./12 cm. Crown of ♂ red (**b**), but yellow in far W ssp. *regina* (**a**). ♀ relatively large with orange-pink legs (cf. ♀ **125.8**). Imm. ♂ as ♀, but crown red/yellow. ♣ Undergrowth of humid lowland forest and second growth. ♪ Call/song: varied; e.g., low, strong "tjowtjow---" (3–5 × "tjow").

126.9 BLUE (or Swallow-tailed) **MANAKIN** (Tangará)

Chiroxiphia caudata L 5.9 in./15 cm. Unmistakable. Note elongated central tail feathers in both sexes. Imm. ♂ (not shown) as ♀, but crown red. ♣ Undergrowth of humid forest and woodland up to 1900 m; only above 500 m in N part of range. ♪ Call: high, short, descending "tjeow" or high, loud, scratchy "iewiew."

126.10 WHITE-THROATED MANAKIN (Dançarino-de-

garganta-branca) *Corapipo gutturalis* L 3.5 in./9 cm. ♂ unmistakable. Note pale chin and belly of ♀. ♣ Low levels in humid forest up to 1100 m. ♣ Humid forest in hilly areas. ♪ Call: extr. high, thin, drawn-out "seee-o-see."

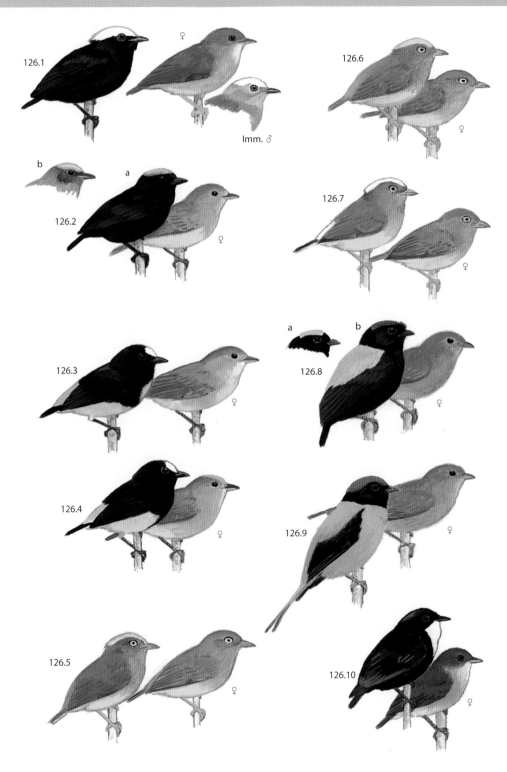

Plate 127

127.1 EASTERN STRIPED MANAKIN (Tangará-ra-

jado) *Machaeropterus regulus* L 3.5 in./
9 cm. Note faint streaking below.
No overlap with **125.9** or **127.2**. ♣
Low levels of humid lowland forest.
♪ Call; mid-high, short, catlike
"tjew." En.

127.2 WESTERN STRIPED MANAKIN *Machaeropterus*

striolatus (Tangará-riscado) L 3.5 in./
9 cm. ♂ unmistakable in range. ♀
resembles ♀ **125.9**, but sides of
chest reddish brown. ♣ Low levels
of humid lowland forest. ♪ Call:
very high, 2-noted "i-tjúw."

NOTE: *Neopelma* Tyrant-Manakins: inconspicuous at low
to mid-levels. Little or no overlap between species, but cf.
131.10 with stronger wing edging and facial pattern. Eye
colors variable and yellow crown streak often not visible.

127.3 SAFFRON-CRESTED TYRANT-MANAKIN

(Fruxu-do-carrasco) *Neopelma chryso-
cephalum* L 5.1 in./13 cm. Not in
range of **127.4**–**127.7**. ♣ Woodland,
stunted forest. Up to 700 m. ♪ Call:
low, nasal "tjew"; song: strange, low,
hurried, accelerating, nasal "tjuut tjuut-tootoo" (as if blow-
ing on paper over a comb).

127.4 SULPHUR-BELLIED TYRANT-MANAKIN

(Fruxu-de-barriga-amarela) *Neopelma
sulphureiventer* L 5.1 in./13 cm. Limited contact with whitish-bellied
127.5. ♣ Humid forest, riverine
belts with bamboo thickets. ♪ Call:
high, slightly nasal "weét"; song: hoarse, 2-noted "vrít-je."

127.5 PALE-BELLIED TYRANT-MANAKIN (Fruxu-

do-cerradão) *Neopelma pallescens* L
5.5 in./14 cm. Only *Neopelma* with
creamy white (not clearly yellowish)
belly. ♣ Woodland, riverine belts.
Up to 700 m. ♪ Call: hurried
"rutrut---," "rut 1–7 ×, each upslurred: song: series of
1 long and 2 short hoarse, froglike "wreh-wrawra" notes.

127.6 WIED'S TYRANT-MANAKIN (Fruxu-baiano)

Neopelma aurifrons L 5.1 in./13 cm.
Differs from **127.7** (note range and
habitat) by shorter tail and less conspicuous crown streak. ♣ Interior of
humid forest; occasionally at edge.
Up to 1000 m. ♪ Song: yodeling "yo-deé-wo-dée," 1st
"dee" (or "tjiw") much higher, 2nd slightly higher. En, R.

127.7 SERRA DO MAR TYRANT-MANAKIN (Fruxu)

Neopelma chrysolophum L 5.1 in./13 cm.
Cf. **127.6**. ♣ Second growth, denser
woodland, forest edge. Avoids forest
interior; 1150–1800 m. ♪ Song: series
of random, of well-separated notes,
such as a slow, staccato "rih-tjew-tjew-tjuh," "rrítju" ("rr"
stressed), "tjuwtju," or "vrrrrrú." En.

127.8 CINNAMON (Neopipo or) **MANAKIN-TYRANT**

(Enferrujadinho) *Neopipo cinnamomea*
L 3.5 in./9 cm. From **141.10** by gray
legs, shorter tail, and crown-patch
(often not visible). ♣ Terra firme up
to 1000 m. ♪ Call: very high, thin,
gliding-down "seeeu"; song: long series of extr. high "fee"
notes, 1st few notes slightly rising in pitch and strength,
then gradually descending (5–7 sec).

127.9 DWARF TYRANT-MANAKIN (Uirapuruzinho)

Tyranneutes stolzmanni L 3.5 in./
9 cm. Tiny, dull, with very short tail
and pale eyes. Cf. **127.10** and
manakins on Pl. **125** and **126**. ♣
Low to mid-levels of humid low-
land forest, mainly interior of terra firme. ♪ Call: very
high, hurried "prutrut---" (3–6 × "rut"); song: curt "zweeh-
wít" ("wít" much higher) or "zweeh-dewít."

127.10 TINY TYRANT-MANAKIN (Uirapuruzinho-do-

norte) *Tyranneutes virescens* L 3.1 in./
8 cm. Very like **127.9** (limited contact), but eyes brown, even shorter
tailed and ♂ with yellow crown-
patch. Cf. manakins on Pl. **125** and
126. ♣ Low to mid-levels of humid lowland forest, mainly
interior of terra firme. ♪ Call/song: high, short, nasal
shiver "wee-de-weet" or quick "better delete."

Plate 128

128.1 BLACK-CAPPED (Manakin or) PIPRITES

(Caneleirinho-de-chapéu-preto) *Piprites pileata* L 4.7 in./12 cm. Unmistakable. ♣ Atlantic forest; often *Araucaria;* 900–2000 m. ♪ Call: very high, nasal "tjew" or low grumbling "tut tut - -"; song: series starting with slow, short "tjew," then high, ringing, hurried "tjeetjee--tju-uh" ("tjee" 4–5 ×, "tju" lower, weak "uh" slightly higher again). R.

128.2 WING-BARRED PIPRITES (Papinho-amarelo)

Piprites chloris L 5.1 in./13 cm. Several sspp.: W *tshudii* (**a**) and NE *clorion* (**b**) shown. No yellow lores or eyering in SE. Note manakinlike shape, yellow throat, wing pattern, and grayish ear coverts. ♣ Dense undergrowth of humid forest and second growth. Up to 1000 m; locally to 1700 m. ♪ Song: low, smooth series of "hoot" notes, after 4–5 hoots interupted by slightly ascending "diderick," together as "hoot-hoot--diderick-hoot-hoot."

128.3 RINGED ANTPIPIT (Estalador-do-norte)

Corythopis torquatus L 5.5 in./14 cm. Unmistakable in most of range by jizz and black (brown in Juv.) chest, but cf. **128.4** (limited contact) with more olive ear coverts and back slightly browner. ♣ On or near the ground in humid forest to 1400 m. ♪ Song: very high, calm "tueet tueet," each "tueet" slightly downslurred.

128.4 SOUTHERN ANTPIPIT (Estalador)

Corythopis delalandi L 5.5 in./14 cm. Cf. **128.3**. ♣ On or near the ground in forest, woodland up to 1000 m. ♪ Song: very high, short, calm, sweet series "weeh-rrrwee-wurr-wiwi" ("rrr" very short, canarylike trills).

128.5 CORRENDERA PIPIT (Caminheiro-de-espora)

Anthus correndera L 5.9 in./15 cm. Note strong streaking of chest and flanks and bold pair of whitish streaks on back. ♣ Pastures, fields, wetlands, grassy roadsides. ♪ Song: in hovering flight, cheerful, unstructured series of twittering, like "fitfit-wrrrruh," "fit-frit-oh-frút," and "fit-frit-oh-wrrrruh---" ("wrrruh" as toneless, nasal trill).

128.6 SHORT-BILLED PIPIT (Caminheiro-de-unha-curta)

Anthus furcatus L 5.5 in./14 cm. Differs from **128.7** by scalier (less streaky) mantle, virtual lack of streaks on flanks, stronger malar, and strongly spotted breast contrasting with whitish belly. ♣ Open areas with short grass. ♪ Song: in flight, very high, slightly varied "writ tjitji-vr-rrrruh-tjuwtjuw--" ("writ" separated from subsequent notes).

128.7 HELLMAYR'S PIPIT (Caminheiro-de-barriga-acanelada)

Anthus hellmayri L 5.5 in./14 cm. Finest breast streaking of all pipits. Note sparse streaks on flank and buff-tinged belly. ♣ Dry, rocky areas, pastures, fields. Up to 2200 m. ♪ Song: from post or in flight, e.g., very/extr. high, short, hurried twitter ending in a nasal drawn-out note, together as "tritfitwitweét-tritfitwit-srèèh," given in 2–3 sec intervals.

128.8 YELLOWISH PIPIT (Caminheiro-zumbidor)

Anthus lutescens L 5.1 in./13 cm. Only pipit in most of its range. Small with diagnostic yellow-tinged underparts. Streaking on underparts mostly restricted to chest; buff streaks on back. ♣ Prefers very short grass in hot open country, lakesides and riversides, agricultural land. ♪ Song: in flight, during ascend silent, when gliding back to ground, nasal, slightly cross-sounding, "sjiieeuuw," starting very high and thin, lowered and becoming nasal.

128.9 OCHRE-BREASTED PIPIT (Caminheiro-grande)

Anthus nattereri L 5.5 in./14 cm. Rich ochre breast contrasting with whitish belly diagnostic. ♣ Open areas, grassland, fields, pastures. Up to 900 m; locally higher. ♪ Song: in flight, very high, sharp, twittering series in 3–6 slightly lowered groups of notes without intervals, ending in a gliding-down "èèèh-èèèh-èèèh." R.

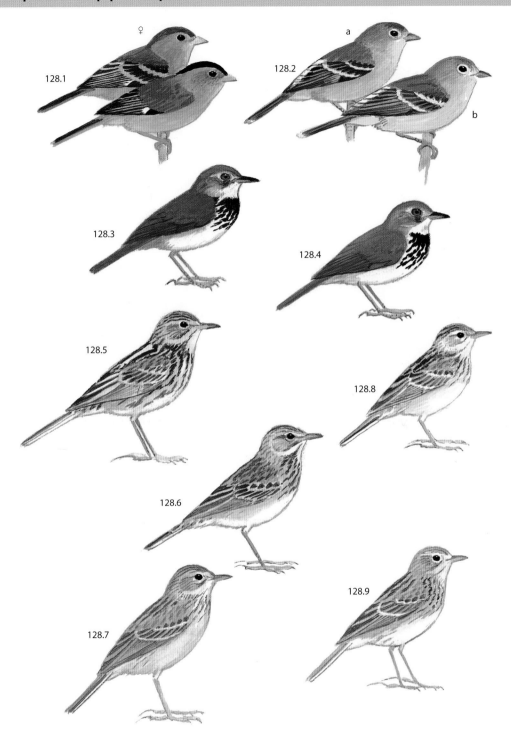

Plate 129

129.1 VARZEA (or Greater) (Mourner or) **SCHIF-FORNIS** (Flautim-ruivo) *Schiffornis major* L 5.9 in./15 cm. Amount of gray in face varyies. More thickset, shorter billed, and less upright stance than Atillas (Pl. **151**). ♣ Várzea up to 300 m. ♪ Song: high, slow, fluted "pjúh puéet," like a wolf whistle.

129.2 THRUSH-LIKE (Mourner or) **SCHIFFORNIS** (Flautim-marrom) *Schiffornis turdina* L 6.3 in./16 cm. Rather featureless; mainly detected by voice. Note large eye. Resembles a large, long-tailed, brownish olive manakin. Cf. **123.10**, **125.10**, and **129.3**. ♣ Low levels in interior of humid forest. Up to 1000 m. ♪ *Note*: A recent study shows that in Brazil, 3 very similar species of *Schiffornis* are involved, differing mainly in voice: *S. veraepacis* (NW Brazil), *S. amazona* (W Amazonia, song: slow, drawn-out "tiuuh-tuweet," 1st part gliding down, 2nd part 2-toned with "weet" much higher and stressed), and *S. turdina* (SE Amazonia and E Brazil).

129.3 GREENISH (Mourner or) **SCHIFFORNIS** (Flautim) *Schiffornis virescens* L 5.9 in./15 cm. Note contrasting rufescent wings and tail, unlike **126.9** and ♀ **129.2**; at higher elevation of **129.2** in area of contact. ♣ Low levels of humid forest, second growth, riverine belt. Up to 1200 m. ♪ Song: variations of very high, thin "tjuuh-witwée" (1st part low and drawn out; 2nd part with 2 decisive, short notes; last one highest).

129.4 CINEREOUS MOURNER (Chorona-cinza) *Laniocera hypopyrra* L 7.9 in./20 cm. Note yellow eye rim. Wing spots diagnostic. May have yellow or orange tufts on sides of breast. ♣ Lower levels of humid forest and woodland ♪ Song: very high, sharp, repeated "usjowée"; "jo" sounding like a short grace note, "wée" rising as if forcefully exhaled.

129.5 BUFF-THROATED PURPLETUFT (Anambezinho) *Iodopleura pipra* L 3.5 in./9 cm. Unmistakable by coloring and size. Often perches on tree tops (as do **129.6** and **129.7**). ♣ Canopy of humid forest, second growth, plantations. Up to 1000 m. ♪ Song: extr. high "weeh-zwee," 1st note slightly higher and longer. En, R.

129.6 DUSKY PURPLETUFT (Anambé-fusco) *Iodopleura fusca* L 4.3 in./11 cm. Note white rump band, vent, and central streak from breast to belly. Cf. **76.9**. ♣ Canopy of humid lowland forest. Often in tops of bare trees. ♪ Voice probably as **129.7**.

129.7 WHITE-BROWED PURPLETUFT (Anambé-decoroa) *Iodopleura isabellae* L 4.7 in./12 cm. Dark with white rump band and stripe on central underparts. Cf. **76.9**. ♣ Canopy of humid lowland forest. Often in tops of bare trees. ♪ Song: extr. high, upslurred "seewee" or single "see."

129.8 BLACK-TAILED TITYRA (Anambé-brancao-de-rabo-preto) *Tityra cayana* L 7.9 in./20 cm. Two sspp.: N and W Nom. (**a**, ♀ shown; ♂ as ♂ **b**) and widespread *braziliensis* (**b**, ♂, ♀). Cf. **129.9**. ♣ Canopy of forest, woodland, second growth, plantations. Up to 1100 m. ♪ Call: curious, dry, toneless series of 1–3 minirattles, like "rrru."

129.9 MASKED TITYRA (Anambé-branco-de-máscara-negra) *Tityra semifasciata* L 7.9 in./20 cm. ♂ from ♂ **129.8** by white tail tip and less black head. ♀ lacks streaking. ♣ Canopy of forest, woodland, second growth, plantations. Lowlands. ♪ Call: dry minirattles, like "rrri."

129.10 BLACK-CROWNED TITYRA (Anambé-branco-de-bochecha-parda) *Tityra inquisitor* L 7.9 in./20 cm. Lack of red to bill diagnostic. Note cinnamon face of ♀. ♣ Canopy of humid forest at edge and clearings, várzea, plantations. ♪ Call: dry minirattles, like "krrru."

129.1

129.2

129.3

129.4

129.5

129.6 ♀

129.7 ♀

♀ a

129.8 b ♀

129.9 ♀

129.10 a b ♀

Plate 130

130.1 SHRIKE-LIKE COTINGA (or Elegant Mourner) (Chibante) *Laniisoma elegans* L 7.1 in./18 cm. Basically unmistakable by black-scalloped yellow underparts. Note black cap of ♂. ♣ Humid forest, mature second growth; 100–900 m. ♪ Song: extr. high, downslurred "piiiieh," repeated with slightly varying pitch and intervals. R.

130.2 WHITE-NAPED XENOPSARIS (Tijerila) *Xenopsaris albinucha* L 5.1 in./13 cm. Differs from ♂ **130.8** (note range) by more slender jizz, whiter underparts, and, often, brown-tinged wings. ♣ Caatinga, dry riverine belts, open areas with scattered trees. Up to 550 m. ♪ Song: extr. high, thin, short, drawn-out, partly trilled twittering.

130.3 GREEN-BACKED BECARD (Caneleiro-verde) *Pachyramphus viridis* L 5.9 in./15 cm. N ssp. *griseigularis* (**a**, ♂ and ♀ without yellow collar) and Nom. (**b**, rest of range in Brazil). Virtually unmistakable, but cf. **154.4.** ♣ Humid forest, woodland, riverine belts, areas with scattered trees. Up to 1000 m. ♪ Song: starting abruptly and hurried, then ascending and slightly decelerating series of 10–15 "dee-dee---" notes or series of ascending "jeh-weé - -" (6–20 ×).

130.4 CHESTNUT-CROWNED BECARD (Caneleiro) *Pachyramphus castaneus* L 5.5 in./14 cm. Gray band from eye to nape diagnostic ♣ Forest, woodland, riverine belts, plantations. Up to 1000 m, locally higher. ♪ Call: extr. high, slightly gliding up and down "tuuit" notes; song: simple series of 4–5 very high "weeu---" notes without intervals.

130.5 WHITE-WINGED BECARD (Caneleiro-preto) *Pachyramphus polychopterus* L 5.9 in./15 cm. Two groups: Amazonian *nigriventris* group (**a**; wing-pattern as **b** in most of range) and E and S Nom. group (**b**). Note black back, white tail tips, and gray not extending clearly above eye in ♂. ♀ with rufescent tail tips and wing edging. Cf. **130.6** and ♂♂ antshrikes (Pl. **104**) with less black crown and different behavior. ♣ Rather open woodland, borders of lowland forest, second growth, riverine belts, mangrove. Normally below 1500 m, but sometimes higher. ♪ Song: high, mellow, waderlike "tih ti-ti-tjuh" (ti-ti-" higher) or "tjew-tjew-tjew-tjeé."

130.6 BLACK-CAPPED BECARD (Caneleiro-bordado) *Pachyramphus marginatus* L 5.5 in./14 cm. ♂ from ♂ **130.5b** by gray extending over eyes as supraloral and mantle usually mottled (rarely all black). ♀ from ♀ **130.5** by rufous crown (at most tinged brown in ♀ **130.5**). ♣ Canopy in interior of humid forest and second growth. Up to 1000 m. ♪ Song: clear "wuh-weet-ohweé"; "weet" slightly higher and "weé" much higher and stressed.

130.7 GLOSSY-BACKED BECARD (Caneleiro-da-guiana) *Pachyramphus surinamus* L 5.1 in./13 cm. Bicolored ♂ and rufous-winged and -crowned ♀ unmistakable. ♣ Canopy of forest and adjacent clearings. Up to 300 m. ♪ Song: very high, rather sharp "wuh-wheeé-wuwuweé"; "wheeé" stressed at end and "wu" voiced 3–6 ×.

130.8 CINEREOUS BECARD (Caneleiro-cinzento) *Pachyramphus rufus* L 5.1 in./13 cm. ♂ resembles **130.2**. ♀♀ distinctive, but cf. **129.1** and Atillas (Pl. **151**). ♣ Forest borders, woodland, semiopen areas with scattered trees. ♪ Song: very high series of "tu" notes as a sharp, descending almost-trill, ending in rising, stressed "tuwít" (2 sec).

130.9 PINK-THROATED BECARD (Caneleiro-pequeno) *Pachyramphus minor* L 6.7 in./17 cm. ♂ distinctive; ♀ from ♀ **130.10** by grayish mantle. ♣ Upperstory of terra firme; occasionally also in várzea. Up to 800 m. ♪ Call: very/extr. high "pweep" and other nasal notes, like "tju-tjuw" (1st "tju" higher, 2nd lower); song: very high, fast, descending, dry "prrrruh" trill.

130.10 CRESTED (or Plain) **BECARD** (Caneleiro-de-chapéu-preto) *Pachyramphus validus* L 7.1 in./18 cm. ♂ large and 2-toned; ♀ has rufous back. ♣ Woodland, forest borders, plantations. Up to 2000 m. ♪ Song: rather silent; sometimes unstructured series of extr./very high, sharp rolling and strident "see" notes.

130.1

130.6

130.2

130.7

130.3 ♂b a ♀b

130.8 ♀

130.4

130.9 ♀

130.5 a b ♀

130.10 ♀

Plate 131

131.1 PLANALTO TYRANNULET (Piolhinho) *Phyllomyias fasciatus* L 4.3 in./11 cm. Three sspp.: Nom. (**a**; C part of range), *brevirostris* (**b**; SE part of range) and *cearae* (not shown; N part of range; resembles **a**, but duller). Note short, stubby, all-black bill (**131.2–131.4** have base of lower mandible pale). Crown duskier or grayer than mantle. ♣ Humid forest, woodland, riverine belts; SL–1800 m, most frequent at 500–800 m. ♪ Song: differs regionally; in SE a slow series of 3–4 slightly descending, plaintive "puh-puh- -" minor-key notes; elsewhere slightly higher-pitched and more distinctly descending series of 3 more major-keyed notes.

131.2 ROUGH-LEGGED TYRANNULET (Piolhinho-chiador) *Phyllomyias burmeisteri* L 4.3 in./11 cm. Relatively thick, short bill with at least base of lower mandible pale. Crown slightly duller olive than back. Cf. **131.1** and **131.4**. ♣ Humid forest, mainly montane. ♪ Call/song: very/extr. high, sharp "tu-weet" or level/slightly descending "tweet-tweet- -" (up to 9 ×, 3 × "tweet"/sec).

131.3 REISER'S TYRANNULET (Piolhinho-do-grotão) *Phyllomyias reiseri* L 4.3 in./11 cm. Note yellow ear coverts and gray-tinged crown. Bill as in **131.4**. ♣ Dry forest, riverine belts.

131.4 GREENISH TYRANNULET (Piolhinho-verdoso) *Phyllomyias virescens* L 4.7 in./12 cm. Short, stubby bill with pale base to lower mandible. Very like **131.3** (note range), but crown and ear coverts olive. Wing bars bolder than in **131.1** and **131.2**; chest also less olive than in **131.2**. ♣ Humid forest and second growth up to 1000 m. ♪ Song: high, sharp, very short, nervous, twittering almost-trill (level, slightly rising or lowering, then rising); also low, chattered, fast "piurrr."

131.5 GRAY-CAPPED TYRANNULET (Piolhinho-serrano) *Phyllomyias griseocapilla* L 4.3 in./11 cm. Note gray head and yellow flanks. ♣ Humid forest and second growth; 750–1850 m, locally down to sea level. ♪ Call: high, clear, drawn-out, rising "weeeew"; song: short series of 1–4 high, clear, whistled "weew- -" notes. En, R.

131.6 SOOTY-HEADED TYRANNULET (Piolhinho-de-cabeça-cinza) *Phyllomyias grise-* *iceps* L 3.9 in./10 cm. Dark sooty crown. Note wing pattern with white restricted to edges of tertials and secondaries. ♣ Edge and clearings of lowland forest. ♪ Song: very high, short, slightly descending, hurried "wit wit-didurip" (1st "wit" slightly higher and distinctly separated).

131.7 FOREST ELAENIA (Maria-pechim) *Myiopagis* *gaimardii* L 4.7 in./12 cm. Differs from ♀ **131.8** by olive face sides and neck. Note horizontal stance. ♣ Forest, riverine belts, woodland. Up to 1000 m or higher. ♪ Call/song: varied; e.g., very high, upslurred "pssweeét."

131.8 GRAY ELAENIA (Guaracava-cinzenta) *Myiopagis* *caniceps* L 4.7 in./12 cm. Stance like **131.1**. Two sspp.: W *cinerea* (**a**, ♂, ♀ shown; ♂ often with olive back) and S and E Nom. (**b**, ♀ shown; ♂ resembles ♂ **a**). ♂♂ of both sspp. distinctive. ♀♀ resembles **131.7**. ♣ Várzea and terra firme up to 1200 m. ♪ Song: series of varying length, starting with 2–4 single/extr. high notes, then gliding down and accelerating to a long trill, slowing down and often finishing with some up-and-down, lilting notes (3–9 sec).

131.9 YELLOW-CROWNED ELAENIA (Guaracava-de-penacho-amarelo) *Myiopagis fla-* *vivertex* L 5.1 in./13 cm. Differs from **131.10** by yellowish wing bars. ♣ Lower levels in várzea up to 300 m. ♪ Song: very high, sometimes fast, loud series, starting with a very high, sweeping note, followed by a short downslurred shiver ("srrr"), then decelerating to "wee-tju," the total as "chee srrr-wee-tju."

131.10 GREENISH ELAENIA (Guaracava-de-crista-alaranjada) *Myiopagis viridicata* L 5.1 in./13 cm. Note lack of wing bars. ♣ Woodland, esp. near streams and clearings, riverine belts, plantations; occasionally in humid forest; SL–1100 m or higher. ♪ Song: simple series of 4–5 very high "feé-oh-weé wit" notes, last one lower pitched (and missing in call).

131.1 a b

131.6

131.2

131.7

131.3

131.8 ♂a ♀a ♀b

131.4

131.9

131.5

131.10

Plate 132

132.1 YELLOW-BELLIED ELAENIA (Guaracava-de-

barriga-amarela) *Elaenia flavogaster*
L 6.7 in./17 cm. Striking bushy crest
often divided in middle, revealing
white. Belly bright or dull yellow.
Cf. similar-sized **132.2** and smaller
132.8 and **132.10**. ♣ Open woodland, second growth,
savanna, scrubby river edges. Up to 1500 m. ♪ Noisy. Call:
shrieking "sreeuw"; song: long, hurried series with rather
unstructured and repetitive notes, such as "wiwí-pèèè- -";
1st part rather sharp, last part nasal and lower.

132.2 LARGE ELAENIA (Guaracava-grande) *Elaenia*

spectabilis L 7.1 in./18 cm. Differs
from **132.1** by 3rd wing bar and by
smaller crest without white. ♣
Clearings and edges of forest, riverine belts, thickets. ♪ Call: loud,
downslurred "Piuw"; song: high, rapid "t-Wrí-oh-wri"
("Wri" higher and stressed).

132.3 NORONHA ELAENIA (Cocoruta) *Elaenia rid-*

leyana L 6.7 in./17 cm. No similar
bird on Noronha. ♣ Scrub, woodland, gardens. ♪ Call: varied; e.g.,
high, descending "tUuuw" in series
with 1.5-sec intervals. En, R.

132.4 WHITE-CRESTED ELAENIA (Guaracava-de-crista-

branca) *Elaenia albiceps* L 5.9 in./
15 cm. Not safely separable from
132.5. ♣ Scrub, woodland, gardens.
♪ Call: strong, very high, "Wiuuw"
or Wijuuw" (1st part stressed and
higher). Generally silent in Brazil.

132.5 SMALL-BILLED ELAENIA (Guaracava-de-bico-

curto) *Elaenia parvirostris* L 5.9 in./
15 cm. Similar to **132.4**. Both have
whitish (not yellowish) mid-belly,
grayish chest often tinged olive,
bold whitish eyering, and little or no
crest. Sp.**132.4** usually has two wing bars and white streak
on crown visible; **132.5** usually has three wing bars and
crown streak often hidden, but these variable in both. Cf.
132.6. ♣ Clearings and edges of forest and woodland.
Also in suburbs. Mainly in lowlands. ♪ Call: varied; dry
"tjip" or chipping "Tjuw" or "ti-sjuw"; song: hurried,
strong "Wee-dr-dee-wuh" note, for example (2nd note a
roll; "Wee" much higher and "wuh" slightly higher).

132.6 OLIVACEOUS ELAENIA (Tuque) *Elaenia meso-*

leuca L 5.9 in./15 cm. No white
crown stripe, unlike **132.4** and
132.5. Unlike **132.4** and **132.5**,
breast more olive than gray. ♣ Interior and borders of humid forest,
second growth, woodland; SL–2000 m. ♪ Call/song:
clapping "Vrih" or "Vri-der," single or in series.

132.7 BROWNISH ELAENIA (Guaracava-do-rio) *Elae-*

nia pelzelni L 7.1 in./18 cm. Browner
and with less distinct wing bars than
132.2 ♣ Tall tree stands along rivers.
Up to 200 m.

132.8 PLAIN-CRESTED ELAENIA (Guaracava-de-

topete-uniforme) *Elaenia cristata* L
5.9 in./15 cm. High crest (without
white) often erect. Not found outside savanna habitat. ♣ Scrub, open
woodland, cerrado. Up to 1500 m.
♪ Call: downslurred "zèr"; song: raspy "zree-zree-zuzu"
or "zreeeh dudu" and variations thereof.

132.9 RUFOUS-CROWNED ELAENIA (Guaracava-de-

topete-vermelho) *Elaenia ruficeps*
L 5.9 in./15 cm. Note small rufous
patch on hindcrown and streaking
below. ♣ Stunted forest, savanna
with sparse palms and bush, riverine
belts, cerrado. Up to 1000 m and higher. ♪ Call: energetic,
rapid "tji-tji-rrrrr" and other rattles and trills as main part
of series that often start with downslurred "Wée-of-."

132.10 LESSER ELAENIA (Chibum) *Elaenia chiriquen-*

sis L 5.5 in./14 cm. Similar to **132.1**,
but smaller, belly always dull yellowish, and undivided crest shorter
(often held flat, causing a squared-
off hindcrown where white is hid-
den). Also cf. **132.8**. ♣ Dry scrub, cerrado, riverine belts,
plantations, cultivated areas. Up to 2000 m. ♪ Call:e.g.,
very high "wíew" or "tjinéw"; song: very high, sharp, hurried "tju-wee tju-weederwee" (all "wee" notes higher).

Plate 133

133.1 HIGHLAND ELAENIA (Tucão) *Elaenia obscura*

L 6.3 in./16 cm. Note short, stubby bill and round head. Differs from **132.2** by more olive, less grayish underparts. ♣ Undergrowth of humid forest and forest patches, second growth; SL–2000 m. ♪ Call: nasal "rrree"; song: high, melodious "the-weedrrr-wee-der-weé"; most prominent is the short roll "drrr" and the higher pitched "wee" at the end.

133.2 SIERRAN ELAENIA (Guaracava-serrana) *Elaenia pallatangae* L 5.9 in./15 cm. Note

narrow white streak on crown. Differs from **132.4** by rather uniform yellow underparts. ♣ Clearings and edge of humid forest, second growth, stunted scrub at exposed spots; 1500–3000 m. ♪ Call: very/extr. high "sreeh."

133.3 GREAT ELAENIA (Guaracava-gigante) *Elaenia dayi* L 7.9 in./20 cm. Dark; largest

elaenia; note round head. ♣ Montane humid forest, woodland, and scrub. No map shown; common at top of Mt. Roraima.

133.4 SUIRIRI FLYCATCHER (Suiriri-cinzento) *Suiriri suiriri* L 6.3 in./16 cm. Three sspp.:

white-bellied S Nom. Chaco Suiriri (**a**), yellow-bellied E and C *affinis* Campo Suiriri (**b**), and NE *bahiae* (not shown; as **b**, but rump not pale). Note stubby all-black bill and gray head. Cf. **133.5** and smaller **134.7–134.9**. ♣ Open woodland, cerrado, dry savanna with some tall scrub. ♪ Call: sharp, nasal "tjef -tjef - "; song: excited chattering in duet, based on low "chet" notes and high "tjuw" notes.

133.5 CHAPADA FLYCATCHER (Suiriri-da-chapada)

Suiriri islerorum L 6.3 in./16 cm. Differs from **133.4b** by much broader, pale tail tip and shorter bill. Pairs lift wings during display (unlike **133.4**). ♣ Cerrado and areas with tall grass. Up to 750 m. ♪ Song: duet, based on high, nasal "tu-reét" notes and very high "mew" notes.

133.6 YELLOW TYRANNULET (Marianinha-amarela)

Capsiempis flaveola L 4.3 in./11 cm. Looks yellow overall, but in NW Brazil with white throat. ♣ Dense thickets and bamboo at edges and in clearings of forest, woodland, lakesides, overgrown pastures, plantations, mangrove. Up to 1500 m. ♪ Song: high, level or slightly upslurred "trrrrri" trill (1–2 sec); also excited cackling, often in duet.

133.7 BEARDED TACHURI (Papa-moscas-canela) *Polystictus pectoralis* L 3.5 in./9 cm. ♂

distinctly marked. ♀ from ♀ (**133.10**) by shorter bill and less contrasting throat. ♣ Dry open areas, savanna with some scrub, cerrado. ♪ Song: perched or in display flight, very high, thin series of about 3 "see sisi" notes, ending in an odd, low, toneless, very short "krrak," together as "see sisi-krrak." R.

133.8 GRAY-BACKED TACHURI (Papa-moscas-de-costas-cinzentas) *Polystictus superciliaris* L 3.9 in./10 cm. Distinct

color pattern. ♣ Rocky, shrubby grassland, deserted pastures; 900–2300 m. ♪ Call: series of thin, compact "eeh-uk"; song: nervous, sustained "tititi---" interrupted by toneless "purrrrrr" trill. En, R.

133.9 TAWNY-CROWNED PYGMY-TYRANT (Barulhento) *Euscarthmus meloryphus* L

3.9 in./10 cm. Rather plain, but crown coloring diagnostic. ♣ Arid scrub, thickets, woodland edges. Mostly from SL–1500 m, sometimes higher. ♪ Call: sharp, very fast "widereet" or explosive "tiwt," frequently repeated.

133.10 RUFOUS-SIDED PYGMY-TYRANT (Maria-corruíra) *Euscarthmus rufomarginatus* L 4.3 in./11 cm. White throat contrasts with rufous flanks and yellowish central belly. ♣ Cerrado and open savanna up to 1000 m. ♪ Call/song: sustained, toneless, fast, dry rattling "pe-tít-rrrut - -" or "tit-tit-tit-rrrut" ("tit-tit" staccato). R.

Plate 134

134.1 YELLOW-CROWNED TYRANNULET (Maria-te-viu) *Tyrannulus elatus* L 4.3 in./11 cm. Note gray head (incl. cheeks) and stubby all-black bill. ♣ Humid forest, second growth, woodland, plantations, suburbs. Up to 1200 m. ♪ Song: 2-noted, clear, plaintive "wih-weér" (or "free beer"), 2nd note higher, shorter, and stressed.

134.2 WHITE-LORED TYRANNULET (Poiaeiro-de-sobrancelha) *Ornithion inerme* L 3.1 in./8 cm. Striking white wing bars composed of drop-shaped spots. ♣ Several types of humid forest, including várzea between SL and 1000 m. ♪ Call/song: varied; e.g., very high, level, accelerating series of 4–7 thin "wit" notes, or a descending "widirrruh" trill.

134.3 SOUTHERN BEARDLESS-TYRANNULET (Risa-dinha) *Camptostoma obsoletum* L 3.9 in./10 cm. Small and active. Four sspp.: widespread Nom/*cinerascens* (**a**, with head grayer than back, whitish yellow underparts and cinnamon to yellowish white wing bars) and N and W *olivaceum/napaeum* (**b**, little or no contrast between head and back, yellow underparts and yellow to white wing bars). Bill rather thick with at least base of lower mandible pale. Bushy crest usually raised and tail often cocked. ♣ Wide variety of open habitats, incl. woodland and towns. Usually avoids interior of forest. Up to 2000 m. ♪ Song: varied; e.g., a very high, rapid, slightly descending series of "slee" notes as "slee-slee---" (2 sec).

134.4 WHITE-THROATED TYRANNULET (Alegrinho-de-garganta-branca) *Mecocerculus leucophrys* L 4.7 in./12 cm. Characteristic vertical stance with long tail. Note wing pattern. ♣ Montane forest and shrub, mainly above 1300 m. ♪ Song: hurried, very short rattles and "pit" notes, normally in unstructured series.

134.5 SOOTY TYRANNULET (João-pobre) *Serpophaga nigricans* L 4.7 in./12 cm. No similar tyrannulet in its range. Appears rather uniform grayish, browner above. Often pumps tail. ♣ At low levels in various open habitats, mainly near water. ♪ Song: dry trill, preceded by "tú-wut" or very high, strident "Weet-tutdrr" ("Weet" forcefully descending).

134.6 RIVER TYRANNULET (Alegrio-do-rio) *Serpophaga hypoleuca* L 4.3 in./11 cm. As **134.5**, but lores white and underparts paler; no overlap in ranges. ♣ Low scrub along rivers and in flood plains. Up to 200 m, locally higher. ♪ Song: series of very high, strong, hurried, happy-sounding twitters.

134.7 WHITE-CRESTED TYRANNULET (Alegrinho) *Serpophaga subcristata* L 4.3 in./11 cm. Belly pale yellow. Normally shows some white between black stripes on crown. ♣ Edges of lowland forest, woodland, riverine belts, cerrado, plantations, pastures; SL–2000 m. ♪ Song: very high, thin, up-and-down series of "teh "notes separating short "tdrrr" rolls; also very high, slightly meandering rattles (4–5 sec).

134.8 WHITE-BELLIED TYRANNULET (Alegrinho-de-barriga-branca) *Serpophaga munda* L 4.3 in./11 cm. Similar to **134.7**, but belly white. Compare **137.7**. ♣ Scrub and woodland, agricultural land. Up to 2800 m in Br season, in N-br season in lowlands. ♪ Song: rapid, dry, staccato, slightly up-and-down series of "dzip"-, "sit"- and "djup" notes, often with bouncing quality.

134.9 GRAY-CROWNED TYRANNULET (Alegrinho-trinador) *Serpophaga/Inezia* sp. L 4.3 in./11 cm. Extr. similar to **134.7**, but with less white and black on crown (this is often hidden in both species). ♣ Woodland, shrub. *Note:* Often referred to as *Serpophaga griseiceps*, but actually represents an undescribed species (2007). R.

134.10 MOUSE-COLORED TYRANNULET (Bagage-iro) *Phaeomyias murina* L 4.7 in./12 cm. Inconspicuous. Resembles smaller **134.3a**, but lacks crest; eyebrow more prominent (cf. **142.10**) and upperparts browner. Pale base to lower mandible, unlike **133.4** and **137.5**. ♣ Arid scrub, cerrado, woodland, riverine belts, suburbs, mangrove. ♪ Song: varied; e.g., very high, strident, sweeping "tuWEEt" ("WEEt" often without "tu"; ascending several pitches).

Plate 135

135.1 CRESTED DORADITO (Tricolino) *Pseudocolopteryx sclateri* L 4.3 in./11 cm. Three wing bars and white streak through bushy crest. ♣ Reeds and other tall vegetation at water up to 500 m. ♪ Call: mellow "wik wik"; song: very high, liquid "wic-wic-wic- -."

135.2 WARBLING DORADITO (Amarelinho-do-junco) *Pseudocolopteryx flaviventris* L 4.3 in./ 11 cm. Note rufous tinge to crown. ♣ Marshes with reed beds. On migration also in other tall, weedy vegetation. ♪ Call: unstructured series of low, nasal, squeaky "cu-bic cu-wik - -" notes.

135.3 SUBTROPICAL DORADITO (Tricolino-olivá-ceo) *Pseudocolopteryx acutipennis* L 4.7 in./12 cm. Brighter green than **135.2** and **135.4** and in different range. ♣ Reeds, marsh, riverine shrub, fields, pastures. Below 700 m outside breeding season. V.

135.4 DINELLI'S DORADITO (Tricolino-pardo) *Pseudocolopteryx dinelliana* L 4.7 in./ 12 cm. Very similar to **135.2**, but differs by more uniform brownish upperparts. ♣ Marsh and shrub up to 500 m. ♪ Song: low, soft "tiderit-zit tiderit-zit - -" sounding like a wooden rattle, except last extr. high "zit." V.

135.5 LESSER WAGTAIL-TYRANT (Papa-moscas-do-sertão) *Stigmatura napensis* L 5.1 in./ 13 cm. NW Nom. shown (**a**) and smaller NE ssp. *bahiae* (**b**, with reduced white at tail tips). Differs from similar **135.6** by size, white (not dark) base of undertail, browner (less gray) upperparts and duller, more buffy yellow underparts. ♣ Grassy and brushy areas near rivers, mainly river islands. Form **b** in NE in arid scrub. Up to 500 m. ♪ Call: high, sharp "Peeh"; song: often in duet; tjilping "Pée-tjer-tjírp," repeated in rapid series.

135.6 GREATER WAGTAIL-TYRANT (Alegrinho-balança-rabo) *Stigmatura budytoides* L 5.9 in./15 cm. Very similar to **135.5**, which see. ♣ Arid scrub, woodland, riverine belts. Up to 1000 m. ♪ Song: often given in duet; high, liquid series of "Wee-tjer- -" from one bird and "tidrrr- -" from the other.

135.7 SLENDER-FOOTED TYRANNULET (Poiaeiro-de-pata-fina) *Zimmerius gracilipes* L 3.9 in./10 cm. Note pale eyes, gray-ish crown, and crisp yellow edging of wing feathers (not wing bars). Often with cocked tail. ♣ Edge, clearings, and interior of humid forest. Up to 500 m, occasionally higher. ♪ Call: very high, decisive "tjev"; song: very high, fast, strident "tu-rrrit" ("rrrit" jumping up).

135.8 CHAPMAN'S BRISTLE-TYRANT (Barbudinho-do-tepui) *Phylloscartes chapmani* L 4.7 in./12 cm. No similar bird in its restricted range. Note upright stance. ♣ Wet montane forest between 1000 and 2000 m.

135.9 SOUTHERN BRISTLE-TYRANT (Barbudinho) *Phylloscartes eximius* L 4.3 in./11 cm. Note distinct facial pattern. From **140.1** by relatively longer tail. Same upright stance as **135.8**. ♣ Borders and interior of humid forest including *Araucaria* woodland. Up to 600 m. ♪ Song: extr. high, energetic, strident, rattling "vrrrrrjeh" trill (1–2 sec). R.

135.10 MINAS GERAIS TYRANNULET (Cara-dourada) *Phylloscartes roquettei* L 4.7 in./12 cm. No similar bird in its restricted range. Rufous lores difficult to see. ♣ Dry forest, tall trees in scrub, riv-erine belts. ♪ Song: low, rattling "tjuddrrr-twit" (1st part slightly descending, 2nd part as a sort of full stop). En, R.

135.1

135.7

135.2

135.8

135.3

135.9

135.4

135.10

a   b   135.6

135.5

Plate 136

136.1 SAO PAULO TYRANNULET (Não-pode-parar)

Phylloscartes paulista L 3.9 in./10 cm. Wing bars more distinct than in **136.2** and only rarely cocks tail. ♣ Borders and interior of humid forest up to 500 m, locally up to 1000 m. ♪ Song: very/extr. high, strident "tits" or "ti-tseet" (repeated). R.

136.2 OUSTALET'S TYRANNULET (Papa-moscas-de-olheiras) *Phylloscartes oustaleti* L

4.7 in./12 cm. Differs from smaller **135.9** by conspicuous yellow eye-rings. ♣ Interior of humid forest, mainly 500–900 m. ♪ Call: short "trrrrri," trill small "tek" notes; song: energetic, high, nasal "tjeu-wí-tjeu-wítja." En, R.

136.3 SERRA DO MAR TYRANNULET (Estalinho)

Phylloscartes difficilis L 4.3 in./11 cm. Unmistakable by green-olive upper-parts strongly contrasting with whitish gray underparts. ♣ Humid forest between 950 and 2150 m. ♪ Song: unstructured, slow series of low "djuw" notes. ♪ Song: very high, sharp yet hoarse, 3-noted "wé-do-die," so fast that 2nd and 3rd note merge if heard from some distance. En, R.

136.4 ALAGOAS (or Long-tailed) **TYRANNULET**

(Cara-pintada) *Phylloscartes ceciliae* L 4.7 in./12 cm. Note long, regularly cocked tail and two wing bars. Only *Phylloscartes* tyrannulet in its tiny range. ♣ Atlantic forest and second growth; 400–550 m. En, R.

136.5 MOTTLE-CHEEKED TYRANNULET (Borbolet-inha-do-mato) *Phylloscartes ventra-lis* L 4.7 in./12 cm. Chin and

supraloral whitish. Note horizontal stance and long, regularly cocked tail like other members of the genus, but unlike **131.1, 131.2,** and **131.4.** ♣ Mainly montane forest, incl. *Araucaria,* second growth, riverine belts. Up to 1500 m, locally higher. ♪ Song: very high, mainly level pitched, twittering trill, which starts hesitantly, acceler-ates, then slows down at the end with some very sharp, very high notes.

136.6 RESTINGA TYRANNULET (Maria-da-restinga)

Phylloscartes kronei L 4.7 in./12 cm. Note clear wing bars, lack of con-trasting blackish auricular-patch (cf. **136.1**), and yellowish face (cf. **136.5,** which occurs at higher altitudes in range of this species). Restricted to lowlands in its small range. ♣ Coastal woodland, second growth, and riverine belts at sea level. ♪ Call: very high "swee"; song: very high, fast, twittering series. En, R.

136.7 BAHIA TYRANNULET (Borboletinha-baiana)

Phylloscartes beckeri L 4.7 in./12 cm. Sides of face pale buff. ♣ Montane forest; 750–1200 m. En, R.

136.8 OLIVE-GREEN TYRANNULET (Borboletinha-guianense) *Phylloscartes virescens* L

4.7 in./12 cm. No eye stripe, only black lore. ♣ Canopy of humid for-est up to 500 m.

136.9 BLACK-FRONTED TYRANNULET (Maria-de-testa-preta) *Phylloscartes nigrifrons*

L 4.7 in./12 cm. Color pattern and horizontal posture distinctive. ♣ Humid montane forest and tall sec-ond growth; 800–1800 m. ♪ Song: series of soft, very high "tji," followed by short dry trill, like "tjítrrrrr" (1 sec).

136.10 BAY-RINGED TYRANNULET (Maria-pequena)

Phylloscartes sylviolus L 4.7 in./12 cm. White eye and buff ocular area diagnostic (the latter some-times reduced). ♣ Edge and interior of lowland forest up to 600 m. ♪ Song: rapid, almost level twittering, sounding (simplified) like "twitwi--twididirit-tjutju"; liquid "twi" tones extr. high; descending "tjutju" low pitched. R.

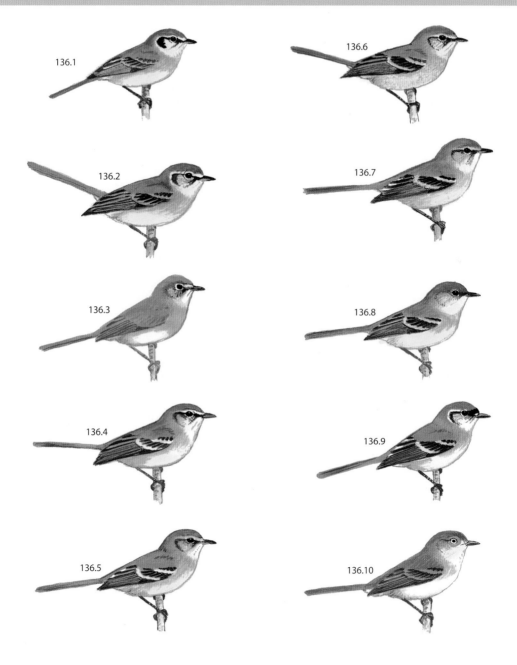

Plate 137

137.1 OCHRE-BELLIED FLYCATCHER (Abre-asa) *Mio-*

nectes oleagineus L 5.1 in./13 cm. Differs from **137.2** by presence of wing bars and pale edges of tertials. Like **137.2** and **137.3**, it often flicks one wing. ♣ Lower levels in várzea and terra firme, second growth, riverine belts, gardens. Up to 1800 m. ♪ Song at dispersed leks: very high, slightly rolling and ascending "preet," repeated and alternated with series of 5–7 low, nasal "tjuw" notes.

137.2 MACCONNELL'S FLYCATCHER (Abre-asa-da-

mata) *Mionectes macconnelli* L 5.5 in./ 14 cm. Differs from **137.1** by plain wings. ♣ Understory of forest, mainly terra firme, less in várzea. Mainly lowlands, but to 2000 m on the tepuis. ♪ Song: unstructured, meandering series of "wrib"notes with inclusions of rattling "tjuw-uhuhuhuhuh" sounds (a bit like a toy trumpet).

137.3 GRAY-HOODED FLYCATCHER (Abre-asa-de-

cabeça-cinza) *Mionectes rufiventris* L 5.5 in./14 cm. Note gray hood and olive back. ♣ Understory of humid forest and second growth up to 1000 m. ♪ Song: slightly descending and accelerating, at the end slightly rising and slowing down series of nasal "tjew" notes.

137.4 SEPIA-CAPPED FLYCATCHER (Cabeçudo) *Lepto-*

pogon amaurocephalus L 5.5 in./ 14 cm. Note dark auricular patch and brown-tinged crown. Regularly lifts one wing. ♣ Forest and woodland. Up to 1100 m. ♪ Call: angry-sounding, slightly rising (or descending) trill; song: very high, nasal trill, at the end bouncing down (2 sec).

137.5 SOUTHERN SCRUB-FLYCATCHER (Guaracava-

modesta) *Sublegatus modestus* L 5.1 in./13 cm. Cf. **137.6**. ♣ Dry to arid habitats with trees and scrub. ♪ Call: very high, thin, nasal "tjíew" or "tjíe-wu"; song: very high, short, strong, sharp warbling series, incorporating call, like "tí-tjuw."

137.6 AMAZONIAN (or Todd's) **SCRUB-FLYCATCHER**

(Sertanejo-escuro) *Sublegatus obscurior* L 5.5 in./14 cm. Differs from **137.5** by slightly longer bill (but still very short and all-black) and more contrasting underparts. ♣ Scrubby clearings, woodland, forest edge; SL–450 m. ♪ Call: upslurred "chuweé"; song: e.g., "Weéh wiwi rru-rru-rru-dru-dru" (1st 2 notes very high and shreeking; "rru" and "dru" in a low, calm tempo).

137.7 PLAIN TYRANNULET (Alegrinho-do-chaco)

Inezia inornata L 3.9 in./10 cm. Very similar to larger **134.7** and **134.8**, but crown plain and base of lower mandible sometimes pale. ♣ Woodland, forest borders, shrubby vegetation at rivers and lakes. ♪ Song: very/extr. high note with stuttering start, rising in strength and pitch, then descending, like "srrreeeeeh."

137.8 AMAZONIAN (Inezia or) **TYRANNULET** (Ama-

relinho) *Inezia subflava* L 4.7 in./ 12 cm. Note prominent and strongly contrasting white "spectacles." Eyes whitish, dark in Imm. (**a**). Lacks gray on chest, unlike **134.7–134.9**, **137.4**, **137.5**, and **137.7**. Also cf. **137.9**. ♣ Shrubby vegetation near water, várzea, swampy forest. Up to 200 m. ♪ Song: varied; e.g., very high, strident, or clear "teweét" notes in very long series or a stream of fluted "tíh-tjuw" ("tíh,"–dry and sometimes doubled; ad "tjuw" fluted).

137.9 PALE-TIPPED (Inezia or) **TYRANNULET** (Ama-

relinho-da-amazônia) *Inezia caudata* L 4.7 in./12 cm. Ad. and Imm. virtually identical to **137.8**, but note range. ♣ Woodland, riverine belts, várzea, mangrove. Up to 400 m. ♪ Song: starts with a very short, crumpled roll and continues with 6–10 very high, descending, loud, sharp "teeuw" notes, each one downslurred.

137.10 MANY-COLORED RUSH-TYRANT (Papa-piri)

Tachuris rubrigastra L 4.3 in./11 cm. Unmistakable in its habitat by color pattern. ♣ Reed beds; SL–2500 m and higher. ♪ Call: high "urk" repeated at 1 ×/sec; song: "wéetj'urr-wéetjuwéetj'urrr," almost double-voiced, with "urr" as a gurgling lower voice.

137.1

137.6

137.2

137.7

137.3

a
137.8

137.4

137.9

137.5

137.10

Plate 138

138.1 RORAIMAN FLYCATCHER (Felipe-do-tepui) *Myiophobus roraimae* L 5.5 in./14 cm. Forest dweller. Note distinctive rufous wing bars. ♣ Lower levels of humid forest on mountain slopes; 500–2000 m.

138.2 BRAN-COLORED FLYCATCHER (Filipe) *Myio-* *phobus fasciatus* L 5.1 in./13 cm. Chest and flanks streaked. ♀♀ black-tyrants (Pl.**145**) with streaked underparts have rufous inner webs of tail feathers (undertail mainly rufous, not dusky) and stronger contrast between rump and back. ♣ Thick vegetatation at forest edge, brushy savanna, pastures with scattered bush, riverine belts; SL–1500 m. ♪ Call: fast "peéh-wdrrrr" (0.5 sec) or with 2nd part drawn out to slow rattle (4 sec); song: sparrow-like "tjur" (1 ×/sec).

138.3 SHARP-TAILED (Grass-)**TYRANT** (Papa-moscas- do-campo) *Culicivora caudacuta* L 3.9 in./10 cm. No other bird with same general color pattern and long thin tail in its habitat. ♣ Dry savanna, cerrado, often at marsh and streams. Up to 1400 m. ♪ Call/song: very high, nasal twittering trill in duet with series of nasal, almost toneless, pumped-out "sree" notes, which gradually gain in strength. R.

NOTE: *Hemitriccus* Tody-Tyrants (Pl. **138** and **139**) have bristles and also flat bills, not unlike *Todirostrum*.

138.4 SNETHLAGE'S (or Tiny) **TODY-TYRANT** (Maria-sebinha) *Hemitriccus minor* L 3.9 in./10 cm. Note long crown feathers. Can have quite yellowish underparts, perhaps associated with different sspp. Nom. is more grayish (esp. on breast); *snethlageae* and *minima* are more yellow. Wing bars less distinct than in very similar **138.9**,**138.10**, and **139.10**. Streaks on throat less dusky than in **138.10** and lores darker than in **138.9**. ♣ Dense vegetation in terra firme and second growth. In W mainly in Igapo. ♪ Call/ song: short, gravelly, downslurred "drrru" trill.

138.5 BOAT-BILLED TODY-TYRANT (Maria-bicudinha) *Hemitriccus josephinae* L 4.3 in./ 11 cm. No wing bars; breast tinged olive. ♣ In vines at edge and clearings of humid forest. ♪ Call/song: high, falling, slightly nasal "pic-pic---" (2–3 × "pic").

138.6 FLAMMULATED PYGMY- (or Bamboo-)**TYRANT** (Maria-de-peito-machetado) *Hemitriccus flammulatus* L 4.3 in./11 cm. Like **138.7** and **138.8**, confined to bamboo, but not in same range. Note drab buff-brown breast. ♣ Bamboo in terra firme and second growth. ♪ Call/song: high, dry "krru" or "krik" with irregular intervals.

138.7 DRAB-BREASTED PYGMY- (or Bamboo-) **TYRANT** (Olho-falso) *Hemitriccus diops* L 4.3 in./11 cm. Differs from **138.8** by distinct white loral spot. Shows indistinct whitish crescent between buffy throat and breast. ♣ Bamboo at edge and in interior of humid forest and second growth up to 1300 m. ♪ Call/song: very high, upslurred, scratchy "krrru," like a mini-rattle.

138.8 BROWN-BREASTED PYGMY- (or Bamboo-) **TYRANT** (Catraca) *Hemitriccus obsoletus* L 4.3 in./11 cm. Loral spot is buff, not white. ♣ Bamboo patches in humid forest and second growth; 1200–2300 m, occasionally lower. ♪ Call/song: irregular series of very high "tic" notes.

138.9 WHITE-EYED TODY-TYRANT (Maria-de-olho- branco) *Hemitriccus zosterops* L 4.3 in./ 11 cm. Very like **138.4**. Belly yellow, unlike **139.10** and clear yellow edging to the primaries, unlike **138.10**. ♣ Terra firme in hilly country up to 850 m. ♪ Call: very high, sharp, dry "pic"; song: very high, short, very dry, sharp, slightly slowing and descending rattling trill.

138.10 ZIMMER'S TODY-TYRANT (Maria-mirim) *Hemitriccus minimus* L 3.9 in./10 cm. Differs from **138.4** by crisper streaks on breast and distinct wing bars. Broad yellow edges of inner wing feathers and darker edge of outer wing feathers causes 2-toned effect on wing, unlike **138.4**, **138.9**, **138.10**. ♣ Stunted forest on poor soil. Up to 450 m. ♪ Song: simple, high, rather sharp "wtttti" trill (fast, upslurred "w" colliding with 1st "t").

Plate 139

139.1 EYE-RINGED TODY-TYRANT (Tiririzinho-do-mato) *Hemitriccus orbitatus* L 4.7 in./ 12 cm. Note distinct face and wing pattern. ♣ Humid forest and second growth between SL and 600 m, occasionally higher. ♪ Song: very high, slightly lowered, "drrrih." En, R.

139.2 JOHANNES'S TODY-TYRANT (Maria-peruviana) *Hemitriccus iohannis* L 4.3 in./ 11 cm. Similar to **139.3**, but no white eyering, streaking below less distinct, and markings on wing more prominent. ♪ Song: high, brisk "tjudrrrri" ("tju" colliding with "d"; "drrrri" rising).

139.3 STRIPE-NECKED TODY-TYRANT (Sebinho-rajado-amarelo) *Hemitriccus striaticollis* L 4.3 in./11 cm. Little overlap in range with **139.2**. Differs from **142.1** by white eyering and indistinct pattern on wing coverts. ♣ Thickets and bamboo in riverine belts and second growth. Up to 700 m. ♪ Song: very high, fast, liquid, yet sharp "Didrdr," "Wic," or sweeping "Wheet."

139.4 HANGNEST TODY-TYRANT (Tachuri-campainha) *Hemitriccus nidipendulus* L 3.9 in./10 cm. Rather plain, greenish above, whitish below, indistinct wing bars. ♣ Woodland and bracken thickets; SL–900 m. ♪ Song: very high, fast, rolling "tidr-de-tidr-de-dir." En.

139.5 PEARLY-VENTED TODY-TYRANT (Sebinho-de-olho-de-ouro) *Hemitriccus margaritaceiventer* L 3.9 in./10 cm. Nom. (**a**) and ssp. *wuchereri* (**b**, with white, more striking wing bars) shown. Cf. **139.6**. ♣ Arid scrub, undergrowth of tall woodland, shrubby pastures, occasionally in riverine belts; SL–1000, locally much higher. ♪ Song: modest, soft yet emphasized series of 6 stepping-down notes, 2nd highest pitched, like "tuc-tíc-tuc-tuc-tuc."

139.6 PELZELN'S TODY-TYRANT (Maria-da-campina) *Hemitriccus inornatus* L 3.5 in./9 cm. As **139.5b**, but not in same range. Note streaks on throat continue over breast. ♣ Stunted woodland. ♪ Song: rather low, modest series of 7–10 well-separated notes, rising at the end and accelerating to a short, upslurred trill.

139.7 BUFF-BREASTED TODY-TYRANT (Maria-do-nordeste) *Hemitriccus mirandae* L 3.9 in./10 cm. Resembles **139.8**, but unique in range. ♣ Highland forest and second growth, at slopes between 600 and 1000 m. ♪ Song: short series of 7–8 sharp, well-accentuated notes, slightly accelerating and ascending. En, R.

139.8 KAEMPFER'S TODY-TYRANT (Maria-catarinense) *Hemitriccus kaempferi* L 3.9 in./10 cm. Note pale edge of tertials and buffy face. No overlap with **139.7**. ♣ Thick undergrowth of lowland forest and second growth. ♪ Song: short, level series of 2–6 short, very high, accentuated, nasal notes. En, R.

139.9 FORK-TAILED PYGMY- (or Tody-) **TYRANT** (Papa-moscas-estrela) *Hemitriccus furcatus* L 4.3 in./11 cm. Unmistakable by face and tail pattern. ♣ Edge of humid forest, often near bamboo. Below 1200 m. ♪ Song: short, dry, hurried, temperamental-sounding rattle, like "t-drrrir" ("t" lower). En, R.

139.10 WHITE-BELLIED TODY-TYRANT (Maria-de-barriga-branca) *Hemitriccus griseipectus* L 4.3 in./11 cm. As **138.9**, but with white belly and different range. Cf. **138.4** and **138.10**. ♣ Terra firme in low and hilly country. ♪ Song: very high, cheerful, sharp but full "Hi Louis."

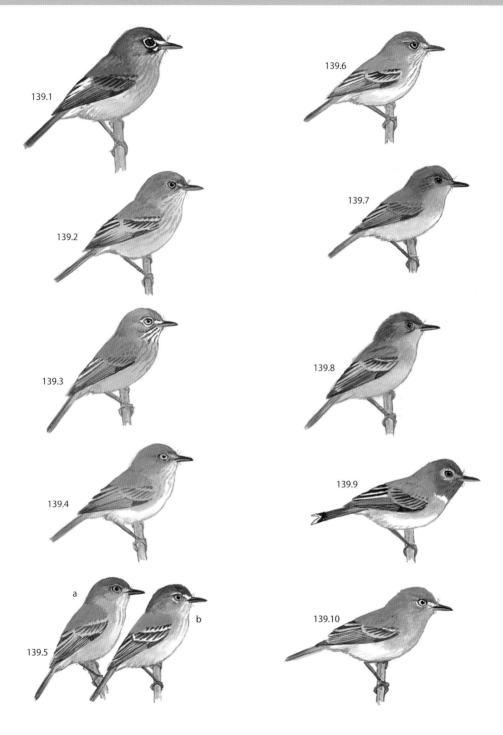

Plate 140

140.1 EARED PYGMY-TYRANT (Miudinho) *Myiornis* *auricularis* L 2.8 in./7 cm. Unmistakable by tiny size and face pattern. ♣ Shrubby growth at edge of humid forest up to 1250 m. ♪ Call: high stressed "pic" notes; song: very high, short, clear trill, often preceded by lower, short "wit," together as "wit-trrruh." *Note*: Pernambuco population might be an undescribed species.

140.2 SHORT-TAILED PYGMY-TYRANT (Caçula) *Myiornis ecaudatus* L 2.4 in./6 cm. Unmistakable by tiny size, very short tail, and head color and patterning. ♣ Edge and clearings of humid forest and second growth up to 950 m. ♪ Call: very high, slightly rasping, yet clear "srreeh-srruw" (last part lower).

140.3 ? SCALE-CRESTED PYGMY-TYRANT (?) *Lophotriccus pileatus* L 3.9 in./10 cm. Should be unmistakable by rufous-with-black crest. ♣ Bamboo stands in forest and second growth; 300 m and higher. ♪ Call: unstructured series of high, "pruk" notes.

140.4 DOUBLE-BANDED PYGMY-TYRANT (Maria- fiteira) *Lophotriccus vitiosus* L 3.9 in./ 10 cm. Two yellowish wing bars and edging of wing. Edging of crest feathers yellowish in W, gray in NE. ♣ Interior and edge of terra firme and várzea, second growth. Up to 800 m. ♪ Call: downslurred, raspy "srrruh."

140.5 LONG-CRESTED PYGMY-TYRANT (Maria- topetuda) *Lophotriccus eulophotes* L 3.9 in./10 cm. Differs from **140.4** by long, different-colored crest, indistinct wing bars, and range. ♣ Bamboo-rich undergrowth of swampy riverine belts and forest edges up to 400 m. ♪ Call: very high, sharp, soft twitter (about 5–6 descending "tic" notes, last one higher).

140.6 HELMETED PYGMY-TYRANT (Caga-sebinho- de-penacho) *Lophotriccus galeatus* L 3.9 in./10 cm. Shorter crest and paler wing bars than **140.4**. ♣ Terra firme and várzea, second growth, savanna woodland. Up to 1100 m. ♪ Call: series of high, staccato "pic" notes.

140.7 PALE-EYED PYGMY-TYRANT (Maria-de-olho- claro) *Atalotriccus pilaris* L 3.9 in./ 10 cm. Differs from **139.5** by greener upperparts and yellowish wash to lower underparts. ♣ Savanna with boulders, woodland, dry forest. Lowlands. ♪ Call: very high, slightly descending, dry "prruh" trill; song: variations of raspy, twittering "prruc-príc-príc-rin."

140.8 BLACK-CHESTED TYRANT (Maria-bonita) *Taeniotriccus andrei* L 4.7 in./12 cm. Unmistakable by coloring of head and wing pattern. ♣ Low levels of terra firme with bamboo or *Cecropia*. Also in várzea. ♪ Call: series of well-spaced, low, emphasized, nasal "tjuw" notes; song: series of widely spaced, alternating "tjuw" and higher "tuweet-tuweet" notes.

140.9 BROWNISH (Flycatcher or) **TWISTWING** (Flautim-pardo) *Cnipodectes subbrunneus* L (♂) 6.3 in./16 cm, (♀) L 5.5 in./14 cm. Grayish crown without crest. ♣ Understory with dense vines and tangles of humid lowland forest. ♪ Song: loud, ringing "tjeuw-tjeuw," each note downslurred.

140.10 RUFOUS TWISTWING (Flautim-rufo) *Cnipo-* *dectes superrufus* L (♂) 8.7 in./22 cm, (♀) 7.9 in./20 cm. Bright rufous overall, without the paler belly of smaller **150.4**. Also cf. Attilas (Pl. **151**), with different bills. ♣ Bamboo thickets in or near humid forest.

140.1

140.2

140.3

140.4

140.5

140.6

140.7

140.8

140.9

140.10

Plate 141

141.1 BLACK-AND-WHITE TODY-TYRANT (Maria-picaça) *Poecilotriccus capitalis* L 3.5 in./ 9 cm. Unmistakable. Note white edges of tertials in ♀. ♣ Scrubby growth, tangled vine, and, often, bamboo at forest edges. ♪ Song: high to very high, hurried, unstructured, rather nasal twittering, often with repetitions of short phrases.

141.2 BUFF-CHEEKED TODY-FLYCATCHER (Maria-do-madeira) *Poecillotriccus senex* L 3.5 in./9 cm. Differs from **141.5** and **141.6** by darker grayish head and more distinct breast streaks. ♣ Low-stature humid forest near rivers and white-sand woodland. ♪ Voice unknown. En.

141.3 RUDDY TODY-FLYCATCHER (Ferreirinho-ferru-gem) *Poecillotriccus russatus* L 3.9 in./ 10 cm. Unmistakable by warm buff face and breast. ♣ Dense thickets at edge of humid forest and second growth at 1200–2500 m. ♪ Song: high, quick, quiet "tid-tdrrrrr," last part as a fast, descending, rattled trill.

141.4 OCHRE-FACED TODY-FLYCATCHER (Tororó) *Poecillotriccus plumbeiceps* L 3.5 in./ 9 cm. No similar bird in its range. Note face pattern and color. ♣ Dense vegetation including bamboo and bracken at edge of forest and in second growth; 750–2750 m. ♪ Call/song: very fast "prrrrur" rattle (1 or 2 ×, 2nd time slightly lower).

141.5 RUSTY-FRONTED TODY-FLYCATCHER (Fer-reirinho-de-cara-parda) *Poecillotriccus latirostris* L 3.5 in./9 cm. Similar to **141.6**, but with rusty-buff ocular area, ochre wing bars, and whitish belly. ♣ Dense shrubby growth at edge of second growth, neglected pastures, along forest edge and at rivers. Up to 1100 m. ♪ Song: short, descending "tdrrrur" rattle, preceded by some "tic" notes.

141.6 SMOKY-FRONTED TODY-FLYCATCHER (Fer-reirinho-de-testa-parda) *Poecillotriccus fumifrons* L 3.5 in./9 cm. Characterized by pale yellow belly and wing bars and by buffy lore. ♣ Dense shrubby vegetation at forest edge and at neglected agricultural land, bush patches in savanna. Up to 400 m. ♪ Song: as **141.5**, but slightly higher pitched.

141.7 SLATE-HEADED TODY-FLYCATCHER (Ferreir-inho-da-capoeira) *Poecillotriccus sylvia* L 3.9 in./10 cm. Note white supraloral and eyering, contrasting with gray crown. Eye color variable. ♣ Shrubby forest edges, overgrown agricultural land, understory of riverine belts. Up to 1100 m. ♪ Song: unstructured series of well-spaced "tic" notes and low, level, rather froglike "prruh-prruh."

141.8 ATLANTIC ROYAL FLYCATCHER (Maria-leque-do-sudeste) *Onychorhynchus swainsoni* L 6.3 in./16 cm. Brighter below than **141.9**, but no overlap in range. ♣ Humid forest; SL–800 m. ♪ Voice as **141.9**. En, R.

141.9 AMAZON ROYAL FLYCATCHER (Maria-leque) *Onychorhynchus coronatus* L 6.3 in./ 16 cm. Note rufous tail and hammerhead jizz. Rarely (crosswise) fanned crest, orange in ♀. Not in range of **141.8**. ♣ Humid forest and woodland, mainly near water. Up to 1000 m. ♪ call: loud, repeated, 2-noted "ée-uh"; mostly silent.

141.10 RUDDY-TAILED FLYCATCHER (Papa-moscas-uirapuru) *Terenotriccus erythrurus* L 3.9 in./10 cm. Differs from **127.8** by pinkish legs, presence of whiskers, and longer tail. ♣ Lower levels of várzea, terra firme, and second growth up to 1200 m. ♪ Call/song: extr. high "fiuw-Fi" ("fiuw" gliding-down, "Fi" emphasized and higher).

141.1
141.2
141.3
141.4
141.5
141.6
141.7
141.8
141.9
141.10

Plate 142

142.1 SPOTTED TODY-FLYCATCHER (Ferreirinho-estriado) *Todirostrum maculatum* L 3.9 in./10 cm. Differs from **139.3** by distinct yellow edging on wing coverts and lack of white eyering. ♣ Dense shrubby vegetation, mainly near water. Also light woodland and gardens. ♪ Song: extr. high, slow, staccato series of evenly spaced, slightly descending notes, often each note doubled in duet; also extr. high, short, dry trills and twitters.

142.2 GRAY-HEADED (or Yellow-lored) **TODY-FLY-CATCHER** (Teque-teque) *Todiro-* *strum poliocephalum* L 3.9 in./10 cm. Note striking yellow lores. Differs from **142.3a** by more extensive lores and lack of white tipping to undertail. ♣ Shrubby edge of humid forest and second growth. Up to 1200 m. ♪ Song extr. high, weak "twit," followed by even higher, energetic "witwit---" ("wit" 4–6 ×). En.

142.3 COMMON TODY-FLYCATCHER (Ferreirinho-relógio) *Todirostrum cinereum* L 3.9 in./10 cm. Dark head. Some individuals have pale yellow lores (**a**). Mantle gray in N. Eyes dark in Juv. ♣ Wide variety of wooded habitats, incl. mangrove. Avoids densely forested regions. Up to 2000 m. ♪ Call/song: series of low, short, dry "trrr-trrr---" trills; a variety of high/very high, single, double, and triple "tic" notes and extr. high "weet-widiwi" (last part as almost-trill).

142.4 PAINTED TODY-FLYCATCHER (Ferreirinho-de-sobrancelha) *Todirostrum pictum* L 3.9 in./10 cm. With yellow or dark (**a**) eye. Note white supraloral and throat. ♣ Canopy and borders of várzea, terra firme, and other types of forest, second growth, and plantations up to 400 m. ♪ Call/song: sequences of irregularly spaced, extr. high "tsit" notes.

142.5 YELLOW-BROWED TODY-FLYCATCHER (Ferreirinho-pintado) *Todirostrum chryso-* *crotaphum* L 3.9 in./10 cm. Eyes dark or (rarely) pale. In Brazil, 5 sspp., all differ from other tody-tyrants in mainly black head with yellow eyebrow/eye stripe. Shown are NW *guttatum* (**a**), NE *illegeri* (**b**), and SW *neglectum* (**c**). Sspp. *similis* (not shown, local in Pará) and *chrysocrotaphum* (not shown, in W) resemble **a**, but black markings on throat reduced or absent. ♣ Canopy of várzea, terra firme, and second growth. Up to 1400 m. ♪ Call/song: unstructured, extr. high series of "pic" notes.

142.6 WHISKERED FLYCATCHER (Assanhadinho) *Myiobius barbatus* L 5.1 in./13 cm. Several sspp.: SE *mastacalis* (**a**) and N and W Nom. (**b**, with dull grayish-olive chest) shown; not shown NE *insignis* and C *amazonicus*, both

of which resemble **b**. Cf. **142.7**. ♣ Understory of humid forest and second growth. In Amazonia mainly in terra firme. Up to 1000 m. ♪ Call: extr. high "tic" notes, given at uneven intervals.

142.7 BLACK-TAILED FLYCATCHER (Assadinho-de-cauda-preta) *Myiobius atricaudus* L 5.1 in./13 cm. Several sspp.: C and NE *connectens* (**a**), coastal NE *snethlagei* (**b**), and SE *ridgewayi* (**c**) shown; not shown is W ssp. *adjacens*, resembling **a**. Sspp. *snethlagei* and *ridgewayi* rather uniform below, unlike **142.7**. Sspp. *connectens* and *adjacens* with chest brownish buff; color often extending slightly onto flanks, unlike overlapping sspp. of **142.7**. ♣ Undergrowth of forest, woodland, second growth. Not usually in terra firme in Amazonia. Up to 1000 m. ♪ Song: series of very/extr. high "see" notes; may be given in a slow, descending series of 4 notes or in a fast, meandering, downslurred series during 2 sec.

142.8 CLIFF FLYCATCHER (Gibão-de-couro) *Hirundinea* *ferruginea* L 6.7 in./17 cm. Nom. (NW, with all-dark upperparts and restricted red in wings) and ssp. *bellicosa* (Swallow Flycatcher, S and E) shown. Unmistakable by shape, posture, and habitat. ♣ At cliffs and other rocky places near tall forest, wooded slopes, fronts of buildings; SL–2000 m. ♪ Call/song: high, very high, or extr. high "Wée-didrrrr" and variations thereof.

142.9 FUSCOUS FLYCATCHER (Guaracavuçu) *Cnemo-* *triccus fuscatus* L 5.5 in./14 cm. Belly white (in E and SC ssp. *bimaculatus*) to yellowish (in SE Nom. and Amazonian *duidae, fuscatior,* and *fumosus*). Lower mandible mainly/all black, except in NW *duidae*, where it is all yellow. All sspp. with pale eyebrow (cf. **134.10**) and two clearly defined cinnamon-buff wing bars. Bill and tail rather long. ♣ Thick undergrowth of forest and woodland, often near water, riverine belts. Below 500 m, occasionally much higher. ♪ Call: e.g., loud, fluted "Weeeuw" or melodious "tee-Tjúw" (2nd note higher pitched and emphasized); song: unstructured but musical, high twittering with characteristic, rapid, slightly descending "wítititit" and slightly nasal "srree."

142.10 EULER'S FLYCATCHER (Enferrujado) *Lathro-* *triccus euleri* L 5.1 in./13 cm. Belly yellowish or white. Lacks eyebrow of **142.10**, and lower mandible always pale. Upperparts browner and wing bars deeper cinnamon-buff than in **144.7** and **144.8**, and perches more upright than **144.3** and **144.4**. ♣ Open undergrowth and borders of humid forest and second growth up to 1500 m. ♪ Song: varied series of 2–5 notes, 1st one normally stressed and slightly longer than slightly descending notes; thereafter "Tjeew-tjuh" or "Tjeew-terduh."

Plate 143

143.1 OLIVACEOUS FLATBILL (Bico-chato-grande)

Rhynchocyclus olivaceus L 5.9 in./ 15 cm. Note yellowish edging of wings and broad bill with pale lower mandible. ♣ Lower levels of humid forest and second growth up to 500 m. ♪ Call: short, very hurried "twee-wi-wi"; song: soft, slightly nasal, cheerful, repeating "wéé-wewee-tewee-wée."

143.2 YELLOW-OLIVE (Flatbill or) **FLYCATCHER**

(Bico-chato-de-orelha-preta) *Tolmomyias sulphurescens* L 5.5 in./14 cm. Note broad bill with pale lower mandible (very tip sometimes dark). Gray-crowned SE Nom. (**a**) has dusky auricular patch, unlike **143.4**. Remaining sspp. have olive crown (**b**; undescribed EC taxon shown, cf. **143.5**) or resemble smaller **143.3** (**c**, *cherrei* from Amapá and Roraima shown), but without pale panel at base of primaries. Eyes usually pale in far N. ♣ Wide range of wooded habitats, from humid forest to woodland, plantations, riverine belts. Not usually inside terra firme in area of overlap with **143.3** and **143.4**. ♣ Wide variety of wooded habitats, from humid forest to woodland; plantations, riverine belts. Not usually inside terra firme in area of overlap with **143.3** and **143.4**. ♪ Call: very high, short whistle; song: extr. high, thin "zee zee."

143.3 YELLOW-MARGINED (or Zimmer's Flatbill or)

FLYCATCHER (Bico-chato-da-copa) *Tolmomyias assimilis* L 5.5 in./ 14 cm. Note broad bill with pale lower mandible, dark eyes, and gray crown. May show pale panel at base of primaries. Cf. **143.2** and **143.4**. ♣ Upperstories of várzea and terra firme, second growth, plantations up to 1000 m or higher. ♪ Call: high, nasal, scratchy "zweeh zweeh - -."

143.4 GRAY-CROWNED (Flatbill or) **FLYCATCHER**

(Bico-chato-de-cabeça-cinza) *Tolmomyias poliocephalus* L 4.7 in./12 cm. Resembles larger **143.3**, but faint or no pale panel at base of primaries, eyes usually pale, and only base of lower mandible pale. ♣ Canopy and edge of humid forest. ♪ Call: very high, gliding-down "fwéeeeh"; song: unstructured series of well-spaced "feeh" notes.

143.5 YELLOW-BREASTED (Flatbill or) **FLYCATCHER**

(Bico-chato-amarelo) *Tolmomyias flaviventris* L 5.1 in./13 cm. Two groups: E Nom. group Ochre-lored Flycatcher (**a**, rather yellow overall with ochre-yellow supraloral and eyering) and W *viridiceps* group Olive-faced Flycatcher (**b**, more olive overall with yellowish supraloral and eyering). Note broad bill and lack of gray to head. Cf. **143.2b** with whitish supraloral and eyering. ♣ Mainly in várzea and riverine belts, but also in terra firme. Up to 1000 m. ♪ Call: extr. high "fweeeh"; song: mid-high, short "fdddddddddit" rattle.

143.6 CINNAMON-CRESTED SPADEBILL (Patinho-escuro)

Platyrinchus saturatus L 3.5 in./ 9 cm. As all spadebills, has very broad bill base. Note absence of facial pattern. ♣ Brushy undergrowth of terra firme up to 900 m. ♪ Call: high, sharp "whit" or "whit-it."

143.7 WHITE-THROATED SPADEBILL (Patinho) *Platy-*

rinchus mystaceus L 3.9 in./10 cm. Some sspp. have pale bill base. Differs from **143.8** by semiconcealed crown patch (smaller or absent in ♀). ♣ Undergrowth of forest, woodland, and riverine belts. ♪ Call: high, sharp "wheet"; song: descending trill; last "whit" note much higher (3 sec).

143.8 GOLDEN-CROWNED SPADEBILL (Patinho-de-coroa-dourada)

Platyrinchus coronatus L 3.5 in./9 cm. Differs from **143.7** by larger crown patch bordered by black line on either side. ♣ Understory of humid forest and second growth. Up to 1000 m, locally higher. ♪ Song: extr. high, slightly lowered, then raised cicadalike trill (2 sec).

143.9 WHITE-CRESTED SPADEBILL (Patinho-de-coroa-branca)

Platyrinchus platy-rhynchos L 4.3 in./11 cm. Richly colored below. Note absence of facial pattern. ♣ Open understory of terra firme up to 500 m. ♪ Call: very high "skuw"; song: buzzing, rising, and descending trill, interrupted in the middle.

143.10 RUSSET-WINGED SPADEBILL (Patinho-gigante)

Platyrinchus leucoryphus L 4.7 in./ 12 cm. Differs from **143.7** by largely rufous wings and longer tail. ♣ Undergrowth of humid Atlantic forest. Up to 1000 m. ♪ Call: high, angry-sounding "tjuw." R.

Plate 144

144.1 OLIVE-SIDED FLYCATCHER (Piui-boreal) *Contopus cooperi* (or *borealis*) L 7.5 in./ 19 cm. Note vest, formed by streaked flanks, which almost touches over breast. ♣ Open forest between 400 and 2500 m. Long sallies from favorite perch. ♪ Call: series of high, run-together "wic" notes with slight accelerations.

144.2 SMOKE-COLORED PEWEE (Piui-de-topete) *Contopus fumigatus* L 6.7 in./17 cm. Note uniform dark color and pointed crest. ♣ Interior, clearings, and edges of montane humid forest between 1000 and 2500 m. ♪ Call: calm series of high, stressed "wic" notes; song: very hgh, slightly gliding-down "wéeuw," often followed by ascending "weer-rút" notes.

144.3 EASTERN WOOD-PEWEE (Piui-verdadeiro) *Contopus virens* L 5.5 in./14 cm. Primary projection longer than in **144.4**, **144.7**, and **148.8**. Faint or no eyering. Perches more upright, wing bars less distinct and more crested than **144.7** and **144.8**. ♣ Forest, second growth, riverine belts, usually below 1500 m. ♪ Call: very high, ascending, mellow "pee-wee" (as in its name).

144.4 TROPICAL PEWEE (Papa-moscas-cinzento) *Contopus cinereus* L 5.5 in./14 cm. Differs from **144.3** by shorter primary projection (1/3 or less of the total tail length), indistinct or absent wing bars, and pale lores (sometimes indistinct). SE Nom. much darker with pale lores often missing. ♪ Call: descending "tjeuuw" or very high, staccato "wic wic -."

144.5 BLACKISH PEWEE (Piui-preto) *Contopus nigrescens* L 5.1 in./13 cm. Uniform dark with slight crest. No overlap with **144.2**. ♣ Canopy or edge of humid foothill forest. ♪ Call: very high, sharp "wic-wic- -"; song: "tjí-juww," lowered in pitch and strength.

144.6 WHITE-THROATED PEWEE (Piui-queixado) *Contopus albogularis* L 5.1 in./13 cm. Differs from **144.5** by white chin. ♣ Edge of humid forest and second growth between 400 and 700 m. ♪ Call: high, dry "wic-wic- -."

144.7 ALDER FLYCATCHER (Papa-moscas-de-alder) *Empidonax alnorum* L 5.9 in./15 cm. Differs from **144.8** only by voice. Two well-marked whitish wing bars. Whitish eyering (sometimes lacking). Primaries only extend slightly past uppertail coverts. Often flicks tail downward. Cf. **144.3**. ♣ Lower levels with dense growth at forest edge and second growth at water. Up to 1100 m. ♪ Call: high, well-separated "tic" notes; song (may sing in Brazil): "vree-zir" (2nd part higher).

144.8 WILLOW (or Traill's) **FLYCATCHER** (Maria-fibiu) *Empidonax traillii* L 5.9 in./ 15 cm. Cf. longer-winged **144.7**. ♣ Wide variety of closed and open habitats, mainly at water. From forest edge to cultivated areas. Normally below 100 m. ♪ Call: upslurred "wic"; song: very high, sharp "Wíc-bew," (2nd part lower). R.

144.9 VERMILION FLYCATCHER (Príncipe) *Pyrocephalus rubinus* L 5.5 in./14 cm. Shown are ♂ and ♀ of S Nom. (**a**, in most of Brazil during N-br. season) and ♀ of N ssp. *saturatus* (**b**). Gray-brown ♀♀ lack clear wing bars (but often show edging) and contrasting rump-patch of ♀♀ black-tyrants, but cf. **145.6b**. ♣ Open habitats often near water, from open woodland and desert scrub to agricultural land. ♪ Call: extr. high "psi"; song: extr. high "tic-tic-psiiieh" (last part may be sharply upslurred).

144.10 AUSTRAL (Patagonian) (or Rufous-backed) **NEGRITO** (Colegial) *Lessonia rufa* L 4.7 in./12 cm. Unmistakable by color pattern and terrestrial behavior. ♣ Open areas with short grass up to 1000 m or higher. ♪ Usually silent.

144.1

144.2

144.3

144.4

144.5

144.6

144.7

144.8

♀a   ♀b

144.9

♀

144.10

Plate 145

145.1 CINEREOUS TYRANT (Maria-preta-acinzen-
tada) *Knipolegus striaticeps* L 5.1 in./
13 cm. ♂ from other ♂ black-
tyrants by dark gray body and darker
blackish hood. No white in open
wing. Note contrasting rufous crown
of ♀. ♣ Woodland and dense forest up to 1000 m or
higher. ♪ Call: extr. high: "tuweet" or "tsic." V. *Note*: all
Knipolegus-tyrants are mostly silent.

145.2 HUDSON'S BLACK-TYRANT (Maria-preta-do-
sul) *Knipolegus hudsoni* L 5.9 in./
15 cm. ♂ shows conspicuous white
flashes in open wing. Differs from
145.7 by smaller size and inconspicuous white spots on lower flank
(often hidden). ♀ lacks contrasting crown of ♀ **145.1** and
bright red eyes of ♀ **145.4**. Also cf. **138.2** and ♀ **144.9**.
♣ Low woodland, scrub, savanna, gardens. Up to 500 m.
♪ Call/song: irregular series of "tic" notes. V.

145.3 AMAZONIAN BLACK-TYRANT (Pretinho-do-
igapó) *Knipolegus poecilocercus* L 5.1 in./
13 cm. ♂ from larger ♂ **145.6** (only
other black-tyrant in range) by
glossy blue-black (not dull black)
plumage. Also cf. ♂ **125.11**. ♀ dis-
tinctive in range, but cf. ♀ **145.6b, 138.2**, and ♀ **144.9**.
Compare ♂ Black Manakin (**125.11**). ♣ Vines and thickets in várzea up to 350 m. ♪ Call: high "tjue" or very
high "pjéeh."

145.4 BLUE-BILLED BLACK-TYRANT (Maria-preta-
de-bico-azulado) *Knipolegus cya-
nirostris* L 5.9 in./15 cm. Note fierce
red eyes of both sexes. ♂ only black-
tyrant in range without white in
open wing. ♀ with stronger, more
extensive barring to underparts than ♀♀ **145.2** and **145.8**.
Also cf. **138.2** and ♀ **144.9**. ♣ Borders of humid forest
and riverine belts up to 2200 m. ♪ Call: extr. high, staccato "whic."

145.5 RUFOUS-TAILED TYRANT (Maria-preta-de-
cauda-ruiva) *Knipolegus poecilurus* L
5.9 in./15 cm. Only *Knipolegus* tyrant
in range and habitat. Differs from
pewees (**144.1–144.6**) by paler eyes
and all-black bill. ♣ Borders of
humid forest and second growth, pastures with some
trees. Between 500 and 2500 m. ♪ Call: very/extr. high,
soft, raspy "zeet-zeet," repeated at 0.5-sec intervals.

145.6 RIVERSIDE TYRANT (Maria-preta-ribeirinha)
 Knipolegus orenocensis L 5.9 in./
15 cm. ♂ resembles ♂ **145.3**. ♀♀
shown of ssp. *xinguensis* (**a**, SE part
of range) and more widespread *sclateri* (**b**); **a** unmistakable in range and
habitat, **b** lacks wing bars of ♀ **145.3** (also cf. ♀ **144.9**).
♣ Semiopen brushy areas at rivers or lakes, with a prefer-
ence for river islands. Up to 300 m. ♪ Call: very high,
stressed "bic."

145.7 CAATINGA (or Brazilian) **BLACK-TYRANT**
(Maria-preta-do-nordeste) *Knipole-
gus franciscanus* L 6.3 in./16 cm. No
 similar black-tyrant in range. ♣ Dry
forest. Mainly near rocky outcrops. En.

145.8 [WHITE-WINGED BLACK-TYRANT (Maria-
preta-bate-rabo) *Knipolegus aterri-
mus*] L 7.1 in./18 cm. ♂ (not shown)
 as ♂**145.7**. No similar black-tyrant
in range. ♣ Woodland, open scrub,
and forest borders. ♪ Song: very/
extr. high, upslurred "sereéh."

145.9 CRESTED BLACK-TYRANT (Maria-preta-de-
penacho) *Knipolegus lophotes* L 7.9 in./
20 cm. Unmistakable by long, thin
 crest. ♣ Open grassy areas with
some tree stands. Up to 1100 m.
♪ Usually silent; flight song very high
"téetwee-twee-tweé" (middle "-twee-" lowest pitched).

145.10 VELVETY BLACK-TYRANT (Maria-preta-de-
garganta-vermelha) *Knipolegus nigerrimus* L 7.1 in./18 cm. Differs from
 145.4 by white wing band in flight.
Note unique throat coloring of ♀.
♣ Open montane areas with some
trees and shrub; 1800–2700 m, locally lower. En.

145.1

♀

145.2

♀

145.3

♀

145.4

♀

145.5

♀a

♂

♀b

145.6

♀

145.7

145.8

♀

145.9

♀

145.10

Plate 146

146.1 SPECTACLED TYRANT (Viuvinha-deóculos)

Hymenops perspicillatus L 5.9 in./ 15 cm. Eye wattle and white in wing diagnostic. ♣ Marsh, natural and cultivated open areas at water; SL–2000 m. ♪ Generally silent; wing buzzes when displaying.

146.2 DRAB WATER-TYRANT (Maria-da-praia) *Och-*

thornis littoralis L 5.1 in./13 cm. Cf. **146.4**. Note pale eyebrow and rather uniform underparts. ♣ Perches low, always at water, esp. at rivers; SL–600 m. ♪ Quiet; occasionally a very high, weak "sweeeh."

146.3 YELLOW-BROWED TYRANT (Suiriri-pequeno)

Satrapa icterophrys L 6.3 in./16 cm. Unmistakable by unique yellow eyebrow, combined with wing pattern. Often in upright stance, like **150.1–150.9**. ♣ Edge of forest, lakes, fields, marsh. Up to 2000 m. ♪ Song: short, fast, nervous, ascending series of 4–5 "wub-wub-weh-weéteet" notes.

146.4 LITTLE GROUND-TYRANT (Gaúcha-d"água)

Muscisaxicola fluviatilis L 5.5 in./ 14 cm. Note slight contrast between belly and chest and white-edged black tail. Cf. **146.2**. ♣ Stands erect between bursts of running in open spots in vegetation near water. Up to 800 m. ♪ Usually silent.

146.5 GRAY MONJITA (Primavera) *Xolmis cinereus* L

9.8 in./25 cm. Unmistakable by red eye and dark malar; as other monjitas perches exposed and shows white flashes in open wings. ♣ Grassland and cerrado, occasionally around settlement. Up to 1200 m. ♪ Call: very high, thin "weéh"; song: very high, soft "weeh-tjuh-teeh."

146.6 BLACK-CROWNED MONJITA (Noivinha-coroada)

Xolmis coronatus L 7.9 in./20 cm. Characterized by black cap. ♣ Open areas with scattered bush and trees. Up to 1500 m.

146.7 WHITE-RUMPED MONJITA (Noivinha-branca)

Xolmis velatus L 7.9 in./20 cm. Not in range of **146.6**; from ♀ **146.9** by wing pattern and lack of white scapulars. ♣ Open areas with scattered bush and trees, usually near water, occasionally near buildings. Up to 1000 m. ♪ Song: nasal, downslurred "njeh," repeated at 1-sec intervals.

146.8 WHITE MONJITA (Noivinha) *Xolmis irupero*

L 7.1 in./18 cm. Unmistakable. ♣ Open areas with scattered bush and trees, usually near marsh or open water. Up to 1000 m. ♪ Song: nasal, downslurred "njieh," repeated at 1-sec intervals.

146.9 BLACK-AND-WHITE MONJITA (Noivinha-de-

rabo-preto) *Xolmis dominicanus* L 7.9 in./20 cm. ♂ from **146.8** by wing pattern; ♀ has contrasting white scapulars. ♣ Marshes and nearby grasslands. Locally in coastal sand dunes. Up to 500 m, occasionally much higher. ♪ Silent. R.

146.10 CHOCOLATE-VENTED TYRANT (Gaúcho-

chocolate) *Neoxolmis rufiventris* L 7.9 in./20 cm. Unmistakable ground dweller. ♣ Grassland and open savanna with some shrub. Also in agricultural areas. Up to 500 m, occasionally much higher. V.

146.1

146.2

146.3

146.4

146.5

146.6

146.7

146.8

146.9

146.10

Plate 147

147.1 STREAMER-TAILED TYRANT (Tesoura-do-brejo) *Gubernetes yetapa* L 13.8 in./ 35 cm (excl. tail streamers). Unmistakable by size and coloring. ♣ Palm groves, open grassy and marshy areas with some scrub. Up to 1000 m. ♪ Call: nasal "dzz."

147.2 SHEAR-TAILED GRAY TYRANT (Tesoura-cinzenta) *Muscipipra vetula* L 7.9 in./ 20 cm. Note long, slender tail. ♣ At borders of humid forest and second growth, mainly between 1000 and 2200 m. ♪ Call: low "duh-djúp."

147.3 PIED WATER-TYRANT (Lavadeira-do-norte) *Fluvicola pica* L 5.1 in./13 cm. No similar bird in its habitat and range. ♣ At edges of marsh, ponds, lakes; below 450 m, sometimes much higher. ♪ Call: high, very short "wic."

147.4 BLACK-BACKED WATER-TYRANT (Lavadeira-de-cara-branca) *Fluvicola albiventer* L 5.5 in./14 cm. Differs from **147.3** by all black mantle. ♣ Marsh, shrub at rivers and other water. Up to 1000 m. ♪ Call: high, dry, very short "wic."

147.5 MASKED WATER-TYRANT (Lavadeira-mas-carada) *Fluvicola nengeta* L 5.9 in./ 15 cm. Distinctly marked. ♣ Marsh, rice fields, shrub at rivers and other water. Up to 300 m, occasionally much higher. ♪ Call: high, sharp "peep."

147.6 WHITE-HEADED MARSH-TYRANT (Freirinha) *Arundinicola leucocephala* L 5.1 in./ 13 cm. Distinctly marked. Note dark wings and tail of ♀. ♣ Marsh and grassy areas along water. Up to 500 m. ♪ Call: very/extr. high, sharp "seet."

147.7 STRANGE-TAILED TYRANT (Tesoura-do-campo) *Alectrurus risora* L 7.9 in./ 20 cm (excl. ♂ tail streamers). ♂ unmistakable (throat is white in N-br plumage); ♀ from ♀ **147.8** by complete breast band. ♣ Grassy areas, marsh, shrub. Up to 500 m. ♪ Probably silent. R.

147.8 COCK-TAILED TYRANT (Galito) *Alectrurus tri-color* L 4.7 in./12 cm (excl. ♂ tail streamers). ♂ unmistakable; ♀ has interrupted breast band. ♣ Open, grassy areas, cerrado, humid savanna. Up to 1100 m. ♪ Mostly silent; soft "tic" notes in flight. R.

147.9 LONG-TAILED TYRANT (Viuvinha) *Colonia colonus* L 5.5 in./14 cm (excl. tail streamers). Unmistakable by pied pattern. ♣ Borders of humid forest, second growth, and riverine belts. Also in plantations. Up to 1200 m, sometimes higher. ♪ Call: e.g., slightly rising, then gliding-down "weé-uw"; song: energetic "freéh-rururu" (2nd part as almost-trill).

147.10 CATTLE TYRANT (Suiriri-cavaleiro) *Machet-ornis rixosa* L 7.9 in./20 cm. Terrestrial behavior and yellow underparts diagnostic. ♣ Open grassy areas with some bush and trees. Up to 300 m, sometimes much higher. ♪ Call: very/extr. high "sreep," single or several joined in fast series and trills.

147.9

147.1

147.6 ♀

147.2

147.8 ♀

147.3

147.7 ♀

147.4

147.10

147.5

Plate 148

148.1 PIRATIC FLYCATCHER (Bem-te-vi-pirata) *Lega-*

tus leucophaius L 6.3 in./16 cm. Differs from **149.4** by rather uniform back, olive rump, and less distinct white wing edging. Also cf. **149.5**. ♣ Forest borders, tall second growth, woodland, riverine belts, cultivation. Mainly below 1000 m. ♪ Call: very high, rapid "wit-tit-di-do"; also very high, drawn-out "feeeeh," repeated irregularly.

148.2 GRAY-CAPPED FLYCATCHER (Bem-te-vi-de-

cabeça-cinza) *Myiozetetes granadensis* L 6.7 in./17 cm. Crown and nape gray. Note short eyebrow. ♣ Variety of humid habitats with trees and shrub in cultivation, at forest edge, near settlements, esp. near water. Lowlands up to 1100 m. ♪ Call: mewing "kew" in long series; song: high "tip-tooh-tetjíw?"

148.3 DUSKY-CHESTED FLYCATCHER (Bem-te-vi-

barulhento) *Myiozetetes luteiventris* L 5.9 in./15 cm. Small with rather plain uniform brownish head. ♣ Canopy and edge of várzea and terra firme and nearby scrubby clearings. Up to 600 m. ♪ Call: very high, strong "ti-keew"; song: mewing "tjew tjew tí-tí-tjew."

148.4 RUSTY-MARGINED FLYCATCHER (Bentevizinho-de-asa-ferrugínea) *Myiozetetes*

cayanensis L 6.7 in./17 cm. Note rufous edging of wing feathers. Differs from **148.5** by yellow, not red, crown-patch and narrower face mask. ♣ Forest borders, riverine belts, shrubby areas, suburbs. Up to 1000 m, locally higher. ♪ Call: very high, drawn-out, nasal "wheeeee."

148.5 SOCIAL FLYCATCHER (Bentevizinho-de-pena-

cho-vermelho) *Myiozetetes similis* L 6.7 in./17 cm. Differs from **148.4** by duller (less black) mask, more olive (less brown) back, orange-red (not orange-yellow) crown-patch (often concealed), and lack of rufous edging on flight feathers. Juv. with rufous edging on flight feathers, but distinct edging to wing coverts dull and pale (unlike **148.4**). ♣ Various open to semiopen habitats with some trees, incl. edge of forest and gardens. Up to 1000 m, occasionally much higher. ♪ Song: very high, sharp, far-carrying "Wée-uw-Wéeer" and similar variations; also "sjeeuw-sjeeuw" or explosive "TFéeuw."

148.6 LESSER KISKADEE (Bentevizinho-do-brejo)

Philohydor (or *Pitangus*) *lictor* L 6.7 in./17 cm. Note long, slender bill. Cf. larger **148.7**. ♣ Shrubs and trees near water, occasionally at mangrove edge. Up to 500 m, locally may be higher. ♪ Call: loud, squeaky, descending "Wréeh-wrée-wruh."

148.7 GREAT KISKADEE (Bem-te-vi) *Pitangus sulphu-*

ratus L 7.9 in./20 cm. Note large size and long, straight bill. Cf. **148.10**. ♣ Any open or semiopen habitat, incl. towns and borders of forest. Up to 1600 m. ♪ Call: loud, plaintive, nasal "Weéeuw"; song: "Kís-ka-dee" (species named after its song).

148.8 YELLOW-THROATED FLYCATCHER (Bem-te-

vi-da-copa) *Conopias parvus* L 6.3 in./16 cm. Note yellow throat. Differs from smaller **148.9** by blacker crown, yellow coronal patch (often concealed), and less contrast between wings and mantle. ♣ Humid forest. Also in tall trees in adjacent areas. Up to 1300 m. ♪ Call/song: high, liquid, musical almost-trill, like "Wee-re-re," diminishing in strength.

148.9 THREE-STRIPED FLYCATCHER (Bem-te-vi-

pequeno) *Conopias trivirgatus* L 5.5 in./14 cm. Note yellow throat and lack of coronal patch. Cf. **148.8**. ♣ Canopy and borders of humid forest. Up to 300 m. ♪ Call/song: high, loud, grating "zeeuw," repeated in irregular series. In SE Brazil, irregular series of "chew-chew-" notes.

148.10 BOAT-BILLED FLYCATCHER (Neinei) *Mega-*

rynchus pitangua L 7.9-9.8 in./20–25 cm. Differs from **148.7** by hefty bill with strongly curved culmen and broad base. ♣ Canopy of várzea at rivers and lakes. Also in a range of other habitats with varying density of trees, including woodland, savanna, plantations. Up to 1500 m. ♪ Call (in two voices by the same bird): high, rapid "er-er-er-wuh" with very low/toneless "zzzzzzzzzr," Also different vocalizations, such as a high, nasal "Wéet-dr-reet."

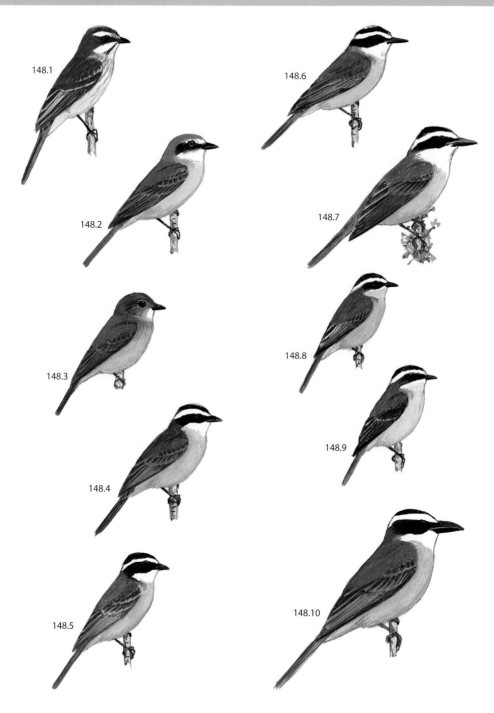

148.1

148.2

148.3

148.4

148.5

148.6

148.7

148.8

148.9

148.10

Plate 149

149.1 STREAKED FLYCATCHER (Bem-te-vi-rajado)

Myiodynastes maculatus L 7.9 in./ 20 cm. Ssp. *solitarius* (**a**) shown and warmer tawny brown Nom. (**b**). Differs from **149.2** by white chin. Also cf. **149.4**. ♣ Forest, woodland, riverine belts, mangrove, caatinga, settlements. Up to 1500 m. ♪ Can be very noisy, giving harsh, nasal calls, like "Wit Wit - -"; dawn song: e.g., strident "Weeh-Weewit."

149.2 SULPHUR-BELLIED FLYCATCHER (Bem-te-

vi-de-barriga-sulfúrea) *Myiodynastes luteiventris* L 7.9 in./20 cm. Dark malar stripes meet over chin. Underparts pale yellow. ♣ Canopy and borders of humid forest and secondary woodland. Up to 1000 m. ♪ Call: short, squeaky "wirít-jeh"; otherwise silent in South America. V.

149.3 SULPHURY FLYCATCHER (Suiriri-de-garganta-

rajada) *Tyrannopsis sulphurea* L 7.9 in./ 20 cm. Differs from **149.9** by shorter bill, shorter, squarish tail, olive-streaked chest sides, and browner wings. ♣ Often (but not always) in palms in borders of forest, savanna, cultivation, towns. Up to 400 m. ♪ Song: mid-high, descending, scratchy, nasal, well-separated "sue sweh tjetjeh" notes, or high, grating "flee ti-tjer-wer" ("flee" very/extr. high and well separated from 2nd part).

149.4 VARIEGATED FLYCATCHER (Peitica) *Empi-

donomus varius* L 7.5 in./19 cm. Prominent white wing edging and rufous tail edging and rump. Smaller billed and less crisply streaked below than **149.1**. ♣ Borders and clearings of forest, woodland, riverine belts, savanna with some trees and bushes, suburbs. Occasionally in terra firme. Up to 1200 m. ♪ Call: very/extr. high, thin "feeee-i."

149.5 CROWNED SLATY FLYCATCHER (Peitica-de-

chapéu-preto) *Griseotyrannus* (or *Empidonomus*) *aurantiocristatus* L 7.1 in./18 cm. Note flat, distinct black crown with semiconcealed yellow patch. ♣ Canopy of humid forest and woodland, open savanna with some tall trees, edges of lowland forest. Up to 1200 m, occasionally higher. ♪ Call/song: extr. high, weak "tseeee" when breeding, otherwise silent.

149.6 EASTERN KINGBIRD (Suiriri-valente) *Tyrannus

tyrannus* L 7.9 in./20 cm. Broad white tail tip diagnostic (less broad in Juv.). ♣ Wide variety of forested and wooded habitats, incl. towns. Not usually in forest interior. Up to 800 m, locally much higher. ♪ Normally silent in South America.

149.7 [GRAY KINGBIRD (Suiriri-cinza) *Tyrannus

dominicensis*] L 7.9 in./20 cm. Note large bill and white underparts. ♣ Canopy and borders of humid forest, savanna, and mangroves. ♪ Call: very high, sharp "pe-Téer."

149.8 WHITE-THROATED KINGBIRD (Suiriri-de-

garganta-branca) *Tyrannus albogularis* L 7.9 in./20 cm. Differs from **149.9** by paler head, which contrasts strongly with the dark mask and white throat. Slight olive cast to chest. ♣ Various open habitats near water, esp. cerrado, open savanna, and riverine woodland. Also near towns in N-br. season. Up to 1000 m. ♪ Voice as **149.4**, but even higher and thinner.

149.9 TROPICAL KINGBIRD (Suiriri) *Tyrannus melan-

cholicus* L 7.9 in./20 cm. Chest olive. Tail forked as in other kingbirds, but unlike **149.3** and **147.10**. ♣ Can be seen anywhere, except inside forest, often near water. Up to 1850 m. ♪ Call: very high, sharp, slightly descending "seedrr," directly continued with sharp, warbling "jtutju---" and similar variations.

149.10 FORK-TAILED FLYCATCHER (Tesourinha)

Tyrannus savana L 7.5 in./19 cm (excl. tail streamers). Unmistakable. No white in tail when streamers have broken off. ♣ Open areas with scattered trees and bushes, including gardens, mangrove, reed beds. Up to 1000 m. ♪ Call: extr. high, weak "tic."

Plate 150

150.1 GRAYISH MOURNER (Vissiá) *Rhytipterna simplex* L 7.9 in./20 cm. Differs from very similar **124.2** by slightly more reddish eyes, often some pink at base of bill, and yellowish cast to the belly. ♣ Upperstory of terra firme, up to 800 m or higher. ♪ Song: varied, esp. in tempo; normally a rising series of sharp "ih" notes, ending in some loud, explosive "Itch" notes. Notes may be well-separated, run-together as a rattle, or decelerating. Last explosive note may be omitted.

150.2 PALE-BELLIED MOURNER (Vissiá-cantor) *Rhytipterna immunda* L 7.5 in./19 cm. Differs from **150.6–150.9** by flanks tinged rusty-buff and grayer, more rounded head (no crest). ♣ Wooded savanna, low várzea. Below 300 m. ♪ Song: 2 well-separated "Réet-je" notes ("Réet" much higher).

150.3 SIRYSTES (Gritador) *Sirystes sibilator* L 7.1 in./18 cm. Sspp. form two groups: widespread white-rumped group (**a**, sspp. *albocinereus* and *subcanescens*) and E and SE gray-rumped group (**b**, Nom. and *atimastus*, note clear edging of wing coverts). ♣ Canopy of forest and woodland. Up to 1000 m. ♪ Call: slightly descending "weeuw-weeuw-weeuw"; song: short, rapid series of 4–7, slightly ascending, fluted "wuh-wíwi-wuh" notes, the last note lowered.

150.4 RUFOUS CASIORNIS (Caneleiro) *Casiornis rufus* L 7.1 in./18 cm. Resembles some Attilas (Pl. **151**) but differently shaped, black bill with pink base. Also cf. Rufous Twistwing (**140.10**). ♣ Woodland, wooded cerrado, riverine belts up to 1500 m. ♪ Call: Very high, downslurred "feeeèh."

150.5 ASH-THROATED CASIORNIS (Caneleiro-enxofre) *Casiornis fuscus* L 7.1 in./18 cm. Less uniform rufous, esp. on upperparts, than **150.4**. ♣ Caatinga, wooded cerrado. Up to 500 m. ♪ Call: Very high, downslurred "tjef." En.

150.6 DUSKY-CAPPED FLYCATCHER (Maria-cavaleira-pequena) *Myiarchus tuberculifer* L 6.3 in./16 cm. Note small size and blackish bill. Cap slightly darker than rest of upperparts. ♣ Interior and clearings of all types of forest, second growth, plantations. Up to 1300 m. ♪ Song: high, plaintive "féeeuw" whistle.

150.7 SWAINSON'S FLYCATCHER (Irré) *Myiarchus swainsoni* L 7.9 in./20 cm. Shown is SE Nom. (**a**, migrates N to NE) and ssp. *phaeonotus* (**b**, only in extr. N, with all-black bill). Both sspp. very similar to **150.9**, but **b** with at least base of lower mandible pale, and localized **a** with paler belly than **150.9a**. ♣ Cerrado, riverine belts, mangrove, and forest. Up to 1800 m. ♪ Call: rasping "srruh"; song: impatient-sounding "put-it-here" ("here" much lower) and variations thereof.

150.8 BROWN-CRESTED FLYCATCHER (Maria-cavaleira-de-rabo-enferrujado) *Myiarchus tyrannulus* L 7.9 in./20 cm. Note rufous in wing and tail (best seen from below). ♣ Dense and open woodland, riverine belts, cerrado. Up to 300 m. ♪ Call/song: e.g., very high short "weert" or a fast, nasal, toneless chatter, like "ée-hè-hè."

150.9 SHORT-CRESTED FLYCATCHER (Maria-cavaleira) *Myiarchus ferox* L 7.1 in./18 cm. Dark Nom. (**a**) and brown ssp. *australis* (**b**, with rufous rump and edges of tail and wing feathers) shown. Note all-black bill. ♣ Clearings and borders of forest, woodland, and agricultural areas. ♪ Call/song: short, fine "prrrrih" trill.

150.1

Imm.

150.2

150.3

a

b

150.4

150.5

a

b

150.6

b

a

150.7

150.8

a

b

150.9

Plate 151

151.1 LARGE-HEADED (or Bamboo) **FLATBILL** (Maria-cabeçuda) *Ramphotrigon megacephalum* L 5.1 in./13 cm. Note habitat and two tawny wing bars. Differs from larger **151.2** by distinct eyebrow. ♣ Interior or edge of humid forest with bamboo. ♪ Song: varied; mournful, slightly lowered "wéeuw" (lowland), 2-noted "wéeh wuw" (distinctly separated), or "wéejuw," 1st note higher, repeated at 1-sec intervals.

151.2 DUSKY-TAILED FLATBILL (Maria-de-cauca-escura) *Ramphotrigon fuscicauda* L 6.3 in./16 cm. Resembles smaller **151.1**, but supraloral indistinct. ♣ Dense undergrowth and bamboo of terra firme and várzea, second growth. Up to 900 m. ♪ Call: slow, fluted "tjuuw-weh" ("tjuuw" gliding down, short "weh" jumping up) or melodious, fluted "pjéeuw pjeé-pjeé-pjuw" ("pjéeuw" lower pitched and descending; last 3 notes higher).

151.3 RUFOUS-TAILED FLATBILL (Bico-chato-de-rabo-vermelho) *Ramphotrigon ruficauda* L 6.3 in./16 cm. Note rufous wing and tail. ♣ Lower levels of várzea and terra firme. Also in wooded savanna. Up to 600 m. ♪ Song: high, slow, mournful "weaeaea-wur."

151.4 BRIGHT-RUMPED ATTILA (Capitão-de-saíra-amarelo) *Attila spadiceus* L 7.9 in./20 cm. Note streaked breast, and bright rump, which is normally paler than occasional bright rump of **151.5–151.9**. Eyes dark to yellow (rarely white as in **151.9**). Shown are normal (**a**) and rufous (**b**) forms. Latter together with gray form (like **a**, but gray head and chest instead of olive) and intermediates form ca. 5% of population. ♣ Clearings and edge of humid forest, second growth, plantations, woodland, bushy savanna, riverine belts. Up to 1500 m, occasionally higher. ♪ Song: loud, resounding series of about 6 whistled, doubled (sometimes tripled) "weéh-duw - -" notes, gaining in strength and pitch.

151.5 GRAY-HOODED ATTILA (Capitão-de-saíra) *Attila**rufus* L 7.9 in./20 cm. Two sspp.: Nom. (**a**) and *hellmayri* (**b**, in Bahia). Ssp. **a** distinctive; **b** from **151.6** and **151.7** by small, white chin. ♣ Humid forest up to 1500 m. ♪ Song: slow series of 4–7 emphasized, fluted "whee" notes, which gradually rise in pitch and strength before the last one, which fades out. En.

151.6 RUFOUS-TAILED ATTILA (Capitão-castanho)*Attila phoenicurus* L 7.1 in./18 cm. Gray hood more sharply demarcated than in **151.7**. ♣ Humid forest (including *Araucaria*) and scrub. Up to 1500 m. ♪ Song: short, quick series of 4 fluted "fee-fee-fifi" notes, the 1st 3 rising in pitch, the 4th falling off.

151.7 CITRON-BELLIED ATTILA (Tinguaçu-de-barriga-amarela) *Attila citriniventris* L 7.1 in./ 18 cm. See brighter **151.6**. ♣ Interior and edge of humid terra firme up to 500 m. ♪ Song: series of 3–8 fluted, more or less staccato notes, which gradually rise until the last one, which falls off, like "piu-piu- - piútwoh."

151.8 CINNAMON ATTILA (Tinguaçu-ferrugem) *Attila**cinnamomeus* L 7.9 in./20 cm. Unmistakable by large pale eye. ♣ Várzea and other types of swamp forest. Also in plantations and mangrove. At rivers and streams. Up to 500 m. ♪ Song: melancholy "pu-peéeeuw" and other similar notes, given in unstructured, calm series.

151.9 DULL-CAPPED (or White-eyed) **ATTILA** (Bate-pára) *Attila bolivianus* L 7.9 in./ 20 cm. Note large whitish eye. ♣ Riverine belts, várzea, and other types of swamp forest at rivers and streams. Up to 500 m. ♪ Song: slow, rising series of about 10–15 fluted notes, which level out in the 2nd half.

151.1

151.2

151.3

151.4 a b

151.5 a b

151.6

151.7

151.8

151.9

Plate 152

152.1 TROPICAL PARULA (Mariquita) *Parula piti-* *ayumi* L 4.3 in./11 cm. Note small size and blue-gray upperparts. ♣ Forest edge, woodland, riverine belts. Up to 2500 m. ♪ Song: variations of very/extr. high, almost-trill, like "zizizizizsisisi-tuh" or "si-si-si-wrrrr-teweh."

152.2 ROSE-BREASTED CHAT (Polícia-do-mato) *Gra-* *natellus pelzelni* L 4.7 in./12 cm. Nom. (**a**) and ssp. *paraensis* (**b**, with less white on flanks and black restricted to forehead) shown. ♀ has pink vent. ♣ Canopy and borders of forest and dense woodland. Up to 850 m. ♪ Call: high, slightly nasal "zjuw"; song: rather hurried series of 5–6 evenly spaced "uweet-uweet- -" notes, often heard in combination.

152.3 AMERICAN REDSTART (Mariquita-de-rabo- vermelho) *Setophaga ruticilla* L 4.7 in./ 12 cm. Unmistakable by color and pattern of often fanned tail. ♣ Forest edge, woodland, shrubby areas, mangrove. Up to 1500 m, occasionally much higher. ♪ Normally silent in South America. V.

152.4 SLATE-THROATED (Redstart or) **WHITESTART** (Mariquita-cinza) *Myioborus minia-tus* L 5.1 in./13 cm. Unmistakable by often fanned, white-edged tail and all-dark (brown-crowned) head. ♣ Montane forest and woodland; 600–2000 m. ♪ Song: very high, thin "ti-ti-tju-tju-tjuw" (sometimes restricted to 1st 2 notes).

152.5 TEPUI (Redstart or) **WHITESTART** (Mariquita- de-cabeça-parda) *Myioborus casta-neocapillus* L 5.1 in./13 cm. Ssp. *duidae* (**a**) and Nom. (**b**, with yellow underparts) shown. Tail like **152.4**. ♣ Forest, second growth, woodland; 1200–2200 m. ♪ Song: thin, accelerating, descending chipping, starting extr. high.

152.6 YELLOW WARBLER (Mariquita-amarela) *Dend-* *roica petechia* (*aestiva*) L 5.1 in./ 13 cm. ♀ from ♀ **152.8**, and ♀ **154.1**, by yellowish undertail. ♣ Semiopen habitats, esp. near water. Up to 1000 m, occasionally higher. ♪ Call: extr. high, dry "chip," but species is probably silent in Brazil.

152.7 BLACKBURNIAN WARBLER (Mariquita-papo- de-fogo) *Dendroica fusca* L 5.1 in./ 13 cm. In ♀ note distinct facial pattern, yellow-tinged throat, and extensive white of undertail. ♣ Forest, woodland, and clearings with scattered trees. Mainly above 1000 m. ♪ Probably silent in Brazil. R.

152.8 BLACKPOLL WARBLER (Mariquita-de-perna- clara) *Dendroica striata* L 5.5 in./ 14 cm. Shown are Ad. ♂, 1st basic ♂ (**a**) and 1st W ♀ (**b**); **a** and **b** rather nondescript, but note wing bars and large white patch on undertail. ♣ Forest borders, clearings with scattered trees, woodland; 500–2500 m. ♪ Probably silent in Brazil.

152.9 [CERULEAN WARBLER (Mariquita-azul) *Dend-* *roica cerulea*] L 4.7 in./12 cm. In ♀ note distinct wing bars, blue-green upperparts, and white patch on undertail. ♣ Canopy of forest and woodland; 500–2000 m. ♪ Probably silent in South America.

152.10 [BLACK-THROATED GREEN WARBLER (Mari- quita-de-garganta-preta) *Dendroica virens*] L 5.1 in./13 cm. ♀ from ♀ **152.7** by blackish breast sides. Accidental visitor. ♪ Probably silent in South America.

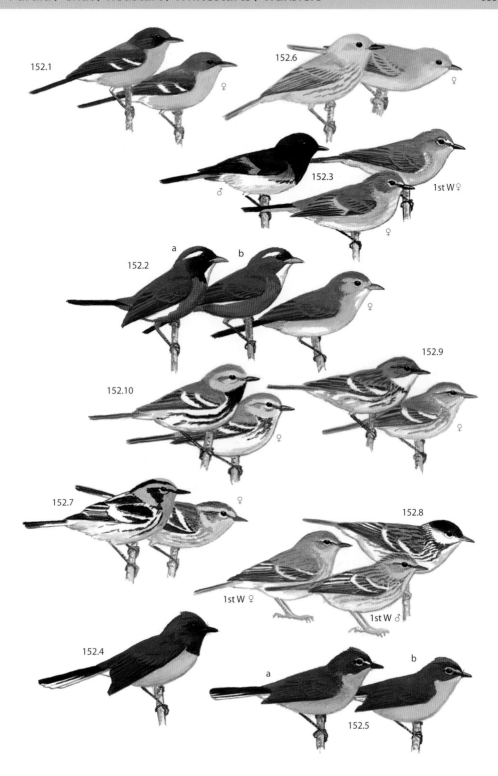

152.1

152.6

♀

152.3

♂

1st W♀

♀

a

b

152.2

♀

152.10

152.9

♀

♀

152.7

♀

152.8

1st W ♀

1st W ♂

152.4

a

b

152.5

Plate 153

153.1 CONNECTICUT WARBLER (Mariquita-de-con-

necticut) *Oporornis agilis* L 5.5 in./
14 cm. Complete white eyering
diagnostic. ♣ Forest borders and
clearings, woodland. Up to 2000 m.
♪ Silent in South America. V.

153.2 NORTHERN WATERTHRUSH (Mariquita-boreal)

Seiurus noveboracensis L 5.9 in./15 cm.
Unmistakable by jizz, habitat, and
streaking below. Bobs rear end when
walking. ♣ Mangrove, woodland
near water. Up to 2000 m. ♪ Call:
very high, metallic "tsic" notes in series of 1 ×/sec. V.

153.3 TWO-BANDED (or Roraima) **WARBLER** (Pula-

pula-de-duas-fitas) *Basileuterus bivit-
tatus* L 5.5 in./14 cm. From **153.4** by
greener face sides. ♣ Shrubby edges
and undergrowth of humid forest
and second growth; 700–1800 m. ♪
Song: extr. high, slightly descending and ascending series,
starting with a few stuttered notes, which gradually accelerate via a trill to a hoarse hiss (2–3 sec).

153.4 GOLDEN-CROWNED WARBLER (Pula-pula)

Basileuterus culicivorus L 5.5 in./14 cm.
Note pale gray eyebrow and yellow
underparts. ♣ Understories of
humid forest and second growth.
Shaded plantations. Up to 1800 m.
♪ Song: varies regionally; in E Brazil, very high "tu-tu-
twit-twit" (2nd "tu" slightly lower); in N Brazil, very high,
slightly descending, thin "wit-wit-wit-witwit."

153.5 WHITE-BELLIED WARBLER (Pula-pula-de-

barriga-branca) *Basileuterus hypo-
leucus* L 5.5 in./14 cm. Note whitish
belly and rufous crown. ♣ Woodland, riverine belts, shrubby foest
edges. ♪ Song: very/extr. high "seeh-
seeh swuh."

153.6 WHITE-BROWED (or -rimmed) **WARBLER** (Pula-

pula-assobiador) *Basileuterus leu-
coblepharus* L 5.5 in./14 cm. Note
white supraloral and partial eyering.
Underparts gray and white. ♣ Forest undergrowth, second growth.
Often near water. Up to 1600 m. ♪ Song: fairly long series
of thin "fee" notes, which start at extr. high level and then
descend very steeply to 5 notes lower (5–6 sec).

153.7 WHITE-STRIPED WARBLER (Pla-pula-de-

sobrancelhau) *Basileuterus leucophrys*
L 5.5 in./14 cm. Note white supraloral and partial eyering. Underparts
gray and white. ♣ Undergrowth at
water in riverine belts. Up to 1000 m.
♪ Call: extr. high tinkling; song: series of pure, fluted
notes, some of these as double notes or short trill "fufu-
fuhfuh-prrrr-pruh" and similar series, with notes varying
in sequence and pitch. En.

153.8 FLAVESCENT WARBLER (Canário-do-mato)

Basileuterus flaveolus L 5.5 in./14 cm.
Note striking yellow eyebrow. Cf. ♀
154.2. ♣ On and near ground in
riverine belts and shrubby clearings.
Up to 1000 m. ♪ Song: double-
voiced series, basically an extr. high series of 5–6 notes of
"fififi-fififi- -" notes; after the 1st two notes, mid-high
"tjeh-tjeh-tjeh-tjeh" is interwoven.

153.9 (Neotropical) **RIVERBANK WARBLER** (Pula-

pula-ribeirinho) *Phaeothlypis rivularis*
L 5.5 in./14 cm. ♣ N ssp. *mesoleuca* (**a**)
and SE Nom. (**b**) shown. Both have
whitish buff underparts. ♣ Near rivers, streams, or swampy areas in for-
est. ♪ Song: starting very high and descending series of
"feew" notes; after the 1st 5–7 notes transformed into
forceful, very loud, level, rattled "tjehtjeh---" (about 7 ×
"tjeh").

153.10 BUFF-RUMPED WARBLER (Pula-pula-de-cauda-

avermelhada) *Phaeothlypis fulvicauda*
L 5.5 in./14 cm. Tail pattern diagnostic. ♣ Near streams and rivers in
forest. Up to 1000 m. ♪ Song: starts
with 1–4 slow or fast introductory
notes, then changes into a series of 10–15 strong, level
"tjewtjew---" notes.

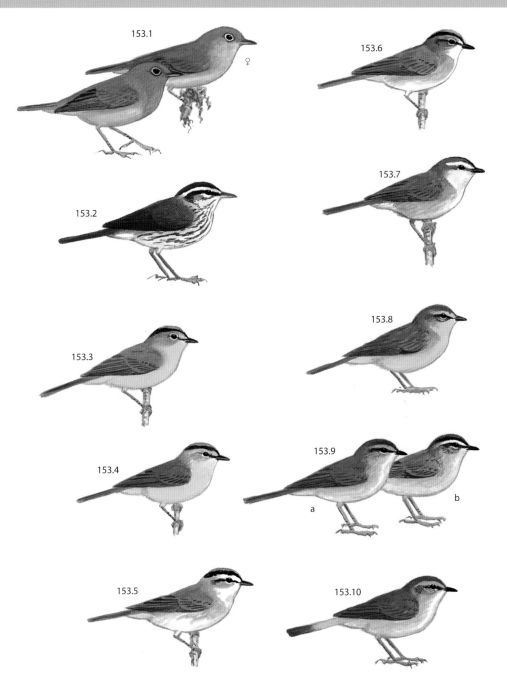

Plate 154

154.1 [**PROTHONOTARY WARBLER** (Mariquita-proto-

notária) *Protonotaria citrea*] L 5.5 in./ 14 cm. Note blue-gray wings and tail. Basal half of undertail with a white patch, unlike in ♀ **152.6**. ♪ Probably silent in South America.

154.2 MASKED YELLOWTHROAT (Pia-cobra) *Geoth-*

lypis aequinoctialis L 5.5 in./14 cm. Note eyering and indistinct supral-oral of ♀. Gray tinge to head of ♀ often absent. ♣ Bushy and grassy fields, marshes, borders of woodland. Often near water. Up to 1500 m. ♪ Song: high, sweet, almost level series, starting with two slow introductory "swee swee" notes, followed by 2–3 short, lilting "feedeweet -" notes, and ending in a distinct flourish, like "wu-wutweet," together as "swee swee feedeweet-feedeweet-wu-wutweet," or variations thereof (e.g., one note is more warbled).

154.3 [**CANADA WARBLER** (Mariquita-do-canadá)

Wilsonia canadensis] L 5.1 in./13 cm. Note eyering and gray upperparts. ♣ Forest undergrowth, second growth; 1000–2000 m. ♪ Probably silent in South America.

154.4 RUFOUS-BROWED PEPPERSHRIKE (Piti-

guari) *Cyclarhis gujanensis* L 5.9 in./ 15 cm. Unmistakable by stout bill and rufous eyebrow in most sspp. (**a**), but rufous restricted to supral-oral in SE ssp. *ochrocephala* (**b**). ♣ Wide variety of wooded and semiopen habitats. Not usu-ally inside dense humid forest. Up to 1500 m. ♪ Song: high, rich, melodious series, like "tjirre-tjú-wu" or rhyth-mic "Tjú-titi-Tjú- -," each series repeated for several min-utes before changing to another.

154.5 SLATY-CAPPED SHRIKE-VIREO (Assobiador-

do-castanhal) *Vireolanius leucotis* L 5.5 in./14 cm. Unmistakable by pale eyes and facial pattern. ♣ Canopy of humid forest. Up to 1800 m. ♪ Song: fluted, gliding-down "téuuw," con-stantly repeated at 1 ×/sec.

154.6 RED-EYED (or Chivi) **VIREO** (Juruviara) *Vireo*

olivaceus L 5.9 in./15 cm. Note black lines bordering eyebrow. N migrant Nom. (**a**, eyes red and vent white; Juv. as **b**) and resident/local migrant *chivi* group (**b**, eyes brown and vent yellow) shown. Cf. **154.7** and **154.8**. ♣ Forest edge, woodland, shrubby clearings, gardens with tall trees. Up to 1500 m, occasionally much higher. ♪ Song (local race): high, chirped "chrrit" or "cheche," constantly repeated 1 ×/1.5 sec; migrant Nom. is silent in South America.

154.7 YELLOW-GREEN VIREO (Juruviara-verde-ama-

relada) *Vireo flavoviridis* L 5.9 in./ 15 cm. Not always safely separable from **154.6**, but flanks are normally richer yellow and less or no black borders around eyebrow. ♣ Canopy and edge of forest and woodland. Up to 1500 m. ♪ Silent in Brazil. R.

154.8 BLACK- (or Brown-) **WHISKERED VIREO**

(Juruviara-barbuda) *Vireo altiloquus* L 5.9 in./15 cm. From **154.6** and **154.7** by narrow dark malar streak, but this is often difficult to see. ♣ Edge and clearings of forest and second growth. Up to 1000 m. ♪ Silent in South America.

154.9 NORONHA VIREO (Juruviara-de-noronha) *Vireo*

gracilirostris L 5.5 in./14 cm. Only vireo on Isla de Noronha. Note long, thin bill and dark eye. ♣ In any habitat on Noronha. ♪ Song: short, chirped "tetjúr." En, R.

154.1

♀

154.6

a

b

154.2

♀

154.7

154.3

♀

b

a

154.8

154.4

154.5

154.9

Plate 155

155.1 RUFOUS-CROWNED GREENLET (Verdinho-coroado) *Hylophilus poicilotis* L 5.1 in./ 13 cm. Note rufous crown. From **155.4** by distinct dusky ear coverts. ♣ Forest, second growth, woodland, scrub. Up to 1800 m. ♪ Song: rapid, high "teweét-teweét- -" (3–6 ×) or rapid "swee-swee- -" (4–5 ×).

155.2 GRAY-CHESTED GREENLET (Verdinho-da-várzea) *Hylophilus semicinereus* L 4.7 in./ 12 cm. Differs from **155.3** by gray, not yellow, breast. ♣ Upperstories and edge of humid forest and clearings up to 400 m. ♪ Song: very high, hurried "wee-wee-wee---" (about 8–20 ×, but often too fast to count).

155.3 LEMON-CHESTED GREENLET (Vite-vite) *Hylo-philus thoracicus* L 4.7 in./12 cm. Two groups: SE Nom. (**a**, Rio de Janeiro Greenlet) and W and N *griseiventris* group (**b**); **a** unique in range, **b** from **155.5** by gray restricted to hindcrown. ♣ In higher levels of the interior and edges of humid forest; **a** also in woodland. Mainly below 600 m. ♪ Song: very high, rapid series of 10–15 × upslurred "tu-Weét - -" notes.

155.4 GRAY-EYED GREENLET (Vite-vite-de-olho-cinza) *Hylophilus amaurocephalus* L 5.1 in./13 cm. Ear-patches less distinct than in **155.1**. ♣ Forest, woodland, caatinga, scrub. Up to 1800 m. ♪ Song: high, rather harsh "see-see" or "teTeé-teTeé-teTeé," and many other variations. En.

155.5 ASHY-HEADED GREENLET (Vite-vite-de-cabeça-cinza) *Hylophilus pectoralis* L 4.7 in./12 cm. Note all-gray head and dark eye. ♣ Woodland, riverine belts, gardens. Up to 400 m. ♪ Song: high, hurried "Wéetje-Wéetje-Wéetje-," rapid "tutjeweé-tutjeweé-tutjeweé," or loud, sharp "WúTjirrrr."

155.6 TEPUI GREENLET (Vite-vite-do-tepui) *Hylo-philus sclateri* L 4.7 in./12 cm. Gray wings and tail diagnostic. ♣ Interior and edge of humid forest; 600–2000 m. ♪ Song: Very high, simple "suwí-tu-èr," ("suwi" sharp and upslurred, "tu-èr" lower, but also ascending) or "suuih tuh" ("suuih" very high, piercing, and gliding down, "tuh" as a low, well-separated full stop).

155.7 BUFF-CHEEKED (or -breasted) **GREENLET** (Vite-vite-camurça) *Hylophilus muscicapinus* L 4.7 in./12 cm. Buff face sides and breast diagnostic. ♣ Forest on poor soils. Up to 600 m. ♪ Song: high, warbling "weet-oh-weeréet."

155.8 BROWN-HEADED GREENLET (Vite-vite-de-cabeça-marrom) *Hylophilus brunneiceps* L 4.7 in./12 cm. From **155.10** by grayish (not yellow) underparts. ♣ Sandy-belt forest, edge of várzea, and savanna woodland. Up to 400 m. ♪ Song: series of steeply gliding down, joined "tiiiiuw- -" notes (about 10 ×).

155.9 TAWNY-CROWNED GREENLET (Vite-vite-uirapuru) *Hylophilus ochraceiceps* L 4.7 in./12 cm. W and C Nom. group (**a**, pale eyes and distinct tawny forecrown) and NE *rubrifrons* group (**b**, brown eyes and less distinctly tawny forecrown) shown. Both are brownish olive above with browner tail. ♣ Undergrowth in interior of humid forest and second growth. Up to 800 m, occasionally much higher. ♪ Song: calm series of well-separated, slightly lowered, drawn-out, penetrating "tieeeh" notes.

155.10 DUSKY-CAPPED GREENLET (Vite-vite-de-barriga-marela) *Hylophilus hypoxanthus* L 4.7 in./12 cm. Note brownish head and dull yellowish underparts. ♣ Upperstory of terra firme. Up to 500 m. ♪ Song: very high, cheerful "is-it-so-wit" or "pichí-soweér."

Plate 156

156.1 WHITE-WINGED SWALLOW (Andorinha-do-rio) *Tachycineta albiventer* L 5.5 in./ 14 cm. White in wing diagnostic. ♣ Areas near water, incl. rivers, lakes, pastures, beaches. Up to 500 m. ♪ Call: toneless, slightly rising "krch" or "wrch."

156.2 WHITE-RUMPED SWALLOW (Andorinha-de-sobre-branco) *Tachycineta leucorrhoa* L 5.1 in./13 cm. White eyebrow difficult to see and therefore not always safely separable from **156.3**. ♣ Open and semiopen areas, often near water. Up to 1000 m. ♪ Call: toneless, short "zzt"; song: jumble of "zzt" and "zr" notes and gurgling, rapidly descending "pri-ri-ri-row."

156.3 CHILEAN SWALLOW (Andorinha-chilena) *Tachy-**cineta meyeni* L 4.7 in./12 cm. Occasionally with short white eyebrow, which never extends over bill. ♣ Open and semiopen areas, often near water. ♪ Call: "pripri."

156.4 BLUE-AND-WHITE SWALLOW (Andorinha-pequena-de-casa) *Pygochelidon* (or *Notiochelidon*) *cyanoleuca* L 5.1 in./ 13 cm. Note dark rump and vent (S migrant ssp. *patagonica* has white of belly extending into black vent). ♣ Open areas in woodland, savanna, forest clearings, towns. Up to 3000 m. ♪ Call: very/extr. high "see," very high, downslurred "tjeuw," and short twitters.

156.5 WHITE-BANDED SWALLOW (Peitoril) *Atticora**fasciata* L 5.9 in./15 cm. Unmistakable. ♣ At rivers in forest. Rarely at lakes and forest clearings. Up to 1000 m. ♪ Call: high "trr"; song: unstructured series of low "prr" notes, or "tetju."

156.6 BLACK-COLLARED SWALLOW (Andoriha-de-coleira) *Pygochelidon* (or *Atticora*) *melanoleuca* L 5.5 in./14 cm. Note dark chest band, rump, and vent. ♣ Near rivers, mainly areas with water rapids. ♪ Call/song: unstructured series of "zt" notes.

156.7 BARN SWALLOW (Andorinha-de-bando) *Hirundo**rustica* L 7.1 in./18 cm. Forked tail with long streamers (often missing). White spots (usually look like a complete band) in tail diagnostic. ♣ Any habitat, except forest interior and heavy woodland. ♪ Mostly silent in South America.

156.8 CLIFF SWALLOW (Andorinha-de-dorso-acane-lado) *Pterochelidon pyrrhonota* L 5.5 in./14 cm. Only swallow with pale buff rump, combined with tawny throat. ♣ Open areas near water in woodland, savanna, forest clearings, towns. Up to 2750 m. ♪ Generally silent in South America.

156 .1

156 .5

156 .2

156 .6

156 .3

156 .7

156 .4

156 .8

Plate 157

157.1 PURPLE MARTIN (Andorinha-azul) *Progne subis* L 7.5 in./19 cm. ♂ not safely separable from ♂ **157.3**. Note, however, the presence of the two spp. in opposite seasons. ♀ from **157.2** and ♀ **157.3** by grayish nuchal collar and forehead. ♣ Wide variety of open and semiopen areas. Often in towns. ♪ Mostly silent in South America.

157.2 GRAY-BREASTED MARTIN (Andorinha-doméstica-grande) *Progne chalybea* L 6.7 in./17 cm. ♀ less glossy blue than ♂. Neck same color as rest of upperparts. Underparts white, chest and throat gray-brown (sometimes bluish). ♣ Open areas in woodland, savanna, forest clearings, towns. Up to 2000 m. ♪ Calls: varied; e.g., "prrrt-prrrt," nasal "tjurt," or gurgling "tjurrt"; song: very/extr. high, scratchy chirping.

157.3 SOUTHERN MARTIN (Andorinha-do-sul) *Progne elegans* L 6.7 in./17 cm. Underparts of ♀ dusky brown with scaly white edging (esp. on lower underparts). Forehead rarely grayish. ♣ Open and semiopen areas. Also in forest clearings. Up to 2500 m.

157.4 BANK SWALLOW (or Sand Martin) (Andorinha-do-barranco) *Riparia riparia* L 4.7 in./12 cm. Resembles **157.5**, but much smaller. Note distinctive erratic and fluttering flight. ♣ Open areas near water. Breeds in freshly cut cliffs, sleeps in reed beds. ♪ Call: toneless "zrt" or "zirrit."

157.5 BROWN-CHESTED MARTIN (Andorinha-do-campo) *Progne tapera* L 6.3 in./16 cm. Large, with brownish upperparts. Note white throat. ♣ Open and semiopen country with trees, including towns. ♪ Call: very high, sharp, dry "zrit-zrit."

157.6 WHITE-THIGHED SWALLOW (Calcinha-branca) *Atticora* (or *Neochelidon*) *tibialis* L 4.7 in./12 cm. Overall dusky with inconspicuous white socks. ♣ Clearings and edge of forest, riverine belts. Up to 1000 m, locally higher. ♪ Call: very high, weak "zip" or "trrrp tiptip."

157.7 TAWNY-HEADED SWALLOW (Andorinha-morena) *Alopochelidon fucata* L 4.7 in./12 cm. Tawny head diagnostic. ♣ Open areas, esp. grassland near water. Up to 1600 m. ♪ Call: extr. high "tjup tjuptup."

157.8 SOUTHERN ROUGH-WINGED SWALLOW (Andorinha-serradora) *Stelgidopteryx ruficollis* L 5.1 in./13 cm. Uniform brownish above with tawny throat. ♣ Open country near water, also in forest clearings. Up to 1000 m, occasionally much higher. ♪ Call: rich, gurgled "wrir," "wirre-wirre-wir," or "zirre-zitzit."

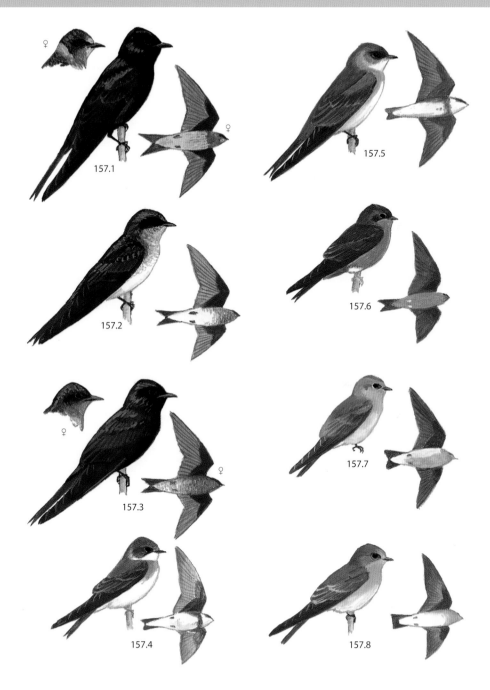

157.1

157.5

157.2

157.6

157.3

157.7

157.4

157.8

Plate 158

158.1 BLACK-CAPPED DONACOBIUS (Japacanim)

Donacobius atricapilla L 7.9 in./20 cm. Two sspp.: widespread Nom. (**a**; Juv. resembles **b**) and *albovittatus* (**b**, far SW). Unmistakable by yellow eye, buff underparts, and black-and-white tail. Skin on sides of throat inflatable (**b**). ♪ Rich repertoire, including high, liquid, rapid "wicwicwic," low, calm "woí-woí-woí," and nasal, mewing "wrèh-wrèh-wrèh." Also duets in two-voiced, liquid "woi-woi-woi" together with toneless scratching, like "zzeh-zzeh-zzeh."

158.2 BICOLORED WREN (Garrincha-dos-lhanos) *Campylorhynchus griseus* L 7.9 in./20 cm.

Unmistakable by broad white subterminal tail band (distinct from below) and white (pale gray or buff-tinged in Juv.) underparts and eyebrow. Bold. ♣ Semiarid woodland and scrub (even in towns). Also palm groves. ♪ Song: basically vocalizes in duet, such as very low, guttural, chattering, mid-high, liquid "wit-tur-trit- -" or low, guttural, chattering "wraf-wratter-vraf-wràh- -."

158.3 THRUSH-LIKE WREN (Catatau) *Campylorhynchus turdinus* L 7.9 in./20 cm. Three

sspp.: *unicolor* (**a**, Pantanal region), Amazonian *hypostictus* (**b**), and E Nom. (not shown, intermediate between **a** and **b**). Note large size, relatively long bill, pale eyebrow, and rather uniform (**a**) or conspicuously dark-spotted (**b**) underparts. ♣ Canopy and edge of humid lowland forest and nearby second growth. Also gallery forest, palm groves, parks. ♪ Call: "kets kets kets-kets," sounding like 2 pebbles struck together; song: low "tjow tjów-tjow-tjow" (2nd part also with 2 × "tjow"), given in duet.

158.4 TOOTH-BILLED WREN (Cambaxirra-cinzenta)

Odontorchilus cinereus L 4.7 in./12 cm. Gnatcatcherlike (Pl. **179**), but note barred tail and brownish tinge to crown. ♣ Canopy of humid forest (esp. terra firme). Up to 500 m. ♪ Song: very high, rattling trill (1 sec) or very/extr. high joined series of 4 "jee" notes.

158.5 SEDGE (or Grass) **WREN** (Corruíra-do-campo)

Cistothorus platensis L 3.9 in./10 cm. Small. Streaked back diagnostic. ♣ Cerrado, grassland, marshes. ♪ Song: partitioned or continuous series of short, very/extr. high notes such as high rattles, sharp trills, sparrowlike "tr-tr-tr-tr," and nasal "zèzèzèzè."

158.6 MOUSTACHED WREN (Garrinchão-pai-avô) *Thryothorus genibarbis* L 6.3 in./16 cm. From

158.7 by more white on face and black-bordered white malar. Differs from **158.8–158.10** by stronger facial markings and plain wings. ♣ Undergrowth of forest, dense vegetation at rivers or lakes, caatinga, palm groves. ♪ Call: nasal, irritated "teeyr"; song: rapid, varied series–(often in duet) with repetitive notes, most notes ending with low "tjow-tjow" or "tjow-tjow-tjow"; also may be "Eeh-wi-tjow-tjow" (3–5 ×) or "fuWeeuh-tjow-tjow" notes.

158.7 CORAYA WREN (Garrinchão-coraia) *Thryothorus coraya* L 5.9 in./15 cm. Black sides of

face (usually with faint white streaks) diagnostic. Chest gray in W. ♣ Undergrowth of humid forest and second growth. Up to 1850 m. ♪ Vocalizations varied. Call: e.g., short, strong rattle; song: strong, rich, continuous series with notes such as characteristic gliding "tuweeit" and short rattles like low, high, or very high "djipdjip---" or "tjiptjiptjip" notes.

158.8 BUFF-BREASTED WREN (Garrinchão-de-barriga-vermelha) *Thryothorus leucotis* L 5.5 in./14 cm. Note barred

wings, distinct white eyebrow, and faintly black-streaked white cheeks. C ssp. *rufiventris* shown; N sspp. less rufescent above. Cf. **158.6**, **158.9**, and **158.10**. ♣ Undergrowth of forest (avoids interior of terra firme), woodland, second growth, mangrove. Prefers areas near water. Up to 950 m. ♪ Call: "fju-djEw" ("fju" high, inhaled); song: continuous, vigorous series of 4–6 × repeated, high, strong, melodious notes, like "Tjer-oh-werrr" or "wur-Tjer."

158.9 FAWN-BREASTED WREN (Garrincha-do-oeste)

Thryothorus guarayanus L 5.5 in./14 cm. Differs from very similar **158.8** (limited contact possible) by stronger marked cheeks, buffier throat, and less rufescent upperparts. ♣ Undergrowth of forest (várzea, semiarid, dry, or riverine), second growth. Prefers areas near water. Up to 400 m. ♪ Song: 3-stepped, calm "tseew tjew tjew" series (1st thin step highest).

158.10 LONG-BILLED WREN (Garrinchão-de-bico-grande) *Thryothorus longirostris* L

5.9 in./15 cm. Resembles **158.8** (limited contact possible), but bill longer. No overlap with **158.9**. ♣ Undergrowth of forest, dense woodland, mangrove, dense shrub. Up to 900 m. ♪ Call: e.g., high, melodious "turrut"; song: calm series of melodious, repeated (2–8 ×) notes, like "Tée-tjur" or "Wée-wit-wudr." En.

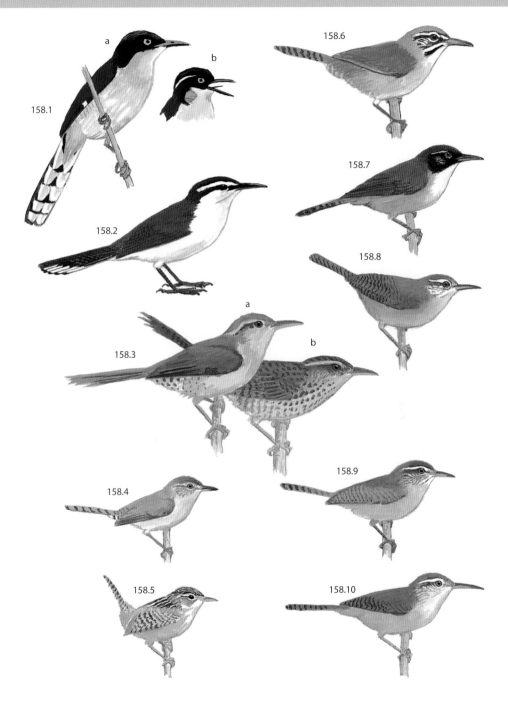

158.1 a b

158.6

158.2

158.7

158.3 a b

158.8

158.4

158.9

158.5

158.10

Plate 159

159.1 GRAY WREN (Garrincha-cinza) *Thryothorus griseus* L 4.7 in./12 cm. Distinctively short tailed and gray. ♣ Tangled undergrowth in clearings and at edge of várzea and woodland. Up to 200 m. En.

159.2 (Southern) **HOUSE WREN** (Corruíra) *Troglodytes (aedon) musculus* L 4.7 in./12 cm. Small. No distinctive features, but note faint grayish buff eyebrow and barred wings and tail. ♣ Virtually any open to semiopen habitat. Often near humans. ♪ Song: highly varied; e.g., short series, often starting with some soft, mumbled, run-together notes, finishing with a short, powerful rattle, like nasal "tju-ru-che-che-WuDDDDR."

159.3 TEPUI WREN (Corruíra-do-tepui) *Troglodytes rufulus* L 4.7 in./12 cm. Gray-throated and gray-breasted ssp. *wetmorei* (**a**, SW part of range) and all-rufous Nom. (**b**, NE part of range) shown. Resembles **159.2**, but more chestnut. ♣ Undergrowth of forest and brushy areas; 1000–2800 m.

159.4 WHITE-BREASTED WOOD-WREN (Uirapuru-de-peito-branco) *Henicorhina leucosticta* L 4.3 in./11 cm. Distinctive facial pattern and short tail. Not in range of larger, longer-tailed **158.6**. ♣ Undergrowth and borders of humid forest; second growth. Up to 1100 m. ♪ Song: short, rapid, powerful, rich series of 2–4 × repeated notes, like high, rapid "fififi-wruh" (1st part higher) or staccato "wéeh-wéeh-wéeh."

159.5 SCALY-BREASTED NIGHTINGALE (or Southern Nightingale) **WREN** (Wren) (Uirapuru-veado) *Microcerculus marginatus* L 4.3 in./11 cm. Contrasting dark brown above, white below with scaled, mottled brown flanks. ♣ Low levels in humid lowland forest. ♪ Song: very beautiful, calm, fluted melody of single, pure notes, as if sung from sheet music.

159.6 FLUTIST WREN (Flautista-do-tepui) *Microcerculus ustulatus* L 4.7 in./12 cm. Uniform dark rufous brown with very short tail. Cf. leaftossers (Pl. **100**). ♣ Low levels in humid forest; 850–2100 m. ♪ Song: as **159.5**; an unbelievable songster, fluting as if calmly varying on an existing song.

159.7 WING-BANDED WREN (Uirapuru-de-asa-branca) *Microcerculus bambla* L 4.7 in./12 cm. Generally unmistakable by wing bands. Cf. ♂ **108.5**. ♣ Low levels in humid forest. Up to 1500 m. ♪ Song: e.g., a rapid series of 5–7, level-pitched, very beautifully fluted notes, long pause, one beautiful note, long pause, then a rapid series of fluted notes.

159.8 MUSICIAN WREN (Uirapuru-verdadeiro) *Cyphorhinus arada* L 5.1 in./13 cm. Three groups: W *modulator* group (**a**, with rufous breast, throat, forecrown, and eyebrow), NE Nom. group (**b**, with white eyebrow and distinctive black-and-white collar) and C ssp. *griseolateralis* (**c**, rather intermediate between **a** and **b**, but grayer below). Note barring to wings, unlike leaftossers (Pl. **100**) and various Antbirds. ♣ Low levels in humid forest. Up to 1000 m. ♪ Song: jumble of low, almost toneless gobbles and much higher series of 4–6 clear, different-pitched, fluted notes.

NOTE: the following 2 species are not members of the wren family, but belong to the gnatcatcher family (Pl. **179**).

159.9 COLLARED GNATWREN (Bico-assovelado-de-coleira) *Microbates collaris* L 4.3 in./11 cm. Unmistakable by facial pattern and very long bill. ♣ Undergrowth of terra firme. Up to 500 m. ♪ Call/song: very high, loud, sharp, gliding-down "péeeee"; also "tjeu-tjeu pueéh-pueéh."

159.10 LONG- (or Straight-)**BILLED GNATWREN** (Bico-assovelado) *Ramphocaenus melanurus* L 4.7 in./12 cm. Very long bill. No barring on tail or wings. ♣ Undergrowth of humid forest, woodland, forest borders. Up to 1500 m. ♪ Song: loud, often shrill, rattling "tu-tutututututu---" trill.

Plate 160

160.1 RUFOUS-BROWN SOLITAIRE (Sabiá-castanho)

Cichlopsis leucogenys L 7.9 in./20 cm. Overall rufous-brown with cinnamon throat and buff vent. Upper mandible black; lower mandible yellow-orange. ♣ Arboreal in humid forest at elevations around 800 m in E; higher in the tepuis. ♪ Song: rapid sequences of inhaled "fff," single "tjuw" and "tjeeh" notes, extr. high "see," and trills and rattles, each sequence 2–3 sec; completely different sequences starting at intervals of 1–1.5 sec. R.

160.2 VEERY (Sabiá-norte-americano) *Catharus fusce-*

scens L 7.1 in./18 cm. Differs from **160.3** and **160.4** by more rufescent color and less distinct spotting below. ♣ Undergrowth of forest, secondary woodland; occasionally cerrado. Shy. ♪ Call: loud, downslurred "weuw." Does not sing in South America.

160.3 GRAY-CHEEKED THRUSH (Sabiá-de-cara-cinza)

Catharus minimus L 7.1 in./18 cm. Cf. **106.4**. ♣ Undergrowth of forest and second growth. Shy. ♪ Call: very/extr. high, thin, slightly raspy "veer." Does not sing in South America.

160.4 SWAINSON'S THRUSH (Sabiá-de-óculos) *Catharus*

ustulatus L 7.1 in./18 cm. Differs from **160.3** by bold buff eyering and lores ("spectacles") and brownish (not grayish) cheeks, but has similar distinct spots on chest. As **160.2** and **160.3**, has pale bar (**a**) across underside of wing. ♣ Mid- to lower levels of forest (esp. near edge), second growth. Shy. ♪ Call: high liquid "wic"; song: e.g., very high, liquid "wir-oh-wir-sreeh-sreeh" and variations.

160.5 YELLOW-LEGGED THRUSH (Sabiá-una) *Tur-*

dus (or *Platycichla*) *flavipes* L 7.9 in./20 cm. ♂ unmistakable. ♀ with plain olive-brown upperparts, faintly streaked throat, and yellow eyering. ♣ Mainly arboreal in humid forest, woodland, and shaded plantations. Up to 2000 m (only above 1000 m in N). ♪ Song: short series (2–8 notes) at 1-sec intervals, like "wioh-wir wee" or "fee-tje-wee fee-tje-wee," many with sharp, extr. high "sjee" overtones; all series loud and energetic, but often rather squeaky.

160.6 PALE-EYED THRUSH (Sabiá-preto) *Turdus* (or

Platycichla) *leucops* L 7.9 in./20 cm. ♂ unmistakable. ♀ resembles ♀ **160.5**, but iris pale gray (or light brown: juv?) and lacks eyering, streaks on throat, and olive tinge above. Also cf. ♀ **160.8**. ♣ Mainly arboreal in humid forest and woodland; 1000–1800 m. ♪ Song: very/extr. high, short series at 1- to 2-sec intervals; each series mainly as a twittered sizzle, occasionally mixed with some lower notes.

160.7 EASTERN SLATY-THRUSH (Sabiá-ferreiro)

Turdus (*nigriceps*) *subalaris* L 7.9 in./20 cm. ♂ gray (sometimes tinged olive); throat distinctly streaked and with white crescent below. ♀ resembles **161.1** (no overlap), but with narrow yellow eyering and bill yellowish brown. Also cf. **161.7b**. ♣ Arboreal in forest (incl. *Araucaria*), tall woodland, high trees in gardens, plantations. Mainly below 1000 m. ♪ Call: e.g., high, slightly upslurred "tweet"; song: short series of 2–6 descending, weak, squeaky notes, given at 5- to 6-sec intervals, like "twee twee sri-sri-sri" or "tur-rit-twee-twee-twee."

160.8 BLACK-HOODED THRUSH (Sabiá-de-cabeça-

preta) *Turdus olivater* L 9.8 in./25 cm. ♂ distinctive. ♀ as ♀ **160.5**, but underparts uniform (belly not paler). ♣ Humid forest, second growth; 900–2600 m. ♪ Call: high, short "twec"; song: double notes like extr. high "seesee" or high, slightly nasal "wecwec" at intervals of 1 sec.

160.9 RUFOUS-BELLIED THRUSH (Sabiá-laranjeira)

Turdus rufiventris L 9.8 in./25 cm. Unmistakable by rufous belly. ♣ Woodland, savanna, second growth, forest edge, shrub, riverine growth, parks, gardens, agricultural areas. Up to 2200 m. ♪ Song: rather long, calm series of fluted notes (like "tju-tju-tjeé tjutu- -," 7–18 sec) at intervals of 2–5 sec. *Note*: This species is the national bird of Brazil.

160.10 PALE-BREASTED THRUSH (Sabiá-barranco)

Turdus leucomelas L 9.8 in./25 cm. Grayish head contrasting with olive-brown back diagnostic, but some ♀♀ without or little gray to head (**a**). ♣ Woodland, second growth, wooded savanna, forest edge, shrub, riverine growth, palm groves, plantations, parks, gardens. Up to 1500 m, locally higher. ♪ Song: as **160.9**, but most notes repeated two or three times.

160.1

160.6

160.2

160.7 ♀

160.3

a

160.8 ♀

160.4

160.9

160.5

♀

160.10

a

Plate 161

161.1 BLACK-BILLED THRUSH (Caraxué-de-bico-preto)

Turdus ignobilis L 7.9 in./20 cm. Dull olive-brown with faintly streaked throat, blackish bill, and no yellow eyering. Cf. ♀ **160.7**, **161.2**, and **161.7b**. ♣ Forest edge, woodland, wooded areas in savanna, plantations, parks, gardens. Up to 2000 m. ♪ Call: soft "wuc" or "wic"; song: loud, shrill, hurried "turre," "tu-re-weét" and similar phrases in series lasting 3–25 sec.

161.2 CREAMY-BELLIED THRUSH (Sabiá-poca) *Turdus*

amaurochalinus L 7.9 in./20 cm. Dull olive-brown with diagnostic dark lores. Throat strongly streaked with white crescent below. Bill yellow (**a**) to dusky (**b**). ♣ Woodland, savanna, second growth, forest edge, shrub, parks, gardens, agricultural areas. Mainly in lowlands. ♪ Song: simple, little varied, yet musical series with short notes, like "tjurre," "wurr," "tjeeh," and "tjut-tjeé."

161.3 LAWRENCE'S THRUSH (Caraxué-de-bico-ama-

relo) *Turdus lawrencii* L 7.9 in./20 cm. Resembles **161.5**, but darker and with yellow eyering and bill (bill dusky in ♀). ♣ Mainly arboreal in humid forest. Inconspicuous. Up to 800 m. ♪ Song: loud, calm, melodious, richly varied series of short and longer notes, mainly perfect imitations of other bird species. May sing for many hours.

161.4 COCOA THRUSH (Sabiá-da-mata) *Turdus fumi-

gatus* L 7.9 in./20 cm. Rich rufous overall with faintly streaked throat, dusky bill, and no eyering. ♣ Humid forest, woodland, shaded plantations, gardens. Inconspicuous. Up to 1000 m. ♪ Song: very long series of short, musical but little-varied, yodeling notes like "tju-you-widuh," without intervals.

161.5 HAUXWELL'S THRUSH (Sabiá-bicolor) *Turdus*

hauxwelli L 7.9 in./20 cm. Very similar to **161.4** (limited overlap), but less rufescent overall, and vent and belly usually whiter. Also cf. **161.3**. ♣ Humid forest and woodland. Inconspicuous. Up to 800 m. ♪ Song: long series of simple, one- or two-noted fluted notes and trills, like "yuyu," "wheét" and "bee-bíh," with very short intervals.

161.6 SPECTACLED (or bare- or yellow- eyed-) **THRUSH**

(Caraxué) *Turdus nudigenis* L 7.9 in./ 20 cm. Unmistakable by broad yellow eyering. ♣ Forest edge, woodland, open areas with scattered woods, plantations, gardens. Up to 1000 m. ♪ Call: squeaky, stepping-up "wur-hèh"; song: series of little-varied notes, like "tjuwur-wirwur" (2nd part higher), given in groups of three.

161.7 WHITE-NECKED THRUSH (Sabiá-coleira) *Tur-

dus albicollis* L 7.9 in./20 cm. Two groups: S and E Nom. group (**a**, with at least lower mandible yellow and flanks rufous; tawny in NE) and Amazonian *phaeopygus* group (**b**, with dusky bill and gray chest/flanks contrasting with brown upperparts). Both with strongly streaked throat with white crescent below and yellow or orange eyering. ♣ Low levels in forest, woodland, second growth. Up to 1500 m. ♪ Song: listless series of hardly varied "wuhuh tíuh" ("tíuh" higher pitched).

161.8 TROPICAL MOCKINGBIRD (Sabiá-da-praia)

Mimus gilvus L 9.8 in./25 cm. Upperparts uniform pale gray. ♣ Semi-open country, savanna, scrub, towns. Mainly near the coast, but up to 1300 m in Roraima. ♪ Call: high, sharp, staccato "tjiptjip"; song: series of short, hurried, 4–6-noted, 2–4 × repeated phrases, like "t'peet-t'peet," "peétje-durr," or "peepeepee-pirreép."

161.9 CHALK-BROWED MOCKINGBIRD (Sabiá-do-

campo) *Mimus saturninus* L 9.8 in./ 25 cm. Browner, more mottled than **161.8** and with distinct blackish postocular streak. Often brownish buff below. ♣ Open areas with trees, scrub, towns. Up to 1000 m. ♪ Call: slightly upslurred "tjer"; song: slow series of high, one-noted to much longer notes, like "wir," "kruts," "wrrrir-wrrrir-wrrrir," "drip-drip," and "uche-uche-uche" at 0.5- to 1-sec intervals.

161.10 WHITE-BANDED MOCKINGBIRD (Calhandra-

de-três-rabos) *Mimus triurus* L 7.9 in./ 20 cm. Note wing pattern and rufescent rump. ♣ Open woodland, open country with scattered trees and bush, settlements. Up to 500 m. ♪ Sustained, leisurely series of upslurred "wrrrh" notes, almost-rattles, squeaks, like "èèèh," shrieks, short rolls, like "trrrr," loud "wééééh" notes, nasal "wèh" notes, and very high "wééh-wééh" notes.

Plate 162

NOTE: Oropendolas and Caciques: nests distinctive and pendulous. All except **162.7** and **162.9** are colonial. Note yellow in tail of the oropendolas (most distinctive from below and in flight).

162.1 GREEN OROPENDOLA (Japu-verde) *Psarocolius* *viridis* L 19.7 in./50 cm (♂), 13.8 in./35 cm (♀). Mainly yellowish olive with pale bill. ♣ Canopy of humid forest. Up to 500 m. ♪ Call: varied; e.g., "tjak tjaktjak" notes; song: fast, rising, gobbling "rrrrrrrrúh," ending in gurgling "ronc-ronc-ronc-ronc."

162.2 BAND-TAILED OROPENDOLA (Japu-de-rabo- verde) *Cacicus latirostris* L 13.8 in./35 cm (♂), 9.8 in./25 cm (♀). Note black terminal band on tail and brown nape. Some birds lack gray on the upper mandible. ♣ River islands and várzea. Up to 300 m.

162.3 RUSSET-BACKED OROPENDOLA (Japu-pardo) *Psarocolius angustifrons* L 17.7 in./45 cm (♂), 13.8 in./35 cm (♀). Dark brownish olive. Note black bill. ♣ Interior and clearings of humid forest, esp. along rivers. Up to 800 m. ♪ Song: short, rapid series of 4 ascending liquid notes "oup-op-pup-póp" (like dripping water).

162.4 CASQUED OROPENDOLA (Japu-de-capacete) *Cacicus oseryi* L 13.8 in./35 cm (♂), 11.8 in./30 cm (♀). Uniform chestnut upperparts. Note swollen pale bill. ♣ Mainly in canopy of terra firme, less so in várzea. Up to 400 m. ♪ Call: varied; e.g., "ugh," like a hoarse, barking dog or a chicken in distress, or parrotlike shrieks, starting very high, then lowered, like "sree-eh" or a liquid "clokclok-wít-je-wèr."

162.5 CRESTED OROPENDOLA (Japu) *Psarocolius* *decumanus* L 17.7 in./45 cm (♂), 13.8 in./35 cm (♀). Large. Very dark with contrasting pale bill and yellow tail, esp. in flight. ♣ Humid forest, woodland, agricultural land with scattered trees. Up to 1200 m. ♪ Song: very complex, including very high, rapid, staccato flutes and liquid curls. Also "blobblob-Tjée-ow" (1st part deeply gobbled).

162.6 OLIVE (or Amazonian) **OROPENDOLA** (Japuaçu) *Psarocolius bifasciatus* L 19.7 in./50 cm (♂), 15.7 in./40 cm (♀). Three sspp.: *yuracares* (**a**, widespread) and Nom. Pará Oropendola (**b**, near Belém) shown. Not shown ssp. *neivae* (Río Tocantins area) intermediate. Note orange-tipped dark bill and pink cheeks. ♣ Canopy and edge of humid forest, mainly terra firme. Up to 500 m. ♪ Call: liquid, hiccupping "wec"; song: rapid, liquid "wdrdrdr-di-drrów" (1st part esp. hard to describe; soft, very short "di" slightly lower).

162.7 SOLITARY BLACK CACIQUE (Iraúna-de-bico- branco) *Procacicus* (or *Cacicus*) *solitarius* L 9.8 in./25 cm. Dark eyes diagnostic. ♣ Dense vegetation at lower levels of edges of forest and woodland, esp. along rivers and lakes. Up to 500 m. ♪ Call: high, sudden "wrèèew"; also short, hoarse rattles; song: series of short, incoherent rattles and very high, squeaky "tjew-tjew-tjee-tjow-tjeh- -."

162.8 RED-RUMPED CACIQUE (Guaxe) *Cacicus hae-* *morrhous* L 11.8 in./30 cm (♂), 7.1 in./25 cm (♀). cm. Note bluish eyes (brown in Imm.) and red rump (often difficult to see when perched). ♣ Forest canopy and borders, woodland. Up to 1000 m. ♪ Call/song: unstructured series of high, hoarse "sreek sreek -" notes (not unlike barking of small dog).

162.9 GOLDEN-WINGED CACIQUE (Tecelão) *Cacicus* *chrysopterus* L 7.9 in./20 cm (♂), 7.1 in./18 cm (♀). Limited overlap with **162.10**, which has yellow vent and blue eyes. Also cf. **165.1**. ♣ Woodland, riverine belts, humid forest. Up to 2000 m. ♪ Call: varied; e.g., mewing "èyeh" or thin, slightly upslurred "whee"; song: short series of liquid single and double notes, often completed by a very high, sharp "sheeshee."

162.10 YELLOW-RUMPED CACIQUE (Xexéu) *Cacicus* *cela* L 11.8 in./30 cm (♂), 7.1 in./25 cm (♀). Note yellow vent and basal third of tail. ♣ Forest borders (esp. várzea), woodland, and areas with scattered trees (incl. towns). Up to 900 m. ♪ Song: unstructured series of single or double croaks and parrotlike chatters.

Plate 163

163.1 FORBES'S BLACKBIRD (Anumará) *Curaeus forbesi*

L 9.8 in./25 cm. Differs from slightly more glossy **163.2** by straighter, longer bill without groove. ♣ Forest edge, marshes, and sugarcane plantations up to 600 m. ♪ Noisy. Call/song: short, dry rattles and series of chattering "twets" notes, often sounding like clicking pebbles. En, R.

163.2 CHOPI BLACKBIRD (Graúna) *Gnorimopsar chopi*

L 9.8 in./25 cm. Like **163.1** with lanceolated feathers on nape and slightly curved bill with groove in lower mandible. ♣ Cultivation, pastures, fields, marsh. Up to 1000 m. ♪ Call/song: loud, explosive "tjouw," single or in unstructured series at varying pitch.

163.3 VELVET-FRONTED GRACKLE (Iraúna-velada)

Lampropsar tanagrinus L 7.9 in./20 cm. Black with slight bluish gloss above. Tail rather long. Note range and habitat. ♣ Várzea, marshy lake edges. Up to 400 m. ♪ Call: dry croaks and "tjew" notes; song: repetitions and variations of very high, rather sharp, yet liquid "tjuw wutwut-tjuweét."

163.4 MOUNTAIN (or Golden-tufted) **GRACKLE** (Iraúna-da-guiana)

Macroagelaius imthurni L 11.8 in./30 cm (♂), 9.8 in./25 cm (♀). Note long tail. Tufts diagnostic (often hidden when perched). ♣ Canopy and edge of humid forest on the tepuis. ♪ Song: high, ascending, gurgling, flowing "tjirrder-t1eh-de-Wúr."

163.5 SCREAMING COWBIRD (Vira-bosta-picumã) *Molothrus rufoaxillaris* L 7.5 in./19 cm.

Sexes similar. Very like ♂ **163.6**, but less glossy and bill shorter. Juv. as **164.1**. ♣ Shrubby areas, pastures, towns. Up to 1000 m. ♪ Call: nasal "chat" or very high "scree"; song: "pruk si-sleé" (1st part low-pitched).

163.6 SHINY COWBIRD (Vira-bosta) *Molothrus bonariensis* L 7.9 in./20 cm. Usually in

groups that contain both the strongly violet-glossed ♂♂ and the dull brownish gray (rarely black) ♀♀. If seen singly (infrequent), cf. ♂ to **163.2**, **163.3**, **163.5**, and ♂ *Tachyphonus* Tanagers (Pl. **169**); cf. ♀ to ♀ **164.9**. ♣ Wide variety of semiopen and open habitats, incl. towns. Spreading with forest clearance. Up to 2000 m. ♪ Song: unstructured, rather quiet series of soft bubbling and very high "sree" notes in hurried phrases.

163.7 GIANT COWBIRD (Iraúna-grande) *Molothrus*

oryzivorus L 15.7 in./40 cm (♂), 11.8 in./30 cm (♀). Large size and thick-necked jizz diagnostic. Eyes pale yellow (**a**) or dark red (**b**). ♣ Wide variety of wooded and forested habitats. Often at river banks. Associated with oropendola and cacique ssp., which it parasitizes. ♪ Song: generally silent, occasionally series of low notes, often transposed in extr. high, loud, chattering "wèh wèhwèh tsjeéptsjeép," or very high, rhythmic, piped "peeeeh peedee-pih."

163.8 CARIB GRACKLE (Iraúna-do-norte) *Quiscalus*

lugubris L 9.8 in./25 cm. (♂), 7.9 in./20 cm. (♀). Unmistakable by wedge-shaped tail. Juv. with dark eyes. ♣ Semiopen areas near the coast, incl. mangrove and towns. Up to 300 m. ♪ Song: very high, gliding-down, partly mewing "tjeeuw" notes, often in "tjeeuw-tjewtjewtjew" series.

163.9 YELLOW-WINGED BLACKBIRD (Sargento) *Agelasticus* (or *Chrysomus*) *thilius* L

7.1 in./18 cm. Yellow shoulder of ♂ diagnostic (no overlap with similar sspp. of **165.1**), but yellow area often small and inconspicuous. ♀ heavily streaked. ♣ Reed beds at marshes and lakes. ♪ Song: varied; short, nasal, hurried phrases, like "titi-tjeuh" or "tiwi-tjew."

163.10 UNICOLORED BLACKBIRD (Carretão) *Agelasticus* (or *Chrysomus*) *cyanopus* L 7.5 in./

19 cm. Note long, straight bill. ♂ uniform glossy black (all races). ♀♀ variable; SC Nom. (**a**, yellowish below, upperparts black and rufous), NE ssp. *xenicus* (**b**, dark brownish black. Imm. male similar), and SE *atroolivaceus* (**c**, brownish with yellow-buff throat). ♂ from other blackbirds and grackles by bill shape and habitat. ♀♀ distinctive; amount of dusky streaking below of ♀ Nom. variable between none and more dense than shown. ♣ Reed beds. Up to 500 m. ♪ Song: calm or hurried series of "chew" notes.

163.1

163.6

Sub ad. ♂

163.2

163.7

a

b

163.3

163.8

♀

163.4

163.9

♀

163.5

163.10

♂

♀c

♀a

♀b

Plate 164

164.1 BAY-WINGED COWBIRD (Asa-de-telha) *Age-*

laioides badius L 7.5 in./19 cm. Generally unmistakable, but Juv. **163.5** very similar. No overlap with **164.2**. ♣ Scrubby areas, pastures, open woodland. ♪ Call: high, sharp "wits"; song: 4–5 sec series of very high twittering, interspersed with short, inhaled trills. En.

164.2 PALE BAYWING (Asa-de-telha-pálido) *Agelaioides*

fringillarius L 7.5 in./19 cm. Often considered a ssp. of **164.1** (no overlap), but paler. ♣ Caatinga forest and woodland, scrubby areas. ♪ Call: sharp "ritz" (as **164.5**). En.

164.3 RED-BREASTED BLACKBIRD (Polícia-inglesa-do-norte)

Sturnella militaris L 7.5 in./19 cm. Cf. **164.4**. ♣ Grassland, pastures, rice fields. Spreading with forest clearance. Up to 1200 m. ♪ Voice similar to **164.12**.

164.4 WHITE-BROWED BLACKBIRD (Polícia-inglesa-do-sul)

Sturnella superciliaris L 7.1 in./18 cm. ♂ from ♂ **164.3** by white eye-stripe. ♀ resembles a large, streaked sparrow with barred tail and reddish tinge below; not reliably separable from ♀ **164.3**. Compare **164.6** and **164.7**. ♣ Grasslands, usually damp. Spreading with forest clearance. Up to 2000 m. ♪ Song: normally starting with "t-zeeeeeee," followed by loose assemblages of soft yet emphasized nasal "thit" and "tjew" notes, toneless, inhaled hisses, and extr. high "seet" notes.

164.5 EASTERN MEADOWLARK (Pedro-ceroulo)

Sturnella magna L 7.9 in./20 cm. Unmistakable by jizz and general color pattern. ♣ Open areas, mainly grassland. ♪ Call: soft, almost toneless "wwwwrwttttu-tjew" trill; song: very high, descending, soft "fee-fee-tju-wuw" and variations.

164.6 PAMPAS (or Lesser Red-breasted) **MEADOWLARK**

(Peito-vermelho-grande) *Sturnella defilippii* L 7.9 in./20 cm. Note long bill and red underparts (less in ♀). ♣ Grassland, susceptible to overgrazing. Up to 500 m.

164.7 BOBOLINK (Triste-pia) *Dolichonyx oryzivorus* L

7.1 in./18 cm. ♂♂ arrive in Brazil in N-br plumage, but moult into Br plumage during northbound migration from March onward. ♀♀ differ from ♀♀ **164.3** and **164.4** by unbarred tails. Note sharp points of tail feathers in all plumages. ♣ Marsh, rice fields, tall grass. Up to 2500 m, normally lower. ♪ Call: metallic-sounding "pink."

164.8 YELLOW-HOODED BLACKBIRD (Iratauá-pequeno)

Chrysomus icterocephalus L 7.1 in./18 cm. ♂ unmistakable; ♀ has diagnostic yellow throat. ♣ Marsh and tall grass at or near rivers. Up to 400 m and above. ♪ Call: low or high "shit"; song: high to extr. high, scratchy or shrill, partly inhaled or nasal phrases, like "sreeeeet-tuituitui."

164.9 CHESTNUT-CAPPED BLACKBIRD (Garibaldi)

Chrysomus ruficapillus L 7.5 in./19 cm. ♂ unmistakable. ♀ nondescript, but note ochre-buff throat, unlike ♀ **163.6**. ♣ Marshes, reed beds, rice fields. Up to 850 m. ♪ Call: "chew" and slow chatter; song: "tip-tip cheeeeeer" (1st part soft and low, 2nd descending part very/extr. high).

164.10 SCARLET-HEADED BLACKBIRD (Cardeal-do-banhado)

Amblyramphus holosericeus L 9.8 in./25 cm. Unmistakable by color pattern. ♣ Extensive reed beds. ♪ Call: soft "cheh cheh -"; song: short phrases like "viti-tju viddertjuuh" ("vi" extr. high and sharp, "tju" slightly nasal).

164.1

N-br. ♂   ♀

164.7

Br. ♂

164.2

♀

164.8

164.3   ♀

♀

164.9

164.4   ♀

164.10

164.5   ♀   164.6   ♀

Plate 165

165.1 EPAULET ORIOLE (Encontro) *Icterus cayanensis*

L 7.9 in./20 cm. Five sspp.: Amazonian Nom. (**a**), E *tibialis* (**b**), and interior SE *valenciobuensi* (**c**) shown; not shown are S *pyrrhopterus* and *periporphyrus*, which resemble **c**. Bill blackish, unlike in caciques (Pl. **162**). Rufous-brown shoulder of **c** often inconspicuous. ♣ Forest edge, woodland, and riverine belts up to 900 m. ♪ Call varied, often harsh "sreeh" or very high "tue"; song: slow series of single notes, like "tjeeuw," "tih," "tjeu," "swee," or "prrru," continuous or organized in 5- to 8-noted groups, given at 1–2 sec intervals.

165.2 MORICHE ORIOLE (Rouxinol-do-rio-negro)

Icterus chrysocephalus L 7.9 in./20 cm. Unmistakable by color pattern. Occasional hybrids with **165.1** occur. ♣ Woodland, forest borders, riverine belts. Associated with palm trees. Up to 900 m. ♪ Song: slow series of often repeated phrases with joined, high/very high "tju," "tutwee," or "wuut" notes.

165.3 YELLOW ORIOLE (João-pinto-amarelo) *Icterus*

nigrogularis L 7.9 in./20 cm. Unmistakable by color pattern. ♣ Arid scrub, woodland, riverine belts, edge of mangrove. Up to 500 m. ♪ Song: melodious series of any length with high to extr. high, fluted notes, joined together or separately emphasized.

165.4 BALTIMORE ORIOLE (Corrupião-de-baltimore)

Icterus galbula L 7.9 in./20 cm. ♀ with olive upperparts and striking white wing bars. ♣ Accidental visitor. ♪ Call: high, decisive "wíc!" or dry rattle. Does not or hardly sings in South America. V.

165.5 CAMPO TROUPIAL (Corrupião) *Icterus jamacaii*

L 9.8 in./25 cm. Differs from **165.6** by black (not orange) crown. Note pale eye and white wing-patch. ♣ Forest edge and borders, caatinga woodland. ♪ Call: "prru"; song: long, slightly out-of-tune series of beautifully fluted, high to very high single notes, sometimes in short, rapid crescendos. En.

165.6 ORANGE-BACKED TROUPIAL (João-pinto)

Icterus croconotus L 9.8 in./25 cm. Note black scapulars and orange crown, nape, and mantle. ♣ Várzea, swamps and other areas near water. In SC also in woodland, even far from water. Up to 500 m.

165.7 SAFFRON-COWLED BLACKBIRD (Veste-

amarela) *Xanthopsar flavus* L 7.5 in./19 cm. ♂ unmistakable. Note yellowish underparts, eyebrow, and shoulder of ♀. ♣ Open marsh and grassland, pastures, fields. Up to 1000 m. ♪ Call: soft, muttered "chuk chukchuk - -"; song: high, unobtrusive, 3-noted phrases, like "t"jee-ohwee." R.

165.8 ORIOLE BLACKBIRD (Iratauá-grande) *Gymno-

mystax mexicanus* L 11.8 in./30 cm (♂), 9.8 in./25 cm (♀). Unmistakable by size and color pattern. ♣ Marshes and semiopen areas near rivers (incl. river islands). Up to 1000 m. ♪ Call: decisive "tsick"; song: unstructured scratchy, drawn-out, rising screeches.

165.9 YELLOW-RUMPED MARSHBIRD (Chopim-

do-brejo) *Pseudoleistes guirahuro* L 9.8 in./25 cm. Differs from **165.10** by all-yellow flanks and rump. ♣ Marsh and grassland up to 1100 m. ♪ Song: short series of alternating loud "wheeet," nasal "tjuh" notes, and short trills.

165.10 BROWN-AND-YELLOW MARSHBIRD (Dragão)

Pseudoleistes virescens L 9.8 in./25 cm. Underparts yellow with broad brown flanks. No rump-patch, unlike **165.1**. ♣ Marsh, moist grassland, fields. Up to 300 m. ♪ Call: low, soft, muttering "pup-purrít-pup-purrít- -."

Plate 166

166.1 BROWN TANAGER (Sanhaçu-pardo) *Orchesticus abeillei* L 7.1 in./18 cm. Unusually colored for a tanager. Differs from **98.7** by stubby bill. ♣ Upperstory of humid forest. Sometimes in tall garden trees; 750–1600 m. ♪ Call: "tsit"; song: extr. high, twittering, like "tittsi-tseeh." En, R.

166.2 CINNAMON TANAGER (Bico-de-veludo) *Schistochlamys ruficapillus* L 7.1 in./18 cm. Unmistakable by color pattern and black mask. ♣ Scrub in caatinga and cerrado, edge of woodland patches, gardens. Up to 1100 m. ♪ Call: nasal "njè"; song: high, simple, fluted "weét-weé-we weét-weé-we - -" ("we" lower).

166.3 BLACK-FACED TANAGER (Sanhaçu-de-coleira) *Schistochlamys melanopis* L 7.1 in./18 cm. Ad. unmistakable. Imm. (**a**) has yellow belly and partial eyering. ♣ Semiopen areas with scattered trees and bush, cerrado, woodland borders. Up to 1500 m. ♪ Song: high, simple "Weeé we-wéetju-wi-wéetju - -" (not always starting with much higher, strong "Weeé").

166.4 WHITE-BANDED TANAGER (Cigarra-do-campo) *Neothraupis fasciata* L 6.3 in./16 cm. Ad. unmistakable. Imm. (**a**, shown at smaller scale) brown above, yellowish buff below. ♣ Cerrado between 500 and 1100 m. ♪ Call: extr. high, excited but soft "chip" notes given by groups; song: simple, cheerful, very high, fluted series including "- - ti-wi-wur - -." R.

166.5 BLACK-GOGGLED TANAGER (Tiê-de-topete) *Trichothraupis melanops* L 6.3 in./16 cm. Unmistakable by color pattern. ♣ Undergrowth of forest, second growth, and riverine belts. Below 1200 m. ♪ Call: extr. high, sharp, emphasized "tcip" or upslurred "pseee"; song: "tseee wer-sit-je" (1st part extr. high, 2nd part mid-high; each note emphasized). Also very long series with buzzes, whistles, short "ps" notes; the same note often repeated many times.

166.6 WHITE-RUMPED TANAGER (Bandoleta) *Cypsnagra hirundinacea* L 6.3 in./16 cm. Paler SW ssp. *pallidigula* (**a**, with short eyebrow) and C rufous-throated Nom. (**b**) shown. ♣ Cerrado and grassland with scattered low trees. Up to 1200 m. ♪ Call: very high, staccato "tchut"; song: excited duets of slightly nasal "tu-Tjúw" from one and a slow rattle from the other bird of a pair.

166.7 MAGPIE TANAGER (Tietinga) *Cissopis leverianus* L 11.8 in./30 cm. Unmistakable by size and pattern. SE ssp. *major* (not shown) has more black on back. ♣ Forest edge and clearings. Up to 1400 m. ♪ Call: sweeping "Péet"; song: e.g., very/extr. high "tsee-ter-tsee-tseet- -," as repeated series.

166.8 BLACK-AND-WHITE TANAGER (Tiê-preto-e-branco) *Conothraupis speculigera* L 6.3 in./16 cm. ♂ with gray rump and flanks. Differs from smaller ♂ **182.1** by bill shape. ♀ rather nondescript with pale yellow underparts and faintly streaked breast. ♣ Woodland, forest edge. Up to 1400 m. ♪ Song: series of stressed "chic-up" notes and "sree-sree" double notes. R.

166.9 CONE-BILLED TANAGER (Tiê-bicudo) *Conothraupis mesoleuca* L 5.5 in./14 cm. ♂ from ♂ **166.8** by range, black flanks, and gray-white bill. ♀ Uniform dark brown with heavy bill. ♣ Gallery woodland, cerrado. ♪ Voice: insufficient information; recording withheld to avoid luring this critically endangered species by playback. En, R.

166.10 RED-BILLED PIED TANAGER (Pipira-de-bico-vermelho) *Lamprospiza melanoleuca* L 6.7 in./17 cm. Unmistakable by pied pattern and red bill (dusky in Juv.) ♣ Canopy and borders of várzea up to 600 m. ♪ Call: e.g., very high "zeezee" or "zeezee-tju" (much lower "tju" probably the answer of the bird's mate).

166.1

166.2

166.3
a

166.4
a

166.5

166.6
a   b

166.7

166.8
♀

166.9
♀

166.10
♀

Plate 167

167.1 ORANGE-HEADED TANAGER (Saí-canário)

 Thlypopsis sordida L 5.1 in./13 cm. Note orange head and gray upperparts. Underparts gray in W. ♣ Riverine belts, woodland, cerrado. Up to 800 m. ♪ Song: e.g., slow, slightly descending series of "chif chef chif chef chih" notes.

167.2 SCARLET-THROATED TANAGER (Carretão)

 Compsothraupis loricata L 7.9 in./ 20 cm. Differs from blackbirds (Pl. **163–165**) by bill shape. ♣ Caatinga, riverine belts, semiopen areas near water. Up to 700 m. ♪ Call/song: slow, unstructured series of harsh "tchaw" notes, given by group. En.

167.3 CHESTNUT-HEADED TANAGER (Cabecinha-

 castanha) *Pyrrhocoma ruficeps* L 5.5 in./ 14 cm. ♂ unmistakable. ♀ olivaceous above with cinnamon-rufous head. ♣ Undergrowth of forest. Up to 1100 m. ♪ Call: extr. high, thin "sit"; song: extr. high, slightly descending "tsee-tsee-tsee-sui-sui."

167.4 HOODED TANAGER (Saíra-de-chapéu-preto)

 Nemosia pileata L 5.1 in./13 cm. ♂ unmistakable. Note bicolored bill and pale lores of ♀. ♣ Open woodland, riverine belts, clearings with scattered trees, plantations. Up to 600 m. ♪ Call: extr. high, thin "tsi"; dawn song: short, very high, thin, rapidly descending "ti-ti-ti-si-sui-sui-seeh."

167.5 CHERRY-THROATED TANAGER (Saíra-apun-

 halada) *Nemosia rourei* L 5.5 in./ 14 cm. Unmistakable. ♣ Canopy of humid forest. En, R.

167.6 GUIRA TANAGER (Saíra-de-papo-preto) *Hemi-*

 thraupis guira L 5.1 in./13 cm. ♂ unmistakable. Note faint yellow eyering of ♀; not safely separable from ♀ **167.7**.♣ Borders of humid forest, woodland, riverine belts. Up to 1500 m, locally higher. ♪ Song: very high, sharp, rapidly descending series of "feet" notes, at the end slowing down to a level "tju-tju-tju."

167.7 RUFOUS-HEADED TANAGER (Saíra-ferrugem)

 Hemithraupis ruficapilla L 5.1 in./ 13 cm. ♂ unmistakable. ♀ similar to ♀ **166.6**. ♣ Forest borders, open woodland, second growth. Up to 1100 m. ♪ Call: very high, dry "zip"; song: very high, level, hurried series of "sisi---" notes, slowing down slightly at the end. En.

167.8 YELLOW-BACKED TANAGER (Saíra-galega)

 Hemithraupis flavicollis L 5.1 in./ 13 cm. ♂ with varying amount of blackish mottling to breast and flank sides unmistakable. ♀ from ♀ **166.6** and **166.7** by yellower underparts and yellow edging of wing feathers. ♣ Forested mountain slopes; 900–1800 m. ♪ Call/song: single or series of nasal, upslurred "sreeeh" notes.

167.9 FULVOUS SHRIKE-TANAGER (Pipira-parda)

 Lanio fulvus L 7.1 in./18 cm. ♂ unmistakable. ♀ most likely confused with ♀♀ *Tachyphonus* tanagers (Pl. **169**). No overlap with **167.10**. ♣ Humid forest, mainly terra firme. Up to 1300 m. ♪ Call: descending "tieuw" or "ti-tieuw."

167.10 WHITE-WINGED SHRIKE-TANAGER (Pipira-

 de-asa-branca) *Lanio versicolor* L 6.3 in./16 cm. ♂ unmistakable. ♀ resembles various ♀♀ *Tachyphonus* tanagers (Pl. **169**). No overlap with **167.9**. ♣ High levels of terra firme. Up to 900 m. ♪ Call: extr. high "sweéh"; song: very high "tjee-tje-wit-je-neet?"

Plate 168

168.1 OLIVE-GREEN TANAGER (Catirumbava) *Ortho-*

gonys chloricterus L 7.1 in./18 cm. Rather large; uniform olive above, yellow below. ♣ Atlantic forest up to 1400 m. ♪ Call: short "tríp" or very high "sreee"; song: short, some-times prolonged, rapid, mid-high twitter, like "wititi---." En.

168.2 GRAY-HEADED TANAGER (Pipira-da-taoca)

Eucometis penicillata L 7.1 in./18 cm. Two spp.: SC *albicollis* (shown) and Amazonian Nom., with grayer throat and darker bill. Differs from smaller **169.5** by crest. ♣ Under-growth of várzea, woodland, riverine belts. Usually near water. Mainly below 600 m. ♪ Call: soft, snappy "bits" notes; song: short, high, musical "wic vri-oh-vri-oh" or longer series of nasal "fuh-tjutju-weeh-te-tju-tetrit- -" notes.

168.3 MASKED CRIMSON TANAGER (Pipira-de-

máscara) *Ramphocelus nigrogularis* L 7.1 in./18 cm. Unmistakable. ♀ slightly duller than ♂. ♣ Várzea, shrubby areas. Mainly near water. ♪ Call: sharp, thin "dzu"; song: high, happy-sounding "tja-tjowee-tja."

168.4 SILVER-BEAKED TANAGER (Pipira-de-más-

cara) *Ramphocelus carbo* L 6.7 in./ 17 cm. ♂ unmistakable; throat of ♀ browner than ♀ **168.5** and darker than ♀ **173.9**. ♣ Forest borders and clearings, towns. Often near water. Up to 1000 m. ♪ Call: high, snappy "chink"; song: very high, hurried, nasal "wutjeweét-tju-tjutju," immediately repeated.

168.5 BRAZILIAN TANAGER (Tię-sangue) *Rampho-*

celus bresilius L 7.1 in./18 cm. ♂ unmistakable. ♀ differs from **168.4** by grayer throat. ♣ Forest borders and clearings (esp. near water), towns. Up to 1000 m. ♪ Call: stac-cato "tju," single or in series.

168.6 BLUE-GRAY TANAGER (Sanhaçu-da-amazônia)

Thraupis episcopus L 6.3 in./16 cm. N Nom. (**a**) and C ssp. *coelestis* (**b**) shown; **a** unique in range; **b** differs-from **168.7** by whitish shoulder. ♣ Semiopen areas, second growth, for-est borders, savanna, towns. Up to 1500 m, occasionally highrer. ♪ Call: partly inhaled, extr. high and nasal notes, like "fuee," "fui-tji" or "tjuw"; song: rapid, nasal twittering, like "tji-the-fu-the-feeéééh-tje-tju."

168.7 SAYACA TANAGER (Sanhaçu-cinzento) *Thraupis*

sayaca L 6.7 in./17 cm. Grayish blue with greenish blue flight-feathers. Cf. **168.6b** and **168.8**. ♣ Open woodland, cultivated areas, towns. Up to 2000 m. ♪ Song: unstructured series of very diverse quality, length, and pitch.

168.8 AZURE-SHOULDERED TANAGER (Sanhaçu-

de-encontro-azul) *Thraupis cyanoptera* L 7.1 in./18 cm. Bill relatively heavy. Not in range of **168.6**. Differs from **168.7** by deep blue shoulder (often concealed), dusky lores, generally bluer above (incl. flight feathers), and turquoise tinge to flanks. ♣ Humid forest and nearby clearings. Up to 1600 m. ♪ Song: e.g., fluted "tweetwee," as a rhythmic interruption of long series of very high, soft twittering. Also slow medleys of "see" and other notes of varying pitch. En, R.

168.9 GOLDEN-CHEVRONED TANAGER (Sanhaçu-

de-encontro-amarelo) *Thraupis ornata* L 7.1 in./18 cm. Yellow shoulders diagnostic. ♣ Humid forest and nearby clearings, gardens. Up to 1750 m. ♪ Song: very/extr. high bursts of short, nervous twittering. En.

168.10 PALM TANAGER (Sanhaçu-do-coqueiro) *Thraupis*

palmarum L 6.7 in./17 cm. Wing pattern with dark flight feathers diagnostic. ♣ Forest, open woodland, second growth, esp. where there are palm trees, towns. Up to 1200 m, locally higher. ♪ Song: bursts of extr. high twittering.

Plate 169

169.1 FLAME-CRESTED TANAGER (Tię-galo) *Tachyphonus cristatus* L 6.3 in./16 cm. ♂ unmistakable by orange-red crest and small throat-patch. ♀ buffy ochre below with whiter throat. Resembles larger ♀ **167.9** and ♀ **168.1**, but smaller billed and belly less yellowish. ♣ Middle and upperlevels of terra firme and várzea. Also nearby clearings. Up to 800 m. ♪ Call: extr. high "tee-tee-tee" or "see-see"; song: very/extr. high "see-see-see-turrr-tirr" series.

169.2 NATTERER'S TANAGER (Pipira-de-natterer) *Tachyphonus nattereri* L 5.9 in./15 cm. To date (2007) only known from two male specimens. Probably a variant of **169.1**, but white shoulder-patch larger and throat black. ♣ Unknown. En.

169.3 YELLOW-CRESTED TANAGER (Tem-tem-de-crista-amarela) *Tachyphonus rufiventer* L 5.9 in./15 cm. ♂ Unmistakable. Dark chest band sometimes missing. Note ochre-yellow underparts and tawny rump of ♀. ♣ Middle and upperstories of terra firme and várzea. Up to 1200 m.

169.4 FULVOUS-CRESTED TANAGER (Tem-tem-de-topete-ferrugíneo) *Tachyphonus surinamus* L 6.3 in./16 cm. Crest of ♂ often concealed. ♀ has conspicuous broken eyering and gray head. ♣ Lower and middle strata of humid forest. Also adjacent clearings. Up to 900 m. ♪ Call: low "turr-turr tjudr truit" and similar notes.

169.5 WHITE-SHOULDERED TANAGER (Tem-tem-de-dragona-branca) *Tachyphonus luctuosus* L 5.5 in./14 cm. ♂ unmistakable by conspicuous white shoulder. ♀ has yellow underparts and gray hood. Cf. larger **168.2**. ♣ Middle and higher levels of terra firme and várzea, second growth, clearings with scattered trees. Up to 1100 m. ♪ Call/song: extr. high "sfeesfeesfee" and very/extr. high, nasal "wheer wheer - -weersrup - -."

169.6 RUBY-CROWNED TANAGER (Tię-preto) *Tachyphonus coronatus* L 6.3 in./16 cm. Note bicolored bill. Ruby crown of ♂ rarely visible. White underwings show in flight. Note relatively dull head and inconspicuous breast streaks of ♀. ♣ Open woodland, dense second growth, plantations, suburbs. Up to 1200 m. ♪ Call: high, bouncing "trit-trit trit- -"; song: simple, high chirping "tjur wdit tjur - -."

169.7 WHITE-LINED TANAGER (Pipira-preta) *Tachyphonus rufus* L 6.7 in./17 cm. ♂ similar to ♂ **169.6**, but no crown-patch; ♀ is uniform rufous. ♣ Semi-open areas with thickets, shrub, and scattered trees. Lowlands–1500 m. ♪ Call: high, sharp "chik"; song: slow, high, sharp "tju-tjed-tju- -."

169.8 RED-SHOULDERED TANAGER (Tem-tem-de-dragona-vermelha) *Tachyphonus phoeniceus* L 5.9 in./15 cm. ♂ similar to ♂ **169.7**, but with red spot on shoulder (usually concealed); ♀ gray (back often browner) with whitish throat. ♣ Savanna, open woodland, riverine belts. Up to 400 m, locally much higher. ♪ Call: low, soft, yet staccato "tuh teh tuh - -."

169.9 BLUE-AND-YELLOW TANAGER (Sanhaçu-papa-laranja) *Thraupis bonariensis* L 6.3 in./16 cm. ♂ unmistakable; ♀ has stubby, bicolored bill, dull ochre-olive underparts, and faint bluish tinge to crown. ♣ Woodland, riverine belts, savanna, agricultural land, towns. Up to 2000 m. ♪ Song: very high, weak "tut-trrit-tut-trree-trut-trrit."

169.10 BLUE-BACKED TANAGER (Pipira-azul) *Cyanicterus cyanicterus* L 6.7 in./17 cm. Unmistakable by color pattern. ♣ Canopy and edge of humid forest. Occasionally in savanna woodland. Up to 500 m. ♪ Call: very high, sharp "feet-feet" or "feet-feet-feet."

169.1

169.2

169.3

169.4

169.5

169.6

169.7

169.8

169.9

169.10

Plate 170

170.1 BLACK-BACKED TANAGER (Saíra-sapucaia)

Tangara peruviana L 5.9 in./15 cm. Differs from **170.2** by black mantle. ♀ not safely separable from ♀ **170.2**. ♣ Coastal forest, woodland, and scrub. Up to 700 m. ♪ Call: extr. high "si." En, R.

170.2 CHESTNUT-BACKED TANAGER (Saíra-preciosa)

Tangara preciosa L 5.9 in./15 cm. ♂ unmistakable; note dusky lores of ♀♀ **170.1** and **170.2**. ♣ Forest (often with *Araucaria*), second growth. Up to 1000 m. ♪ Call: extr. high "seeee"; song: very/extr. high "tutututu---tsrrrr," starting as fast stutter and changing to rattled, slightly downslurred trill.

170.3 BURNISHED-BUFF TANAGER (Saíra-amarela)

Tangara cayana L 5.5 in./14 cm. Two main groups; *flava* group (**a**, widespread) and Nom. group (**b**, N of Ri. Amazonas). ♀♀ duller and lack black of ♂♂. ♣ Cerrado, with scattered trees, riverine belts, forest borders, gardens. Up to 1800 m. ♪ Call: extr. high, down-gliding "seeee"; song: "trup tree see-si-si---," accelerating to an almost-trill.

170.4 BRASSY-BREASTED TANAGER (Saíra-lagarta)

Tangara desmaresti L 5.1 in./13 cm. Unmistakable by green coloring of upperparts and by brassy breast. ♣ Humid Atlantic forest, second growth. Mainly 500–1800 m. ♪ Call: extr. high "feefee-wi"; song: extr. high "iiiiiiiii." En.

170.5 GILT-EDGED TANAGER (Saíra-douradinha)

Tangara cyanoventris L 5.1 in./13 cm. Unmistakable by yellow head and turquoise-blue breast. ♣ Humid Atlantic forest, second growth; 400–1000 m. ♪ Call: extr. high "tseé" and soft twittering. En.

170.6 GREEN-AND-GOLD TANAGER (Saíra-ouro)

Tangara schrankii L 4.7 in./12 cm. Distinctly patterned and colored. Note complicated face mask. ♣ Canopy and borders of terra firme and várzea; also in adjacent clearings. Up to 900 m. ♪ Call: extr. high "zit"; song: series of "zit" notes, occasionally changing in tempo.

170.7 YELLOW-BELLIED TANAGER (Saíra-de-barriga-amarela)

Tangara xanthogastra L 4.7 in./12 cm. Note yellow belly and overall spotting. ♣ Canopy and borders of terra firme and várzea; also in adjacent clearings. Up to 1000 m. ♪ Call: extr. high "sit-sit- -."

170.8 SPOTTED TANAGER (Saíra-negaça)

Tangara punctata L 4.7 in./12 cm. Differs from **170.7** by whitish belly. Differs from **170.9** by bluish white ocular area. ♣ Canopy and borders of terra firme and várzea; also in adjacent clearings; 500–1500 m. ♪ Call: extr. high "tip."

170.9 SPECKLED TANAGER (Saíra-pintada)

Tangara guttata L 4.7 in./12 cm. Note uniform turquoise wing edging and yellow head. ♣ Canopy and borders of terra firme and várzea; also in adjacent clearings. Mainly 700–1700 m. ♪ Call: extr. high (just audible) "tic" notes and short trills.

170.10 DOTTED TANAGER (Saíra-carijó)

Tangara varia L 4.3 in./11 cm. Small. ♂ has bluish wings and faint spots on chest. ♀ uniformly green with slightly yellow-tinged belly. Juv. **170.7** has yellower underparts, and Juvs. **170.8** and **1790.9** have paler underparts (esp. chest). Also cf. ♀ **176.5**. ♣ Canopy and borders of terra firme and várzea; also in adjacent clearings. Up to 300 m. ♪ Call: extr. high (just within ear reach) "tic" notes and "sisisi."

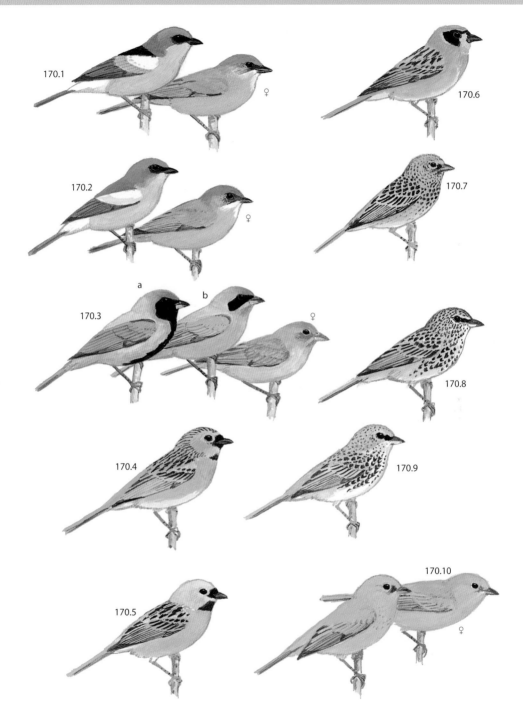

170.1

170.2 ♀

170.3 a b ♀

170.4

170.5

170.6

170.7

170.8

170.9

170.10 ♀

Plate 171

171.1 BLACK-HEADED TANAGER (Saíra-de-cabeça-preta) *Tangara cyanoptera* (*whitelyi*) L 5.1 in./13 cm. ♂ distinctly patterned; ♀ with gray streaks on throat and breast. ♣ Forest borders, clearings with scattered trees, second growth, plantations; 700–2300 m. ♪ Call: extr. high, rapid, descending "pic-pic-pic."

171.2 BLUE-NECKED TANAGER (Saíra-de-cabeça-azul) *Tangara cyanicollis* L 5.1 in./13 cm. Unmistakable by color pattern. ♣ Woodland, gardens, cultivations. Up to 2000 m. ♪ Call: extr. high "tsee tsee-tsee - -" at varying speed.

171.3 MASKED TANAGER (Saíra-mascarada) *Tangara nigrocincta* L 4.7 in./12 cm. Unmistakable by color pattern. ♣ Forest borders, shrubby clearings. Up to 900 m. ♪ Call: extr. high "tic tic - -."

171.4 OPAL-RUMPED TANAGER (Saíra-diamante) *Tangara velia* L 5.1 in./13 cm. NE Nom. (**a**, with dark underparts) and SE ssp. *cyanomelas* Silvery-breasted Tanager (**b**, with straw-yellow front and pale blue underparts). Rufous belly diagnostic. ♣ Canopy and borders of humid forest. Also in nearby clearings. Up to 500 m, rarely higher. ♪ Call: extr. high, fine "tic tic - -."

171.5 OPAL-CROWNED TANAGER (Saíra-opala) *Tangara callophrys* L 5.5 in./14 cm. Unmistakable by pale front, eyebrow, and rump. ♣ Canopy and borders of terra firme and várzea; also in adjacent clearings. Up to 500 m.

171.6 PARADISE TANAGER (Sete-cores-da-amazônia) *Tangara chilensis* L 5.1 in./13 cm. NE ssp. *paradisea* (**a**, NW *coelicolor* similar) and W Nom. (**b**, with all-red rump) shown. ♣ Canopy and borders of terra firme and várzea; also in adjacent clearings. Up to 1500 m. ♪ Call: extr. high, slighly rising, inhaled "feeee"; also communal chirping.

171.7 SEVEN-COLORED TANAGER (Pintor-verdadeiro) *Tangara fastuosa* L 5.1 in./13 cm. Unmistakable in its small range. ♣ Humid forest up to 550 m. ♪ Call: high, nasal "tjeu" and chattering in duet. En, R.

171.8 GREEN-HEADED TANAGER (Saíra-sete-cores) *Tangara seledon* L 5.1 in./13 cm. Unmistakable in its range. ♣ Humid forest interior and borders, second growth, gardens. Up to 1300 m. ♪ Call: soft, extr. high twittering; also nasal contact calls.

171.9 RED-NECKED TANAGER (Saíra-militar) *Tangara cyanocephala* L 5.1 in./13 cm. Unmistakable by red neck. Nom. (**a**) and isolated ssp. *cearensis* (**b**, smaller, with dark throat-patch and blue uppertail coverts) shown. ♣ Humid forest and forest borders. Mainly 400–1000 m. ♪ Call: extr. high, sharp twittering, sometimes developing into a short, rolling song.

171.10 SWALLOW TANAGER (Saí-andorinha) *Tersina viridis* L 5.9 in./15 cm. ♂ and ♀ unmistakable by general color pattern and by flank barring. Erratic, sometimes numerous but may be absent for more than a year. ♣ Humid forest borders, woodland. Up to 1500 m, occasionally higher. ♪ Call: extr. high, slightly rising "sreee" or "t'sreee"; song: rapid series of alternating, extr. high "fee" and low, dry "teh."

Plate 172

172.1 DIADEMED TANAGER (Sanhaçu-frade) *Stepha-* *nophorus diadematus* L 7.5 in./19 cm. Unmistakable by small red crest in front of white cap. ♣ Borders of montane forest, woodland, gardens, tall bush in marsh. Up to 2400 m. ♪ Call: dry "witch"; song: high, rich, slightly hurried, short series with notes of varying pitch, in which "tjú-o"Weét" is frequently used, esp. as ending (4–5 sec).

172.2 FAWN-BREASTED TANAGER (Saíra-viúva) *Pip-* *raeidea melanonota* L 5.5 in./14 cm. Distinctly colored and patterned. Note all-buff underparts. ♣ Forest, woodland, riverine belts, bushy pastures. Up to 2050 m. ♪ Song: extr. high, rather slow series of "si" notes (2–3 sec).

172.3 TURQUOISE TANAGER (Saíra-de-bando) *Tan-* *gara mexicana* L 5.5 in./14 cm. Unmistakable by yellow to creamy yellow underparts. ♣ Forest borders and clearings, woodland, gardens, plantations. Up to 500 m, higher in the tepuis. ♪ Call: extr. high, almost inaudible "si" at about 1-sec intervals.

172.4 WHITE-BELLIED TANAGER (Cambada-de- chaves) *Tangara brasiliensis* L 5.5 in./ 14 cm. Unmistakable. Often considered a ssp. of **172.3** (no overlap), but underparts whitish. ♣ Forest borders and clearings, woodland, gardens, plantations. Up to 500 m. ♪ Call: extr. high "stri" at about 1-sec intervals.

172.5 BAY-HEADED TANAGER (Saíra-de-cabeça- castanha) *Tangara gyrola* L 4.7 in./ 12 cm. NE Nom. (**a**; W S sspp. rather similar) and C ssp. *albertinae* (**b**) shown. Essentially unmistakable. ♣ Canopy and borders of humid forest, clearings, and gardens with tall trees. Up to 1600 m. ♪ Call: soft "tjeu" or rapid "trip-trip-trip"; song: rapid "tictictic-tjùw."

172.6 RED-CRESTED CARDINAL (Cardeal) *Paroaria* *coronata* L 7.5 in./19 cm. Note crest and gray back. ♣ Semiopen areas with scrub and scattered trees. Often near water. Up to 500 m. ♪ Song: slow series of repeated and varied "tuweet you tutju-ru-ru" (intervals of about 1 sec within and between notes).

172.7 RED-CAPPED CARDINAL (Cardeal-da-amazônia) *Paroaria gularis* L 6.7 in./17 cm. Note bicolored bill. C ssp. *cervicalis* (not shown) as **a**, but lacks black around the eyes. Juv. (**b**) with dark bill, browner back, and buffy brown face and throat. ♣ Open and semiopen areas near water. Up to 400 m. ♪ Dawn song: "weé-tju."

172.8 RED-COWLED CARDINAL (Cardeal-do-nordeste) *Paroaria dominicana* L 7.1 in./18 cm. Only cardinal in its range. Note pied pattern on back and wings. Juv. as Juv. **172.7**, but with paler bill. ♣ Caatinga woodland and scrubby areas. Up to 1200 m. ♪ Song: series of high, strong, clear "tju, weetju" notes and short almost-rolls. En (also introduced to Fernando de Noronha).

172.9 YELLOW-BILLED CARDINAL (Cavalaria) *Paro-* *aria capitata* L 6.7 in./17 cm. Note pinkish orange bill and legs and near-complete white collar. Juv. resembles Juv. **172.7**. ♣ Marsh, flooded grassland, lake shores, river edges. Up to 500 m. ♪ Very high, continuous "tju-weé-tju-tju-weé-tju-tju-weé-tju."

172.10 CRIMSON-FRONTED CARDINAL (Cardeal- de-goiás) *Paroaria baeri* L 6.7 in./ 17 cm. Nom. (**a**) and black-throated ssp. *exinguensis* (**b**) shown. Sides of neck lack white. Red in head pattern rather obscure. ♣ Open and semiopen areas near water. Up to 400 m. En.

172.1

172.2

♀

172.3

172.4

172.5
a
b

172.6

172.7
a
b

172.8

172.9

172.10
a
b

Plate 173

173.1 BANANQUIT (Cambacica) *Coereba flaveola* L
4.3 in./11 cm. Note pronounced eyebrow and down-curved bill. ♣ Any habitat with trees (incl. towns). Avoids interior of dense humid forest. Up to 2000 m. ♪ Song: very/extr. high, rapid twittering with a lot of inhaled and nasal notes.

173.2 DULL-COLORED GRASSQUIT (Cigarra-parda)
Tiaris obscurus L 4.3 in./11 cm. Sexes alike. Resembles **173.3**, but paler grayish brown and bill usually bicolored (dark above, yellowish below). Does not usually associate with seedeaters; look for groups or pairs that only contain ♀-plumaged individuals. ♣ Shrubby clearings and borders of woodland. ♪ Song: simple, very/extr. high, hurried "seesee-fili-sree." R.

173.3 SOOTY GRASSQUIT (Cigarra-do-coqueiro) *Tiaris*
fuliginosus L 4.7 in./12 cm. Sooty, not glossy black; ♀ dull olive-brown with whitish belly; bill slender and conical (compared to *Sporophila* seedeaters) and usually dark, occasionally bicolored. Cf. **173.2**. ♣ Shrubby or grassy clearings of woodland and forest. Up to 1500 m. ♪ Song: simple, extr. high, fast variations on "zizi-tsuur-sjree."

173.4 OLIVE-BACKED TANAGER (Pipira-olivácea)
Mitrospingus oleagineus L 7.5 in./19 cm. No similar bird in its range. Note gray extending over bill. ♣ Humid forest on the tepuis; 900–1800 m. ♪ Call/song: single notes or series of nasal, upslurred "sreeeh" notes.

173.5 HEPATIC TANAGER (Sanhaçu-de-fogo) *Piranga*
flava L 7.1 in./18 cm. Widespread *flava* group Lowland Hepatic Tanager shown. Not shown darker *lutea* group Highland Hepatic Tanager (NW Roraima and N Amazonas) with clear, dark lores. Note bicolored bill (blackish above, bone-gray below). ♣ Open forest, woodland, open areas with scattered trees, cerrado. Up to 2000 m. ♪ Voice varies geographically; call: in N, "chuh" or rapid, descending, dry "chu-tr-ti-tr-ti"; in rest of Brazil is soft "tjeh"; song: slow, unstructured series of "tjuw," "tjep," and "weeh" notes.

173.6 SUMMER TANAGER (Sanhaçu-vermelho) *Piranga*
rubra L 7.1 in./18 cm. Differs from **173.5** by longer, dusky horn-colored bill. Lacks dark lores of highland form of **173.5**. Often recorded 1st year male (**a**) shown. ♣ Open woodland, tall second growth, riverine belts, suburbs, parks. Lower mountain slopes. ♪ Call: descending, dry, almost-rattle, like "pi-tri-chi-chu-chuh."

173.7 SCARLET TANAGER (Sanhaçu-escarlate) *Piranga*
olivacea L 6.7 in./17 cm. ♂ changes from N-br (**a**) to red Br plumage between January and April. ♀ from ♀♀ **173.5** and **173.6** by dusky wings. ♣ Woodlands, suburbs, orchards. Up to 2200 m. ♪ Call: "chi-ding" (1st part toneless, 2nd part high with sound quality of two softly colliding bottles).

173.8 WHITE-WINGED TANAGER (Sanhaçu-de-asa-
branca) *Piranga leucoptera* L 4.7 in./12 cm. Unmistakable by wing bars. ♣ Canopy and edge of forest, woodland, clearings with scattered trees; 1000–2000. ♪ Call: e.g., "wuts-weeét" note (1st part almost toneless, 2nd part much higher); song: slow series of extr. high "seeet" notes.

173.9 RED-CROWNED ANT-TANAGER (Tię-do-
mato-grosso) *Habia rubica* L 7.1 in./18 cm. Shown are brick-red ♂, C ssp. *hesterna* ♀ (**a**), and E Nom. group ♀ (**b**). Note orange crown-patch (sometimes hidden) and whitish underparts in ♀ **a** (underparts buffier in NW *rhodinolaema*, dingy olive-brown in SW *peruviana*). ♀ **b** lacks whitish throat of ♀ **169.1** and streaked chest of ♀ **169.6**. ♣ Undergrowth and borders of humid forest. Up to 900 m. ♪ Call: "chatchat," given singly or in fast series; dawn song: slow series of alternating high "wi" notes and low "wu" notes (each note single or doubled, or long series of low "wu" notes).

173.10 YELLOW CARDINAL (Cardeal-amarelo) *Gubernatrix cristata* L 7.9 in./20 cm. Unmistakable by crest. ♣ Open woodland, semiopen scrub. Up to 700 m. ♪ Song: slow, loud series of high "weé-tjou" and "tou-weé-tjou." R.

173.5

173.4

♀

173.6

♀

a

173.1

173.7

N-br. ♂

♀

173.8

♀

173.10

173.3

173.9

♀a

♂

♀b

♀

173.2

Plate 174

174.1 BLACK-BACKED GROSBEAK (Rei-do-bosque)

Pheucticus aureoventris L 7.9 in./ 20 cm. Unmistakable by general color pattern. ♣ Areas with scattered trees and scrub and woodland. Up to 2000 m and higher. ♪ Call: high, slightly hoarse "djip"; song: high, lilting "weé-de-weét wir weé-oh-wír" and variations. V.

174.2 YELLOW-GREEN GROSBEAK (Furriel) *Caryo-*

thraustes canadensis L 7.1 in./18 cm. Black-fronted ssp. *frontalis* (**a**) and yellow-fronted *brasiliensis* (**b**) shown. Unmistakable by small face mask. ♣ Upperstory of humid forest. Up to 900 m. ♪ Call: high, slightly nasal "tjew-tjew" or "njew"; song: high, level, nasal "weetje-weetju."

174.3 YELLOW-SHOULDERED GROSBEAK (Furriel-

de-encontro) *Parkerthraustes humeralis* L 6.3 in./16 cm. Unmistakable by head pattern and yellow shoulder. ♣ Canopy and edge of humid forest; 200–1000 m. ♪ Call: extr. high, thin "feetjuh."

174.4 RED-AND-BLACK GROSBEAK (Bicudo-encar-

nado) *Periporphyrus erythromelas* L 7.9 in./20 cm. Note black hood. ♣ Lower levels of humid forest. Up to 1000 m. ♪ Song: mid-high, rich, fluted "tuweé-tjuh-tejèh-tjuh" ("weé" and "jèh" emphasized and drawn out).

174.5 SLATE-COLORED GROSBEAK (Bico-encarnado)

Saltator grossus L 7.9 in./20 cm. Unmistakable by combination of white bib and red bill. ♣ Mainly upperstory in interior of humid forest. Up to 1200 m. ♪ Song: "weetju-weetju-tjuwí" (1st "weetju" higher, "tjuwí" drawn up) or "weetju-Witwuh."

174.6 BLACK-THROATED GROSBEAK (Pimentão)

Saltator fuliginosus L 7.9 in./20 cm. Differs from **174.5** by black throat and different range. ♣ Mainly upperstory of humid Atlantic forest. Up to 1200 m. ♪ Song: often in two parts with long interval, "Weétju-pjerur tjur -wur wír" ("Weét" in 1st and "wír" in 2nd part highest).

174.7 GLAUCOUS-BLUE (or Indigo) **GROSBEAK**

(Azulinho) *Cyanoloxia glaucocaerulea* L 5.5 in./14 cm. Note short bill. Note male plumage suffused with gray and stubby bill. ♀ from ♀ **174.9** and ♀ **184.1** by bill shape. ♣ Forest borders, second growth. Up to 900 m. ♪ Song: very high, short, hurried warbling (2–4 sec).

174.8 BLUE-BLACK GROSBEAK (Azulão-da-amazônia)

Cyanocompsa cyanoides L 6.3 in./ 16 cm. Note habitat. ♂ from ♂ **183.7** by slightly heavier bill and straighter culmen. ♀ uniform chocolate brown. Cf. ♀ **184.2** and ♀ **184.4**. ♣ Undergrowth of humid forest and woodland. Up to 1000 m. ♪ Call: dry, short "bits"; song: descending series, starting very high with some piercing notes, changing to fluted notes, and ending in a short warble, together as "fee-fee-feet-witwit-witwit-sifsif-tji-rèr."

174.9 ULTRAMARINE GROSBEAK (Azulão) *Cyano-*

compsa brissonii L 6.3 in./16 cm. ♂ very like ♂ **174.8**. ♀ from ♀ **174.7** by bill shape and from ♀ **174.8** by paler fulvous-brown underparts. Also cf. ♀ **184.4**. ♣ Semiarid woodland and scrub. Up to 1500 m. ♪ Call: nasal "tjiw"; song: very high, level at first or gradually descending, melodious, warbling series, with "tju-sweét" note.

174.1 ♀

174.2
a
b

174.3

174.4 ♀

174.5 ♀

174.6 ♀

174.7 ♀

174.8 ♀

174.9 ♀

Plate 175

175.1 GRAYISH SALTATOR (Sabiá-congá) *Saltator coerulescens* L 7.9 in./20 cm. Several S and C sspp. (**a**) and N sspp. (**b**). Differs from other saltators by short eyebrow and gray upperparts. ♣ Dry woodland, pastures with scattered trees, riverine belts, second growth. Up to 1000 m. ♪ Song: beautiful and very varied phrases of about 4–8 strong, clear notes given at 10-sec intervals, like "tjuw-tjuw-tjuw-wú" (repeated "tjuw" characteristic).

175.2 BUFF-THROATED SALTATOR (Tempera-viola) *Saltator maximus* L 7.9 in./20 cm. Differs from **175.4** by short eyebrow. ♣ Forest borders and canopy, scrubby clearings, second growth. Up to 1200 m. ♪ Song: long series of variations on high "tjúrewur wutjewúr."

175.3 GOLDEN-BILLED SALTATOR (Bico-duro) *Saltator aurantiirostris* L 7.9 in./20 cm. White eyebrow starts just above eye. ♣ Dry woodland and scrub. Up to 1500 m. ♪ Song: very high "witjer-Weétjer" and slight variations thereof.

175.4 GREEN-WINGED SALTATOR (Trinca-ferro-verdadeiro) *Saltator similis* L 7.9 in./20 cm. Less brilliant green above than **175.2**. Differs from **175.2** by long eyebrow. Also cf. ♀ **175.5**. ♣ Woodland; forest borders, and clearings. Up to 1200 m. ♪ Song: loud "djeu-TjewTjew-Tjéu" and variations, some notes with nasal quality.

175.5 THICK-BILLED SALTATOR (Bico-grosso) *Saltator maxillosus* L 7.9 in./20 cm. From **175.4** by buff (not white) throat, greener ear coverts, and heavier bill. ♣ Canopy and borders of humid forest and woodland. Up to 2200 m. Rare in lowlands. ♪ Call: high, quiet "wicwic"; song: high, clear "wir-te-Jú-wir-tjuh-Wír" (ending abruptly).

175.6 BLACK-THROATED SALTATOR (Bico-de-pimenta) *Saltator atricollis* L 7.9 in./20 cm. No other bird with its pattern in range. ♣ Cerrado and caatinga; 700–1300 m. ♪ Call: high "bits," sounding like as clicking pebbles; song: very high, hurried, mellow warbling "weet-jewir-p-weetjewir -" (the total 3 sec).

175.7 EUROPEAN GOLDFINCH (Pintassilgo-europeu) *Carduelis carduelis* L 5.1 in./13 cm. Unmistakable by pattern and voice. ♣ Gardens, agricultural areas with scattered trees and shrub. ♪ Song: high, fast, very liquid, mellow warbling. I.

175.8 [EUROPEAN GREENFINCH (Verdilhão-comum) *Carduelis chloris*] L 5.9 in./15 cm. Bulky appearance and striking yellow wingstripe in flight diagnostic. ♣ Agricultural areas with woodland and tree patches, gardens. ♪ Call: hoarse "sreeeeeh." I.

175.9 HOUSE SPARROW (Pardal) *Passer domesticus* L 5.9 in./15 cm. ♂ unmistakable. Note long, pale eyebrow of ♀. ♣ Urban areas. ♪ Call/song: well-known chirping "ching." I.

175.10 COMMON WAXBILL (Bico-de-lacre) *Estrilda astrild* L 4.7 in./12 cm. Unmistakable by small size and color pattern. ♣ Urban areas. I.

Plate 176

176.1 WHITE-BELLIED DACNIS (Saí-de-barriga-branca) *Dacnis albiventris* L 4.3 in./11 cm. Yellow-eyed ♂ darker blue than ♂ **176.2** and with edged wing feathers. ♀ from ♀ **176.2** by pale brownish eyes, greener upperparts, and yellower underparts. ♣ Canopy and borders of humid forest. Up to 400 m. ♪ Call/song: probably extr. high, very fine twittering.

176.2 BLACK-FACED DACNIS (Saí-de-máscara-preta) *Dacnis lineata* L 4.3 in./11 cm. Note yellow eyes. ♂ unmistakable by black nape and white mid-belly. ♀ brownish above with buff-white to white belly. ♣ Canopy and edge of humid forest, clearings with scattered trees, woodland. Up to 1400 m.

176.3 YELLOW-BELLIED DACNIS (Saí-amarela) *Dacnis flaviventer* L 4.7 in./12 cm. ♂ unmistakable; note breast mottling and red eye of ♀. ♣ Canopy and borders of terra firme and várzea; also in adjacent clearings with scattered trees. Up to 500 m, sometimes higher. ♪ Call: high, rather loud, upslurred "weéh."

176.4 BLACK-LEGGED DACNIS (Saí-de-pernas-pretas) *Dacnis nigripes* L 4.3 in./11 cm. ♂ from ♂ **176.5** by more solid blue in wings and by dusky legs. ♀ unmistakable in range. ♣ Humid forest and woodland. Up to 1700 m. En, R.

176.5 BLUE DACNIS (Saí-azul) *Dacnis cayana* L 4.7 in./12 cm. Note pinkish legs. Broad blue edging to wing feathers of ♂. ♀ green with bluish head. ♣ Forest borders, second growth, woodland, riverine belts. Up to 1400 m. ♪ Call: high "tjit."

176.6 GREEN HONEYCREEPER (Saí-verde) *Chlorophanes spiza* L 5.1 in./13 cm. ♂ unmistakable. ♀ green with bicolored bill. ♣ Canopy and borders of terra firme and várzea, second growth. Up to 1500 m. ♪ Call: high to mid-high twittering "tit" or "tit-wut."

176.7 SHORT-BILLED HONEYCREEPER (Saí-de-bico-curto) *Cyanerpes nitidus* L 3.5 in./9 cm. Legs reddish. ♂ with blue mantle and black "beard." ♀ from ♀ **176.8** by dark lores and blue supraloral. ♣ Canopy and borders of terra firme and várzea; also in adjacent clearings with scattered trees. Up to 400 m.

176.8 PURPLE HONEYCREEPER (Saí-de-perna-amarela) *Cyanerpes caeruleus* L 4.3 in./11 cm. Yellowish legs diagnostic; note blue moustache of ♀. ♣ Canopy and borders of terra firme and várzea; also in adjacent clearings with scattered trees. Up to 1200 m. ♪ Call: extr. high "zrree."

176.9 RED-LEGGED HONEYCREEPER (Saíra-beija-flor) *Cyanerpes cyaneus* L 4.7 in./12 cm. Yellow underwings diagnostic. ♂ shows blue throat and contrasting cap. ♀ has no blue or buff on head. ♣ Forest borders, second growth, clearings with scattered trees, shaded plantations, gardens. Up to 2000 m. ♪ Call/song: high, nasal, slightly lowered "tjew."

176.1

176.2 ♀

176.6

176.7 ♀

176.3 ♀

176.8 ♀

176.4 ♀

176.9

N-br. ♂

♀

176.5 ♀

Plate 177

177.1 PLUMBEOUS EUPHONIA (Gaturamo-anão)

Euphonia plumbea L 3.5 in./9 cm. Small. More gray than blue, not cobalt blue as **177.10**. ♣ Savanna woodland, forest edge. Up to 1000 m. ♪ Call: very high "swee-swee"; song: series of "swee-swee," alternating with short jumbles of rapid, rich twitters.

177.2 PURPLE-THROATED EUPHONIA (Fim-fim)

Euphonia chlorotica L 3.9 in./10 cm. ♂ with yellow underparts and crown-patch extending back to rear edge of eye. ♀ Nom. (**a**) has yellow forehead and grayish underparts with yellowish flanks and vent. Nape/crown often tinged gray. ♀ ssp. *cyanophora* (**b**; far NW) with less white below. ♣ Forest edge, second growth, riverine belts, caatinga, scrub. Up to 1200 m, locally much higher. ♪ Call/song: rapid or drawn-out high, clear "feebee."

177.3 FINCH'S EUPHONIA (Gaturamo-capim)

Euphonia finschi L 3.9 in./10 cm. ♂ has yellow up to above eye and no white in tail. ♀ with yellow-tinged forehead, unlike ♀ **177.4**. ♣ Forest interior and borders. Up to 1200 m. ♪ Song: very high, clear "fee-bee-bee."

177.4 VIOLACEOUS EUPHONIA (Gaturamo-verdadeiro)

Euphonia violacea L 4.3 in./11 cm. ♂ with yellow throat and white in undertail. Cf. ♂ **177.5**. ♀ not safely separable from ♀ **177.5**, but thicker-billed than ♀ **177.2b** and ♀ **177.3**. ♣ Forest borders, riverine belts, gardens. Seldom in open, arid areas. Up to 1000 m. ♪ Call: very high, sharp "tweet"; song: varied; e.g., very high, sharp "fee-fee-fee-fee"; also high, rapid twittering with nasal "tjew" and short trills and rattles.

177.5 THICK-BILLED EUPHONIA (Gaturamo-de-bico-grosso)

Euphonia laniirostris L 4.3 in./11 cm. Note yellow throat. SC Nom. (**a**, undertail like **177.4**) and W and NC ssp. *melanura* (**b**, with all-dark undertail and richer yellow underparts) shown. Both with cap that extends farther back (past the eye) than in ♂ **177.4**. ♀♀ of the two sspp. not reliably separable from ♀ **177.4**. ♣ Humid and arid areas. Forest borders, woodland, gardens, agricultural areas with scattered trees. Up to 1200 m, occasionally higher. ♪ Call: sudden, sharp "wit"; song: series of staccato "wic" rattles and other rapid sequences of "wuc" and "wee" notes.

177.6 GREEN-THROATED (or -chinned) **EUPHONIA** (Cais-cais)

Euphonia chalybea L 4.3 in./11 cm. ♂ with dark chin, yellow throat, and small yellow forehead patch. Note thick bill, gray from ear patch to belly, and olive-yellow chin, flanks, and vent in ♀. ♣ Forest borders and clearings with tall trees. Up to 500 m. ♪ Call: mid-high, dry, rapid "ditditditdit"; song: short, simple warble with partly inhaled "tif" notes. R.

177.7 GOLDEN-RUMPED EUPHONIA (Gaturamo-rei)

Euphonia cyanocephala L 4.3 in./11 cm. Unmistakable by blue crown. ♣ Forest borders and clearings with tall trees, gardens; 500–2800 m, occasionally lower. ♪ Call: very high "teeuw" or low, nasal "tjur"; song: level series of "tjur," mixed with and alternating with very high twittering.

177.8 WHITE-VENTED EUPHONIA (Gaturamo-de-barriga-branca)

Euphonia minuta L 3.5 in./9 cm. White vent diagnostic. Yellow on forehead stops just before eye. ♀ with complete yellow chest band and white throat and vent. ♣ Canopy and borders of terra firme and várzea; also in adjacent clearings. Up to 1000 m. ♪ Song: short, very high, rich "tuweét-ver-ver" or "weet-weet-vr."

177.9 ORANGE-BELLIED EUPHONIA (Fim-fim-grande)

Euphonia xanthogaster L 4.3 in./11 cm. ♂ with orange-tinged underparts and forecrown patch extending past eyes. Note buff-yellow vent, gray nape and orange cast to forehead of ♀. ♣ Humid forest, second growth. Up to 2000. ♪ Call/song: rapid, nasal "wutwutwutwut" or "djeu-djeu."

177.10 RUFOUS-BELLIED EUPHONIA (Gaturamo-do-norte)

Euphonia rufiventris L 4.3 in./11 cm. ♂ with yellow-orange underparts and no forehead patch. Note tawny vent of ♀. ♣ Canopy and borders of terra firme and várzea. Up to 1100 m. ♪ Call: very high, rapid, dry, scratchy "scree-scree-scree."

Plate 178

178.1 GOLDEN-BELLIED (or White-lored) **EUPHO-**

NIA (Gaturamo-verde) *Euphonia chrysopasta* L 4.3 in./11 cm. Unmistakable by white lores, which make bill look heavier. ♣ Canopy and borders of terra firme and várzea; also in adjacent clearings. Up to 900 m. ♪ Call: very high, sharp "wits"; song: e.g., high, mellow, rapid "wiwi-ju-wer-wur-wur" or explosive "tjú-wer-whé-wer."

178.2 GOLDEN-SIDED EUPHONIA (Gaturamo-preto)

Euphonia cayennensis L 4.3 in./11 cm. Unmistakable by yellow flanks, contrasting with remaining all-black plumage. ♀ with pale grayish central underparts incl. vent. ♣ Canopy and borders of humid forest. Up to 600 m. ♪ Call: dry, rattling "sree-sree" or slightly rising, rapid "wuh-wuh-wuh-wú."

178.3 CHESTNUT-BELLIED EUPHONIA (Ferro-velho)

Euphonia pectoralis L 4.3 in./11 cm. Unmistakable by rufous underparts of ♂ and tawny vent of ♀. ♣ Canopy and borders of forest. Up to 1300 m. ♪ Call: low, rattling, scratchy "wru-wru-wru-wru-wru."

178.4 BLUE-NAPED CHLOROPHONIA (Bandeirinha)

Chlorophonia cyanea L 4.7 in./12 cm. Nom. (**a**) and green-fronted ssp. *cyanea* (**b**) shown. Unmistakable by thickset jizz and color pattern. ♣ Canopy and borders of humid forest; also in adjacent clearings; 500–2000 m. ♪ Call: high, plaintive "pweeeh."

178.5 GREATER FLOWER-PIERCER (Fura-flor-grande)

Diglossa major L 6.7 in./17 cm. No similar bird in range. Note rufous vent. ♣ Humid forest and shrubby clearings in the tepuis; 1300–2800 m. ♪ Call: extr. high, fine "fi"; song: duet; one bird giving low, scratchy notes, the other giving high, tinkling notes.

178.6 SCALED FLOWER-PIERCER (Fura-flor-escamado)

Diglossa duidae L 5.5 in./14 cm. No similar bird in range; note bill shape. ♣ Humid forest and shrubby clearings in the tepuis; 1400–2300 m.

178.7 CHESTNUT-VENTED CONEBILL (Figuinha-de-rabo-castanho)

Conirostrum speciosum L 4.3 in./11 cm. ♂♂ of S and E Nom. (**a**) and N ssp. *amazonum* (**b**) shown. Chestnut vent of ♂ diagnostic. ♀ with olivaceous back and grayish head. ♣ Open woodland, riverine belts, várzea. Up to 1000 m. ♪ Call/song: soft "sru-tee-sru-tee - -."

178.8 BICOLORED CONEBILL (Figuinha-do-mangue)

Conirostrum bicolor L 4.7 in./12 cm. Bluer above than **178.9** and with buff cast to underparts. Juv. (not shown) resembles ♀ **154.1**, but duller and without white undertail patch. Also cf. ♀ **152.6**. ♣ Mangrove, open woodland, shrub at rivers. Up to 200 m. ♪ Call: high "bits"; song: unstructured twittering, including "- -fjeu tjeuw - -."

178.9 PEARLY-BREASTED CONEBILL (Figuinha-ama-zônica)

Conirostrum margaritae L 4.7 in./12 cm. Underparts pure gray. ♣ Woodland and scrub near rivers. Up to 100 m.

178.1

178.2

178.3

178.4

a

b

♀

178.5

178.6

178.8

178.7

a

b

♀

178.9

Plate 179

179.1 TROPICAL GNATCATCHER (Balança-rabo-de-chapéu-preto) *Polioptila plumbea* L 4.7 in./12 cm. ♂ unmistakable by cap and slender jizz. ♀ of NE ssp. *atricapilla* (not shown) very like ♀ **179.6**. Differs from **179.2** by different range. ♣ Open woodland, forest borders, clearings with scattered trees, mangrove. Up to 1200 m. ♪ Call: mewing "neuh"; song: varies by region; e.g., very high, hurried series of sharp "seep" notes (sometimes less rapid and slightly descending at the end).

179.2 CREAMY-BELLIED GNATCATCHER (Balança-rabo-leitoso) *Polioptila lactea* L 4.7 in./12 cm. Not in range of **179.1** ♣ Canopy and borders of forest and woodland. Up to 500 m. ♪ Call: nasal, slightly lowered "njeuh"; song: series of 6–7 thin "weet" notes. R.

NOTE: The following three species (**179.3**–**179.5**) were considered conspecific until 2007. Note lack of white in wing. No overlap in ranges. ♣ Canopy and edge of humid forest up to 500 m.

179.3 GUIANAN GNATCATCHER *Polioptila guianensis* L 4.3 in./11 cm. Distinct eyering, contrasting gray breast, and all-white outer tail feathers. ♣ Canopy and edge of humid forest up to 500 m.

179.4 PARÀ GNATCATCHER *Polioptila paraensis* L 4.3 in./11 cm. Very pale overall, indistinct eyering, breast and throat white, inner webs of outer two pair of tail feathers black at base. ♣ Canopy and edge of humid forest up to 500 m. ♪ Call: "wheet" or "wheet'r."

179.5 RIO NEGRO GNATCATCHER *Polioptila facilis* L 4.3 in./11 cm. No eyering, pale gray throat, partly black outer tail feathers. ♣ Canopy and edge of humid forest up to 500 m.

179.6 MASKED GNATCATCHER (Balança-rabo-de-máscara) *Polioptila dumicola* L 5.1 in./13 cm. Two sspp.: S Nom. (**a**) and C ssp. *berlepschi* (**b**, ♂ shown). ♂♂ unmistakable by black mask. ♀ from ♀ **179.1** ssp. *atricapilla* by white lores and supraloral. ♣ Cerrado, open woodland, riverine belts. Up to 2400 m. ♪ Song: varied; e.g., very/extr. high, almost level, rapid "fu-fu-fu-fu-fi-fi-" or slower "fee-fee-fee- -."

179.7 ORANGE-FRONTED YELLOW-FINCH (Canário-do-amazonas) *Sicalis columbiana* L 4.7 in./12 cm. Two sspp. in Brazil: EC *leopoldinae* (**a**) and Amazonian *goeldii* (**b**). Differs from **179.11** by size, dusky lores, and virtual lack of streaking (even in ♀♀ and Imms.). ♣ Riverine belts, settlements. Forages on ground. Up to 300 m. ♪ Call: high, nasal "sjirp," "tjirip," or very high, clear "tjic."

179.8 STRIPE-TAILED YELLOW-FINCH (Canário-rasteiro) *Sicalis citrina* L 4.7 in./12 cm. White patches in undertail of both sexes diagnostic. Note unstreaked yellow crown of ♂. ♀ with yellowish underparts and streaks on chest and flanks. Juv. similar to ♀, but yellow only on central underparts. ♣ Savanna, grassland, and open farmland. Up to 3000 m. ♪ Song: hurried, slightly nasal series in two parts; 1st very high, sharp "tseeptseep- -" (3–5 ×), 2nd lower-pitched, clearer "tue-tue- -" (4–8 ×).

179.9 GRASSLAND YELLOW-FINCH (Tipio) *Sicalis* *luteola* L 4.7 in./12 cm. Very like **179.10**, but chest more olive and no overlap in range. ♣ Grassland, edge of marshes, fields. Mainly near sea level, but up to 2000 m in far NW. ♪ Song: simple, very high, decelerating series of 7–9 "teuw" notes, starting as almost-trill.

179.10 MISTO YELLOW-FINCH *Sicalis luteiventris* L 5.1 in./13 cm. ♂ with finely streaked crown and yellow supraloral and ocular region. Differs from ♂ **179.7** (which is often considered a ssp.) by distribution and by more distinct grayish olive tinge to chest. Also cf. ♂ **179.8**. ♀ with streaked upperparts and plain underparts; similar to ♀ **179.9**. ♣ Open to semiopen areas with grass. Up to 2500 m.

179.11 SAFFRON FINCH (Canário-da-terra-verdadeiro) *Sicalis flaveola* L 5.5 in./14 cm. Relatively large. Two sspp: E *brasiliensis* (**a**, ♂ shown; ♀ is duller and has no orange on crown) and SE and SC ssp. *pelzelni* (**b**, ♂ and ♀). In ♀ **b**, note whitish underparts with streaked chest and flanks. Juv. of both sspp. resemble ♀ **b**. Imm. with yellow collar. ♣ Semiopen areas with scattered bush and trees, agricultural land, suburbs, cities. Up to 1000 m, locally higher. ♪ Song: calm, simple series of single and double notes with an occasional short trill, like "tjuw-tjew-witju-zree-u"u-wèh-djuw- -."

179.1   ♀

179.3   ♀

179.2   ♀

179.4

179.6 a   ♀

b

179.5

179.7
a   b   ♀

179.9   ♀

179.8   ♀

179.11
♂b
Imm. ♂

179.10   ♀

♀b
♂a

Plate 180

180.1 PURPLISH JAY (Gralha-do-pantanal) *Cyanocorax cyanomelas* L 15.7 in./40 cm. Dull purplish (often appears all dark). ♣ Woodland, riverine belts, scrub. Up to 1000 m. ♪ Call: series of mid-high, raucous "wreh-wreh" ("wreh" up to 4 ×/phrase).

180.2 AZURE JAY (Gralha-azul) *Cyanocorax caeruleus* L 15.7 in./40 cm. Shiny azure-blue (sometimes greener). ♣ Humid forest, often with *Araucaria*. Up to 1000 m. ♪ Call: noisy, high "eur eur eur tjef-tjef-tjef- -," "tjef" much higher." R.

180.3 VIOLACEOUS JAY (Gralha-violácea) *Cyanocorax violaceus* L 15.7 in./40 cm. Note whitish nape. No similar jay in range. ♣ Várzea, mainly at edges and in clearings with tree stands, often along rivers and lakes. Up to 1000 m. ♪ Call: very high, loud, ringing, lowered "djeeuw-djeeuw-djeeuw."

180.4 AZURE-NAPED JAY (Gralha-de-nuca-azul) *Cyanocorax heilprini* L 13.8 in./35 cm. Note white tail tips. ♣ Forest edge, second growth, woodland, wooded savanna. Up to 250 m. ♪ Call as **180.3**, but might be slightly higher pitched.

180.5 CURL-CRESTED JAY (Gralha-do-campo) *Cyanocorax cristatellus* L 13.8 in./35 cm. Note dark eye and stiff crest. ♣ Cerrado, riverine belts, savanna with low trees. Up to 1100 m. ♪ Call; loud, descending "wèèèèuh" shrieks.

180.6 CAYENNE JAY (Gralha-da-guiana) *Cyanocorax cayanus* L 13.8 in./35 cm. Not in range of **180.7** and **180.8**. ♣ Wooded savanna, humid forest. Up to 1100 m. ♪ Call: high, loud, slightly downslurred "tjuwtjuw tjuwtjuw -."

180.7 PLUSH-CRESTED JAY (Gralha-picaça) *Cyanocorax chrysops* L 13.8 in./35 cm. Nom. (**a**) and dark-necked ssp. *diesingii* (**b**) shown. Note crest on hind crown, esp. large in **b**. ♣ Woodland and nearby scrub, forest. Up to 1100 m. ♪ Call: very high "tjuw?" or bouncing, rapid "rututut."

180.8 WHITE-NAPED JAY (Gralha-cancã) *Cyanocorax cyanopogon* L 13.8 in./35 cm. No overlap with **180.6**. Differs from **180.7** by duller upperparts and whiter nape. ♣ Woodland, scrub, riverine belts or patches. Up to 1100 m. ♪ Call: e.g., series of a high "creucreu" notes. En.

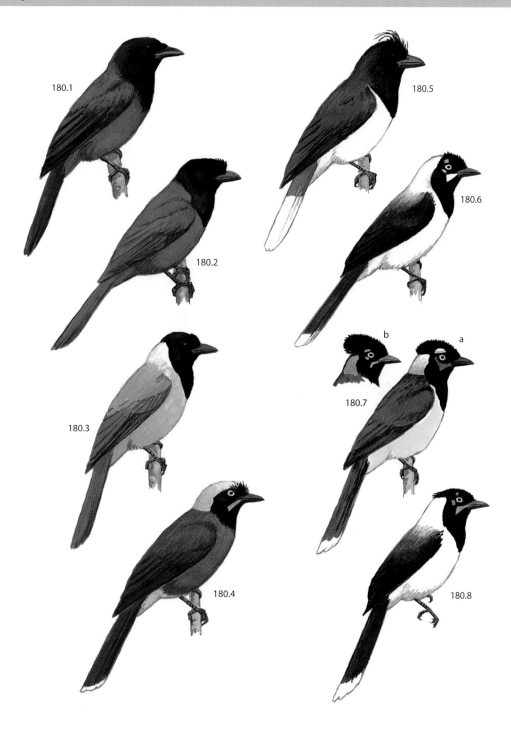

180.1

180.5

180.2

180.6

180.3

b

a

180.7

180.4

180.8

Plate 181

NOTE: ♂♂ of most *Sporophila* species in full ♂ plumage are normally outnumbered by individuals that look like ♀♀; this is because ♂♂ attain full Ad. plumage only after 2–3 years, but it might also be possible that some ♂♂ keep the ♀ plumage for life.

181.1 BUFFY-FRONTED SEEDEATER (Pixoxó) *Sporo-* *phila frontalis* L 5.1 in./13 cm. Large with indistinct wing bars in both sexes. Lower mandible significantly higher than upper mandible. Imm. ♂ lacks white forehead of Ad. ♂. ♣ Forest and adjacent second growth, mainly with bamboo. Up to 1500 m. ♪ Song: loud, fast, staccato "tje-te-tetrrít." R.

181.2 TEMMINCK'S SEEDEATER (Cigarra-verdadeira) *Sporophila falcirostris* L 4.3 in./11 cm. Both sexes very like **181.3** (no overlap), but ♂ usually without malar. Differs from **181.5a** by bill shape and less distinct wing markings in ♂. ♣ Forest edge and second growth, often with bamboo. Up to 1200 m. ♪ Song: very/extr. high, buzzing "t'tsrrrrr" trill (1–1.5 sec). R.

181.3 SLATE-COLORED SEEDEATER (Cigarrinha-do- norte) *Sporophila schistacea* L 4.3 in./ 11 cm. Lower mandible twice as high as upper. Culmen slightly curved or straight. ♂ with rich yellow bill and (usually) a white malar and single wing bar. ♀ with blackish bill and whitish buff belly. Cf. **181.4** and **181.5**. ♣ Woodland, forest edge and clearings, often with bamboo or seeding grasses. Up to 1500 m. ♪ Song: extr. high almost-rattle, like "wseeef-sisi-sisitititititeh."

181.4 GRAY SEEDEATER (Papa-capim-cinza) *Sporo-* *phila intermedia* L 4.3 in./11 cm. Culmen strongly curved. ♂ with yellow or flesh-colored bill. Rarely with white malar, but never shows wing bar. ♀ with blackish bill and whitish-buff belly. Cf. **181.3** and **181.5**. ♣ Open grassy and bushy habitats, less at forest borders and in clearings. Up to 500 m. ♪ Song: continuous, rapid, very high warbling in which every note is repeated 3–4 × (e.g., "tjitjitji" or "weetweetweet") or replaced by short trills.

181.5 PLUMBEOUS SEEDEATER (Patativa) *Sporophila* *plumbea* L 4.3 in./11 cm. ♂ with black bill (often yellow in SE, **a**) and white chin. ♀ with dark bill (lower mandible often paler) and whitish buff belly. Cf. **181.2–181.4**. ♣ Savanna, edge of riverine forest. Mainly near water. Up to 1400 m. ♪ Song: very high warbling in short series including 2–3 repeated notes such as "tjeutjeu," "kuwerber," "sisisi," or "witje-witje."

181.6 CAQUETA SEEDEATER (Papa-capim-de-caquetá) *Sporophila murallae* L 4.3 in./11 cm. ♂ from ♂ **181.7** by faint wing bars and range. ♀ like ♀ **181.7**. ♣ Grassy and shrubby areas, forest borders, river islands. Up to 400 m. ♪ Song: very high, up-and-down series of single, slightly hurried, nasal "tju", "tji", "wir," and "sir" notes.

181.7 WING-BARRED SEEDEATER (Coleiro-do-norte) *Sporophila americana* L 4.3 in./11 cm. ♂ with broad upper wing bar and narrow, faint lower wing bar. Black collar often incomplete. Cf. ♂♂ **181.6** and **183.8**. ♀ resembles **182.2**, but darker and belly whitish buff. ♣ Grassy and shrubby areas, fields, towns. Up to 400 m. ♪ Voice as **181.6**.

181.8 RUSTY-COLLARED SEEDEATER (Coleiro-do- brejo) *Sporophila collaris* L 4.7 in./ 12 cm. Nom. (**a**) and ssp. *malanocephalo* (**b**) shown. Unmistakable by general color pattern and black pectoral band. ♀ with two wing bars, whitish wing speculum, and contrasting whitish throat. ♣ Grassy and shrubby areas near water. Rarely on the ground. Up to 500 m. ♪ Song: rather slow series of nasal "tjer," "tjih," and "tjuw" notes.

181.9 LESSON'S SEEDEATER (Estrela-do-norte) *Sporo-* *phila bouvronides* L 4.3 in./11 cm. ♂ as ♂ **181.10**, but no white in crown and upper chest often mottled black. ♀ as ♀ **181.10**. ♣ Grassy and shrubby places, esp. at water. Up to 800 m. ♪ Song: high, slightly accelerating "tjetjetuter'r'rr," trill but might be silent in Brazil.

181.10 LINED SEEDEATER (Bigodinho) *Sporophila* *lineola* L 4.3 in./11 cm. ♂ with white cheeks and crown stripe. ♀ with yellowish bill (upper mandible usually darker) and contrasting whitish belly; from ♀ **181.9** only by range/season. Also cf. ♀ **182.5**. ♣ Grassy and shrubby areas, often near water. Up to 1200 m ♪ Song: rapid descending series, starting very high, the total sounding as "tweet-tweet-tititi'tw'tirrr."

Plate 182

182.1 BLACK-AND-WHITE SEEDEATER (Papa-capim-preto-e-branco) *Sporophila luctuosa* L 4.3 in./11 cm. ♂ black above with white wing speculum and spot below eye. Cf. ♂♂ **182.2** and **166.8**. ♀ like ♀ **182.2**. ♣ Grassy and

shrubby areas. ♪ Song: e.g., "wreu-chi-checheche" (1st part raspy, 2nd part soft and modest).

182.2 YELLOW-BELLIED SEEDEATER (Baiano) *Sporophila nigricollis* L 4.3 in./11 cm. ♂ with yellowish-white underparts, black hood, and olive back. Cf. ♂♂ **182.3** and **182.4**. ♀ (with dark bill and yellowish buff belly) inseparable

from ♀♀ **182.1** and **182.3**. ♪ Song: short, descending series of 5–7 notes in a sort of up-and-down cadence, starting very high, like "wheeét-jtutju-wír tjutju-wírwirr" (last "wirr" characteristically low).

182.3 DUBOIS'S SEEDEATER (Papa-capim-de-costas-cinzas) *Sporophila ardesiaca* L 4.3 in./11 cm. ♂ from ♂ **182.2** by gray back and white belly; ♀♀ of the two inseparable. ♣ Shrubby and grassy places, roadsides. Up to 800 m. En.

182.4 HOODED SEEDEATER (Papa-capim-do-banal) *Sporophila melanops* L 4.3 in./11 cm. ♂ from ♂ **182.2** by black hood not extending to chest. ♀ unknown. ♣ Unknown. *Note*: Only known from a single specimen; possibly a hybrid or a variant of **182.2**. En, possibly extinct.

182.5 DOUBLE-COLLARED SEEDEATER (Coleirinho) *Sporophila caerulescens* L 4.3 in./11 cm. ♀ with bicolored bill (dusky above, yellowish below) and whitish buff belly. Cf. ♀♀ **181.10** and **173.3**. ♣ Semiopen and shrubby areas, agricultural land. Rare in extensive grassland. Up to 1200 m. ♪ Song: short, rapid, very high warble, occasionally with an inhaled rattle.

182.6 WHITE-THROATED SEEDEATER (Golinho) *Sporophila albogularis* L 4.3 in./11 cm. ♂ with white throat and black collar. ♀ with dark bill and whitish belly. ♣ Caatinga, shrubby woodland borders. Up to 1200 m. ♪ Song: high, short series of "tuteé," "tjif," and "tjew" notes. En.

182.7 BLACK-AND-TAWNY SEEDEATER (Caboclinho-do-sertão) *Sporophila nigrorufa* L 3.9 in./10 cm. ♂ distinctly bicolored. ♀ similar to ♀ **182.10**, but bill slightly heavier. ♣ Grassy areas, mainly near water. Lowlands. ♪ Song: slow phrases of 1–7 notes, like high "tjuuuh," "tji-wtjiwtjiw," "fjeeh," and "tjuh-tureeh." R.

182.8 WHITE-BELLIED SEEDEATER (Chorão) *Sporophila leucoptera* L 4.7 in./12 cm. Nom. (**a**) and gray-flanked ssp. *cinereola* (**b**) shown. Rather large. ♂ distinctly bicolored with a yellow to pink bill. ♀ with heavy, dark bill and whitish belly. ♣ Grassy areas with scattered bush. Mainly near water. Up to 800 m. ♪ Song: long series of drawn-out, gliding-up "tuweét" notes.

182.9 RUDDY-BREASTED SEEDEATER (Caboclinho-lindo) *Sporophila minuta* L 3.9 in./10 cm. ♂ from ♂♂ **182.10** and **183.5** by lack of wing speculum, gray extending over ear coverts, and range. ♀ with yellowish brown bill and no wing speculum. Cf. **183.4**. ♣ Open grassy fields, savanna, roadsides. Up to 1600 m. ♪ Song: short series of very high, variable notes, like "weelee-weelee-diterlee-weelee."

182.10 TAWNY-BELLIED SEEDEATER (Caboclinho-de-barriga-vermelha) *Sporophila hypoxantha* L 3.9 in./10 cm. ♂ with rufous-tawny underparts and rump; paler than ♂ **183.5**. ♀ with buff underparts, white wing speculum, and yellowish dusky bill; virtually inseparable from ♀♀

183.1, **183.2**, **183.4**, **183.6**, and **183.8**. ♣ Tall grass, roadsides, marsh. Up to 1100 m. ♪ Call: varied; e.g., "ziu," "tsee," or "zreee" notes; song: short, calm series of 6–9 varied, high to very high, raspy "weetju wee-tzju sher-tju-sisi" notes.

Plate 183

183.1 DARK-THROATED SEEDEATER (Caboclinho-de-papo-escuro) *Sporophila ruficollis* L 4.3 in./11 cm. ♂ unmistakable by dark throat. ♀ like ♀ **182.10**. ♣ Tall grass, open shrubby areas. Often near water. Up to 1200 m. R.

183.2 MARSH SEEDEATER (Caboclinho-de-papo-branco) *Sporophila palustris* L 3.9 in./10 cm. ♂ unmistakable by white throat. ♀ like ♀ **182.10**. ♣ Tall grass near marsh. Up to 1100 m. ♪ Song: short series of varied, very high notes, like "sjee wee-tju-wee-tju." R.

183.3 [NAROSKY'S SEEDEATER (Caboclinho-de-coleira-branca) *Sporophila zelichi*] L 3.9 in./10 cm. Resembles **183.2**, but mantle and edges of wing feathers rufous. ♣ Grassland at water.

183.4 CHESTNUT-BELLIED SEEDEATER (Caboclinho-de-peito-castanho) *Sporophila castaneiventris* L 3.9 in./10 cm. ♂ with median underparts rufous. ♀ resembles ♀ **182.9**. ♣ Grassy and bushy clearings, marsh, lawns. Up to 500 m. ♪ Song: rapid, rather long, varied series, starting with very high, clear warbling, then slightly descending to more nasal twittering.

183.5 RUFOUS-RUMPED (or Gray-and-chestnut) **SEEDEATER** (Caboclinho-de-sobre-ferrugem) *Sporophila hypochroma* L 3.9 in./10 cm. ♂ mainly chestnut; from ♂ **183.9b** by gray cap. ♀ like ♀ **182.10**. ♣ Tall grassland and savanna, mainly near water. Up to 1100 m. ♣ Tall grass near marsh. Up to 1100 m. ♪ Song: series of very high, varied, clear notes, like "teetje wee-wir tee-tji-wee." R.

183.6 CHESTNUT SEEDEATER (Caboclinho-de-chapéu-cinzento) *Sporophila cinnamomea* L 3.9 in./10 cm. ♂ mainly chestnut; from ♂ **183.9b** by gray cap. ♀ like ♀ **182.10**. ♣ Tall grass near marsh. Up to 1100 m. R.

183.7 BLACK-BELLIED SEEDEATER (Caboclinho-de-barriga-preta) *Sporophila melanogaster* L 3.9 in./10 cm. Unmistakable by coloring of underparts. ♀ like ♀ **182.10**. ♣ Tall grassland (incl. marshes) and scrub. Up to 1100 m. ♪ Call: "see-u"; song: very high twittering, interspersed with "see-u" call. En, R.

183.8 WHITE-NAPED SEEDEATER (Papa-capim-de-coleira) *Dolospingus fringilloides* L 5.5 in./14 cm. Large. Pointed and conical bill pale in ♂, dark in ♀. Cf. ♂ **181.7**. ♣ Open scrubby forest and nearby savanna. Up to 250 m. ♪ Song: rapid strings of double or triplet notes, like "wee-wee-wee-sree-sree-sree-tuweé-tuweé-tuweé."

183.9 CAPPED SEEDEATER (Caboclinho) *Sporophila bouvreuil* L 3.9 in./10 cm. ♂♂ range from whitish to rufous according to age and race, but note black cap. Shown are Imm. ♂ ssp. *pileata* (**a**, in S) and Ad. Nom. (**b**, in E and N). ♀ like ♀ **182.10**. ♣ Savanna with tall grass, open cerrado. Up to 1100 m. ♪ Song: calm series of mostly double notes with distinct intervals, like "wree-wree wru-wru tjee-tju surr tjer-tjer- -."

183.10 CHESTNUT-BELLIED (or Lesser) **SEED-FINCH** (Curió) *Sporophila* (or *Oryzoborus*) *angolensis* L 5.1 in./13 cm. ♂ unmistakable. ♀ with less heavy bill than ♀♀ **184.1** and **184.3** and upperparts tinged olive, unlike ♀♀ **184.1**, **174.7**, and **174.9**. ♣ Scrubby and grassy clearings and edge of forest or woodland. Up to 1500 m. ♪ Song: series mainly based on strong "- - tjeu-tjeu-tjeu - -."

183.1 ♀

183.2 ♀

183.3

183.4 ♀

183.5 ♀

183.6 ♀

183.7 ♀

183.8 ♀

a b 183.9 ♀

183.10 ♀

Plate 184

184.1 BLACKISH-BLUE SEEDEATER (Negrinho-do-mato) *Amaurospiza moesta* L 5.1 in./ 13 cm. Bill rather conical. ♂ slaty blue; cf. ♂ **184.5**. ♀ warm tawny-brown; cf. ♀♀ **183.10** and **174.7**. ♣ Undergrowth of forest and woodland, mainly with bamboo. Up to 1600 m. ♪ Song: short, rapid warble, like "tjeu-tjeu-wi-tutju." R.

184.2 LARGE-BILLED SEED-FINCH (Bicudinho) *Spo-**rophila* (or *Oryzoborus*) *crassirostris* L 5.5 in./14 cm. Very similar to larger **184.4**. ♣ Tall grassland and scrub, incl. forest borders. Often near water. Up to 500 m. ♪ Song: short, animated series of rather nasal twittering, often introduced by a few "fjeu- -" notes.

184.3 PARAMO SEEDEATER (Patativa-da-amazônia) *Catamenia homochroa* L 5.5 in./14 cm. Note rufous vent in both sexes. ♂ slaty gray, ♀ streaked above (also below in imm.). ♣ Low stunted forest and scrubby growth; 1600–2500 m. ♪ Song: calm, peculiar series of 2–6 very long, fluted "puuuh-piiiih- -" notes, level or very differently pitched.

184.4 GREAT-BILLED (or Greater Large-billed) **SEED-****FINCH** (Bicudo) *Sporophila* (or *Oryzoborus) maximiliani* L 6.3 in./ 16 cm. Bill enormous. Very similar to **184.2**, but slightly larger bill with a dull, bony texture (not shiny smooth). ♀ with olive tinge above, unlike ♀♀ **174.8** and **174.9**. Also cf. ♀ **183.10**. ♣ Tall grass and scrub in damp or wet places. Up to 1100 m. ♪ Song: calm series of very high, varied notes, trills, and rattles. R.

184.5 BLUE-BLACK GRASSQUIT (Tiziu) *Volatinia* *jacarina* L 4.3 in./11 cm. Note pointed bill. ♂ glossy blue-black with white underwing often evident in flight; cf. ♂♂ **184.1**, **173.3**, and larger *Tachyphonus* tanagers (Pl. **169**). Sub-Ad. ♂ (**a**) variably speckled. ♀ with streaked chest and flanks; cf. ♀♀ **185.2** and **185.3**. ♣ Various open to semiopen habitats, incl. towns. Up to 2000 m. ♪ Song: simple, 2-noted "zeé-dji," repeated constantly.

184.6 COAL-CRESTED FINCH (Mineirinho) *Charito-**spiza eucosma* L 4.7 in./12 cm. ♂ unmistakable. Note cinnamon-buff underparts and laid-back crest in ♀. ♣ Cerrado up to 1200 m. ♪ Song: simple, very high, hurried, warbled "sree-o-wee," repeated at 1-sec intervals. R.

184.7 (Gray) PILEATED FINCH (Tico-tico-rei-cinza) *Coryphospingus pileatus* L 5.1 in./ 13 cm. Note striking eyering and gray coloring above. ♣ Dry scrub, woodland, forest borders, roadsides; 1000 m. ♪ Song: calm, 2-noted phrase, 1st part extr. high, fast gliding-up "sweéf," 2nd part mid-high "trru" or "tudu," together as "sweéf-trru," repeated 8–10 ×.

184.8 RED-CRESTED FINCH (Tico-tico-rei) *Corypho-**spingus cucullatus* L 5.5 in./14 cm. Eyering and reddish overall coloring diagnostic. ♣ Arid scrub, dry woodland, agricultural land. Up to 1500 m. ♪ Song: structure as **184.7**, but 1st part much lower pitched and 2nd part more sounding like a short "turr" trill

184.9 MOURNING SIERRA-FINCH (Canário-andino-negro) *Phrygilus fruticeti* L 7.1 in./ 18 cm. Unmistakable by size, color pattern, and striking wing bars. Note rufescent ear coverts of ♀. ♣ Arid scrub. ♪ Song: simple series of 3–6 "t'weet-nrrr-t'weet-ehhh-uch-trr" notes ("t'weet" very high, fluted; "nrrr" and "ehhh" with peculiar nasal quality). V.

Plate 185

185.1 BLACK-MASKED FINCH (Tico-tico-de-máscara-negra) *Coryphaspiza melanotis* L 5.5 in./14 cm. ♂ unmistakable. ♀ with yellow shoulder and white-tipped tail (easily visible from below). ♣ Tall grassland, often with bushes. Up to 1200 m. ♪ Song: simple, hurried "witwit-sre-sreésreéje" ("witwit" high, rest extr. high). R.

185.2 UNIFORM FINCH (Cigarra-bambu) *Haplospiza unicolor* L 5.1 in./13 cm. Note habitat. Uniform gray ♂ unique. ♀ from ♀ **184.5** by more conical bill and streaked throat. ♣ Bamboo-rich undergrowth of humid forest. Up to 1400 m. ♪ Song: extr. high, 2-noted, rapid "swee-wee."

185.3 BLUE (or Yellow-billed Blue) **FINCH** (Campainha-azul) *Porphyrospiza caerulescens* L 5.1 in./13 cm. ♂ unmistakable. Note yellowish bill (culmen dusky), rufescent back and streaked underparts of ♀. ♣ Open cerrado. Up to 1100 m. ♪ Song: simple but pleasant, calm, very high "feét-feét-teu feét-feét-teu" ("teu" lower pitched). R.

185.4 COMMON DIUCA-FINCH (Diuca) *Diuca diuca* L 6.7 in./17 cm. Unmistakable by general pattern. ♀ slightly more brown than ♂. ♣ Shrub, cultivation, gardens. ♪ Song: calm, high, slightly rising, fluted "tuit weet weet-tui"; each note emphasized. V.

185.5 WEDGE-TAILED GRASS-FINCH Canário-do-campo *Emberizoides herbicola* L 7.9 in./20 cm. From **185.7** and **185.8** by strongly pointed tail feathers, buffier underparts, and yellower (less orange) bill. Compare **185.6**. ♣ Areas with tall grass and some scattered bush. Up to 1500 m. ♪ Song: simple, varied, clear series of 2–4 very high level, upslurred, or lowered "teet-weer" or "zt-toweeé" notes.

185.6 LESSER (or Gray-cheeked) **GRASS-FINCH** Canário-do-brejo *Emberizoides ypiranganus* L 7.1 in./18 cm. Resembles **185.5**, but grayer cheeks contrast with white throat. ♣ Marsh and wet grassland. Up to 900 m. ♪ Song: mid-high, raspy, rapid "ch-ch-ch-ch- -" (about 10 × "ch"; the total slightly lowered at the end).

185.7 GREAT PAMPA-FINCH (Sabiá-do-banhado) *Embernagra platensis* L 8.7 in./22 cm. Note dusky face. ♣ Tall grassland, often with bushes. ♪ Song: 2-noted series of soft "tut" notes, followed by very high, slightly descending "tjeeert" or "tut-téer-téer."

185.8 PALE- (or Buff-) **THROATED PAMPA-** (or Serra-) **FINCH** (Rabo-mole-da-serra) *Embernagra longicauda* L 8.7 in./22 cm. From **185.7** by white partial eyering and supraloral. Also cf. **185.5**. ♣ Dry scrub, lightly wooded areas, agricultural land with scattered palms. Often in rocky areas; 700–1300 m. ♪ Song: 2-noted, strong "tut-twieer" ("tut" soft, "twieer" higher and upslurred). En, R.

185.9 RUFOUS-COLLARED SPARROW (Tico-tico) *Zonotrichia capensis* L 5.9 in./15 cm. Rufous collar diagnostic, but lacking in Imm., which has spotted chest. ♣ Any open to semiopen habitat, incl. towns. Up to 3000 m. ♪ Call: high "tjip"; song: calm, very high series of 4–6 notes, like "tu-tjeé-tuwu-weé" or "tju-weeét tjutju."

185.1

185.2 ♀

185.3 ♀

185.4 ♀

185.9

185.5

185.6

185.7

185.8

Plate 186

186.1 BLACK-AND-RUFOUS WARBLING-FINCH

(Quem-te-vestiu) *Poospiza nigrorufa* L 5.9 in./15 cm. Note mainly rufous underparts and long eyebrow. No overlap with **186.2a**. ♣ Usually near water in open woodland; also in gardens. Up to 900 m. ♪ Song: "sweet-sweet-je sweet-sweet-je sweet-sweet-je" ("sweet" extr. high and sharp).

186.2 RED-RUMPED WARBLING-FINCH (Quete) *Poo-*

spiza lateralis L 5.9 in./15 cm. Two sspp.: Nom. Buff-throated Warbling-Finch (**a**; N part of range; supraloral often faint) and ssp. *cabanisi*, Gray-throated Warbling-Finch (**b**; N to São Paulo). Red rump diagnostic. Imm. **b** (shown) with yellow throat and eyebrow. ♣ Forest borders, open woodland. Up to 1800 m; Nom. not in lowlands. ♪ Song: very high chirping, like "tseep-típ-teh-tsíp- -."

186.3 BLACK-CAPPED WARBLING-FINCH (Capa-

cetinho) *Poospiza melanoleuca* L 5.1 in./13 cm. Unmistakable in range. Imm. resembles **186.4**, best distinguished by range. ♣ Dry woodland and shrub, often near water. ♪ Song: simple "tweet treet weet treet - -" chirping.

186.4 CINEREOUS WARBLING-FINCH (Capacetinho-

do-oco-do-pau) *Poospiza cinerea* L 5.1 in./13 cm. Note small, dark mask. Cf. ♂ **179.6**. ♣ Deciduous woodland, cerrado; 600–1100 m. ♪ Song: very high "tip-chik-chik-tip-chik- -." En, R.

186.5 BAY-CHESTED WARBLING-FINCH (Peito-

pinhão) *Poospiza thoracica* L 5.5 in./14 cm. From **186.2** by different facial pattern and gray rump. ♣ Montane forest, esp. at edges and clearings with scattered trees and bush; 800–1500 m. ♪ Call: extr. high, weak "tsic tsic - -" at irregular intervals. En.

186.6 GRASSLAND SPARROW (Tico-tico-do-campo)

Ammodramus humeralis L 5.1 in./13 cm. Eyering and yellow supraloral diagnostic. ♣ Tall grassy savanna, cerrado. Up to 1700 m. ♪ Song: variable; 1 or 2 drawn-out, nasal, fluted notes at 2-sec intervals, sometimes followed by a short, tinkling trill.

186.7 YELLOW-BROWED SPARROW (Cigarrinha-do-

campo) *Ammodramus aurifrons* L 5.5 in./14 cm. From **186.6** by extensive yellow of face and no white eyering. ♣ Open grassy habitats, roadsides, large clearings. Up to 1000 m, locally higher. ♪ Song: soft, toneless, buzzing "zrrr-zrrrr" trill.

186.8 DICKCISSEL (Papa-capim-americano) *Spiza*

americana L 5.9 in./15 cm. Sparrow-like, esp. in 1st basic plumage (**a**, note indistinct streaks on chest), but yellow eyebrow in all plumages. Note rusty shoulder of adults (less in ♀). Black bib reduced or lacking in N-br. ♂. ♣ Grassy areas up to 1000 m. ♪ Call: raspy "drrt" or "bzzt". V.

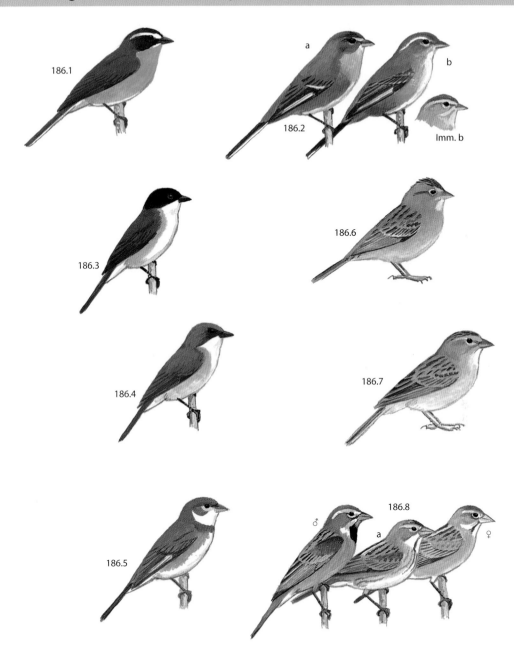

Plate 187

187.1 BLACK-STRIPED SPARROW (Tico-tico-cantor)

Arremonops conirostris L 6.7 in./ 17 cm. Unmistakable by head pattern. ♣ Dense undergrowth of humid woodland, weedy fields, shaded plantations. Up to 1500 m. ♪ Song: nice, musical, fluted series, starting with "weét tjuw -," followed by several "weét-trill" and "weét-tjuwtjuwtjuw" notes.

187.2 TEPUI BRUSH-FINCH (Tico-tico-do-tepui) *Atlapetes personatus* L 7.1 in./18 cm. Distinctive in range. Nom. (shown)

only ssp. confirmed in Brazil, but rufous-throated and rufous-chested *jugularis* may occur in extr. N Amazonas. ♣ Mainly at forest borders and in clearings; 1000–2500 m. ♪ Song: very high "Tjiu-chachacha" ("cha" rapid, 2–4 ×) or "Tjuw-sisisisi"; these and other vocalisations often as duet.

187.3 YELLOW-FACED SISKIN (Pintassilgo-do-nordeste) *Carduelis yarrellii* L 3.9 in./ 10 cm. From **187.4** by smaller black area on head; ♀ by yellower under-

parts and more uniform greenish head. ♣ Caatinga, second growth, forest edge, plantations, towns. Up to 550 m. ♪ Song: low, hurried, nasal warbling with chatters, soft rattles, and trills (3–20 sec). En, R.

187.4 HOODED SISKIN (Pintassilgo) *Carduelis magellanica* L 4.3 in./11 cm. Cf. **187.3**. More extensive range. ♣ Woodland,

grassland with scattered trees, towns. Up to 2500 m. ♪ Song: long series of rather low, hurried, chattered warbling, like("wur-wirre-tsjetsje- -."

187.5 LONG-TAILED REED-FINCH (Tico-tico-do-banhado) *Donacospiza albifrons* L 5.9 in./15 cm. Note facial pattern

and long tail. ♀ shows slightly more distinct streaks on mantle. ♣ Reed beds and scrubby areas near water. Up to 900 m.

187.6 SAFFRON-BILLED SPARROW (Tico-tico-de-bico-amarelo) *Arremon flavirostris* L 6.3 in./16 cm. Combination of black chest band and orange-yellow bill with black culmen diagnostic. Nom.

(**a**, N part of range), SE ssp. *polionotus* (**b**) and ssp. *devillei* (**c**, SW part of range) shown. ♣ Dry woodland and shrub. Up to 1400 m. ♪ Song: extr. high, rapid "tjew sjew-sjew-sjew-sjew."

187.7 PECTORAL SPARROW (Tico-tico-de-bico-preto) *Arremon taciturnus* L 5.9 in./15 cm. All-black bill diagnostic. Yellow shoulder-patch relatively large. ♣

Undergrowth of humid forest and second growth. Up to 1500 m; mainly in lowlands in area of overlap with **187.9**. ♪ Song: extr. high, hissed "ssee-ssee-ssee."

187.8 HALF-COLLARED SPARROW (Tico-tico-do-mato) *Arremon semitorquatus* L 5.9 in./ 15 cm. Upper mandible black, lower mandible yellow. From **187.9** also

by grayer flanks and larger black spots on sides of chest. ♣ Undergrowth of humid forest and second growth. Up to 1200 m; usually not in lowlands in area of overlap with **187.8**. ♪ Song: very to extr. high "zui-zee" and variations. En.

187.9 SAO FRANCISCO SPARROW (Tico-tico-do-são-francisco) *Arremon franciscanus* L 5.9 in./15 cm. Bill yellow with black culmen. Cf. **187.8**. ♣ Thick

scrub in caatinga. ♪ Song: extr. high "tsutititi---" ("tititi---" as almost-trill). En, R.

Protected Areas of Brazil

The protected areas of Brazil are organized into a system of about 60 national parks, 23 biological reserves, 7 ecological reserves, 21 ecological stations, 19 environmental protection areas, and 48 national forests (as of July 2007). The map indicates the national parks (NPs); a list of the other categories of protected areas can be found on the Internet (http://www.parks.it/world/BR/Eindex.html). A survey of National Parks and Nature Reserves, that is regularly updated, can be found on the Web site http://www.nationalparks-worldwide.info/brazil.htm. You might also want to check Arthur Grosset's Web site (http://www.arthurgrosset.com/sitenotes/brazil.html), which gives site notes for Brazil.

1. Abrolhos Marine NP
2. Amazônia NP
3. Aparados da Serra NP
4. Araguaia NP
5. Araucárias NP
6. Brasília NP
7. Cabo Orange NP
8. Campos Gerais NP
9. Caparaó NP
10. Cavernas do Peruaçu NP
11. Chapada das Mesas NP
12. Chapada Diamantina NP
13. Chapada dos Guimarães NP
14. Chapada dos Veadeiros NP
15. Descobrimento NP
16. Emas NP
17. Fernado de Noronha Marine NP
18. Grande Sertão Veredas NP
19. Iguaçu NP
20. Ilha Grande NP
21. Itatiaia NP
22. Jaú NP
23. Jericoacoara NP
24. Lagoa do Peixe NP
25. Lençóis Maranhenses NP
26. Monte Pascoal NP
27. Monte Roraima NP
28. Nascentes do Rio Parnaíba NP
29. Pacaás Novos NP
30. Pantanal Matogrossense NP
31. Pau Brasil NP
32. Pedra Azul NP

33. Pico da Neblina NP
34. Pontões Capixabas NP
35. Restinga de Jurubatiba NP
36. Saint-Hilaire/Lange NP
37. São Joaquim NP
38. Sempre Vivas NP
39. Serra da Bocaina NP
40. Serra da Bodoquena NP
41. Serra da Canastra NP
42. Serra da Capivara NP
43. Serra da Cutia NP
44. Serra da Mocidade NP
45. Serra das Confusões NP
46. Serra de Itabaiana NP

47. Serra do Cipó NP
48. Serra do Divisor NP
49. Serra do Itajaí NP
50. Serra do Pardo NP
51. Serra dos Órgãos NP
52. Serra Geral NP
53. Sete Cidades NP
54. Supcragüi NP
55. Tijuca NP
56. Tumucumaque NP
57. Ubajara NP
58. Vale do Catimbau NP
59. Viruá NP
60. Xingu NP

Sociedade Brasileira de Ornitologia (SBO)
(http://www.ararajuba.org.br/sbo_eng/index_eng.htm)

The Brazilian Ornithological Society (SBO) was founded in 1987, with the mission of promoting the scientific study and conservation of Brazilian birds. The society is open to the participation of anyone, in Brazil or abroad, interested in Brazilian birds. The SBO publishes the periodical *Revista Brasileira de Ornitologia* (*The Brazilian Journal of Ornithology*), every 6 months. It is a scientific journal committed exclusively to articles and notes on aspects of the biology of Brazilian birds. The journal is intended to promote the flow of information among the members.

Comitê Brasileiro de Registros Ornitológicos (CBRO)
(http://www.cbro.org.br/CBRO/map.htm)

The Brazilian Ornithological Records Committee (CBRO) was created as a forum to discuss and publish data related to the distribution of birds in Brazil. The CBRO reviews and updates available information about avian distribution in Brazil and consolidates and publishes its conclusions on the Internet in the form of a checklist. There is no need to join the CBRO formally. Anyone can take part in the CBRO's work as a collaborator, joining in the discussions of the matters on the agenda, publicizing the work of the committee, writing notes for publication, and carrying out the CBRO's recommendations.

Museums in Brazil

The following museums have very large and important collections of bird skins:

- Museu de Zoologia da Universidade de São Paulo (MZUSP) (http://www.usp.br/prc/catalogomuseus/english/mz_apresentacao.htm)
- Museu Paraense Emilio Goeldi (http://www.museu-goeldi.br/)
- Museu Nacional do Rio de Janeiro (http://www.museum.com/jb/museum?id=23121)

Sociedade para a Conservação das Aves do Brasil—SAVE Brasil
(www.savebrasil.org.br)

Sociedade para a Conservação das Aves do Brasil—SAVE Brasil—is a not-for-profit civil society, based in São Paulo, with special emphasis on the conservation of birds in Brazil. SAVE Brasil is part of the BirdLife International alliance, present in more than 100 countries and territories worldwide. Following BirdLife International principles, SAVE Brasil works through a participatory approach and develops and implements conservation strategies and actions involving scientific research, raising awareness, environmental education, sustainable development, and public policies, especially related to the creation of protected areas. In 2006 SAVE Brasil published the book *Important Bird Areas in Brazil: Part I, Atlantic Forest Region*, which describes the 163 most important sites for birds (IBAs) along 15 Brazilian states within the Atlantic Forest Domain. Eighty-three percent of Brazilian threatened species occur in these states. BirdLife/SAVE Brasil identified 16 priority areas for immediate action because they hold significant numbers of one or more species at risk of extinction. Current efforts brought a renewed attention to some of these areas and the hope of survival for some of the most threatened species in the world.

BirdLife International (http://www.birdlife.org/)

Birdlife International is a global partnership of conservation organizations that strives to conserve birds, their habitats, and global biodiversity, working with people toward sustainable use of natural resources. BirdLife partners operate in more than 100 countries and territories worldwide

The American Ornithologists' Union (AOU) (http://www.aou.org/)

Founded in 1883, the American Ornithologists' Union is the oldest and largest organization in the New World devoted to the scientific study of birds. Although the AOU primarily is a professional organization, its membership of about 4,000 includes many amateurs dedicated to the advancement of ornithology. AOU publishes *The Auk*, a quarterly journal of ornithology that presents articles dealing with ornithological research.

South American Classification Committee, American Ornithologists' Union (http://www.museum.lsu.edu:80/~Remsen/SACCBaseline.html)

The South American Classification Committee is an official committee of the American Ornithologists' Union, whose mission is to create a standard classification, with English names, for the bird species of South America. This classification is subject to constant revision by the proposal system to allow incorporation of new data.

Neotropical Bird Club (NBC) (www.neotropicalbirdclub.org)

The NBC aims to

• Foster an interest in the birds of the Neotropics among birdwatchers throughout the world

- Increase awareness of the importance of support for conservation in the Neotropics
- Mobilize the increasing number of enthusiastic birdwatchers active in the region to contribute to the conservation of Neotropical birds
- Provide a forum for the publication of articles and notes about Neotropical birds, their identification, and their conservation and thus enhance information exchange
- Channel efforts toward priority species and sites, drawing attention to conservation needs
- Publicize the activities of local groups and individuals and improve liaison and collaboration between these people and other birdwatchers.

The journal *Cotinga* features news, notices, recent publications, expedition results, reviews, and preliminary or interim publication of studies on Neotropical birds by contributors from all parts of the world in English, Spanish, and Portuguese. The NBC also publishes an annual birding magazine, *Neotropical Birding*, which includes articles on identification and good birding sites across the region. The NBC is open to all, and the club welcomes new members. Further details can be obtained from the secretary at secretary@neotropicalbirdclub.org.

NatureServe (http://www.natureserve.org/index.jsp)

NatureServe is an organization that provides, on a nonprofit basis, scientific information for conservation action in the United States, Canada, Latin America, and the Caribbean.

Bibliography and Further References

FIELD GUIDES

Robert S. Ridgely, Guy Tudor. *The Birds of South America* (New York: Oxford University Press)

    Volume I, *Jays – Finches* (1989)

    Volume II, *Ovenbirds – Cotingas* (1994)

Tomas Sigrist. *Aves do Brasil* (AvisBrasilis, 2006)

Deodato Souza. *All the Birds of Brazil* (Dall, 2002)

FIELD GUIDES FOR ADJACENT REGIONS

James F. Clements, Naom Shany, Dana Gardner, and Eustace Barnes. *A Field Guide to the Birds of Peru* (Barcelona: Lynx Edicions, 2001)

Steven L. Hilty, William L. Brown, Guy Tudor. *A Guide to the Birds of Colombia* (Princeton, NJ: Princeton University Press, 1986)

Steven L. Hilty, John A. Gwynne, Guy Tudor. *Birds of Venezuela* (Princeton, NJ: Princeton University Press, 2003)

Alvaro Jaramillo, Peter Burke, and David Beadle. *Birds of Chile* (London: Christopher Helm, 2003)

Tito Narosky and Dario Yzurieta. *Birds of Argentina & Uruguay, A Field Guide* (Buenos Aires: Vazquez Mazzini, 2003)

Robert S. Ridgely, Paul J. Greenfield. *The Birds of Ecuador* (London: Christopher Helm, 2001)

Homas S. Schulenberg, Douglas F. Stotz, Daniel F. Lane, John P. O'Neill, Theodore A. Parker III: *Birds of Peru* (London: Christopher Helm, 2007)

David Sibley. *The North American Bird Guide* (Kent, UK: Pica Press, 2000)

HANDBOOKS

J. del Hoyo, A. Elliott, J. Sargatal, D. Christie, eds. *Handbook of the Birds of the World* (Barcelona: Lynx Edicions)

    Vol. 1, *Ostrich – Ducks* (1992)

    Vol. 2, *New World Vultures – Guineafowl* (1994)

    Vol. 3, *Hoatzin – Auks* (1996)

    Vol. 4, *Barn-owls – Hummingbirds* (1997)

    Vol. 5, *Sandgrouse – Cuckoos* (1999)

    Vol. 6, *Mousebirds – Hornbills* (2001)

    Vol. 7, *Jacamars – Woodpeckers* (2002)

    Vol. 8, *Broadbills – Tapaculos* (2003)

    Vol. 9, *Cotingas – Pipits and Wagtails* (2004)

    Vol. 10, *Cuckoo-shrikes – Thrushes* (2005)

Vol. 11, *Old World Flydatchers – Old World Warblers* (2006)

Vol. 12, *Picathartes – Tits and Chickadees* (2007)

(Other volumes yet to be published.)

Helmut Sick. *Birds in Brazil* (Princeton, NJ: Princeton University Press, 1993)

BOOKS ON BIRD GROUPS

David Brewer, Barry Kent MacKay. *Wrens, Dippers and Thrashers* (London: Christopher Helm, 2001)

Michael Brooke, John Cox. *Albatrosses and Petrels across the World* (New York: Oxford University Press, 2004)

C. Byers, U. Olsson, and J. Curson. *Buntings and Sparrows* (Kent, UK: Pica Press, 1995)

P. Chantler and G. Driessens. *Swifts* (Kent, UK: Pica Press, 1995)

N. Cleere and D. Nurney. *Nightjars* (Kent, UK: Pica Press, 1998)

P. Clement, A. Harris, and J. Davis, *Finches and Sparrows* (London: Christopher Helm, 1993)

Peter Clement and Ren Hathway. *Thrushes* (Helm, 2000)

Jon Curson, David Quinn, and David Beadle. *New World Warblers* (London: Christopher Helm, 1995)

James Ferguson-Lees and David A. Christie. *Raptors of the World* (London: Christopher Helm, 2001)

C. H. Fry, K. Fry, and A. Harris. *Kingfishers, Bee-eaters and Rollers* (London: Christopher Helm, 1992)

David Gibbs, Eustace Barnes, and John Cox, *Pigeons and Doves* (Kent, UK: Pica Press, 2001)

Rolf Grantsau, *Die Kolibris Brasiliens* (Espressão e cultura, 1988)

J. Hancock and J. Kushlan. *The Herons Handbook* (London: Croom Helm, 1984)

S. Harrap and D. Quinn. *Tits, Nuthatches & Treecreepers* (London: Christopher Helm, 1996)

P. Harrison. *Seabirds* (London: Croom Helm, 1983)

P. Hayman, J. Marchant, and T. Prater. *Shorebirds* (London: Christopher Helm, 1986)

Morton L. Isler and Phyllis R. Isler. *Tanagers* (London: Christopher Helm, 1999)

Alvaro Jaramillo and Peter Burke. *New World Blackbirds* (London: Christopher Helm, 1999)

Tony Jupiter and Mike Parr. *Parrots* (Kent, UK: Pica Press, 1998)

Claus König, Friedhelm Weick, and Jan-Hendrik Becking. *Owls* (Kent, UK: Pica Press, 1999)

S. Madge and H. Burn. *Wildfowl* (London: Christopher Helm, 1988)

S. Madge and H. Burn. *Crows and Jays* (London: Christopher Helm, 1999)

K. M. Olsen and H. Larsson. *Skuas and Jaegers* (Kent, UK: Pica Press, 1997)

Lester Short, Jennifer Horne, and Albert E. Gilbert. *Toucans, Barbets and Honeyguides* (New York: Oxford University Press, 2001)

B. Taylor and B. van Perlo. *Rails* (Kent, UK: Pica Press, 1998)

Angela Turner and C. Rose, *Swallows and Martins* (London: Christopher Helm, 1998)

H. Winkler, D. A. Christie, and D. Nurney. *Woodpeckers* (Kent, UK: Pica Press, 1995)

BIRD SOUNDS

Peter Boesman. *Birds of Brazil MP3 Sound Collection* (Westernieland: Birdsounds.nl, 2006. MP3-CD)

Peter Boesman. *Birds of Venezuela MP3 Sound Collection* (Westernieland: Birdsounds.nl, 2006. MP3-CD)

Niels Krabbe and Jonas Nilsson. *Birds of Ecuador* (Westernieland: Birdsongs BV, 2003. DVD-ROM)

Curtis A. Marantz and Kevin J. Zimmer. *Bird Voices of Alta Floresta and Southeastern Amazonian Brazil* (Ithaca NY: Cornell Laboratory of Ornithology, 2006.S. Set of 6 CDs)

Sjoerd Mayer. *Birds of Bolivia 2.0* (Westernieland: Birdsongs BV, 2000. CD-ROM)

John V. Moore, Paul Coopmans, Robert S. Ridgely, and Mitch Lysinger. *The Birds of Northwest Ecuador,* Vol. 1: *The Upper Foothills and Subtropics* (San Jose CA: John V. Moore Nature Recordings, 1999. Set of 3 CDs)

Houghton Mifflin and the Cornell Laboratory of Ornithology/Interactive Audio: *Peterson Field Guides, Westen Bird Songs* (Ithaca NY: Cornell Laboratory of Ornithology, 1990. Set of 2 CD's)

Heinz Remold. *The Land Birds of Southeast Brazil, Disc 2: Furnarids – Sharpbill* (Brookline NY: Heinz Remold, 2001. CD-ROM)

Heinz Remold. *The Land Birds of Southeast Brazil, Disc 3: Swallows – Icterids with the Pigeons, Parrots and Woodpeckers* (Brookline NY: Heinz Remold, 2006. CD-ROM)

Thomas S. Schulenberg, Curtis A. Marantz, and Peter H. English. *Voices of Amazonian Birds; Birds of the Rainforest of Southern Peru and Northern Bolivia,* Vol. 1: *Tinamous through Barbets* (Ithaca NY: Cornell Laboratory of Ornithology, 2000. CD)

Thomas S. Schulenberg, Curtis A. Marantz, and Peter H. English. *Voices of Amazonian Birds; Birds of the Rainforest of Southern Peru and Northern Bolivia,* Vol. 2: *Toucans through Antbirds* (Ithaca NY: Cornell Laboratory of Ornithology, 2000. CD)

Thomas S. Schulenberg, Curtis A. Marantz, and Peter H. English. *Voices of Amazonian Birds; Birds of the Rainforest of Southern Peru and Northern Bolivia,* Vol. 3: *Ground Antbirds through Jays* (Ithaca NY: Cornell Laboratory of Ornithology, 2000. CD)

THE INTERNET

Arthur Grosset's Web page. http://www.arthurgrosset.com/ (photos of neotropical and other birds)

Atualidades Ornithologicas. http://www.ao.com.br/ (Brazilian Ornithological Web Site)

Checklist of the Birds of Brazil. Comitê Brasileiro de Registros Ornitológicos. http://www.cbro.org.br/CBRO/map.htm

Classification of the bird species of South America. South American Classification Committee, American Ornithologists' Union. Composite species list with Scientific and English names created by Sjoerd Mayer. Updated November 16, 2008. http://www.museum.lsu.edu/~Remsen/SACCList.html

Fatbirder. http://www.fatbirder.com/links_geo/america_south/brazil.html (birding in Brazil)

Handbook of Birds of the World, Lynx Edicions. http://www.hbw.com/ibc/ (video clips of birds worldwide)

Mango Verde. http://www.mangoverde.com/birdsound/index.html (photos of birds worldwide)

NatureServe. http://www.natureserve.org/infonatura/ (distribution maps of neotropical birds)

Xeno-Canto America. http://www.xeno-canto.org/perc_map.php (voice recordings of neotropical birds)

Information and photos of almost every bird species can also be found on the Internet by typing its English, Portuguese, or scientific name in the dialog window of any search engine.

TINAMOUS

27.8   Yellow-legged Tinamou (*Crypturellus noctivagus*)

26.9   Lesser Nothura (*Nothura minor*)

CURRASOW & GUANS

30.3   Buff-browed Chachalaca (*Ortalis superciliaris*)

29.1   White-crested Guan (*Penelope pileata*)

29.2   Chestnut-bellied Guan (*Penelope ochrogaster*)

29.3   White-browed Guan (*Penelope jacucaca*)

31.2   Alagoas Curassow (*Mitu mitu*)

31.7   Red-billed Curassow (*Crax blumenbachii*)

EAGLES, HAWKS & ALLIES

19.2   White-collared Kite (*Leptodon forbesi*)

20.5   White-necked Hawk (*Leucopternis lacernulatus*)

RAILS

34.1   Little Wood-Rail (*Aramides mangle*)

PIGEONS & DOVES

44.5   Blue-eyed Ground-Dove (*Columbina cyanopis*)

PARROTS

47.2   Indigo Macaw (*Anodorhynchus leari*)

47.4   Spix's Macaw (*Cyanopsitta spixii*)

47.8   Golden Parakeet (*Guarouba guarouba*)

48.3   Jandaya Parakeet (*Aratinga jandaya*)

48.4   Golden-capped Parakeet (*Aratinga auricapillus*)

48.8   Cactus Parakeet (*Aratinga cactorum*)

49.1   Blue-throated Parakeet (*Pyrrhura cruentata*)

49.4   Pearly Parakeet (*Pyrrhura lepida*)

49.7   White-eared Parakeet (*Pyrrhura leucotis*)

49.9   Gray-breasted Parakeet (*Pyrrhura griseipectus*)

50.1   Hellmayr's Parakeet (*Pyrrhura amazonum*)

50.2   Deville's Parakeet (*Pyrrhura lucianii*)

50.4   Pfrimer's Parakeet (*Pyrrhura pfrimeri*)

51.8   Brown-backed Parrotlet (*Touit melanonota*)

51.9   Golden-tailed Parrotlet (*Touit surdus*)

52.1   Plain Parakeet (*Brotogeris tirica*)

54.6   Vulturine Parrot (*Gypopsitta vulturina*)

54.7   Bald Parrot (*Gypopsitta aurantiocephala*)

53.4   Red-browed Parrot (*Amazona rhodocorytha*)

53.5   Red-tailed Parrot (*Amazona brasiliensis*)

52.8   Kawall's Parrot (*Amazona kawalli*)

CUCKOOS

55.8   Scaled Ground-Cuckoo (*Neomorphus squamiger*)

OWLS

57.9   Pernambuco Pygmy-Owl (*Glaucidium mooreorum*)

NIGHTJARS

61.1   Bahian Nighthawk (*Nyctiprogne vielliardi*)

62.4   Pygmy Nightjar (*Caprimulgus hirundinaceus*)

HUMMINGBIRDS

64.3   Margaretta's Hermit (*Phaethornis margarettae*)

64.8   Dusky-throated Hermit (*Phaethornis squalidus*)

65.2.2   Maranhão Hermit (*Phaethornis maranhaoensis*)

65.5   Minute Hermit (*Phaethornis idaliae*)

65.6   Broad-tipped Hermit (*Anopetia gounellei*)

65.10   Hook-billed Hermit (*Glaucis dohrnii*)

66.1   Saw-billed Hermit (*Ramphodon naevius*)

67.4   Long-tailed Woodnymph (*Thalurania watertonii*)

69.8   Sombre Hummingbird (*Aphantochroa cirrochloris*)

70.8   Brazilian Ruby (*Clytolaema rubricauda*)

71.3   Hooded Visorbearer (*Augastes lumachella*)

71.4   Hyacinth Visorbearer (*Augastes scutatus*)

71.8   Stripe-breasted Starthroat (*Heliomaster squamosus*)

JACAMARS

75.5   Three-toed Jacamar (*Jacamaralcyon tridactyla*)

NEW WORLD BARBETS

76.4   Brown-chested Barbet (*Capito brunneipectus*)

PUFFBIRDS

75.9   Chestnut-headed Nunlet (*Nonnula amaurocephala*)

78.4   Spot-backed Puffbird (*Nystalus maculates*)

78.7   Crescent-chested Puffbird (*Malacoptila striata*)

WOODPECKERS

81.7   Spotted Piculet (*Picumnus pygmaeus*)

81.8   Varzea Piculet (*Picumnus varzeae*)

82.3   Tawny Piculet (*Picumnus fulvescens*)

82.4 Ochraceous Piculet (*Picumnus limae*)
83.7 Yellow-eared Woodpecker (*Veniliornis maculifrons*)
84.8 Kaempfer's Woodpecker (*Celeus obrieni*)

OVENBIRDS (INCL. WOODCREEPERS)

87.3 Brigida's Woodcreeper (*Hylexetastes brigidai*)
87.6 Carajás Woodcreeper (*Xiphocolaptes carajaensis*)
87.8 Moustached Woodcreeper (*Xiphocolaptes falcirostris*)
88.1 Hoffmann's Woodcreeper (*Dendrocolaptes hoffmannsi*)
88.10 Spix's Woodcreeper (*Xiphorhynchus spixii*)
89.4 Scaled Woodcreeper (*Lepidocolaptes squamatus*)
89.5 Wagler's Woodcreeper (*Lepidocolaptes wagleri*)
90.2 Striolated Tit-spinetail (*Leptasthenura striolata*)
90.4 Itatiaia Spinetail (*Oreophylax moreirae*)
90.6 Cipo Canastero (*Asthenes luizae*)
91.4 Long-tailed Cinclodes (*Cinclodes pabsti*)
91.6 Wing-banded Hornero (*Furnarius figulus*)
92.1 Pinto's Spinetail (*Synallaxis infuscata*)
92.3 Bahia Spinetail (*Synallaxis whitneyi*)
93.4b Araguaia Spinetail (*Synallaxis simoni*)
94.1 Pallid Spinetail (*Cranioleuca pallida*)
94.5 Gray-headed Spinetail (*Cranioleuca semicinerea*)
94.7 Scaled Spinetail (*Cranioleuca muelleri*)
95.1 Red-shouldered Spinetail (*Gyalophylax hellmayri*)
95.2 Striated Softtail (*Thripophaga macroura*)
95.7 Orange-eyed Thornbird (*Phacellodomus erythrophthalmus*)
96.8 Pink-legged Graveteiro (*Acrobatornis fonsecai*)
97.1 Caatinga Cachalote (*Pseudoseisura cristata*)
97.8 White-collared Foliage-gleaner (*Anabazenops fuscus*)
97.10 Pale-browed Treehunter (*Cichlocolaptes leucophrus*)
98.9 Alagoas Foliage-gleaner (*Philydor novaesi*)
99.3 Pará Foliage-gleaner (*Automolus paraensis*)
100.10 Great Xenops (*Megaxenops parnaguae*)

ANTBIRDS

102.2 Silvery-cheeked Antshrike (*Sakesphorus cristatus*)
102.3 Glossy Antshrike (*Sakesphorus luctuosus*)
103.3 Caatinga Barred Antshrike (*Thamnophilus capistratus*)
104.9 Planalto Slaty Antshrike (*Thamnophilus pelzelni*)
104.10 Sooretama Slaty Antshrike (*Thamnophilus ambiguus*)
105.2 Rondonia Bushbird (*Clytoctantes atrogularis*)

105.5 Rufous-backed Antvireo (*Dysithamnus xanthopterus*)
105.6 Plumbeous Antvireo (*Dysithamnus plumbeus*)
106.1 Klages's Antwren (*Myrmotherula klagesi*)
106.7 Star-throated Antwren (*Myrmotherula gularis*)
107.4 Rio de Janeiro Antwren (*Myrmotherula fluminensis*)
107.7 Salvadori's Antwren (*Myrmotherula minor*)
107.9 Unicolored Antwren (*Myrmotherula unicolor*)
107.10 Alagoas Antwren (*Myrmotherula snowi*)
108.3 Band-tailed Antwren (*Myrmotherula urosticta*)
108.9 Orange-bellied Antwren (*Terenura sicki*)
109.1 Bahia Antwren (*Herpsilochmus pileatus*)
109.7 Pectoral Antwren (*Herpsilochmus pectoralis*)
109.10 Caatinga Antwren (*Herpsilochmus sellowi*)
110.1 Narrow-billed Antwren (*Formicivora iheringi*)
110.4 Serra Antwren (*Formicivora serrana*)
110.5 Restinga Antwren (*Formicivora littoralis*)
110.6 Black-hooded Antwren (*Formicivora erythronotos*)
110.8 Sincorá Antwren (*Formicivora grantsaui*)
110.9 Paraná Antwren (*Stymphalornis acutirostris*)
110.10 São Paulo Antwren (*Stymphalornis* sp.)
111.1 Ferruginous Antbird (*Drymophila ferruginea*)
111.3 Rufous-tailed Antbird (*Drymophila genei*)
111.4 Ochre-rumped Antbird (*Drymophila ochropyga*)
111.7 Scaled Antbird (*Drymophila squamata*)
111.10 Fringe-backed Fire-eye (*Pyriglena atra*)
112.2 Rio de Janeiro Antbird (*Cercomacra brasiliana*)
112.5 Bananal Antbird (*Cercomacra ferdinandi*)
113.1 Slender Antbird (*Rhopornis ardesiacus*)
113.6f Spix's Warbling Antbird (*Hypocnemis striata*)
114.6c Rufous-faced Antbird (*Schistocichla rufifascies*)
114.10 Pale-faced Antbird (*Skutchia borbae*)
115.2 White-bibbed Antbird (*Myrmeciza loricata*)
115.3 Squamate Antbird (*Myrmeciza squamosa*)
116.3 Scalloped Antbird (*Myrmeciza ruficauda*)
117.3 Harlequin Antbird (*Rhegmatorhina berlepschi*)
117.6 White-breasted Antbird (*Rhegmatorhina hoffmannsi*)
117.7 Bare-eyed Antbird (*Rhegmatorhina gymnops*)

ANTPITTAS

118.3 Such's Antthrush (*Chamaeza meruloides*)
119.6 White-browed Antpitta (*Hylopezus ochroleucus*)

GNATEATERS

118.7 Hooded Gnateater (*Conopophaga roberti*)
118.9 Black-cheeked Gnateater (*Conopophaga melanops*)
118.10 Black-bellied Gnateater (*Conopophaga melanogaster*)

TAPACULOS

120.2 Serra do Mar Tapaculo (*Scytalopus speluncae*)
120.4 Marsh Tapaculo (*Scytalopus iraiensis*)
120.5 Diamantina Tapaculo (*Scytalopus diamantinensis*)
120.6 Bahia Tapaculo (*Scytalopus psychopompus*)
120.7 White-breasted Tapaculo (*Scytalopus indigoticus*)
120.8 Brasilia Tapaculo (*Scytalopus novacapitalis*)
120.10 Slaty Bristlefront (*Merulaxis ater*)
120.11 Stresemann's Bristlefront (*Merulaxis stresemanni*)

COTINGAS

121.1 White-winged Cotinga (*Xipholena atropurpurea*)
121.2 White-tailed Cotinga (*Xipholena lamellipennis*)
121.8 Banded Cotinga (*Cotinga maculata*)
122.3 Black-and-gold Cotinga (*Tijuca atra*)
122.4 Gray-winged Cotinga (*Tijuca condita*)
124.3 Cinnamon-vented Piha (*Lipaugus lanioides*)
124.5 Kinglet Calyptura (*Calyptura cristata*)
124.8 Hooded Berryeater (*Carpornis cucullata*)
124.9 Black-headed Berryeater (*Carpornis melanocephala*)
129.5 Buff-throated Purpletuft (*Iodopleura pipra*)

MANAKINS

123.6 Araripe Manakin (*Antilophia bokermanni*)
123.7 Pin-tailed Manakin (*Ilicura militaris*)
126.5 Opal-crowned Manakin (*Lepidothrix iris*)
126.6 Golden-crowned Manakin (*Lepidothrix vilasboasi*)
127.1 Eastern Striped Manakin (*Machaeropterus regulus*)
127.6 Wied's Tyrant-Manakin (*Neopelma aurifrons*)
127.7 Serra do Mar Tyrant-Manakin (*Neopelma chrysolophum*)

TYRANT-FLYCATCHERS

131.5 Gray-capped Tyrannulet (*Phyllomyias griseocapilla*)
132.3 Noronha Elaenia (*Elaenia ridleyana*)
133.8 Gray-backed Tachuri (*Polystictus superciliaris*)
135.10 Minas Gerais Tyrannulet (*Phylloscartes roquettei*)
136.2 Oustalet's Tyrannulet (*Phylloscartes oustaleti*)
136.3 Serra do Mar Tyrannulet (*Phylloscartes difficilis*)
136.4 Alagoas Tyrannulet (*Phylloscartes ceciliae*)
136.6 Restinga Tyrannulet (*Phylloscartes kronei*)
136.7 Bahia Tyrannulet (*Phylloscartes beckeri*)

139.1 Eye-ringed Tody-Tyrant (*Hemitriccus orbitatus*)
139.4 Hangnest Tody-Tyrant (*Hemitriccus nidipendulus*)
139.7 Buff-breasted Tody-Tyrant (*Hemitriccus mirandae*)
139.8 Kaempfer's Tody-Tyrant (*Hemitriccus kaempferi*)
139.9 Fork-tailed Pygmy-Tyrant (*Hemitriccus furcatus*)
141.2 Buff-cheeked Tody-Flycatcher (*Poecilotriccus senex*)
141.8 Atlantic Royal Flycatcher (*Onychorhynchus swainsoni*)
142.2 Yellow-lored Tody-Flycatcher (*Todirostrum poliocephalum*)
145.7 Caatinga Black-Tyrant (*Knipolegus franciscanus*)
145.9 Velvety Black-Tyrant (*Knipolegus nigerrimus*)
150.5 Ash-throated Casiornis (*Casiornis fuscus*)
151.5 Gray-hooded Attila (*Attila rufus*)

NEW WORLD WARBLERS

153.7 White-striped Warbler (*Basileuterus leucophrys*)

VIREOS & ALLIES

154.9 Noronha Vireo (*Vireo gracilirostris*)
155.4 Gray-eyed Greenlet (*Hylophilus amaurocephalus*)

WRENS

158.10 Long-billed Wren (*Thryothorus longirostris*)
159.1 Gray Wren (*Thryothorus griseus*)

NEW WORLD BLACKBIRDS

163.1 Forbes' Blackbird (*Curaeus forbesi*)
164.1 Pale Baywing (*Agelaioides fringillarius*)
165.5 Campo Troupial (*Icterus jamacaii*)

TANAGERS

166.1 Brown Tanager (*Orchesticus abeillei*)
166.9 Cone-billed Tanager (*Conothraupis mesoleuca*)
167.2 Scarlet-throated Tanager (*Compsothraupis loricata*)
167.5 Cherry-throated Tanager (*Nemosia rourei*)
167.7 Rufous-headed Tanager (*Hemithraupis ruficapilla*)
168.1 Olive-green Tanager (*Orthogonys chloricterus*)
168.8 Azure-shouldered Tanager (*Thraupis cyanoptera*)
169.2 Natterer's Tanager (*Tachyphonus nattereri*)

English–Portuguese Dictionary

See also

- The Portuguese names in the species accounts
- The key to the distribution maps (p. 15)
- "Parts of a Bird" (p. xiii)
- "Symbols. Abbreviations, and Glossary" (p. 25)

The following is a small collection of the main terms and words used in the captions for features and habitat. Note that the basic form of the words is presented with addition of the most frequent suffixes or endings in parentheses.

(Inglês–Português)
Veja também

- os nomes do português das espécies descritas
- a chave dos mapas de distribuição (p. 15)
- 'partes de um pássaro' (p. xiii)
- 'símbolos e abreviaturas' (p. 25)

O seguinte é uma relação dos termos e das palavras principais usados nos subtítulos de cada espécie, suas características e habitat. Note que a relação de palavras básicas está seguida dos sufixos mais freqüentes entre parênteses.

above	acima de	begin(ning)	comecar
absence/absent	ausência	behavior	comportamento
abundant	abundante	behind	atrás de
accent(uate, ed)	ênfase, acentuado	below	abaixo
accident(al, ally)	acidente	belt(s)	correia
active	ativo	bend	curvatura
adjacent	adjacente	between	entre
age	idade	beware	cuidado
always	sempre	beyond	além de
amber	âmbar	bill(s, ed)	bico
among	entre	bird(s)	pássaro
ant	formiga	bit	pedacinho
any	alguns	black(ish, er, est)	preto
appear(s, ance)	aparecer	blotch(es, ed)	mancha
arid	árido	blue/bluish	azul
army ants	grupo grande formigas	blurry	desfocado
around	em torno	body	corpo
attain(ed, ing)	alcancar	bold(er)	bem definido
average	média	bordered	limitado
avoid(s)	evitar	border(s)	margem
away	afastado	both	ambos
azure	azul	brackish	água suavemente salgada
backside	parte traseira	branch	filial
band(s)	faixa	brassy	amarelo metálico
bar(s, red, ring)	barra	breed(s, er, ing)	raça
bare	descoberto	bright(er, est)	claro
beach(es)	praia	brilliant	brilhante
beat(s)	batida	broad(er, est, ly)	largo
because	porque	broken	quebrado
become(s)	tornar-se	brown(er, est, ish)	marrom
before	antes	brush(y)	arbusto baixo denso

buff(ier, iest, y, ish)	lustre	differ(s, ent, ently, ing, ence)	difirir
build	configuração	direct(ly)	direto
bulky	volumoso	discover(ed)	descobrir
burned	queimado	distance	distância
bush(es, y)	arbusto	distinct(ly, ive, ively)	distinto
call(s)	atendimento	ditch(es)	valeta
calm	calma	dot(ted)	pintas
canopy	dossel	double	dobro
cap	topo da cabeça	doubtful(ly)	duvidoso
case(s)	caso	down	para baixo
cast	molde	drop(s)	gota
cattle	gado	dry/drier/driest	seco
caused	causado	due	esperado
change/changing	mudar	dull(er, est)	sem graça
characterize(d)	caracterizar	dusky/duskier/duskiest	meio escuro
chestnut	castanha	dweller	morador
chocolate	chocolate	e.g.	por exemplo
cinnamon	canela	each	cada um
city/cities)	cidade	earth	terra
clean	limpo	easy/easily	fácil
clearing(s)	clareiro	edge,(s, ed)/edging	borda
cliff(s)	penhasco	elegant	elegante
close (r, st,ly)	próximo	emerald	verde esmeralda
coast(al)	costa	entire	inteiro
cocked	?	erect	ereto
collar	colar	eroded	erosão
colony/colonies/colonial	colônia	even	uniforme
color(s, ed, ing)	cor	example(s)	exemplo
common(er, est, ly)	comum	exclusive(ly)	exclusivo
compact	compacto	expose(d)	exposto
compare(d)	comparar com	extend(s, ing)	estender
complete(ly)	completo	extension(s)	extensão
complicate(d)	complicado	extensive(ly)	extensivo
conceal(ed)	escondir	face/facial	cara
consider(ed)	considerar	fact	fato
conspicuous	conspícuo	faint(ly)	fraco
contrast(s, ing)	contraste	fair(ly)	razoável
coppery	cúprico	fall(en)	queda
corner(s)	esquina	fan(ned)	leque
correct(ly)	correto	far	distante
country	país	farmland	terra de cultivo
cover	tampa	fast	rápido
crescent(s)	crescente	feather(s, ing)	pena
crosswise	transversalmente	featureless	sem características
crown(ed)	coroa	feed(s, ing)	alimentação
cryptic	enigmático	feel	sentir
cultivation(s)	cultivo	feet	pés
curve(d)	curva	fern(s)	samambaia
cut(ting)	corte	few(er)	poucos
dark(er, est, ish)	escuro	field(s)	campo
dead	morto	fierce	feroz
deep(er)	profundo	find/found	encontrar
dense (r, ly)	denso	fine(ly)	delicado
depict(ed)	descrever	fish(es, ing)	peixes

flash(es)	claráo	hybrid(s)	híbrido
flat(ter, est)	plano	illustrated	ilustrado
flesh	pele	immediate(ly)	imediatamente
fly(ing)/flies	voar	include(s)/including	Incluir, inclusive
flight	vôo	incomplete	incompleto
flooded	inundado	inconspicuous	discreto
flood plains	alagado	inland	interior
floor	fundo	inner	interno
fold(ed)	dobra	insect(s)	inseto
foliage	folhagem	inseparable	inseparável
follow(s)	seguir	inspect	inspecionar
foreside	fachada	intersect(s)	cruzar-se
forest(s, ed)	floresta	involve(d)	envolver
fork(ed)	bifurcação	island(s)	ilha
form(s, ed, ing)	forma	joint(ed)	conjunto
frequent	freqüente	just	somente
fresh	fresco	keel(ed)	quilha
fringe/fringing	franja	keep(s, ing)	deter
from/by	de/par	know(n)	saber
front	parte dianteira	labeled	etiquetado
full(y)	completo	lack(s, ing)	faltar
gallery	galeria	lagoon(s)	lagoa
garden(s)	jardim	lake(s)	lago
general(ly)	geralmente	land	terra
give/giving	dar	landscape(s)	paisagem
glide(s)/gliding	deslizar	large(r, st)	grande
glossy/glossier	lustroso	last/latter	último
golden	dourado	layer(s)	camada
grass(es, y, land)	grama/campo	lead(s, ing)	na frente
gray(er, est, ish)	cinzento	least	menos
green(er, est)	verde	leave(s)	deixar
groove(s)	ranhura	leg(s)	perna
ground(s)	chão	lengthwise	longitudinalmente
group(s)	grupo	less	menos
grove(s)	bosque	level(s)	nível
grow(th)	crescer	life	vida
half	meio	light(er, est, ly)	claro
halfway	na metade	like	como
hang(s, ing)	pendurar	limit(ed)	limitar
harbor(s)	porto	line(s)/lining	linha
hard(ly)	duro	little	pouco
head(s)	cabeça	local(ly)	local
hear(s, d)	ouvir	localize(d)	localizado
heavy/heavier/heaviest	pesado	long(er, est)	longo
hedge(s)	cerca viva	look(s, ing)	olhar
hence	por isso	low(er, est, ed)	baixo
hidden	escondido	lowland(s)	planície
high(er, est)	elevado	main(ly)	principal
highlands	paises montanhosos	margin(s)	margem
hind	traseiro	mark(ing, ings)	marca
hold/held	segurar	maroon	marrom
hood	capa	marsh(es, y)	pântano
humid	úmido	mask	máscara
hunt(s, ing)	caçar	may	pode ser que

medium	mediano	park(s)	parque
meet(s)	encontrar	part(s)	parte
method	método	partial	parcial
mid-	no meio de	partly	em parte
middle	médio	pasture(s)	pasto
might	poder (possibilidade)	patch(es)	manchas
migrate(s)	migrar	patrol(s)	patrulha
miss(ing)	perder	pattern(s, ed, ing)	desenho
moist	úmido	peak(s)	pico
montane	montanha	pearl	pérola
more	mais	perch(es, ed)	poleiro
most(ly)	a maioria	pied	multicor
mottle(d)/mottling	cores misturadas	pink(ish)	cor-de-rosa
moult(s, ing)	mudar de penas	plac(s, d)	lugar
mountain(s)	montanha	plain	liso
much	muito	plantation(s)	plantação
mud	lama	plant(s)	planta
mud flat	planície enlameada	point(ed)	ponto
narrow(er, est, ly)	estreito	pond(s)	lagoa
near(ly, by)	perto	pool(s)	poça
nest(s)	ninho	poor	deficiente
never	nunca	positive(ly)	positivo
night	noite	possible/possibly	possível
nocturnal	noturno	prefer(s, ring)	prefirir
notched	entalhado	probable/probably	provável
number	número	project(s, ing)	projetar
obvious	óbvio	pump(ing)	bomba
occur(s)	ocorrer	purple/purplish	roxo
ochraceous	alaranjado	quite	quase
ochre	cor de ocre	raise(d)	levantar
ocular	ocular	ranch(land)	rancho
offshore	sobre o mar	range(s)	área
often	frequentemente	rapid	rápido
old(er, est)	velho	rare(r, st, ly)	raro
olive	verde-oliva	rather	um tanto
only	somente	reach(es, ing)	alcançar
open	aberto	rear	parte traseira
orange	laranja	reason(s)	razão
other(wise)	se não	recall(ing)	recordar
out	fora de	record(s, ing)	gravar
outcrop(s)	saliencia	red(der, dest, dish)	vermelho
outer(most)	exterior	reduce(d)	reduzir
outnumber(ed)	exceder em número	reed beds	habitat com juncos
outside	fora	reed(s, y)	junco
over	sobre	reef(s)	recife
overall	total	region(s)	região
overgrown	coberto de vegetação	relative(ly)	relativo
overhanging	pender sobre	reliable/reliably)	confiável
overlap	sobreposto	remarkable	notável
paint(ed)	pintura	replace(d)	substituir
pair	par	resemble(s, ing)	parecer com
pale(r, st)	pálido	respond	responder
palm(s)	palmito	retain(ed)	reter
panel	painel	retract(ed)	retratar

rich(er, est, ly)	rico	shrubbery	moite de arbustos
ridge(s)	cume	shut	fechado
rim(s, med)	borda	shy	tímido
ring(ed)	anel	side(s)	lado
river(s)	rio	similar	semelhante a
riverine	vale	single	solteiro
roadside(s)	beira da estrada	size(s, d)	tamanho
rock(s, y)	rocha	skin	pele
roof(s)	telhado	slender	delgado
roost(s, ing)	pernoitar	slight(ly)	um pouco
round(er, est, ed)	redondo	slope(s)	inclinação
Rufous, rufescent	vermelho marronzado	small(er, est)	pequeno
run(s, ning)	correr	smear/smudge	mancha
rush(es)	junco	soar(s, ing)	pairar
rusty	oxidado	soil(s)	terra
safe(ly)	seguro	solid	sólido
saline	salgado	some	alguns
sally(ing)	voar com objetivo	sometimes	às vezes
salty	salgada	somewhat	um tanto
same	mesmo	song	canção
sand(y)	areia	sooty	sooty
sandbar(s)	banco de areia	space(s)	espaço
scale(d)/scaling	pintadinho	sparse(ly)	escasso
scallop(ed, ing)	tipo de marcação	species	espécie
scarce(ly)	escasso	speckle(s, d)	salpico
scatter(ed)	dispersar	spectacles	óculos
scrub(bed, by)	cerrado	spot(s, ted, ting, ty)	pintadinho
sea	mar	spread(s, ing)	espelhar
seam	emenda	square/squarish	quadrado
season	estação	stage(s)	estágio
second(ly)	segundo	stance	postura
secretive	meio escondido	stand(s)	posição
sedge(s)	junco	staring	olhar fixamente
see(s, n)	ver	start(s, ing)	começar
seed(ing)	semente	status	categoria
seem(s, ingly)	parecer	steep	íngreme
settlement(s)	estabelecimento	stem(s)	caule
several	diversos	stiff	duro
shade(d)	máscara	still	ainda
shadow	sombra	stony	pedregoso
shaft(s)	haste	(upper-, under-)story/stories	andar
shallow	raso	straight(er, est)	em linha reta
shape(d)	forma	strat(um, a)	camada
share(s, d)	dividir	straw	palha
sharp(ly)	afiado	streak(s, ed, ing, y)	listras
shelf	prateleira	stream(s)	córrego
shiny	brilhante	strict(ly)	estrito
ship(s)	barco	striking	impressionante
shore(s)	costa	stripe(s, ing)	listra
short(er, est)	curto	strong(ly)	forte
should	deve	stubb(y, ier, iest)	pequeno
shoulder	ombro	stunted	atrofiado
show(s, n, ing)	mostrar	subterminal	subterminal
shrub(by)	arbusto	surface	superfície

surrounding(s)	arredores	upper	superior
sustain(ed)	sustentar	upright	ereto
swamp(s, y)	pântano	upturned	virado para cima
swarm(s)	enxame	urban	urbano
swim(s)	nadar	use	usar
tail(s, ed)	cauda	vagrant	visitante
tall(er, est)	alto	variable	variável
tangle(s, d)	emaranhado	variation	variação
tawny	tipo de marrom	variety	variedade
thick	densamente	vary/varies/varying	variar
thicket(s)	grosso	very	muito
thickset	troncudo	vinaceous	cor de vinho
thigh(s)	coxa	vine(s)	planta trepadeira
thin	fino	violet	violeta
throat(s, ed)	garganta	virtually	praticamente
through	através	visible	visível
throughout	durante todo	visitor	visitante
tidal	movimento das marés	voice	voz
tinge(d)	matiz	walk(s, ing)	andar
tiny	minúsculo	warm	morno
tip(s, ped)	ponta	wash/thin layer of color	revestimento fino
together	junto	water(s)	água
tone(s, d)	tom	web(s) of feather	vexilo
touch(es)	tocar	wedge	cunha
town(s)	cidade	well	bem
trail(ing)	arrastar	wet	molhado
translucent	translúcido	wetlands	pantanais
trawler(s)	traineira	whereas	visto que
tree(s)	árvore	which	qual
treeless	sem árvores	while	enquanto
tuft(s)	tufo	whisker(s)	bigodes
turquoise	turquesa	white, (r, st)/whitish)	branco
twice	duas vezes	wide	largamente
type(s)	tipo	widespread	espalhado
typical(ly)	típico	window(s)	janela
un-	des-/in-	wing(s, ed)	asa
under-	sob-	wire(s)	fio
undergrowth	plantas baixas	wood(s, ed)	madeira/bosque
underneath	debaixo de	woodland	mata
underside	lado de baixo	world	mundo
undulating	ondulante	wrist(s)	pulso
unless	a menos que	year(s)	ano
unlike(ly)	desigual/diferente	yellow(er, est, ish)	amarelo
unmistakable	inconfundível		

Index

The first part of a number refers to the plate number, and the second part to the number of a species on that plate. The names are printed as in the captions, with English names in bold capitals, Portuguese in regular type, and scientific names in italics.